HEBDEN :

CHEMISTRY 11

A WORKBOOK FOR STUDENTS

by

James A. Hebden, Ph. D.

Hebden :
Chemistry 11
A Workbook for Students

Twenty Third Printing – April 2015

Copyright © 1998, James A. Hebden

Hebden Home Publishing
Kamloops, B.C.
CANADA

Distributor: Western Campus Resources Inc.
485 Mountain Highway
North Vancouver, BC V7J 2L3
Telephone: (604)-988-1055 ; toll free: 1-800-995-5283
Fax: (604)-988-3309 ; toll free fax: 1-877-977-4539
e-mail: info@textbookscanada.ca

ISBN   978-0-9682069-1-1

Printed in Canada by Hignell Book Printers

PREFACE

This book covers the entire British Columbia Chemistry 11 curriculum as revised in 1996. Some material from my book Chemistry: Theory and Problems, Book One (McGraw–Hill Ryerson, 1980) has also been included, with permission.

This book has been designed for student use and field tested for several years. My students have found the notes and exercises included in this book to be of great use. The final form of this book was greatly influenced by the suggestions and comments of many students. It is hoped that this book will be of use to other teachers and students alike. When students miss a class, having to learn the material on their own is often a frustrating experience for both students and teacher. It is my hope that the notes, explanations and exercises in this book will make it easier to "catch up" (or to work ahead).

DISCLAIMER

The chemical laboratory has hazards, both expected and unexpected. This Workbook does not outline procedures for any chemical experiments. It is beyond the scope of this Workbook to identify specific laboratory hazards or provide protocols to avoid them. The information in this Workbook relating to the safe handling of chemicals, chemical solutions, chemistry equipment and safety equipment is intended to provide a general guide and background that fosters sound safety practices in the laboratory and is not a substitute for proper and specific classroom instruction in chemistry safety procedures. In every case, students must be properly supervised, trained in laboratory procedures and made aware of specific hazards in about-to-be-performed laboratory experiments.

ACKNOWLEDGEMENTS

The support, advice and encouragement of my wife, Frances, has played a major role in the creation of this book. Her continued suggestions and help with the entire project, from initial concept through to final editing, have made possible an otherwise almost impossible task.

The experienced advice, mentoring and friendship of Gordon Gore is greatly appreciated and acknowledged. His encouragement and humour were of enormous help in all stages of the preparation of this book. He truly defines the word "educator".

The cartoons in this book were drawn by the highly talented Ehren Stillman ("ZimBoBwe"), of Mission, B.C. The cartoons have enriched this book immeasurably and helped to illustrate the human side of chemistry.

The legions of students and teachers who gave me feedback and suggestions on earlier versions of this book are gratefully acknowledged.

COVER PHOTOGRAPH

Some of the main themes of Chemistry 11 are highlighted in the cover photograph. The molecular model shows the bonding in a diamond crystal. The combustion reaction is giving off heat and light and the broad leaves of the plant are engaged in photosynthesis while producing organic compounds. Photosynthesis is the reverse of a combustion reaction.

The design of the cover by Loren Phillips is gratefully acknowledged.

PERMISSIONS

Data from the tables

> Periodic Table of the Elements
> Standard Atomic Weights
> Physical Constants of Organic Compounds
> Physical Constants of Inorganic Compounds
> Conversion Factors
> Density of Various Solids
> Elements in Sea Water
> Enthalpy of Combustion of Selected Organic Compounds
> Strengths of Chemical Bonds
> Table of the Isotopes, and
> Ionization Potentials of Atoms and Atomic Ions

have been reprinted with permission from the "HandBook of Chemistry and Physics", 73rd edition, 1992. Copyright CRC Press, Boca Raton, Florida © 1992. Permission to use this data is gratefully acknowledged.

Permission to use some of the material in "Chemistry: Theory and Problems, Book One", has been granted by McGraw–Hill Ryerson Limited.

The permission of the British Columbia Ministry of Education, Skills and Training to use the layout of the Tables contained in the "Examinations and Assessment Branch Chemistry Data Booklet" is gratefully acknowledged.

The table "Electronegativities of the Elements" on page 200 is reproduced from L. Pauling, *The Nature of the Chemical Bond and the Structure of Molecules and Crystals*, Cornell University Press, Ithica, New York, 1960. Permission to use this table is gratefully acknowledged.

TABLE OF CONTENTS

UNIT V : THE MOLE CONCEPT

UNIT VI : CHEMICAL REACTIONS

UNIT VII : CALCULATIONS INVOLVING REACTIONS (STOICHIOMETRY)

UNIT VIII : ATOMS AND THE PERIODIC TABLE

UNIT IX : SOLUTION CHEMISTRY

UNIT X : ORGANIC CHEMISTRY

Answers

Glossary

Tables

Chemistry 11 is intended to give students an understanding of many principles of modern chemistry. Since not all students taking Chem 11 go on to take Chem 12, Chem 11 is a "survey course" which covers the "basics". Some of the topics are covered in previous science courses but the present course extends those topics and introduces many new ones. After completing Chem 11 you should be able to understand the chemistry underlying many of the natural processes around you, as well as much of what you read in magazines or newspapers.

Chemistry 11 also acts as a stepping stone to Chemistry 12 and beyond that to university or college science courses. One of the most enjoyable parts of Chem 11 is the laboratory work. You will be taught the proper procedures for working safely in the laboratory, for handling chemicals and for using specialized chemical equipment. Much of the pleasure of chemistry is found in the variety of colour changes you will see and the manner in which crystals grow, gases and solids suddenly form, and energy is given off or absorbed. In true experimental work, you should experience a sense of wonder, awe and surprise. Chemistry is fun!

UNIT I : SAFETY IN THE CHEMICAL LABORATORY

In Chemistry 11 you will be taught how to deal with chemicals and chemical equipment in a safe manner: compliance with all safety procedures will be strictly enforced. You will be shown how to use safety equipment and the emergency procedures to follow in the unlikely event of an accident. Then it will be up to you to work safely. Unsafe behavior and "fooling around" in a lab are not funny – they are STUPID and endanger your classmates and yourself.

Before each experiment you will be told the **special** precautions to be observed with the chemicals and equipment to be used. At all times, **general** safety procedures must be followed and you must know how to use the available protective and safety equipment.

In the event of **ANY** emergency, your teacher must be notified. However, it is not necessary to get your teacher's attention and permission **BEFORE** using emergency equipment; a quick yell as you go for the equipment will notify everyone that an emergency has arisen.

I.1. EMERGENCY EQUIPMENT

The following five pieces of equipment are only intended for use in the event of an emergency. STUDENTS DO NOT HAVE TO ASK PERMISSION TO USE ANY EMERGENCY EQUIPMENT, but must be prepared to justify why they used the equipment. Not all schools will necessarily have all the equipment listed.

> You should sketch a good map which includes your chemistry room, the surrounding hallways, the designated fire exit for the room, and the location where you are to assemble once the building is evacuated during a fire drill.

A. FIRE EXTINGUISHERS

Location:
> Indicate on your map the location of
> a) **all** the fire extinguishers in your laboratory.
> b) the closest fire extinguisher **outside** the laboratory.

When to use: Generally, your teacher will use the fire extinguisher, but if your teacher is absent temporarily or can't get to an extinguisher in time you may need to use it. If, in your opinion, the fire is uncontrolled and small enough to be put out with a fire extinguisher, use one. (Other students must immediately leave the room and someone must pull the fire alarm.) IF YOU DOUBT THAT THE FIRE IS SMALL ENOUGH THAT A FIRE EXTINGUISHER WILL DO THE JOB, quickly leave the room (someone should turn off the main gas supply for the room if that can be done safely), close the door behind you, pull the fire alarm and evacuate the building. Don't try to be a hero; fighting a substantial fire **MUST** be left to trained fire–fighters.

How to use: Take the extinguisher to the location of the fire, grab the extinguisher by the handle and yank the safety pin out of the side of the handle with a sharp pull.

   a) Small extinguishers
   - If the extinguisher has a fixed "horn", aim the horn at the **BASE** of the flames and pull the trigger, sweeping the spray back and forth over the area in flames.
   - If the extinguisher has a hose and nozzle secured to the extinguisher body by clips, remove the hose from the clips so that you can hold the extinguisher in one hand and direct the spray with the other. Aim the nozzle at the **BASE**

of the flame and pull the trigger, sweeping the spray back and forth over the area in flames.

b) Large extinguishers can be set on their base and their hose freed from the retaining clips, leaving both hands free to pull the trigger and direct the spray.

Time and distance of effectiveness: Large extinguishers will spray for about 20 s; smaller ones for about 10 s. You have to get within 4–5 m (12–15 ft) for the spray to be effective, so don't waste the extinguisher contents with "practice sprays" or spray from too far away.

Comments: Do not spray the contents of an extinguisher on a person! The spray from some types of extinguishers can instantly freeze flesh or drive powder into the eyes or lungs. (A fire blanket is used when a person's clothing or hair has caught fire.) The extinguishers available in a high school chemistry laboratory usually are "general purpose" ones which spray out powdered baking soda and can be used with the chemical, electrical and general fires which might occur.

B. FIRE BLANKET

Location: | Indicate on your map the location of the fire blanket in the lab. |

When to use: There are two possible situations where a fire blanket should be used.

a) A fire blanket should be used when a student's clothing or hair catches fire. The blanket must be used **very quickly** in order to minimize injury.

b) A fire blanket can be used to smother burning material on the floor or a bench, provided the fire can be approached with sufficient safety to allow the blanket to be placed over the entire area involved. Since both a blanket and extinguisher can be used on a small fire, use whichever one you can get to most quickly.

How to use: Pull the cord at the bottom of the fire blanket "tube" to get the blanket out.
- A student on fire must "stop, drop and roll". Throw the fire blanket over the student as soon as possible. Once the fire is out, remove any burned clothing (unless it has melted onto the skin). It is very important to get burned skin cooled as soon as possible.
- If there is a small fire on a lab bench or the floor, the fire blanket may be thrown carefully over the area involved in flames. Be careful not to knock over any beakers or flasks containing flammable materials if they are close to the flames.

Comments: A standing person burns like a candle ... but MUCH QUICKER. If you catch on fire, immediately drop to the floor and roll around. If you panic and run around, someone must get the fire blanket and wrap it around you, get you on the floor and roll you in the blanket until the fire is out. Sometimes it may be necessary to get you onto the floor and roll you around while the fire blanket is coming.

C. EYEWASH FOUNTAIN OR EYEWASH STATION

Location: | Indicate on your map the location of the eyewash fountain or eyewash station. |

When to use: The eyewash MUST be used any time a chemical or solution gets into eyes.

How to use: As soon as something gets in your eye, yell for help and **HURRY** to the eyewash; if you cannot see, yell for someone to help you.

a) **Use of an Eyewash Fountain:** Push the vertical paddle back with your hand and put your face down into the stream of water so that water strikes your eyes DIRECTLY. You **MUST** keep your eyes **OPEN** in the stream of water, blinking rapidly to help wash underneath the lids. Keep washing the eyes for at least 5 minutes, unless it is just a harmless substance (how do you know?); toward the end of this time the eyes may be sore just from the cold water, but pain is better than blindness. If you are panicking someone may have to hold your head in the fountain and help by giving you encouragement and reminders of what to do.

b) **Use of an Eyewash Bottle:** If possible, get to a sink so that water can be splashed up into your eyes. Then lie on your back so that the people administering first aid can slowly drip liquid from an eyewash bottle into the affected eye(s). This washing should continue for at least 10 minutes.

In all cases someone must call for help. If your teacher and/or medical aide deems it necessary, you will be prepared for transport to a medical facility.

Comments:

a) Contact lenses must be removed for proper cleaning. You may have to wash the "contacts" out if they can't be quickly "popped out". In general, do a quick preliminary wash, then pop out the contacts and wash thoroughly.

b) You have less than one second to get DILUTE acid or base out of your eyes before damage starts to occur — don't waste time getting to the eyewash. When you yell, **everyone** must get out of the way and move obstacles out of your way.

c) Medical treatment will usually be required to assess the extent of harm to your eyes.

d) If there is reason to suspect you have glass in your eyes as well as chemicals, the situation becomes complicated and more serious. If, while your eyes are being washed in the eyewash fountain or with the eyewash bottle, you feel a foreign object in your eyes, call for help. The first aid attendant may attempt to remove the object. If the object cannot be removed, both your eyes will be bandaged to prevent you from blinking and you will be transported on your back as soon as possible to a medical facility.

D. EMERGENCY SHOWER

Location: Indicate on your map the location of the emergency shower.

When to use: The shower is used when hazardous chemicals spray over large areas of the body.

How to use: There are two common types of emergency showers in use. One involves an overhead shower having a pull–ring, while the other is a hand–held shower with an on–off handle. Either stand under the shower head and pull down on the ring or turn the on–off handle and hold the shower head so as to spray water liberally over the affected area. If a hazardous liquid chemical or solution soaks into your clothing, the affected clothing **must** be removed after the washing process. Your teacher will discuss with you the procedures which must be followed to protect the modesty of students. Do not worry if water gets on the floor (but be careful not to slip). Any clothing removed should be thoroughly washed before being put on again. Someone may be able to assist with a change of clothing such as "gym" clothes.

E. ACID-BASE NEUTRALIZING SOLUTION

(This is not actually "equipment" but is a specialized solution to help control the harmful effects of certain accidents. There is no need to alert everyone in the room that you are using the solution.)

Location: Indicate on your map the location of the neutralizing solution.

When to use: Use this solution whenever an acidic or basic ("caustic") solution has come in contact with your skin. DO NOT USE IT IN YOUR EYES – use the eyewash if something gets in your eyes. If unsure as to whether a solution is acidic or basic, ask your teacher for instructions or use the neutralizing solution just to be safe. The solution usually consists of a dilute solution of sodium acetate and acetic acid ("vinegar"), and is more or less harmless to the skin for short periods of exposure.

How to use: First wash the affected area with large amounts of water and then pour some of the neutralizing solution on the affected area and gently wash the skin with the solution. If the skin felt slippery before applying the neutralizing solution, the chemical which contacted the skin was a base and prolonged washing of the skin must take place to help get all of the base removed: basic solutions tend to "eat their way" under the top layers of the skin. After washing with the neutralizing solution, continue to wash with warm soapy water.

SOME FINAL NOTES ON EMERGENCIES

a) Priorities

If more than one piece of equipment is needed or more than one problem has arisen, tend to the most serious problem first.
- a person on fire (immediately life–threatening), then
- a person with chemicals or glass in their eyes (threatens permanent blindness), then
- a person soaked with chemicals (harm to skin; generally a slower reaction due to natural protective oils on skin)

b) Sources of First–Aid Assistance

List the people trained to provide first aid in your school.

I.2. PROTECTIVE EQUIPMENT

The purpose of protective equipment is to protect you from the effects of hazardous chemicals or material BEFORE any problems arise.

A. SAFETY GOGGLES

Location: Indicate on your map where the safety goggles are stored.

When to use: Safety goggles **MUST** be used whenever chemicals are being used or glass–working is being performed. Goggles must be put on **PRIOR** to handling any chemicals or glass and must not be removed until **AFTER** you have disposed of or put away all chemicals or glass. **Putting on safety goggles at the start of a lab period MUST become an automatic reflex!**

How to use: Goggles must fit snugly; if a lens is loose or a strap is broken, get a replacement pair and give the defective pair to your teacher. Goggles must not simply be held on the face with a hand, moved up onto your forehead, or left to dangle around your neck.

B. FUME HOODS

Location: Indicate on your map the location of the fume hoods.

When to use: The fume hoods must be used whenever poisonous or offensive odours are being produced. At no time should such odours be allowed to enter the classroom. Do not carry a reaction mixture out of the fume hood to show your teacher or partner; instead ask them to come to the fume hood. Normally, the instructions for a experiment will specify the use of a fume hood, if required, as part of the procedure.

How to use: Learn where the On/Off buttons for the fume hood are located (they generally are below or beside the fume hoods). It is **NOT** necessary to pull down the sliding glass partition during usage; the hoods are supposed to have sufficient draft to keep fumes out of the room even when the sliding glass is fully up. The only time it should be necessary to pull down the glass is when a reaction may spatter out of its container or a strong draft is required to accelerate an evaporation process. If you pull down the glass and try to work with your hands extended under the glass your cramped movements may endanger you if something unexpected suddenly causes you to try to jerk your hands out.

I.3. IN CASE OF FIRE

a) The FIRST and most important thing to do is to back out of harm's way and evaluate the situation.

b) Next, warn the teacher and other students with a shout.

c) ***CONTROLLED FIRES***: If a fire is controlled, in the sense that it is contained in a beaker, flask or test tube, the fire can often be put out by placing a watch glass or inverted beaker over the top of the container and smothering the fire. **Be VERY careful not to spill the contents.** If unsure that you want to attempt such a maneuver, simply call for help. DO NOT PANIC – even if NOTHING is done the fire normally will burn itself out. If the fire involves a small amount of burning liquid on a benchtop and might take a minute or so to burn itself out, the fire blanket can be used carefully to smother the fire.

d) ***UNCONTROLLED FIRES***: If the fire is not minor and will possibly continue to spread, everyone must immediately evacuate the room except those who may be using a fire extinguisher. If possible, someone should turn off the main gas supply in the room. Also, someone must pull the fire alarm to start the evacuation of the building. The door must be left closed after the last person is out.

Important: Students **must** quickly go to the designated assembly point so that a roll call can be made to check that everyone has safely made it out of the building. You must NOT go elsewhere to "visit with friends" since your teacher is required to be know whether you are safely out of the building. Your whereabouts MUST be known so as to guarantee your life is not in danger!

I.4. SOME LABORATORY HAZARDS

	HAZARD	NATURE OF HAZARD	HOW TO DEAL WITH HAZARD
1.	Spilled chemicals	Chemical burns	Notify teacher for cleanup instructions, but keep away in the meantime.
2.	Broken glass	Cuts; chemicals in cuts	Notify teacher for cleanup instructions if chemicals are mixed with the glass. Otherwise, use broom / dustpan provided and put in special receptacle for broken glass.
3.	Burning chemicals in container	Burns	Step back and notify class, then deal with the fire as outlined above ("IN CASE OF FIRE; CONTROLLED FIRES").
4.	Chemicals on hands	Chemical burns; skin irritation or allergic reaction	Wash off immediately under fast–running water. Then use NEUTRALIZING SOLUTION if the chemicals are an acid, a base or have properties unknown to you.
5.	Being asked to smell chemical vapours	Strong odours may injure nasal passages	Holding the container in front of you, dilute the smell by gently "wafting" the odour to your nose with a wave of the hand over the container and toward the nose.
6.	Bunsen burners	Burns; fires	Tie long hair back or use elastics; don't keep burner gas on for more than a few seconds if burner won't start (seek help rather than filling the room with flammable gas).
7.	Loose hair or "floppy" clothing / accessories	Burns or chemical spillage; equip–ment knocked onto floor	Tie long hair back or use elastics; remove ties or tuck into shirt front; secure or remove loose clothing accessories such as scarves or dangling jewelry. Wide, loose sleeves should be secured at the wrist by an elastic.

I.5. DISPOSAL OF CHEMICALS

1. Disposal of Unused Chemicals

Never put unused chemicals back into their original containers! If you have taken too much of a chemical, ask if anyone else in your class can use it or ask your teacher for disposal instructions. Putting chemicals back into their original container poses two problems:
  • the chemical may be put in the wrong container, spoiling the chemicals or starting a reaction.
  • the chemicals may be contaminated by using glassware that was not perfectly clean and dry.

2. Disposal of Used Chemicals

You will be given instructions as to how to dispose of the chemicals used in each experiment. The sink or waste paper basket is NOT to be used unless so instructed. Many of the chemicals you will use are harmless to the environment, but some are extremely destructive. Let's take care, eh!

YOU DON'T NEED PERMISSION TO USE SAFETY EQUIPMENT

I.6. GENERAL RULES OF SAFE LABORATORY CONDUCT

1. There **MUST** be no horseplay in the lab.
2. There **MUST** be no running in the lab. Always look where you are going and don't turn around quickly; you may spill chemicals being carried by someone else. Notify people if you are passing behind them with a container of chemicals, so that they know not to make any sudden moves.
3. You must not carry out unauthorized experiments. For example, you must not mix chemicals in other than the way in which you were told.

To summarize: you must always have a "conscious safety attitude".

A "CONSCIOUS SAFETY ATTITUDE" means you should always think about the possible safety–related consequences of any action you are planning.

QUESTIONS:

1. What is the first thing you must do in each of the following situations?
   (a) A burning liquid spills on your clothing.
   (b) An unknown solution sprays into your eyes.
   (c) The chemical in a beaker on your lab bench catches fire.
   (d) A beaker full of liquid chemical falls onto the floor, breaking the beaker and spreading the chemical.
   (e) You get a few millilitres of acid or base on your hands.

2. You are having trouble getting a Bunsen burner to light and after 15 seconds the gas still won't ignite. What should you do at this point?

3. When using a fire extinguisher, where should you aim the spray?

4. How should you handle a controlled fire in the laboratory?

5. Why is it not necessary to ask permission before using emergency equipment?

6. How long will a small fire extinguisher continue to spray?

7. If a chemical sprays into a student's eyes and simultaneously a flaming liquid sprays on his clothes, what should be done first?

8. A beaker full of acid drops on the floor. In addition to the danger from getting acid on your hands, why shouldn't you attempt to pick up the pieces of glass with your hands?

Safety Notes:

UNIT II : INTRODUCTION TO CHEMISTRY

Before you learn how to make stinks and bangs in your chemistry lab, there are a few tiny little details to attend to ... such as how to read the scales on the equipment you will be using, how to handle the units used in Chemistry 11 and how to decide how good your data is. This unit gives you the background needed for the remainder of Chemistry 11.

II.1. UNIT CONVERSIONS

This section shows how to use a mathematical method called Unit Conversions which will be used extensively in Chemistry 11 and 12. Initially, you will be solving relatively easy problems. **Avoid the temptation to solve the problems by your own method; you should learn the Unit Conversion method.** OK, let's get on with the game.

If eggs are $\dfrac{\$1.44}{1\,doz}$, another way to say this is that eggs are $\dfrac{1\,doz}{\$1.44}$.

> The statement "$1.44 per dozen" allows us to RELATE or CONNECT one amount ($1.44) to another amount (1 dozen). Both
>
> $$\frac{\$1.44}{1\,doz} \quad \text{and} \quad \frac{\$1.44}{1\,doz}$$
>
> make the same connection implied by the statement:
>
> $$\$1.44 = 1\,doz$$
>
> where the "=" sign here is interpreted as "**IS EQUIVALENT TO**".

Definition: A **CONVERSION FACTOR** is a fractional expression relating or connecting two different units.

Examples:

STATEMENT FORM	CONVERSION FACTORS
1 min = 60 s	$\dfrac{1\ min}{60\ s}$ and $\dfrac{60\ s}{1\ min}$
$1 = 100 ¢	$\dfrac{\$1}{100\ ¢}$ and $\dfrac{100\ ¢}{\$1}$

Look at one of the conversion factors that relate "minutes" to "seconds".

$\dfrac{1\ min}{60\ s}$ → the TOP part
  EQUALS
  → the BOTTOM part

Dividing "1 min" by something **EQUAL TO** 1 min produces **a fraction with a value equal to "1"**. Multiplying any expression by this conversion factor is equivalent to multiplying by "1" and therefore WILL NOT CHANGE THE VALUE of the expression. The next example shows how a conversion factor is used.

EXAMPLE: **How many minutes are there in 3480 seconds?**

$$\text{\# of minutes} = 3480 \text{ s} \times \frac{1 \text{ min}}{60 \text{s}} = \textbf{58 min}$$

Both "60 s" and "1 min" are the same length of time (multiplying by the conversion factor didn't change the VALUE of the time). However, the units are different after using the conversion factor: the question starts with a *large number* of **SMALL** time units and ends up with a *small number* of **LARGE** time units.

The method of unit conversions uses conversion factors to change the units associated with an expression to a different set of units.

Every unit conversion problem has three major pieces of information which must be identified:
   i)   the unknown amount and its UNITS,
   ii)   the initial amount and its UNITS, and
   iii)   a conversion factor which relates or connects the initial UNITS to the UNITS of the unknown.

INCREDIBLY, VITALLY IMPORTANT NOTE!

In all the calculations which follow you must **ALWAYS** include the units, for they are the "major players" in the calculation. If you are tempted to omit or "forget about" the units, DON'T! The course you fail could be Chem 11!

EXAMPLES: a)   **What is the cost of 2 doz eggs if eggs are $1.44/doz?**

The first thing to do is tear this problem apart and analyze the information it contains.

What is the cost	of 2 doz eggs	if eggs are $1.44/doz
UNKNOWN AMOUNT	INITIAL AMOUNT	CONVERSION STATEMENT

The **UNKNOWN AMOUNT** and its **UNIT:**
- The unknown is identified in *the phrase which asks the question*. In this problem the UNKNOWN is the "cost".
- Since the only unit of "cost" mentioned in the problem is **dollars** ($1.44/doz), use this unit with the unknown amount.

         UNKNOWN AMOUNT = # of dollars

The **INITIAL AMOUNT** and its **UNIT:**
- It is in a PHRASE CONNECTED OR DIRECTLY RELATED TO THE PHRASE CONTAINING THE UNKNOWN — "What is the cost *of* 2 doz eggs ...". Notice that in this case the word "of" connects the unknown amount to the initial amount.
- It is a number with a **SINGLE UNIT** ("doz"). The only other number mentioned, $1.44/doz, involves two units.

         INITIAL AMOUNT = 2 doz

The **CONVERSION STATEMENT:**
- involves TWO DIFFERENT UNITS ("$" and "doz"), AND
- is a separate statement which does not involve a question.

The conversion statement gives the information needed to make the conversion factor. The possible conversion factors are

$$\frac{\$1.44}{1 \text{doz}} \quad \text{and} \quad \frac{\$1.44}{1 \text{doz}} \ .$$

PUTTING EVERYTHING TOGETHER completes the unit conversion. (If you follow what happens here, fine. Otherwise, don't worry; you will be shown how to "put everything together" next.)

$$\text{\# of dollars} = 2 \ \cancel{doz} \times \frac{\$1.44}{1 \ \cancel{doz}} = \$2.88$$

Notice that the unit "doz" cancels

b) If a car can go 80 km in 1 h, how far can the car go in 8.5 h?

Again, dissect the sentence.

If a car can go 80 km in 1 h,	how far can the car go	in 8.5 h?
CONVERSION STATEMENT	UNKNOWN AMOUNT	INITIAL AMOUNT

The **UNKNOWN AMOUNT and its UNIT:** The part of the sentence which asks the question ("how far can the car go") implies that the unknown is a distance. Since the only unit of distance mentioned is "km" ("80 **km** in one hour"), use this as the distance unit.

UNKNOWN AMOUNT = # of kilometres

The **INITIAL AMOUNT and its UNIT:** The initial amount, 8.5 h, is connected directly to the unknown — "how far can the car go **in** 8.5 h" — and has a single unit ("h").

INITIAL AMOUNT = 8.5 h

The **CONVERSION STATEMENT:** This statement is recognized because it
  • makes a statement involving a number with no question asked or implied, AND
  • mentions two different units (km and h).
The possible conversion factors are

$$\frac{80 \ km}{1 \ h} \quad \text{and} \quad \frac{1 \ h}{80 \ km} \ .$$

PUTTING EVERYTHING TOGETHER in a complete unit conversion:

$$\text{\# of kilometers} = 8.5 \ \cancel{h} \times \frac{80 \ km}{1 \ \cancel{h}} = \textbf{680 km} \ .$$

Again, note that the unit "h" cancels.

EXERCISE:

1. For each of the following problem statements identify   • the unknown amount and its unit,
                                                            • the initial amount and its unit, and
                                                            • the conversion factors and their units.
    (You aren't required to put everything together and solve the problem yet ... that comes next.)

    a) If a chemical costs $50 per gram, what is the cost of 100 g of the chemical?
    b) Computer disks cost $6.00 for 10 disks. How many disks can you buy for $36.00?
    c) Cork has a density of 0.35 g/mL. What is the volume of 20 g of cork?
    d) If 3 kiwi fruit sell for $1, how many kiwi fruit can you buy for $5?
    e) If 4 bims are worth 5 tuds, how many bims can you buy for 30 tuds?
    f) A farmer trades 2 cows for 7 goats. At this rate, how many goats can he get for 10 cows?
    g) One mole of oxygen has a mass of 32 g. What is the mass of 5.5 moles of oxygen?
    h) One molecule of sulphur contains 8 sulphur atoms. How many sulphur molecules can be made from 104 sulphur atoms?
    i) How long must an electrical current of 35 coulombs/s flow in order to deliver 200 coulombs?
    j) What temperature increase is caused by 100 kJ of heat if 4.18 kJ of heat causes a $1^{\circ}C$ increase in temperature?

HOW TO PUT EVERYTHING TOGETHER

The method of unit conversions may seem a little awkward at first, but later it will allow you to solve some complicated problems **in one line. Also, it is "SELF–CHECKING", allowing you to check the "correctness" of your results**!

The general form of a unit conversion calculation is shown below.

> **(UNKNOWN AMOUNT) = (INITIAL AMOUNT) X (CONVERSION FACTOR)**

EXAMPLES: a) **If 0.200 mL of gold has a mass of 3.86 g, what is the mass of 5.00 mL of gold?**

The **UNKNOWN AMOUNT and its UNIT:** The question asks "What is the mass", which suggests finding "# of grams".

The **INITIAL AMOUNT and its UNIT** is "5.00 mL", which is tied to the unknown amount ("What is the mass") by the connector "of".

The **CONVERSION STATEMENT** is "If 0.200 mL of gold has a mass of 3.86 g". The amounts being connected are   0.200 mL and 3.86 g.

Now to solve the problem. Put the **unknown amount** on the **left** side of an "=" sign to identify what you are trying to find.

> # of grams =

Then put the **initial amount and unit** on the **right** side of the "=" sign.

> # of grams = 5.00 mL

Next multiply the initial value by a conversion factor. Construct the conversion factor from the conversion statement as follows.

The conversion statement connects "0.200 mL" and "3.86 g"; possible conversion factors are

$$\frac{0.200 \text{ mL}}{3.86 \text{ g}} \quad \text{and} \quad \frac{3.86 \text{ g}}{0.200 \text{ mL}} .$$

Use the conversion factor which has "0.200 mL" on the bottom. **THE PURPOSE OF PLACING "0.200 mL" ON THE BOTTOM OF THE FRACTION IS TO ALLOW THE UNIT "mL" TO** *CANCEL*.

$$\text{\# of grams} = 5.00 \text{ mL} \times \frac{3.86 \text{ g}}{0.200 \text{ mL}}$$

Finally, carry out the multiplication and finish the problem.

$$\text{\# of grams} = 5.00 \text{ mL} \times \frac{3.86 \text{ g}}{0.200 \text{ mL}} = \textbf{96.5 g}$$

This problem started with the unit "mL" and eventually **converted** to the unit "g"; hence the term "***Unit Conversion***". To show that everything has been done properly, notice that the procedure started with "# of grams" on the left, and found 96.5 g as an answer.

The conversion statement allows you to make two possible conversion factors:

$$\frac{0.200 \text{ mL}}{3.86 \text{ g}} \quad \text{and} \quad \frac{3.86 \text{ g}}{0.200 \text{ mL}} .$$

The required conversion factor was BUILT by arranging the fraction in such a way as to cancel the initial unit "mL". If the other conversion factor had been used (that is, the fraction was built upside–down), the calculation would have given:

$$\text{\# of grams} = 5.00 \text{ mL} \times \frac{0.200 \text{ mL}}{3.86 \text{ g}} = 0.259 \frac{(\text{mL})^2}{\text{g}} = \text{a mess!!!}$$

Therefore, whenever you multiply the initial value by a conversion factor you have to ask yourself:

> "WHICH WAY DO I HAVE TO WRITE THE CONVERSION FACTOR IN ORDER TO ALLOW THE INITIAL UNITS TO CANCEL PROPERLY?"

b) If 0.200 mL of gold has a mass of 3.86 g, what is the volume occupied by 100.0 g of gold?

The **UNKNOWN AMOUNT and its UNIT:** The question asks "what is the volume", which suggests finding "# of millilitres".

The **INITIAL AMOUNT and its UNIT** are "100.0 g", which is tied to the unknown amount ("what is the volume") by the connector "occupied by".

As in the previous example, the **CONVERSION STATEMENT** is "If 0.200 mL of gold has a mass of 3.86 g". The amounts being connected are 0.200 mL and 3.86 g.

Now to solve the problem. Start with the **unknown amount** on the **left** side of an "=" sign.

$$\text{\# of millilitres} =$$

Then put the **initial amount and unit** on the **right** side of the "=" sign.

$$\text{\# of millilitres} = 100.0 \text{ g}$$

Construct a conversion factor from the conversion statement such that the starting unit "g" is cancelled by having "3.86 g" on the bottom.

$$\text{\# of milliliters} = 100.0 \text{ g} \times \frac{0.200 \text{ mL}}{3.86 \text{ g}}$$

Finally, carry out the multiplication and finish the problem:

$$\text{\# of milliliters} = 100.0 \text{ g} \times \frac{0.200 \text{ mL}}{3.86 \text{ g}} = \textbf{5.18 mL}$$

Again, notice that the problem tried to find "# of millilitres" and found 5.18 mL as an answer. Also, note that the conversion factor used in this problem, 0.200 mL/3.86 g, was the inverse of the conversion factor used in the problem above, 3.86 g/0.200 mL. **The way the conversion factor is used depends on which unit is to be cancelled.**

SUMMARY OF THE PROCEDURE TO BE USED WITH UNIT CONVERSIONS

1. Identify the unknown amount and its unit. Write these down on the left–hand side of an "=" sign.

2. Identify the initial amount and its unit. Write these down on the right–hand side of the "=" sign.

3. Identify the conversion factor. Multiply the initial amount by the conversion factor in such a way that one of the units in the conversion factor cancels the unit of the initial amount.

4. Complete the problem by multiplying and/or dividing the amounts on the right–hand side.

EXERCISE:

2. Solve the following using the method of unit conversions.

    a) If there are 6.02×10^{23} atoms in 1 mol of atoms, how many atoms are there in 5.5 mol of atoms?

    b) If one mole of a gas has a volume of 22.4 L, how many moles are there in 25.0 L of gas?

    c) If one mole of nitrogen has a mass of 28 g, how many moles of nitrogen gas are in 7.0 g of nitrogen gas?

    d) How many seconds must an electrical current of 35 coulombs/s flow in order to deliver 200.0 coulombs?

    e) A quiet sound exerts a pressure of 4×10^{-8} kPa ("kPa" = kilopascals, an SI pressure unit). What is this pressure in atmospheres if 1 atmosphere is 101.3 kPa?

    f) A large nugget of naturally occurring silver metal has a mass of 3.20×10^4 troy ounces. What is the mass in kilograms if 1 troy ounce is equivalent to 0.0311 kg?

    g) A reaction is essentially complete in 5.0×10^{-4} s. If one millisecond (1 ms) equals 10^{-3} s, how many milliseconds does the reaction take?

    h) If 1 mol of octane produces 5450 kJ of heat when burned, how many moles of octane must be burned to produce 15 100 kJ of heat?

    i) Our fingers can detect a movement of 0.05 micron. If 1 micron is 10^{-3} mm, what is this movement expressed in millimetres (mm)?

    j) If concentrated hydrochloric acid has a concentration of 11.7 mol/L, what volume of hydrochloric acid is required in order to have 0.0358 mol of hydrochloric acid?

MULTIPLE UNIT CONVERSIONS

So far, hopefully, so good. All of the problems above involve a single conversion factor, which leads to the question "What happens when there is *more than one* conversion factor involved in a problem?" In fact, you have already run into such problems in everyday life if you have ever tried to solve a problem such as "How many seconds are there in 1 day?" Consider the following examples.

EXAMPLES: **(a) If eggs are $1.44/doz, and if there are 12 eggs/doz, how many individual eggs can be bought for $4.32?**

Analyzing this problem —

The UNKNOWN AMOUNT is "how many individual eggs can be bought".

The INITIAL AMOUNT is $4.32.

There are two conversion statements: "eggs are $1.44/doz", and
                                        "there are 12 eggs/doz".

The overall connection which is required is   **($) ⟶ (eggs).**

The first conversion statement, $1.44 = 1 doz, makes the connection

($) ⟶ (doz) .

The second conversion statement, 12 eggs = 1 doz, makes the connection

(doz) ⟶ (eggs) .

Combining the conversion statements gives the overall connection

($) ⟶ (doz) ⟶ (eggs)

which is the connection required (in bold, above).

To start, set up the problem as usual.

# of eggs = $4.32

Now, apply the first conversion factor, which cancels the unit "$".

$$\text{\# of eggs} = \$4.32 \times \frac{1\,doz}{\$1.44}$$

So far, cancelling the unit "$" on the right side leaves the unit "doz". The unit change
($) ⟶ (doz) is accomplished. Now apply the second conversion factor, which cancels
the unit "doz" and accomplishes the unit change (doz) ⟶ (eggs).

$$\text{\# of eggs} = \$4.32 \times \frac{1\,\cancel{doz}}{\$1.44} \times \frac{12\,eggs}{1\,\cancel{doz}} = \textbf{36 eggs}$$

Notice that both the units "$" and "doz" are cancelled.

(b) **The automobile gas tank of a Canadian tourist holds 39.5 L of gas. If 1 L of gas is
equal to 0.264 gal in the United States ("gal" is the symbol for "gallon", a measure
of volume used in the U.S.), and gas is $1.26/gal in Dallas, Texas, how much will it
cost the tourist to fill his gas tank in Dallas?**

UNKNOWN AMOUNT = # of dollars

INITIAL AMOUNT = 39.5 L

Required connection: (L) ⟶ ($)

Conversion statements available: 1 L = 0.264 gal   and   1 gal = $1.26

Connections available through the conversion statements:

(L) ⟶ (gal)   and   (gal) ⟶ ($)

Using the conversion statements together gives the required overall connection.

(L) ⟶ (gal) ⟶ ($)

Using both conversion statements solves the problem. One statement, 1 L = 0.264 gal,
allows the cancelling of the initial unit, "L". The other statement, 1 gal = $1.26, allows the
cancelling of the unit "gal" which was introduced by the first conversion factor.

$$\text{\# of dollars} = 3.95\,\cancel{L} \times \frac{0.264\,gal}{1\,\cancel{L}} \times \frac{\$1.26}{1\,gal} = \textbf{\$13.1}$$

At the end, the units "L" and "gal" have been cancelled, leaving the required unit, "$".

EXERCISES:

3. An old barometer hanging on the wall of a mountain hut has a reading of 27.0 inches of mercury.
    If 1 inch of mercury equals 0.0334 atm ("atmospheres") and 1 atm = 101.3 kPa ("kilopascals"), what is
    the pressure reading of the barometer, in kilopascals?

4. It requires 334 kJ of heat to melt 1 kg of ice.
    (a) The largest known iceberg had a volume of about 3.1×10^{13} m^3. How much heat was
        required to melt the iceberg if 1 m^3 of ice has a mass of 917 kg?
    (b) The explosive "TNT" releases 1.51×10^4 kJ of energy for every kilogram of TNT which
        explodes. Provided that all the energy of an explosion went into melting the ice, how many
        kilograms of TNT would be needed to melt the iceberg in part (a) of this question?

5. Sugar costs $0.980/kg. 1 t = 1000 kg. How many tonnes ("t") of sugar can you buy for $350?

6. The Cullinan diamond, the largest diamond ever found, had an uncut volume of 177 mL. If 1 mL of
    diamond has a mass of 3.51 g and 1 carat = 0.200 g, how many carats was the Cullinan diamond?

7. How many kilometres ("km") will a car travelling at 120 km/h go in: (a) 0.25 h?   (b) 12 min?

8. Solve the following, using the fact that beakers cost $8.40 per dozen.
   (a) Harry drops 3 dozen beakers. How much will the Chemistry teacher charge Harry?
   (b) Harry drops another 5 dozen beakers (clumsy!). If Burger Bob's hamburgers cost $1.50 each, how many hamburgers could clumsy Harry have bought for the same amount of money as he has to pay for the second batch of beakers?
   (c) Harry does not learn very quickly, and breaks a third batch of beakers. If he has to pay $13.30, what is the number of beakers he breaks the third time? (Express your answer in actual numbers of beakers, rather than in "dozens of beakers".)

9. An ancient Celtic chicken farmer wished to purchase a gift for his wife. The gift was worth 2 horses. At the local market, 3 horses were worth 5 cows, 1 cow was worth 4 hogs, 3 hogs were worth 4 goats, and 1 goat cost 9 chickens. How much was the gift going to cost the farmer, who had to pay in chickens?

10. If 1 yard = 3 feet, 1 foot = 12 inches and 1 centimetre = 0.3937 inch, how many centimetres are there in 5 yards?

In addition to the above, there is a specialized type of unit conversion which you must be able to perform: METRIC CONVERSIONS. Before starting on these conversions, let's review metric usage.

II.2. SI UNITS

The International System (SI) of metric units has numerous "base units", although only a few are used in Chemistry 11. A "base unit" is a basic unit of measurement; all other units are multiples of the base units, or combinations of base units.

A. SOME SELECTED BASE UNITS IN THE INTERNATIONAL SYSTEM (SI)

Quantity	Written Unit	Unit Symbol
length	metre	m
mass	gram *	g *
time	second	s
amount of substance	mole	mol

  * The actual base unit for mass in the SI system is the kilogram (kg), which is an inconsistent base unit, but for the purposes of Chemistry 11 the gram (g) is considered to be the base unit.

B. SOME ADDITIONAL UNITS USED

Quantity	Written Unit	Unit Symbol
volume	litre	L
mass	tonne	t

C. MULTIPLES OF BASE UNITS

Written Prefix	Prefix symbol	Equivalent exponential
mega	M	10^6
* kilo	K	10^3
deci	D	10^{-1}
* centi	C	10^{-2}
* milli	M	10^{-3}
micro	μ	10^{-6}

(The prefixes preceded by a "*" are those used most frequently in Chemistry 11.)

D. SOME IMPORTANT EQUIVALENCES

$$1 \text{ mL} = 1 \text{ cm}^3$$
$$1 \text{ m}^3 = 10^3 \text{ L}$$
$$1 \text{ t} = 10^3 \text{ kg}$$

EXAMPLES: (a) Re–write the expression "5 kilograms" using
   • PREFIX and UNIT SYMBOLS, and
   • an EXPONENTIAL EQUIVALENT.

The **prefix symbol** which stands for "kilo" is "k" and the **unit symbol** which stands for "grams" is "g".

Therefore: 5 kilograms = 5 kg.

The **exponential equivalent** of "kilo" and "k" is "10^3"

Therefore: 5 kilograms = 5×10^3 g.

(b) Re–write the expression "2 ms" using
   • a WRITTEN PREFIX and UNIT, and
   • an EXPONENTIAL EQUIVALENT.

The **written prefix** which is equivalent to "m" is "milli" and the **written unit** which is equivalent to "s" is "seconds".

Therefore: 2 ms = 2 milliseconds.

The **exponential equivalent** of "milli" and "m" is "10^{-3}"

Therefore: 2 ms = 2×10^{-3} s.

(c) Re–write the expression "2.7×10^{-2} m" using
   • a WRITTEN PREFIX and UNIT, and
   • a PREFIX SYMBOL .

The **written prefix** equivalent to "10^{-2}" is "centi", and the **written unit** which is equivalent to "m" is "metres".

Therefore: 2.7×10^{-2} m = 2.7 centimetres.

The **prefix symbol** which stands for "10^{-2}" is "c"

Therefore: 2.7×10^{-2} m = 2.7 cm.

The following multiples are used very infrequently and do not have to be memorized. They are only included for the purpose of completeness. (Like, you never can tell when they might come in handy.)

Written Prefix	Prefix symbol	Equivalent exponential
yotta	Y	10^{24}
zetta	Z	10^{21}
exa	E	10^{18}
peta	P	10^{15}
tera	T	10^{12}
giga	G	10^{9}
hecto	h	10^{2}
deka	da	10^{1}
nano	n	10^{-9}
pico	p	10^{-12}
femto	f	10^{-15}
atto	a	10^{-18}
zepto	z	10^{-21}
yocto	y	10^{-24}

EXERCISES:

11. Re–write the following using PREFIX and UNIT SYMBOLS, and EXPONENTIAL EQUIVALENTS.

(a) 2.5 centimetres   (c) 25.2 millimoles   (e) 0.25 megalitres
(b) 1.3 kilograms   (d) 5.1 decigrams   (f) 6.38 micrograms

12. Re–write the following using WRITTEN PREFIXES and UNITS, and EXPONENTIAL EQUIVALENTS.

(a) 2.5 mm   (c) 1.9 kmol   (e) 9.94 cg
(b) 6.5 dL   (d) 4 Mt   (f) 1.25 μs

13. Re–write the following using PREFIX SYMBOLS, and WRITTEN PREFIXES and UNITS.

(a) 4.5×10^{-3} mol   (c) 0.50×10^{-6} L   (e) 8.85×10^{6} t
(b) 1.6×10^{3} m   (d) 2.68×10^{-1} g   (f) 7.25×10^{-2} m

14. Express   (a) 50 cm^3 in millilitres   (b) 22.5 t in kilograms   (c) 0.125 m^3 in litres

II.3. METRIC CONVERSIONS

Metric conversions involve using unit conversions between prefix symbols and exponential equivalents.

EXAMPLES: (a) Write a conversion statement between **cm** and **m.**

Since "c" stands for "10^{-2}" then   1 cm = 10^{-2} m.

(b) Write a conversion statement between **ms** and **s.**

Since "m" stands for "10^{-3}" then   1 ms = 10^{-3} s.

EXERCISE:

15. Write conversion statements between each of the following.

(a) kg and g   (d) dm and m   (g) kL and L   (j) cL and L
(b) Mm and m   (e) cs and s   (h) μs and s   (k) dmol and mol
(c) μL and L   (f) mmol and mol   (i) Mg and g   (l) mg and g

EXAMPLE: **How many micrometres are there in 5 cm?**

Unknown amount = # of μm

Initial amount = 5 cm

You can write your own conversion statements between μm and m, and cm and m because the prefixes **micro** (μ) and **centi** (c) are mentioned in the problem statement.

1 μm = 10^{-6} m   These statements can be combined to make the connections below.
1 cm = 10^{-2} m   (μm) $\longrightarrow$ (m) $\longrightarrow$ (cm)

The conversion is now straightforward.

$$\# \text{ of } \mu m = 5 \text{ cm} \times \frac{10^{-2} \text{ m}}{1 \text{cm}} \times \frac{1 \mu m}{10^{-6} \text{ m}} = \mathbf{5 \times 10^4 \; \mu m}$$

The diagram below shows the manner in which a given base unit (for example, meters) is related to the important prefix symbols.

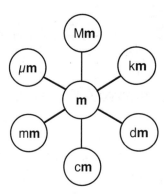

As can be seen, all the prefix symbols are directly related to the "central" base unit. (The central unit "m" also could be any other base unit such as g, s or mol.) In order to connect any two metric prefixes, first connect the initial prefix symbol to the base unit and then connect the base unit to the prefix symbol of the unknown.

EXAMPLE: **Express 8 kg in milligrams.**

Unknown amount = # of mg

Initial amount = 8 kg

Since the prefix symbols "k" (kilo) and "m" (milli) are mentioned in the problem statement, write down the conversion statements.

$1 \text{ kg} = 10^3 \text{ g}$ These statements can be combined to make the connections below.
$1 \text{ mg} = 10^{-3} \text{ g}$ (kg) $\longrightarrow$ (g) $\longrightarrow$ (mg)

Carry out the conversion.

$$\# \text{ of mg} = 8 \text{ kg} \times \frac{10^3 \text{ g}}{1 \text{kg}} \times \frac{1 \text{mg}}{10^{-3} \text{ g}} = 8 \times 10^6 \text{ mg}$$

EXAMPLE: **Express 5 Mg/mL in kilograms/litre.**

Unknown amount = # of $\dfrac{\text{kg}}{\text{L}}$

Initial amount = $\dfrac{5 \text{ Mg}}{\text{mL}}$

This problem requires the conversion of both the numerator and the denominator. Again, write conversion statements for each metric prefix mentioned.

$1 \text{ kg} = 10^3 \text{ g}$
$1 \text{ Mg} = 10^6 \text{ g}$
$1 \text{ mL} = 10^{-3} \text{ L}$

Treat the top and bottom of the initial fraction separately.

- to convert the top: (Mg) $\longrightarrow$ (g) $\longrightarrow$ (kg)
- to convert the bottom: (mL) $\longrightarrow$ (L)

Depending on how comfortable you are with conversion factors, you can carry out the overall conversion in two ways.

a) **The 3–step method**:

   1st: Convert the top (ignoring the bottom).

$$\text{\# of kg} = 5\ Mg \times \frac{10^6\ g}{1\,Mg} \times \frac{1\,kg}{10^3\ g} = 5 \times 10^3\ kg$$

   2nd: Convert the bottom (ignoring the top).

$$\text{\# of L} = 1\ mL \times \frac{10^{-3}\ L}{1\ mL} = 1 \times 10^{-3}\ L$$

   3rd: Divide the converted top amount by the converted bottom amount.

$$\text{\# of}\ \frac{kg}{L} = \frac{5 \times 10^3\ kg}{1 \times 10^{-3}\ L} = 5 \times 10^6\ \frac{kg}{L}$$

b) **The 1–step method**:   Simply convert the top and then the bottom (or vice versa), applying all the conversion factors one after another.

   • arbitrarily, first convert **Mg** to **g** : $\text{\# of}\ \dfrac{kg}{L} = \dfrac{5\,Mg}{1\ mL} \times \dfrac{10^6\ g}{1\,Mg}$

   • then immediately convert **g** to **kg** : $\text{\# of}\ \dfrac{kg}{L} = \dfrac{5\,Mg}{1\ mL} \times \dfrac{10^6\ g}{1\,Mg} \times \dfrac{1\,kg}{10^3\ g}$

   • then convert the BOTTOM by cancelling the **mL** on the bottom of the initial amount with **mL** in the top of a final conversion factor

$$\text{\# of}\ \frac{kg}{L} = \frac{5\,Mg}{1\ mL} \times \frac{10^6\ g}{1\,Mg} \times \frac{1\,kg}{10^3\ g} \times \frac{1\ mL}{10^{-3}\ L} = \mathbf{5 \times 10^6\ \frac{kg}{L}}$$

Sneaky Short–Cut

   Situations which simply require changing from prefix symbol form to base unit form can use a direct substitution of the exponential equivalent for the prefix symbol. This procedure helps to eliminate writing one conversion factor in longer problems.

   EXAMPLE: If aluminum is worth $0.00116/g, what is the cost of 725 kg of aluminum?

$$\text{\# of dollars} = 725 \times 10^3\ g \times \frac{\$0.00116}{g} = \mathbf{\$870}$$

   "725 kg" is simply written as "725 x 10^3 g", eliminating the conversion factor $\dfrac{10^3\ g}{1\ kg}$.

EXERCISES:

16. (a) If 1 mg = 10^{-3} g and 1 Mg = 10^6 g, how many milligrams are there in 0.25 Mg?
   (b) If 1 μs = 10^{-6} s and 1 cs = 10^{-2} s, how many centiseconds are there in 10 μs?
   (c) If 1 mm = 10^{-3} m and 1 cm = 10^{-2} m, how many millimetres are there in 15.8 cm?
   (d) If 1 kg = 10^3 g and 1 mg = 10^{-3} g, how many kilograms are there in 250 mg?
   (e) If 1 dL = 10^{-1} L and 1 kL = 10^3 L, how many decilitres are there in 0.5 kL?

17. Convert the following

(a) 3 s into milliseconds	(f) 2 L into decilitres	(k) 1 year into seconds
(b) 50.0 mL into litres	(g) 7 μs into milliseconds	(l) 1 mg/dL into grams per litre
(c) 2 L into microlitres	(h) 51 kg into milligrams	(m) 1 cm/μs into kilometres/second
(d) 25 kg into grams	(i) 3125 μL into kilolitres	(n) 1 cg/mL into decigrams/litre
(e) 3 Mm into metres	(j) 1.7 μg into centigrams	(o) 5 cg/ds into milligrams/second

18. Light travels at a rate of 3.00×10^8 m/s.

    (a) It takes light 8.3 min to travel from the surface of the sun to the earth. What is the distance of the earth from the sun?

    (b) The moon is 3.8×10^5 km from the earth. What time will pass between the instant an astronaut on the moon speaks and the instant his voice is heard on earth? (His voice travels by modulated laser beam at the speed of light.)

    (c) A robot vehicle is travelling on the surface of Mars while Mars and Earth are at their closest approach (7.83×10^7 km). Suddenly, a video camera on the robot shows a yawning crevasse dead ahead! How many minutes will it take for an electronic signal travelling at the speed of light to go from Earth to Mars in order to tell the robot to stop immediately?

19. (Care: Nasty!) A measurement is given as 9.0 lb/in^3. If 1 kg = 2.2 lb and 1 m = 39 in, convert the measurement into kg/m^3.

OPTIONAL EXERCISES:

20. If sugar is $9.80 for 10 kg, what is the cost of: (a) 90.0 kg of sugar?   (b) 6.00 tonnes of sugar?

21. If 1 inch = 2.54 cm, what is the length, in centimetres, of a 20.0 inch rod? What is the length, in metres, of a 36 inch ruler?

22. Express 90 μg in centigrams.

23. A car travels at a constant speed of 105 km/h.
    (a) How many hours does it take to go 450 km?
    (b) How many seconds does it take to go 2.0×10^2 m?
    (c) How many kilometres are traveled in 10.0 min?
    (d) How many centimetres are traveled in 1.00 ms?

24. If 1 L of granite has a mass of 5.50 kg,
    (a) what is the mass of 7.00 L of granite?
    (b) what is the volume occupied by 22 kg of granite?
    (c) what is the mass, in grams, of 5.00 mL of granite?

25. The SI unit of energy is the joule (unit symbol = J). If 0.334 kJ of energy is required to melt 1.00 g of ice and 1 kJ = 1000 J then:
    (a) what mass of ice can be melted by 10.0 kJ of heat?
    (b) how many kilojoules of heat are required to melt 50.0 g of ice?
    (c) how many joules of heat are required to melt 2.00 kg of ice?

26. Express 80.0 Mg in micrograms.

27. Express 2 cL/ms in kilolitres/second.

28. Express 50.0 mL/min in microlitres/second.

DERIVED QUANTITIES

Definitions: A **DERIVED QUANTITY** is a number made by combining two or more other values.

A **DERIVED UNIT** is a unit which is made by combining two or more other units.

EXAMPLE: The heat change occurring when the temperature of a water sample increases is given by

$$\Delta H = c \cdot m \cdot \Delta T$$

where: ΔH = the change in heat ; "Δ" is the Greek letter "delta" and is used to indicate "the change in" (ΔH is measured in joules, **J**).

m = the mass of water being heated (measured in grams, **g**),

ΔT = the temperature change of the water (measured in degrees Celsius, $^\circ$**C**)

and c = a derived quantity called the specific heat capacity, which can be calculated by rearranging the above equation.

$$c = \frac{\Delta H}{m \cdot \Delta T}$$

The units of **c** are derived by substituting the units of each symbol into the equation. For example, using the values: $\Delta H = 4.02 \times 10^4$ J , $m = 175$ g   and $\Delta T = 55.0^\circ$C   gives

$$c = \frac{4.02 \times 10^4 \text{ J}}{175 \text{ g} \times 55.0^\circ\text{C}} = 4.18 \ \frac{\text{J}}{\text{g} \cdot ^\circ\text{C}} \ .$$

Therefore, **c** is a **derived quantity**, having **derived units**, found by combining three other quantities (ΔH, m and ΔT) and their units.

EXERCISE:

29. Find the derived value and units for

(a) the molar concentration, **c**, using the equation $c = \dfrac{n}{V}$,

where: $n = 0.250$ mol   and $V = 0.500$ L.

(b) the Universal Gas Constant, **R**, using the equation $R = \dfrac{P \cdot V}{n \cdot T}$,

i) where $P = 1$ atm, $V = 22.4$ L, $n = 1$ mol   and $T = 273$ K   (K is the temperature on the Kelvin scale).

ii) where $P = 202.6$ kPa, $V = 24.45$ L, $n = 2$ mol   and $T = 298$ K.

(c) the entropy change for the boiling of water , Δ**S**, using the equation $\Delta H = T \cdot \Delta S$,

where: $\Delta H = 44.0$ kJ   and $T = 373$ K. (Hint: you will have to rearrange the equation first.)

(d) the kinetic energy of hydrogen gas at 0°C, **KE**, using the equation $KE = \frac{1}{2} m \cdot v^2$,

where: $m = 3.35 \times 10^{-27}$ kg   and $v = 1692 \ \dfrac{\text{m}}{\text{s}}$.

II.4. DENSITY

Definitions: **Mass** = the quantity of matter in an object

Density = the mass contained in a given volume of a substance

In other words, density is mass divided by volume.

$$d = \frac{m}{V}$$

where: d = the density
m = the mass
V = the volume

EXERCISE:

30.   If "m" is measured in grams, and "V" is measured in litres, what are the units of "d"?

Density calculations involve direct substitution of information into the density equation, after rearranging the equation to solve for the unknown.

EXAMPLES: (a) **An iron bar has a mass of 19 600 g and a volume of 2.50 L. What is the iron's density?**

Substitute the given values into the density equation.

$$d = \frac{m}{V} = \frac{19600g}{2.50L} = \textbf{7.84 x 10}^3 \textbf{ g/L}$$

(b) **If mercury has a density of 13 600 g/L, what volume (in millilitres) is occupied by 425 g of mercury?**

First, rearrange the density equation to solve for V

$$V = \frac{m}{d}$$

and then substitute the given information.

$$V = \frac{m}{d} = \frac{425g}{13600g/L} = 0.0313 \text{ L}$$

Finally, perform a unit conversion to express the answer in millilitres.

$$V = 0.0313 \text{ L x } \frac{1 \text{ mL}}{10^{-3} \text{ L}} = \textbf{31.3 mL}$$

Note: You could also start the problem by using a unit conversion – a density is actually a conversion factor: 1 L = 13 600 g.

$$\text{\# of litres} = 425 \text{ g x } \frac{1 \text{ L}}{13600g} = 0.0313 \text{ L}$$

IMPORTANT FACT:

> For water at 4°C –
>   **d = 1000.0 g/L**
> or **d = 1.0000 g/mL**

Note that measuring the volume of a sample of water allows you to immediately know its mass, and vice versa. Density can be translated into a conversion statement.

1 g = 1 mL (this is **ONLY** TRUE for water at 4°C, but is quite close for other temperatures)

For example, 50 mL of water will have a mass of 50 g.

Another important fact is: **LESS DENSE LIQUIDS AND OBJECTS FLOAT ON LIQUIDS HAVING A GREATER DENSITY** (in other words, corks float in water and rocks don't). This fact is summarized below.

> Objects will sink in a liquid if
> $d_{OBJECT} > d_{LIQUID}$.
>
> Objects will float in a liquid if
> $d_{OBJECT} < d_{LIQUID}$.

EXERCISES:

31. A 3.50 mL chunk of boron has a mass of 8.19 g. What is the density of the boron?

32. An iron bar has a mass of 125 g. If iron's density is 7.86×10^3 g/L, what volume does the bar occupy?

33. A block of beeswax has a volume of 200.0 mL and a density of 961 g/L. What is the mass of the block?

34. Alcohol has a density of 789 g/L. What volume of alcohol is required in order to have 46 g of alcohol?

35. A gas called neon is contained in a glass bulb having a volume of 22.4 L. If the density of the neon is 0.900 g/L, what is the mass of the neon in the bulb?

36. A 70.0 g sphere of manganese (density = 7.20×10^3 g/L) is dropped into a graduated cylinder containing 54.0 mL of water. What will be the water level indicated after the sphere is inserted?

37. A 25.0 mL portion of each of W, X, Y and Z is poured into a 100 mL graduated cylinder. Each of the 4 compounds is a liquid and will not dissolve in the others. If 55.0 mL of W have a mass of 107.3 g, 12.0 mL of X have a mass of 51.8 g, 42.5 mL of Y have a mass of 46.8 g and 115.0 mL of Z have a mass of 74.8 g, list the layers in the cylinder from top to bottom.

38. Explain why boats made of iron are able to float. The density of iron is 7.86×10^3 g/L.

39. If the density of copper is 8.92×10^3 g/L and the density of magnesium is 1.74×10^3 g/L, what mass of magnesium occupies the same volume as 100.0 g of copper?

40. The sun has a volume of 1.41×10^{30} L, an average density of 1.407 g/mL, and can be thought of as more or less pure hydrogen. If the sun consumes 4.0×10^6 t of hydrogen per second, how many years will it take at this rate to burn all of the hydrogen? Hint: use the results of exercise 17(k). The sun will actually cease burning its hydrogen in far less time than indicated by this simple calculation.

41. (OPTIONAL: A Stinker!) A hollow cylinder, closed at both ends, has a volume of 250.0 mL and contains 4.60 g of argon gas. A 90.0 g cube of sodium (density = 970.0 g/L) is inserted into the tube in such a way that no gas escapes. What is the density of the gas afterwards?

II.5. SIGNIFICANT FIGURES AND EXPERIMENTAL UNCERTAINTY

When **COUNTING** a small number of objects it is not difficult to find the **EXACT** number of objects. On the other hand, when a property such as mass, time, volume or length is **MEASURED** you can *never* find the exact value. It is possible to find a mass, say, very precisely but it is *impossible* to find an object's exact mass.

All measurements have a certain amount of "uncertainty" associated with them. The purpose of this section is to show you how to correctly report and use the results of the experimental measurements you will be making in Chemistry 11.

You will need to learn   (a) how to find and report the uncertainty associated with each measurement, and

(b) the number of digits which can be claimed when reporting results and carrying out calculations with the results.

Let's look at the rules of the game.

SIGNIFICANT FIGURES

A. | A **significant figure** is a **measured** or **meaningful digit.** |

> **EXAMPLE:** If a stopwatch is used to time an event and the elapsed time is 35.2 s, then the measurement has 3 significant figures (3, 5 and 2). If the stopwatch can only be read to 0.1 s then it is silly to claim that the time according to the stopwatch is 35.**2168497** s. Since the stopwatch cannot measure the time to 7 decimal places, the last digits (**168497**) have **no significance** – in other words these last digits are "imagined" or a joke.

> **EXAMPLE:** A balance gives a reading of 97.53 g when a beaker is placed on it. This first reading has 4 significant figures since the measurement contains 4 digits. The beaker is then put on a different balance, giving a reading of 97.5295 g. In this second case there are more significant figures to the measurement (6 significant figures).

SPECIAL NOTE: When a *measurement* is reported it is usual to assume that in numbers such as

10, 1100, 120, 1000, 12 500

any zeroes at the end are NOT SIGNIFICANT WHEN NO DECIMAL POINT IS SHOWN. That is, we assume the last digits are zeroes because they are rounded off to the nearest 10, 100, 1000, etc. The number of significant digits in the above examples are shown in parentheses, below.

10 (1), 1100 (2), 120 (2), 1000 (1), 12 500 (3)

To complicate matters, SI usage dictates that a decimal point cannot be used without a following digit. For example, 10.0 and 100.0 are legal examples of SI usage with 3 and 4 significant digits respectively, but 10. and 100. are "illegal" ways of showing numbers. If you need to show that a number has been measured to 3 significant figures and has a value of 100 or that the number 1000 has actually been measured to 4 significant figures, the solution is to use exponential notation.

$$1.00 \times 10^2 = 100 \quad \text{(to 3 significant figures)}$$
$$1.000 \times 10^3 = 1000 \quad \text{(to 4 significant figures)}$$

EXERCISE:

42. How many significant figures do each of the following measurements have?

    (a) 1.25 kg   (c) 11 s   (e) 1.283 cm   (g) 2 000 000 years

    (b) 1255 kg   (d) 150 m   (f) 365.249 days   (h) 17.25 L

B.

> An **ACCURATE** measurement is a measurement that is close to the CORRECT or ACCEPTED value. (The closer to the correct/accepted value, the more accurate the measurement.)
>
> A **PRECISE** measurement is a reproducible measurement. In general, the more precise a measurement, the more SIGNIFICANT DIGITS it has.

Notes: 1. The accuracy of a measuring instrument depends on whether the instrument is properly "calibrated". For example, if a reference mass of 50.000 g is put on an electronic balance and the balance gives a reading of 48.134 g, the balance is not accurate. A special adjustment on the electronic balance is then used to make the balance give a reading of 50.000 g, in agreement with the reference mass. This adjustment process is called a "calibration".

         2. For the purposes of Chemistry 11, "high precision" shall be used to mean a "high number of significant figures". In general, it is reasonable to assume that if an instrument in good operating condition can give a reading to 8 significant figures a first time, it will give the same (and therefore reproducible) measurement a second time — provided what is being measured does not change. (There are cases where an instrument can record many digits but not give reproducible results as the result of "machine malfunction" or random errors, but these are ignored for our purposes.)

EXAMPLES: Assume the **CORRECT** width of a room is 5.32000 m.

- A measurement of 5.3 m is **ACCURATE but not VERY PRECISE.** (The value "5.3" is very close to correct as far as its significant figures go, but there are not many significant figures so the value is not very precise)

- If several measurements with some device consistently give the width as 5.45217 m, the measurements are **PRECISE but not ACCURATE.** (Apart from the initial "5" none of the significant digits are correct, so the measurements lack accuracy. The measurements DO have several significant figures, however, so they are precise.)

- If a measurement is consistently given as 5.32001 m, it is **ACCURATE and PRECISE.** (The measured value has many significant figures, so it is precise, and the measured digits agree very well with the correct value, so the measurement is accurate.)

- If a measurement is 7.1 m, it is **not ACCURATE and not PRECISE.** (There are very few significant figures, so the measurement is not very precise, and all the digits are in error so the measurement is not accurate.)

EXERCISES:

43. Assume you have a balance which gives very precise measurements. What might be true about the balance in order that its readings would be precise but not accurate?

44. A "calibration weight" has a mass of exactly 1.000 000 g. A student uses 4 different balances to check the mass of the weight. The results of the weighings are shown below.

> mass using balance A = 0.999 999 g   mass using balance C = 3.0 g
> mass using balance B = 1.00 g   mass using balance D = 0.811 592 g

(a) Which of the balances give accurate weighings?
(b) Which of the balances give precise weighings?
(c) Which balance is both accurate and precise?

45. An atomic clock is used to measure a time interval of 121.315 591 s. Assume you have to measure the same time interval. Give an example of a time interval you might actually measure if your measurement is:
(a) not accurate, but is precise.   (c) both inaccurate and imprecise.
(b) not precise, but is accurate.   (d) both accurate and precise.

C. | The **number** of significant figures is equal to all the **certain** digits PLUS the **first uncertain** digit.

EXAMPLE: In the figure at the right, the liquid level is somewhere between 42 and 43 mL. You know that it is at least 42 mL, so you are "certain" about the first two digits. As a guess, the volume is about 42.6 mL; it could be 42.5 or 42.7 but 42.6 seems reasonable. There is some "significance" to this last, guessed digit. It is somewhat uncertain, **but** not completely so. For example, the reading is NOT 42.1 or 42.9. As a result, there are two CERTAIN digits (4 and 2) and one uncertain–but–still–significant digit (6) for a total of THREE significant figures.

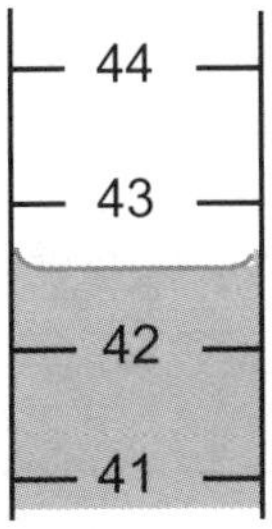

```
 _  44  _
 
 _  43  _
 ⌣
 _  42  _
 
 _  41  _
```

NOTE: If you are given a measurement without being told something about the device used to obtain the measurement, assume that the LAST DIGIT GIVEN IS SOMEWHAT UNCERTAIN.

EXERCISE:

46. How many "certain" digits are contained in each of the following measurements?
(a) 45.3 s   (b) 125.70 g   (c) 1.85 L   (d) 2.121 38 g

D. | "**Defined**" numbers and "**counting**" numbers are assumed to be **PERFECT** so that they are "exempt" from the rules applying to significant figures.

Defined or counted values involve things which cannot realistically be subdivided and must be taken on an "all–or–nothing" basis.

EXAMPLES: When "1 book" or "4 students" is written, it means exactly "1 book" and "4 students", not 1.06 books and 4.22 students.

The conversion factor   1 kg = 1000 g   is used to define an exact relationship between grams and kilograms, so that the numbers involved are assumed to be perfect.

EXERCISE:

47. In the space following each value below put "M" if the value was likely obtained by a **M**easurement, or "C" if the value was probably determined by **C**ounting.
(a) 4 comets   (b) 45 seconds   (c) 6.5 litres   (d) 12 TV sets   (e) 12 grams

HOW TO READ A SCALE

Before learning more about uncertainty, you must first be able to read a scale properly.

IMPORTANT: The following terms are used –

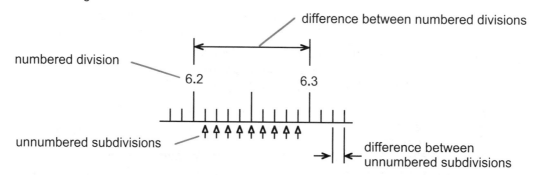

Both the numbered divisions and unnumbered subdivisions are **CALIBRATED** DIVISIONS because the overall scale has been "marked off" or "calibrated" at regular intervals.

If the unnumbered subdivisions *were numbered*, they would be labelled as shown below.

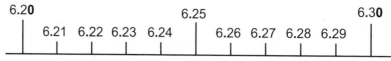

The "numbered divisions" would then read "6.20" and "6.30", rather than "6.2" and "6.3". The unnumbered subdivisions allow two more decimal places to be read. For example, the numbered divisions above differ in the first decimal place and the unnumbered subdivisions allow a reading to the second decimal place. The estimated distance between unnumbered subdivisions allows a reading to the third decimal place.

EXAMPLES: **(a) What is the value of (i) and (ii) on the following centimetre scale?**

The first two digits of (i) are 6.2 and the first two digits of (ii) are 6.3. The problem is to read the next two digits for each point.

FIRST: Find the difference between each NUMBERED DIVISION.
In the above example: 6.3 – 6.2 = 0.1 cm.

SECOND: Find the number of unnumbered subdivisions between numbered divisions and calculate the value of each unnumbered subdivision. Each numbered division above has 10 subdivisions and each unnumbered sub–division is
$$\frac{0.1 \text{ cm}}{10} = 0.01 \text{ cm}$$

Since the unnumbered subdivisions have a value of 0.01 cm, the value at (i) is a little more than 6.21 cm and the value at (ii) is a little more than 6.37 cm.

THIRD: Estimate how far along their respective unnumbered subdivisions (i) and (ii) are; this gives a reading to the next decimal place, which is the uncertain digit.

Reading at (i):   The 3 certain digits are "6.21". The pointer is half–way from 6.21 to 6.22, so the uncertain 4th digit is probably a "5". Therefore, the reading is **6.215 cm**.

Reading at (ii):   The 3 certain digits are "6.37". The pointer is $^3/_{10}$ of the way from 6.37 to 6.38, so the uncertain 4th digit is probably a "3". Therefore, the reading is **6.373 cm**.

(b) What is the value of (i) and (ii) on the following centimetre scale?

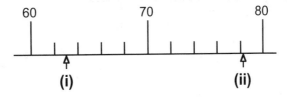

The value of (i) lies between 60 and 70 cm; the value of (ii) lies between 70 and 80 cm.

FIRST: The difference between numbered divisions is 10 cm.

SECOND: There are 5 subdivisions between each numbered division, so each unnumbered subdivision is equal to

$$\frac{10 \text{ cm}}{5} = 2 \text{ cm}$$

THIRD: Pointer (i) lies between 62 and 64, and pointer (ii) is between 78 and 80.

Reading at (i):   The pointer is about half–way ($^5/_{10}$) between 62 and 64. Therefore the reading is more than 62 cm by $^5/_{10}$ of 2 cm (the subdivision value).

reading = 62 cm + 0.5 x 2 cm = **63.0 cm**

(The numbered divisions differ by "tens", the unnumbered subdivisions are read to the "ones" and an estimate between unnumbered subdivisions are read to "tenths".)

Reading at (ii):   The pointer is about $^1/_{10}$ of the way from 78 to 80. Therefore the reading is more than 78 by $^1/_{10}$ of 2 cm.

reading = 78 cm + 0.1 x 2 cm = **78.2 cm**

EXERCISE:

48. In each of the following, determine the reading as follows. *Note:* all measurements are in "cm".
    i)   Find the difference between each numbered division.
    ii) Find how many unnumbered subdivisions lie between each numbered division and calculate the value of the intervals between each unnumbered subdivision.
    iii) Estimate the value at the pointer (you will have to estimate how far the pointer is from one unnumbered subdivision to the next).

(a)

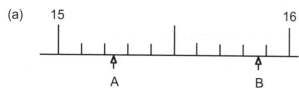

A = _____

B = _____

(b)

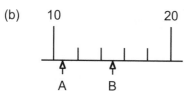

A = _____

B = _____

(c)

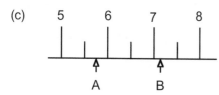

A = _____

B = _____

(d)

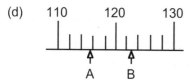

A = _____

B = _____

(e)

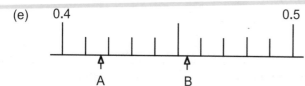

A = _____

B = _____

There is one last problem associated with reading scales that must be examined: **what to do when the "pointer" is exactly on one of the markings.**

EXAMPLE: Look at the centimetre ruler and indicated values below.

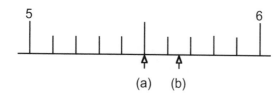

The pointer at (a) seems to indicate a value of 5.5 cm but that is *not* the correct value. Look at the pointer at (b). Since the value at (b) is about 5.65, both the value at (a) and (b) can be guessed to the nearest **0.01 cm**. The value for (a) must be given as **5.50 cm.**

BE VERY CAREFUL WHEN A VALUE APPEARS TO COINCIDE EXACTLY WITH A MARKING ON A MEASURING DEVICE. The following procedure should help when such a situation occurs.

THE PROCEDURE FOR CORRECTLY READING MEASURING SCALES WHEN A POINTER IS EXACTLY ON A NUMBERED DIVISION

• Determine the value that the measurement seems to have.

• Pretend you have a value in between two of the unnumbered subdivisions on your measuring device.

• Determine how many decimal places you could read off the measuring device at the "in–between value".

• Add a sufficient number of zeroes to the actual reading to give you the correct number of decimal places for your reading.

In the example above, the intervals between unnumbered subdivisions can be read to 0.01 cm; that is, to 2 decimal places. The reading appears to be 5.5, which is only 1 decimal place, so an extra zero is added to get the value: **5.50 cm.** Similarly, consider the value of the measurement below.

The value seems to be 5 cm, but the previous example shows that an "in–between value" can be read to 0.01 cm (2 decimal places) and so 2 extra zeroes are added to arrive at the final reading: **5.00 cm.**

EXERCISES:

49. Determine the readings on the following centimetre rulers.

(a)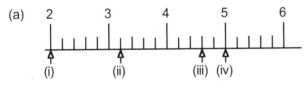

Reading at (i)   = _____

Reading at (ii) = _____

Reading at (iii) = _____

Reading at (iv) = _____

(b)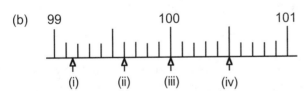

Reading at (i)   = _____

Reading at (ii) = _____

Reading at (iii) = _____

Reading at (iv) = _____

50.   Determine the volume readings of the following burettes. **Care!** The numbers *increase* going *down* the scale.

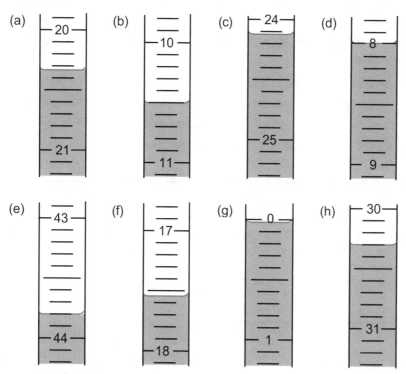

EXPERIMENTAL UNCERTAINTY

Having seen how to deal with significant figures and make proper readings, the next step is to learn about experimental uncertainty.

Definition: The experimental uncertainty is the estimated amount by which a measurement might be in error.

E.   When adding an uncertainty to a measurement, the uncertainty goes after the measured value but before the unit.

EXAMPLE: Assume that a measured temperature is 39.6°C and the uncertainty in the measurement is ± 0.1°C (Part F shows how to estimate the uncertainty). The measurement and uncertainty are shown below.

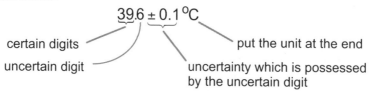

certain digits

uncertain digit

put the unit at the end

uncertainty which is possessed by the uncertain digit

NOTE: **If the uncertain digit is in the first decimal place, the uncertainty will be in the first decimal place also.**

INTERPRETATION OF UNCERTAINTIES

When a measurement is said to be 39.6 ± 0.1°C, this implies that the actual value most likely lies in the range from (39.6 – 0.1)°C to (39.6 + 0.1)°C; that is, from 39.5°C to 39.7°C.

Similarly the measurement 15.55 ± 0.02 mL implies a volume in the range from 15.55 – 0.02 = 15.53 mL to 15.55 + 0.02 = 15.57 mL.

If only the range of probable values is known, for example 88.0 g to 89.0 g, the uncertainty is simply one–half of the stated range.

$$\text{range} = 89.0 - 88.0 \quad = 1.0 \text{ g}$$
$$\text{uncertainty} = {}^1\!/_2 \, (1.0) \quad = 0.5 \text{ g}$$

The measurement reported is the MIDPOINT of the range, plus/minus the uncertainty. The midpoint of the range is simply the AVERAGE of the endpoints of the range.

$$\text{midpoint} = {}^1\!/_2 \, (88.0 + 89.0) = 88.5 \text{ g}$$

Therefore, the reported measurement is   **88.5 ± 0.5 g.**

Similarly, if the range is 15.0 g to 15.5 g then the midpoint of the range is 15.3 g (to one decimal point) and the uncertainty is ${}^1\!/_2 \, (0.5) = 0.3$ g (to one decimal point). [Yes, 15.3 ± 0.3 g predicts the range as 15.0 – 15.6 g, but the range, midpoint and uncertainty are all recognized as simply "good guesses".]

IMPORTANT: The place values (tens, units, first decimal, etc.) of the experimental uncertainty and the first uncertain digit of a measurement must agree with each other.

EXAMPLES: 15.5°C ± 0.01°C is *wrong* because the measurement is only read to the nearest 0.1°C, which means the first decimal place is uncertain. An uncertainty of 0.01°C implies the measurement can be read with at least partial certainty to the second decimal place.

5.52 ± 0.01 mL is *correct* because the last (uncertain) digit in the measurement and the uncertainty quoted are both to the second decimal place.

EXERCISES:

51.   Write the following measurements and uncertainties in the correct form.
   (a) A balance gives a mass reading of 51.32 g. The balance has an uncertainty of 0.01 g.
   (b) A student records a volume of 55 mL with an uncertainty of 1 mL.
   (c) A measurement is in the range from 452 g to 458 g.
   (d) A measurement is in the range from 0.5128 g to 0.5132 g.
   (e) Several people time the same event. Their times range from 98.2 s to 99.5 s.
   (f) A series of white mice have masses ranging from 48.9 g to 50.6 g.

52.   What is the range of values possible for the following?
   (a) 15.25 ± 0.01 mL   (b) 110.0 ± 0.2 mL   (c) $1.528 \times 10^{-6} \pm 0.005 \times 10^{-6}$ s

F. | **NORMALLY USE UNCERTAINTIES TO THE NEAREST 0.1 OF THE SMALLEST UNNUMBERED SUBDIVISION.** *If* you can only estimate a value to the nearest ±0.2 or even ±0.5 of the smallest unnumbered subdivision, feel free to do so, but be prepared to justify your decision. (Sometimes values are hard to read.)

Now that you know HOW to read a scale, estimating the uncertainty is relatively easy.

EXAMPLE: Look at the centimetre scale below.

The pointer indicates a value of 6.214, and the last digit ("4") is somewhat uncertain. **The place value (third decimal place) of the experimental uncertainty and the first uncertain digit of a measurement must agree with each other.** Therefore the value and uncertainty are

6.214 ± 0.001 cm .

EXAMPLE: The value on the scale below is 2.26 cm and $^1/_{10}$ of an unnumbered subdivision is 0.02 cm.

Therefore, the value and uncertainty are   **2.26 ± 0.02 cm .**

EXERCISES:

53.   Record values for the experimental uncertainty encountered in using the following apparatus.

Apparatus	Difference between numbered divisions	# of unnumbered subdivisions between numbered divisions	Smallest unnumbered subdivision	Uncertainty of measurement
thermometer				
10 mL graduated cylinder				
25 mL graduated cylinder				
100 mL graduated cylinder				
250 mL graduated cylinder				
50 mL burette				
clock				
balance				
Other:				
Other:				
Other:				

54.   Determine the uncertainty for each of the measurements in exercises 48–50, and record the measurement, uncertainty and units in the correct fashion.

G. | **Leading** zeroes are **not** significant. |

> *EXAMPLE:* The mass "25 g" has 2 significant figures. Using a unit conversion to express 25 g in kilograms gives
>
> $$\text{\# of kg} = 25 \text{ g} \times \frac{1 \text{ kg}}{10^3 \text{ g}} = 0.025 \text{ kg} .$$
>
> A more precise measurement was not performed so the measurement must still have two significant figures, the 2 and 5. The leading zeroes (in bold) in **0.0**25 kg are NOT SIGNIFICANT. Notice that re–expressing 25 g in megagrams increases the number of leading zeroes — 0.000 025 Mg — but the leading zeroes are not significant.

The number of leading zeroes depends on the size of the unit used to express the measured value, and is *not related* to the precision, accuracy or number of significant figures.

H. | **Trailing** zeroes are **all** assumed to be significant and must be justified by the precision of the measuring equipment. |

> *EXAMPLE:* The zeroes at the end of the following 2 numbers are called "trailing zeroes".
>
> 25.00 g   represents the precision of a common lab balance (4 significant figures in this case)
>
> 25.000 000 g   represents a highly precise microbalance (8 significant figures)
>
> A balance precise to at least 0.000 001 g is required in order to ensure that the trailing zeroes in 25.000 000 g are zeroes and not some other digits.
>
> (If a balance capable of making a measurement to ± 0.01 g is used and the result is written as "35.6 g", it is not correct to say "*Oh, I forgot to record the second decimal place, it must have been a zero.*" In fact, any reading from "35.60 g" to "35.69 g" was equally possible. Write "35.60 g" only when the balance actually shows "0" in the second decimal place.)

EXCEPTION: Recall that a number which is written without a decimal and has been rounded off to the nearest 100 (say) does not claim that the last zeroes are significant.

> *Example:* In 38 500 g the trailing zeroes are NOT SIGNIFICANT.

To summarize all the comments on leading and trailing zeroes —

There are two ways to count the number of significant figures.

EXPRESS THE NUMBER IN SCIENTIFIC NOTATION AND THEN COUNT ALL THE DIGITS.

Or even simpler:

starting from the left side of the number, ignore all "leading zeroes" and only start counting at the first NON–ZERO digit. Once you start counting, continue until you run out of digits.

EXAMPLE: $0.000\ 035\ 000 = 3.5000 \times 10^{-5}$, and therefore the number has 5 significant figures.

EXERCISE:

55. State the number of significant figures in each of the following.

(a) 3570   (c) 41.400   (e) 0.000 572   (g) 41.50×10^{-4} (i) $1.234\ 00 \times 10^{8}$

(b) 17.505   (d) 0.51   (f) 0.009 00   (h) $0.007\ 160 \times 10^{5}$ (j) $0.000\ 410\ 0 \times 10^{7}$

I. | After **MULTIPLYING** or **DIVIDING** numbers, round off the answer to the **LEAST NUMBER OF SIGNIFICANT FIGURES** contained in the calculation.

EXAMPLE: 2.00 x $3.000\,00$ = 6.00

3 significant   6 significant   3 significant
figures   figures   figures

Since the calculation involves a lower precision number (3 significant figures) and a higher precision number (6 significant figures), the precision of the result is limited by the LEAST precise number involved. The answer has only 3 significant figures.

When multiplying 2 numbers like 5.0×20.0 you must be careful how you write the answer.

$5.0 \times 20.0 = 100$ **IS WRONG!**

In this case a 2 significant figure number (5.0) is being multiplied by a 3 significant figure number (20.0), so the answer is only allowed to have 2 significant figures. Since "100" implies 1 significant figure, you MUST change to EXPONENTIAL FORM to properly show that the answer has 2 significant figures.

$5.0 \times 20.0 = 1.0 \times 10^2$

EXAMPLE: $\dfrac{15.55 \times 0.012}{24.6} = 0.0076$

This example involves numbers with 4, 3 and 2 significant figures. Since the least precise number, 0.012, has only 2 significant figures, the answer is rounded off to 2 significant figures.

EXAMPLE: $\dfrac{2.4000}{8.000} = 0.3000$

If you perform this calculation on your calculator, the result shown will be "0.3". **BUT,** the answer must have 4 significant figures, so three ZEROES are added to indicate that the answer is "0.3000" to 4 significant figures.

EXAMPLE: $\dfrac{2.56 \times 10^5}{8.1 \times 10^8} = 3.2 \times 10^{-4}$

The exponential parts of the numbers do not contribute to the number of significant figures. This calculation has a 3 significant figure number, 2.56×10^5, divided by a 2 significant figure number, 8.1×10^8. Putting these numbers into a calculator, and rounding the final answer to 2 significant figures, gives 3.2×10^{-4}.

IMPORTANT: YOU MUST **ALWAYS** PERFORM CALCULATIONS TO THE MAXIMUM NUMBER OF SIGNIFICANT FIGURES ALLOWED BY YOUR CALCULATOR AND **ONLY** YOUR FINAL ANSWER SHOULD BE ROUNDED OFF TO THE CORRECT NUMBER OF SIGNIFICANT FIGURES.   ROUNDING OFF **INTERMEDIATE** ANSWERS OFTEN PRODUCES INCORRECT RESULTS.

If you cannot keep all your calculated values in your calculator (or its memory), then always round off intermediate results so as to keep at least ONE "SIGNIFICANT FIGURE" more than you will eventually use in your final result.

EXERCISE:

56. Perform the indicated operations and give the answer to the correct number of significant figures.

   (a) 12.5 x 0.50   (e) $(6.40 \times 10^8) \times (5 \times 10^5)$ (i) 4.75 x 5

   (b) 0.15 x 0.0016   (f) 4.37×10^3 / 0.008 560 0   (j) 0.000 01 / 0.1000

   (c) 40.0 / 30.0000   (g) 51.3 x 3.940   (k) 7.4 / 3

   (d) 2.5 x 7.500 / 0.150   (h) 0.51×10^{-4} / 6×10^{-7} (l) 0.000 43 x 0.005 001

J. | After **ADDING** or **SUBTRACTING** numbers, round off the answer to the **LEAST NUMBER OF DECIMAL PLACES** contained in the calculation.

The idea behind this rule is simple. The number with the least number of decimal places is least precise and limits the precision of the final result.

EXAMPLE:

```
    12.5|6  cm
 + 125.8|▓  cm
 ───────────────
   138.3|6  cm
```

The second value, 125.8 cm, is only precise to the 1st decimal place so the final answer is rounded off to one decimal place: **138.4 cm.**

EXAMPLE:

```
    41.037 6|▓   g
  - 41.037 5|84  g
  ────────────────
    0.000 0|16  g
```

Since the least precise number has 4 decimal places, the answer must be rounded to 4 decimal places: **0.0000 g.** This answer is interpreted to mean there is no significant difference between the numbers being subtracted.

EXAMPLE: $1.234 \times 10^6 + 4.568 \times 10^7 = ?$

Since the exponents are different, one of the exponents must be changed to the size of the other. Arbitrarily, change the smaller exponent so that it equals the larger one.

1.234×10^6 becomes 0.1234×10^7

(Since the exponent becomes one power of 10 larger (10^6 becomes 10^7), the number in front is made one power of 10 smaller to compensate.)

Now the numbers are added.

```
   0.123|4  x 10^7
 + 4.568|▓  x 10^7
 ─────────────────
   4.691|4  x 10^7
```

Since the second number is only known to the third decimal place (in its present exponential form), the answer is rounded to the third decimal place.

Answer = **4.691×10^7**

Note: When an uncertain number is multiplied or divided by an exact (counting) number, the result obeys the rules for adding or subtracting the uncertain number. In other words, the answer is rounded to the same number of decimal places as the uncertain number.

EXAMPLES: The weights of 3 boys are: 51.0 kg, 52.4 kg and 49.8 kg. The average of their weights is

$$\frac{(51.0 + 52.4 + 49.8)}{3} = \textbf{51.1 kg}$$

DO NOT try to restrict the answer to 1 significant figure, because "3 boys" is an exact (counting) number rather than a "1 significant figure" number.

A Canadian nickel has a mass of 4.53 g. The mass of three such nickels is:

3 x 4.53 = 13.59 g   (the "3" is exact; both "4.53" and "13.59" have 2 decimal places)

IN SUMMARY

When **multiplying** or **dividing** two numbers, the result is rounded to the least number of significant figures used in the calculation.

When **adding** or **subtracting** two numbers, the result is rounded to the least number of decimal places used in the calculation.

EXERCISES:

57. Perform the indicated operations and give the answer to the correct number of significant figures.
(a) $15.1 + 75.32$
(b) $178.904\ 56 - 125.8055$
(c) $4.55 \times 10^{-5} + 3.1 \times 10^{-5}$
(d) $0.000\ 159 + 4.0074$
(e) $1.805 \times 10^{4} + 5.89 \times 10^{2}$
(f) $0.000\ 048\ 1 - 0.000\ 817$
(g) $7.819 \times 10^{5} - 8.166 \times 10^{4}$
(h) $45.128 + 8.501\ 87 - 89.18$
(i) $0.0589 \times 10^{-6} + 7.785 \times 10^{-8}$
(j) $89.75 \times 10^{-12} + 6.1157 \times 10^{-9}$

58. Perform the indicated operations and give the answer to the correct number of significant figures.
(a) $7.95 + 0.583$
(b) $1.99 / 3.1$
(c) $4.15 + 1.582 + 0.0588 - 35.5$
(d) $1200.0 / 3.0$
(e) $5.31 \times 10^{-4}/3.187 \times 10^{-8}$
(f) $45.9 - 15.0025$
(g) 375.59×1.5
(h) $5.1076 \times 10^{-3} - 1.584 \times 10^{-2} + 2.008 \times 10^{-3}$
(i) $1252.7 - 9.4 \times 10^{2}$
(j) $0.024\ 00 / 6.000$

Mixed calculations involving the addition, subtraction, multiplication and/or division of uncertain values are treated in a step–by–step manner, as shown in the next example.

EXAMPLE: Perform the indicated operations and give the answer to the correct number of significant figures.

$$50.35 \times 0.106 - 25.37 \times 0.176 = ?$$

First: Evaluate the multiplications (and divisions, if present). All digits given by the calculation are shown, with significant figures shown in bold.

$$50.35 \times 0.106 = \mathbf{5.337}1$$
$$25.37 \times 0.176 = \mathbf{4.465}\ 12$$

Second: Perform all additions and subtractions last. The results of the two multiplications are subtracted from each other. Since both of the multiplications are good to the second decimal place, the final result is rounded to the second decimal place.

$$\mathbf{5.337}1 - \mathbf{4.465}\ 12 = -\mathbf{0.871}\ 92$$

Therefore the answer is rounded to **0.87**.

EXERCISE:

59. In the following mixed calculations perform multiplications and divisions before doing the additions and subtractions. Keep track of the number of significant figures at each stage of a calculation.

(a) $25.00 \times 0.1000 - 15.87 \times 0.1036$

(b) $35.0 \times 1.525 + 50.0 \times 0.975$

(c) $(0.865 - 0.800) \times (1.593 + 9.04)$

(d) $\dfrac{(0.3812 + 0.4176)}{(0.0159 - 0.0146)}$

(e) $\dfrac{3.65}{0.3354} - \dfrac{6.14}{0.1766}$

(f) $\dfrac{5.3 \times 0.1056}{0.1036 - 0.0978}$

(g) $(0.341 \times 18.64 - 6.00) \times 3.176$

(h) $9.34 \times 0.071\ 46 - 6.88 \times 0.081\ 15$

UNIT III : THE PHYSICAL PROPERTIES AND PHYSICAL CHANGES OF SUBSTANCES

III.1. SOME BASIC DEFINITIONS IN SCIENCE

In this course you will be asked to describe substances in many different ways. To make sure that we are using a common vocabulary, some important terms first must be defined and agreed upon.

Definitions: **QUALITATIVE** information is *NON–NUMERICAL* information.

QUANTITATIVE information is *NUMERICAL* information.

Example	Qualitative Description	Quantitative Description
Your height	tall, short	5' 10" , 180 cm
Your weight	normal, heavy	110 lb, 123 kg
Chemistry 11 mark	awesome, fail	100%, 55/200

(Qualitative and quantitative information serve different purposes. "The boy is five feet tall" is a quantitative statement which makes no judgement about the boy's height. If the boy was only six years old, the qualitative statement "the boy was extraordinarily tall" would let us know that an unusual situation existed.)

An **OBSERVATION** is *qualitative* information collected through the direct use of our senses.

An **INTERPRETATION** (or "inference") is an attempt to put meaning into an observation.

A **DESCRIPTION** is a *list* of the properties of something.

DATA is *quantitative* information which is experimentally–determined or obtained from references.

An **EXPERIMENT** is a test or a procedure that is carried out in order to discover a result.

A **HYPOTHESIS** is a SINGLE, UNPROVEN assumption or idea which attempts to explain why nature behaves in a specific manner. When initially put forward, hypotheses are tentative but, if they survive testing, eventually gain general acceptance.

A **THEORY** is a set of hypotheses that ties together a large number of observations of the real world into a logically consistent and understandable pattern. In other words, a theory is a TESTED, REFINED and EXPANDED explanation of why nature behaves in a given way.

A **LAW** is a broad generalization or summary statement which describes a large amount of experimental evidence stating how nature behaves when a particular situation occurs.

Some Additional Comments about Hypotheses, Theories and Laws

The following are general characteristics of HYPOTHESES.
- Hypotheses are normally single assumptions.
- Hypotheses are narrow in their scope of explanation.
- When originally proposed, hypotheses are tentative (being based on suggestive but VERY incomplete evidence) but may become generally accepted after more complete testing.

The following are general characteristics of THEORIES.
- Theories are composed of one or more underlying hypotheses.
- Theories are broad in scope and may have subtle implications which are not foreseen when they are proposed because they provide explanations for entire "fields" of related behaviour.

- Theories are sometimes called **models** because they often provide a concrete way to examine, predict and test the workings of nature.
- A theory can't be "proven" but at some point it may have such a tremendous record of explanation and prediction that we place a high probability on its correctness as a model capable of describing reality.
- Theories must be "falsifiable"; that is, they must make ***testable predictions*** about the behaviour of the system under NEW conditions.   (If a theory makes no predictions then it is not "wrong", but it **is** discarded as useless.)

The following are general characteristics of LAWS.
- Laws summarize the results of many experiments or observations and state what will happen when a specific situation occurs.
- Laws do NOT try to explain WHY something occurs.
- Laws are NOT "proven theories", as sometimes is erroneously stated. Laws are often stated before any theory exists as to WHY the law is true. In the past, new experiments have occasionally shown a particular law to be invalid, causing an upheaval in scientific thought while new theories were proposed to explain the new observations.

Examples of hypotheses

1.   All gases are made up of tiny, fast–moving particles.
2.   The tiny particles in a gas transfer some or all of their energy of movement when they collide with one another or the walls of their container.
3.   The tiny particles in a gas act like miniature billiard balls and the entire system undergoes no net change in energy when particles collide.

Notice that all the above hypotheses are assumptions about the way gases exist and behave.

Examples of theories

The **KINETIC THEORY OF GASES** states that gases act as they do because they are made up of point–like particles which are constantly moving, colliding and exchanging energy.

   The KINETIC THEORY OF GASES is the result of combining the three hypotheses above. Pressure is explained as a result of the collision of gas particles with the walls of the container. Temperature is defined in terms of the average velocity of the moving particles.

The **ARRHENIUS THEORY OF ACIDS AND BASES** is the result of combining the following hypotheses.
- Some substances can break up in water to form positive and negative charged particles called ions.
- Acids are substances which break up in water to form an ion of H^+ and a negative ion.
- Bases are substances which break up in water to form an ion of OH^- and a positive ion.
- The reaction between an acid and a base is the result of the H^+ from the acid combining with the OH^- from the base to produce water.
- When an acid and a base react, the left–over positive and negative ions combine to produce a substance called a salt.

Examples of laws

BOYLE'S LAW states that if the temperature is unchanged, then the greater the pressure applied to a sample of gas, the smaller its volume.

CHARLES' LAW states that if the applied pressure is unchanged, then the greater the temperature of a gas sample, the greater its volume.

EXERCISES:

1. Give a quantitative description of   (a) a length of time.   (b) a temperature.

2. Give a qualitative description of   (a) a length of time.   (b) a temperature.

3. Which parts of the description in the following passage are quantitative and which are qualitative?

    Copper is a reddish–coloured element with a metallic lustre. It is an excellent conductor of heat and electricity, melts at 1085°C and boils at 2563°C. Archeological evidence shows that it has been mined for the past 5000 years and presently is considered to be one of the most important metals available. Copper is insoluble in water and virtually all other solvents, reacts easily with nitric acid but only slightly with sulphuric and hydrochloric acids. It has a density of 8.92 g/mL, which makes it more dense than iron.

4. "I observed that the long tube had a bright white glow". Give at least two different interpretations that could explain why the tube had a bright white glow. Propose a simple experiment that would help you to decide which of your interpretations is most likely to be correct.

5. What is the difference between
    (a) "observations" and "data"?   (c) "observation" and "interpretation"?
    (b) "observation" and "description"?

6. Which of the following can be incorrect?
    (a) data   (b) observations   (c) interpretations   (d) hypotheses   (e) theories   (f) laws

7. Ideally, experiments should be done to find out WHAT HAPPENS when a procedure is performed, NOT to confirm an expected result. What might happen if an experiment is carried out with the intention of proving that what you think will happen does, in fact, happen?

8. The tiny "protons" inside an atomic nucleus behave in a weird way if a beam of high energy particles is fired at them. One way to explain such behaviour of protons is to assume protons are made up of extremely small particles called "quarks". Is this assumption a hypothesis, theory or law?

9. A person proposes that the world was created 15 minutes ago, in such a way that it looks as if it has been here for billions of years, including a created set of memories which makes us believe we have existed individually for many years. Is this "proposition" an acceptable theory?

10. "Whatever you throw out in the trash today, you will need desperately within four days." Assuming that this whimsical statement is true, is it stated as a hypothesis, a theory, or a law?

11. Explain the important differences between   (a) a hypothesis and a theory.   (b) a theory and a law.

12. You have two 4 L cans, **A** and **B**, (shown at right). They are sealed with rubber stoppers. A piece of black rubber tubing **T** goes through the stopper in can **A**, over to can **B** and through its stopper. A piece of bent glass tubing **G** goes through the stopper in can **A**. Finally, a glass funnel **F** goes through the stopper in can **B**. The exposed end of **G** is about 3 cm above the funnel top. When about 300 mL of water is poured down the funnel into can **B**, water is seen to rise up glass tube **G**, pour out the tip and into the funnel. At this point no more water is poured into the funnel, but water continues to pour out of tube **G**. After a litre of water has come out, the outpouring still has not slowed down.

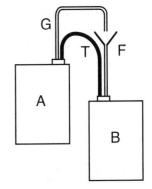

    (a) Based on these observations, propose a model for the interior of the cans. Hint: will the water keep flowing forever?

    (b) Apart from actually taking out the stoppers and looking in the cans, what further experiments could you propose to test your model?

III.2. THE PHYSICAL PROPERTIES OF MATTER

What is "Chemistry" anyway? Chemistry is such a broad field that sometimes it is said that "Chemistry is what chemists do". Before giving a better definition for Chemistry, a special term must be defined.

Definition: **MATTER** =   anything that has mass and occupies space. (Matter is what makes up the universe, other than energy.)

A better definition of Chemistry can now be given.

> **CHEMISTRY is the science concerned with the properties, composition and behaviour of matter.**

This section extensively examines the physical properties of matter; later sections examine the composition and behaviour of matter.

Definitions: A **SUBSTANCE** is something with a unique and identifiable set of properties.

Therefore, two objects with different properties must be made of different substances.

A **PHYSICAL PROPERTY** of a substance is a property that can be found without creating a new substance.

Example: Density, colour, hardness and melting temperature are physical properties.

A **CHEMICAL PROPERTY** is the ability of a substance to undergo chemical reactions and change into new substances, either by itself or with other substances.

Example: One chemical property of hydrogen is its ability to burn in air and produce water; another is its ability to react with chlorine gas and produce hydrogen chloride.

A physical property can be either **INTENSIVE** or **EXTENSIVE**.

Definitions: An **EXTENSIVE** property of a substance is a physical property which depends on the amount of the substance present.

Example: Mass and volume are extensive properties. The more substance you have (the more its EXTENT), the greater the mass and volume it occupies.

Extensive properties are NOT used to identify substances. For example, a 5 g chunk of material could be dirt or gold.

An **INTENSIVE** property of a substance is a physical property which depends solely on the nature of the substance, and NOT on how much of the substance is present.

Example: Density and melting temperature are intensive properties. Pure gold always has the same density and melting temperature, regardless of amount.

Intensive properties are used to identity a substance.

EXERCISES:

13. Which of the following statements describe physical properties and which describe chemical properties?
   (a) Glass is transparent.   (d) Copper conducts electricity.
   (b) Salt melts at 801°C.   (e) Fumes from ammonia and hydrochloric acid mix to produce
   (c) Adding lye to fat makes soap.   a white smoke.

14. Give an example of something which is observable but which does not contain matter.

15. Which of the following are intensive properties and which are extensive?
     (a) shape   (c) length   (e) electrical conductivity   (g) hardness
     (b) smell   (d) colour   (f) time required to dissolve a solid

---

Matter exists in THREE COMMON states or "phases": **solid, liquid** and **gas.** The three common phases of matter each have a unique set of properties which allow a given substance to be classified as one of a solid, liquid or gas.

(a) **Solids** are rigid, do not readily change their shape, and experience very small changes in volume when heated or subjected to pressure.

(b) **Liquids** conform to the shapes of their containers and experience only slight changes in volume when heated or subjected to pressure.

(c) **Gases** conform to the shapes of their containers and experience drastic changes in volume when heated or subjected to pressure.

Liquids can be seen as an "intermediate" phase between a solid and a gas when you consider that
  • both **solids** and **liquids** undergo only slight changes in volume when heated or subjected to pressure
  • both **liquids** and **gases** conform to the shapes of their containers.
Therefore, liquids share some properties with both solids and gases.

The space which exists between molecules is quite different in solids, liquids and gases.

In a solid, all of the particles are packed into a given volume in a highly organized and rigid manner which requires particles to be in direct contact with each other. So, solids are not compressible.

  Example: The volume occupied by 28.0 g of solid nitrogen is 27.3 mL.

In a liquid, the particles remain in close contact with each other but have sufficient room to slide past one another easily and prevent an organized packing. Because of the close contact between particles, liquids are not compressible.

  Example: The volume occupied by 28.0 g of liquid nitrogen is 34.6 mL.

In a gas,   the particles are widely separated and only contact each other during collisions. Because the wide separation of particles can be decreased, gases are compressible.

  Example: The volume occupied by 28.0 g of gaseous nitrogen at room temperature ($20^{\circ}C$) and one atmosphere pressure is 24 000 mL (24 L).

The table below shows that liquids are an intermediate phase between solids and gases.

	solid	liquid	gas
volume occupied	small	small	large
movement allowed in substance	small	large	very large

There are also several EXOTIC states of matter. You do not have to know them but you may find them of some interest.

- **PLASMA** – A plasma is a gas made of charged particles such as electrons and naked atomic nuclei at extremely high temperatures ($10^7\,^\circ$C). Examples are: lightning, the interior of stars, and neon lights.

- **SUPERCONDUCTIVE STATE** – Superconductive material allows electricity to flow without ANY resistance. An electrical pulse flowing in a superconducting loop can theoretically flow forever. Previously, the superconductive material had to be at very low temperatures ($-250\,^\circ$C), but exciting new discoveries have found superconductors which operate close to room temperature. These may allow new types of electronic devices and supercomputers to be created.

- **SUPERFLUID STATE** – A special type of helium (He–3) at $-272\,^\circ$C has no frictional forces. If set in motion, the helium keeps moving at a constant rate. A container of He–3 also spontaneously self-siphons out of its container if it can eventually reach a lower level.

- **SUPERCONDENSED STATES** – These states are found in collapsed stars. In "white dwarf" stars the atoms are squeezed into a solid having a density of about 50 000 g/mL; in "neutron stars" the electrons, protons and neutrons are crushed together until the nuclear particles touch and effectively coalesce into a giant "neutron" with a density of 2×10^{14} g/mL; in a "black hole" matter is pushed together so tightly that it is crushed out of existence in our universe.

New Superconductor Discovered

In order to continue examining physical properties, a few additional definitions are required.

Definitions: **HARDNESS** is the ability of a solid to resist abrasion or scratching.

MALLEABILITY is the ability to be rolled or hammered into thin sheets.

DUCTILITY is the ability to be stretched or drawn into wires.

LUSTRE is the manner in which a solid surface reflects light. Lustres can vary from metallic to adamantine (diamond–like), glassy, oily, pearly, silky or dull.

VISCOSITY is the *resistance* of a fluid to flow.

DIFFUSION is the intermingling of fluids as a result of motion within the fluid (this applies to both gases and liquids).

VAPOUR is the gaseous material formed by the evaporation of a substance which boils above room temperature.

> *Example*:   Acetone is a liquid which boils at 56°C. The acetone that evaporates at room temperature (25°C) is called a "vapour".
>
> Oxygen boils far below room temperature and therefore is called a "gas" at room temperature.

VAPOUR PRESSURE is the pressure created by the vapour evaporating from a liquid. (Vapour pressure is abbreviated as VP.)

Note: The **BOILING TEMPERATURE** of a liquid (which you understand to a certain extent, and which will be properly defined later) is often called the "boiling point" and is abbreviated as **BP**.

Similarly, the **MELTING TEMPERATURE** of a solid is often called the "melting point" and is abbreviated as **MP**.

EXERCISE:

16.   Colour is a physical property that MAY distinguish between two solids, two liquids, or two gases. Suggest as many other physical properties as you can which might also distinguish between two
(a) solids.   (b) liquids.   (c) gases.

AN INVESTIGATION OF: VAPOUR PRESSURE, EVAPORATION RATE, DIFFUSION RATE, VISCOSITY, AND GAS COMPRESSIBILITY

For each experiment below, read the description of results and answer the questions which follow.

EXERCISES:

17.   A sample of liquid butanol at room temperature is put into a pressure–measuring device and the vapour pressure created by the evaporation of vapour from the butanol is found to be 0.9 kPa. When a few millilitres of butanol are placed in an open evaporating dish on an electronic balance, the balance shows that the mass of butanol remains almost unchanged for several minutes. A thermometer placed in boiling butanol registers a temperature of 117°C. When the series of measurements is repeated with liquid acetone, the vapour pressure is found to be 31 kPa and the boiling temperature is found to be 56°C. When acetone is placed in an open evaporating dish on an electronic balance, the mass of acetone is found to decrease quickly and steadily.

(a) Which substance, butanol or acetone, has the higher vapour pressure?
(b) What relationship exists between a liquid's boiling temperature and its vapour pressure?
(c) What relationship exists between a liquid's vapour pressure and its evaporation rate?
(d) What would you expect to be true about the vapour pressure of iron metal?
(e) Diethyl ether ("hospital ether") boils at 35°C. Compare the expected evaporation rate and vapour pressure of diethyl ether to acetone.

18.   A few crystals of a water–soluble dye are dropped simultaneously into a basin containing hot water and a basin containing cold water. The dye spreads out quickly in the basin of hot water and much more slowly in the cold water. In a second experiment, a few dark purple crystals of iodine are sealed into an upright 30 cm glass tube at 50°C. After a few minutes a faint purple cloud of gaseous iodine is seen just above the iodine crystals, but the purple colour remains close to the bottom. Next, iodine crystals are sealed in a similar tube at 100°C. The purple gas formed spreads relatively quickly throughout the entire tube. In a third experiment, a 30 cm glass tube sealed with cotton batting at both ends has gaseous hydrogen chloride injected into one end while simultaneously gaseous ammonia is injected into the other end. After about 30 s, a white ring is seen inside the tube, as shown below. The white ring is solid ammonium chloride, produced when gaseous ammonia meets and reacts with gaseous hydrogen chloride.

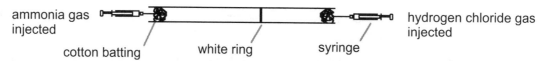

ammonia gas injected   cotton batting   white ring   syringe   hydrogen chloride gas injected

(a) Propose a general relationship between temperature and diffusion rate.

(b) Which gas travels faster through air: ammonia or hydrogen chloride?

(c) The ammonia molecule is lighter than the hydrogen chloride molecule. What relationship appears to exist between a molecule's mass and the speed with which it travels? (In other words, what relationship appears to exist between a molecule's mass and its diffusion rate?)

19. Small steel pellets are simultaneously dropped down three glass tubes, each of which is one metre long and each of which contains a different liquid: hexane, carbon tetrachloride and glycerol. A pellet drops very quickly to the bottom of the tube containing hexane. A pellet drops quickly to the bottom of the tube containing carbon tetrachloride, but less quickly than in the tube of hexane. A pellet passing through the tube containing glycerol seems to "take forever" to reach the bottom. When 25 mL samples of each of carbon tetrachloride, glycerol and hexane are poured into the same tube, three distinct layers are seen. The carbon tetrachloride is found on the bottom, the glycerol lies in the middle and the hexane floats on top.

(a) Rank the liquids – hexane, glycerol and carbon tetrachloride – from lowest to highest viscosity.

(b) Rank the liquids – hexane, glycerol and carbon tetrachloride – from lowest to highest density.

(c) What relationship appears to exist between the viscosity and density of a liquid?

20. (a) If you use a tire pump to pump up a bicycle tire, what happens to the pressure exerted on the gas in the pump when you push down on the pump handle?

(b) What happens to the gas volume in the pump when you push down on the pump handle?

(c) Complete the following statement.

When the pressure on a gas increases, the volume of the gas _____.

(d) If you scoop up some freshly–fallen snow and compress it between your hands, what happens to the volume of the snow when you
   (i) apply pressure, and   (ii) release the pressure?

(e) If you squeeze a sponge in your hands, what happens to the volume of the sponge when you
   (i) apply pressure, and   (ii) release the pressure?

(f) What can you conclude about the ability of a gas sample to "recover" when an externally applied pressure is released?

ADDITIONAL EXERCISES:

21. Does corn syrup have a high or low viscosity? Does gasoline have a high or low viscosity? If you heat up a glass of syrup, what happens to the viscosity of the syrup?

22. Which of the following are extensive properties and which are intensive properties?
   (a) viscosity   (c) the pressure exerted by helium in a balloon
   (b) the time required to melt a sample of ice

23. Ice evaporates at a very slow rate. What can you conclude about the vapour pressure of ice?

24. Which of solids, liquids and gases can possess each of the properties below? There may be more than one phase possible in each case.
   (a) the ability to flow rapidly   (d) the ability to melt
   (b) transparency   (e) the ability to create a vapour pressure
   (c) the ability to be easily compressed

25. Which phase of matter can be described as occupying a relatively small volume and allowing a large movement of the particles within the phase?

26. The volumes occupied by 32.0 g of oxygen are (in no particular order): 27.9 mL, 22.4 L and 22.4 mL for its different phases. What is the volume occupied by   (a) solid oxygen?   (b) gaseous oxygen?

27. A balloon is filled with air and sealed. **At this point the balloon is neither expanding nor shrinking.**
    (a) Is the pressure inside the balloon greater than, equal to or less than the atmospheric pressure pushing on the outside of the balloon? [Hint: What happens if the atmospheric pressure rises?]
    (b) What would you expect to observe if you put a filled balloon in a sealed glass tank and then created a vacuum in the tank?

28. Water vapour is more viscous than chlorine gas. What can you predict regarding the density of water vapour versus chlorine gas?

29. (a) Harry is sitting three metres away from Harriet in a cold room. John is sitting three metres away from Juanita in a warm room. Will Juanita smell John's aftershave lotion before or after Harriet smells Harry's identical aftershave lotion? Why?
    (b) Assume Harry and John wore different aftershave lotions, but were in rooms having the same temperature. What physical property would determine whether the scent of John's aftershave would reach Juanita before the scent of Harry's aftershave reached Harriet?

30. Viscosity is measured in "poise". The viscosities of argon gas and chlorine gas are 222 micropoise and 133 micropoise respectively at 25°C. Will a small plastic sphere fall faster in argon or chlorine gas?

31. If the boiling temperature of chloroform is 62°C, should gaseous chloroform at room temperature be called a "gas" or a "vapour".

32. Glycerol has a lower vapour pressure than does ethanol at room temperature. Which of glycerol and ethanol has the lower boiling point?

III.3. THE CLASSIFICATION OF MATTER

The physical properties possessed by substances are used to classify the substances into various categories.

Definitions: A **SYSTEM** is the part of the universe being studied in a given situation.

A **PHASE** is any part of a system which is uniform in both its composition and properties.

Phases in a system are distinct REGIONS separated from each other by VISIBLE BOUNDARIES (although sometimes a microscope is needed to see the boundaries).

EXAMPLE: When a copper rod is placed in water, all the points within the copper have the same properties, and all the points within the water have the same properties. In this TWO PHASE system there is a distinct boundary where the copper stops and the water exists.

Before proceeding, a few more definitions are needed. You should recall these definitions from previous science courses, but they are included here for completeness.

Definitions: An **ELEMENT** is a substance which cannot be separated into simpler substances as a result of any chemical process.

Examples: silver metal, copper metal, hydrogen gas

An **ATOM** is the smallest possible unit of an element which retains the fundamental properties of the element.

Examples: silver (Ag), copper (Cu), hydrogen (H)

A **MOLECULE** is a cluster of two or more atoms held together strongly by electrical forces.

Examples: water (H_2O), ethanol (CH_3CH_2OH), table sugar ($C_{12}H_{22}O_{11}$)

An **ION** is an atom or molecule which possesses an electrical charge.

Examples: sodium ion (Na^+), chloride ion (Cl^-), nitrate ion (NO_3^-)

A **PARTICLE** is a general term used to describe a small bit of matter such as an atom, molecule or ion.

The following scheme is generally accepted for classifying substances.

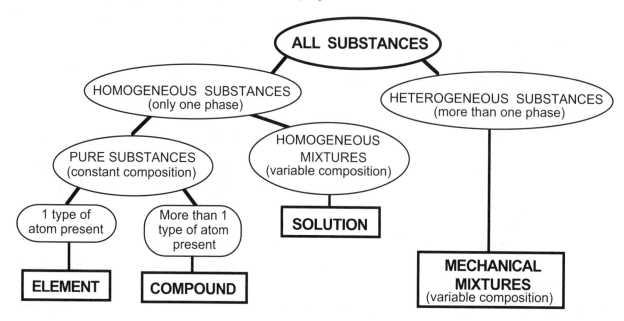

The following terms are used to classify matter. (Refer to the above classification diagram as the terms below are discussed.)

1. A **HOMOGENEOUS** substance is a substance consisting of only one phase.

    Examples: air, water, salt water, a piece of iron

2. A **HETEROGENEOUS** substance is a substance consisting of more than one phase.

    Examples: a human being, a pencil, gravel

3. A **PURE SUBSTANCE** is a substance that is homogeneous and has an unchangeable composition.

    Examples: sugar, water, copper, iron

4. A **MIXTURE** is a system made up of two or more substances, such that the relative amounts of each substance can be VARIED.

    Examples: salt dissolved in water, alcohol dissolved in water

    "Mixture" is a general term which includes both heterogeneous mixtures (better known as "mechanical mixtures") and homogeneous mixtures (better known as "solutions").

5. A **MECHANICAL MIXTURE** is a heterogeneous mixture of two or more substances.

    Examples gravel, sand and iron filings, a pencil

    Note: ALL HETEROGENEOUS substances are MECHANICAL MIXTURES, and vice versa.

6. A **SOLUTION** is a homogeneous mixture of two or more substances.

    There are several different types of solutions.

Type of Solution	Example
gas–in–gas solution	air (oxygen, nitrogen, etc.)
gas–in–liquid solution	soda pop
liquid–in–liquid solution	water and alcohol
solid–in–liquid solution	salt water
solid–in–solid solution	alloys (metals melted together)

Definition: A **SOLVENT** is the component in a solution which exists in the greater quantity.

> *Example*: When salt is dissolved in water, WATER is the SOLVENT.

Definition: Solutions in which the solvent is WATER are called "**AQUEOUS**" solutions. (The term "aqueous" comes from the Latin word for water, "aqua".)

> The symbol "aq" is added after the chemical symbol for a compound to indicate that the compound is in **AQUEOUS SOLUTION.**

> *Example*: NaCl(aq) = aqueous sodium chloride, or salt water.

Definition: A **SOLUTE** is the component in a solution which exists in the smaller quantity.

> *Example*: When salt is dissolved in water, SALT is the SOLUTE.

IMPORTANT: When water exists in a solution, it is conventional to call water the "solvent", even if it exists in the lesser quantity. For example, in a solution which is 60% alcohol and 40% water, the water is still considered to be the solvent.

7. As defined previously, an **ELEMENT** is a substance which cannot be separated into simpler substances as a result of any chemical process. In other words, an element is a pure substance in which all the atoms are of the same type.

> *Examples:* The substances shown on the periodic table (such as H, C, N, O) are elements.

8. A **COMPOUND** is a pure substance made of two or more types of atoms. **Only one type of molecule is present in a compound.**

> *Examples:* salt (sodium chloride) = NaCl, sugar = $C_{12}H_{22}O_{11}$, water = H_2O

The table below shows how the terms *atom, element, molecule* and *compound* are used.

If a single particle is a/an:	Then a large–scale, visible collection of these particles is called:
atom *or* molecule made of identical atoms	element
molecule made of different atoms	compound

THE DIFFERENCE IN PHYSICAL PROPERTIES BETWEEN DIFFERENT CLASSIFICATIONS OF MATTER

Pure substances (elements and compounds)

> In a given state (solid, liquid or gas), pure substances will have unchanging, uniform properties.

> > *Example:* Salt (sodium chloride, NaCl) has a density of 2.16 g/mL, melts at $801^{\circ}C$, and is colourless.

Homogeneous mixtures

> For a particular composition, a homogeneous mixture has uniform, unchanging physical properties.

> > *Example:* One litre of an aqueous solution containing **50.0 g** of salt freezes at $-1.62^{\circ}C$, is clear and colourless and has a density of 1.035 g/mL.

> If the composition of a homogeneous mixture is changed, a new set of physical properties results. The properties of this new mixture are uniform and unchanging if the composition does not change.

> > *Example:* One litre of an aqueous solution containing **100.0 g** of salt freezes at $-3.29^{\circ}C$, is clear and colourless and has a density of 1.068 g/mL.

Heterogeneous mixtures

The substances which make up a heterogeneous mixture (that is, a mechanical mixture) will each have their own, unique set of physical properties. In general, the physical properties of each substance present will have no effect on the physical properties of the other substances present.

Example: If a mixture of water and iron is heated, first the water will boil at its usual boiling temperature and the iron will melt later at its own, high melting point.

IN SUMMARY

Pure substance – unchanging, uniform physical properties

Homogeneous mixture – changeable composition, but each particular composition has unchanging, uniform physical properties

Heterogeneous mixture – each component present has different physical properties, regardless of composition

As can be seen, a specific homogeneous mixture has a constancy of properties in common with pure substances, and a variable composition in common with heterogeneous mixtures.

EXERCISES:

33. Classify each of the following as one of an atom, a molecule or an ion.
    (a) S^{2-} (b) O_2 (c) Sb   (d) O   (e) Al^{3+} (f) NH_3

34. A clear glass bottle contains white sand, some nails, salt water with some dye dissolved in it, and a layer of gasoline on top. How many phases are present in this system (excluding the bottle and lid)?

35. What should you see if a system is   (a) heterogeneous?   (b) homogeneous?

36. Classify each of the following as one of heterogeneous or homogeneous.
    (a) a diamond   (b) a tree   (c) a hen's egg   (d) a cup of coffee (apart from the cup)

37. Assume you have a 10 g piece of pure gold. Should you refer to the gold as an atom or an element?

38. In what way are a true solution and a compound similar? In what way do they differ?

39. Which of an element, compound, solution or mechanical mixture are possible classifications for the following? (There may be more than one answer for each example.)
    (a) a clear liquid which can be boiled away to leave a white solid
    (b) a collection of solid particles, some of which are white and some of which are red
    (c) a solid which melts at $170^{\circ}C$
    (d) a gas
    (e) a liquid
    (f) a liquid which boils away completely at $136^{\circ}C$. When the liquid is strongly heated in a closed container, a yellow gas and a black solid are produced.

40. Which substance is the solute in each of the following?
    (a) water containing 5% acetic acid (this mixture is commonly called "vinegar")
    (b) tincture of iodine (a small amount of solid iodine mixed with alcohol)
    (c) a mixture containing 60% alcohol and 40% chloroform
    (d) a solution containing 900 g of silver nitrate and 100 g of water.

41. Which of sugar, dirt and air are pure substances and which are mixtures?

42. Potassium chloride, KCl, is used as a "salt substitute". What is meant by "KCl(aq)"?

43. How many phases are present in a regular pencil?

44. Classify each of the following as a mixture or a compound.
    (a) alcohol, CH_3CH_2OH (c) soda pop   (e) CH_3OH in H_2O
    (b) a pizza   (d) baking soda ($NaHCO_3$)

III.4. THE PHYSICAL SEPARATION OF SUBSTANCES

There are many methods which can be used to separate one substance from another. All the methods examined in this section take advantage of differences in the physical properties of the substances involved. (Some advanced techniques rely on using differing chemical properties of the substances involved, but these techniques produce different chemical substances and are not considered here.)

A. HAND SEPARATION

A **MECHANICAL MIXTURE** can often be separated by *hand* or by the use of a *sieve* or *magnet*.

Example: Collectors in the past picked rubies out of the gravel in the streams of Burma by hand.

Sieves are used to separate fossilized dinosaur bone fragments from sand and gravel.

Magnets are used during recycling operations to separate the iron from a mixture of finely chopped iron, plastic, aluminum and copper.

B. FILTRATION

Filtration allows the separation of liquids from solids; that is, the separation of **MECHANICAL MIXTURES** involving liquids and solids.

Note: Filtration *cannot* be used to separate DISSOLVED solids from a liquid. Therefore, you can't remove the salt from a salt water solution by filtration methods. Filtration only works when the solid particles present are big enough to be seen; smaller particles (such as dissolved salt) simply pass right through the filter paper.

The material which remains behind on **FILTER PAPER** is called the **RESIDUE,** and the liquid which passes through filter paper is called the **FILTRATE.**

Example: Sand can be filtered out of a sand/sea water mixture. After the filtration, the sand is the residue and the sea water is the filtrate.

C. EVAPORATION

Evaporation involves allowing the liquid in a **SOLID–IN–LIQUID SOLUTION** to evaporate or to be boiled away, leaving the solid.

Example: Evaporation of the water from salt water is used in the commercial production of salt on several seacoasts.

D. DISTILLATION

When a **LIQUID–IN–LIQUID SOLUTION** is heated in a distillation setup (illustrated below), the liquid with the lowest boiling temperature boils first. The vapour produced is at the exact boiling temperature of the liquid and ascends to the top of the **DISTILLATION FLASK,** passes a thermometer, enters the side–arm of the flask and contacts the cold inner surface of the **CONDENSER.** The gas cools and CONDENSES back into a liquid, dropping out the end of the condenser as a purified liquid called a **DISTILLATE.** If the liquids present have boiling temperatures which are quite close to each other, one or more re–distillations of the distillate caught in the "receiving vessel" may be required in order to produce pure compounds. If the boiling temperatures are well separated, a single distillation may be sufficient to produce very pure products. In some cases, the liquid remaining in the distillation flask may be the desired liquid and the distillation is used to remove an unwanted solvent. Occasionally, a solid–in–liquid solution may be distilled to quickly separate the liquid from the solid, but liquid–in–liquid distillation is much more common.

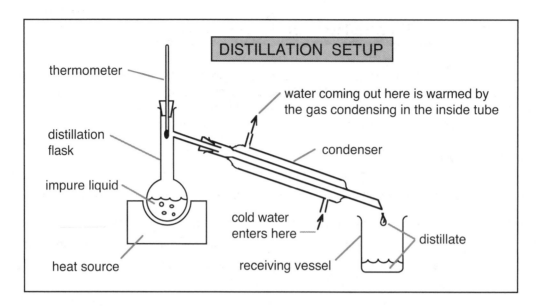

E. SOLVENT EXTRACTION

There are two ways in which this technique can be used.

Extraction of a solid from a MECHANICAL MIXTURE of solids

This method uses a liquid that dissolves one or more of the solids present but leaves others undissolved. In the ideal case, only two solids will be present so that the desired solid is either

(i)   left behind, or
(ii) dissolved and subsequently separated by simple evaporation of the solvent.

In "less–than–ideal" cases, different solvents may have to be used and numerous cycles involving extraction, evaporation of the solvent and re–extraction are required. If no suitable solvent can be found after extensive experimentation, the extraction procedure cannot be used.

Example: Add water to a sand/sugar mixture to extract the sugar and leave the sand behind.

Extraction of a dissolved liquid or solid from a LIQUID SOLUTION

Before going further, two related special terms are needed.

Definitions: Two liquids are **MISCIBLE** if they are mutually soluble in each other in all proportions.

> *Example*: Water and alcohol dissolve each other in all proportions and thus are MISCIBLE.

Two liquids are **IMMISCIBLE** if they are INSOLUBLE in each other.

> *Example*: Water and vegetable oil do not mix with each other and are IMMISCIBLE.

"Partial miscibility" situations also exist. For example, water and chloroform are partially soluble in each other. Most liquids mutually dissolve to at least a very small extent so that "IMMISCIBLE" implies that only tiny amounts of the liquids dissolve in each other.

To carry out solvent extraction on a solution with one or more solid and/or liquid substances dissolved in a liquid solution, a solvent must possess TWO important experimentally–determined properties.

• the added solvent is IMMISCIBLE with the solvent already present.
• the added solvent dissolves one or more desired substances from the solution and leaves unwanted substances behind (or vice versa).

Depending on the relative densities of the solution and added solvent, the added solvent may form a layer above or below the original solution, as shown below.

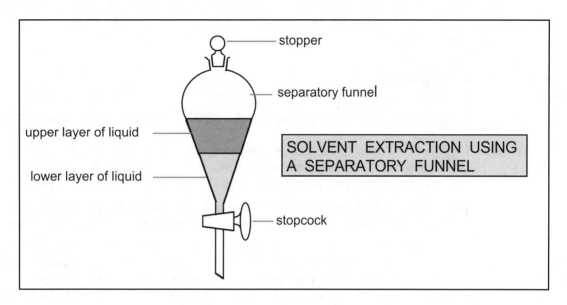

After a solvent is added to a solution, the mixture is shaken in a **SEPARATORY FUNNEL**. Some substances are more soluble in the added solvent than they are in the original solvent and pass from the original solvent into the added solvent. The added solvent is then drained from the original solution and a second quantity of solvent is added to the solution. After being shaken, more of the **remaining** desired substances go into the added solvent and also can be drained.

Assume 80% of a desired substance leaves the original solution and moves to the added solvent each time the extraction process is carried out. The calculation to find the amount transferred from solution to solvent is based on **the amount left behind**. After ONE extraction, 20% of the desired substance is **left** in the original solution. After TWO extractions, 20% of the first 20% is **left**. That is

$$20\% \text{ of } 20\% = 0.20 \times 0.20 = 0.04 = 4\%$$

of the desired substance is left in the original solution. After THREE extractions there is

$$0.20 \times 0.20 \times 0.20 = 0.008 = 0.8\% \text{ left, and so on.}$$

Again, as with the previous extraction method, only experimentation can determine if a suitable solvent exists so that solvent extraction is possible. (A special guideline for solubility called "Like dissolves like" will be learned later, when solutions are studied more extensively.)

F. RECRYSTALLIZATION

Recrystallization is a variation on the method of EVAPORATION in which the solid in a **SOLID–IN–LIQUID** solution is separated in a pure and crystalline state. A **SATURATED** solution of a desired solid is prepared in a suitable solvent. (A SATURATED solution is a solution that has dissolved all of the solid that it can. In other words, all the solvent present is required just to keep all the solid dissolved.) The two most common ways to prepare a saturated solution are adding a solid to a solvent at room temperature until no more solid dissolves and adding just enough hot solvent to dissolve the solid. The solvent is then allowed to slowly evaporate or slowly cool, and as it does some of the desired solid comes out of solution as **CRYSTALS**. (The solvent is **not** allowed to evaporate completely.) The resulting crystals are often extremely pure. The recrystallization method is used when a solid consists mostly of the desired material and small amounts of one or more impurities. The saturated solution should only be saturated with respect to the desired substance; there should be only small amounts of impurities present so as to prevent more than one substance forming crystals at the same time. Once crystals have formed, they are separated from the remaining solution by **HAND SEPARATION** (if only a few large crystals have formed) or more frequently by **FILTRATION** (when a mass of small crystals has formed). The term "**fractional crystallization**" is sometimes used to describe the process of purifying a substance by recrystallization. (The word "fractional" is added to emphasize the fact that several different chemicals may be present but the crystallization process separates out or "fractionates" the desired substance from the impurities.)

G. GRAVITY SEPARATION

This method is used to separate desired solids from a MECHANICAL MIXTURE, based on their **DENSITY**.

Example: Gold pans are used to trap dense particles of gold (density = 19.3 g/mL) and allow less dense rock and gravel (average density = 2–3 g/mL) to be removed. Gold in streams is often found in cracks in the underlying bedrock since it rapidly sinks under the lighter sand and gravel.

Mechanical shakers agitate a mixture of low and high density materials, allowing the high density substances to sink to the bottom and the low density substances to move to the top.

In the "froth flotation" process, finely pulverized ores are stirred into tubs of liquid through which fine air bubbles are blown. A "frothing agent" dissolved in the liquid produces a foam as the air passes through the stirred ore–liquid mixture. Rock particles rich in a desired ore are trapped in the froth, carried to the surface and removed by skimming off the foam. Rock particles having little or no ore content sink to the bottom and are eventually discarded.

Another gravity separation method involves the use of a **CENTRIFUGE,** which whirls a test tube around at extremely high speeds forcing finely dispersed solids to the bottom of the test tube. (The closed end of the test tube faces away from the central rotating axis; the huge force arising as a result of the rotation pushes the solids to the bottom of the tube.)

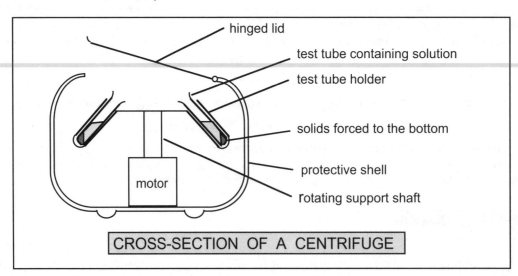

hinged lid

test tube containing solution

test tube holder

solids forced to the bottom

protective shell

rotating support shaft

motor

CROSS-SECTION OF A CENTRIFUGE

Centrifuges are frequently used when a chemical reaction forms small amounts of solid particles in a solution and the solid must be separated. A solid formed in a liquid solution as a result of a chemical reaction is called a **PRECIPITATE.**

Note: Both filtration and centrifuging can produce a separation with similar solid–in–liquid mechanical mixtures. However, filtration works best with relatively large volumes of liquid, whereas a centrifuge works best with volumes that can be held in a small test tube.

H. PAPER, COLUMN and THIN LAYER CHROMATOGRAPHY

Each of **PAPER, COLUMN** and **THIN LAYER CHROMATOGRAPHY** works similarly and is used to separate **small** amounts of **SOLID–IN–LIQUID SOLUTIONS** containing two or more dissolved solids which are coloured or can be reacted to form colours. *Paper chromatography* uses a sheet of absorbent paper and *thin layer chromatography* **(TLC)** uses a thin absorbent layer of dried silica gel on a sheet of glass or plastic. (Column chromatography is discussed below.) A drop of the solid–in–liquid mixture is put near one end of a chromatography sheet and allowed to dry. Another liquid, the "**developing solvent**", is allowed to absorb into the lower end of the chromatographic sheet containing the mixture and the liquid is absorbed up the sheet. A "*solvent front*" is seen as the liquid slowly moves upwards.

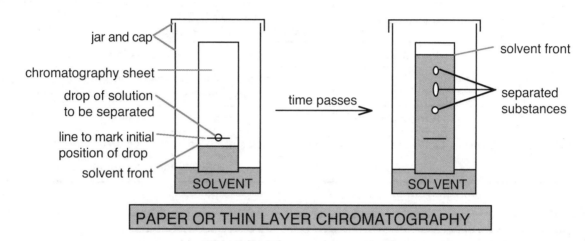

jar and cap

chromatography sheet

drop of solution to be separated

line to mark initial position of drop

solvent front

SOLVENT

time passes

solvent front

separated substances

SOLVENT

PAPER OR THIN LAYER CHROMATOGRAPHY

As the solvent is absorbed up the sheet, two opposing tendencies come into play: the dissolved solids tend to stay absorbed onto the sheet *but* the solids also tend to dissolve in the solvent. Chemicals which have a greater tendency to stick to the sheet and less tendency to dissolve in the solvent travel only a short distance up the sheet. Solids which have a greater tendency to dissolve in the solvent will travel almost as fast as the upward–flowing *solvent front*. After drying the sheet, the areas containing the separated solids can be individually cut out (if using a paper sheet) or scraped off (if using a silica gel TLC sheet). Each individual solid can then be dissolved out of the paper or silica gel, and the solvent evaporated to leave the solid in its pure form.

In column chromatography (shown at the right), a tube is packed with an absorbent material called the "**stationary phase**". This absorbent material is a porous solid such as powdered silica gel or resin beads. The solution containing the mixture of dissolved solids (the "**mobile phase**") is poured on top of the stationary phase. Finally, a "**developing solvent**" is poured in the top of the column. As with paper chromatography, the solvent spreads out and separates the components in the mixture. The components which have the greatest tendency to dissolve in the solvent and the least tendency to adhere to the stationary phase will "drip" out the bottom first. All that has to be done is to collect each "fraction", containing a specific separated component dissolved in the solvent, as it emerges from the bottom.

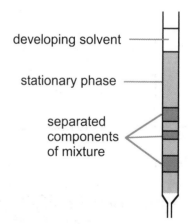

developing solvent

stationary phase

separated components of mixture

Frequently, chromatography can be used to separate apparently colourless solids **IF** the solids are capable of "fluorescing" (glowing) when exposed to ultraviolet light.

Final Note: All three of the chromatography methods discussed above have their advantages and disadvantages. It is beyond the scope of this introductory course to decide when each one should be used. They are all treated as interchangeable methods for the present purposes.

A SYNOPSIS OF SEPARATION METHODS

Rather than attempting to give a "one–method–does–all" recipe, it is preferable to see what separation methods ("tools") can be used when you are confronted with particular situations.

A. Mechanical Mixtures

MIXTURE	METHOD	WHEN TO USE METHOD
SOLID in SOLID	Hand separation	Large chunks present among other solids
	Gravity separation	The density of the desired solids is much different from the density of the other solids
	Solvent extraction	One solid preferentially dissolves in a particular solvent
	Chromatography	The solids are coloured, present in small amounts and are soluble in some solvent or mixture of solvents
SOLID in LIQUID	Hand separation	A few large pieces of solid are present in the liquid
	Gravity separation	Solid particles are present in a *small* amount of liquid
	Filtration	Solid particles are present in a *large* amount of liquid

B. Solutions

MIXTURE	METHOD	WHEN TO USE METHOD
SOLID in LIQUID	Evaporation	The solid is wanted and the liquid is not
	Distillation	The liquid is wanted; the solid may or may not be wanted
	Solvent extraction	An immiscible added solvent preferentially dissolves at least one but not all of the solids present
	Recrystallization	One dissolved solid is much less soluble than the others present (if any); the liquid is not wanted
	Chromatography	Small amounts of more than one coloured solid are present; the liquid present is not wanted
LIQUID in LIQUID	Distillation	Two or more liquids are present and have different boiling temperatures
	Solvent extraction	An immiscible added solvent preferentially dissolves at least one but not all of the liquids present

EXERCISES:

45. A red–brown solution of bromine in water (density = 1.01 g/mL) is poured into a separatory funnel. Trichloroethane (density = 1.34 g/mL) is added and the mixture shaken thoroughly. Afterwards, two liquid layers are seen in the funnel: a clear layer of water and a reddish–orange layer of bromine in trichloroethane. Which layer will be on the top?

46. (a) If you wished to completely remove and save the liquid from a solid–in–liquid solution, which separation method(s) could be used?
    (b) If you wished to completely remove and *not* save the liquid from a solid–in–liquid solution, which separation method(s) could be used?

47. Which separation method(s) could be used to separate the following?
    (a) two miscible liquids
    (b) two immiscible liquids
    (c) a flour–like solid floating around in water
    (d) a mixture of three water–soluble dyes
    (e) a mixture of sand, salt and water

48. Copper(II) sulphate, potassium nitrate and sodium chloride are solids which dissolve in water to about the same extent. If a mixture contains about 100 g of copper(II) sulphate, 0.5 g of potassium nitrate and 0.1 g of sodium chloride, which separation method(s) might be used to recover most of the copper(II) sulphate from the mixture?

49. A single solvent extraction removes 90% of a desired chemical from a solution. What percentage of the chemical is *left* in the solution after two successive extractions?

50. A single solvent extraction removes 60% of a desired chemical from a solution. What percentage of the chemical would be *removed* from the solution after four successive extractions?

51. Why shouldn't the solvent completely evaporate in the recrystallization method of purification?

52. When an aqueous alum solution is left uncovered some of the water present evaporates, forming perfect alum crystals. The perfect crystals are scattered among many imperfect crystals. What separation technique(s) can be used to separate the perfect crystals from the rest of the mixture?

53. How can you separate all the components in a mixture containing sand, iron filings, water, gasoline, red water–soluble dye and blue water–soluble dye? In pure form the dyes are powders.

54. How can you separate a mixture of white sand (density = 2.2 g/mL), black sand (density = 5.2 g/mL), liquid methanol (MP = –94°C, BP = 65°C), and liquid hexanol (MP = –47°C, BP = 158°C)? Methanol and hexanol are miscible.

55. How can you separate a mixture of the three solids: potassium sulphate (MP = 1069°C, soluble in water, insoluble in alcohol), calcium carbonate (MP = greater than 1000°C, insoluble in water, insoluble in alcohol) and naphthalene (MP = 81°C, insoluble in water, soluble in alcohol)?

56. How can you separate a mixture of liquid chloroform (density = 1.48 g/mL, BP = 62°C, soluble in alcohol, insoluble in water), water (BP = 100°C), sugar (decomposes at 185°C, soluble in water, insoluble in alcohol and chloroform), powdered aluminum(insoluble in water, alcohol and chloroform) and liquid benzene (boils at 80°C, soluble in chloroform and alcohol, insoluble in water)? [Hint: what phases or layers will be observed in this mixture?]

57. You have a few milligrams of a mixture of powdered crystals containing green copper(II) chloride, pink cobalt(II) chloride and yellow iron(III) chloride. Suggest a method to separate the mixture.

58. How could you separate a mixture consisting of 500 kg of white sand (density = 2.2 g/mL), 50 kg of pennies (density = 8.96 g/mL), 10 kg of small nails (density = 7.86 g/mL) and 1 kg of fine platinum granules (density = 21.45 g/mL)? The sand and platinum granules are the same size.

III.5. PHASE CHANGES

If substances just sat around and did nothing, not only would there be very little for chemists to do (which would be a terrible shame) but there would be no chemists in the first place. In fact, life would not exist and the universe would be a pretty dead place ... if a universe existed at all.

Definitions: A **CHEMICAL CHANGE** is a change in which new substances are formed.

A CHEMICAL CHANGE produces a set of chemicals which is DIFFERENT from the set of chemicals which existed before the change.

A **PHYSICAL CHANGE** is a change in the **PHASE** of a substance, such that no new substances are formed.

A PHYSICAL CHANGE does NOT change the SET of chemicals involved.

IMPORTANT: Chemical changes are frequently accompanied by physical changes. For example, hydrogen **gas** and oxygen **gas** react to form **liquid** water. Therefore, a reference to a chemical change implies that the *primary* change is chemical, but a physical change may occur as a result.

In general, continued heating of a solid produces the following temperature behaviour.

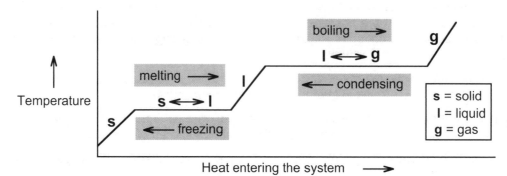

Note: The temperature does not change during a phase change (such as melting and boiling).

Definitions: **MELTING TEMPERATURE** is the temperature at which a solid changes into the liquid phase.

FREEZING TEMPERATURE is the temperature at which a liquid changes into the solid phase.

At the MELTING/FREEZING temperature the solid and liquid phases co–exist.

BOILING TEMPERATURE is the temperature at which a liquid changes into the gas phase.

CONDENSATION TEMPERATURE is the temperature at which a gas changes into the liquid phase.

At the BOILING/CONDENSING temperature the liquid and gas phases co–exist.

As time goes on, heat is constantly entering the substance represented in the above graph.

• *On the sloping portions of the graph* – all the heat is used to warm the substance so the temperature rises.

• *On the level portions of the graph* – the substance contains so much heat energy that it cannot absorb more heat and stay in the same phase. The added heat is used, for example, to break up the solid and allow a liquid to form. All the heat is used to change phase so the temperature doesn't change and the graph levels off.

The diagram below shows what happens during the melting process.

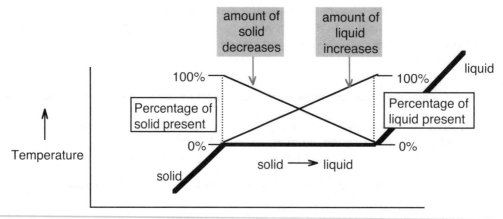

There is a steady decrease in the amount of solid as the amount of liquid increases. At the start of the phase change the substance is 100% solid, then more and more liquid forms. Eventually, the last bit of solid melts and the phase change is complete.

Special note: When 1 g of candle wax is *burned* about 10 000 joules of heat are produced; when 1 g of liquid wax **solidifies** about 40 joules of heat are produced. This is typical of the differences between the energy involved in physical changes (for example, the solidification of wax) and chemical changes (for example, the burning of wax). In general:

> The amount of heat involved in a physical change is much less than the amount involved in a chemical change.

EXERCISES:

59. Classify each of the following as either a chemical change (primarily) or a physical change.
    (a) the formation of fog
    (b) burning a cigarette
    (c) the sprouting of a seed
    (d) the rusting of iron
    (e) mixing yellow and blue paint to make green paint
    (f) separating an alcohol–water mixture into water and alcohol

60. Benzene melts at $6^\circ C$ and boils at $80^\circ C$. Plot a graph showing the temperature–vs–time behaviour of benzene as its temperature is raised from $0^\circ C$ to $100^\circ C$. Label the axes and indicate the phases present on each portion of the graph. No scale needs to be specified for the time axis.

61. Water freezes at $0^\circ C$ and boils at $100^\circ C$. Plot a graph showing the temperature–vs–time behaviour of steam as its temperature is lowered from $120^\circ C$ to $-20^\circ C$. Label the axes and indicate the phases present on each portion of the graph. No scale needs to be specified for the time axis.

62. Some substances undergo a special type of phase change called **sublimation** in which they go directly from the **solid phase** to the **gas phase,** without melting. (The reverse process, in which a gas changes directly into a solid, is called **deposition**.) Ammonium carbamate sublimes at $60^\circ C$. Plot a graph showing the temperature–vs–time behaviour of ammonium carbamate as its temperature is raised from $0^\circ C$ to $100^\circ C$. Label the axes and indicate the phases present on each portion of the graph. No scale needs to be specified for the time axis.

63. A sample of ice was melted by a steady supply of heat and after 20 minutes was completely melted. What was the approximate composition of the sample after (a) 5 minutes? (b) 10 minutes?

III.6. THE ROLE OF KINETIC ENERGY IN PHYSICAL CHANGES

All molecules are constantly in motion.

Definition: **KINETIC ENERGY** (KE) is the energy that molecules possess as a result of their motion.

There are three types of kinetic energy which a *molecule* can possess.

   (a) **Rotational Energy** (E_{ROT}) – causes a molecule to rotate around one of its axes; bond lengths and bond angles don't change.

      EXAMPLE: There are three ways in which a water molecule can rotate.

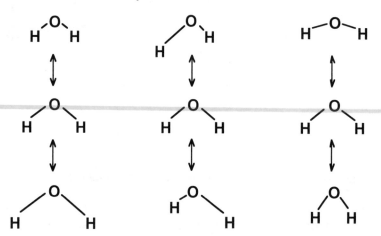

   (b) **Vibrational Energy** (E_{VIB}) –   changes the bond lengths and/or angles between atoms in a molecule

      EXAMPLE: Some of the numerous ways in which water can vibrate are shown below.

   (c) **TRANSLATIONAL ENERGY** (E_{TRANS}) – causes the molecule to travel in a straight line from place to place, but has no effect on bond lengths and angles.

      EXAMPLE:

                                                   — wall

Special Note: Vibrational energy refers to relative movement of two atoms *within* a molecule. Separate molecules in a crystal can oscillate back and forth, bumping into a neighbour on the left, rebounding to hit a neighbour on the right, and so on in a continuous manner, but these molecular oscillations are the result of *translational* energy, not *vibrational* energy.

PRACTICAL APPLICATIONS OF KINETIC ENERGY CHANGES

1. MICROWAVE OVENS supply energy which causes the water molecules in food and liquids to vibrate. As molecules absorb energy and bump into each other, the food "heats up".

2. In INFRARED (IR) SPECTROSCOPY, molecules absorb infrared (heat) energy. ("Infrared" is pronounced "infra–red".) IR energy is just light energy with less energy than red light; if white light is passed through a prism, the light energies are spread out as shown below.

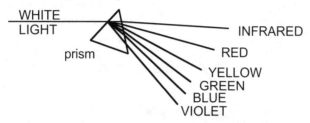

A thermometer held to the side of the red light (in the path of the IR light) shows a temperature increase — IR energy is heat energy. Different molecules have differing sets of bonds (which vibrate in a unique way) and absorb different sets of "infrared" energies. IR spectroscopy is used to help identify unknown molecules. A simplified IR spectrophotometer is shown below.

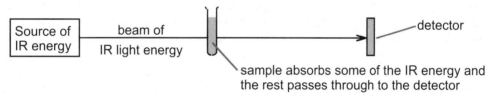

The frequency of the infrared light is slowly changed and the amount of energy absorbed at each different frequency is automatically plotted, producing the typical "spectrum" below. ("Frequency" measures how energetic the light is.)

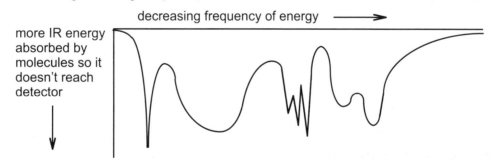

Initially, the sample absorbs none of the energy passing through it (the detector registers 100% of the energy). Then, as the frequency increases, first one bond in the molecule and then another absorbs energy when the frequency of the IR source is exactly that required to make the bond VIBRATE. As a result, the amount of energy reaching the detector decreases each time a bond absorbs energy. Each downward "valley" comes from a specific type of vibration of a particular chemical bond.

Every different molecule has its own "fingerprint"; by comparing the spectrum of an "unknown" molecule with the spectra of known molecules the unknown can be identified.

THE ROLE OF KINETIC ENERGY IN PHASE CHANGES

The temperature–vs–energy graph is related to kinetic energy changes as shown below.

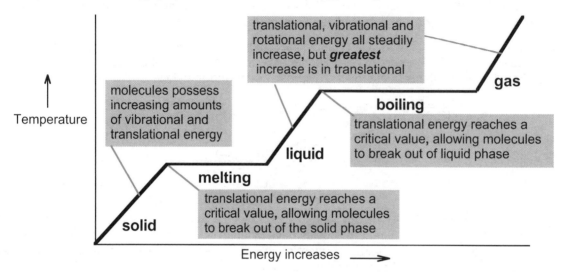

In the solid state, the increase in E_{VIB} and E_{TRANS} causes the molecules to oscillate back and forth, bumping into their neighbours with increasing frequency and force. Eventually, the translational energy increases to the point where molecules can overcome the bonds holding them to their neighbours in the solid: at this point the substance is at its melting temperature. The molecules now have the maximum energy they can possess and still remain connected to one another; any additional energy increases their E_{TRANS} and allows them to separate from one another. In other words, the molecules can pull away from one another and the solid melts.

As the molecules in the liquid state receive additional energy, they move faster and faster. A thermometer will register this increase in translational energy as an increase in temperature. (The molecules bump into the thermometer and transfer some of their energy to the thermometer.)

The process occurring at the boiling temperature is similar to what happens at the melting point, except that the energy added to molecules at their boiling temperature enables them to completely escape from their neighbours and fly off into the gas phase. Energy added to molecules in the gas phase makes them move faster still, causing an increase in temperature.

EXERCISES:

64. What is the overall effect of adding heat to any sample of particles, regardless of its phase or state?

65. Assuming that an isolated atom acts like a mathematical point (which has no volume, diameter, or front and back), which of the 3 types of kinetic energy can apply to an ISOLATED ATOM?

66. Which of the three types of kinetic energy is most important in causing phase changes?

67. Which of the three types of kinetic energy are possessed by a "frisbee" thrown between two people?

68. Which of the three types of kinetic energy do not change the shape of a molecule?

69. Predict what should happen to the viscosity of a liquid as temperature increases, and state why.

70. The infra–red spectra of methanol $\begin{bmatrix} \text{H} \\ | \\ \text{H-C-O-H} \\ | \\ \text{H} \end{bmatrix}$ and ethanol $\begin{bmatrix} \text{H} \quad \text{H} \\ | \quad | \\ \text{H-C-C-O-H} \\ | \quad | \\ \text{H} \quad \text{H} \end{bmatrix}$ are similar

    in many ways but not identical. Why might the spectra be **similar**?

71. What happens to the volume occupied by a substance as its translational kinetic energy increases from a very small to a very large value?

UNIT IV : INORGANIC NOMENCLATURE

Every field of study has its own language. Learning the language of Chemistry starts by learning the names of the elements and their compounds. Two of the major fields of Chemistry are organic chemistry and inorganic chemistry. Organic chemistry is the study of carbon compounds while inorganic chemistry is the study of the elements and "non–organic" compounds. The term "**inorganic nomenclature**" refers to the naming of elements and inorganic compounds. Previous science courses have taught you to name many elements and inorganic compounds. This unit will extend your knowledge of inorganic nomenclature.

IV.1. THE CHEMICAL ELEMENTS

The table below is only a partial list of the elements, but represents the elements which will be of interest in Chemistry 11 and 12. (The complete list of elements is found in the tables *Periodic Table of the Elements* and *Atomic Masses of the Elements*, at the back of this book.)

Name	Symbol	Name	Symbol	Name	Symbol	Name	Symbol
aluminum	Al	cobalt	Co	manganese	Mn	silicon	Si
antimony	Sb	copper	Cu	mercury	Hg	silver	Ag
argon	Ar	fluorine	F	molybdenum	Mo	sodium	Na
arsenic	As	francium	Fr	neon	Ne	strontium	Sr
astatine	At	gallium	Ga	nickel	Ni	sulphur	S
barium	Ba	germanium	Ge	nitrogen	N	tellurium	Te
beryllium	Be	gold	Au	oxygen	O	thallium	Tl
bismuth	Bi	helium	He	palladium	Pd	tin	Sn
boron	B	hydrogen	H	phosphorus	P	titanium	Ti
bromine	Br	indium	In	platinum	Pt	tungsten	W
cadmium	Cd	iodine	I	polonium	Po	uranium	U
calcium	Ca	iron	Fe	potassium	K	vanadium	V
carbon	C	krypton	Kr	radium	Ra	xenon	Xe
cesium	Cs	lead	Pb	radon	Rn	zinc	Zn
chlorine	Cl	lithium	Li	rubidium	Rb		
chromium	Cr	magnesium	Mg	selenium	Se		

Some comments about the elements may help you to learn their names and symbols.

a) The first letter in the symbol is ALWAYS in upper case (capitals). Second letters, if present, are ALWAYS in lower case.

   Example: Pt, Te, Be, Cl

b) Many elements just use the first two letters of the element's name as the element's symbol.

   Example: Al, Bi, Li.

c) When the first two letters have already been used with some other element, the first and third letters are used.

   Example: Ar = **ar**gon
   As = **ars**enic (can't use Ar)
   At = **ast**atine (can't use As)

d) Elements which were known in ancient times or which have names taken from substances known in ancient times have symbols derived from their Latin names.

Element	Latin name	Symbol
antimony	stibium	Sb
copper	cuprum	Cu
gold	aurum	Au
iron	ferrum	Fe
lead	plumbum	Pb
mercury	hydragyrum	Hg
potassium	kalium	K
silver	argentum	Ag
sodium	natrium	Na
tin	stannum	Sn

e) A few elements have single letter symbols.

   Example: B, C, F, H, I, K, N, O, P, S, U, V, W

f) Some elements and their symbols frequently cause problems with students. The following might be of some help keeping things straight.

   Au & Ag :   Au comes from **Au**rum, meaning shining or **gold**en dawn
   Ag comes from **Arg**ent, and "argent" in French means "money or **silver**"

   Mg & Mn :   Look at the first and third letters – **M**a**g**nesium = Mg   and   **M**a**n**ganese = Mn

   W :   Comes from "**W**olfram", the European name for tungsten

   F :   This is a **single–letter** symbol. Don't add an "l" as is found with chlorine, Cl!

   P & K :   Be careful with this pair, they are easy to confuse –
   K = potassium (from "**K**alium") and   P = **P**hosphorus

   Ra & Rn :   Radium was found first, by Mme. Curie, so it gets to use the Ra combination for its symbol. Radon was found later, so it used the first and last letters of its name, **R**ado**n**.

Self–Test: For each of the following, give the name of the element if the symbol is given and give the symbol if the name is given.

(a) sodium _____   (k) cadmium _____

(b) K _____   (l) Be _____

(c) thallium _____   (m) arsenic _____

(d) Hg _____   (n) Mo _____

(e) silicon _____   (o) platinum _____

(f) Kr _____   (p) Cu _____

(g) fluorine _____   (q) tungsten _____

(h) Cr _____   (r) Pb _____

(l) sulphur _____   (s) astatine _____

(j) Cs _____   (t) B _____

METALS and NONMETALS

Previous science courses told you what the terms "metal" and "nonmetal" mean. Unit VIII of this course systematically examines the properties of the metals and nonmetals, but because the present unit deals with the naming of compounds made from metals and nonmetals it is necessary to quickly refresh your memory with respect to where the metals and nonmetals are located on the periodic table.

The compounds used in the examples and exercises which follow are selected from the metals in white boxes (below) and the nonmetals in shaded boxes. The elements in outlined boxes are not used in any of the examples or exercises which follow (although you should know the names and symbols for later purposes).

H																	He
Li	Be											B	C	N	O	F	Ne
Na	Mg											Al	Si	P	S	Cl	Ar
K	Ca	Sc	Ti	V	Cr	Mn	Fe	Co	Ni	Cu	Zn	Ga	Ge	As	Se	Br	Kr
Rb	Sr	Y	Zr	Nb	Mo	Tc	Ru	Rh	Pd	Ag	Cd	In	Sn	Sb	Te	I	Xe
Cs	Ba	La	Hf	Ta	W	Re	Os	Ir	Pt	Au	Hg	Tl	Pb	Bi	Po	At	Rn
Fr	Ra																

IV.2. NAMING INORGANIC COMPOUNDS

Going across the periodic table, the following correspondence is found between the columns of the table and the charges of the ions formed by the elements in the columns. (There are some exceptions, but assume the values below unless otherwise indicated.)

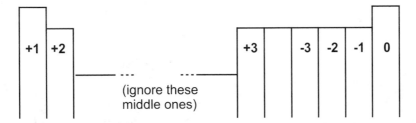

+1	+2	(ignore these middle ones)	+3	-3	-2	-1	0

You should memorize the following ion charges.

H^+							
Li^+	Be^{2+}					O^{2-}	F^-
Na^+	Mg^{2+}		Al^{3+}			S^{2-}	Cl^-
K^+	Ca^{2+}	(ignore these middle ones)					Br^-
Rb^+	Sr^{2+}						I^-
Cs^+	Ba^{2+}						

IMPORTANT: Metals form **POSITIVE** ions.

Nonmetals form **NEGATIVE** ions (Hydrogen is generally an exception).

Definitions: An **ANION** is an ion with a NEGATIVE charge.
> *Example:* Cl^-, NO_3^-

A **CATION** is an ion with a POSITIVE charge.
> *Example:* Al^{3+}, NH_4^+

> MEMORY AID: "**CAT**ions are **PUSS**itive"

A **MONATOMIC** species is made up of only ONE atom.
> *Example:* Ne, He, Li^+, Cl^-

A **DIATOMIC** species is made up of two atoms (which may be the same or different types).
> *Example:* O_2, IBr, NO, Br_2, ClO^-, Hg_2^{2+}

A **TRIATOMIC** species is made up of three atoms.
> *Example:* O_3, NO_2, NOCl, H_2O, I_3^-

A **POLYATOMIC** species is made up of many atoms ("poly" means "more than ONE").

> **Note:** This is a general term and applies to any species having more than one atom.
> *Example:* H_3PO_4, $H_2PO_4^-$, NO_3^-, NH_3, HS^-, NO

EXERCISE:

1. In the space after each of the following species, indicate which of the terms below apply to each species. There is more than one term which applies to each species.

> N (neutral),   C (a cation),   A (an anion)
> M (monatomic),   D (diatomic),   T (triatomic),   P (polyatomic)

(a) SO_4^{2-} _____

(b) H_2O _____

(c) Sr^{2+} _____

(d) OH^- _____

(e) NH_4^+ _____

(f) Ar _____

NAMING MONATOMIC IONS

A. Naming monatomic metal ions: Use the name of the metal and add the word "ion".

> **Example:**   Sodium metal (Na) forms the sodium ion (Na^+)
> Aluminum metal (Al) forms the aluminum ion (Al^{3+})

The Stock System of naming metal ions: If a metal ion has more than one possible charge, the charge is indicated by a Roman numeral, in parentheses, immediately following the name.

> **Example:** Fe^{3+} = iron(III) ion , Fe^{2+} = iron(II) ion , U^{6+} = uranium(VI) ion , U^{3+} = uranium(III) ion

EXERCISES:

2.   Write the names of the following ions using the Stock system of notation.
(a) Cu^+ (b) Cr^{3+} (c) W^{6+}

3.   Write the formula of the following ions to show their charges.
(a) cobalt(III) ion   (b) nickel(II) ion   (c) vanadium(V) ion

B. Naming monatomic non–metal ions: Take off the original ending of the element's name and put on an **"ide"** ending. (The ending **ide** means the ion has a negative charge and has no attached atoms such as oxygen included with the ion.)

Element name	Element symbol	Ion name	Ion symbol
fluor**ine**	F	fluor**ide**	F^-
chlor**ine**	Cl	chlor**ide**	Cl^-
brom**ine**	Br	brom**ide**	Br^-
iod**ine**	I	iod**ide**	I^-
ox**ygen**	O	ox**ide**	O^{2-}
sulph**ur**	S	sulph**ide**	S^{2-}
nitr**ogen**	N	nitr**ide**	N^{3-}
phosph**orus**	P	phosph**ide**	P^{3-}

NAMING POLYATOMIC IONS

The rules for naming polyatomic ions are somewhat complicated and are not part of the Chemistry 11 course. The table **Names, Formulae and Charges of Some Common Ions** at the back of this book lists the ions which will be encountered in Chemistry 11 and 12. Although you are not required to memorize the table of ions, it is **strongly recommended that you do memorize** the names, formulae and charges of the following commonly encountered ions. (Failure to memorize them will cost you a great deal of time during both Chemistry 11 and 12, especially on tests.)

carbonate = CO_3^{2-}	chromate = CrO_4^{2-}	phosphate = PO_4^{3-}	acetate = CH_3COO^-
nitrate = NO_3^-	dichromate = $Cr_2O_7^{2-}$	hydroxide = OH^-	ammonium = NH_4^+
sulphate = SO_4^{2-}	permanganate = MnO_4^-		

CONSTRUCTING THE FORMULA OF AN IONIC COMPOUND, GIVEN THE NAME OF THE COMPOUND

Definition: An **IONIC COMPOUND** is a compound made up of ions.

This section shows how to write the formula for an ionic compound given the name of the compound.

> **IMPORTANT:** Compounds are **NEUTRAL MOLECULES.** Therefore
> (the sum of the "+" ion charges in the molecule) = (the sum of the "–" ion charges in the molecule)

The translation of a chemical name into a chemical formula is a simple process with three rules.

1. **Write the formula for the positive ion first and write the formula for the negative ion second.**
   (In a chemical name, the **POSITIVE** ion is *always* written **FIRST** and the **NEGATIVE** ion is *always* **SECOND.** All you do is translate the words in the chemical name into ions in the order they are given.)

   For example: Tin(IV) oxide is translated as $Sn^{4+} O^{2-}$

2. **"Criss–cross" the numbers in front of the charges on the ions.** (If no number is shown, use a "1". The result of the "criss–crossing" operation shown in the example below is to take
   $2(Sn^{4+}) = 8$ "+" charges, and $4(O^{2-}) = 8$ "–" charges, so that
   (the number of "+" charges) = (the number of "–" charges).

   For example: $Sn^{4+}_{2} \diagdown\!\!\!\!\diagup O^{2-}_{4}$

3. **Tidy up the formula in a three–part process.**
   • If both subscripts can be evenly divided by "2" (or "3", occasionally), do so.
   • Omit the superscripted charges.
   • Omit any subscript which is a "1".

   For example: $Sn^{4+}_{2} \diagdown\!\!\!\!\diagup O^{2-}_{4}$ $\xrightarrow{\text{divide subscripts by 2}}$ $Sn^{4+}_{1} O^{2-}_{2}$ $\xrightarrow[\text{a value of "1"}]{\text{omit charges and superscripts with}}$ $Sn O_2$

EXAMPLES:

a) **sodium chloride :** sodium ion = Na^+ , chloride ion = Cl^-
   Criss–cross the charges – $Na^+_1 Cl^-_1$ – eliminate charges and any subscripts equal to "1": **NaCl**

b) **potassium oxide :** potassium ion = K^+ , oxide ion = O^{2-}
   Criss–cross the charges – $K^+_2 O^{2-}_1$ – eliminate charges and any subscripts equal to "1": **K$_2$O**

c) **calcium phosphide :** calcium ion = Ca^{2+} , phosphide ion = P^{3-}
   Criss–cross the charges – $Ca^{2+}_3 P^{3-}_2$ – and eliminate charges: **Ca$_3$P$_2$**

d) **tin(IV) sulphate :** tin(IV) ion = Sn^{4+} , sulphate ion = SO_4^{2-}
   Criss–cross the charges: $Sn^{4+}_2 (SO_4^{2-})_4$ [note that the entire sulphate ion is taken 4 times]
   divide subscripts by 2 – $Sn^{4+}_1 (SO_4^{2-})_2$ – eliminate charges and subscripts equal to "1": **Sn(SO$_4$)$_2$**

e) **iron(II) phosphate :** iron(II) ion = Fe^{2+} , phosphate ion = PO_4^{3-}
   Criss–cross the charges – $Fe^{2+}_3 (PO_4^{3-})_2$ – and eliminate charges: **Fe$_3$(PO$_4$)$_2$**

f) **ammonium sulphate :** ammonium ion = NH_4^+ , sulphate ion = SO_4^{2-}
   Criss–cross charges – $(NH_4^+)_2 (SO_4^{2-})_1$ – eliminate charges and subscripts equal to "1": **(NH$_4$)$_2$SO$_4$**

g) **mercury(I) chloride :**   mercury(I) ion = Hg_2^{2+} ,   chloride ion = Cl^-

Criss–cross charges − $\left(Hg_2^{2+}\right)_1 Cl_2^-$ − eliminate charges and subscripts equal to "1": **Hg_2Cl_2**

Note: You **CAN'T** divide subscripts by 2 to get HgCl since the mercury(I) ion is Hg_2^{2+} , **not** Hg^+.

EXERCISE:

4.   Write the formula for the following compounds. You should use your table of *Names, Formulae, and Charges of Some Common Ions* to help identify the ions present.

(a) tin(IV) sulphate
(b) ammonium oxalate
(c) lithium oxide
(d) copper(I) nitride
(e) mercury(I) nitrite
(f) iron(III) hydroxide
(g) silver sulphate

(h) lead(II) perchlorate
(i) chromium(III) oxide
(j) manganese(II) fluoride
(k) potassium dihydrogen phosphate
(l) uranium(IV) sulphate
(m) ammonium dichromate
(n) copper(I) phosphate

(o) calcium hypochlorite
(p) sodium hydrogen sulphite
(q) magnesium permanganate
(r) tungsten(V) bromide
(s) ammonium phosphate
(t) mercury(II) acetate

CONSTRUCTING THE NAME OF AN IONIC COMPOUND, GIVEN THE FORMULA OF THE COMPOUND

The reverse procedure to that used in the previous section is relatively straight–forward.

Metal ions often have more than one possible charge and the trick is deciding on the charge a metal ion has in a particular compound. For the purposes of this unit, you can assume that negative ions always have only one possible charge, which is the one shown in the table *Names, Formulae and Charges of Some Common Ions*.

The translation of a compound formula into a compound name involves two possible situations.

1. **If the first ion in the compound only has one possible charge, simply write the names of the ions one after another.** (Omit the word "ion" from the names.)

Example: **$ZnCl_2$:** Zn^{2+} = zinc ion, Cl^- = chloride ion   and the name is   **zinc chloride** .

2. **If the first ion is a metal known to possess more than one possible charge OR a metal which is not on the table, "un–criss–cross" the subscripts and use them as charges.** Remember that the first ion has a positive charge and the second has a negative charge.

Example: **PbO_2 :** un–criss–crossing the subscripts gives $(Pb^{2+})_1(O^{1-})_2$.

Next, if the known charge on the negative ion is double (or triple) the charge calculated by the un–criss–crossing process then double (or triple) the charges calculated for both the positive and negative ions. [This process allows for the possibility that the subscripts in the molecule were divided by 2 or 3 when the compound formula was written.]

Example: Since oxide ion is O^{2-}, the charges are doubled to give $(Pb^{4+})_1(O^{2-})_2$.

Last, use Stock notation to write the positive ion's name, followed by the negative ion's name.

Example: $(Pb^{4+})_1(O^{2-})_2$ is named   **lead(IV) oxide.**

EXAMPLES:

a) **Ag_2SO_4 :** Ag^+ = silver ion , SO_4^{2-} = sulphate ion

Ag^+ is the only ion of silver so the compound name is: **silver sulphate.**

b) **Cu_2O :** Since Cu has more than one possible ion charge start by un–criss–crossing subscripts.

$(Cu^{1+})_2\, O^{2-}$

O^{2-} is the correct charge for oxygen so that copper has a +1 charge and the compound name is: **copper(I) oxide.**

c) **FeS:**   Since Fe has more than one possible ion charge start by un–criss–crossing subscripts.

$$Fe^{1+} S^{1-}$$

The charge on S should be S^{2-}, not S^{1-}, so that all charges are multiplied by 2: $Fe^{2+} S^{2-}$.
Therefore the compound name should be: **iron(II) sulphide.**

d) **Fe$_2$(HPO$_4$)$_3$:**   Since Fe has more than one possible charge start by un–criss–crossing subscripts.

$$(Fe^{3+})_2 \ (HPO_4^{2-})_3$$

HPO_4^{2-} is the correct charge for the monohydrogen phosphate ion so that the compound name is: **iron(III) monohydrogen phosphate.**

e) **U(SO$_4$)$_2$:**   Since uranium is not in the table its charge must be worked out.
Un–criss–crossing the subscripts gives

$$U^{2+} \ (SO_4^-)_2 \ .$$

But the charge on sulphate should be 2– so that the charges are multiplied by 2.

$$U^{4+} \ (SO_4^{2-})_2$$

The name of the compound is: **uranium(IV) sulphate.**

You must memorize the "common name" of two compounds: **H$_2$O = water**   and   **NH$_3$ = ammonia.**

EXERCISE:

5.   Write the name of the following compounds.

    (a) Ag$_3$PO$_4$ (e) (NH$_4$)$_2$CO$_3$ (i)   (NH$_4$)$_2$S   (m) LiClO$_2$ (q) SnO$_2$

    (b) Al$_2$(SO$_4$)$_3$ (f)   VCl$_3$ (j)   NH$_4$HCO$_3$ (n) Na$_2$HPO$_4$ (r) ZnCr$_2$O$_7$

    (c) Fe$_2$S$_3$ (g) Hg$_2$CO$_3$ (k) FeC$_2$O$_4$ (o) Al(OH)$_3$ (s) V$_2$O$_5$

    (d) CuCl   (h) CuSO$_4$ (l)   Mg(HSO$_3$)$_2$ (p) CrI$_3$ (t) Sr$_3$N$_2$

NAMING HYDRATES

When a crystal of an ionic compound is grown by evaporation from aqueous solution, frequently it is found that the crystal structure will include water molecules.

EXAMPLE: When copper(II) sulphate is crystallized from water, the resulting crystals have the formula

$$CuSO_4 \cdot 5H_2O \ .$$

This formula shows that 5 water molecules are included with (or attached to) every $CuSO_4$. In other words, $CuSO_4 \cdot 5H_2O$ can be thought of as "$CuSO_4 + 5H_2O$".

Molecules which include water molecules in their crystal structures are called **HYDRATES.** The naming of hydrates is straightforward and relies on using a prefix to tell how many water molecules are attached.

Memorize the following prefixes and the numbers they represent.

Prefix used	# of water molecules	Prefix used	# of water molecules
mono	1	hexa	6
di	2	hepta	7
tri	3	octa	8
tetra	4	nona	9
penta	5	deca	10

EXAMPLE: $CuSO_4 \cdot 5H_2O$ = copper(II) sulphate pentahydrate

$Zn(CH_3COO)_2 \cdot 2H_2O$ = zinc acetate dihydrate

$Ca(NO_3)_2 \cdot 4H_2O$ = calcium nitrate tetrahydrate

EXERCISE:

6.   Write the name of the following hydrated compounds.

(a) $FeBr_3 \cdot 6H_2O$ (d) $CoF_2 \cdot 4H_2O$ (g) $Na_2SO_4 \cdot 10H_2O$

(b) $Li_2Cr_2O_7 \cdot 2H_2O$ (e) $Na_2CO_3 \cdot H_2O$ (h) $Ni_3(PO_4)_2 \cdot 8H_2O$

(c) $Al_2O_3 \cdot 3H_2O$ (f) $Na_2S \cdot 9H_2O$ (i) $MgHPO_4 \cdot 7H_2O$

7.   Write the formula for the following hydrated compounds.

(a) iron(III) phosphate octahydrate   (d) chromium(II) oxalate monohydrate

(b) cadmium(II) nitrate tetrahydrate   (e) nickel(II) chloride hexahydrate

(c) copper(II) phosphate trihydrate   (f) aluminum nitrate nonahydrate

NAMING COMPOUNDS BY USING THE PREFIX-NAMING SYSTEM

Definitions: A **BINARY COMPOUND** is a compound made of two different types of atoms.

Example: SO_2, Na_2S, NaCl and $SnCl_4$ are binary compounds.

A **TERNARY COMPOUND** is a compound made of three different types of atoms.

Example: H_2SO_4, KOH, $NaNO_3$ and $KMnO_4$ are ternary compounds.

The PREFIX–NAMING SYSTEM of naming is generally reserved for binary compounds in which THERE ARE TWO DIFFERENT **NONMETALS** INVOLVED.

The rules for using the prefix–naming system (P_2S_3 is used to illustrate the rules)

1.   Each compound name is made of two words, each with a suitable prefix.

The prefixes used are shown in the table below.

Prefix used	# of atoms	Prefix used	# of atoms
mono	1	tetra	4
di	2	penta	5
tri	3	hexa	6

2.   The first word is just the name of the first element, with a prefix to indicate how many of these atoms exist in each molecule.

Example: The first word in the name for P_2S_3 will be **diphosphorus**.

3.   The second name is the name of the second element, with an "ide" ending on the element's name and a prefix to indicate how many of these atoms exist in each molecule.

Example: The second word in the name for P_2S_3 will be **trisulphide**.

Therefore the complete name of P_2S_3 is **diphosphorus trisulphide**.

4.   **EXCEPTION:** if there is **only one** of the **first** atom, do not use any prefix for that atom.

Example: CO_2 is carbon dioxide, NOT monocarbon dioxide.

EXAMPLES: CS_2 = carbon disulphide SO = sulphur monoxide
  Si_2I_6 = disilicon hexaiodide N_2O_4 = dinitrogen tetroxide ("tetraoxide" is clumsy)

EXERCISE:

8. Name the following using the prefix–naming system.
   (a) NO_2 (b) ClF_3 (c) S_4N_2 (d) P_2O_6 (e) N_2O_3 (f) SF_4 (g) BrF (h) SF_6

9. Write the formula for the following compounds.
   (a) sulphur trioxide
   (b) phosphorus pentachloride
   (c) xenon hexafluoride
   (d) oxygen difluoride
   (e) carbon monoxide
   (f) carbon tetrachloride
   (g) tetraphosphorus trisulphide
   (h) dinitrogen pentasulphide
   (i) trisilicon tetranitride

SOME COMMON ACIDS

A compound is called an "acid" if the compound has a chemical formula starting with "H". All of the following acids are assumed to be dissolved in water; that is, they are "aqueous solutions".

HF = hydrofluoric acid H_2SO_4 = sulphuric acid HNO_3 = nitric acid
HCl = hydrochloric acid H_2SO_3 = sulphurous acid HNO_2 = nitrous acid
HBr = hydrobromic acid H_3PO_4 = phosphoric acid $HC_2H_3O_2$ or CH_3COOH = acetic acid
HI = hydroiodic acid

Some additional facts about these acids:
   HF is used to "etch" or "frost" glass ,
   HCl is present in "stomach acid" and is also called "muriatic acid",
   HNO_3 is a very corrosive acid which reacts with most metals,
   H_2SO_4 is the acid used in automobile batteries,
   H_2SO_3 is one of the principle components of acid rain ,
   H_3PO_4 is present in most Cola beverages,
   A 5% solution of CH_3COOH is called "vinegar".

Some compounds form acidic solutions but are usually found as gases and are named as "hydrogen" compounds.

EXAMPLES: H_2S = hydrogen sulphide HCN = hydrogen cyanide

SUMMARY : HOW TO PICK THE CORRECT METHOD FOR NAMING A COMPOUND

The first element or ion in a formula is used to decide on the method.

If the first element or ion in the formula is:	Then:
hydrogen	write the name of the acid if the substance is listed under "SOME COMMON ACIDS". use "hydrogen" as the first name and add the name of the anion which follows the "H" if the acid is NOT in the list.
a non–metal (and the formula doesn't contain NH_4)	use the prefix–naming system
a species listed in the table **Names, Formulae, and Charges of Some Common Ions**	use the name of the cation listed, followed by the name of the anion.
a metal not listed in the table **Names, Formulae, and Charges of Some Common Ions**	use the Stock system (Roman numerals) for the cation, followed by the name of the anion.

IV.3. EXTENSION : THE COLOURS OF SOME COMMON AQUEOUS IONS

The following coloured ions are encountered frequently in chemistry so that the ability to recognize these ions by their colour is a useful skill for you to acquire. **For the purposes of Chemistry 11 and 12, any ions not shown in the list below should be assumed to be colourless** unless told otherwise.

Ion	Colour	Ion	Colour	Ion	Colour
Fe^{2+}	pale green	MnO_4^-	purple	$Cr_2O_7^{2-}$	bright orange
Fe^{3+}	dull yellow	Ni^{2+}	bright green	Cu^{2+}	blue (**)
Co^{2+}	pink–red (**)	CrO_4^{2-}	bright yellow	Mn^{2+}	very pale pink (*)

(*) Mn^{2+} is pale pink in crystals and concentrated aqueous solutions but colourless in dilute solution

(**) these ions have the indicated colour **only** if water of hydration is present in their crystals or they are in aqueous solutions

EXERCISES:

10. A bright yellow solution is mixed with a blue solution to produce a new compound. Suggest a formula and name for the compound.

11. A freshly–made solution is pale green but gradually becomes yellow after exposure to the air for a few hours. Which metal ion is originally present in solution and which ion exists after a few hours?

12. What colour do you expect the following compounds to be?
    (a) sodium carbonate (c) copper(II) sulphate (e) lithium dichromate
    (b) sodium permanganate (d) copper(I) sulphate (f) manganese chloride crystals

13. Potassium carbonate solution is added to a bright green solution to produce a new compound. Suggest a formula and name for the compound.

COMBINED EXERCISES FOR INORGANIC NAMING

Write the correct name for each of the following.

14. MgO
15. $CuSO_4$
16. $NaCH_3COO$
17. NH_4NO_2
18. $MoCl_5$
19. $LiOH \cdot H_2O$
20. $PtCl_4$
21. NH_4ClO_4
22. AlN
23. $KMnO_4$
24. Cu_2SO_4
25. H_2SO_4
26. $Na_2CO_3 \cdot 10H_2O$

27. Na_2SO_3
28. $Pb(HSO_4)_4$
29. WF_6
30. NaH_2PO_4
31. BaS
32. NH_4ClO_2
33. $Fe(ClO)_2$
34. $Sn(CN)_2$
35. KrF_2
36. Na_3PO_4
37. CaS
38. $Mn(SCN)_2$
39. $AgMnO_4$

40. $Pt_2O_3 \cdot 3H_2O$
41. PBr_5
42. $Cu(CH_3COO)_2$
43. $Al(ClO_4)_3$
44. NH_3
45. Al_2S_3
46. $NaOH$
47. $Ba(HS)_2 \cdot 4H_2O$
48. N_2O
49. HNO_3
50. $CsHCO_3$
51. Cu_2S
52. C_3S_2

53. $Cu(NO_3)_2 \cdot 6H_2O$
54. $Co(ClO_3)_2$
55. Mn_2O_3
56. $Zn(CH_3COO)_2$
57. CH_3COOH
58. $MnPO_4$
59. $Cr(NO_3)_3 \cdot 9H_2O$
60. $Sr(ClO)_2$
61. VN
62. $Pb(C_2O_4)_2$
63. CoF_3
64. $BaSO_4$
65. $CuCr_2O_7$

66. NI_3
67. $CrBr_2$
68. Mg_3P_2
69. $FeSO_4 \cdot 5H_2O$
70. $Ca(OH)_2$
71. H_3PO_4

72. $RaSO_4$
73. KHC_2O_4
74. Cl_2O
75. TiO_2
76. $NiSO_4 \cdot 7H_2O$
77. $Mg(ClO_2)_2$

78. $PbCl_4$
79. $Fe(HC_2O_4)_3$
80. I_2O_5
81. $Hg(NO_3)_2$
82. $Zn(OH)_2$
83. H_2S

84. XeO_3
85. $TiCl_2$
86. HF
87. $Sn(CrO_4)_2$
88. $Co_3(PO_4)_2 \cdot 8H_2O$
89. PtS_2

Write the chemical formula for each of the following.

90. silver chloride
91. sulphur dioxide
92. iron(III) oxalate
93. beryllium oxide
94. lead(II) acetate decahydrate
95. potassium chromate
96. mercury(I) acetate
97. molybdenum(III) chloride
98. ammonia
99. gold(III) sulphide
100. silver dichromate
101. calcium acetate
102. chromium(III) oxalate
103. calcium nitrite
104. difluorine dioxide
105. molybdenum(V) oxide
106. silicon tetrafluoride
107. cadmium(II) acetate
108. mercury(II) chloride
109. lithium hydrogen sulphite
110. acetic acid
111. magnesium chlorate hexahydrate
112. phosphorus trifluoride
113. copper(II) iodide
114. calcium nitride
115. magnesium hydroxide
-116. molybdenum(V) sulphide trihydrate
117. iron(II) dihydrogen phosphate
118. carbon tetraiodide
119. zinc sulphate
120. mercury(I) sulphide
121. sulphurous acid
122. iron(II) fluoride octahydrate
123. magnesium hydrogen sulphate
124. aluminum sulphide
125. radium carbonate
126. xenon tetrafluoride

127. sodium oxide
128. barium phosphate
129. mercury(I) nitrate dihydrate
130. sodium hypochlorite
131. gold(I) cyanide
132. tin(IV) bromide
133. hydroiodic acid
134. tetrasulphur tetranitride
135. iron(II) hydroxide
136. copper(I) fluoride
137. tin(II) hydrogen carbonate
138. dinitrogen pentoxide
139. zinc hydrogen sulphite
140. zinc perchlorate hexahydrate
141. gold(III) nitrate
142. manganese(III) sulphate
143. hydrochloric acid
144. chromium(II) oxide
145. zinc hydrogen sulphide
146. molybdenum(VI) sulphide
147. iron(III) carbonate
148. iodine pentafluoride
149. manganese(IV) oxide
150. hydrogen cyanide
151. iron(III) sulphate nonahydrate
152. potassium nitrite
153. chromium(III) phosphide
154. nickel(II) hydroxide
155. chlorine tetroxide
156. mercury(II) thiocyanate
157. nitrous acid
158. lead(II) carbonate
159. sodium hydrogen oxalate
160. aluminum bromide hexahydrate
161. lead(II) iodide
162. silver oxide
163. manganese(IV) monohydrogen phosphate

Mo_3S

UNIT V : THE MOLE CONCEPT

V.1. ATOMIC MASSES AND AVOGADRO'S HYPOTHESIS

Experimental work by the English chemist John Dalton (1766–1844) was concerned with how much of one element could combine with a given amount of another element. He put forth the following hypotheses.

- Molecules are made up of "atoms" of various elements.
- If compound B contains twice the mass of element X as does compound A, then compound B must contain twice as many atoms of X.
- Simple compounds are made up of only one atom of each of the two elements making up the compound. (Dalton was aware that this hypothesis might be quite wrong but he had no way of knowing how many atoms were actually contained in a compound.)

Dalton did not attempt to figure out the mass of an individual atom of any element. Instead he simply assigned an **arbitrary mass** to each element, assuming that hydrogen was the lightest element and therefore could be assigned a mass of "1". Since his experiments found that C was 6 times heavier than H, C was assigned a mass of 6. Similarly, O was 16 times heavier than H and was assigned a mass of 16. In this way, Dalton eventually was able to calculate "relative masses" for several different elements.

EXAMPLE: The reaction between 2.74 g of hydrogen gas and 97.26 g of chlorine gas makes 100 g of hydrogen chloride. Assuming hydrogen chloride contains one atom each of hydrogen and chlorine, the chlorine atom is

$$\frac{97.26\,g}{2.74\,g} = 35.5 \text{ times heavier than the hydrogen.}$$

Since hydrogen is assigned a mass of "1", chlorine has a mass of "35.5".

EXERCISE:

1. Assume a chemist working in 1810 tries to duplicate some of Dalton's results, published a year or two earlier, and obtains the following results (expressed in the modern mass unit, grams).

    11.1 g of hydrogen gas react with 88.9 g of oxygen gas
    46.7 g of nitrogen gas react with 53.3 g of oxygen gas
    42.9 g of carbon react with 57.1 g of oxygen gas

    Assuming a mass of "1" for hydrogen, calculate the relative masses of oxygen, nitrogen and carbon. (Don't be surprised if the values you calculate are not what you would expect from the periodic table. Not all the molecules produced in reactions involve 1:1 combinations of atoms, which was a problem plaguing early chemists for many years.)

Dalton's atomic mass scale was partly in error because not all of the molecules he studied actually contained only one atom of each element. For example, it is now known that a molecule of hydrogen contains two hydrogen atoms. Dalton's mass scale was just being introduced when the French chemist Joseph Gay–Lussac began to study how gases reacted. Gay–Lussac reacted pairs of gases at the same temperature and pressure and found the following results.

    1 L of hydrogen gas reacts with 1 L of chlorine gas to make 2 L of HCl(g)
    1 L of nitrogen gas reacts with 3 L of hydrogen gas to make 2 L of NH_3(g)
    2 L of carbon monoxide gas react with 1 L of oxygen gas to make 2 L of CO_2(g)

By itself, Gay–Lussac's data did not seem to be related to the puzzle of how to determine atomic masses. But then the Italian chemist Amadeo Avogadro proposed the following explanation for Gay–Lussac's data.

> Avogadro's Hypothesis: Equal volumes of different gases, at the same temperature and pressure, contain the same number of particles.

In other words, if **1 L** of gas A reacts with **1 L** of gas B, then there are exactly as many particles of A present as B. Therefore, the molecule formed by reacting A with B has **one atom** of A for every **one atom** of B, and the formula of the product molecule is: **AB**. Similarly, if **2 L** of gas A reacts with **1 L** of gas B then there will be TWICE as many atoms of A as of B, so that 2 atoms of A will combine with 1 atom of B to form **A$_2$B**.

(The ability of Avogadro's Hypothesis to reconcile experimental data from weight and volume measurements was not recognized and accepted until forty years after Avogadro's Hypothesis was put forward.)

EXERCISE:

2. If 1.0 L of nitrogen gas reacts with 3.0 L of chlorine gas when both gases are at the same temperature and pressure, how many chlorine molecules are present for every nitrogen molecule in the reaction? Suggest a formula for the compound formed and name the compound.

3. Experimentally it is found that 1.5 L of gaseous sulphur react with 3.0 L of gaseous oxygen at the same temperature and pressure. Suggest a possible formula and name for the compound formed.

4. At room temperature and pressure, 250 mL of chlorine gas reacted completely with 750 mL of fluorine gas. Suggest a possible formula and name for the compound formed in the reaction.

5. If 1.0 L of unknown gas X contains 3.0 x 10^{23} molecules at a certain temperature and pressure, how many molecules are present in 5.0 L of oxygen gas at the same temperature and pressure?

V.2. THE MOLE

Consider the following problem. One atom of iron and one atom of sulphur react to make one molecule of iron(II) sulphide, FeS. How can large amounts of iron and sulphur be reacted so as to use all the iron and sulphur and not have any of either element left over? Obviously, equal numbers of iron atoms and sulphur atoms must be mixed together, but how? Equal volumes of the elements can't be reacted together because iron and sulphur are not normally gases and the solids have different densities. The easiest way to measure large amounts of solids is to measure their masses.

The mass of one iron atom is 9.27 x 10^{-23} g and the mass of one sulphur atom is 5.33 x 10^{-23} g. Such tiny masses are impossible to measure on a balance; the most accurate balances available can only detect masses greater than about 10^{-12} g.

Let's re–think the problem: all that is really wanted is to make some FeS, starting with Fe and S, without having any leftover starting materials. The number of molecules of FeS being made is not important. Probably the only thing about the amount of FeS which might be of concern is the actual mass of FeS which can be made.

The periodic table shows that the atomic mass of Fe is 55.8 u and the atomic mass of S is 32.1 u. ("u" is the unit symbol which stands for "unified atomic mass unit".) The masses of Fe and S atoms are in the ratio:

$$\frac{\text{mass Fe}}{\text{mass S}} = \frac{55.8 \text{ u}}{32.1 \text{ u}}.$$

Provided equal numbers of Fe and S atoms are used, the masses of Fe and S are always in a 55.8 : 32.1 ratio.

For example: $\dfrac{\text{mass of 1000 Fe atoms}}{\text{mass of 1000 S atoms}} = \dfrac{1000 \times 55.8 \text{ u}}{1000 \times 32.1 \text{u}} = \dfrac{55.8}{32.1}$

Conversely, if the masses of Fe and S are in a 55.8 : 32.1 ratio, there are equal numbers of Fe and S atoms.

Aha! The masses shown on the periodic table can be used directly if they are **measured in GRAMS**. It is easy to weigh out and react 55.8 **g** of Fe with 32.1 **g** of S. This solves our problem for everyday lab work and introduces the concept of a **MOLE**.

Definitions: A **MOLE** is the number of carbon atoms in exactly 12 g of carbon.

[Strictly speaking, the mole is the number of particles in exactly 12 g of a particular variety ("isotope") of carbon having a mass of 12 ("C–12"). Another variety of carbon has a mass of 13 ("C–13"). Naturally–occurring samples of carbon are mostly C–12 with small amounts of C–13 mixed in, so that the average mass of the naturally–occurring mixture is 12.011.]

The **MOLAR MASS** is the mass of ONE MOLE of particles.

This definition leads to the following statement.

> **The molar mass of an element is the mass shown on the periodic table, expressed in grams.**

EXAMPLES:

Element	Atomic mass shown on periodic table	Molar mass of element
C	12.0	12.0 g
Fe	55.8	55.8 g
S	32.1	32.1 g

FINDING THE MOLAR MASS OF A COMPOUND

Finding the molar mass of a species simply involves using the periodic table to look up the mass of every atom involved, adding up the masses of the atoms and expressing the resulting mass in "grams".

IMPORTANT: Unless specifically asked to use more precise values, always use masses rounded off to **one decimal place.** The masses of the elements are given in the *Periodic Table of the Elements* and the table *Atomic Masses of the Elements* at the back of this book.

EXAMPLES: To calculate the molar mass of $C_{12}H_{22}O_{11}$ add the masses of 12 C's, 22 H's and 11 O's.

$$
\begin{aligned}
12\,C &= 12 \times 12.0 &= 144.0\ g \\
22\,H &= 22 \times 1.0 &= 22.0\ g \\
11\,O &= 11 \times 16.0 &= 176.0\ g \\
\hline
\text{molar mass} &&= \textbf{342.0 g}
\end{aligned}
$$

To calculate the molar mass of $(NH_4)_2SO_4$, recall that "$(NH_4)_2$" represents **2** NH_4 groups.

$(NH_4)_2SO_4 = 2 \times (N + 4 \times H) + S + 4 \times O = 2$ N's $+ 8$ H's $+ 1$ S $+ 4$ O's

$$
\begin{aligned}
2\,N &= 2 \times 14.0 &= 28.0\ g \\
8\,H &= 8 \times 1.0 &= 8.0\ g \\
1\,S &= 1 \times 32.1 &= 32.1\ g \\
4\,O &= 4 \times 16.0 &= 64.0\ g \\
\hline
\text{molar mass} &&= \textbf{132.1 g}
\end{aligned}
$$

To calculate the molar mass of **Cu(NO3)2•6H2O**, recall that the "**•6H2O**" indicates that six water molecules are attached to the $Cu(NO_3)_2$ molecule to make a hydrate.

$$Cu(NO_3)_2•6H_2O = Cu + 2\ NO_3 + 6\ H_2O = Cu + 2 \times (N + 3 \times O) + 6 \times (2 \times H + O)$$
$$= 1\ Cu + 2\ N's + 12\ O's + 12\ H's$$

$$1\ Cu = 1 \times 63.5 = 63.5\ g$$
$$2\ N = 2 \times 14.0 = 28.0\ g$$
$$12\ O = 12 \times 16.0 = 192.0\ g$$
$$12\ H = 12 \times 1.0 = 12.0\ g$$
$$\overline{}$$
$$molar\ mass = \textbf{295.5 g}$$

EXERCISES:

6. Calculate the molar mass of each of the following.

(a) NO	(e) CH_4	(i) $FeCl_3$	(m) CH_3COOH
(b) H_2O	(f) $AgNO_3$	(j) SnC_2O_4	(n) $CH_3CH_2CH_2CH_3$
(c) NH_3	(g) $Ca(OH)_2$	(k) $Sn(C_2O_4)_2$	(o) $Ni(H_2O)_2(NH_3)_4Cl_2$
(d) CO_2	(h) $Al(NO_3)_3$	(l) $(NH_4)_3PO_4$	(p) $Al_2(SO_4)_3$

7. Calculate the molar mass of each of the following.

(a) $Co_3(AsO_4)_2•8H_2O$ (b) $Pb(C_2H_3O_2)_2•3H_2O$ (c) $MgSO_4•7H_2O$ (d) $KAl(SO_4)_2•12H_2O$

CALCULATIONS RELATING THE NUMBER OF MOLES AND THE MASS OF A SUBSTANCE

The use of the MOLAR MASS allows the calculation of the mass of a given number of moles of a substance and the calculation of the number of moles in a given mass of a substance.

Note: Recall that the unit symbol for "mole" is **"mol"**.
          Example: three moles = 3 mol

Under **no** circumstances must you use any other unit symbol for the unit "mole", because all other possibly–suitable abbreviations (m, mo, M, Mo) already have special meanings in chemistry. Using any unit symbol besides "mol" will cause you great confusion later on in this course.

The following conversion factors are used to relate the number of moles to the mass of material present.

> **1 mol** of X has a mass of **(molar mass of X) g**
>
> produces the conversion factors
>
> $$\frac{1 \ mol}{(molar \ mass \ of \ X) \ g} \quad or \quad \frac{(molar \ mass \ of \ X) \ g}{1 \ mol}$$

EXAMPLE: **What is the mass of 3.25 mol of CO_2?**

molar mass of CO_2 = 44.0 g = mass of 1 mol of CO_2

mass of CO_2 = 3.25 mol x $\dfrac{44.0 \ g}{1 \ mol}$ = **143 g**

EXAMPLE: **What is the mass of 1.36×10^{-3} mol of SO_3?**

molar mass of SO_3 = 80.1 g = mass of 1 mol of SO_3

mass of SO_3 = 1.36×10^{-3} mol x $\dfrac{80.1 \ g}{1 \ mol}$ = **0.109 g**

EXAMPLE: **How many moles of N_2 are there in 50.0 g of N_2?**

molar mass of N_2 = 28.0 g = mass of 1 mol of N_2

# of moles = 50.0 g x $\dfrac{1 \ mol}{28.0 \ g}$ = **1.79 mol**

EXAMPLE: **How many moles of CH_3OH are there in 0.250 g of CH_3OH?**

molar mass of CH_3OH = 32.0 g = mass of 1 mol of CH_3OH

# of moles = 0.250 g x $\dfrac{1 \ mol}{32.0 \ g}$ = **7.81×10^{-3} mol**

The units of molar mass are actually **g/mol**. This suggests that the molar mass can be calculated by dividing the mass of a substance by the number of moles contained in the substance.

EXAMPLE: **If 0.140 mol of acetylene gas has a mass of 3.64 g, what is the molar mass of acetylene?**

molar mass = $\dfrac{3.64 \ g}{0.140 \ mol}$ = **26.0 g/mol**

EXERCISES:

8. Calculate the mass of the following.
    (a) 1.00 mol of NH_4Cl (e) 0.0125 mol of XeF_4 (h) 7.90×10^{-4} mol of H_2SO_3
    (b) 4.50 mol of NH_4Cl (f) 2.60 mol of CH_3CH_3 (i) 1.00×10^{-3} mol of $NaOH$
    (c) 3.25 mol of PCl_3 (g) 3.25×10^2 mol of NH_3 (j) 1.75×10^{-4} mol of Fe
    (d) 0.00355 mol of Na_2HPO_4

9. Calculate the number of moles in the following.
    (a) 17.0 g of H_2SO_4 (d) 0.125 mg of CuS (g) 55.2 mg of Cl_2 (j) 0.0845 g of $KMnO_4$
    (b) 91.5 g of H_2O (e) 4.50 kg of CH_4 (h) 128.2 g of SO_2
    (c) 53.0 g of C (f) 225 g of $(NH_4)_2SO_4$ (i) 2955 kg of Ag

10. Calculate the molar mass of each of the substances mentioned in the following.
    (a) A 0.250 mol sample of methane has a mass of 4.00 g.
    (b) A 0.00248 mol sample of cholesterol has a mass of 0.947 g.
    (c) The mass of 6.47×10^{-4} mol of diamond is 7.76 mg.
    (d) A 3.44×10^{-5} mol sample of a particular protein has a mass of 74.8 g.

CALCULATIONS RELATING THE NUMBER OF MOLES AND THE VOLUME OF A GAS

Calculations involving gas volumes are simplified by the previously–mentioned Avogadro's Hypothesis.

> **Avogadro's Hypothesis:** Equal volumes of different gases, at the same temperature and pressure, contain the same number of particles.

Before proceeding, some additional definitions are needed.

Definition: The **MOLAR VOLUME** of a gas is the volume occupied by one mole of the gas.

<u>S</u>TANDARD <u>T</u>EMPERATURE AND <u>P</u>RESSURE (<u>STP</u>) = 0°C and 101.3 kPa.

Avogadro's Hypothesis is interpreted to mean: **all gas samples with the same pressure, temperature and number of particles occupy identical volumes. This restatement implies that equal numbers of moles of every gas at STP occupy identical volumes.**

Experimentally–determined fact:

> 1 mol of ANY GAS at STP has a volume of 22.4 L.

In other words **the MOLAR VOLUME of *any gas* at STP is 22.4 L.**

> Conversion factor: $\dfrac{1 \text{ mol}}{22.4 \text{ L}}$ or $\dfrac{22.4 \text{ L}}{1 \text{ mol}}$

NOTE: These conversion factors **ONLY apply to gases and only at STP.**

EXAMPLE: **What is the volume occupied by 0.350 mol of $SO_2(g)$ at STP?**

$$\text{\# of litres} = 0.350 \text{ mol} \times \frac{22.4 \text{ L}}{1 \text{ mol}} = \textbf{7.84 L}$$

EXAMPLE: **How many moles of gas are contained in a balloon with a volume of 10.0 L at STP?**

$$\text{\# of moles} = 10.0 \text{ L} \times \frac{1 \text{ mol}}{22.4 \text{ L}} = \textbf{0.446 mol}$$

EXERCISES:

11. Calculate the volume at STP occupied by the following.
     (a) 12.5 mol of NH_3(g)   (b) 0.350 mol of O_2(g)   (c) 4.25 mol of HCl(g)

12. Calculate the number of moles in the following gases at STP.
     (a) 85.9 L of H_2(g)   (b) 375 mL of SO_3(g)   (c) 5.00 mL of OCl_2(g)

CALCULATIONS RELATING THE NUMBER OF MOLES AND THE NUMBER OF PARTICLES

The **MOLE** is the fundamental unit in chemistry for measuring the **AMOUNT OF SUBSTANCE** in the sense of "number of particles of the substance". The preceding sections showed how to perform calculation based on the mass and the volume of a mole of a substance, but a question which you might have is "how many particles ARE THERE in one mole"?

Experimentally–measured value: | **1 mol = 6.02 x 10^{23}** |

This value, 6.02×10^{23}, is called **AVOGADRO'S NUMBER**. (No, Avogadro didn't discover it; it was named in his honour.)

Notice that there are NO UNITS attached to "6.02×10^{23}", simply because it is just a number. (This is similar to the same way that "dozen" stands for the number "12".)

EXERCISES: (These exercises are not important but may help you gain some idea of the enormity of Avogadro's Number.)

13. Assume that you distribute Avogadro's Number of dollars evenly among each of the 4.5×10^9 people on Earth. Further, assume that everyone spends ONE THOUSAND dollars each second, day and night. What percentage of each person's wealth will have been spent after one year?

14. The total land area of the earth is 1.49×10^8 km^2. The cross–sectional area of a penny is 3.61 cm^2 (1 km^2 = 10^{10} cm^2) and the thickness of a penny is 1.50 mm. If a mole of pennies is distributed evenly over the total land area of the earth, how thick a layer will be formed?

In general, chemists have little interest in the actual numbers of molecules involved in a reaction. However, on occasion, the number of particles is required, so let's examine the calculations involved.

| Conversion factor: $\dfrac{1 \text{ mol particles}}{6.02 \times 10^{23} \text{ particles}}$ or $\dfrac{6.02 \times 10^{23} \text{ particles}}{1 \text{ mol particles}}$ |

EXAMPLE: **How many molecules are there in 0.125 mol of molecules?**

$$\text{\# of molecules} = 0.125 \text{ mol} \times \frac{6.02 \times 10^{23} \text{ molecules}}{1 \text{ mol}} = \textbf{7.53 x 10}^{22} \textbf{ molecules}$$

EXAMPLE: **How many moles of N atoms are there in 5.00 x 10^{17} N atoms?**

$$\text{\# of moles} = 5.00 \times 10^{17} \text{ atoms} \times \frac{1 \text{ mol}}{6.02 \times 10^{23} \text{ atoms}} = 8.31 \times 10^{-7} \text{ mol}$$

EXAMPLE: **A light source emits 8.50 x 10^{17} photons per second. (A photon is a "particle of light".) How many moles of photons are emitted by the light source in one minute?**

$$\text{\# of moles} = 1 \text{ min} \times \frac{60 \text{ s}}{1 \text{ min}} \times \frac{8.50 \times 10^{17} \text{ photons}}{1 \text{ s}} \times \frac{1 \text{ mol}}{6.02 \times 10^{23} \text{ photons}}$$
$$= 8.47 \times 10^{-5} \text{ mol}$$

Note: The above three examples don't depend on whether the particles are atoms, molecules, or whatever. The calculations just deal with the numbers of particles.

Avogadro's Number is also used to find the molar mass of particles if the mass of one particle is known.

EXAMPLE: **A particular variety of carbon atom has a mass of 2.16 x 10^{-23} g/atom. What is the mass of a mole of this variety of carbon atom?**

$$\text{mass} = 2.16 \times 10^{-23} \frac{g}{\text{atom}} \times \frac{6.02 \times 10^{23} \text{ atoms}}{1 \text{ mol}} = 13.0 \frac{g}{\text{mol}}$$

IMPORTANT: If the actual mass of the particles involved is given in grams (or kilograms, etc.), then multiplying the mass by Avogadro's Number gives the mass of a mole of such particles, as found in the preceding example.

$$\text{mass of 1 mol in grams} = (6.02 \times 10^{23}) \times (\text{individual mass of atom in grams})$$

When a particle's atomic symbol is found on the periodic table, just use the mass of the particle given in the periodic table and simply attach the unit "g" to get the molar mass (as you did when you first learned how to find the molar mass).

COMBINED EXERCISES:

15. Calculate the number of moles contained in the following.
    (a) 10.6 L of $SO_2(g)$ at STP   (e) 0.950 kg of NaOH
    (b) 7.50 x 10^{21} molecules of HNO_3 (f) 25.0 mL of $N_2(g)$ at STP
    (c) 425 mg of $Ca(OH)_2$ (g) 5.50 x 10^{25} molecules of CCl_4
    (d) 4.25 x 10^{12} molecules of Fe_2O_3 (h) 0.120 L of $NO_2(g)$ at STP

16. Calculate the volume of the following gases at STP.
    (a) 0.235 mol of $B_2H_6(g)$ (b) 9.36 mol of $SiH_4(g)$ (c) 2.55 x 10^3 mol of $C_2H_6(g)$

17. Calculate the mass of each of the following.
    (a) 0.125 mol of $CO_2(g)$ at STP   (c) 6.54 x 10^{-4} mol of HCN(g) at STP
    (b) 5.48 mol of $FeCl_3(s)$ (d) 15.4 mol of $Ni(OH)_2(s)$

18. Calculate the mass of 1 mol of each of the following.
    (a) $Na_2B_4O_7 \cdot 10H_2O$
    (b) Grandma Smith, an average grandmother, having a mass of 52 kg. (Express your answer in kilograms.)
    (c) a bismuth atom with a mass of 3.52 x 10^{-22} g
    (d) an electron having a mass of 9.1 x 10^{-28} g.
    (e) $Cu_3(OH)_2(CO_3)_2$
    (f) a book having a mass of 1.34 kg

19. An unknown gas sample contains only one of the compounds SO_3, CH_4, NF_3 or C_2H_2. If 1 molecule of the gas has a mass of 1.18×10^{-22} g, which type of molecule is contained in the sample?

20. General Saunders "Kamloops Fried Chicken" features the "Super Barrel", containing 2 mol of chickens (cut up and deep fried). How many drumsticks are contained in the Super Barrel? How many drumsticks, wings and thighs are in the Super Barrel altogether?

V.3. MULTIPLE CONVERSIONS BETWEEN MOLES, MASS, VOLUME AND NUMBER OF PARTICLES

Before jumping into the middle of some complex conversion factor calculations, a simple process must be understood: **how to find the number of atoms in a given number of molecules.**

This calculation simply involves counting the number of atoms in one molecule and then multiplying by the number of molecules involved.

EXAMPLE: **How many atoms are there in 5 molecules of $CuSO_4 \cdot 5H_2O$?**

1 molecule of $CuSO_4 \cdot 5H_2O$ contains 21 atoms (check this!)

# of atoms = 5 molecules x 21 $\dfrac{\text{atoms}}{\text{molecule}}$ = **105 atoms**

EXAMPLE: **How many HYDROGEN atoms are there in 30 molecules of H_3PO_4?**

1 molecule of H_3PO_4 contains 3 atoms of H, so that:

# of atoms of H = 30 molecules x $\dfrac{3 \text{ atoms of H}}{1 \text{ molecule}}$ = **90 atoms**

EXERCISE:

21. How many atoms are contained in 1 molecule of each of the following?
   (a) CH_3CO_2H (c) $(CH_3)_2CO$ (e) $C_{15}H_{22}O_6N_2S$
   (b) NH_4Cl (d) $(NH_4)_2SO_4$ (f) $Ni(H_2O)_4(NH_3)_2Cl_2$

The previous sections showed how to perform single–step conversions between moles and any of mass, volume, or number of particles. This section shows how to convert between mass and volume, number of particles and mass, and so on. The box below summarizes the conversion factors needed.

CONVERSION	CONVERSION FACTOR
MOLES ⟷ NUMBER OF PARTICLES	$\dfrac{6.02 \times 10^{23} \text{ particles}}{1 \text{ mol particles}}$ or $\dfrac{1 \text{ mol particles}}{6.02 \times 10^{23} \text{ particles}}$
MOLES ⟷ MASS	$\dfrac{(molar\ mass)\ \text{g}}{1 \text{ mol}}$ or $\dfrac{1 \text{ mol}}{(molar\ mass)\ \text{g}}$
MOLES ⟷ VOLUME (gases at STP)	$\dfrac{22.4 \text{ L}}{1 \text{ mol}}$ or $\dfrac{1 \text{ mol}}{22.4 \text{ L}}$
MOLECULES ⟷ ATOMS	$\dfrac{(atom\ count)\ \text{atoms}}{1 \text{ molecule}}$ or $\dfrac{1 \text{ molecule}}{(atom\ count)\ \text{atoms}}$

In the following calculations, keep the diagram below in mind. The mole is "central" to all conversions between mass, particles and volume: each calculation goes from **STARTING UNIT** to **MOLES** to **FINAL UNIT.**

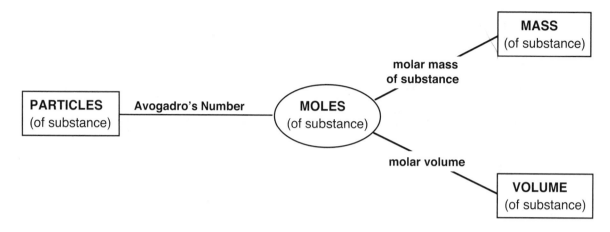

EXAMPLE: **What is the volume occupied by 50.0 g of NH₃(g) at STP?**

    (Plan: Convert MASS to MOLES and then to VOLUME)

$$\text{volume} = 50.0 \text{ g} \times \frac{1 \text{ mol}}{17.0 \text{ g}} \times \frac{22.4 \text{ L}}{1 \text{ mol}} = \textbf{65.9 L}$$

    Note: The first step involved converting the given amount (50.0 g) into moles.

EXAMPLE: **What is the mass of 1.00×10^{12} atoms of Cl?**

    (Plan: Convert # OF ATOMS to MOLES and then to MASS)

$$\text{mass} = 1.00 \times 10^{12} \text{ atoms} \times \frac{1 \text{ mol}}{6.02 \times 10^{23} \text{ atoms}} \times \frac{35.5 \text{ g}}{1 \text{ mol}} = \textbf{5.90} \times \textbf{10}^{-11} \textbf{ g}$$

    Note: The first step was to convert the given amount (1.00×10^{12} atoms) into moles.

EXAMPLE: **How many oxygen atoms are contained in 75.0 L of SO₃(g) at STP?**

    The calculation starts with a volume of SO₃ **MOLECULES**, converts to moles of SO₃ **MOLECULES,** then to the number of **MOLECULES** and finally the molecules are broken into the required number of **ATOMS.** Only if you are originally given a volume of ATOMS will you be able to go directly from moles of ATOMS to the number of ATOMS.

$$\text{# of O-atoms} = 75.0 \text{ L} \times \frac{1 \text{ mol}}{22.4 \text{ L}} \times \frac{6.02 \times 10^{23} \text{ molecules}}{1 \text{ mol}} \times \frac{3 \text{ O-atoms}}{1 \text{ molecule}}$$

$$= \textbf{6.05} \times \textbf{10}^{24} \textbf{ O-atoms}$$

EXERCISES:

22. Find the mass, in grams, of each of the following.

    (a) 2×10^6 CO molecules   (e) 125 He atoms   (i) 3.45 mL of O₂(g) at STP

    (b) 1.25 L of NH₃(g) at STP   (f) 1 Ag atom   (j) 1.00×10^8 L of H₂(g) at STP

    (c) 5×10^{14} N₂ molecules   (g) 4.15×10^{15} CH₄ molecules

    (d) 1 KOH molecule   (h) 175 N atoms

23. How many atoms are contained in each of the following?
   (a) 1.00 mol of NH_4Cl (e) 12 g of H_2O_2 (i) 125 g of CH_3Cl
   (b) 2.5 mol of $O_3(g)$ (f) 55.0 mL of N_2O (g) at STP (j) 8.30×10^{-4} mL of $BF_3(g)$ at STP
   (c) 8.00 g of Fe   (g) 40.0 g of K   (k) 6.5×10^{-6} g of Kr
   (d) 15.0 L of Ar(g) at STP (h) 5.0 g of NaCl   (l) 9.5×10^{-3} g of NH_3

24. What volume at STP is occupied by each of the following?
   (a) 16.5 g of $AsH_3(g)$ (e) 8.65×10^{21} molecules of $SO_2(g)$
   (b) 5.65×10^{22} molecules of $POF_3(g)$ (f) 6.98×10^{15} atoms of Xe(g)
   (c) 0.750 g of $O_3(g)$ (g) 28.4 mg of $H_2Te(g)$
   (d) 9.04×10^{24} atoms of He(g)   (h) 3.25 kg of $C_2H_6(g)$

So far, the **volumes** used all refer to a gaseous substance at STP. If **DENSITY** is mentioned at any point in a problem, you should immediately recall that $d = {}^m/_V$ and understand the following points.

- **If the volume of a solid or liquid is the unknown,** calculate the volume from $V = {}^m/_d$. If the mass is not known, find the mass from the moles of the substance present. If the **molar volume** is the unknown, the molar mass is used in the calculation. **(Note that you cannot use the molar volume of a gas, 22.4 L, when calculating the volume of a liquid or solid.)**

- **If the density is unknown,** you will need both mass and volume to calculate: $d = {}^m/_V$. The mass can be found if the number of moles is known. If neither the mass nor volume is given, the density of a gas at STP can be found by using the mass of 1 mol and the volume of 1 mol at STP.

- **If the number of moles is unknown,** use the density and volume to calculate $m = d \cdot V$ and then convert the mass to moles.

- **If the molar mass of a gas at STP is unknown,** the data given is usually the mass and volume of a small amount of gas. In this case, find the density of the gas using the given mass and volume and then combine the density with the volume of 1 mol (22.4 L) to find the mass of 1 mol.

EXAMPLE: **What is the volume occupied by 3.00 mol of ethanol, $CH_3CH_2OH(l)$? (d = 0.790 g/mL)**

    Note: Plan the calculation by working from the final unit to the starting unit. You are asked for the VOLUME, and since ethanol is not a gas you can't use "22.4 L". DENSITY relates VOLUME to MASS. In turn, MASS is related to the starting unit, MOLES.

$$\text{\# of millilitres} = 3.00 \text{ mol} \times \frac{46.0 \text{ g}}{1 \text{ mol}} \times \frac{1 \text{ mL}}{0.790 \text{ g}} = \textbf{175 mL}$$

EXAMPLE: **How many moles of Hg(l) are contained in 100 mL of Hg(l)? (d = 13.6 g/mL)**

    (Plan: Convert VOLUME to MASS and then to MOLES)

$$\text{\# of moles} = 100 \text{ mL} \times \frac{13.6 \text{ g}}{1 \text{ mL}} \times \frac{1 \text{ mol}}{200.6 \text{ g}} = \textbf{6.78 mol}$$

EXAMPLE: **What is the density of $O_2(g)$ at STP?**

    The calculation requires a suitable mass and volume. There are NO numbers given with which to work, but ... the term "STP" suggests a volume of 22.4 L for one mole of gas and the mass of one mole of $O_2(g)$ is 32.0 g.

$$\text{density} = \frac{m}{V} = \frac{\text{mass of 1 mol}}{\text{volume of 1 mol}} = \frac{32.0 \text{ g}}{22.4 \text{ L}} = \textbf{1.43} \frac{\textbf{g}}{\textbf{L}}$$

EXAMPLE: **A 2.50 L bulb contains 4.91 g of a gas at STP. What is the molar mass of the gas?**

The density of the gas is found from the given mass and volume.

$$d = \frac{4.91 \text{ g}}{2.50 \text{ L}} = 1.964 \text{ g/L}$$

Since 1 mol of a gas at STP has a volume of 22.4 L, the mass of 1 mol is given by

$$\text{molar mass} = m = d \cdot V = 1.964 \frac{g}{L} \times 22.4 \text{ L} = \textbf{44.0 g}$$

EXAMPLE: **Al_2O_3(s) has a density of 3.97 g/mL. How many atoms of Al are in 100 mL of Al_2O_3?**

(Plan: Convert VOLUME to MASS, then to MOLES, then to # of MOLECULES and finally to # OF ATOMS)

$$\text{\# of atoms} = 100 \text{ mL} \times \frac{3.97 \text{ g}}{1 \text{ mL}} \times \frac{1 \text{ mol}}{102.0 \text{ g}} \times \frac{6.02 \times 10^{23} \text{ molecules}}{1 \text{ mol}} \times \frac{2 \text{ Al atoms}}{1 \text{ molecule}}$$

$$= \textbf{4.69} \times \textbf{10}^{\textbf{24}} \textbf{ atoms}$$

EXERCISES:

25. What is the density of CO_2(g) at STP?

26. How many atoms of N are there in 30.0 g of NH_4NO_3?

27. The density of CCl_4(l) is 1.59 g/mL. How many molecules of CCl_4 are there in 2.50 L of CCl_4?

28. If 1.35 L of diborane gas has a mass of 1.67 g at STP, what is the molar mass of diborane?

29. What is the density of gaseous ethane, C_2H_6, at STP?

30. What volume of C_6H_6(l) contains 8.50×10^{24} atoms of C? (density of C_6H_6(l) = 0.877 g/mL)

31. If 250.0 mL of silane gas at STP has a mass of 0.358 g, what is the molar mass of silane? If silane is made of silicon and hydrogen atoms, suggest a molecular formula for silane.

32. Carbon disulphide, CS_2 , is a liquid having a density of 1.26 g/mL. What volume is occupied by 4.50×10^{22} molecules of CS_2?

33. What is the molar volume of quartz, SiO_2? density = 2.64 g/mL.

34. What is the density of gold if 0.02780 mol of gold has a volume of 0.2836 mL?

SUMMARY PROBLEMS

35. How many atoms are there in each of the following?
     (a) 5 molecules of $C_6H_2Cl_4$ (b) 10 molecules of $Co(ClO_4)_2 \cdot 6H_2O$

36. How many molecules are there in each of the following?
     (a) a flask containing 50.0 mL of NH_3(g) at STP   (c) 75.0 g of sugar, $C_{12}H_{22}O_{11}$
     (b) a plastic bag containing 25.0 L of Cl_2(g) at STP   (d) 125 mg of white phosphorus, P_4

37. What is the volume occupied by each of the following gases at STP?
     (a) 10.0 g of H_2S(g)   (c) 5.0×10^{20} molecules of BrF(g)
     (b) 15.0 mg of SbH_3(g)   (d) 8.5×10^{25} molecules of B_2H_6(g)

38. What is the mass of each of the following?
     (a) 1 atom of Au   (c) 250.0 mL of C_3H_6(g) at STP
     (b) 1.5×10^{15} molecules of AgCl   (d) 2.00 L of SF_6(g) at STP

39. How many moles are in each of the following?
    (a) 5.00 g of $C_{10}H_8$ (c) 6.00 L of $NO_3F(g)$ at STP   (e) 4.55×10^{12} atoms of Pt
    (b) 525 mg of K_3PO_4 (d) 1.00 mL of $O_3(g)$ at STP   (f) 6.02×10^{16} molecules of PCl_5

40. What is the molar mass of each of the following?
    (a) a protein molecule having a mass of 1.25×10^{-17} g
    (b) 0.179 mol of a substance having a mass of 74.0 g
    (c) a molecule of anthracene having a mass of 2.96×10^{-22} g
    (d) $Na_2S_2O_3 \cdot 5H_2O$
    (e) 0.0229 mol of a substance having a mass of 2.13 g
    (f) $Co_2Fe(CN)_6$

41. (a) What is the density of $PH_3(g)$ at STP?
    (b) What is the molar volume of gold? (density = 19.31 g/mL)
    (c) How many moles are contained in 1.25 mL of $CS_2(l)$? (density = 1.26 g/mL)
    (d) What is the density of liquid octane, C_8H_{18}, if 0.100 mol of octane has a volume of 16.2 mL?
    (e) What is the density of $NOCl(g)$ at STP?
    (f) What volume is occupied by 0.0875 mol of silver if silver has a density of 10.5 g/mL?
    (g) What is the density of $CuSO_4 \cdot 5H_2O$ if 0.0275 mol of $CuSO_4 \cdot 5H_2O$ has a volume of 3.01 mL?
    (h) How many moles are contained in 7.50 L of $C_2H_5OH(l)$? (density = 0.789 g/mL)
    (i) If 750.0 mL of gaseous fluoromethane has a mass of 1.14 g at STP, what is the molar mass of fluoromethane?
    (j) What is the volume occupied by 0.0155 mol of NaCl? (density of NaCl = 2.17 g/mL)
    (k) If 1.25 L of disilane gas at STP has a mass of 3.47 g, what is the molar mass of disilane?
    (l) What is the molar volume of lithium? (density = 0.534 kg/L)

42. (a) How many atoms are there in 2 molecules of $Hg(IO_3)_2$?
    (b) What volume at STP is occupied by 1.45×10^{30} molecules of $COF_2(g)$?
    (c) How many molecules are there in 64.0 g of FeS(s)?
    (d) How many moles are in 25.0 mL of HCN(g) at STP?
    (e) What volume at STP is occupied by 43.5 g of $ClF_3(g)$?
    (f) How many moles are in 2.75×10^{23} atoms of Fe?
    (g) How many molecules are there in 125 mL of NOCl(g) at STP?
    (h) What is the mass of 3.01×10^{22} atoms of Pt ?
    (i) What is the molar mass of $HClO_4 \cdot 2H_2O$?
    (j) What is the density of $CH_2F_2(g)$ at STP?
    (k) What is the mass of 25.0 mL of Kr(g) at STP ?
    (l) What is the molar volume of iridium metal, Ir? (density = 22.42 g/mL)
    (m) What is the molar mass of 0.0139 mol of a substance having a mass of 0.888 g?
    (n) What is the density of acetic acid, CH_3COOH, if 0.250 mol of CH_3COOH has a volume of 14.3 mL?
    (o) How many moles are in 85.0 mg of CuSCN?
    (p) What volume is occupied by 0.145 mol of ruby, Al_2O_3 , if ruby has a density of 3.97 g/mL?
    (q) What is the molar mass of an atomic particle with a mass of 9.11×10^{-28} g?
    (r) If 135 L of cyanogen gas has a mass of 313 g at STP, what is the molar mass of cyanogen?
    (s) If the density of HgS is 8.10 g/mL, how many moles are in a cylinder filled with 50.0 mL of HgS?

43. (a) What volume at STP is occupied by 5.75×10^{10} molecules of $SbH_3(g)$?
    (b) How many molecules are there in 75.0 L of $O_3(g)$ at STP?
    (c) What is the mass of 2.50 L of $PF_5(g)$ at STP?
    (d) What is the molar mass of $Al_2(C_2O_4)_3 \cdot 4H_2O$?
    (e) How many moles are in 15.0 L of $HN_3(g)$ at STP?
    (f) What is the mass of 1 molecule of $(NH_4)_2SO_4$?

(g) What is the density of $C_4H_8(g)$ at STP?

(h) What is the molar mass of a molecule having a mass of 6.23×10^{-22} g?

(i) How many atoms are there in 3 molecules of $CH_3COOCH_2CH_3$?

(j) If 5.54 mL of carbon oxysulphide gas has a mass of 14.9 mg at STP, what is the molar mass of carbon oxysulphide?

(k) How many moles are in 125 g of PbC_2O_4?

(l) What is the molar mass of 0.546 mol of a substance having a mass of 73.1 g?

(m) How many moles are in 1.85×10^{24} molecules of CsI?

(n) What is the volume of 0.0694 mol of molybdenite, MoS_2 , having a density of 4.80 g/mL?

(o) How many molecules are there in 5.00 g of $OF_2(g)$?

(p) What is the density of a calcite crystal, $CaCO_3$, if 0.0316 mol of $CaCO_3$ has a volume of 1.167 mL?

(q) How many moles of sugar, $C_{12}H_{22}O_{11}$, are contained in 100.0 mL of sugar? (density = 1.58 g/mL)

(r) What volume at STP is occupied by 275 mg of $GeH_4(g)$?

(s) What is the molar volume of mercury? (density = 13.55 g/mL)

V.4. PERCENTAGE COMPOSITION

The **PERCENTAGE COMPOSITION** is the percentage (by mass) of the species in a chemical formula.

EXAMPLE: **What is the percentage composition of CH_4?**

Assume there is 1 mol of the compound.   molar mass = 16.0 g
total mass of C in compound = 12.0 g
total mass of H in compound =   4.0 g

% of C in compound = $\dfrac{12.0 \text{ g}}{16.0 \text{ g}}$ x 100% = **75.0%**

% of H in compound = $\dfrac{4.0 \text{ g}}{16.0 \text{ g}}$ x 100% = **25.0%**

EXAMPLE: **What is the percentage composition of H_2SO_4?**

Assume there is 1 mol of the compound.   molar mass = 98.1 g
 total mass of H in compound = 2 x 1.0 g =   2.0 g
total mass of S in compound = 1 x 32.1 g = 32.1 g
total mass of O in compound = 4 x 16.0 g = 64.0 g

% of H in compound = $\dfrac{2.0 \text{ g}}{98.1 \text{ g}}$ x 100% = **2.0%**

% of S in compound = $\dfrac{32.1 \text{ g}}{98.1 \text{ g}}$ x 100% = **32.7%**

% of O in compound = $\dfrac{64.0 \text{ g}}{98.1 \text{ g}}$ x 100% = **65.2%**

EXAMPLE: **What is the percentage of water in $CuSO_4 \cdot 5H_2O$?**

Assume there is 1 mol of the compound.   molar mass = 249.6 g
total mass of H_2O in compound = 5 x 18.0 g = 90.0 g

% of H_2O in molecule = $\dfrac{90.0 \text{ g}}{249.6 \text{ g}}$ x 100% = **36.1%**

EXERCISES:

44. Calculate the percentage composition of the following.
   (a) C_2H_6 (d) $C_2H_4O_2$ (g) $CaCl_2{\cdot}2H_2O$ (j) $C_{17}H_{15}N_3O_2Cl$ (m) $C_2H_4N_2O_4$
   (b) $FeCl_2$ (e) $CaCO_3$ (h) $(NH_4)_3PO_4$ (k) $Sn(SO_4)_2{\cdot}2H_2O$ (n) $K_3Fe(CN)_6$
   (c) $FeCl_3$ (f) $NaOH$ (i) $Ag(NH_3)_2Cl$ (l) $(NH_4)_2Sn(OH)_6$

45. Calculate the percentage of the bold species in each of the following.
   (a) $CaCl_2{\cdot}2\mathbf{H_2O}$ (c) $Ce_2(C_2O_4)_3{\cdot}9\mathbf{H_2O}$ (e) $Cr(\mathbf{NH_3})_6Cl_3{\cdot}H_2O$ (g) $Cu(\mathbf{C_2H_3O_2})_2{\cdot}2NH_3$
   (b) $NiSO_4{\cdot}7\mathbf{H_2O}$ (d) $Al_2(SO_4)_3{\cdot}18\mathbf{H_2O}$ (f) $Cr(NH_3)_6Cl_3{\cdot}\mathbf{H_2O}$ (h) $Fe_2(\mathbf{SO_4})_3{\cdot}9H_2O$

V.5. EMPIRICAL AND MOLECULAR FORMULAE

The **EMPIRICAL FORMULA** is sometimes called the **SIMPLEST FORMULA** and is the smallest whole–number ratio of atoms which represents the molecular composition of a species.

EXAMPLE: All of CH_2 , C_2H_4 , C_3H_6 , C_4H_8 and C_5H_{10} contain twice as many H's as C's and therefore the empirical formula (the simplest ratio) for all these molecules is **CH_2** .

Finding the empirical formula is essentially the opposite procedure to determining the percentage composition of a compound.

EXAMPLE: **What is the empirical formula of a compound consisting of 80.0% C and 20.0% H?**

Note that neither the chemical formula nor molar mass is known. Assume you have 100 g of the compound, so that:

mass of C = 80.0 % of 100 g = 80.0 g
mass of H = 20.0 % of 100 g = 20.0 g .

For the moment, ignore the right–hand column below. Use the masses of each element present to determine the number of moles of each element.

$$\text{moles of C} = 80.0 \text{ g} \times \frac{1 \text{ mol}}{12.0 \text{ g}} = 6.67 \text{ mol} \qquad \overset{\div 6.67}{1}$$

$$\text{moles of H} = 20.0 \text{ g} \times \frac{1 \text{ mol}}{1.0 \text{ g}} = 20 \text{ mol} \qquad 3$$

Since "100 g" was an arbitrary (but convenient) mass, the numbers of moles calculated have no real significance. However, the **RATIO** which exists between the numbers of moles *is* significant. To find the smallest whole–number ratio, divide both "6.67" and "20" by the **SMALLER** number, that is, "6.67". The results of this division are shown in the right–hand column above.

According to these "simplest ratio" values, you can now say that carbon and hydrogen atoms are present in the ratio:

1 C : 3 H

and the simplest way to express the chemical formula is: **CH_3** .

Note that the percentage composition of C_2H_6 is found as follows.

Molar mass = 30.0 g

% of C in compound = $\dfrac{24.0 \text{ g}}{30.0 \text{ g}}$ x 100% = 80.0%

% of H in compound = $\dfrac{6.0 \text{ g}}{30.0 \text{ g}}$ x 100% = 20.0%

Therefore, both CH_3 and C_2H_6 contain 80.0% C and 20.0% H, and both have three times as many hydrogen atoms as carbon atoms. The **SIMPLEST** ratio which describes the relative number of carbons and hydrogens is

C_1H_3 or simply **CH_3**.

EXAMPLE: **A compound contains 58.5% C, 7.3% H and 34.1% N. What is the empirical formula of the compound?**

Assume 100.0 g of the compound is taken.

mass of C = 58.5 g , mass of H = 7.3 g , mass of N = 34.1 g

$\div 2.44$

moles C = 58.5 g x $\dfrac{1 \text{ mol}}{12.0 \text{ g}}$ = 4.88 mol | 2

moles H = 7.3 g x $\dfrac{1 \text{ mol}}{1.0 \text{ g}}$ = 7.3 mol | 2.99 ≈ 3

moles N = 34.1 g x $\dfrac{1 \text{ mol}}{14.0 \text{ g}}$ = 2.44 mol | 1

Hence the empirical formula is **C_2H_3N**.

EXAMPLE: **What is the empirical formula of a compound containing 81.8% C and 18.2% H?**

Assume 100.0 g of the compound is taken.

mass of C = 81.8 g , mass of H = 18.2 g

$\div 6.82$ x 3

moles C = 81.8 g x $\dfrac{1 \text{ mol}}{12.0 \text{ g}}$ = 6.82 mol | 1 | 3

moles H = 18.2 g x $\dfrac{1 \text{ mol}}{1.0 \text{ g}}$ = 18.2 mol | 2.67 | 8

Note that a third column is added to the above calculation. Dividing the calculated number of moles by the smallest number of moles present (6.82) leaves a fraction (2.67) in the second column. This is a problem because the empirical formula is a WHOLE–NUMBER ratio. Since the ".67" ending of 2.67 indicates the presence of a fraction involving "thirds", clear the fraction by multiplying the values in the second column by 3, so as to produce the whole–number values in the third column.

Therefore the empirical formula is **C_3H_8**.

IMPORTANT: You must be able to recognize the following fractions and their decimal equivalents.

$$0.20 = {}^1/_5 \qquad 0.40 = {}^2/_5 \qquad 0.67 = {}^2/_3$$
$$0.25 = {}^1/_4 \qquad 0.50 = {}^1/_2 \qquad 0.75 = {}^3/_4$$
$$0.33 = {}^1/_3 \qquad 0.60 = {}^3/_5 \qquad 0.80 = {}^4/_5$$

SNEAKY TRICK: You don't have to re-write fractions such as 2.67 in the form ${}^8/_3$. All you have to do is to recognize that numbers such as 2.67, 1.33, 5.67 and 3.33 involve **THIRDS** and simply multiply the fraction by **3** to clear the fraction. Similarly, numbers like 1.75, 2.25 and 3.75 involve **QUARTERS,** so that multiplying by **4** will clear such fractions.

INCREDIBLY, VITALLY IMPORTANT NOTE:

Always carry out calculations to 3 or 4 digits and NEVER round off intermediate values. The numbers 3.60, 3.67, 3.75 and 3.80 are very close to one another and improper round-off of calculations will cause you to multiply by the wrong number when trying to "clear fractions".

EXAMPLE: **What is the empirical formula of a compound containing 39.0% Si and 61.0% O?**

Assume 100.0 g of the compound is taken.

mass of Si = 39.0 g , mass of O = 61.0 g

$$\text{moles Si} = 39.0 \text{ g} \times \frac{1 \text{ mol}}{28.1 \text{ g}} = 1.39 \text{ mol}$$

	÷ 1.39	x 4
Si	1	4
O	2.74 ≈ 2.75	11

$$\text{moles O} = 61.0 \text{ g} \times \frac{1 \text{ mol}}{16.0 \text{ g}} = 3.81 \text{ mol}$$

The empirical formula is **Si_4O_{11}**.

EXERCISE:

46. Find the empirical formula for the following compounds.

(a) 15.9% B, 84.1% F
(b) 87.5% Si, 12.5% H
(c) 43.7% P, 56.3% O
(d) 77.9% I, 22.1% O
(e) 77.7% Fe, 22.3% O

(f) 70.0% Fe, 30.0% O
(g) 72.4% Fe, 27.6% O
(h) 46.3% Li, 53.7% O
(i) 24.4% C, 3.39% H, 72.2% Cl
(j) 26.6% K, 35.4% Cr, 38.0% O

(k) 21.8% Mg, 27.9% P, 50.3% O
(l) 3.66% H, 37.8% P, 58.4% O
(m) 46.2% C, 7.69% H, 46.2% O
(n) 50.5% C, 5.26% H, 44.2% N

FINDING THE MOLECULAR FORMULA

If the empirical formula can be found, it is straightforward to calculate the molar mass of the empirical formula; that is, the **empirical mass.**

The first example in this section pointed out that all of CH_2 , C_2H_4 , C_3H_6 , C_4H_8 and C_5H_{10} have identical empirical formulae. Since all of these compounds have formulae which are whole-number multiples of CH_2 , then the molar mass of all of the compounds must be a whole-number multiple of the empirical mass of CH_2 .

Let   N = the WHOLE NUMBER multiple of the empirical mass.

$$\text{multiple} = N = \frac{\text{molar mass}}{\text{empirical mass}}$$

Since the molar mass is a multiple of the empirical mass, then the molecular formula must be the same multiple of the empirical formula:

> molecular formula = N x (empirical formula) .

Before proceeding, we must examine the methods for finding the molar mass which are available to us.

A SUMMARY OF METHODS FOR FINDING THE MOLAR MASS

(a) *Finding the Molar Mass from the Density of a Gas at STP*

If: density of gas X = $1.43 \, \dfrac{g}{L}$ (at STP)

then: mass of 1 mol of X = $1.43 \, \dfrac{g}{L} \times \dfrac{22.4 \, L}{1 \, mol}$ = **32.0** $\dfrac{g}{mol}$.

(b) Finding the Molar Mass from the Mass and Volume of a Gas at STP

If you are told: "0.0425 L of gas X at STP has a mass of 0.135 g"

then: density of gas X = $\dfrac{0.135 \, g}{0.0425 \, L}$ = 3.176 g/L

and: molar mass of X = $3.176 \, \dfrac{g}{L} \times \dfrac{22.4 \, L}{1 \, mol}$ = **71.2 g/mol**

(c) *Finding the Molar Mass if the Mass of a Certain Number of Moles is Given*

If you are told: "0.0250 mol of X has a mass of 1.775 g"

then: molar mass = $\dfrac{1.775 \, g}{0.0250 \, mol}$ = **71.0** $\dfrac{g}{mol}$

(d) *Finding the Molar Mass if the Molar Mass is Given as a Multiple of a Known Molar Mass*

If you are told: X has a molar mass which is 1.64 times that of CO_2

then: molar mass CO_2 = 44.0 g/mol

and: molar mass of X = 1.64 x 44.0 g/mol = **72.2 g/mol**

EXAMPLE: **A molecule has an empirical formula of HO and a molar mass of 34.0 g.   What is the molecular formula?**

> empirical mass of HO = 17.0 g
>
> $N = \dfrac{molar \ mass}{empirical \ mass} = \dfrac{34.0 \ g}{17.0 \ g} = 2$

and: molecular formula = 2 x (empirical formula) = 2 x (HO) = H_2O_2

EXAMPLE: A gas has the empirical formula POF_3. If 0.350 L of the gas at STP has a mass of 1.62 g, what is the molecular formula of the compound?

empirical mass of POF_3 = 104.0 g

$$\text{density of gas} = \frac{1.62 \text{ g}}{0.350 \text{ L}} = 4.63 \; \frac{g}{L}$$

$$\text{mass of 1 mol gas} = 4.63 \; \frac{g}{L} \; x \; \frac{22.4 \text{ L}}{1 \text{ mol}} = 104 \; \frac{g}{mol}$$

$$N = \frac{\text{molar mass}}{\text{empirical mass}} = \frac{104.0 \text{ g}}{104 \text{ g}} = 1$$

So that: molecular formula = 1 x (empirical formula) = **POF_3**

EXAMPLE: The empirical formula of a compound is SiH_3. If 0.0275 mol of compound has a mass of 1.71 g, what is the compound's molecular formula?

empirical mass = 31.1 g

$$\text{molar mass} = \frac{1.71 \text{ g}}{0.0275 \text{ mol}} = 62.2 \; \frac{g}{mol}$$

$$N = \frac{62.2 \text{ g}}{31.1 \text{ g}} = 2$$

and: molecular formula = 2 x (empirical formula) = 2 x (SiH_3) = **Si_2H_6**

EXERCISES:

47. A gas has the empirical formula CH_2. If 0.850 L of the gas at STP has a mass of 1.59 g, what is the molecular formula?

48. A gas has the percentage composition: 30.4% N and 69.6% O. If the density of the gas is 4.11 g/L at STP, what is the molecular formula of the gas?

49. A compound has an empirical formula C_5H_{11}. If 0.0275 mol of the compound has a mass of 3.91 g, what is the molecular formula of the compound?

50. A gas has an empirical formula CH. If 450 mL of the gas at STP has a mass of 0.522 g, what is the molecular formula?

51. When a sample of nickel carbonyl is heated, 0.0600 mol of a gas containing carbon and oxygen is formed. The gas has a mass of 1.68 g and is 42.9% C. What is the molecular formula of the gas?

52. A gas sample is analyzed and found to contain 33.0% Si and 67.0% F. If the gas density is 7.60 g/L at STP, what is the molecular formula of the gas?

53. A gas has the percentage composition: 78.3% B and 21.7% H. A sample bulb is filled with the unknown gas and weighed. The mass of unknown gas is found to be 0.986 times the mass of a sample of nitrogen gas, $N_2(g)$, in the same bulb under the same conditions of temperature and pressure. What is the molecular formula of the unknown gas?

54. A gas has an empirical formula CH_2. If 0.500 L of the gas at STP has a mass of 0.938 g, what is the molecular formula of the compound?

55. A sample of gas has an empirical formula of O and has a molar mass which is 3 times that of CH_4. What is the molecular formula of the gas?

V.6. MOLAR CONCENTRATION

This section is concerned with the idea of "concentration" and how to work with solutions of different concentrations. Everything in this section involves a simple idea: **knowing the concentration of a solution provides a way to find how much of a particular substance exists in a given volume of the solution.**

Definitions: The **CONCENTRATION** of a substance in solution is the amount of the substance which exists in a given volume of the solution.

    A **CONCENTRATED** solution has a relatively high concentration. (There is a large amount of substance dissolved in the solution.)

    A **DILUTE** solution has a relatively low concentration. (Very little substance is dissolved in the solution.)

NOTE: The terms "concentrated" and "dilute" are comparative and do not have precise meanings. Frequently, concentrated solutions are SATURATED solutions, or solutions with the "maximum possible concentration". Dilute solutions can be formed when large amounts of some solvent (normally water) are added to a concentrated solution in order to produce a lower concentration.

Chemists frequently use the "mole" to describe the amount of a substance in a solution.

Definition: The **MOLAR CONCENTRATION** or **MOLARITY** of a substance in solution is the number of moles of the substance contained in 1 L of *solution*.

    Note: This definition refers to "1 L of SOLUTION", not "1 L of SOLVENT". For example, 1 L of a concentrated solution of KBr(aq) may contain 550 g of KBr and 825 mL of water.

EXAMPLE: **If 2.0 L of solution contain 5.0 mol of NaCl, what is the molarity of the NaCl?**

$$\text{molar concentration} = \frac{5.0 \text{ mol}}{2.0 \text{ L}} = 2.5 \ \frac{\textbf{mol}}{\textbf{L}}$$

NOTES: 1. The unit symbol for "**mol/L**" is "**M**".
    2. When expressed in words, the unit symbol "**M**" is written as "**molar**".
    3. The short–hand symbol for "**molar concentration of ...**" is a set of brackets: **[...]**

EXAMPLES: If a 1.0 L of solution contains 2.5 mol of NaCl, the molar concentration can be expressed in several equivalent ways (shown below).

$$\text{molar concentration of NaCl} = 2.5 \ \frac{\text{mol}}{\text{L}} = 2.5 \text{ M}$$

[NaCl] = 2.5 M

The molarity of the sodium chloride is 2.5 molar.

MAKING UP SOLUTIONS

VOLUMETRIC FLASKS are used to obtain accurate volumes of solutions (see Figure 1, at right). Volumetric flasks are manufactured in specific volumes: 10 mL, 25 mL, 50 mL, 100 mL, 250 mL, 500 mL, 1000 mL, 2000 mL, etc. Generally, the volumes are accurate to about ± 0.1%. The following procedure is used for making up an aqueous solution.

Add the required amount of chemical to a flask having an appropriate volume. Then add distilled water until the flask is about one–half to two–thirds full. Cap the flask and shake it until the chemical has completely dissolved. Then add distilled water until the bottom of the meniscus (curved separation between water and air) just touches the etched line on the flask's neck (Figure 2). In order to get the last bit of water in accurately, it is advisable to use a small dropper. Finally, re–cap the flask and shake thoroughly until no wavy lines (resembling the heated air seen above a hot road) can be seen in the solution.

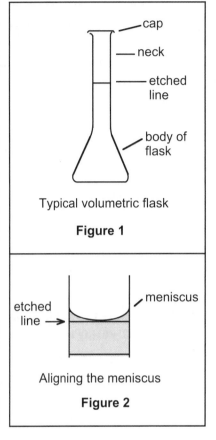

Typical volumetric flask

Figure 1

Aligning the meniscus

Figure 2

EXERCISES:

56. You have been asked to make 1.000 L of 1.000 M NaCl solution. Why shouldn't you add 1.000 L of water first and then add the NaCl to be dissolved?

57. You are making up a solution and accidentally add a bit too much liquid, so that the liquid level is about 2 mm above the etched line on the neck of the volumetric flask. What should you do at this point?

58. What practical problems arise if a solution is not thoroughly mixed?

The definition of molar concentration leads directly to the equations below.

molar concentration = $\dfrac{\textbf{moles}}{\textbf{volume}}$ where: c = molar concentration, in mol/L

n = number of moles

or: $c = \dfrac{n}{V}$ V = volume, in litres

EXAMPLE: **What is the [NaCl] in a solution containing 5.12 g of NaCl in 250.0 mL of solution?**

Plan: In order to find molarity (c), the moles (n) and volume (V) are needed. A volume is given and the mass given can be converted to moles.

$$\text{moles of NaCl} = 5.12 \text{ g} \times \frac{1 \text{ mol}}{58.5 \text{ g}} = 0.0875 \text{ mol}$$

and: $$[\text{NaCl}] = c = \frac{n}{V} = \frac{0.0875 \text{ mol}}{0.2500 \text{ L}} = \textbf{0.350 M}$$

EXAMPLE: **What mass of NaOH is contained in 3.50 L of 0.200 M NaOH?**

Plan: The molarity (c) and volume (V) are given so moles (n) can be found. Moles can then be converted to mass.

Solving $c = \dfrac{n}{V}$ for n gives $n = c \cdot V$

then: moles NaOH = 0.200 $\dfrac{mol}{L}$ x 3.50 L = 0.700 mol

and: mass NaOH = 0.700 mol x $\dfrac{40.0\ g}{1\ mol}$ = **28.0 g**

EXAMPLE: **What is the molarity of pure sulphuric acid, H_2SO_4 , having a density of 1.839 g/mL?**

Notice that density and molarity both have units of amount/volume

where: density = $\dfrac{amount\ (as\ mass)}{volume}$ and   molarity = $\dfrac{amount\ (as\ moles)}{volume}$.

Therefore, a unit conversion can be used to convert from an amount expressed in "grams" to an amount expressed in "moles" (and vice versa).

$$[H_2SO_4] = \dfrac{1.839\ g}{0.001\ L} \times \dfrac{1\ mol}{98.1\ g} = \textbf{18.7 M}$$

EXAMPLE: **What is the molarity of the $CaCl_2$ in a solution made by dissolving and diluting 15.00 g of $CaCl_2 \cdot 6H_2O$ to 500.0 mL?**

When $CaCl_2 \cdot 6H_2O$ dissolves in water $CaCl_2 \cdot 6H_2O(s) \longrightarrow CaCl_2(aq) + 6\ H_2O(l)$

the moles of $CaCl_2$ produced equals the moles of $CaCl_2 \cdot 6H_2O(s)$ dissolved.

$$[CaCl_2] = [CaCl_2 \cdot 6H_2O] = \dfrac{15.00\ g}{0.5000\ L} \times \dfrac{1\ mol}{219.1\ g} = \textbf{0.1369 M}$$

EXERCISES:

59. Calculate the molar concentration of the following solutions.
     (a) 0.26 mol of HCl in 1.0 L of solution   (d) 25.0 g of NaCl in 250.0 mL of solution
     (b) 2.8 mol of HNO_3 in 4.0 L of solution   (e) 1.50 g of $CoBr_2 \cdot 6H_2O$ in 600.0 mL of solution
     (c) 0.0700 mol of NH_4Cl in 50.0 mL of solution   (f) 10.0 g of $Cr(NO_3)_3 \cdot 9H_2O$ in 325 mL of solution

60. What is the actual experimental procedure you would use to prepare the following solutions?
     (a) 1.00 L of 3.00 M NH_4Cl (e) 2.75 L of 0.0120 M NaOH
     (b) 500.0 mL of 0.250 M $Hg(NO_3)_2$ (f) 2.00 L of 0.0300 M $CuSO_4$, starting with $CuSO_4 \cdot 5H_2O(s)$
     (c) 125 mL of 0.500 M $Ba(NO_3)_2$ (g) 50.0 mL of 0.225 M BaI_2 , starting with $BaI_2 \cdot 2H_2O(s)$
     (d) 250.0 mL of 0.100 M $SbCl_3$

61. How many moles of $AlCl_3$ are contained in 350.0 mL of 0.250 M $AlCl_3$?

62. What volume of 2.40 M HCl can be made from 100.0 g of HCl?

63. How many moles of $Sr(NO_3)_2$ are contained in 55.0 mL of 1.30×10^{-3} M $Sr(NO_3)_2$?

64. What volume of 2.8×10^{-2} M NaF contains 0.15 g of NaF?

65. The density of water at $4^\circ C$ is 1.000 kg/L. What is the molar concentration of H_2O in pure water at $4^\circ C$? (Hint: how many moles of H_2O are contained in 1 L?)

66   The density of acetic acid, $CH_3COOH(l)$, is 1049 g/L. What is the molarity of pure acetic acid?

67. The molar concentration of pure $HClO_4(l)$ is 17.6 M. What is the density of pure $HClO_4$?

68. The molarity of $CS_2(l)$ is 16.6 M. What is the density of $CS_2(l)$?

69. How many grams of $CaCl_2$ are contained in 225 mL of 0.0350 M $CaCl_2$ solution?

70. How many grams of Na_3PO_4 are contained in 3.45 L of 0.175 M $Na_3PO_4 \cdot 12H_2O$?

71. Acetone has a density of 0.790 g/mL. What mass of acetone and benzoic acid, C_6H_5COOH, is required to make 350.0 mL of a 0.0100 M solution of benzoic acid dissolved in acetone? Ignore the contribution which the benzoic acid makes to the volume. Based on your answer, why does it seem appropriate that you can ignore the contribution made by benzoic acid to the total volume?

DILUTION CALCULATIONS

The following set of exercises is designed to help you develop an intuitive approach to working with molarity calculations involving dilution and mixing of solutions. To make sure you don't get on the "wrong track", you should check each answer before proceeding to the next question or part of a question.

EXERCISES:

72. Assume you have been given a can of orange juice concentrate. Let:

    concentration of juice in can = 1 OJ   (1 orange juice unit) .

    You are probably aware of the fact that mixing one can of concentrated orange juice with one can of water produces orange juice that is "one half of full strength", so that:

    $$\text{diluted concentration} = \frac{1}{2} \text{ full strength} = \frac{1}{2} \text{ OJ} \qquad \text{(1 Orange Juice unit)}$$

    What diluted concentration, in OJ's, will you have if you mix

    (a) one can of orange juice with two cans of water?
    (b) one can of orange juice with three cans of water?
    (c) one can of orange juice with nine cans of water?
    (d) two cans of orange juice with two cans of water?
    (e) two cans of orange juice with eight cans of water?
    (f) three cans of orange juice with five cans of water?

73. Summarize the results of exercise 72 by writing a general equation for the diluted concentration of orange juice produced by mixing **C** cans of concentrated orange juice and **W** cans of water.

74. Now let's pretend that you are not mixing concentrated orange juice with water, but instead are mixing concentrated orange juice with concentrated apple juice.

    Let: concentration of apple juice = 1 AJ.

    (a) Does the fact that you are now adding apple juice instead of water to the orange juice change the AMOUNT of orange juice already present? Is the total volume different when one can of orange juice is mixed into one can of apple juice instead of one can of water? Is the orange juice diluted more (or less) if apple juice is added instead of water?
    (b) Let's change our viewpoint for a moment. Pretend we are now interested in how much the apple juice is being diluted, rather than how much the orange juice is diluted. Remembering that the concentration of the apple juice is 1 AJ, what is the diluted concentration of the apple juice when one can of apple juice is mixed with one can of orange juice?
    (c) Separately calculate the diluted concentration of orange juice, in OJ' ş and the diluted concentration of apple juice, in AJ's, when the following are mixed.
       i)   One can of orange juice is mixed with one can of apple juice.
       ii) One can of orange juice is mixed with two cans of apple juice.

    iii) One can of orange juice is mixed with three cans of apple juice.
    iv) Two cans of orange juice is mixed with three cans of apple juice.
    v) Five cans of orange juice is mixed with five cans of apple juice.
    vi) Four cans of orange juice is mixed with six cans of apple juice.

75. Summarize the results of exercise 74 by writing two general equations: one for the diluted concentration of orange juice and one for the diluted concentration of apple juice. Assume that **O** cans of orange juice and **A** cans of apple juice are mixed together.

76. How would you modify your equations in exercise 75 if the original concentrations were 0.8 OJ and 0.7 AJ instead of 1 OJ and 1 AJ?

77. OK, now we investigate the results of mixing two different brands of orange juice. El Cheapo Orange Drink Concentrate has a concentration which is 0.50 OJ. The other brand, Expensive Orange Juice Concentrate, has a concentration which is 1.0 OJ. *The mixing of the two different brands means the addition of the cans of one brand will DILUTE the concentration of the other brand, similar to the way that the apple juice and orange juice diluted each other.*

    Assume you mix TWO cans of El Cheapo (having a concentration of 0.50 OJ) with THREE cans of Expensive (having a concentration of 1.0 OJ).

    a) What is the concentration of the El Cheapo orange juice, after mixing?
    b) What is the concentration of the Expensive orange juice, after mixing?
    c) What is the total concentration of orange juice, expressed in OJ's, in the mixture?
    d) What is the total concentration of orange juice produced when five cans of Expensive Concentrate is mixed with three cans of El Cheapo Concentrate?
    e) What is the total concentration of orange juice produced when four cans of Expensive Concentrate is mixed with seven cans of El Cheapo Concentrate?

Now that you have explored the deep mysteries of orange and apple juice, let's apply this knowledge to chemical solutions having concentrations measured in moles / litre.

When two solutions are mixed, the resulting mixture has a total volume and total number of moles equal to the sum of the individual volumes and individual numbers of moles of chemical found in the separate solutions.

In other words –
$$\text{molarity of mixture} = \frac{\textbf{total moles of chemical in which we are interested}}{\textbf{total volume of mixture}}$$

A. SIMPLE DILUTION OF A CHEMICAL IN SOLUTION

Assume: **initial concentration of solution** (in more concentrated form) = c_{CONC}
        initial volume of solution (in more concentrated form) = V_{CONC}
        diluted concentration (after water is added) = c_{DIL}
        diluted volume (after water is added) = V_{DIL}

The "diluted volume" can also be thought of as the "total volume after dilution".

Since $c = \dfrac{n}{V}$ then $n = c \cdot V$

which means   moles of chemical in concentrated solution = $n_{CONC} = c_{CONC} \times V_{CONC}$
and   moles of chemical in diluted solution = n_{DIL} = $c_{DIL} \times V_{DIL}$.

But the amount of the chemical is not changed when the solution is diluted, only the concentration of the chemical is changed. Therefore moles of concentrated chemical = moles of diluted chemical

or: $n_{CONC} = n_{DIL}$

so that: $c_{CONC} \times V_{CONC} = n_{CONC} = n_{DIL} = c_{DIL} \times V_{DIL}$.

FINAL EQUATION:

$$c_{CONC} \times V_{CONC} = c_{DIL} \times V_{DIL}$$

or

$$c_{DIL} = c_{CONC} \times \frac{V_{CONC}}{V_{DIL}}$$

Aha! Look at the second equation in the box, above. It is our "orange juice dilution equation"!

EXAMPLE: **If 200.0 mL of 0.500 M NaCl is added to 300.0 mL of water, what is the resulting [NaCl] in the mixture?**

Since $[NaCl]_{DIL}$ and c_{DIL} have the same meaning, then

$$[NaCl]_{DIL} = [NaCl]_{CONC} \times \frac{V_{CONC}}{V_{DIL}} = 0.500 \text{ M} \times \frac{200.0 \text{ mL}}{(200.0 + 300.0) \text{ mL}} = \textbf{0.200 M}$$.

B. MIXING TWO SOLUTIONS HAVING DIFFERENT CONCENTRATIONS OF THE SAME CHEMICAL

This is the equivalent problem to mixing El Cheapo orange juice and Expensive orange juice. One solution dilutes the other solution, and vice versa. In the calculations below, one solution is arbitrarily "#1" and the other "#2". In order to get an accurate answer you must keep extra digits in the intermediate answers, rounding only the final answer to the correct number of significant digits.

> **Treat mixtures of two solutions as two separate "single dilutions" and then add the results of the individual single dilutions to get the overall concentration of the mixture as was done when mixing El Cheapo and Expensive brands of orange juice in exercise 77.**

EXAMPLE: **If 300.0 mL of 0.250 M NaCl is added to 500.0 mL of 0.100 M NaCl, what is the resulting [NaCl] in the mixture?**

Arbitrarily, let solution #1 be 0.250 M NaCl and solution #2 be 0.100 M NaCl.

$$[NaCl]_{DIL} (\#1) = [NaCl]_{CONC} (\#1) \times \frac{V_{CONC} (\#1)}{V_{DIL}} = 0.250 \text{ M} \times \frac{300.0 \text{ mL}}{800.0 \text{ mL}} = 0.09375 \text{ M}$$

$$[NaCl]_{DIL} (\#2) = 0.100 \text{ M} \times \frac{500.0 \text{ mL}}{800.0 \text{ mL}} = 0.06250 \text{ M}$$

$$[NaCl] \text{ (total)} = [NaCl]_{DIL} (\#1) + [NaCl]_{DIL} (\#2) = 0.09375 + 0.06250 = \textbf{0.156 M}$$

Note: The final concentration lies between the original concentrations of the two NaCl solutions: 0.100 M < **0.156 M** < 0.250 M. Obviously the mixture's concentration cannot be greater than the most concentrated solution involved or less than the least concentrated solution used.

C. MAKING DILUTE SOLUTIONS FROM CONCENTRATED SOLUTIONS

Again, this calculation is based on the fact that the moles of chemical in the diluted solution equals the moles of chemical poured from the concentrated solution. That is, $n_{CONC} = n_{DIL}$.

$$\boxed{c_{CONC} \times V_{CONC} = c_{DIL} \times V_{DIL}}$$

EXAMPLE: **What volume of 6.00 M HCl is used in making up 2.00 L of 0.125 M HCl?**

The equation: $c_{CONC} \times V_{CONC} = c_{DIL} \times V_{DIL}$

is rearranged to solve for the volume of concentrated solution required.

$$V_{CONC} = \frac{c_{DIL} \times V_{DIL}}{c_{CONC}} = \frac{0.125 \text{ M} \times 2.00 \text{ L}}{6.00 \text{ M}} = \textbf{0.0417 L}$$

EXAMPLE: **A student mixes 100.0 mL of water with 25.0 mL of a sodium chloride solution having an unknown concentration. If the student finds the molarity of the sodium chloride in the diluted solution is 0.0876 M, what is the molarity of the original sodium chloride solution?**

The diluted volume is 100.0 mL + 25.0 mL = 125.0 mL

Therefore $c_{CONC} = c_{DIL} \times \dfrac{V_{DIL}}{V_{CONC}} = 0.0876 \text{ M} \times \dfrac{125.0 \text{ mL}}{25.0 \text{ mL}} = \textbf{0.438 M}$

EXERCISES:

78. If 20.0 mL of 0.75 M HBr is diluted to a total volume of 90.0 mL, what is the molar concentration of the HBr in the resulting solution?

79. What is the molar concentration of the KOH solution resulting from mixing 55 mL of 0.15 M KOH and 75 mL of 0.25 M KOH?

80. If 1 drop (0.050 mL) of 0.20 M NaBr is added to 100.00 mL of water, what is the molarity of the NaBr in the resulting solution?

81. What is the molar concentration of the HNO_3 solution resulting from mixing 5.0 mL of 3.5 M HNO_3 and 95 mL of 0.20 M HNO_3?

82. Concentrated HNO_3 is 15.4 M. How would you prepare 2.50 L of 0.375 M HNO_3?

83. Concentrated H_3PO_4 is 14.6 M. How would you prepare 45.0 L of 0.0600 M H_3PO_4?

84. If 300.0 mL of solution A contains 25.0 g of KCl and 250.0 mL of solution B contains 60.0 g of KCl, what is the molarity of the KCl in the solution resulting from mixing solutions A and B?

85. If 500.0 mL of 0.750 M NaCl is boiled down until the final volume is reduced to 300.0 mL, what is the final molarity of the NaCl? (Assume no salt is lost during the boiling process.)

86. How would you prepare 250.0 mL of 0.350 M HCl, starting with 6.00 M HCl?

87. What mass of NaCl is needed to prepare 500.0 mL of 0.400 M NaCl?

88. What is the concentration of the NaOH solution produced by mixing 125.0 mL of 0.250 M NaOH with 200.0 mL of 0.175 M NaOH?

89. What volume of 12.0 M NaOH is required in order to prepare 3.00 L of 0.750 M NaOH?

90. What is the concentration of $CaCl_2$ produced when 55.0 mL of 0.300 M HCl is mixed with 80.0 mL of 0.550 M $CaCl_2$?

91. When 350.0 mL of 0.250 M $MgCl_2$ is boiled down to a final volume of 275.0 mL, what is the molarity of the $MgCl_2$ in the resulting solution?

92. If 20.0 mL of 0.350 M NaCl and 75.0 mL of 0.875 M NaCl are mixed and the resulting solution is boiled down to a volume of 60.0 mL, what is the molarity of the NaCl in the final solution?

93. A solution is made by mixing 100.0 mL of 0.200 M $BaCl_2$ and 150.0 mL of 0.400 M NaCl. What is the concentration of sodium chloride in the final solution?

94. If 75.0 mL of 0.200 M Na_3PO_4 is added to 25.0 mL of 0.800 M K_3PO_4, what is the concentration of Na_3PO_4 in the mixture?

AN OVERVIEW OF MOLARITY PROBLEMS

The 5 basic types of molarity problems and the equations relevant to the problems are shown below.

A. Making a solution with a given concentration

$$c = \frac{n}{V}, \quad \text{where} \quad n = \text{mass (g)} \times \frac{1 \text{ mol}}{\text{molar mass (g)}}$$

You may also be given moles (or mass) and concentration, and be asked to find the volume, or some variation of this problem.

B. Dilution of a single solution

$$c_{DIL} = c_{CONC} \times \frac{V_{CONC}}{V_{DIL}}$$

C. Mixing two solutions

$$c_{DIL} (\#1) = c_{CONC} (\#1) \times \frac{V_{CONC} (\#1)}{V_{DIL}} \quad \text{and} \quad c_{DIL} (\#2) = c_{CONC} (\#2) \times \frac{V_{CONC} (\#2)}{V_{DIL}}$$

$$c \text{ (total)} = c_{DIL} (\#1) + c_{DIL} (\#2)$$

D. Converting a density to a molarity and vice versa

$$c = d \frac{\text{(g)}}{\text{(L)}} \times \frac{1 \text{ mol}}{\text{molar mass (g)}} \quad \text{and} \quad d = c \frac{\text{(mol)}}{\text{(L)}} \times \frac{\text{molar mass (g)}}{1 \text{ mol}}$$

E. Making a dilute solution from a concentrated solution

$$c_{CONC} \times V_{CONC} = c_{DIL} \times V_{DIL}$$

(Note that this is essentially the same as type B, above.)

MOLARITY REVIEW PROBLEMS

95. What is the molarity of each of the following solutions?
    (a) 5.62 g of $NaHCO_3$ is dissolved in enough water to make 250.0 mL
    (b) 184.6 mg of K_2CrO_4 is dissolved in enough water to make 500.0 mL
    (c) 0.584 g of oxalic acid ($H_2C_2O_4$) is diluted to 100.0 mL

96. What is the actual experimental procedure you would use to make
    (a) 1.00 L of 0.100 M NaCl, starting with solid NaCl?
    (b) 250.0 mL of 0.09000 M KBr, starting with solid KBr?
    (c) 500.0 mL of 0.125 M $Ca(NO_3)_2$, starting with solid $Ca(NO_3)_2 \cdot 3H_2O$?

97. What is the concentration of the solution produced when
    (a) 125 mL of 3.55 M LiOH is mixed with 475 mL of 2.42 M LiOH?
    (b) 150.0 mL of water is added to 200.0 mL of 0.250 M NaCl?
    (c) 100.0 mL of 12.0 M KBr is mixed with 950.0 mL of 0.200 M KBr?
    (d) 75 mL of water is mixed with 5.0 mL of 2.50 M KBr?
    (e) 50.0 mL of water is mixed with 850.0 mL of 0.1105 M HCl?
    (f) 50.0 mL of 0.125 M HCl is mixed with 75.0 mL of 0.350 M HCl?

98. What is the molarity of the solution produced when
    (a) 250.0 mL of 0.750 M KBr is boiled down to a volume of 175.0 mL?
    (b) 350.0 mL of water and 75.0 mL of 0.125 M $NaNO_3$ are mixed and boiled down to 325.0 mL?
    (c) 150.0 mL of 0.325 M LiBr and 225.0 mL of 0.500 M LiBr are mixed and boiled to 275.0 mL?

99. What mass of solid solute is present in
    (a) 5.0 L of 2.5 M KBr?   (b) 225 mL of 0.135 M MgI_2?   (c) 350.0 mL of 0.250 M NaCl?

100. What is the molarity of the following pure liquids?
    (a) C_8H_{18}, d = 0.7025 g/mL   (b) CH_3COCH_3, d = 789.9 g/L   (c) $POCl_3$, d = 1.675 g/mL

101. What is the density of the following pure liquids?
    (a) SbF_5, molarity = 13.8 M   (b) S_2Cl_2, molarity = 12.73 M   (c) C_6H_5CHO, molarity = 9.825 M

102. (a) What volume of 3.00 M HCl is required to make up 5.00 L of 0.250 M HCl?
    (b) What volume of 15.4 M HNO_3 is needed to make up 500.0 mL of 0.100 M HNO_3?
    (c) What volume of 0.150 M HCl can be made from 250.0 mL of 5.00 M HCl?
    (d) What concentration of NaCl solution is made by diluting 3.00 L of 0.850 M NaCl to 12.5 L?
    (e) A solution is made in such a way that when 100.0 mL of the solution is diluted to 5.00 L, the resulting mixture has a concentration of 0.100 M. What is the molarity of the original solution?
    (f) What mass of KBr is contained in 500.0 mL of 0.235 M KBr?
    (g) What volume of 0.550 M HCl contains 50.0 g of HCl?
    (h) How many moles of LiCl are contained in 5.50 L of 0.850 M LiCl?
    (i) What is the concentration of $CaCl_2$ produced when 75.0 g of $CaCl_2$ is diluted to 950.0 mL?
    (j) What is the density of pure liquid $CHBr_3$ (molarity = 11.4 M)?
    (k) What volume of 0.0675 M $Ba(NO_3)_2$ contains 2.55 g of $Ba(NO_3)_2$?
    (l) How many moles of $FeCl_3$ are contained in 1.50 L of 0.368 M $FeCl_3$?
    (m) What is the molarity of $SnCl_2$ produced when 25.00 g of $SnCl_2 \cdot 2H_2O$ is diluted to 750.0 mL?
    (n) What volume of 0.995 M HCl is required to make 3.50 L of 0.0450 M HCl?
    (o) What is the molarity of NaCl made by mixing 185.0 mL of water with 55.0 mL of 0.543 M NaCl?
    (p) What mass of $BaCl_2 \cdot 2H_2O$ is required to make up 1.35 L of 0.250 M $BaCl_2$?
    (q) What is the concentration of $CaCl_2$ produced by mixing 145 mL of 0.550 M $CaCl_2$ with 55 mL of 0.135 M $CaCl_2$?
    (r) What is the molarity of pure liquid C_6H_6 (d = 0.8787 g/mL)?

UNIT VI : CHEMICAL REACTIONS

VI.1. INTRODUCTION TO CHEMICAL EQUATIONS

Various types of evidence indicate that chemical reactions occur. Although no single piece of evidence may be conclusive, when several changes are found they generally give clear evidence of a reaction. Some examples of changes that frequently accompany a chemical reaction are:

- the temperature may change
- different coloured materials may be formed
- new phases may be formed.

In general, a chemical reaction is said to occur when the starting chemical species form different chemicals.

Definition: A **CHEMICAL REACTION EQUATION** is an equation that shows the chemicals used up and produced during a chemical reaction.

The general form of a chemical equation is: **REACTANTS $\longrightarrow$ PRODUCTS**

A **CHEMICAL WORD EQUATION** uses **words** to describe the REACTANTS and PRODUCTS.

EXAMPLE: "Sodium and chlorine react to form sodium chloride." This can be restated using CHEMICAL SYMBOLS.

$$2\,Na + Cl_2 \longrightarrow 2\,NaCl$$

The numbers in front of the symbols are called **COEFFICIENTS** and refer to the numbers of molecules of each species involved in the reaction.

During a chemical reaction the reactants are changed and replaced by products. This means that the interpretation of "$\longrightarrow$" is "as time passes". That is:

REACTANTS EXIST, then as time passes PRODUCTS EXIST.

VI.2. THE CONSERVATION LAWS

Definitions: A **SYSTEM** is the part of the universe being studied in a particular situation.

A system is **CLOSED** if nothing can enter or leave the system.

A system is **OPEN** if things can enter and leave the system.

EXAMPLES: If an experiment examines how a beaker full of hot liquid cools down with time, the "system" is the beaker and its contents.

If an experiment involves a beaker of hot liquid, cooling and transferring its heat to air inside a box, the "system" consists of the beaker, the hot liquid and the air in the box. (Depending on the type of experiment, the box may or may not be thought of as part of the system.)

A beaker full of boiling water is an example of an open system if the beaker and water are considered to be the "system" and the beaker is on a hot plate. Heat is able to enter the beaker and water (the system) and water vapour is able to escape.

A sealed glass tube containing hot water is an example of a system that is **closed with respect to mass.** No material can get in or out of the sealed tube.

EXERCISES:

1. Give an example of a system which is
    (a) closed with respect to light.
    (b) open with respect to light and closed with respect to mass.
    (c) closed with respect to sound.
    (d) open with respect to mass and closed with respect to light.
    (e) closed with respect to heat.

2. Is it possible to have a system that is completely closed with respect to everything? Why?

Definition: A quantity is **CONSERVED** if the quantity does not change during a reaction. (That is, the system is CLOSED with respect to the quantity.)

A **CONSERVATION LAW** is an experimentally observed law which states what is CONSERVED (unchanged) in a special set of circumstances.

Four conservation laws are important to Chemistry 11 and 12.

The **LAW OF CONSERVATION OF MASS**
The total mass in a closed system does not change during a chemical reaction.

The **LAW OF CONSERVATION OF ATOMS**
The total number and type of atoms in a closed system does not change during a chemical reaction.

The **LAW OF CONSERVATION OF ELECTRICAL CHARGE**
The total electrical charge in a closed system does not change during a chemical reaction.

The **LAW OF CONSERVATION OF ENERGY**
The total energy in a closed system does not change during a chemical reaction. (The relative amounts of the various types of energy may change, but the total amount of energy is unchanged.)

EXERCISES:

3. You rip a piece of paper into several pieces.
    a) What is CONSERVED with respect to the paper?
    b) What is NOT CONSERVED with respect to the paper?
    c) One piece of paper is taken away. What is now conserved and what isn't?

4. Which conservation laws are being broken in the following situations? (Note that conservation laws may not necessarily be broken in every case.)

    a) $Fe + S \longrightarrow CuS$

    b) 7.0 g of nitrogen gas are reacted with 8.0 g of oxygen gas to make 16.0 g of nitrogen monoxide.

    c) $Fe^{3+} + S^{2-} \longrightarrow FeS$

    d) $2\ Ag^+ + SO_4^{2-} \longrightarrow Ag_2SO_4$

    e) $3\ Cr + O_2 \longrightarrow Cr_2O_3$

    f) At STP, 71.0 g of chlorine gas and 64.0 g of oxygen gas produce 135 g of chlorine dioxide gas.

5. Which of the following are conserved in a chemical reaction?
    (a) phase   (b) numbers of atoms   (c) volume   (d) moles of molecules

6. Show that each of the following reactions obey the laws of conservation of atoms and of mass.

    (a) $CH_4 + 2\ O_2 \longrightarrow CO_2 + 2\ H_2O$ (b) $NaOH + HCl \longrightarrow NaCl + H_2O$

VI.3. BALANCING CHEMICAL REACTION EQUATIONS

If a chemical equation is **BALANCED**, then **mass, atoms,** and **electrical charge** are **CONSERVED. In Chemistry 11, the act of balancing an equation will be confined to making sure that ATOMS ARE CONSERVED; that is, having the same number of each type of atom on each side of the equation.**

The following example shows the essential ideas behind the balancing process.

EXAMPLE: **Balance the equation   __ H_2S + __ $PbCl_2$ $\longrightarrow$ __ PbS + __ HCl .**

Start with an atom which is involved in only **one species on each side of the equation** and assign coefficients which balance (give equal numbers of) the atom. In this equation, Pb, S, Cl and H occur only once on each side of the equation. Arbitrarily, start the balancing with ONE Pb.

$$\_\_\ H_2S + 1\ PbCl_2 \longrightarrow 1\ PbS + \_\_\ HCl$$

This FIRST placement of coefficients is THE ONLY TIME you should have to write in TWO coefficients in order to balance an atom. From this point on, you should only need to place a single coefficient in the equation in order to balance another atom.

(We say that the Pb's have now been "balanced" because the same, definite number of atoms ("1") exists on both sides of the equation as a result of the coefficients used.)

The balanced atoms are part of molecules which involve other atoms. Select **ONE** of the "other atoms" which now occurs **ONCE MORE** in the equation without a coefficient in front of it. (S and Cl are atoms in molecules containing Pb.) For example, the "1" in front of PbS not only defines the number of Pb's but also the number of S atoms: 1 S is on the right so 1 S must be selected on the left. Add a single coefficient in front of the other molecule containing S.

$$1\ H_2S + 1\ PbCl_2 \longrightarrow 1\ PbS + \_\_\ HCl$$

Continue this "find an atom which occurs once without a coefficient in front of it and balance it" procedure. Arbitrarily, balance H by placing a coefficient in front of HCl.

$$1\ H_2S + 1\ PbCl_2 \longrightarrow 1\ PbS + 2\ HCl$$

Finally, double check that all the atoms are balanced. A good place to start is with Cl because this last atom was balanced by default. (That is, no attempt was made to balance Cl.)

The balancing of an equation is not a difficult process, but it does take practice to be able to carry out the process in a quick, efficient manner. Because the types of equations you will encounter are so varied, it is difficult to list a "hard–and–fast" set of rules which guarantees automatic success. Nevertheless, the following suggestions will help you achieve success in balancing the equations encountered in Chemistry 11. (Examples will follow to show how these suggestions are applied.)

a) Quickly scan the equation to identify atoms that occur in only one species on each side of the equation. One of these atoms **must** be your starting point.

b) Metal atoms often dictate what happens in the reaction, so that normally they should be balanced first. If there are no metal atoms, look for anything present besides H and O. H and O are often found several times throughout an equation and frequently can't be balanced until most of the other atoms are balanced.

c) Once a coefficient is put in front of a species in order to balance a particular atom, at least one other atom in the species now has this same coefficient. Look on the other side of the equation to see if this other atom appears once more in the equation without a coefficient in front of it. Once such an atom has been found, balance that atom by placing a coefficient in front of the species containing the atom. Continue this process until a coefficient has been put in front of every molecule.

d) Until you have put a number in front of a species, assume you have **ZERO** atoms or molecules of that species. In other words, treat a BLANK as a ZERO.

e) Try to balance entire groups (eg. SO_4 , PO_4 , NO_3 , etc.), if possible.

f) If an atom is part of a diatomic element, such as "O" in O_2 , notice that:

$$2\ \text{O–atoms} = 1\ O_2$$
$$1\ \text{O–atom} = {}^1/_2\ O_2$$
$$5\ \text{O–atoms} = {}^5/_2\ O_2$$
$$\text{"x" O–atoms} = {}^x/_2\ O_2 .$$

g) If a fraction (eg. $^1/_2$) occurs during the balancing, multiply the equation by the whole number (eg. 2) which eliminates the fraction.

EXAMPLE: **Balance __ $(NH_4)_3PO_4$ + __ NaOH $\longrightarrow$ __ Na_3PO_4 + __ NH_3 + __ H_2O .**

Na, N and PO_4 all occur in just one species on each side and can be used to start the balancing procedure. Arbitrarily, start with the metal, Na.

$$\text{__ } (NH_4)_3PO_4 \quad + \textbf{3}\ NaOH \qquad \textbf{1}\ Na_3PO_4 + \text{__}\ NH_3 + \text{__}\ H_2O$$

The coefficents (in bold) were found by "criss–crossing" the subscripts of the Na's on either side, as shown.

> **Note:** Show **all** the assigned coefficents, even if they are 1's, so as to indicate the atoms in the molecule are "balanced so far". (The coefficients are a "HANDS OFF" sign to prevent you from indiscriminately changing the balancing you have achieved to this point.) If you wish, you can omit coefficients having a value of "1" in your **final** answer.

There are many equivalent ways to proceed from this point; what follows is simply one way. Since there is **1** PO_4 group on the right side, put a **1** in front of the "$(NH_4)_3PO_4$".

$$1\ (NH_4)_3PO_4 + 3\ NaOH \longrightarrow 1\ Na_3PO_4 + \text{__}\ NH_3 + \text{__}\ H_2O$$

Since there are **3** N atoms on the left side, place a **3** in front of the NH_3 .

$$1 \ (NH_4)_3PO_4 + 3 \ NaOH \longrightarrow 1 \ Na_3PO_4 + 3 \ NH_3 + \_\_ \ H_2O$$

Finally, arbitrarily balance the O's. Ignore the O's in the PO_4 group because they are already balanced. There are 3 other O's on the left (**3 NaOH**), so put a **3** in front of the H_2O.

$$1 \ (NH_4)_3PO_4 + 3 \ NaOH \longrightarrow 1 \ Na_3PO_4 + 3 \ NH_3 + 3 \ H_2O$$

As a final check, notice that the H's are also balanced: 15 H's on each side.

EXAMPLE: Balance $\quad \_\_ \ C_{19}H_{17}NO_3 + \_\_ \ O_2 \longrightarrow \_\_ \ CO_2 + \_\_ \ H_2O + \_\_ \ N_2$.

No metal atoms are present, so arbitrarily start with "C". (N and H are also possible choices.)

$$1 \ C_{19}H_{17}NO_3 + \_\_ \ O_2 \longrightarrow 19 \ CO_2 + \_\_ \ H_2O + \_\_ \ N_2$$

Since 1 N is on the left side, 1 N is required on the right and therefore put "$1/2$" in front of the N_2

$$1 \ C_{19}H_{17}NO_3 + \_\_ \ O_2 \longrightarrow 19 \ CO_2 + \_\_ \ H_2O + {}^1/_2 \ N_2$$

To clear the fraction in front of the N_2, double all the numbers assigned to this point.

$$2 \ C_{19}H_{17}NO_3 + \_\_ \ O_2 \longrightarrow 38 \ CO_2 + \_\_ \ H_2O + 1 \ N_2$$

Neither H nor O are balanced, but there are still two molecules containing O that have no coefficient so far, so H is balanced next. There are 34 H's on the left side, so 34 H's are needed on the right. Since the H's on the right come in pairs (H_2O), put a **17** in front of the H_2O.

$$2 \ C_{19}H_{17}NO_3 + \_\_ \ O_2 \longrightarrow 38 \ CO_2 + 17 \ H_2O + 1 \ N_2$$

Next, balance the O's: on the right side there are   (38 x 2) + (17 x 1) = 93 O's .
On the left side, 6 O's are assigned (2 x 3) and therefore (93 – 6 =) 87 more are needed. Since the O's come in pairs, put ${}^{87}/_2$ in front of the O_2 .

$$2 \ C_{19}H_{17}NO_3 + {}^{87}/_2 \ O_2 \longrightarrow 38 \ CO_2 + 17 \ H_2O + 1 \ N_2$$

Finally, clear the fraction "${}^{87}/_2$" by doubling all the coefficients.

$$4 \ C_{19}H_{17}NO_3 + 87 \ O_2 \longrightarrow 76 \ CO_2 + 34 \ H_2O + 2 \ N_2$$

Re–check to make sure that all the atoms are balanced – mistakes can happen.

EXAMPLE: Balance $\quad \_\_ \ Cr_2(SO_4)_3 + \_\_ \ KI + \_\_ \ KIO_3 + \_\_ \ H_2O \longrightarrow \_\_ \ Cr(OH)_3 + \_\_ \ K_2SO_4 + \_\_ \ I_2$.

Any of Cr, SO_4 or H are possible starting points. Arbitrarily start with the metal, Cr.

$$1 \ Cr_2(SO_4)_3 + \_\_ \ KI + \_\_ \ KIO_3 + \_\_ \ H_2O \longrightarrow 2 \ Cr(OH)_3 + \_\_ \ K_2SO_4 + \_\_ \ I_2$$

Having balanced the Cr's, either of H or SO_4 (which are part of the molecules $Cr_2(SO_4)_3$ and $Cr(OH)_3$) can now be balanced. Arbitrarily, balance the SO_4's next. There are 3 SO_4's on the left so 3 K_2SO_4 are required on the right.

$$1 \ Cr_2(SO_4)_3 + \_\_ \ KI + \_\_ \ KIO_3 + \_\_ \ H_2O \longrightarrow 2 \ Cr(OH)_3 + 3 \ K_2SO_4 + \_\_ \ I_2$$

The only atom which now can be balanced by adding a single coefficient is H. Since 6 H's are on the right, and H's come in pairs in the H_2O on the left, then 3 H_2O's are needed.

$$1 \ Cr_2(SO_4)_3 + \_\_ \ KI + \_\_ \ KIO_3 + 3 \ H_2O \longrightarrow 2 \ Cr(OH)_3 + 3 \ K_2SO_4 + \_\_ \ I_2$$

Next, the O's must be balanced (K and I still appear in more than one "unbalanced" molecule). Discounting the O's in the SO_4 groups, there are 6 O's on the right. On the left, 3 O's are now accounted for (in H_2O), so that another 3 are required, in the form of 1 KIO_3 .

$$1 \, Cr_2(SO_4)_3 + \underline{} \, KI + 1 \, KIO_3 + 3 \, H_2O \longrightarrow 2 \, Cr(OH)_3 + 3 \, K_2SO_4 + \underline{} \, I_2$$

The K's can now be balanced. There are 6 K's on the right, and 1 K is already accounted for on the left (in KIO_3), so an additional 5 K are required on the left, in the form of 5 KI.

$$1 \, Cr_2(SO_4)_3 + 5 \, KI + 1 \, KIO_3 + 3 \, H_2O \longrightarrow 2 \, Cr(OH)_3 + 3 \, K_2SO_4 + \underline{} \, I_2$$

Finally, there is a total of 6 I's on the left so that 3 I_2 is required on the right.

$$1 \, Cr_2(SO_4)_3 + 5 \, KI + 1 \, KIO_3 + 3 \, H_2O \longrightarrow 2 \, Cr(OH)_3 + 3 \, K_2SO_4 + 3 \, I_2$$

Re–check to make sure that all the atoms are correctly balanced.

EXAMPLE: **Balance** $\underline{}$ **$MoCl_3$ +** $\underline{}$ **O_2 +** $\underline{}$ **AgCl** $\longrightarrow$ $\underline{}$ **$MoCl_4$ +** $\underline{}$ **Ag_2O** .

Any of Mo, O and Ag are possible starting points. Arbitrarily start with Mo.

$$1 \, MoCl_3 + \underline{} \, O_2 + \underline{} \, AgCl \longrightarrow 1 \, MoCl_4 + \underline{} \, Ag_2O$$

Now that Mo is balanced, Cl exists only once in the equation without a coefficient in front of it. Since there are 3 Cl's on the left and 4 on the right, one more Cl is required on the left.

$$1 \, MoCl_3 + \underline{} \, O_2 + 1 \, AgCl \longrightarrow 1 \, MoCl_4 + \underline{} \, Ag_2O$$

Next, 1 Ag is assigned on the left so 1 Ag is needed on the right. Since Ag comes in pairs in Ag_2O, take $\frac{1}{2}$ of this molecule.

$$1 \, MoCl_3 + \underline{} \, O_2 + 1 \, AgCl \longrightarrow 1 \, MoCl_4 + \tfrac{1}{2} \, Ag_2O$$

Clear the fraction by doubling the assigned coefficients to this point.

$$2 \, MoCl_3 + \underline{} \, O_2 + 2 \, AgCl \longrightarrow 2 \, MoCl_4 + 1 \, Ag_2O$$

Next, there is 1 O assigned on the right so 1 O is required on the left. Since O comes in pairs in the molecule O_2 , take $\frac{1}{2}$ of this molecule.

$$2 \, MoCl_3 + \tfrac{1}{2} \, O_2 + 2 \, AgCl \longrightarrow 2 \, MoCl_4 + 1 \, Ag_2O$$

Finally, clear the fraction by doubling all coefficients.

$$4 \, MoCl_3 + 1 \, O_2 + 4 \, AgCl \longrightarrow 4 \, MoCl_4 + 2 \, Ag_2O$$

Re–check to make sure that all the atoms are correctly balanced.

EXERCISES: Balance the following chemical reaction equations.

7. $\underline{}$ Sn + $\underline{}$ O_2 $\longrightarrow$ $\underline{}$ SnO

8. $\underline{}$ H_2 + $\underline{}$ Cl_2 $\longrightarrow$ $\underline{}$ HCl

9. $\underline{}$ N_2 + $\underline{}$ H_2 $\longrightarrow$ $\underline{}$ NH_3

10. $\underline{}$ Na + $\underline{}$ H_2O $\longrightarrow$ $\underline{}$ NaOH + $\underline{}$ H_2

11. $\underline{}$ NH_3 + $\underline{}$ O_2 $\longrightarrow$ $\underline{}$ N_2 + $\underline{}$ H_2O

12. $\underline{}$ C_6H_{14} + $\underline{}$ O_2 $\longrightarrow$ $\underline{}$ CO_2 + $\underline{}$ H_2O

13. $\underline{}$ KNO_3 $\longrightarrow$ $\underline{}$ KNO_2 + $\underline{}$ O_2

14. __ CaC_2 + __ O_2 $\longrightarrow$ __ Ca + __ CO_2

15. __ C_5H_{12} + __ O_2 $\longrightarrow$ __ CO_2 + __ H_2O

16. __ K_2SO_4 + __ $BaCl_2$ $\longrightarrow$ __ KCl + __ $BaSO_4$

17. __ KOH + __ H_2SO_4 $\longrightarrow$ __ K_2SO_4 + __ H_2O

18. __ $Ca(OH)_2$ + __ NH_4Cl $\longrightarrow$ __ NH_3 + __ $CaCl_2$ + __ H_2O

19. __ C + __ SO_2 $\longrightarrow$ __ CS_2 + __ CO

20. __ Mg_3N_2 + __ H_2O $\longrightarrow$ __ $Mg(OH)_2$ + __ NH_3

21. __ V_2O_5 + __ Ca $\longrightarrow$ __ CaO + __ V

22. __ Na_2O_2 + __ H_2O $\longrightarrow$ __ $NaOH$ + __ O_2

23. __ Fe_3O_4 + __ H_2 $\longrightarrow$ __ Fe + __ H_2O

24. __ Cu + __ H_2SO_4 $\longrightarrow$ __ $CuSO_4$ + __ H_2O + __ SO_2

25. __ Al + __ H_2SO_4 $\longrightarrow$ __ H_2 + __ $Al_2(SO_4)_3$

26. __ Si_4H_{10} + __ O_2 $\longrightarrow$ __ SiO_2 + __ H_2O

27. __ NH_3 + __ O_2 $\longrightarrow$ __ N_2H_4 + __ H_2O

28. __ $C_{15}H_{30}$ + __ O_2 $\longrightarrow$ __ CO_2 + __ H_2O

29. __ BN + __ F_2 $\longrightarrow$ __ BF_3 + __ N_2

30. __ $CaSO_4{\cdot}2H_2O$ + __ SO_3 $\longrightarrow$ __ $CaSO_4$ + __ H_2SO_4

31. __ $C_3H_7N_2O_7$ + __ O_2 $\longrightarrow$ __ CO_2 + __ H_2O + __ N_2

32. __ $C_7H_{16}O_4S_2$ + __ O_2 $\longrightarrow$ __ CO_2 + __ H_2O + __ SO_2

33. __ Na + __ ZnI_2 $\longrightarrow$ __ NaI + __ $NaZn_4$

34. __ $HBrO_3$ + __ HBr $\longrightarrow$ __ H_2O + __ Br_2

35. __ Al_4C_3 + __ H_2O $\longrightarrow$ __ $Al(OH)_3$ + __ CH_4

36. __ $Ca(NO_3)_2{\cdot}3H_2O$ + __ LaC_2 $\longrightarrow$ __ $Ca(NO_3)_2$ + __ $La(OH)_2$ + __ C_2H_2

37. __ CH_3NO_2 + __ Cl_2 $\longrightarrow$ __ CCl_3NO_2 + __ HCl

38. __ $Ca_3(PO_4)_2$ + __ SiO_2 + __ C $\longrightarrow$ __ $CaSiO_3$ + __ CO + __ P

39. __ Al_2C_6 + __ H_2O $\longrightarrow$ __ $Al(OH)_3$ + __ C_2H_2

40. __ NaF + __ CaO + __ H_2O $\longrightarrow$ __ CaF_2 + __ $NaOH$

41. __ LiH + __ $AlCl_3$ $\longrightarrow$ __ $LiAlH_4$ + __ $LiCl$

42. __ CaF_2 + __ H_2SO_4 + __ SiO_2 $\longrightarrow$ __ $CaSO_4$ + __ SiF_4 + __ H_2O

43. __ $CaSi_2$ + __ $SbCl_3$ $\longrightarrow$ __ Si + __ Sb + __ $CaCl_2$

44. __ TiO_2 + __ B_4C + __ C $\longrightarrow$ __ TiB_2 + __ CO

45. __ NH_3 + __ O_2 $\longrightarrow$ __ NO + __ H_2O

46. __ SiF_4 + __ $NaOH$ $\longrightarrow$ __ Na_4SiO_4 + __ NaF + __ H_2O

47. __ NH_4Cl + __ CaO $\longrightarrow$ __ NH_3 + __ $CaCl_2$ + __ H_2O

48. __ $NaPb$ + __ C_2H_5Cl $\longrightarrow$ __ $Pb(C_2H_5)_4$ + __ Pb + __ $NaCl$

49. __ Be$_2$C + __ H$_2$O $\longrightarrow$ __ Be(OH)$_2$ + __ CH$_4$

50. __ NpF$_3$ + __ O$_2$ + __ HF $\longrightarrow$ __ NpF$_4$ + __ H$_2$O

51. __ NO$_2$ + __ H$_2$O $\longrightarrow$ __ HNO$_3$ + __ NO

52. __ LiAlH$_4$ + __ BF$_3$ $\longrightarrow$ __ LiF + __ AlF$_3$ + __ B$_2$H$_6$

Optional Mind–Benders: Good Luck – you will need it!

53. __ Cu + __ HNO$_3$ $\longrightarrow$ __ Cu(NO$_3$)$_2$ + __ NO + __ H$_2$O

54. __ FeCl$_2$ + __ KNO$_3$ + __ HCl $\longrightarrow$ __ FeCl$_3$ + __ NO + __ H$_2$O + __ KCl

55. __ KMnO$_4$ + __ HBr $\longrightarrow$ __ MnBr$_2$ + __ Br$_2$ + __ KBr + __ H$_2$O

56. __ K$_2$Cr$_2$O$_7$ + __ HCl $\longrightarrow$ __ KCl + __ CrCl$_3$ + __ H$_2$O + __ Cl$_2$

VI.4. WRITING PHASES IN REACTION EQUATIONS AND USING CHEMICAL WORD EQUATIONS

Besides showing the number and type of molecules, a chemical reaction equation can also show the phases in which the reactants and products exist. The phases of chemicals are shown by including the following symbols in parentheses immediately after the chemical formula.

s = solid , l = liquid , g = gas , aq = aqueous (which means "dissolved in water")

EXAMPLES: $2 \, Hg(l) + O_2(g) \longrightarrow 2 \, HgO(s)$
          liquid   gas   solid

$AgNO_3(aq) + NaCl(aq) \longrightarrow NaNO_3(aq) + AgCl(s)$

(which means silver nitrate and sodium chloride are dissolved in water to produce a solution of sodium nitrate and solid silver chloride)

IMPORTANT: Memorize the fact that **seven** of the elements form **diatomic molecules**.

MEMORY AID: There are 7 diatomic elements "in the shape of a seven plus one."
Look at the representation of the periodic table below to see what this phrase means.

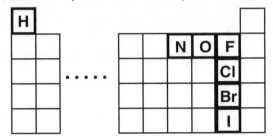

See how the elements **N, O, F, Cl, Br** and **I** are arranged in the shape of a "**7**". The element "**H**" is by itself (this is the "**plus one**"). Therefore, the seven diatomic elements are N_2 , O_2 , F_2 , Cl_2 , Br_2 , I_2 and H_2 .

The following examples show how chemical word equations are translated into chemical equations involving phases.

Note: The words "crystals", "powder" and "precipitate" all mean the phase is a **solid**. *Precipitate* is used to refer to a solid formed when two liquid or aqueous solutions react.

EXAMPLES: a)   Solid sodium reacts with chlorine gas to produce solid sodium chloride.

$2 \, Na(s) + Cl_2(g) \longrightarrow 2 \, NaCl(s)$

b)   Liquid water reacts with powdered sodium oxide to produce aqueous sodium hydroxide.

$H_2O(l) + Na_2O(s) \longrightarrow 2 \, NaOH(aq)$

c)   Aqueous hydrochloric acid reacts with calcium carbonate crystals, producing aqueous calcium chloride, gaseous carbon dioxide and liquid water.

$2 \, HCl(aq) + CaCO_3(s) \longrightarrow CaCl_2(aq) + CO_2(g) + H_2O(l)$

EXERCISES:

57.   Translate the following word equations into chemical symbols and balance the resulting equations. Do not include the phases.
  (a)   potassium + water $\longrightarrow$ potassium hydroxide + hydrogen
  (b)   strontium + water $\longrightarrow$ strontium hydroxide + hydrogen
  (c)   aluminum and chlorine react to produce aluminum chloride
  (d)   copper(I) oxide and carbon react to form copper and carbon dioxide
  (e)   ammonia and sulphuric acid form ammonium sulphate

In each of the following write a balanced chemical equation, including the phases.

58. Liquid phosphoric acid reacts with aqueous barium hydroxide to give water and a precipitate of barium phosphate.

59. Solid aluminum oxide and aqueous sulphuric acid produce water and aqueous aluminum sulphate.

60. Nitrogen trifluoride gas and hydrogen gas react to form nitrogen gas and gaseous hydrogen fluoride.

61. Powdered sodium carbonate and aqueous hydrobromic acid react to form carbon dioxide gas, aqueous sodium bromide and water.

62. Sodium nitrate crystals and solid sodium metal react to form solid sodium oxide and nitrogen gas.

63. Gaseous boron trichloride reacts with steam to yield solid boron trihydroxide and hydrogen chloride gas.

64. Gaseous xenon hexafluoride reacts violently with water to form solid xenon trioxide and gaseous hydrogen fluoride.

VI.5. TYPES OF CHEMICAL REACTIONS

There are five major types of chemical reactions of importance in Chemistry 11. This section shows how to identify the various types of reactions and write the products expected from a given set of reactants. (Because many chemical reactions are very complicated and the products of a reaction sometimes are difficult or impossible to predict without performing an experiment, only simple examples are considered in this section.)

Type 1: **Synthesis (or Combination)**

A **SYNTHESIS** or **COMBINATION** reaction involves the **combination** of two or more substances to form (or "**synthesize**") a compound.

EXAMPLES: $C(s) + O_2(g) \longrightarrow CO_2(g)$
$H_2(g) + Cl_2(g) \longrightarrow 2\ HCl(g)$
$2\ Sb(s) + 3\ Br_2(l) \longrightarrow 2\ SbBr_3(s)$

In general, a synthesis / combination is represented by the equation:
$A + B \longrightarrow AB$.

YOU ONLY HAVE TO PREDICT PRODUCTS WHEN THE REACTANTS ARE TWO ELEMENTS.

What to look for: Two ELEMENTS react

How to predict products: Assume the product is a compound made of the two elements joined together and the compound is made of ions. Use the most common charges for each ion.

EXAMPLE: $H_2(g) + F_2(g) \longrightarrow 2\ HF(g)$ (based on H = +1, F = −1)

Type 2: **Decomposition**

A **DECOMPOSITION** reaction involves breaking down a molecule into simpler substances.

EXAMPLES: $2\ Ag_2O(s) + heat \longrightarrow 4\ Ag(s) + O_2(g)$
$2\ HgO(s) + heat \longrightarrow 2\ Hg(l) + O_2(g)$
$2\ NO(g) + heat \longrightarrow N_2(g) + O_2(g)$

In general, a decomposition reaction can be thought of as the reverse of a combination reaction:
$AB \longrightarrow A + B$.

What to look for: A SINGLE COMPOUND on the reactant side

How to predict products: YOU WILL ONLY HAVE TO PREDICT PRODUCTS WHEN THE ORIGINAL COMPOUND BREAKS INTO THE ELEMENTS WHICH MAKE IT UP.

EXAMPLE: $2 H_2O(l) \longrightarrow 2 H_2(g) + O_2(g)$ (water is decomposed by electricity)

Type 3: **Single Replacement**

A **SINGLE REPLACEMENT** involves replacing **one** atom in a compound by another atom.

EXAMPLES: $CuCl_2(aq) + Fe(s) \longrightarrow FeCl_2(aq) + Cu(s)$
$Cl_2(aq) + 2 KI(aq) \longrightarrow I_2(aq) + 2 KCl(aq)$
$2 AgNO_3(aq) + Cu(s) \longrightarrow 2 Ag(s) + Cu(NO_3)_2(aq)$

In general, a single replacement reaction is represented by the reaction:

$A + BX \longrightarrow B + AX$.

What to look for: An ELEMENT reacts with a COMPOUND

How to predict products: The COMPOUND contains a metal followed by a nonmetal.
- If the reacting ELEMENT is a **metal**, let it "trade places" with the **metal** atom in the COMPOUND.
- If the ELEMENT is a **nonmetal**, let it "trade places" with the **nonmetal** atom in the COMPOUND.

EXAMPLES: $CuI_2 + Br_2 \longrightarrow CuBr_2 + I_2$ (nonmetal replaces nonmetal)
$CuI_2 + Fe \longrightarrow FeI_2 + Cu$ (metal replaces metal)

Type 4: **Double Replacement (or Metathesis)**

A **DOUBLE REPLACEMENT** or **METATHESIS** reaction involves an exchange of atoms or groups between two different compounds.

EXAMPLES: $AgNO_3(aq) + NaCl(aq) \longrightarrow AgCl(s) + NaNO_3(aq)$
$2 NaCl(aq) + H_2SO_4(aq) \longrightarrow 2 HCl(g) + Na_2SO_4(aq)$
$Ba(NO_3)_2(aq) + Na_2SO_4(aq) \longrightarrow BaSO_4(s) + 2 NaNO_3(aq)$

In general, a double replacement / metathesis reaction is represented by the equation:

$AB + XY \longrightarrow AY + XB$.

What to look for: Two COMPOUNDS react

How to predict products: Assume the reactants are made up of ions. Make up products by having the positive ions (which are always written first) "swapping partners". Pay special attention to the ion charges when predicting the formula of the product formed.

EXAMPLE: $Cu(NO_3)_2(aq) + Na_2S(aq) \longrightarrow CuS(s) + 2 NaNO_3(aq)$

Since both reactants are normally aqueous compounds, the reason a reaction occurs is that one ion from each reacting compound joins together to form a new compound which either is insoluble in water (such as CuS, above) or is water itself (as shown in the neutralization reaction below).

NOTE: A special type of DOUBLE REPLACEMENT reaction involves the reaction of an **ACID** with a **BASE**. **(An acid has a chemical formula starting with "H", and a base has a chemical formula ending with "OH".)**

Examples: HCl, H_2SO_4 , HNO_3 and H_2S are acids

  Na**OH**, K**OH**, Ca**(OH)**$_2$ and Fe**(OH)**$_3$ are bases

This special type of double replacement sometimes is called a **water forming reaction** but it is more commonly called a **NEUTRALIZATION** reaction. A neutralization reaction involves the reaction between the **H** in an acid and the **OH** in a base to make **H$_2$O**.

Examples: $HCl(aq) + NaOH(aq) \longrightarrow NaCl(aq) + H_2O(l)$

  $H_2SO_4(aq) + 2\ KOH(aq) \longrightarrow K_2SO_4(aq) + 2\ H_2O(l)$

Besides water, the other product of an acid–base reaction is a SALT.

Definition: A **SALT** is an ionic compound that is neither an acid nor a base. That is; a salt is an ionic substance whose formula does not start with "H" or end with "OH".

In general: **AN ACID PLUS A BASE GIVES A SALT PLUS WATER** .

Example: $HNO_3 + KOH \longrightarrow KNO_3 + H_2O$
   acid   base   salt   water

Writing a neutralization reaction is quite simple. Consider the following.

  $H_3PO_4 + Ba(OH)_2 \longrightarrow$?

The actual reaction which is taking place in **all** acid–base neutralizations is just:

  $H^+ + OH^- \longrightarrow H_2O$.

Therefore, start by making sure that the numbers of H's and OH's involved are equal. Since the H_3PO_4 has 3 H's and the $Ba(OH)_2$ has 2 OH's, "criss–cross" the number of H's and OH's to obtain the coefficients in front of the acid and base.

  2 $H_3PO_4 +$ **3** $Ba($**OH**$)_2 \longrightarrow$?

Now, there are 6 H's and 6 OH's and therefore the reaction will produce 6 H_2O's.

  2 $H_3PO_4 +$ **3** $Ba($**OH**$)_2 \longrightarrow$ **6** H_2O + ?

To write the formula of the salt produced, collect together the remaining positive and negative ions and form them into a SINGLE COMPOUND with the positive ion written first; there are 3 Ba's and 2 PO$_4$'s on the reactant side so the final equation is:

  2 $H_3PO_4 +$ **3** $Ba(OH)_2 \longrightarrow 6\ H_2O +$ **Ba$_3$(PO$_4$)$_2$** .

When all of the acid and base present have neutralized each other, so that no excess of either acid or base remains, the resulting solution is said to be **NEUTRAL**.

Type 5:   Combustion of Hydrocarbons

COMBUSTION is a general term referring to the rapid reaction of a substance with oxygen to produce substantial amounts of heat, and usually a flame. A special and very important case of combustion involves organic compounds; that is, compounds whose formula starts with carbon.

When a **HYDROCARBON** (a compound made of C and H) undergoes **COMBUSTION**, the process involves the reaction of the hydrocarbon with oxygen to produce carbon dioxide and water.

EXAMPLE: $C_5H_{12}(l) + 8\ O_2(g) \longrightarrow 5\ CO_2(g) + 6\ H_2O(l)$

In general, the combustion (burning) of a hydrocarbon is given by the equation:

  Hydrocarbon + $O_2 \longrightarrow CO_2 + H_2O$

What to look for: A hydrocarbon reactant

How to predict products: Add $O_2(g)$ to the hydrocarbon, then write the products as $CO_2(g)$ and $H_2O(l)$. (See special notes, below)

Special notes:

1. Burning an organic compound containing OXYGEN does not change the balancing procedure.

$$C_5H_{12}O_2 + 7\,O_2 \longrightarrow 5\,CO_2 + 6\,H_2O$$

2. Burning an organic compound containing SULPHUR produces $SO_2(g)$.

$$C_5H_{12}S + 9\,O_2 \longrightarrow 5\,CO_2 + 6\,H_2O + SO_2$$

Sulphur dioxide reacts with water to form sulphurous acid

$$SO_2(g) + H_2O(l) \longrightarrow H_2SO_3(aq)$$

and sulphurous acid is a major component of acid rain.

SUMMARY OF REACTION TYPES

TYPE	HOW TO RECOGNIZE REACTANTS	HOW TO PREDICT PRODUCTS
Synthesis or Combination	2 Elements	Combine elements into one compound
Decomposition	One compound	Break compound into its elements
Single Replacement	Element + Compound	Interchange metals (or nonmetals) present
Double Replacement	Compound + Compound	Interchange positive ions in compounds
Neutralization (special case of double replacement)	Acid + Base	Water is one product; remaining ions combine to form a salt
Combustion of Hydrocarbon	(A substance whose formula starts with "C") + O_2	CO_2 + H_2O (if H present) + SO_2 (if S present)

EXERCISES:

65. Complete and balance the following neutralization equations.
    (a) $H_2SO_4 + NaOH$
    (b) $H_3PO_4 + KOH$
    (c) $H_2SO_4 + Fe(OH)_3$
    (d) $H_4P_2O_7 + Ca(OH)_2$
    (e) $H_2SO_4 + Ba(OH)_2$

66. Balance the following equations and classify each reaction as one of: synthesis, decomposition, single replacement, double replacement, neutralization or combustion.
    (a) $C_2H_2 + O_2 \longrightarrow CO_2 + H_2O$
    (b) $Mg + CuSO_4 \longrightarrow MgSO_4 + Cu$
    (c) $Na + O_2 \longrightarrow Na_2O$
    (d) $Fe(NO_3)_3 + MgS \longrightarrow Fe_2S_3 + Mg(NO_3)_2$
    (e) $N_2O \longrightarrow N_2 + O_2$
    (f) $Sn(OH)_4 + HBr \longrightarrow H_2O + SnBr_4$
    (g) $Cl_2 + KI \longrightarrow KCl + I_2$
    (h) $Al + S \longrightarrow Al_2S_3$
    (i) $C_6H_{12}O_6 + O_2 \longrightarrow CO_2 + H_2O$
    (j) $HF + Fe(OH)_3 \longrightarrow FeF_3 + H_2O$
    (k) $H_2O_2 \longrightarrow H_2O + O_2$
    (l) $FeCl_2 + K_2S \longrightarrow FeS + KCl$
    (m) $Ca + O_2 \longrightarrow CaO$
    (n) $H_2SO_4 + NaOH \longrightarrow Na_2SO_4 + H_2O$
    (o) $C_2H_5OH + O_2 \longrightarrow CO_2 + H_2O$
    (p) $Cr + SnCl_4 \longrightarrow CrCl_3 + Sn$
    (q) $Pb(NO_3)_2 + K_2CrO_4 \longrightarrow PbCrO_4 + KNO_3$
    (r) $Fe + I_2 \longrightarrow FeI_2$
    (s) $C_3H_6OS_2 + O_2 \longrightarrow CO_2 + H_2O + SO_2$
    (t) $MgCl_2 \longrightarrow Mg + Cl_2$
    (u) $Co(NO_3)_2 + H_2S \longrightarrow CoS + HNO_3$
    (v) $H_4P_2O_7 + KOH \longrightarrow K_4P_2O_7 + H_2O$
    (w) $Mg + HCl \longrightarrow H_2 + MgCl_2$
    (x) $HI \longrightarrow H_2 + I_2$

67. Complete and balance the following reactions and classify each equation as one of: synthesis, decomposition, single replacement, double replacement, neutralization or combustion.
    (a) $HNO_3 + Sr(OH)_2 \longrightarrow$
    (b) $C_6H_4(OH)_2 + O_2 \longrightarrow$
    (c) $Zn + Ni(NO_3)_2 \longrightarrow$
    (d) $AlCl_3 + Na_2CO_3 \longrightarrow$
    (e) $Al + O_2 \longrightarrow$
    (f) $Ba(OH)_2 + H_2SO_4 \longrightarrow$
    (g) $NO_2 \longrightarrow$
    (h) $Cl_2 + CaBr_2 \longrightarrow$
    (i) $C_9H_{20}O_4S_2 + O_2 \longrightarrow$
    (j) $ZnSO_4 + SrCl_2 \longrightarrow$
    (k) $Zn + S_8 \longrightarrow$
    (l) $NH_3 \longrightarrow$
    (m) $HCl + KOH \longrightarrow$
    (n) $ICl \longrightarrow$
    (o) $Na_3PO_4 + Ca(OH)_2 \longrightarrow$
    (p) $C_4H_8S + O_2 \longrightarrow$
    (q) $Mg + ZnSO_4 \longrightarrow$
    (r) $Li + O_2 \longrightarrow$

VI.6. ENERGY CHANGES IN CHEMICAL REACTIONS

Molecules are held together by **CHEMICAL BONDS.** In order to break a bond, energy has to be added to the bond. (This should make sense: it takes energy to break a piece of string — which is held together by chemical bonds.)

EXAMPLE: The reaction $HCl + energy \longrightarrow H + Cl$ is shown graphically below.

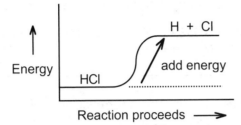

Therefore, the separated atoms (H and Cl) contain more energy than the original molecule (HCl).

Conversely, if two atoms join together, they must **give off their excess energy** in order to allow them to "stick" together, rather than simply colliding and flying apart again.

EXAMPLE: The reaction $H + Cl \longrightarrow HCl + energy$ is shown graphically below. Note that this reaction is the **opposite** of the above reaction.

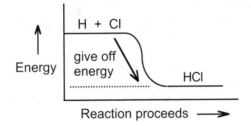

Therefore, if a reaction takes in **more** energy to **break** bonds than it **gives off** to **form** bonds, the reaction will require a NET INPUT OF ENERGY.

Conversely, if a reaction takes in **less** energy to **break** bonds than it **gives off** to **form** bonds, the reaction will GIVE OFF ENERGY.

Definition: An EXOTHERMIC reaction **GIVES OFF** heat to its surroundings. (Heat EXITS from the reactants.)

    EXAMPLE: $CH_4 + 2 O_2 \longrightarrow CO_2 + 2 H_2O + 891$ kJ

Note: The coefficients always refer to "moles" when the heat involved is expressed in kilojoules ("kJ") of energy. The prediction of the amount of heat involved in a reaction is beyond the scope of Chemistry 11.

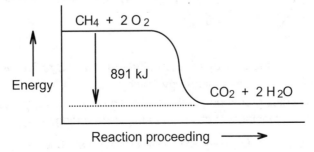

EXERCISES:

68. You can think of the above reaction as occuring in two steps. (The reaction DOES NOT go this way, but it is convenient to pretend.)

   Step 1: $CH_4 + 2 O_2 \longrightarrow C + 4 H + 4 O$ (the reactants are broken down to individual atoms)

   Step 2: $C + 4 H + 4 O \longrightarrow CO_2 + 2 H_2O$ (the individual atoms are assembled into products)

   (a) Does step 1 absorb or give off energy?
   (b) Does step 2 absorb or give off energy?
   (c) Since the overall reaction is exothermic, which step involves more energy: step 1 or step 2?

69. The energy needed to break an H–Cl bond is 432 kJ: $HCl + 432 \text{ kJ} \longrightarrow H + Cl$. How many kilojoules of energy are given off in the reaction: $H + Cl \longrightarrow HCl + \_\_ \text{ kJ}$? Why?

Definition: An ENDOTHERMIC reaction **ABSORBS** heat from its surroundings. (Heat ENTERS the reaction.)

   EXAMPLE: $KClO_3(s) + 41.4 \text{ kJ} \longrightarrow K^+(aq) + ClO_3^-(aq)$

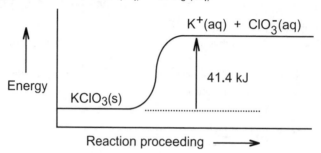

Reaction proceeding ⟶

As shown in exercise 68, a chemical reaction involves breaking and forming bonds as reactants form products. Each type of bond requires a different amount of energy during the breaking process, so that changing the reactants into products (that is, replacing one set of bonds with a different set of bonds) means the products have a different energy from the reactants.

 • If **more** energy is used to break the bonds in the reactants than is given off producing the bonds in the products, the reaction is ENDOTHERMIC.

 • If **less** energy is used to break the bonds in the reactants than is given off producing the bonds in the products, the reaction is EXOTHERMIC.

A distinction MUST be made between the reacting chemicals and their surroundings.

In an EXOTHERMIC reaction, the chemicals give off energy to their surroundings.

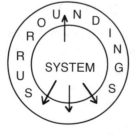

(The arrows show heat flowing from the system to the surroundings.)

Since the **surroundings absorb the energy** given off, the **surroundings feel WARMER.** The reactant molecules in this case contain a great deal of energy (such as sugar, $C_{12}H_{22}O_{11}$, and oxygen below). As the reaction occurs, the molecules produced (such as CO_2 and H_2O) contain less energy, so that the excess energy contained in the reactants is given off to the surroundings in the form of HEAT.

   $C_{12}H_{22}O_{11} + 12 O_2 \longrightarrow 12 CO_2 + 11 H_2O + 5638 \text{ kJ}$
   sugar

In an ENDOTHERMIC reaction, the chemicals absorb energy from their surroundings.

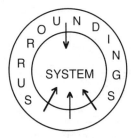

Since the **surroundings lose energy** to the reactants, the **surroundings feel COOLER.** For example, an ice cube absorbs heat from your hand in order to melt. Your hand then feels cooler. The reactant molecules in an endothermic reaction contain relatively little energy (such as CO_2 and H_2O, below); when sufficient energy is added to the reactants they can form high–energy product molecules (such as sugar). The following reaction shows the overall reaction involved in PHOTOSYNTHESIS; the energy absorbed comes from sunlight (note the oxygen which is produced by the photosynthesis reaction; the photosynthesis reaction is the opposite of the combustion reaction).

$$12\ CO_2 + 11\ H_2O + 5638\ kJ \longrightarrow \underset{\text{sugar}}{C_{12}H_{22}O_{11}} + 12\ O_2$$

EXERCISES:

70. Is the burning of wood exothermic or endothermic?

71. Is the melting of sugar exothermic or endothermic?

72. A beaker becomes warm when a reaction occurs in it. Are the chemicals in the beaker gaining or losing energy? Is the reaction endothermic or exothermic?

73. Which contain more energy in an endothermic reaction: the reactants or products?

74. In an exothermic reaction, do you have to add or remove energy in order to allow products to form?

Definitions: **ENTHALPY**, H, is the HEAT contained in a system.

ΔH = the change in enthalpy during a reaction.

$\Delta H = H_{PRODUCTS} - H_{REACTANTS}$,

where: $H_{REACTANTS}$ = the heat energy contained in the reactant
$H_{PRODUCTS}$ = the heat energy contained in the products

EXERCISE:

75. Is $\Delta H > 0$ or $\Delta H < 0$ for an endothermic reaction? Is $\Delta H > 0$ or $\Delta H < 0$ for an exothermic reaction?

Exothermic and endothermic reactions can be shown in alternate ways.

$$\textbf{ENDOTHERMIC} \begin{cases} A + 50\,kJ \rightarrow B \\ or: A \rightarrow B \; ; \; \Delta H = +50\,kJ \end{cases}$$

Similarly : $$\textbf{EXOTHERMIC} \begin{cases} C \rightarrow D + 80\,kJ \\ or: C \rightarrow D; \; \Delta H = -80\,kJ \end{cases}$$

MEMORY AID: The two possible signs for a number are **+** and **−** (and we generally say "positive" before saying "negative").
Therefore we can use the memory aid:

+ → −

which can be interpreted as

if HEAT is on the **LEFT,** then ΔH = **+**
if HEAT is on the **RIGHT,** then ΔH = **−** .

EXERCISES:

76.   Draw an energy diagram having ΔH = +25 kJ.

77.   Draw an energy diagram having ΔH = −50 kJ.

78. ΔH = −50 kJ for the reaction: F $\longrightarrow$ G . Re–write this equation to show the 50 kJ properly on the reactant or product side.

79.   If a reaction absorbs 30 kJ of heat, what is ΔH for the reaction?

80.   If P $\longrightarrow$ Q + 25 kJ, what is ΔH for the reaction? Which have more energy, the reactants or products?

UNIT VII : CALCULATIONS INVOLVING REACTIONS (STOICHIOMETRY)

The reaction between phosphoric acid, H_3PO_4, and potassium hydroxide, KOH, can produce three different products based on the relative amounts of H_3PO_4 and KOH used. Specifically:

$$H_3PO_4 + KOH \longrightarrow KH_2PO_4 + H_2O$$
$$H_3PO_4 + 2\,KOH \longrightarrow K_2HPO_4 + 2\,H_2O$$
$$H_3PO_4 + 3\,KOH \longrightarrow K_3PO_4 + 3\,H_2O\,.$$

Each of the products KH_2PO_4, K_2HPO_4 and K_3PO_4, has different properties and different uses. For example, KH_2PO_4 is used in baking powder, K_2HPO_4 is used in some fertilizers and antifreezes, and K_3PO_4 is used in liquid soaps.

After examining the equations above, two questions which might come to mind are:

    (i) how can we make a particular one of the three products?
    (ii) what amounts of H_3PO_4 and KOH are required to make a specific amount of K_2HPO_4, for example.

The answers to these questions lie in the study of "stoichiometry".

Definition: **STOICHIOMETRY** = the relationship between the amount of reactants used in a chemical reaction and the amounts of products produced by the reaction.

By studying stoichiometry, we will see how to predict the amount of a specific product created when a given amount of reactant is used.

VII.1. THE MEANING OF THE COEFFICIENTS IN A REACTION EQUATION

The coefficients in the equation $2\,H_2 + O_2 \longrightarrow 2\,H_2O$

tell us that two hydrogen molecules react with one oxygen molecule to produce two molecules of water. However, the equation is also balanced when written as

$$200\,H_2 + 100\,O_2 \longrightarrow 200\,H_2O$$

or even $2 \times (6.02 \times 10^{23})\,H_2 + 1 \times (6.02 \times 10^{23})\,O_2 \longrightarrow 2 \times (6.02 \times 10^{23})\,H_2O\,.$

This latter equation is equivalent to writing

$$2\,mol\ H_2 + 1\,mol\ O_2 \longrightarrow 2\,mol\ H_2O$$

or simply $2\,H_2 + O_2 \longrightarrow 2\,H_2O$

where the coefficients can now refer to the amount of molecules, measured in moles, which are involved in the reaction.

Thus, the ratio $\dfrac{H_2}{O_2} = \dfrac{2}{1}$ is maintained using either: $\dfrac{2\ \text{molecules } H_2}{2\ \text{molecules } O_2}$

                or: $\dfrac{2\ \text{mol } H_2}{2\ \text{mol } O_2}\,.$

EXAMPLE: Consider the reaction equation $N_2 + 3\,H_2 \longrightarrow 2\,NH_3$.

a) How many molecules of N_2 are required to react with 15 molecules of H_2?

Since 1 molecule of N_2 reacts with 3 molecules of H_2, then:

$$\text{\# of molecules of } N_2 = 15 \text{ molecules } H_2 \times \frac{1 \text{ molecule } N_2}{3 \text{ molecules } H_2} = 5 \text{ molecules} .$$

IMPORTANT: Use completely–labelled units (eg. "molecule N_2" not just "molecule") so as to know which coefficient goes on top and which goes on the bottom of the conversion factor.

b) How many moles of NH_3 are produced when 18 mol of H_2 are reacted?

Since 3 mol of H_2 produce 2 mol of NH_3, then:

$$\text{\# of moles of } NH_3 = 18 \text{ mol } H_2 \times \frac{2 \text{ mol } NH_3}{3 \text{ mol } H_2} = \textbf{12 mol} .$$

EXERCISES:

1. In the reaction $2\,C_2H_6 + 7\,O_2 \longrightarrow 4\,CO_2 + 6\,H_2O$

    a)   how many oxygen molecules react with 6 molecules of C_2H_6?

    b)   how many H_2O molecules are produced when 12 molecules of C_2H_6 react?

    c)   how many moles of oxygen molecules are needed to produce 18 mol of CO_2 ?

    d)   how many moles of CO_2 are produced when 13 mol of C_2H_6 are used up?

2. In the reaction $3\,Fe + 4\,H_2O \longrightarrow Fe_3O_4 + 4\,H_2$

    a)   how many molecules of Fe_3O_4 are produced when 12 atoms of Fe react?

    b)   how many moles of Fe are required to produce 16 mol of H_2?

    c)   how many H_2 molecules are made when 40 molecules of Fe_3O_4 are produced?

    d)   how many moles of H_2O are required to react with 14.5 mol of Fe?

3. How many moles of $H_2O(g)$ are produced when 9.6 mol of $O_2(g)$ react according to the equation
    $2\,H_2(g) + O_2(g) \longrightarrow 2\,H_2O(g)$?

4. Consider the equation $3\,I_2(g) + 6\,F_2(g) \longrightarrow 2\,IF_5(g) + I_4F_2(g)$.

    a)   How many moles of $I_4F_2(g)$ are produced by 5.40 mol of $F_2(g)$?
    b)   How many moles of $F_2(g)$ are required to produce 4.50 mol of $IF_5(g)$?
    c)   How many moles of $I_2(g)$ are required to react with 7.60 mol of $F_2(g)$?

5. CARE! A student decomposes some hydrogen peroxide, H_2O_2 , according to the equation
    $2\,H_2O_2 \longrightarrow 2\,H_2O + O_2$.

    If a total of 0.125 mol of reactants and products are involved in the reaction, how many moles of O_2 are produced?

VII.2. STOICHIOMETRY CALCULATIONS INVOLVING MOLES, MASS, GAS VOLUME AND MOLECULES

Stoichiometry calculations allow us to find how much of chemical #1 is involved in a chemical reaction based on the amount of chemical #2 involved. A typical problem might read something like:

"How many grams of chemical #1 must be reacted in order to produce 25 g of chemical #2?"

The relationship between the moles of chemical #1 and the moles of chemical #2 is central to each calculation. (You practised working with this relationship in exercises 1–5.) A good way to visualize the connection between the two chemicals mentioned is as follows: the central part of each calculation is seen as a **bridge** between the moles of the two chemicals mentioned in the problem.

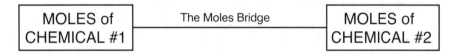

The following general diagram shows the kinds of "connections" which can be made when performing stoichiometry calculations.

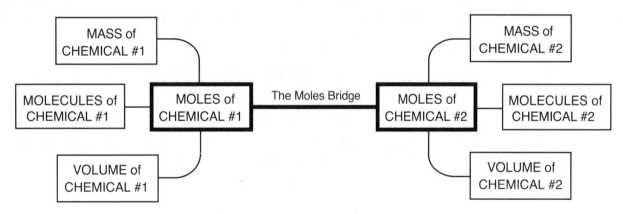

General Diagram For Stoichiometric Calculations

Before crossing the "moles bridge" the initial units for chemical #1 (given as a number of molecules, mass or gas volume at STP) must be converted to **MOLES** of chemical #1. After crossing the moles bridge, "moles of chemical #2" is converted to the units needed for chemical #2 (number of molecules, mass or volume).

EXAMPLES: The combustion of propane, C_3H_8, proceeds according to the following equation.

$$C_3H_8(g) + 5\ O_2(g) \longrightarrow 3\ CO_2(g) + 4\ H_2O(l)$$

a) What mass of CO_2 is produced by reacting 2.00 mol of O_2?

> **PLAN:** The "central" calculation is the conversion from moles of O_2 to moles of CO_2
> $$5\ mol\ O_2 = 3\ mol\ CO_2 .$$
> Since the initial data is given as moles of O_2, first convert **moles of O_2** to **moles of CO_2** and then convert moles of CO_2 to mass of CO_2.

$$\text{mass of } CO_2 = 2.00\ \text{mol } O_2 \times \frac{3\ \text{mol } CO_2}{5\ \text{mol } O_2} \times \frac{44.0\ \text{g } CO_2}{1\ \text{mol } CO_2} = \textbf{52.8 g}$$

b) **What mass of C_3H_8 is required to produce 100.0 g of H_2O?**

> **PLAN:** The initial data is the mass of H_2O. First, convert the mass of H_2O to moles of H_2O. Then, apply the central conversion factor which converts moles of H_2O to moles of C_3H_8 :
>
> $$1 \text{ mol } C_3H_8 = 4 \text{ mol } H_2O.$$
>
> Finally, convert moles of C_3H_8 to mass of C_3H_8 .

$$\text{mass of } C_3H_8 = 100.0 \text{ g } H_2O \times \frac{1 \text{mol } H_2O}{18.0 \text{ g } H_2O} \times \frac{1 \text{ mol } C_3H_8}{4 \text{ mol } H_2O} \times \frac{44.0 \text{ g } C_3H_8}{1 \text{ mol } C_3H_8} = \textbf{61.1 g}$$

c) **If a sample of propane is burned what mass of $H_2O(l)$ is produced if the reaction also produces 50.0 L of $CO_2(g)$ at STP?**

> **PLAN:** The fact that both species mentioned are products is no problem; the problem still deals with two species in a reaction. The starting data is a volume (50.0 L of CO_2) so start by converting from litres to moles. Then apply the conversion factor connecting moles of CO_2 to moles of H_2O:
>
> $$3 \text{ mol } CO_2 = 4 \text{ mol } H_2O.$$
>
> Finally convert from moles of H_2O to mass of H_2O, since that was the unknown in the problem statement.

$$\text{mass of } H_2O = 50.0 \text{ L } CO_2 \times \frac{1 \text{ mol } CO_2}{22.4 \text{ L } CO_2} \times \frac{4 \text{ mol } H_2O}{3 \text{ mol } CO_2} \times \frac{18.0 \text{ g } H_2O}{1 \text{ mol } H_2O} = \textbf{53.6 g}$$

d) **A propane burner is used in an auditorium as part of a chemistry demonstration. What volume of $O_2(g)$ at STP is consumed from the auditorium air if the burner produces 10.0 L of $CO_2(g)$ at STP during the demonstration?**

> **PLAN:** Again, the central calculation requires connecting the two species mentioned:
>
> $$5 \text{ mol } O_2 = 3 \text{ mol } CO_2.$$
>
> Since the starting data is in litres and the unknown is in litres, the conversion sequence is:
>
> $$\text{litres } CO_2 \longrightarrow \text{ moles } CO_2 \longrightarrow \text{ moles } O_2 \longrightarrow \text{ litres } O_2$$

$$\text{Volume of } O_2 = 10.0 \text{ L } CO_2 \times \frac{1 \text{ mol } CO_2}{22.4 \text{ L } CO_2} \times \frac{5 \text{ mol } O_2}{3 \text{ mol } CO_2} \times \frac{22.4 \text{ L } O_2}{1 \text{ mol } O_2} = \textbf{16.7 L}$$

e) **A sample of porous, gas–bearing rock is crushed and 1.35×10^{-6} g of $C_3H_8(g)$ is extracted from the powdered rock. How many molecules of CO_2 are produced if the gas sample is burned in the presence of an excess of $O_2(g)$?**

NOTE: The phrase "an excess of O_2" contains two pieces of information. First, you know some O_2 is included in the reaction and C_3H_8 doesn't burn without oxygen (because it couldn't). Second, you don't have to worry about the amount of O_2 being used but can simply assume that there is enough to make all the C_3H_8 present react.

$$\text{\# of } CO_2 \text{ molec} = 1.35 \times 10^{-6} \text{ g } C_3H_8 \times \frac{1 \text{mol } C_3H_8}{44.0 \text{ g } C_3H_8} \times \frac{3 \text{mol } CO_2}{1 \text{mol } C_3H_8} \times \frac{6.02 \times 10^{23} \text{ molec } CO_2}{1 \text{mol } CO_2}$$

$$= \textbf{5.54} \times \textbf{10}^{\textbf{16}} \textbf{ molecules}$$

EXERCISES:

6. Consider the reaction $4 NH_3(g) + 5 O_2(g) \longrightarrow 6 H_2O(g) + 4 NO(g)$.

    a) What mass of $NO(g)$ is produced when 2.00 mol of $NH_3(g)$ are reacted with excess $O_2(g)$?
    b) What mass of $H_2O(g)$ is produced when 4.00 mol of $O_2(g)$ are reacted with excess $NH_3(g)$?
    c) What volume of $NH_3(g)$ at STP is required to react with 3.00 mol of $O_2(g)$?
    d) What volume of $NH_3(g)$ at STP is required to produce 0.750 mol of $H_2O(g)$?

7. Pentane, C_5H_{12}, burns according to the reaction $C_5H_{12}(l) + 8 O_2(g) \longrightarrow 5 CO_2(g) + 6 H_2O(l)$.

    a) What mass of $CO_2(g)$ is produced when 100.0 g of $C_5H_{12}(l)$ is burned?
    b) What mass of $O_2(g)$ is required to produce 60.0 g of $H_2O(l)$?
    c) What mass of $C_5H_{12}(l)$ is required to produce 90.0 L of $CO_2(g)$ at STP?
    d) What volume of $O_2(g)$ at STP is required to produce 70.0 g of $CO_2(g)$?
    e) What volume of $O_2(g)$ at STP is required to produce 48.0 L of $CO_2(g)$ at STP?
    f) What mass of $H_2O(l)$ is made when the burning of C_5H_{12} gives 106 L of $CO_2(g)$ at STP?

8. Tetraethyl lead, $Pb(C_2H_5)_4$, is an "antiknock" ingredient which was added to some gasolines. Tetraethyl lead burns according to the equation

    $$2 Pb(C_2H_5)_4(l) + 27 O_2(g) \longrightarrow 2 PbO(s) + 16 CO_2(g) + 20 H_2O(l).$$

    a) What volume of $O_2(g)$ at STP is consumed when 100.0 g of $PbO(s)$ are formed?
    b) How many molecules of CO_2 are formed when 1.00×10^{-6} g of tetraethyl lead is burned?
    c) How many molecules of H_2O are formed when 135 molecules of O_2 react?
    d) What volume of $O_2(g)$ at STP, in millilitres, is required to react with 1.00×10^{15} molecules of tetraethyl lead?

9. Nitromethane, a fuel occasionally used in some drag racers, burns according to the reaction

    $$4 CH_3NO_2(l) + 3 O_2(g) \longrightarrow 4 CO_2(g) + 6 H_2O(l) + 2 N_2(g).$$

    a) What mass of H_2O is produced when 0.150 g of CH_3NO_2 is burned?
    b) What combined volume of gas at STP is produced if 0.316 g of CH_3NO_2 is burned?
    c) What volume of $O_2(g)$ at STP is required to produce 0.250 g of CO_2?
    d) What mass of H_2O is produced when 0.410 g of CO_2 is produced?

10. A sample of high purity silicon is prepared by strongly heating a mixture of hydrogen and silicon tetrachloride in a sealed tube:

    $$SiCl_4(g) + 2 H_2(g) \longrightarrow Si(s) + 4 HCl(g) .$$

    If exactly 1.00 g of silicon is required, what mass of each of $SiCl_4$ and H_2 must react?

11. Hydrazine, N_2H_4, is a rocket fuel which is prepared according to the reaction

    $$2 NH_3(aq) + NaOCl(aq) \longrightarrow N_2H_4(aq) + NaCl(aq) + H_2O(l) .$$

    NaOCl is common "bleach" and $NH_3(aq)$ is produced by passing $NH_3(g)$ into water. If 1.25×10^4 kg of hydrazine is required, how many litres of ammonia gas (at STP) is required in the reaction?

12. One of the most efficient drying agents known is P_4O_{10}. In fact, P_4O_{10} will even remove water from pure H_2SO_4 to produce SO_3 :

    $$P_4O_{10}(s) + 6 H_2SO_4(l) \longrightarrow 4 H_3PO_4(aq) + 6 SO_3(g).$$

    Pure $H_2SO_4(l)$ has a density of 1.84 g/mL. If 25.0 mL of $H_2SO_4(l)$ react, what mass of P_4O_{10} also reacts and what volume of $SO_3(g)$ at STP is produced?

Tough and Nasty Problems! (Only real Chemists should attempt these!)

13. Ozone, O_3 , in the upper atmosphere protects the earth from the sun's harmful ultraviolet radiation. One step in the destruction of the ozone layer by chlorine–containing compounds is

$$Cl(g) + O_3(g) \longrightarrow ClO(g) + O_2(g).$$

The volume of the ozone in the upper atmosphere is estimated to be 1.5×10^{15} L at STP. Each Cl atom is continually "recycled" so as to be capable of destroying an average of about 1.0×10^5 molecules of ozone. What mass of Cl atoms would be required to use up the available ozone if the ozone were not "regenerated"?

14. What is the molar mass of Q if 0.150 mol of R_4 and 143.8 g of Q_2 react completely to yield RQ_3 as the only product?

15. Mercury(II) oxide, HgO, decomposes when heated: $2 HgO(s) \longrightarrow 2 Hg(l) + O_2(g)$.   What mass of HgO decomposes to yield one–third as many atoms as there are in 100.0 g of neon gas?

16. When 7.682 g of $XZO_3(s)$ is heated, 2.208 g of O_2 and 5.474 g of XZ(s) are formed. When XZ is mixed with $AgNO_3$, all the XZ reacts to form 8.639 g of AgZ(s). Find the molar masses of X and Z.

VII.3. STOICHIOMETRY CALCULATIONS INVOLVING MOLAR CONCENTRATION

Recall that molar concentration calculations involve the use of the equation

$$c = \frac{n}{V} \; .$$

Stoichiometry calculations are based on the relationship between the moles (or molecules) of one chemical and the moles (or molecules) of a second chemical. The rearranged form of the above equation,

$$n = c \cdot V,$$

allows the moles of two chemicals to be related by means of their concentrations and volumes. (Molarity calculations can also be mixed with the types of calculations used in the previous section.)

IMPORTANT: If a VOLUME is mentioned, and the problem involves a molarity, DO NOT assume that "22.4 L" should be used. The use of "22.4 L" is justified only if the substance being referred to is a **gas** AND if the key phrase "**at STP**" is mentioned along with the volume.

EXAMPLES: Tums™ is an antacid composed primarily of calcium carbonate (chalk), and stomach acid is a dilute solution of hydrochloric acid. The neutralization reaction between $CaCO_3$ and stomach acid is represented by the equation:

$$CaCO_3(s) + 2 \, HCl(aq) \longrightarrow CaCl_2(aq) + CO_2(g) + H_2O(l).$$

a) **A tablet of Tums™ has a mass of 0.750 g. What volume of stomach acid having [HCl] = 0.0010 M is neutralized by a 0.750 g portion of $CaCO_3$?**

> **PLAN:** Since the acid volume is unknown, the calculation begins with the known mass of the $CaCO_3$. The mass of $CaCO_3$ is converted to moles of $CaCO_3$ and then to moles of HCl. The moles and molarity of the HCl then allow calculation of the required volume.

$$\text{moles of HCl} = 0.750 \text{ g } CaCO_3 \times \frac{1 \text{ mol } CaCO_3}{100.1 \text{ g } CaCO_3} \times \frac{2 \text{ mol HCl}}{1 \text{ mol } CaCO_3} = 0.0150 \text{ mol}$$

$$\text{volume of HCl} = \frac{n}{c} = \frac{0.0150 \text{ mol}}{0.0010 \text{ mol/L}} = \textbf{15 L}$$

b) **What volume of $CO_2(g)$ at STP is produced if 1.25 L of 0.0055 M HCl reacts with an excess of $CaCO_3$?**

> **PLAN:** The moles of HCl can be found from the molarity and volume. The moles of CO_2 can be found from the moles of HCl and the volume of CO_2 is found from the moles of CO_2 (using the molar volume of a gas at STP).

$$\text{moles of HCl} = 0.0055 \, \frac{\text{mol}}{\text{L}} \times 1.25 \text{ L} = 0.006875 \text{ mol}$$

$$\text{volume of } CO_2 = 0.006875 \text{ mol HCl} \times \frac{1 \text{ mol } CO_2}{2 \text{ mol HCl}} \times \frac{22.4 \text{ L } CO_2}{1 \text{ mol } CO_2} = \textbf{0.077 L}$$

A special process called TITRATION is used to find the unknown concentration of a chemical in solution.

Definitions: **TITRATION** is a process in which a measured amount of a solution is reacted with a known volume of another solution (one of the solutions has an unknown concentration) until a desired **EQUIVALENCE POINT** is reached.

The **EQUIVALENCE POINT** (or "**STOICHIOMETRIC POINT**") is the point in a titration where the ratio of the moles of each species involved exactly equals the ratio of the coefficients of the species in the balanced reaction equation.

EXAMPLE: When sulphuric acid reacts completely with sodium hydroxide, the reaction equation is

$$H_2SO_4 + 2\,NaOH \longrightarrow Na_2SO_4 + 2\,H_2O.$$

Assume a beaker contains 0.0250 mol of H_2SO_4 . A graduated tube called a **burette** is used to slowly add NaOH solution. At the instant that 0.0500 mol of NaOH has been added, that is, the equivalence point has been reached, the titration process is stopped.

Ratio of coefficients in equation = Ratio of moles actually present	
$\dfrac{2\ NaOH}{1\ H_2SO_4} = \dfrac{2}{1}$	$\dfrac{0.0500\ \text{mol NaOH}}{0.0250\ \text{mol } H_2SO_4} = \dfrac{2}{1}$

(The equivalence point is recognized by the fact that a special coloured dye called an **indicator** changes colour at the point that the acidic solution is exactly neutralized by the added NaOH.)

EXAMPLES: Consider the reaction $H_3PO_4 + 2\,KOH \longrightarrow K_2HPO_4 + 2\,H_2O.$

a) **If 19.8 mL of H_3PO_4 with an unknown molarity react with 25.0 mL of 0.500 M KOH, according to the above reaction, what is the molarity of the H_3PO_4?**

> **PLAN:** The concentration and volume of KOH is given, so that moles of KOH can be found. The moles of H_3PO_4 can be calculated from the moles of KOH. Finally, the moles of H_3PO_4 and volume of H_3PO_4 are used to calculate the $[H_3PO_4]$.

$$\text{moles of KOH} = n = c{\cdot}V = 0.500\ \frac{\text{mol}}{\text{L}} \times 0.0250\ \text{L} = 0.0125\ \text{mol}$$

$$\text{moles of } H_3PO_4 = 0.0125\ \text{mol KOH} \times \frac{1\ \text{mol } H_3PO_4}{2\ \text{mol KOH}} = 0.00625\ \text{mol}$$

$$[H_3PO_4] = \frac{0.00625\ \text{mol}}{0.0198\ \text{L}} = \textbf{0.316 M}$$

b) **What volume of 0.200 M KOH is required to react with 125 mL of 0.250 M H_3PO_4 in order to produce a solution of K_2HPO_4?**

> **PLAN:** This calculation is very similar to the previous one. The moles of H_3PO_4 can be found from the volume and concentration. The moles of KOH can be found from the moles of H_3PO_4 and finally, since both the moles and concentration of the KOH will be known, the volume can be found.

$$\text{moles of } H_3PO_4 = n = c{\cdot}V = 0.250\ \frac{\text{mol}}{\text{L}} \times 0.125\ \text{L} = 0.03125\ \text{mol}$$

$$\text{moles of KOH} = 0.03125\ \text{mol } H_3PO_4 \times \frac{2\ \text{mol KOH}}{1\ \text{mol } H_3PO_4} = 0.0625\ \text{mol}$$

$$\text{volume of KOH} = \frac{n}{c} = \frac{0.0625 \text{ mol}}{0.200 \text{ mol}/\text{L}} = \textbf{0.313 L}$$

EXERCISES:

17. A student wants to put 50.0 L of hydrogen gas at STP into a plastic bag by reacting excess aluminum metal with 3.00 M sodium hydroxide solution according to the reaction

$$2 \text{ Al(s)} + 2 \text{ NaOH(aq)} + 2 \text{ H}_2\text{O(l)} \longrightarrow 2 \text{ NaAlO}_2\text{(aq)} + 3 \text{ H}_2\text{(g)}.$$

What volume of NaOH solution is required?

18. What volume of 0.250 M HCl is required to completely neutralize 25.0 mL of 0.318 M NaOH? [Hint: what is the balanced equation for the reaction between HCl and NaOH?]

19. A technician analyzes a sample of water from the "tailings" pond of a mine for the presence of mercury. After treating and concentrating the water sample, the technician carries out the titration reaction

$$\text{Hg}^{2+} + 2 \text{ Cl}^- \longrightarrow \text{HgCl}_2\text{(s)}.$$

A 25.0 mL sample of water containing mercury reacts with 15.4 mL of 0.0148 M Cl^- (as NaCl).
a) What is the molar concentration of the mercury in the water sample?
b) What mass of HgCl_2 is formed in the reaction?

20. A 10.0 mL sample of a saturated solution of Ca(OH)_2 is titrated with 23.5 mL of 0.0156 M HCl.
a) What is the molarity of the Ca(OH)_2 in the saturated solution?
b) What mass of Ca(OH)_2 is dissolved in 250.0 mL of saturated Ca(OH)_2?

21. A student titrates a 2.00 mL sample of hydrogen peroxide solution, $\text{H}_2\text{O}_2\text{(aq)}$, according to the reaction

$$2 \text{ MnO}_4^- \text{ (aq)} + 5 \text{ H}_2\text{O}_2\text{(aq)} + 6 \text{ H}^+\text{(aq)} \longrightarrow 2 \text{ Mn}^{2+}\text{(aq)} + 5 \text{ O}_2\text{(g)} + 8 \text{ H}_2\text{O(l)}.$$

The supply bottle of H_2O_2 is labelled as "3.00% by volume" (3.00 mL of H_2O_2 per 100 mL of solution), which the student calculates to have $[\text{H}_2\text{O}_2] = 1.24$ M.
a) What volume of 0.0496 M MnO_4^- is required for the titration?
b) What volume of $\text{O}_2\text{(g)}$ at STP is produced during the reaction?

22. A 1.00 mL sample of pure phosphoric acid, H_3PO_4 , is titrated with 43.8 mL of 0.853 M NaOH according to the reaction

$$2 \text{ NaOH} + \text{H}_3\text{PO}_4 \longrightarrow \text{Na}_2\text{HPO}_4 + 2 \text{ H}_2\text{O}.$$

a) What is the molar concentration of pure H_3PO_4?
b) Calculate the density of pure H_3PO_4 .

23. The iron present in a sample of iron ore is converted to Fe^{2+} and titrated with dichromate ion

$$\text{Cr}_2\text{O}_7^{2-} + 6 \text{ Fe}^{2+} + 14 \text{ H}^+ \longrightarrow 2 \text{ Cr}^{3+} + 6 \text{ Fe}^{3+} + 7 \text{ H}_2\text{O}.$$

If 17.6 mL of 0.125 M dichromate ion is required to titrate a 25.0 mL sample of Fe^{2+} solution,
a) what is the molarity of the Fe^{2+}? b) what mass of iron is present in the 25.0 mL sample?

24. Prior to analyzing a fertilizer sample containing NH_4NO_3 , a chemist makes a test solution by dissolving 15.5 g of pure NH_4NO_3 and diluting it to 500.0 mL. If the chemist wishes to carry out the titration reaction

$$\text{NH}_4\text{NO}_3\text{(aq)} + \text{NaOH(aq)} \longrightarrow \text{NH}_3\text{(g)} + \text{H}_2\text{O(l)} + \text{NaNO}_3\text{(aq)}$$

such that the reaction requires 25.0 mL of NaOH when 10.0 mL of the NH_4NO_3 solution is titrated,
a) what is the molarity of the NaOH she should use?
b) what volume of $\text{NH}_3\text{(g)}$ at STP would be produced?

25. CARE! The CO_2 content of a 10.0 L sample of air at STP is determined as follows. The air is pumped through a flask containing 25.0 mL of 0.0538 M $Ba(OH)_2$, precipitating the CO_2 present as $BaCO_3$:

$$Ba(OH)_2(aq) + CO_2(g) \longrightarrow BaCO_3(s) + H_2O(l).$$

a) How many moles of $Ba(OH)_2$ are present in the original $Ba(OH)_2$ solution?

b) Only a small amount of the $Ba(OH)_2$ present reacts with the added CO_2. The remaining, unreacted, $Ba(OH)_2$ is titrated with hydrochloric acid according to the equation

$$Ba(OH)_2 + 2\ HCl \longrightarrow BaCl_2 + 2\ H_2O.$$

If the titration requires 23.0 mL of 0.104 M HCl, how many moles of $Ba(OH)_2$ remain in the $Ba(OH)_2$ solution after reaction with the CO_2 in the air?

c) How many moles of $Ba(OH)_2$ are reacted by the CO_2?

d) How many moles of CO_2 are in the sample of air?

e) How many litres of CO_2 at STP are contained in the 10.0 L sample of air? What percentage of the air sample's volume is CO_2?

VII.4. STOICHIOMETRY OF EXCESS QUANTITIES

The stoichiometry calculations in the previous section assume that a given reactant is completely used up during a reaction. Nevertheless, reactions frequently are carried out in such a way that one or more of the reactants actually are present in EXCESS amounts. Some reasons for having an excess amount include:

(i) deliberately adding an excess of one reactant to make sure all of a second reactant is used (the second reactant may be too expensive to waste or harmful to the environment if left unreacted).

(ii) unavoidably having a reactant in excess because a limited amount of another reactant is available.

EXAMPLE: **If 20.0 g of $H_2(g)$ react with 100.0 g of $O_2(g)$ according to the reaction**

$$2\ H_2(g) + O_2(g) \longrightarrow 2\ H_2O(l)\ ,$$

which reactant is present in excess and by how many grams?

A simple way to find the excess reactant is to calculate the mass of some **arbitrarily–selected product**. In this case, you can find how much H_2O can be formed.

$$\text{mass of } H_2O \text{ (based on } H_2) = 20.0 \text{ g } H_2 \times \frac{1 \text{ mol } H_2}{2.0 \text{ g } H_2} \times \frac{2 \text{ mol } H_2O}{2 \text{ mol } H_2} \times \frac{18.0 \text{ g } H_2O}{1 \text{ mol } H_2O} = \textbf{180.0 g}$$

$$\text{mass of } H_2O \text{ (based on } O_2) = 100.0 \text{ g } O_2 \times \frac{1 \text{ mol } O_2}{32.0 \text{ g } O_2} \times \frac{2 \text{ mol } H_2O}{1 \text{ mol } O_2} \times \frac{18.0 \text{ g } H_2O}{1 \text{ mol } H_2O} = \textbf{112.5 g}$$

There is enough H_2 to make 180.0 g of H_2O, but only enough O_2 to make 112.5 g, so that the O_2 **sets a limit** on the amount of H_2O formed. Therefore, O_2 is called the **LIMITING REACTANT**. Since there is only enough O_2 to make 112.5 g of H_2O, not all of the H_2 can be used and H_2 is called the **EXCESS REACTANT**.

To find the mass of H_2 in excess, find the mass of H_2 which actually reacts based on either the mass of limiting reactant (O_2), or the mass of a product (H_2O) formed by the limiting reactant. Then, subtract the mass of H_2 which reacts from the starting mass of H_2. We **arbitrarily** find the mass of H_2 used by starting with the mass of the limiting reactant, O_2.

$$\text{mass of } H_2 \text{ reacted} = 100.0 \text{ g } O_2 \times \frac{1 \text{ mol } O_2}{32.0 \text{ g } O_2} \times \frac{2 \text{ mol } H_2}{1 \text{ mol } O_2} \times \frac{2.0 \text{ g } H_2}{1 \text{ mol } H_2} = \textbf{12.5 g}$$

And: mass of H_2 (in excess) = mass H_2 (at start) − mass H_2 (reacted) = 20.0 − 12.5 = **7.5 g**

EXAMPLE: If 56.8 g of $FeCl_2$, 14.0 g of KNO_3 and 40.0 g of HCl are mixed and allowed to react according to the equation

$$3\, FeCl_2 + KNO_3 + 4\, HCl \longrightarrow 3\, FeCl_3 + NO + 2\, H_2O + KCl$$

a)   which chemical is the LIMITING reactant?

Arbitrarily find the mass of NO which can be produced by each of the three reactants.

$$\text{mass of NO (based on } FeCl_2) = 56.8\text{ g } FeCl_2 \times \frac{1\text{ mol } FeCl_2}{126.8\text{ g } FeCl_2} \times \frac{1\text{ mol NO}}{3\text{ mol } FeCl_2} \times \frac{30.0\text{ g NO}}{1\text{ mol NO}}$$

$$= \textbf{4.48 g}$$

$$\text{mass of NO (based on } KNO_3) = 14.0\text{ g } KNO_3 \times \frac{1\text{ mol } KNO_3}{101.1\text{ g } KNO_3} \times \frac{1\text{ mol NO}}{1\text{ mol } KNO_3} \times \frac{30.0\text{ g NO}}{1\text{ mol NO}}$$

$$= \textbf{4.15 g}$$

$$\text{mass of NO (based on HCl)} = 40.0\text{ g HCl} \times \frac{1\text{ mol HCl}}{36.5\text{ g HCl}} \times \frac{1\text{ mol NO}}{4\text{ mol HCl}} \times \frac{30.0\text{ g NO}}{1\text{ mol NO}} = \textbf{8.22 g}$$

Since the KNO_3 produces the **least** amount of NO, KNO_3 is the **LIMITING REACTANT**. Therefore, **both** $FeCl_2$ and HCl are **IN EXCESS**.

b)   how many grams of each "excess reactant" are actually present in excess?

First find the mass of $FeCl_2$ and HCl which actually react, **arbitrarily based on the mass of the limiting reactant** KNO_3. Then calculate the mass of each reactant left over. (The mass of NO or any other product could have been used instead of the mass of KNO_3.)

$$\text{mass of } FeCl_2 \text{ (used)} = 14.0\text{ g } KNO_3 \times \frac{1\text{ mol } KNO_3}{101.1\text{ g } KNO_3} \times \frac{3\text{ mol } FeCl_2}{1\text{ mol } KNO_3} \times \frac{126.8\text{ g } FeCl_2}{1\text{ mol } FeCl_2}$$

$$= 52.7\text{ g}$$

mass of $FeCl_2$ in excess = 56.8 − 52.7 = **4.1 g**

$$\text{mass of HCl (used)} = 14.0\text{ g } KNO_3 \times \frac{1\text{ mol } KNO_3}{101.1\text{ g } KNO_3} \times \frac{4\text{ mol HCl}}{1\text{ mol } KNO_3} \times \frac{36.5\text{ g HCl}}{1\text{ mol HCl}} = 20.2\text{ g}$$

mass of HCl in excess = 40.0 − 20.2 = **19.8 g**

EXERCISES:

26. What mass of CS_2 is produced when 17.5 g of C are reacted with 39.5 g of SO_2 according to the equation

$$5\, C + 2\, SO_2 \longrightarrow CS_2 + 4\, CO\text{ ?}$$

What mass of the excess reactant will be left over?

27. What mass of NO is produced when 87.0 g of Cu are reacted with 225 g of HNO_3 according to the equation

$$3\, Cu + 8\, HNO_3 \longrightarrow 3\, Cu(NO_3)_2 + 2\, NO + 4\, H_2O\text{ ?}$$

What mass of the excess reactant will be left over?

28. What mass of P_4 is produced when 41.5 g of $Ca_3(PO_4)_2$, 26.5 g of SiO_2 and 7.80 g of C are reacted according to the equation

$$2\, Ca_3(PO_4)_2 + 6\, SiO_2 + 10\, C \longrightarrow P_4 + 6\, CaSiO_3 + 10\, CO\text{ ?}$$

How many grams of each excess reactant will remain unreacted?

29. What mass of Br_2 is produced when 25.0 g of $K_2Cr_2O_7$, 55.0 g of KBr and 60.0 g of H_2SO_4 are reacted according to the equation

$$K_2Cr_2O_7 + 6\ KBr + 7\ H_2SO_4 \longrightarrow 4\ K_2SO_4 + Cr_2(SO_4)_3 + 3\ Br_2 + 7\ H_2O\ ?$$

   How many grams of each excess reactant will remain unreacted?

30. What volume of $CO_2(g)$ at STP can be made when 0.0250 L of $C_5H_{12}(l)$ (density = 626.0 g/L), is reacted with 40.0 L of $O_2(g)$ at STP, according to the equation

$$C_5H_{12}(l) + 8\ O_2(g) \longrightarrow 5\ CO_2(g) + 6\ H_2O(l)\ ?$$

31. If 50.0 mL of 0.100 M HCl is allowed to react with 30.0 mL of 0.200 M NaOH according to the reaction

$$HCl + NaOH \longrightarrow NaCl + H_2O,$$

   which reactant is in excess?

32. If 0.250 g of $Ba(OH)_2$ is mixed with 15.0 mL of 0.125 M HBr, what mass of $BaBr_2$ can be formed?

$$Ba(OH)_2 + 2\ HBr \longrightarrow BaBr_2 + 2\ H_2O$$

VII.5. EXTENSION : PERCENTAGE YIELD AND PERCENTAGE PURITY

Sometimes 100% of the expected amount of products cannot be obtained from a reaction. The term "Percentage Yield" is used to describe the amount of product actually obtained as a percentage of the expected amount. There are two major reasons for this reduced yield of products.

   i)   The reactants may not all react. This can occur either because:
   • not all of the pure material actually reacts, or
   • the reactants may be less than 100% pure.

   ii) Some of the products are lost during procedures such as solvent extraction, filtration and crystallization, which are needed to physically separate and purify the products.

If you know the expected amount of a product based on a stoichiometry calculation and measure the actual mass of product formed, you can calculate the **PERCENTAGE YIELD** of the reaction as follows.

$$PERCENTAGE\ YIELD = \frac{mass\ of\ product\ obtained}{mass\ of\ product\ expected} \times 100\ \%$$

Another way in which less than the "expected" amount of a product is produced is to start with reactants which are less than 100% pure. In this case, the **PERCENTAGE PURITY** of the REACTANT is calculated as follows.

$$PERCENTAGE\ PURITY = \frac{mass\ of\ pure\ reactant}{mass\ of\ impure\ reactant} \times 100\ \%$$

Regardless of the reason why less products than expected are produced, one of two situations is always true.

1. **The *actual amount* of PRODUCTS FOUND is LOWER than the *value expected* from a simple stoichiometry calculation which assumes 100% yield and/or 100% purity.**

   This suggests the use of a simple two–step sequence to treat all percentage yield/purity calculations which require finding the amount of a **PRODUCT.**

   a. Ignore any percentage yields or purities and calculate the "amount of product expected" using a standard stoichiometry calculation.

   b. **Multiply the "amount of product expected" by the decimal equivalent of the percentage yield or purity.** (This brings the "amount of product expected" **down** to the "actual amount found" and allows for losses of product.)

2. **The *actual amount* of REACTANTS NEEDED to produce a specific amount of product is GREATER than the *value expected* from a simple stoichiometry calculation which assumes 100% yield and/or 100% purity.**

   Again, this suggests using a two-step process to treat all percentage yield/purity calculations which require finding the amount of a **REACTANT.**

   a. Ignore any percentage yields or purities and calculate the "amount of reactant needed" using a standard stoichiometry calculation.

   b. **Divide the "amount of reactant needed" by the decimal equivalent of the percentage yield or purity.** (Dividing by a decimal smaller than 1 increases the "amount of reactant needed". This **increase** in the amount of reactant needed compensates for the losses which occur when the reactant forms products.)

Percentage yield calculations fall into three categories.
   • Find the percentage yield, given the mass of reactant used and mass of product formed.
   • Find the mass of product formed, given the mass of reactant used and the percentage yield.
   • Find the mass of reactant used, given the mass of product formed and the percentage yield.

There is more than one way to carry out the following calculations. As stated above (in the boxes) we initially assume a purity or yield equal to 100% and then compensate for less than 100% yield/purity in a final step of the calculation.

EXAMPLE 1: **When 15.0 g of CH_4 is reacted with an excess of Cl_2 according to the reaction**
$$CH_4 + Cl_2 \longrightarrow CH_3Cl + HCl,$$
a total of 29.7 g of CH_3Cl is formed. What is the percentage yield of the reaction?

First find the mass of CH_3Cl expected (assuming a 100% yield).

$$\text{mass of } CH_3Cl = 15.0 \text{ g } CH_4 \times \frac{1 \text{ mol } CH_4}{16.0 \text{ g } CH_4} \times \frac{1 \text{ mol } CH_3Cl}{1 \text{ mol } CH_4} \times \frac{50.5 \text{ g } CH_3Cl}{1 \text{ mol } CH_3Cl} = 47.34 \text{ g}$$

Now: $\text{percentage yield} = \frac{\text{mass obtained}}{\text{mass expected}} \times 100\% = \frac{29.7 \text{ g}}{47.34 \text{ g}} \times 100\% = \textbf{62.7\%}$

EXAMPLE 2: **What mass of K_2CO_3 is produced when 1.50 g of KO_2 is reacted with an excess of CO_2 according to the reaction**

$$4 KO_2(s) + 2 CO_2(g) \longrightarrow 2 K_2CO_3(s) + 3 O_2(g),$$

if the reaction has a 76.0% yield?

First calculate the mass of K_2CO_3 produced (assuming a 100% yield).

$$\text{mass of } K_2CO_3 = 1.50 \text{ g } KO_2 \times \frac{1 \text{ mol } KO_2}{71.1 \text{ g } KO_2} \times \frac{2 \text{ mol } K_2CO_3}{4 \text{ mol } KO_2} \times \frac{138.2 \text{ g } K_2CO_3}{1 \text{ mol } K_2CO_3} = 1.458 \text{ g}$$

Now introduce the fact that the percentage yield is only 76.0%, which reduces the mass of K_2CO_3 expected.

$$\text{actual mass of } K_2CO_3 = 76.0\% \text{ of } 1.458 \text{ g} = 0.760 \times 1.458 \text{ g} = \mathbf{1.11 \text{ g}}$$

EXAMPLE 3: **What mass of CuO is required to make 10.0 g of Cu according to the reaction**

$$2 NH_3 + 3 CuO \longrightarrow N_2 + 3 Cu + 3 H_2O$$

if the reaction has a 58.0% yield?

First calculate the mass of CuO required (assuming a 100% yield).

$$\text{mass of CuO} = 10.0 \text{ g Cu} \times \frac{1 \text{ mol Cu}}{63.5 \text{ g Cu}} \times \frac{3 \text{ mol CuO}}{3 \text{ mol Cu}} \times \frac{79.5 \text{ g CuO}}{1 \text{ mol CuO}} = 12.52 \text{ g}$$

Since the mass of reactant needed is based on a 58.0% yield, divide by 58.0% (actually, 0.580 as a decimal equivalent) to increase the amount of reactant and compensate for the losses which occur when the reactants form products.

$$\text{actual mass of CuO needed} = \frac{12.52 \text{ g}}{0.580} = \mathbf{21.6 \text{ g}}$$

Similar to percentage yield calculations, percentage purity calculations fall into three categories.

- Find the percentage purity, given the mass of reactant used and mass of product formed.
- Find the mass of product formed, given the mass of reactant used and the percentage purity.
- Find the mass of reactant used, given the mass of product formed and the percentage purity.

EXAMPLE 1: **If 100.0 g of FeO produce 12.9 g of pure Fe according to the reaction**

$$2 FeO + 2 C + O_2 \longrightarrow 2 Fe + 2 CO_2,$$

what is the percentage purity of the FeO used?

First calculate the mass of pure FeO which forms 12.9 g of Fe.

$$\text{mass of FeO} = 12.9 \text{ g Fe} \times \frac{1 \text{ mol Fe}}{55.8 \text{ g Fe}} \times \frac{2 \text{ mol FeO}}{2 \text{ mol Fe}} \times \frac{71.8 \text{ g FeO}}{1 \text{ mol FeO}} = 16.6 \text{ g}$$

and: $\text{percentage purity} = \dfrac{\text{mass of pure FeO}}{\text{mass of impure FeO}} \times 100\% = \dfrac{16.6 \text{ g}}{100.0 \text{ g}} \times 100\% = \mathbf{16.6\%}$

EXAMPLE 2: **What mass of pure sodium carbonate, Na_2CO_3, is formed by heating and decomposing 5.00 kg of 79.4% pure "trona", $Na_5(CO_3)_2(HCO_3)\cdot 2H_2O$, according to the equation**

$$2 Na_5(CO_3)_2(HCO_3)\cdot 2H_2O(s) \longrightarrow 5 Na_2CO_3(s) + CO_2(g) + 5 H_2O(l) ?$$

Assume that the trona is 100% pure and find the mass of Na_2CO_3 expected.

$$\text{mass of } Na_2CO_3 = 5.00 \times 10^3 \text{ g} \times \frac{1 \text{ mol trona}}{332.0 \text{ g trona}} \times \frac{5 \text{ mol } Na_2CO_3}{2 \text{ mol trona}} \times \frac{106.0 \text{ g } Na_2CO_3}{1 \text{ mol } Na_2CO_3}$$

$$= 3.991 \times 10^3 \text{ g}$$

Now introduce the fact that the trona is only 79.4% pure, reducing the amount of pure product formed.

$$\text{mass } Na_2CO_3 = 0.794 \times 3.991 \times 10^3 \text{ g} = \mathbf{3.17 \times 10^3 \text{ g}}$$

EXAMPLE 3: **What mass of impure zinc metal having a purity of 89.5% is required to produce 975 mL of hydrogen gas at STP according to the reaction**

$$Zn(s) + 2\ HCl(aq) \longrightarrow ZnCl_2(aq) + H_2(g)\ ?$$

First, find the mass of 100% pure zinc required.

$$\text{mass of Zn} = 0.975\ \text{L}\ H_2 \times \frac{1\ \text{mol}\ H_2}{22.4\ \text{L}\ H_2} \times \frac{1\ \text{mol}\ Zn}{1\ \text{mol}\ H_2} \times \frac{65.4\ \text{g}\ Zn}{1\ \text{mol}\ Zn} = 2.847\ \text{g}$$

Since the zinc was impure, divide by 89.5% (actually, 0.895 as a decimal equivalent) so as to increase the calculated mass of metal used and compensate for the fact that not all the metal used was zinc.

$$\text{mass of impure Zn} = \frac{2.847\ \text{g}}{0.895} = \textbf{3.18 g}$$

EXERCISES:

33. The roasting of siderite ore, $FeCO_3$, produces iron(III) oxide:
$$4\ FeCO_3 + O_2 \longrightarrow 2\ Fe_2O_3 + 4\ CO_2\ .$$

   a) A 15.0 g $FeCO_3$ sample is 42.0% pure. What mass of Fe_2O_3 can the sample produce?

   b) A second sample of $FeCO_3$, with a mass of 55.0 g, is roasted so as to produce 37.0 g of Fe_2O_3. What is the percentage purity of the $FeCO_3$?

   c) A 35.0 g sample of pure $FeCO_3$ produces 22.5 g of Fe_2O_3. What is the percentage yield of the reaction?

   d) What mass of siderite ore with a purity of 62.8% is needed to make 1.00 kg of Fe_2O_3?

34. A 100.0 g sample of impure FeS_2 is roasted to produce Fe_2O_3 and SO_2 :
$$4\ FeS_2(s) + 11\ O_2(g) \longrightarrow 2\ Fe_2O_3(s) + 8\ SO_2(g).$$
If 4.50 L of $SO_2(g)$ is collected at STP, what percentage of FeS_2 is in the sample?

35. A student reacts 25.0 mL of benzene (C_6H_6, density = 0.879 g/mL) with a "nitrating mixture" containing excess nitric acid to make 18.0 mL of nitrobenzene ($C_6H_5NO_2$, density = 1.204 g/mL) according to the equation
$$C_6H_6 + HNO_3 \longrightarrow C_6H_5NO_2 + H_2O.$$

   a) What is the percentage yield of the reaction?

   b) What mass of C_6H_6 is left unreacted?

36. The reaction $SiO_2(s) + 4\ HF(g) \longrightarrow SiF_4(g) + 2\ H_2O(g)$ produces 2.50 g of H_2O when 12.20 g of SiO_2 is treated with a small excess of HF.

   a) What mass of SiF_4 is formed?

   b) What mass of SiO_2 is left unreacted?

   c) What is the percentage yield of the SiF_4?

37. When 5.000 kg of malachite ore containing 4.30% of malachite, $Cu_2(OH)_2CO_3$, is heated, the product is copper (II) oxide:
$$Cu_2(OH)_2CO_3 \longrightarrow CO_2 + 2\ CuO + H_2O\ .$$

   a) If the reaction has an 84.0% yield, how many grams of CuO are produced?

   b) If the decomposition reaction has an 87.0% yield, what mass of ore containing 3.70% malachite is required to produce 100.0 g of CuO?

38. A mine produces a silver ore named argentite, Ag_2S. The ore is smelted according to the overall reaction

$$Ag_2S + C + 2\,O_2 \longrightarrow 2\,Ag + CO_2 + SO_2 .$$

a) A 250.0 kg load of argentite ore contains 0.135% pure Ag_2S. What mass of silver metal can be produced from the load of ore?

b) A 76.4 g test sample of ore from a new ore vein produces 0.261 g of pure silver. What is the percentage of pure argentite in the ore?

c) A sample of pure Ag_2S has a mass of 152.6 g. When smelted, the sample produces 117.4 g of pure Ag. What is the percentage yield of the smelting process?

d) What mass of ore containing 0.795% Ag_2S is required to produce a 50.0 kg ingot of silver metal?

e) If 89.2% of the Ag_2S present is extracted from 3.50×10^4 kg of ore containing 1.86% Ag_2S, what mass of silver metal can be produced?

UNIT VIII : ATOMS AND THE PERIODIC TABLE

It seems everyone knows what atoms are and accepts the idea that they are the building blocks of everything around us, but consider the following. As late as 1900, Europe's leading chemist, Wilhelm Ostwald, published a famous and respected textbook of chemistry which never once referred to atoms because the concept of "atoms" was thought to be useless in his opinion. In addition, it was not until 1932 that the neutron was found (although its existence had long been suspected). In other words, when your grandparents were young, school chemistry texts were largely silent on what made up an atom because the latest news from the research journals had yet to come into common knowledge.

This unit briefly examines the path leading to the discovery of what makes up an atom, and then examines the ways in which the inner structure of the atom explains the concept of nuclear isotopes, the form of the periodic table, the fact that many elements behave and react in a predictable manner, and the manner in which atoms combine with each other.

VIII.1. THE STRUCTURE OF THE ATOM

A. EARLY MODELS OF THE ATOM

a)   The Atomic Models of the Early Greeks and Medieval Alchemists

The earliest suggestion that atoms might exist came in the 5th century B.C. when Democritus expanded on the ideas of his teacher and stated that the differences between substances were the direct result of differences in the size and shape of tiny, uniform, uncuttable particles.

In the 4th century BC, Aristotle rejected this idea and proposed that earthly matter had no properties itself and that various combinations of simple properties existed in this undifferentiated "matter" to create every substance known. The four properties which could exist were

moist, dry, heat and cold.

These properties were contained in various proportions by four major elements

water, air, fire and earth,

that made up everything our senses could detect. For example, the element "fire" had the properties of "hot" and "dry".

AIR	moist	WATER
hot		cold
FIRE	dry	EARTH

Early Greek "periodic table"

(Greek students didn't have a long list of elements to memorize for Alchemy 11 !)

Aristotle's theories of matter and properties were meant as philosophical analogies and were not intended to suggest that one could actually extract and purify the properties from a substance.

Some later versions of Aristotle's theory stated that matter could be infinitely subdivided and other versions stated that a non–dividable smallest particle of each type of substance existed. The important point to note is that all the Greek theories were essentially philosophical and moralistic in nature and did little or nothing to suggest a direction for experimental work (which was thought to be misleading and not worth carrying out since it was believed that nature could best be understood by philosophers, not experimenters, because experimental results were often ambiguous and misleading).

During the middle ages, a great deal of practical chemical knowledge accumulated from the investigations of arab and european alchemists. This large body of experimental work contained information on the separation of metals from ores and numerous types of distillations. From this body of work the idea that matter existed as "corpuscles" which were subject to various attractions and repulsions eventually emerged, but again the ideas were mainly philosophical in nature. So little chemical knowledge existed that there was no chemical industry as such and little day to day usage of any chemicals other than those which existed naturally in the form of food or beverages.

b) Dalton's Atomic Theory

In 1808, John Dalton reintroduced the idea of atoms and supported his atomic theory on a firm experimental foundation. Dalton's atomic theory can be stated as follows.

  i) Elements are made up of extremely small particles called atoms.
  ii) The atoms making up a particular element are all identical and different types of atoms have different properties.
  iii) Each chemical compound is unique and consists of a particular combination of specific types of atoms put together in a distinctive way.
  iv) Chemical reactions involve the reshuffling of the atoms in a compound to make new compounds. The new compounds are made from the same atoms which were present in the original compound.

These hypotheses explained three fundamental laws which had been recognized, if not explicitly stated, for some time.

The Law of Definite Proportions (also called the **Law of Constant Composition**): Every pure sample of a particular compound always contains the same proportion by mass of the elements in the compound. (This law was explained by Dalton's 2nd and 3rd hypotheses.)

The Law of Multiple Proportions: When different masses of one element combine with a specific mass of a second element, the mass ratios of the first element are small whole number ratios. For example, when 1.00 g of copper is reacted with different amounts of oxygen, two different compounds can be formed in which there are 0.126 g and 0.252 g of oxygen present. The ratio of the oxygen masses in these compounds is

$$\frac{0.252}{0.126} = \frac{2}{1} \;.$$

(These experimental observations are explained by Dalton's 3rd hypothesis.)

The Law of Conservation of Mass: The mass of the reactants equals the mass of the products. (This law was explained by Dalton's 4th hypothesis.)

In addition to his atomic theory, Dalton made a huge contribution to chemistry by showing how to calculate the atomic masses of the atoms involved in a reaction and how to find the number of each type of atom in the molecules. This allowed accurate analyses of compounds and the prediction of the amounts of each reactant needed to make a given product.

c) The Thomson Model of the Atom

By the end of the nineteenth century a large amount of chemical research had been carried out and interpreted in terms of atoms and molecules, although there was little direct evidence for atoms. Nevertheless, by the middle of the nineteenth century evidence began to emerge, not for the direct existence of atoms but for the even smaller particles which make up atoms.

The first piece of the puzzle regarding the composition of the atom fell into place in 1897 when J.J. Thomson discovered that atoms contain negatively–charged particles which he called "corpuscles" and were later named "electrons". Later, he showed that positively–charged particles could also be obtained from atoms. Because individual atoms are electrically neutral, Thomson hypothesized that atoms must possess both positive and negative charges. Although he did not know why such a positive charge might exist, he proposed that the atom consisted of a ball of positive charge with negative charges distributed throughout the ball, as shown below.

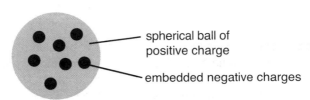

This model was later nicknamed "the plum pudding model" because it resembled an English pudding which has raisins spread through its interior. In a magnetic field, the oscillation of electrons back and forth through the positive charge explained many puzzling experimental observations. Although the Thomson model was later disproved, it was consistent with the data available at the time and represented an elegant model having a great deal of explaining power. Thomson found that the electron possessed a mass as well as a charge and showed that the charge (e) to mass (m) ratio was

$$\frac{e}{m} = -1.76 \times 10^{8} \text{ coulombs/gram,} \quad \text{where a coulomb is a unit of electrical charge.}$$

Later work by Robert Milliken in 1909 showed that an electron's mass is a tiny 9.11×10^{-28} g.

EXERCISES:

1. The ancient Greek view of nature was based on an experimental approach to acquiring knowledge. Support or contradict this statement.

2. Suggest a possible reason why most investigations of the alchemists were concerned with the separation of metals from ores.

3. How did the work of Dalton allow an expansion of chemical manufacturing?

4. Early chemists believed that atoms were indivisible and had no internal structure. What effect did the work of Thomson have on such ideas?

5. The term "berthollide" describes a compound in which the amounts of the elements present can be changed over a substantial range. For example, samples of FeS may actually have formulas such as $Fe_{0.943}S$ or $Fe_{0.896}S$. Such compounds were unknown in Dalton's time. Which, if any, of the Laws of Definite Proportions, Multiple Proportions and Conservation of Mass are violated by the existence of the berthollides?

6. Show that the following four oxides of nitrogen obey the Law of Multiple Proportions.

Compound #	Mass of N (g)	Mass of O (g)
1	0.3160	0.0903
2	0.3160	0.3611
3	0.3160	0.7223
4	0.3160	0.5417

B. THE RUTHERFORD-BOHR MODEL OF THE ATOM

Within a short time after Thomson published his model, a fairly detailed and accurate picture of the atom's structure emerged. Even as Thomson was investigating the atom, other workers were finding other pieces of the atomic puzzle, although where the pieces fit was not immediately clear.

Henri Becquerel (1896) was trying to study light emission by minerals when he found that energy was given off by uranium–containing minerals, even when they were not exposed earlier to light (that is, the minerals were not re–emitting previously–absorbed light). He had accidentally discovered radioactivity, that is, the ability to spontaneously "radiate" energy.

Marie and Pierre Curie (1898) followed up on Becquerel discovery and separated various radio-active elements (notably radium and polonium) and studied their properties. They coined the term "radioactive decay".

The greatest contribution to the study of the atom was made by **Sir Ernest Rutherford**, a New Zealander who worked for nine years making fundamental discovery after discovery in Montreal before moving to Manchester, England. The following summary of his work reveals why he was awarded the Nobel Prize in chemistry in 1908.

a) *Discovered the alpha, beta and gamma particles* (1899 and later). Initially, Rutherford found two new types of particles. One particle was easily stopped by a thin piece of metal — he called this the "alpha" (α) particle — and the other particle penetrated a much greater thickness of metal — he called this the "beta" (β) particle. Beta particles eventually were found to be high energy electrons emitted directly from the atomic nucleus. He later detected gamma (γ) particles and found them to be high energy radiation given off by the nucleus.

The table below shows the ability of alpha, beta and gamma particles to pass through various substances. Although alpha particles do not penetrate tissue, they deliver sufficient energy to ionize molecules and cause severe damage to individual cells. A gamma particle can penetrate great distances through tissue, but does not cause much ionization to occur.

Maximum penetrating power of alpha, beta and gamma particles			
PARTICLE	Penetration in dry air	Penetration in tissue	Penetration in lead
alpha (α)	4 cm	0.05 mm	0 mm
beta (β)	6–300 cm	0.06–4 mm	0.3 mm
gamma (γ)	over 4 km	over 5 m	over 30 cm

b) *Correctly interpreted the nature of radioactivity* (1902). He showed that new elements were formed as a result of the radioactive decay of an element.

c) *Discovered the true nature of the alpha particle* (1908). He showed that α–particles were simply He^{2+} ions.

d) *Discovered the atomic nucleus* (1911). When he bombarded a piece of thin gold foil with alpha particles, most of the particles went straight through, which meant that atoms were mostly empty space. A few of the heavy alpha particles bounced straight back, which meant that there was a very tiny region in the atom where most of the mass was concentrated: the nucleus. When expressed as a multiple of the charge on the electron, the nucleus was found to have a positive charge that was effectively equal to the atomic number of the atom. He postulated that the nucleus contained all the protons and most of the mass of the atom.

e) *Predicted the existence of the neutron* (1920). As soon as Rutherford found that the atomic nucleus contained protons, he had a serious problem. Protons have a mass of 1 and a charge of +1. The helium nucleus was known to have a total charge of +2, which implied that it contained 2 protons, but it also had a mass of 4. He therefore suggested that the nucleus must contain neutral particles (neutrons) having a mass of 1, so as to account for the extra mass of He^{2+}.

THE RUTHERFORD MODEL OF THE ATOM

Rutherford proposed that the atom consists of a tiny, positively charged nucleus surrounded by a cloud of negatively–charged electrons. The nucleus contains almost all the mass of the atom and consists of protons and neutrons. The number of electrons surrounding the nucleus equals the number of protons in the nucleus, so as to make the atom electrically neutral.

In 1932, **J. Chadwick** discovered the neutron predicted by Rutherford.

The following table summarizes the properties of the three major atomic particles. (There are actually well over a hundred known elementary particles, but they are unimportant for our purposes.)

The Properties of the Atomic Particles				
PARTICLE	SYMBOL	CHARGE	MOLAR MASS (g)	WHERE FOUND
electron	e^-	–1	0.000 549	outside nucleus
proton	p	+1	1.007 825	inside nucleus
neutron	n	0	1.008 665	inside nucleus

Rutherford's work was concerned with the atomic nucleus and was not overly concerned with what the electrons were doing. Once he found that electrons had to exist outside the nucleus, others had to deal with the problem of electron behaviour. The "planetary" model of electron behaviour suggested that electrons whirled around the nucleus, in the same manner that the planets revolve around the sun. The problem was that the movement of negatively–charged electrons around the positively– charged nucleus would cause the electrons to radiate energy as they passed through the electric and magnetic fields surrounding the nucleus and quickly collapse into the nucleus. The fact that this radiation and collapse did not occur meant that something was very wrong with the planetary model.

Niels Bohr (1913) came up with a simple equation that could predict the peculiar pattern of energies which can be produced by a hydrogen atom. In order to derive his equation, he had to make some special assumptions about the way electrons in an atom behaved. (The consequences of Bohr's work is examined in more detail in section F, "The Electronic Structure of the Atom".)

> **THE BOHR MODEL OF THE ATOM**
>
> Bohr proposed that the electrons in an atom are restricted to having certain specific energies and are restricted to following specific paths called "orbits" at a fixed distance from the nucleus. Electrons were only allowed to emit or absorb energy when they moved from one orbit to another.

Bohr's theory of the atom assumed that Rutherford's ideas were correct and tried to describe what the electrons were doing. The overall picture describing the atom required a combination of the ideas of both Rutherford and Bohr, so that the overall picture is sometimes called the **Rutherford–Bohr model** of the atom. Bohr's theory eventually ran into a problem when it was found that the theory could not be made to work with any atom having more than one electron. Since that time, the notion of an orbit followed by the electrons in an atom has been discarded. Nevertheless, the Bohr–Rutherford model of the atom is still useful for developing the ideas encountered in this unit.

EXERCISES:

7. Why did Rutherford's discovery of the atomic nucleus cause Thomson's "plum pudding" model of the atom to be abandoned?

8. What problem did the discovery of the neutron solve?

9. Does the Rutherford atomic model conflict with Dalton's atomic theory? Explain your answer.

10. According to Rutherford's model of the atom, what existed in the nucleus of the atom?

11. Which of alpha, beta and gamma particles could pass completely through
    (a) a thin piece of cardboard?   (b) an elephant?

12. How does the data in the table "The Properties of the Atomic Particles" support Rutherford's statement that the nucleus of the atom contains almost all the mass of the atom.

C. ATOMIC NUMBER AND ATOMIC MASS

The chemical elements are differentiated from one another by the number of protons in the nucleus.

EXAMPLE: H has 1 proton in its nucleus
                  He has 2 protons in its nucleus
                  Li has 3 protons in its nucleus

         Conversely   any atom containing 1 proton must be hydrogen, H
                      any atom containing 2 protons must be helium, He
                      any atom containing 3 protons must be lithium, Li

Definition: The **ATOMIC NUMBER** of an atom is the number of protons in its nucleus.

The fact that each proton has a +1 charge suggests an alternate way to define the atomic number.

The **ATOMIC NUMBER** of an atom is the charge on its nucleus.

A **neutral** atom has NO OVERALL CHARGE, which means the number of positive charges due to the protons in the nucleus must equal the number of negatively–charged electrons surrounding the nucleus. In other words:

> In a neutral atom
> **number of electrons = number of protons.**

There are three pieces of information which usually are shown for each element on the periodic table.

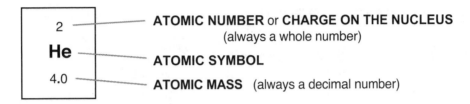

2	**ATOMIC NUMBER** or **CHARGE ON THE NUCLEUS** (always a whole number)
He	**ATOMIC SYMBOL**
4.0	**ATOMIC MASS** (always a decimal number)

EXAMPLE: The atomic number of Na is 11. This means the following statements are also true.

Na has 11 protons in its nucleus.
Any atom containing exactly 11 protons is an atom of Na.
The charge on the nucleus of a sodium atom is +11.
A neutral sodium atom has 11 electrons.

> If electrons are added to or subtracted from a neutral atom, the resulting particle is called an **ION**.

Note: Electrons have a **NEGATIVE** charge so –
      ADDING a **NEGATIVE** charge produces a **NEGATIVE** ion, and
      TAKING AWAY a **NEGATIVE** charge produces a **POSITIVE** ion.

EXAMPLES: If an extra electron is added to a neutral F atom, then:

number of protons   = 9
number of electrons = 9 + 1 (extra) = 10

so that: total charge on nucleus =   +9
total charge of electrons = −10
_____

total charge on atom   =   −1   and the ion is written as: F^- .

If two electrons are removed from a neutral Ba atom, then:

number of protons   = 56
number of electrons = 56 − 2 (removed) = 54

so that: total charge on nucleus = +56
total charge of electrons = −54
_____

total charge on atom   =   +2   and the ion is written as: Ba^{2+} .

EXAMPLE: How many electrons are possessed by N^{3-}?

N^{3-} has 3 **more** electrons than a neutral atom of N. Since a neutral atom of N has 7 electrons (its atomic number equals the number of electrons), then:

number of electrons on N^{3-} = 7 + 3 = **10** .

How many electrons are possessed by Sn^{4+}?

Sn^{4+} has 4 **fewer** electrons than a neutral atom of Sn. Since a neutral atom of Sn has 50 electrons, then:

number of electrons on Sn^{4+} = 50 − 4 = **46** .

EXERCISES:

13. How many protons are in the nucleus of each of the following?
     (a) Be   (b) U   (c) Mn

14. How many electrons are there in a neutral atom of each of the following?
     (a) C   (b) Fe   (c) Ar

15. How many electrons are there on each of the following?
     (a) Na^{+} (c) V^{3+} (e) Cl^{-} (g) Sb^{3-} (i) H^{-}
     (b) Mg^{2+} (d) O^{2-} (f) Al^{3+} (h) Fe^{2+} (j) As^{3-}

16. What is the ion produced when
     (a) two electrons are added to S?   (f) two electrons are removed from Mn^{2+}?
     (b) two electrons are removed from Ca?   (g) an electron is removed from V^{4+}?
     (c) an electron is added to Cl?   (h) two electrons are added to Sb^{-} ?
     (d) three electrons are removed from Al?   (i) an electron is removed from O^{2-} ?
     (e) an electron is added to Cr^{3+}?

17. What is the charge on the nucleus of each of the following?
     (a) Mg   (b) Ne   (c) K^{+} (d) S^{2-}

Since both neutrons and protons have a molar mass of approximately 1 g, then the total mass of an atom will be determined by the total number of protons **and** neutrons. (The electrons are too light to make an appreciable contribution to the mass of an atom.)

Definition: The **ATOMIC MASS** of an atom is the total number of protons and neutrons.

Since   **atomic number = (# of protons)**
and   **atomic mass   = (# of protons) + (# of neutrons)**

then | **number of neutrons = (atomic mass) – (atomic number)** |

If the values for the atomic mass and atomic number must be shown with the atomic symbol, the following super/subscript symbol is used.

atomic mass ———— $^{23}_{11}\text{Na}$
atomic number ——

This symbol is sometimes written as

^{23}Na (since all sodium atoms have an atomic number of 11)

or even   **Na–23**   (which avoids having to write the atomic mass as a superscript).

Hint: If you get confused as to whether the top number in the superscript/subscript symbol is an atomic mass or atomic number, remember that atomic mass is always greater than or equal to atomic number (because there are more protons and neutrons than there are just protons).

EXAMPLE: Find the number of protons, neutrons and electrons possessed by the following atoms.

a) $^{27}_{13}$**Al**   Since the atom is neutral, then   (# of p) = (# of e⁻) , and

number of protons = atomic number = **13**
number of electrons = **13**
number of neutrons = (atomic mass) – (atomic number) = 27 – 13 = **14**.

b) $^{75}_{33}$**As**⁺   Since the atom has a single "+" charge, then

number of protons = **33**
number of electrons = 33 – 1 = **32**   (the "+" charge indicates one electron is **removed**)
number of neutrons = (atomic mass) – (atomic number) = 75 – 33 = **42**.

EXERCISES:

18. Using the data in the table "**The properties of the atomic particles**" write super/subscript symbols for the proton, neutron and electron. (Assume the mass of the electron is effectively zero when writing its symbol and let its atomic number be its charge, –1.)

19. Fill in the following table. Show both the atomic number and atomic mass of the "particle".

Particle	Atomic Number	Atomic Mass	Number of protons	Number of neutrons	Number of electrons
$^{52}_{24}$Cr					
$^{222}_{86}$Rn					
	31			39	31
			13	14	13
		197		118	76
		75	33		36
			83	126	78

D. ISOTOPES

If a **proton** ($_1^1p$) is accelerated to extremely high velocities and strikes the nucleus of an atom, the proton may be absorbed by the "target" nucleus to produce a new element.

EXAMPLE: $_9^{19}F + {_1^1}p \longrightarrow {_{10}^{20}}Ne$ (note that the atomic numbers and atomic masses are added)

On the other hand, adding a **neutron** ($_0^1n$) to an element's nucleus simply produces a heavier version of the same element.

EXAMPLE: $_9^{19}F + {_0^1}n \longrightarrow {_9^{20}}F$

Definition: **ISOTOPES** are atomic species having the same atomic number but different atomic masses.

EXERCISES:

20. "Heavy water" has the formula D_2O, where "D" is an isotope of hydrogen. A chemist has two samples: one contains pure "ordinary" water and the other contains pure "heavy" water. Measuring the mass and volume of each sample gives the following results.

    volume of ordinary water = 25.00 mL   volume of heavy water = 25.00 mL
    mass of ordinary water   = 25.00 g   mass of heavy water   = 27.65 g

    Since isotopes only differ in their masses and have similar atomic diameters, the samples of heavy and ordinary water contain equal numbers of molecules.
    (a) How many times heavier than an ordinary water molecule is a heavy water molecule?
    (b) If ordinary water has a molar mass of 18.0 g, what is the molar mass of heavy water?
    (c) The formula of heavy water is D_2O. Since "O" has a molar mass of 16.0 g, what is the molar mass of the isotope "D"?
    (d) Write the formula for D, showing the atomic mass and atomic number as super/subscripts.
    (e) How many electrons, protons and neutrons does a neutral atom of D possess? How many electrons, protons and neutrons does a neutral atom of H possess? Suggest why D is called "heavy hydrogen".

21. You have two different samples of $H_2S(g)$. Sample 1 has a density of 1.539 g/L at 0°C and is made from hydrogen and sulphur having a molar mass of 1.008 g and 32.066 g respectively. Sample 2 has a density of 1.670 g/L at the same temperature and pressure and is made from hydrogen with a molar mass of 1.008 g and an artificially–created isotope of sulphur. What is the molar mass of the artificial sulphur?

There are three different isotopes of hydrogen, each of which has a special name.

$_1^1H$ = H = ORDINARY HYDROGEN (called "protium" on rare occasions)

$_1^2H$ = D = DEUTERIUM (sometimes called "heavy" hydrogen)

$_1^3H$ = T = TRITIUM (sometimes called "radioactive" hydrogen)

No other isotopes have special names.

Shad quickly realizes how "heavy water" got its name

-Zimbobwe

EXERCISE:

22. Complete the table. Show the atomic number and atomic mass in the "Symbol" column.

	Symbol	Atomic Mass	Atomic Number	Number of protons	Number of neutrons	Number of electrons
(a)		84	36			36
(b)				35	45	35
(c)		127	53			54
(d)			27		32	27
(e)	Zn				36	
(f)	Cd^{2+}	112				
(g)				38	50	36
(h)	$X^{2-} =$				75	54
(i)	$X^{3+} =$	103				42
(j)	$X^{3-} =$		33		42	

E. NATURAL MIXTURES OF ISOTOPES

The molar mass of chlorine is 35.5 g. Since there can't be 0.5 of a proton or neutron, then "35.5 g" **must** represent an **AVERAGE** value for a **MIXTURE** of isotopes. (Similarly, "the typical Canadian family has 2.5 children" is a statement referring to an average — how else do you get half a child?)

EXAMPLE: Experiments show that chlorine is a mixture which is 75.77% Cl–35 and 24.23% Cl–37. If the precise molar mass of Cl–35 is 34.968 852 g and of Cl–37 is 36.965 903 g, what is the average molar mass of the chlorine atoms in such a mixture?

Assume there are exactly 100 moles of the mixture.

Then   # of moles of Cl–35 = 0.7577 x 100 mol = 75.77 mol

# of moles of Cl–37 = 0.2423 x 100 mol = 24.23 mol

$$\text{mass of Cl–35} = 75.77 \text{ mol} \times \frac{34.968\ 852 \text{ g}}{1 \text{ mol}} = 2649.59 \text{ g}$$

$$\text{mass of Cl–37} = 24.23 \text{ mol} \times \frac{36.965\ 903 \text{ g}}{1 \text{ mol}} = 895.68 \text{ g}$$

total mass of mixture = 2649.59 + 895.68 = 3545.27 g

$$\text{average molar mass of mixture} = \frac{3545.27 \text{ g}}{100 \text{ mol}} = \mathbf{35.453 \ \frac{g}{mol}}$$

Note: It is not necessary to take 100 mol of a mixture. You can assume that **one mole of "average" atoms** is used, having a composition which is 75.77 % Cl–35 and 24.23 % Cl–37. The above calculation is then simplified.

$$\text{mass of Cl–35 in mixture} = 0.7577 \text{ mol} \times 34.968\ 852 \ \frac{g}{mol} = 26.4959 \text{ g}$$

$$\text{mass of Cl–37 in mixture} = 0.2423 \text{ mol} \times 36.965\ 903 \ \frac{g}{mol} = 8.9568 \text{ g}$$

and   total mass of mixture = 26.4959 + 8.9568 = **35.453 g**

This mass agrees with the value of 35.453 g found experimentally for naturally occurring chlorine because exact masses were used for Cl–35 and Cl–37. If you are NOT given the exact molar masses of the isotopes, but instead are told, for example, that

$$^{35}\text{Cl} = 75.77\% , \quad ^{37}\text{Cl} = 24.23\%$$

then use the atomic masses "35" and "37".

Average mass = 0.7577 x 35 + 0.2423 x 37 = 35.485 g

This average mass is less exact but still satisfactory for most purposes.

EXERCISES:

23. The following mixtures of isotopes are found in nature. Calculate the expected molar mass of a sample of each mixture.

(a) ^{10}B = 18.8%, ^{11}B = 81.2%

(b) ^{69}Ga = 60.0%, ^{71}Ga = 40.0%

(c) ^{107}Ag = 51.8%, ^{109}Ag = 48.2%

(d) ^{70}Ge = 20.5%, ^{72}Ge = 27.4%, ^{73}Ge = 7.8%, ^{74}Ge = 36.5%, ^{76}Ge = 7.8%

(e) ^{64}Zn = 48.9%, ^{66}Zn = 27.8%, ^{67}Zn = 4.1%, ^{68}Zn = 18.6%, ^{70}Zn = 0.6%

(f) ^{90}Zr = 51.5%, ^{91}Zr = 11.2%, ^{92}Zr = 17.1%, ^{94}Zr = 17.4%, ^{96}Zr = 2.8%

(g) ^{92}Mo = 15.8%, ^{94}Mo = 9.0%, ^{95}Mo = 15.7%, ^{96}Mo = 16.5%, ^{97}Mo = 9.5%, ^{98}Mo = 23.8%, ^{100}Mo = 9.6%

24. Natural samples of carbon contain 98.90% C–12 (mass = 12.000 000) and 1.10% C–13 (mass = 13.003 355). What is the molar mass of the mixture of carbon isotopes, expressed to 3 decimal places?

25. Naturally occurring silicon consists of 92.23% Si–28 (mass = 27.976 927 g), 4.67% Si–29 (mass = 28.976 495 g) and 3.10% Si–30 (mass = 29.973 770 g). What is the expected average molar mass of a sample of natural silicon, expressed to 4 decimal paces?

F. THE ELECTRONIC STRUCTURE OF THE ATOM

(a) ENERGY LEVEL DIAGRAMS

When a hydrogen atom is irradiated with energy, some of the energy is absorbed and then re-emitted. If the light emitted by hydrogen atoms is passed through a prism (or a diffraction grating, which acts similar to a prism) and then onto a strip of photographic film, the "**line spectrum**" below is observed.

In 1913 Niels Bohr proposed a model which explained why the hydrogen atom's line spectrum looks like it does and why only certain energies are observed in the spectrum. He proposed that the electron in a hydrogen atom only exists in specific energy states. These energy states are associated with specific circular orbits which the electron can occupy around the atom. When an electron absorbs or emits a specific amount of energy it instantaneously moves from one orbit to another; the greater the energy the farther the orbit from the atomic nucleus.

Definition: An **ENERGY LEVEL** is a specific amount of energy which an electron in an atom can possess.

The energy levels of hydrogen have the pattern shown below. ("n" is the number of the energy level.) The actual number of energy levels is very large; only a few are shown.

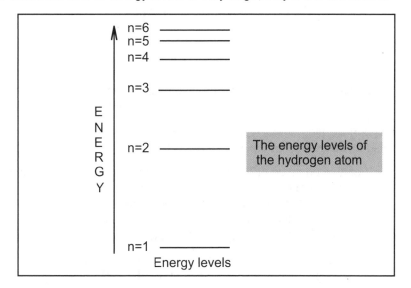

The pattern of lines in the spectrum reflects the energy level pattern. The observed spectrum represents *energy level differences* occurring when an electron in a higher energy level gives off energy and drops down to a lower level. The energy difference between two particular energy levels is called the **QUANTUM** of energy associated with the transition between the two levels.

A few years after Bohr published his theories on electron orbits, several significant changes were made to his basic ideas. The Theory of Quantum Mechanics which finally emerged is beyond the scope of this course, but one change in Bohr's theory must be mentioned. The notion of electrons orbiting a nucleus along a specific path in a well defined orbit had to be abandoned and replaced by the idea that different electrons, depending on their energies, simply occupy particular regions of space called "orbitals".

Definition: An **ORBITAL** is the actual region of space occupied by an electron in a particular energy level.

The Energy Level Diagram for Hydrogen

Experimental studies show that the lowest set of energy levels for hydrogen is arranged as follows. Each dash represents the energy possessed by a particular orbital in the atom. The letters s, p, d and f refer to four different "types" of orbitals which are discussed later.

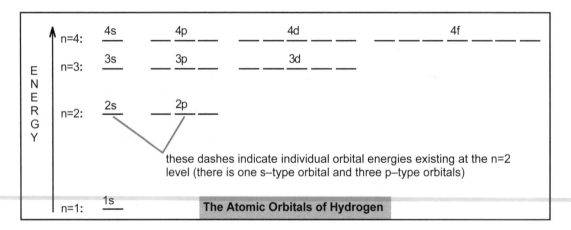

The Atomic Orbitals of Hydrogen

Definitions: A **SHELL** is the set of all orbitals having the same n–value.

For example, the 3rd shell consists of the 3s, 3p and 3d orbitals.

A **SUBSHELL** is a set of orbitals of the same type.

For example, the set of five 3d–orbitals in the 3rd shell is a subshell.

As can be seen on the above energy level diagram, all the orbitals for a hydrogen atom with a given value of n have the same energy (this is not true for atoms with more than one electron).

The rules governing which types of orbitals can occur for a given energy level, and how many orbitals of a given type can exist, are given below.

    i)   For a given value of "n", n different types of orbitals are possible.
        • for n = 1: only the s–type is possible.
        • for n = 2: the s– and p–types are possible.
        • for n = 3: the s–, p– and d–types are possible.
        • for n = 4: the s–, p–, d– and f–types are possible.

    ii)   An s–type   subshell consists of   ONE s–orbital.
           A   p–type   subshell consists of THREE p–orbitals.
           A   d–type   subshell consists of   FIVE d–orbitals.
           An f–type   subshell consists of SEVEN f–orbitals.

The Energy Level Diagram for Polyelectronic Atoms

The energy level diagram for hydrogen must be modified to describe any other atom. Fortunately, the modified diagram below can be used for **ALL** polyelectronic atoms (atoms having more than one electron).

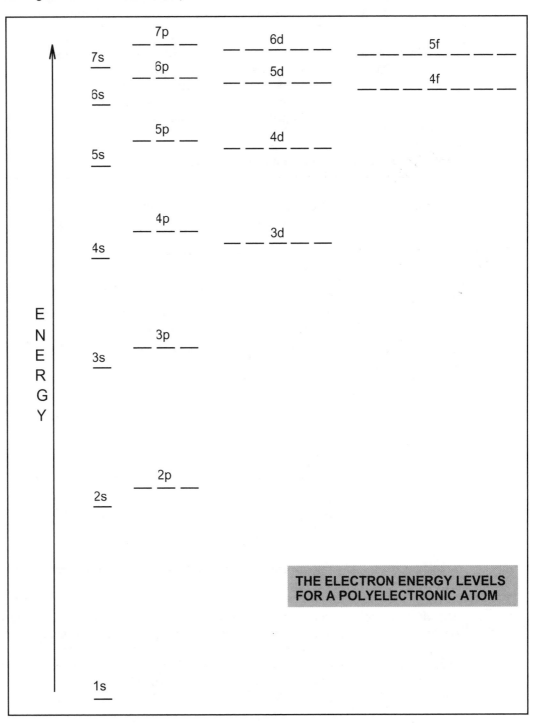

THE ELECTRON ENERGY LEVELS
FOR A POLYELECTRONIC ATOM

(b) ELECTRON CONFIGURATIONS

The addition of electrons to the orbitals of an atom follows 2 simple rules.

> 1. As the atomic number increases, electrons are added to the available orbitals. To ensure the LOWEST POSSIBLE ENERGY for the atom, electrons are added to the orbitals having the lowest energy first.
>
> 2. A maximum of 2 electrons can be placed in each orbital. This means there can be a MAXIMUM of: • 2 electrons in an s–type subshell
>   • 6 electrons in a   p–type subshell
>   • 10 electrons in a   d–type subshell
>   • 14 electrons in an f–type subshell.

i)   Writing Electron Configurations for Neutral Atoms

Definition: An **ELECTRON CONFIGURATION** is a description of which orbitals in an atom contain electrons and how many electrons are in each orbital.

Hydrogen has 1 electron, which goes in the *lowest* (1s) energy level. As a result, H has the electron configuration
$$H\,(\,1s^1\,)\,,$$ which is read as "Hydrogen, one s one".

Helium has 2 electrons. Since an orbital can have up to 2 electrons, both electrons go in the 1s orbital and helium has the electron configuration
$$He\,(\,1s^2\,)\,,$$ which is read as "Helium, one s two".

At this point the first electron shell is completely filled. The first electron shell, having $n=1$, consists of only *one* orbital, the **1s**.

Lithium has 3 electrons. The first 2 electrons go in the 1s orbital; the 3rd goes into the 2s orbital (which has the next–higher energy). The electron configuration of Li is
$$Li\,(\,1s^2\,2s^1\,)\,.$$

Similarly:

$$Be\,(\,1s^2\,2s^2\,) \qquad\qquad O\,(\,1s^2\,2s^2\,2p^4\,)$$
$$B\,(\,1s^2\,2s^2\,2p^1\,) \qquad\quad F\,(\,1s^2\,2s^2\,2p^5\,)$$
$$C\,(\,1s^2\,2s^2\,2p^2\,) \qquad\quad Ne\,(\,1s^2\,2s^2\,2p^6\,)$$
$$N\,(\,1s^2\,2s^2\,2p^3\,)$$

At this point the 2nd shell (all orbitals with $n = 2$) has been filled and the 2nd shell is said to be **CLOSED** (as in "closed to further filling").

The diagram below shows how the periodic table can be interpreted in terms of electron orbitals. Elements in the first two columns are adding one or two electrons to successive s–orbitals (1s, 2s, etc.). Elements in the last six columns are adding up to six electrons to successive p–orbitals (2p, 3p, etc.). The transition metals in the center of the table are adding up to ten electrons to successive d–orbitals (3d, 4d, etc.). (The lanthanides and actinides involve filling the 4f and 5f orbitals respectively.)

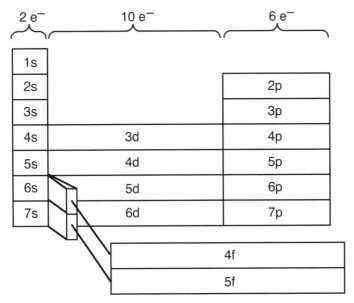

The electron configuration of most elements can be easily determined by using this "orbital version" of the periodic table.

EXAMPLE: **Silicon**, Si, has 14 electrons. The first 2 electrons are placed in the 1s orbital, which completes the first shell. The next 8 electrons fill the second shell: 2 electrons go in the 2s orbital and 6 electrons go in the 2p orbitals. The remaining 4 electrons go into the third shell: 2 electrons go into the 3s orbital and the remaining 2 electrons go into 3p orbitals. Altogether, the electron configuration of Si is written as follows.

$$Si\ (\ 1s^2\,2s^2\,2p^6\,3s^2\,3p^2\,)$$

Technetium, Tc, has 43 electrons and lies in the "4d" block of orbitals. All intervening orbitals are filled before getting to the 4d orbitals.

$$Tc\ (\ 1s^2\,2s^2\,2p^6\,3s^2\,3p^6\,4s^2\,3d^{10}\,4p^6\,5s^2\,4d^5\,)$$

EXERCISE:

26. Predict the electron configuration of the following.

(a) P	(d) Br	(g) K	(j) Xe	(m) Ga
(b) Ti	(e) Sr	(h) Cd	(k) Cs	(n) Mn
(c) Co	(f) Ar	(i) Ca	(l) Pb	(o) Zr

ii) Core Notation

The set of electrons belonging to a given atom can be divided into two subsets: the CORE electrons and the OUTER electrons.

Definition: The **CORE** of an atom is the set of electrons with the configuration of the nearest noble gas (He, Ne, Ar, Kr, etc.) having an atomic number LESS than that of the atom being considered.

The **OUTER** electrons consist of all electrons outside of the core. Since core electrons normally don't take part in chemical reactions, they are not always explicitly included when writing the electron configuration of an atom.

CORE NOTATION is a way of showing the electron configuration in terms of the core and the outer electrons. The rules for writing an electron configuration using core notation are straight-forward. The use of core notation is illustrated below using aluminum, Al.

- Locate the atom and note the noble gas at the end of the row above the element.

    Example: Ne is the noble gas at the end of the row *above* Al.

- Start to write the electron configuration as usual, but replace the part of the electron configuration corresponding to the configuration of the noble gas with the symbol for the noble gas in square brackets: [...]. Follow the core symbol with the electron configuration of the remaining outer electrons.

    Example: Al($1s^2 2s^2 2p^6$ $3s^2 3p^1$)   becomes   Al([Ne] $3s^2 3p^1$)
                         CORE   OUTER   CORE   OUTER

More examples:

Full notation	Core notation
S ($1s^2 2s^2 2p^6 3s^2 3p^4$)	S ([Ne] $3s^2 3p^4$)
Rb ($1s^2 2s^2 2p^6 3s^2 3p^6 4s^2 3d^{10} 4p^6 5s^1$)	Rb ([Kr] $5s^1$)
Kr ($1s^2 2s^2 2p^6 3s^2 3p^6 4s^2 3d^{10} 4p^6$)	Kr ([Ar] $4s^2 3d^{10} 4p^6$)

Hint: If you are given the electron configuration of an element in the 3rd or greater row, and are asked to re-write the configuration in core notation, look backwards from the end of the electron configuration to find a "p^6"; this is the end of the core electrons.

EXCEPTION: If you are asked to write the core notation for a noble gas such as krypton, you must show the electron configuration as

Kr([Ar] $4s^2 3d^{10} 4p^6$)

rather than   Kr([Kr])   (you don't get away that easily!)

EXERCISE:

27. Re-write the electron configurations in the previous exercise using core notation.

iii) Electron Configuration Exceptions

There are two exceptions to the configurations of elements up to Kr. Instead of finding

Cr ([Ar] $4s^2 3d^4$)   ; "d^4" is one electron short of a half-filled subshell

and   Cu ([Ar] $4s^2 3d^9$)   ; "d^9" is one electron short of a filled subshell,

the actual electron configurations for Cr and Cu are found to be

Cr ([Ar] $4s^1 3d^5$)   ; "$4s^1$" and "$3d^5$" are two half-filled subshells

and   Cu ([Ar] $4s^1 3d^{10}$)   ; "$4s^1$" is a half-filled subshell, and "$3d^{10}$" is a filled subshell.

The electron configuration exceptions of Cr, Cu and a few other atoms and ions indicate that

a filled or exactly half-filled d-subshell is especially stable.

Because of this extra stability, an atom or ion that is one electron short of a "d^5" or "d^{10}" configuration may have an electron configuration in which one electron is shifted from the filled s-subshell having the highest energy into the unfilled d-subshell. That is:

$4s^2 3d^4$ becomes $4s^1 3d^5$
$4s^2 3d^9$ becomes $4s^1 3d^{10}$.

iv) Writing Electron Configurations for Ions

i) **NEGATIVE IONS** – To write the electron configuration of a NEGATIVE ION, add electrons to the last unfilled subshell, starting where the neutral atom left off.

Example: $O\,(\,[He]\,2s^2\,2p^4\,)\,+\,2\,e^-\,\longrightarrow\,O^{2-}\,(\,[He]\,2s^2\,2p^6\,)$

$S\,(\,[Ne]\,3s^2\,3p^4\,)\,+\,\ e^-\,\longrightarrow\,S^-\,(\,[Ne]\,3s^2\,3p^5\,)$

ii) **POSITIVE IONS** – The electron configurations of POSITIVE IONS involve two rules.

> 1. Electrons in the outermost shell (largest n–value) are removed first.
> 2. If there are electrons in both the s– and p–orbitals of the outermost shell, the electrons in the p–orbitals are removed first.
>
> These rules are equivalent to the following statement.
>
> Write the core notation for the atom, remove electrons in the order:
>
> **p–electrons** before **s–electrons** before **d–electrons** .

The outermost electrons are removed preferentially. In addition, the electrons in the highest–energy outermost orbital require the least amount of extra energy in order to be completely removed from the atom and therefore are first to be removed.

Examples: $Sn\,(\,[Kr]\,5s^2\,4d^{10}\,5p^2\,)\,\longrightarrow\,2\,e^-\,+\,Sn^{2+}\,(\,[Kr]\,5s^2\,4d^{10}\,)$
   • 5p is removed before 5s

$Sn\,(\,[Kr]\,5s^2\,4d^{10}\,5p^2\,)\,\longrightarrow\,4\,e^-\,+\,Sn^{4+}\,(\,[Kr]\,4d^{10}\,)$
   • 5p and 5s are removed before 4d

$V\,(\,[Ar]\,4s^2\,3d^3\,)\,\longrightarrow\,2\,e^-\,+\,V^{2+}\,(\,[Ar]\,3d^3\,)$
   • 4s is removed before 3d (4s is OUTSIDE 3d)

EXERCISE:

28. Predict the electron configuration of the following ions, using core notation.

(a) H^- (c) Br^- (e) Ti^{2+} (g) Mn^{2+} (i) Fe^{3+} (k) Ru^{3+}
(b) Sr^{2+} (d) N^{3+} (f) N^{2-} (h) Ge^{4+} (j) Ge^{2+} (l) Sb^{3+}

v) Predicting the Number of Valence Electrons

Definition: **VALENCE ELECTRONS** are electrons which can take part in chemical reactions.

In other words:

VALENCE ELECTRONS are all the electrons in an atom *EXCEPT* those in the
   • core, or
   • in filled d– or f–subshells.

EXAMPLES: $Al\,(\,[Ne]\,3s^2\,3p^1\,)$ has 3 valence electrons: "$3s^2\,3p^1$"

$Ga\,(\,[Ar]\,4s^2\,3d^{10}\,4p^1\,)$ has 3 valence electrons (omit the filled $3d^{10}$)

$Pb\,(\,[Xe]\,6s^2\,4f^{14}\,5d^{10}\,6p^2\,)$ has 4 valence electrons (omit the filled $4f^{14}$ and $5d^{10}$)

$Xe\,(\,[Kr]\,5s^2\,4d^{10}\,5p^6\,)$ has ZERO valence electrons (noble gas configuration)

EXERCISE:

29. How many valence electrons do the following contain?

(a) O   (d) Ca   (g) Te   (j) Xe^{2+} (m) Tc^{4+} (o) O^-

(b) P   (e) Xe   (h) Cl^- (k) Zn^{2+} (n) Sb^{3+} (p) Nb^{3+}

(c) V   (f) Hg   (i) I^{5+} (l) Ge^{4+}

VIII.2. THE PERIODIC TABLE

A. EARLY ATTEMPTS TO ORGANIZE THE ELEMENTS : MASS CONFUSION

By 1817 chemists had discovered 52 elements; by 1863 that number had risen to 62. Observed similarities in chemical properties, combined with the analysis work of Dalton, prompted chemists to try to find a way to organize the elements according to their most obvious property: their mass. Because there were several different ways to measure atomic mass, resulting in different masses frequently being assigned for the same element, it was impossible to organize the elements in any consistent manner. A way to organize the elements had to wait until chemists learned to refine their ideas, separate pure elements from available minerals and compounds, find better methods of analysis, and invent the equipment needed to aid them in their work.

The earliest attempt to organize the elements came between 1817 and 1827 when Johann Döbereiner noticed **triads** of substances in which the average mass of two substances equalled the mass of a third substance. For example:

$$\text{mass of SrO} \approx {}^1/_2 (\text{mass of CaO} + \text{mass of BaO})$$
$$104 \approx {}^1/_2 (56 + 153)$$

Numerous triads were discovered but little came of the efforts other than to convince chemists that some scheme of organization should be possible.

By 1857, William Odling pointed out that the known elements could be divided into 13 groups, based on their physical and chemical properties. The table below shows some of Odling's groups, which coincide with many of the columns in the modern periodic table.

Group	Elements in Group
1	F, Cl, Br, I
2	O, S, Se, Te
3	N, P, As, Sb, Bi
4	B, Si, Ti, Sn
5	Li, Na, K
6	Ca, Sr, Ba
7	Mg, Zn, Cd
8	Cr, Mn, Co, Fe, Ni, Cu
9	Hg, Pb, Ag
10	Pd, Pt, Au

Then, between 1863 and 1866, John Newlands showed that by assigning hydrogen an arbitrary mass of 1 and ordering the known elements by their masses, every eighth element shared a common set of properties. He called this the "law of octaves", analogous to musical octaves. For example, Li, Na and K had similar properties. (Before you object that if Li is counted as element #1 in its group then Na is element #9 and K is element #17, you should know that the noble gases were not discovered until the 1890's. Therefore, Newlands counted Li as element #1 in its group, Na was element #8 and K was element #15.) Newlands' work was actually quite elegant and a fundamental breakthrough, but he was repeatedly criticized for changing the way he ordered the elements. Also, he was unable to predict the properties of yet–to–be–discovered elements.

In 1869, the Russian chemist Dimitri Mendeleev published a method of organizing the elements according to both their masses and their properties. Although Mendeleev's work was similar in some ways to the work of others working to organize the elements, he worked in isolation, almost unaware of the efforts of others. (Lothar Meyer made the same discovery in the same year but because Meyer's results were published a year later the credit for the discovery goes to Mendeleev. Ironically, It was not until Meyer's publication referred to Mendeleev's results that the Russian chemist's publication was finally noticed.) Mendeleev showed that when the elements are listed according to masses, certain properties recur PERIODICALLY. He took an inspired step and broke the list into a series of rows, as shown below, such that elements in one row are directly over elements with similar properties in other rows. He called each horizontal row a PERIOD and each vertical column a GROUP.

Row	Group I	Group II	Group III	Group IV	Group V	Group VI	Group VII	Group VIII
1	H = 1							
2	Li = 7	Be = 9.4	B = 11	C = 12	N = 14	O = 16	F = 19	
3	Na = 23	Mg = 24	Al = 27.3	Si = 28	P = 31	S = 32	Cl = 35.5	
4	K = 39	Ca = 40	— = 44	Ti = 48	V = 51	Cr = 52	Mn = 55	Fe = 56, Co = 59 Ni = 59, Cu = 63
5	(Cu = 63)	Zn = 65	— = 68	— = 72	As = 75	Se = 78	Br = 80	
6	Rb = 85	Sr = 87	?Yt = 88	Zr = 90	Nb = 94	Mo = 96	— = 100	Ru = 104, Rh = 104 Pd = 106, Ag = 108
7	(Ag = 108)	Cd = 112	In = 113	Sn = 118	Sb = 122	Te = 125	I = 127	
8	Cs = 133	Ba = 137	?Di = 138	?Ce = 140	—	—	—	— — — —
9	(—)	—	—	—	—	—	—	
10	—	—	?Er = 178	?La = 180	Ta = 182	W = 184	—	Os = 195, Ir = 197 Pt = 198, Au = 199
11	(Au = 199)	Hg = 200	Tl= 204	Pb = 207	Bi = 208	—	—	
12	—	—	—	Th = 231		U = 240	—	

In certain cases, he interchanged elements when their properties dictated that an element should be placed in a particular group in spite of contrary indications by its mass. Mendeleev's genius was evident in the way he left gaps in his table for elements which he proposed had yet to be discovered; for example, the elements with masses 44, 68, 72 and 100. Moreover, he was able to predict the properties of these elements and their compounds so accurately that when the elements were eventually discovered the match between predicted and observed properties was remarkably close. In one instance, a property of a newly discovered element differed significantly from that predicted by Mendeleev. So confident was he in the predictive abilities of his table that he requested that the property be remeasured. The new measurement was almost exactly as suggested by Mendeleev. This ability to predict chemical and physical properties convinced chemists that they finally had the tool they had long sought. THE PERIODIC TABLE ALLOWED CHEMISTS TO ORGANIZE AND UNDERSTAND THEIR DATA, AND PREDICT NEW PROPERTIES.

EXERCISE:

30. This exercise will allow you to recreate some of the predictions of Mendeleev. The year is
     1880. The element germanium (Ge) will not be discovered for several years, but its existence
     was predicted by Mendeleev in 1871. Some properties of the elements above, below and on
     either side of germanium on the periodic table are shown below. You are asked to predict the
     properties of germanium using the properties of its neighbours and whatever mathematical
     methods seem appropriate to you.

	Al	Si	P
Atomic mass	27.1	28.1	31.0
Density (g/mL)	2.70	2.33	1.82
Density of oxide (g/mL)	3.97	2.65	2.14
Formula of chloride	$AlCl_3$	$SiCl_4$	$PCl_3(l)$, $PCl_5(g)$
Density of chloride (g/mL)	2.44	1.48	1.57 (liquid)
Colour	silvery white	grey	pale yellow
Lustre	metallic	metallic	waxy

	Ga	Ge	As
Atomic mass	69.7		74.9
Density (g/mL)	5.90		5.73
Density of oxide (g/mL)	5.88		3.87
Formula of chloride	$GaCl_3$		$AsCl_3$
Density of chloride (g/mL)	2.47		2.16
Colour	silvery		steel grey
Lustre	metallic		dull metallic

	In	Sn	Sb
Atomic mass	114.8	118.6	121.8
Density (g/mL)	7.31	7.28	6.69
Density of oxide (g/mL)	7.18	6.95	5.67
Formula of chloride	$InCl_3$	$SnCl_2$, $SnCl_4$	$SbCl_3$, $SbCl_5$
Density of chloride (g/mL)	3.46	3.95, 2.23	3.14, 2.34
Colour	silvery white	silvery white	bluish–white
Lustre	metallic	metallic	metallic

B. THE MODERN PERIODIC TABLE

As more and better data became available, chemists made a significant change to Mendeleev's
method of organizing the elements. The modern periodic table is organized according to **ATOMIC
NUMBERS** rather than **ATOMIC MASSES**. This immediately solved problems where different isotopic
abundances caused the masses to be "out of order" as is seen with the elements Ar and K, Co and Ni,
and Te and I. The Periodic Law below summarizes the organization of the periodic table.

The Periodic Law: The properties of the chemical elements recur periodically when the elements are arranged from lowest to highest atomic numbers.

The previous section dealing with electron configurations showed how the various "blocks" of elements
(corresponding to the filling of s, p, d and f orbitals) give the periodic table its characteristic shape. This
section will identify the major groups of elements within the periodic table and then examine the trends
in selected physical and chemical properties which exist within the table and why those trends exist.

(a) THE MAJOR DIVISIONS WITHIN THE PERIODIC TABLE

The modern form of the periodic table is a visual presentation of the elements which allows the relationship between the elements to be easily seen. The basic arrangement of the table and the terms used in describing the features of the table are as follows.

Definitions: A **PERIOD** is the set of all the elements in a given **row** going **across** the table.

A **GROUP** or **FAMILY** is the set of all the elements in a given **column** going **down** the table.

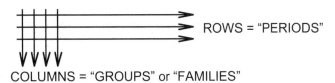

COLUMNS = "GROUPS" or "FAMILIES"

There are several special groups, rows and "blocks" of elements.

- The **REPRESENTATIVE ELEMENTS** are the "main groups" of elements, as shown on the diagram below.

- The **TRANSITION METALS** are the central block of elements which separate the two blocks of the representative elements.

- The **ALKALI METALS** = the elements in the first column (except hydrogen)

- The **ALKALINE EARTH METALS** = the elements in the second column

- The **HALOGENS** = the elements in the column headed by fluorine (ions are called "halides")

- The **NOBLE GASES** = the elements in the column headed by helium

- The **LANTHANIDES** = the elements in the row shown underneath the main part of the table, starting with *lanthanum*

- The **ACTINIDES** = the elements in the row shown underneath the main part of the table, starting with *actinium*

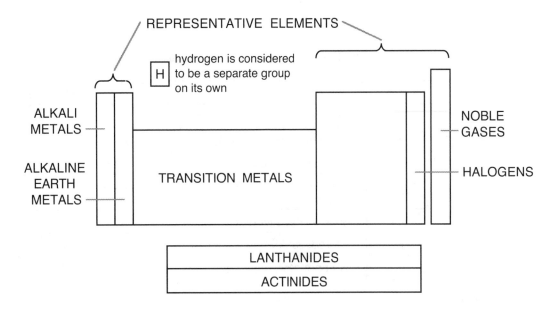

EXERCISES:

31. State the chemical family or group to which each of the following elements belongs.
    (a) radon   (c) iron   (e) iodine   (g) lithium
    (b) calcium   (d) cesium   (f) zinc   (h) chlorine

32. Give the symbols for two other elements in the same family as the following.
    (a) Na   (b) Ar   (c) Mg   (d) Br

33. Give the symbols for two other elements in the same period as the following.
    (a) C   (b) S

(b) METALS, NONMETALS AND SEMICONDUCTORS

In addition to the above groups, rows and blocks, there is another way of classifying elements: according to the metallic character of the element.

The properties of metals

Metals
- reflect light when polished (are shiny and have a "metallic lustre").
- are opaque.
- are good conductors of electricity and heat.
- are generally, but not always, flexible when in thin sheets.
- are generally *malleable* (can be hammered or rolled into thin sheets) and *ductile* (can be drawn or stretched into wires).
- are usually solid at room temperatures (mercury is an exception).

The properties of nonmetals

Non–metals
- are gases, liquids or brittle solids at room temperature.
- are poor heat and electrical conductors.
- if solids, are dull to lustrous in appearance and opaque to translucent.

EXERCISE:

34. Classify each of the following samples as one of:
    - a METAL (has the properties of a metal),
    - a NONMETAL (has the properties of a nonmetal), or
    - a MIXTURE of metallic and nonmetallic properties.

SAMPLE	PROPERTIES	CLASSIFICATION
A	Pale yellow gas, nonconductor	
B	Conductor, shiny, hard, silvery, malleable	
C	Nonconductor, yellow, looks waxy, soft, brittle	
D	Hard, silvery–grey, brittle, somewhat shiny, fair conductor	
E	Liquid, shiny, silvery, conductor	
F	Dark red, liquid, nonconductor	
G	Fair conductor, brittle, dull grey	

As can be seen from the above exercise, metallic character is not "all or nothing".   There are elements which share some of the properties of both metals and nonmetals.

The nonmetals can be divided into two subgroups:
- nonmetals with very low electrical conductivities, and
- nonmetals with fair to moderate electrical conductivities.

Definition: A **SEMICONDUCTOR** is a nonmetal having an electrical conductivity which increases with temperature.

Notes: a) SEMICONDUCTORS were formerly called *metalloids* or *semimetals* because they have properties which resemble metals more than nonmetals. The term "metalloid" is no longer used by chemists, but is included here because of continued usage in many textbooks.

b) The important difference between metals and semiconductors is that the electrical conductivity of metals DECREASES with increasing temperature whereas the electrical conductivity of semiconductors INCREASES with increasing temperature. The study of semiconductors is beyond the scope of Chemistry 11.

The division of the elements in the periodic table into metals, nonmetals and semiconductors shown below is accepted by most chemists.

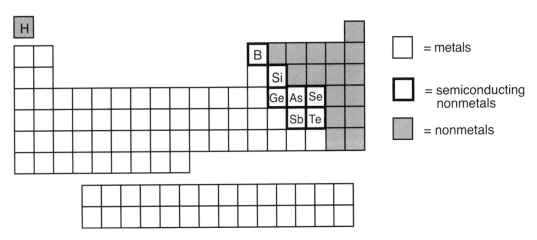

There are two important trends in the periodic table which exist among the elements.

i) | The properties of the elements change from metallic to nonmetallic going from left to right across the table.

EXAMPLE: Examining the elements of the third period,

Na, Mg, Al, Si, P, S, Cl, Ar,

the following properties are found.

Na, Mg and Al are silvery metals (conduct electricity).

Si is a blue–grey semiconductor with a somewhat metallic lustre. Its chemical properties are those of a non metal but its physical and electrical properties are those of a semiconductor.

P is a nonmetal which exists in three main forms or "allotropes": white, red and black. The white and red forms are nonconductors but the black form is a conductor.

S, Cl and Ar are nonmetals.

ii) | Elements become more metallic (or better metals) going down a family in the periodic table. |

EXAMPLE: Examining the elements of group 14,

C, Si, Ge, Sn and Pb,

the following properties are found.

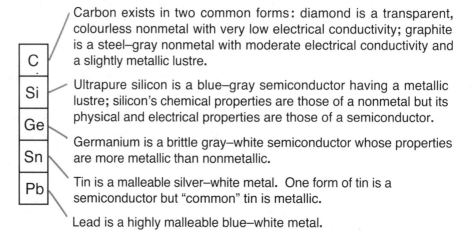

Carbon exists in two common forms: diamond is a transparent, colourless nonmetal with very low electrical conductivity; graphite is a steel–gray nonmetal with moderate electrical conductivity and a slightly metallic lustre.

Ultrapure silicon is a blue–gray semiconductor having a metallic lustre; silicon's chemical properties are those of a nonmetal but its physical and electrical properties are those of a semiconductor.

Germanium is a brittle gray–white semiconductor whose properties are more metallic than nonmetallic.

Tin is a malleable silver–white metal. One form of tin is a semiconductor but "common" tin is metallic.

Lead is a highly malleable blue–white metal.

The diagram below summarizes the above two trends in the periodic table.

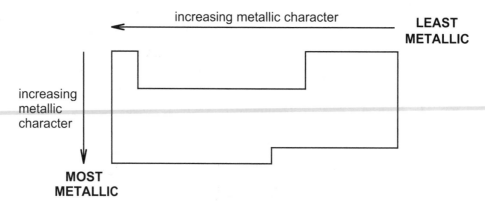

EXERCISES:

35. On which side of the periodic table do you find the nonmetals?

36. Which member of each of the following pairs is more metallic?
     (a) B or Ga   (b) Ge or S   (c) Br or Sn   (d) Mg or P   (e) As or Bi

37. Arrange the following in order from most metallic to least metallic: P, Ca, F, Si, Ge.

38. Which member of each of the following pairs would you expect to be a better electrical conductor?
     (a) Sb or P   (b) K or I   (c) Ge or As   (d) B or Al   (e) Tl or S   (f) Sb or Te

39. Match the following elements with the best description. Use the process of elimination by making the most obvious matches first.
     (a) P   (i)   brittle; steel–grey; partially reflective; fair conductor
     (b) Ba   (ii) soft; silvery-white; reflective; good conductor
     (c) Sb   (iii) waxy yellow solid; translucent; poor conductor
     (d) Ar   (iv) brittle; bluish-white; reflective; fair conductor
     (e) As   (v)   colourless gas; extremely poor conductor

VIII.3. CHEMICAL BONDING

A. THE ELECTRONIC NATURE OF CHEMICAL BONDING

(a) THE ELECTROSTATIC FORCES BETWEEN CHARGED PARTICLES

Definition: An **ELECTROSTATIC FORCE** is a force existing as a result of the attraction or repulsion between two charged particles.

All bonding is based on the experimentally–derived relationships of electrostatics shown below.

---

1. Opposite charges attract each other. (In other words, a positive and a negative charge attract each other.)
2. Like charges repel each other. (In other words, two positive charges repel each other, as do two negative charges.)
3. The greater the distance between two charged particles, the smaller the attractive (or repulsive) force existing between them.
4. The greater the charge on two particles, the greater the force of attraction (or repulsion) between them.

The above electrostatic relationships are used to explain the trends in physical and chemical properties examined in this unit.

(b) ELECTRON SHELLS REVISITED

Each "period" on the periodic table represents a different layer of electrons; that is, a different "electron shell".
- The 1st shell has 2 electrons and therefore the 1st period has 2 elements
- The 2nd shell has 8 electrons and therefore the 2nd period has 8 elements
- The 3rd shell has 8 electrons and therefore the 3rd period has 8 elements

(*Note:* for the purposes of this section, the transition metals, lanthanides and actinides are IGNORED.)

Going from left to right across a given period, **the atomic number (that is, the number of protons in the nucleus) increases, and the positive charge on the nucleus increases.** This increase in atomic number also brings an increase in the number of electrons surrounding the nucleus. **All the electrons in a given shell can be assumed to have the same average distance from the nucleus.**

EXERCISES:

40. What should happen to the atomic radius as the number of electron "shells" increases? Why? **What should happen to the atomic radius going down a group?**

41. What happens to the size of the positive nuclear charge "felt" by the electrons surrounding the nucleus in an element, going from left to right across a row of the table? What effect would you expect this change in charge to have on the average distance between the nucleus and a given electron going across the table? **What should happen to the radii of the elements, going from left to right ACROSS a row of the periodic table?** (This point is *very important*!)

Definitions: An **OPEN SHELL** is a shell containing less than its maximum number of electrons.

A **CLOSED SHELL** is a shell containing its maximum number of electrons.

Example: The third shell, starting with Na and ending with Ar, can hold a maximum of 8 electrons: $3s^2 3p^6$. The atoms from Na to Cl have less than 8 electrons in their third shell, so that their outermost shell is **OPEN**. The atom Ar has its outermost (third) shell full with 8 electrons, and therefore its third shell is **CLOSED**.

EXERCISES:

42. Fill in the blanks using the words "OPEN" or "CLOSED". The entries in the 1st and 3rd columns refer to the TOTAL NUMBER of electrons possessed by an atom.

If an atom has:	Then its outermost shell is:	If an atom has:	Then its outermost shell is:
1 electron		10 electrons	
2 electrons		11 electrons	
3 electrons		16 electrons	
8 electrons		18 electrons	

43. Which family of elements appears to possess only CLOSED SHELLS? Which elements have open shells?

44. Which of the following have an OPEN SHELL and which have ALL SHELLS CLOSED?
    - (a) Cl
    - (b) Ne
    - (c) Mg
    - (d) Si
    - (e) Na^+
    - (f) Cl^-
    - (g) O^-
    - (h) Ca^{2+}
    - (i) I
    - (j) Al^+

(c) VALENCE ELECTRONS REVISITED

Previously, valence electrons were defined as all the electrons in an atom except those in the core or in filled d– or f–subshells. This definition can be rephrased in a different way.

Definition: **VALENCE ELECTRONS** are the electrons in OPEN SHELLS.

Note: "valence" is used here as an **adjective**, modifying "electrons"

Valence electrons are "reactable electrons". The NOBLE GASES have *NO* valence electrons and are *NOT REACTIVE*. Similarly, F and Na *HAVE* valence electrons and *ARE REACTIVE*.

EXAMPLES: When counting valence electrons: Li has 1, Be has 2 and B has 3.
Similarly: K has 1, Ca has 2 and Ga has 3.

The valence electrons of transition metal atoms will not be considered in this section, so that the maximum number of valence electrons in a given period (row) for our purposes is 7.

EXAMPLE: The number of valence electrons in the third period can be counted as follows (recall that Kr has a full shell).

atom	K	Ca	Ga	Ge	As	Se	Br	Kr
# of electrons	1	2	3	4	5	6	7	0

EXERCISE:

45. Fill in the number of valence electrons corresponding to each atom.

atom	# of valence electrons	atom	# of valence electrons
F		Pb	
Ne		Pb^{2+}	
Na		S^-	
Ne^+		S^{2-}	

(d) THE VALENCE OF AN ATOM

Isolated atoms have their electrons placed in s, p, d and f orbitals, as was discussed in the section "*The Electronic Structure of the Atom*". However, when an atom is involved in a chemical bond some of the atom's orbitals are modified to allow electrons to be shared between adjacent atoms. (The nature of these modified orbitals is beyond the scope of this course. The number of modified orbitals, and the manner in which they are modified, varies from molecule to molecule.)

We will make no distinction between modified and unmodified electron orbitals in this section. The only important fact is that there are a total of FOUR orbitals into which electrons can be placed (since there are four orbitals – an "s" and three "p" orbitals – in each period). [The transition metals are ignored in this course when dealing with chemical bonding.] Three rules dictate how valence electrons are put into these modified orbitals.

 • Each individual orbital holds up to 2 electrons.
 • Since electrons repel each other, each electron added goes into a vacant orbital, if possible.
 • Only after each orbital contains one electron will the addition of successive electrons require electrons to become "paired up".

EXERCISE:

46. (a) Use the rules outlined above to place the required number of valence electrons for each atom into each diagram below. Show each electron as a "dot". The four elipses surrounding each atom represent the four orbitals available to receive electrons.
Note: Ignore the electrons in the 1st shell; show only the electrons in the 2nd shell.

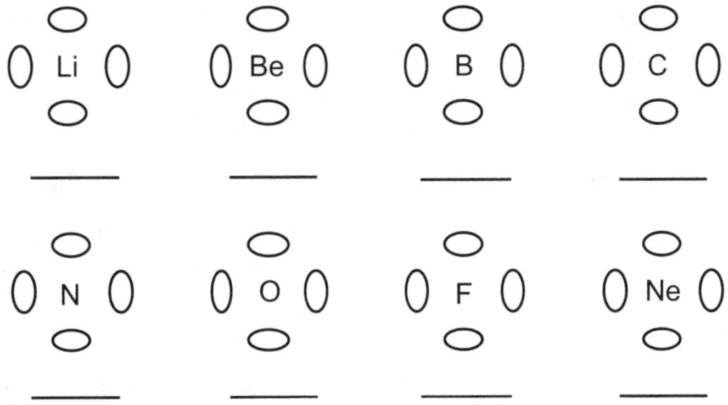

   (b) Experiments show that "paired-up" electrons usually do NOT react; only **UNPAIRED** electrons normally take part in bonding and chemical reactions. On the space provided below each atom in part (a) write the number of unpaired electrons possessed by each atom.

Definition: **VALENCE** (as a noun) = the number of electrons which are *normally* available for bonding.

= **the number of unpaired electrons on the atom.**

Valence is sometimes called the **COMBINING CAPACITY.**

EXERCISE:

47. Fill in the table below.

atom	H	He						
valence								
atom	Li	Be	B	C	N	O	F	Ne
valence								
atom	Na	Mg	Al	Si	P	S	Cl	Ar
valence								

(e) IONIZATION ENERGY

In order to form a **positive** ion, an electron must be removed from a neutral atom.

EXAMPLE: $Li + energy \longrightarrow Li^+ + e^-$

Definition: **IONIZATION ENERGY** is the energy required to remove an electron from a neutral atom. (The electron removed is the outermost and therefore most easily removed electron and is always a valence electron unless the atom has a closed shell.)

EXERCISES:

48. (a) What happens to the distance between the nucleus and outermost electrons going **down** a chemical family?
     (b) What happens to the electrostatic attraction of the nucleus to an electron in the outermost shell going **down** a family?
     (c) What happens to the ionization energy going **down** a family?

49. (a) What happens to the distance between the nucleus and the outermost electrons going left to right **across** a period? (Hint: see exercise 41.)
     (b) What happens to the nuclear charge going **across** the period?
     (c) What happens to the electrostatic attraction of the nucleus to an electron in the outermost shell going **across** a period?
     (d) What happens to the ionization energy going **across** the period?

50. Place arrowheads in the correct direction on the horizontal and vertical lines below.

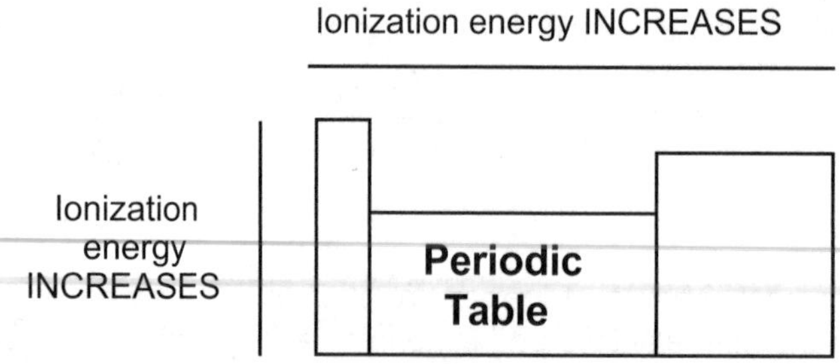

Ionization energy INCREASES

Ionization energy INCREASES

Periodic Table

51. Which member of each of the following pairs should have a greater ionization energy?
     (a) Br or Cl   (b) Al or Cl   (c) Ne or Xe   (d) Mg or Ba   (e) F or Ne   (f) Rb or I

AN EXTENSION TO "IONIZATION ENERGY"

The ionization energies (IE) of the first 20 elements are given in the table below.

Atom	Atomic #	IE (kJ)	Atom	Atomic #	IE (kJ)	Atom	Atomic #	IE (kJ)
H	1	1312	O	8	1314	P	15	1012
He	2	2372	F	9	1681	S	16	1000
Li	3	520	Ne	10	2081	Cl	17	1251
Be	4	899	Na	11	496	Ar	18	1521
B	5	801	Mg	12	738	K	19	419
C	6	1086	Al	13	578	Ca	20	590
N	7	1402	Si	14	787			

EXERCISE:

52. Plot the ionization energy versus atomic number on the following graph and connect each point to the next with a straight line. Then answer the following questions.

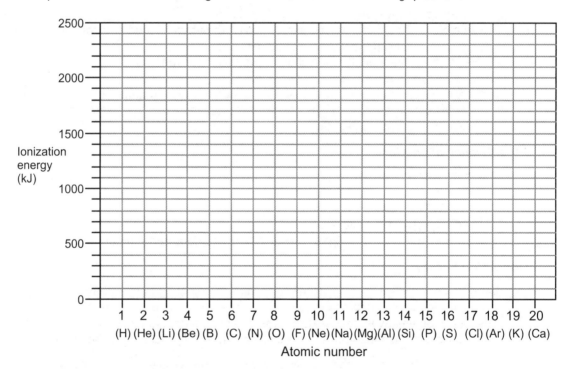

(a) Why are the ionization energies for He, Ne and Ar so high?

(b) Why do the ionization energies decrease going from He to Ne to Ar?

(c) Why is there a general increase in ionization energy going from Li to Ne?

(d) "Filled subshells and half–filled subshells have a special stability which requires extra energy to be applied before electron removal can occur". This general statement is supported by the existence of the electron configuration exceptions found for Cu and Cr. What experimental evidence exists in the graph "ionization energy versus atomic number" to support this general statement?

SUMMARY I: From "THE ELECTROSTATIC FORCES BETWEEN CHARGED PARTICLES" to "IONIZATION ENERGY"

This summary lists the important points which should be known about the preceding five sections.

The Electrostatic Forces Between Charged Particles

Like charges repel each other; unlike charges attract.
The closer together two charged particles, the greater the force between them.
The greater the charge on two particles, the greater the force between them.

Electron Shells Revisited

Each PERIOD (ROW) in the periodic table corresponds to a different ELECTRON SHELL.
The MORE SHELLS an atom has, the BIGGER the size of the atom.
Going DOWN the periodic table, the atoms get BIGGER.
Going from LEFT TO RIGHT across the periodic table, the atoms get SMALLER.
A CLOSED SHELL has the same number of electrons as a NOBLE GAS.
An OPEN SHELL is any shell which is not closed; that is, does not have the same number of electrons as a noble gas.

Valence Electrons Revisited

Valence electrons are electrons in OPEN SHELLS.
Valence electrons are counted by simply finding the atom desired and counting from left to right in the row containing the atom until you get to the atom.
Ignore the transition metals when counting valence electrons.
Noble gases have ZERO valence electrons.
If an atom has a charge, add one valence electron for every negative charge and subtract one for every positive charge. If the result of the addition or subtraction has the same number of electrons as a noble gas, the valence is ZERO.

The Valence of an Atom

The VALENCE OF AN ATOM (or ION) is the number of unpaired electrons possessed by the atom (or ion).
The VALENCE of successive atoms going from left to right across the periodic table (other than H and He) follows the pattern:
                          1, 2, 3, 4, 3, 2, 1, 0.   (Ignore transition metals.)

Ionization Energy

Ionization energy is the energy required to take one electron from a neutral atom.
The ionization energy decreases going down a family in the periodic table.
The ionization energy increases going from left to right across a period.
Overall, Helium has the greatest ionization energy and Francium has the least.

SUMMARY EXERCISES:

53. Consider two atoms: O and Te.
     (a) Which atom has a larger atomic radius?
     (b) Which atom has the larger ionization energy?
     (c) Which atom has more shells?
     (d) How many valence electrons does Te have?
     (e) What is the valence of Te?
     (f) Which atom has a greater electrostatic attraction between its nucleus and outermost electrons: O or Te?

54. Which ion pair has a greater electrostatic attraction between ions: Li^+ and F^- or Na^+ and Cl^-?

55. Consider two atoms: Ga and Br.
    (a) Which atom has a larger atomic radius?
    (b) Which atom has the larger ionization energy?
    (c) Which atom has more shells?
    (d) How many valence electrons does each atom have?
    (e) What is the valence of each atom?
    (f) Which atom has a greater electrostatic attraction between its nucleus and outermost electrons?

56. Which of the following have open shells?
    (a) Se   (b) Br^- (c) Sr^+ (d) Kr^+ (e) Xe   (f) Sb^{3-} (g) Ge

B. TYPES OF CHEMICAL BONDING

SPECIAL NOTE: The following *must* be remembered when examining trends down or across the periodic table.

When going **DOWN** a family in the periodic table, properties are affected by the **INCREASING SIZE** of the atoms and the **INCREASING DISTANCE** between the nuclei and the valence electrons.

When going **ACROSS** a period in the periodic table, properties are affected by the **DIFFERING VALENCE, NUCLEAR CHARGE** and **CHARGE ON THE SPECIES.**

(a) IONIC BONDING

Definition: An **IONIC BOND** is formed by the attraction of *positive ions* to *negative ions*.

An ionic bond is formed when an electron from one atom is transferred to another atom, so as to create one positive ion and one negative ion.

Definition: A **LEWIS STRUCTURE**, also called an "electron dot diagram", is a diagram showing how the *VALENCE* electrons are distributed in an atom, ion or molecule.

EXAMPLE: The diagram below uses Lewis Structures to show how atoms of Li and F combine to form Li^+ and F^- ions. The "dots" around the atoms represent valence electrons.

$$Li \cdot \quad + \quad \cdot F : \quad \xrightarrow[\text{electron from Li}]{\text{F takes valence}} \quad Li^+ \quad : F^- : $$

The electrostatic attraction between the + and − charges holds the ions together.

EXAMPLE: The reaction between atoms of Ca and O is illustrated below, using Lewis Structures.

$$\cdot Ca \cdot \quad + \quad \cdot O : \quad \xrightarrow[\text{electrons from Ca}]{\text{O takes 2 valence}} \quad Ca^{2+} \quad : O^{2-} : $$

A very simple fact makes it easier to deal with charged spheres.

If a sphere possesses a charge, the charge can be assumed to be **concentrated at the centre of the sphere**, rather than being spread over the sphere's surface or throughout its volume.

To see the importance of the above fact, assume that two charged spheres touch one another.

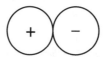

All the electrostatic attraction now depends on the distance separating the central charges:
the greater the distance, the smaller the attraction.

How to predict when an IONIC BOND will form.

IONIC BONDS are formed when elements from *opposites sides* of the periodic table are combined. That is, when a **METAL** and a **NONMETAL** are combined.

EXAMPLE: NaCl involves an ionic bond; Na is a metal and Cl is a nonmetal.

BrCl does not involve an ionic bond because both Br and Cl are nonmetals.

EXERCISE:

57. Which of the following atom pairs would you expect to form ionic bonds when they join?
    (a) Ba and S   (b) P and Cl   (c) Ca and O   (d) Rb and I   (e) O and H   (f) S and O

Interlude: ELECTRONEGATIVITY

The concept of ELECTRONEGATIVITY explains *why* Li and F form ions in the first place.

Definition: The **ELECTRONEGATIVITY** of an atom is the tendency of the atom to attract electrons from a neighbouring atom.

The exercises below are designed to help you examine why electronegativity exists and what trends in electronegativity occur in the periodic table. The investigation centres on the atoms Li, F and I.

EXERCISES:

58. This exercise compares Li and F.
    (a) Which atom is larger: Li or F?   (Hint: see exercise 41.)
    (b) Which atom has the stronger attraction to the outer electrons on a neighbouring atom, based only on the atomic radius?
    (c) Which atom has the greater nuclear charge?
    (d) Which atom can attract electrons from an adjacent atom most strongly, based on both size and nuclear charge?
    (e) Summarize the above by filling in the blank below.

    IN GENERAL, when going from *left* to *right* across the periodic table the electronegativity of the atoms will _____ .

59. This exercise compares F and I.
    (a) Which atom is larger: F or I?
    (b) Which atom has a stronger attraction to the outer electrons of another atom?
    (c) Summarize the above by filling in the blank below.

    IN GENERAL, when going down a family of the periodic table the electronegativity of the atoms will _____ .

60. Place arrowheads in the correct direction on the horizontal and vertical arrows below.

Electronegativity INCREASES

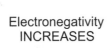 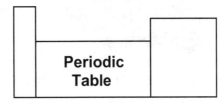

Electronegativity INCREASES

Periodic Table

61. (a) Ignoring the noble gases, which atom is the most electronegative?
    (b) Ignoring the noble gases, which atom is the least electronegative?
    (c) Which is more electronegative: K or Be?
    (d) Which is more electronegative: Pb or S?

If an atom has a **HIGH** electronegativity, it **strongly attracts** electrons from a **NEIGHBOURING ATOM** and may completely remove an electron from the neighbouring atom. This high attraction to a neighbouring atom's electrons also means that **atoms with a high electronegativity STRONGLY ATTRACT THEIR OWN VALENCE ELECTRONS**. As a result, these valence electrons are difficult to remove and the atom has a **HIGH IONIZATION ENERGY**.

If an atom has a *LOW* electronegativity, it has *little attraction* to the electrons of a *NEIGHBOURING ATOM* and little tendency to remove electrons from a neighbour. Such an atom also has a relatively small attraction to its *OWN VALENCE ELECTRONS*. Therefore, these valence electrons are relatively easy to remove and the atom has a *LOW IONIZATION ENERGY*.

(Note the similarity between the trends in exercises 50 and 60.)

Overall then, when Li and F approach each other, F has a great tendency to remove an electron from Li, and Li has little tendency either to remove an electron from F or hold onto its own valence electron. As a result, Li loses an electron to form Li^+ and F gains an electron to form F^-.

OK, now back to the IONIC BOND. The strength of such bonds can be estimated by examining the *MELTING TEMPERATURES* of ionic compounds.

The experimentally–determined melting temperature of LiF is $845^{\circ}C$. Some other ionic substances and their melting temperatures are:

$$NaF = 993^{\circ}C , \quad KCl = 770^{\circ}C \quad and \quad LiCl = 605^{\circ}C.$$

These high melting temperatures support the following conclusion.

IONIC BONDS are *VERY STRONG*, so that compounds held together by ionic bonds have *HIGH MELTING TEMPERATURES*.

In other words, a great deal of energy must be added to break ionic bonds. For example:

$$LiF + 1030 \text{ kJ/mol} \longrightarrow Li^+ + F^-.$$

Note: The formula for solid lithium fluoride is written as LiF(s), which might suggest that the Li and F are neutral atoms joined to make LiF. In fact, solid LiF is actually an "ionic lattice" in which ions are packed together in an orderly arrangement to make a crystal of LiF, as shown below.

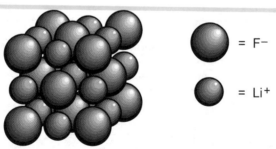

Going across the periodic table, a simple rule governs the charge created when an atom forms an ion.

In general, when an atom forms an ion the atom loses or gains sufficient electrons to attain a closed shell.

EXAMPLES:

$$Na \longrightarrow e^- + Na^+$$
1 valence e^- closed shell

$$Cl + e^- \longrightarrow Cl^-$$
7 valence e^-'s   closed shell

The most common charges found when going across the periodic table are shown below. [Elements in column 14 (C, Si, Ge, Sn and Pb) are not included because C, Si and Ge do not form simple ionic compounds and Sn and Pb are metals which most readily form +2 ions and only rarely, if ever, form +4 ions.]

Column in Periodic Table	1	2	13	14	15	16	17	18
Charge on ion	+1	+2	+3		−3	−2	−1	0

EXERCISES:

62. (a) Which compound has the smaller distance between the nuclei of the two ions involved: NaCl or KBr?
    (b) What happens to the force of electrostatic attraction between the two ions in an ionic bond as the ions get smaller?
    (c) What happens to the strength of an ionic bond as the ions involved get smaller? What happens to the melting temperature?

63. Mg^{2+} and Na^+ have roughly the same ionic radius. O^{2-} and F^- have roughly the same ionic radius. Which substance should have a higher melting temperature: NaF or MgO? Why?

64. Which member of each following pair would you expect to have the higher melting point?
    (a) CaO or RbI   (c) LiF or NaCl   (e) RbI or KCl
    (b) BeO or BN   (d) CsCl or BaS   (f) BeO or MgS

Interlude: INVESTIGATING THE SIZE OF AN ION RELATIVE TO THE SIZE OF A NEUTRAL ATOM

Exercise 40 showed that atoms increase in size going down a family in the periodic table and exercise 41 showed that atoms decrease in size going from left to right across the table. The exercises below investigate what happens to the size of an atom if electrons are added or removed to form an ion.

EXERCISES:

65. **NEGATIVE IONS:** Assume extra electrons are added to a neutral atom of O to make O^{2-}. The resulting ion has the same positive nuclear charge and an increased number of negative electrons surrounding the nucleus.
   (a) What happens to the amount of electrostatic repulsion existing between the electrons?
   (b) What happens to the volume occupied by the electrons due to the change in the amount of electron–electron repulsion?
   (c) Fill in the appropriate word.

NEGATIVE IONS are _____ than the corresponding neutral atom.

66. **POSITIVE IONS:** Assume electrons are removed from a neutral atom of Mg to make Mg^{2+}. The resulting ion has the same positive nuclear charge and a decreased number of negative electrons surrounding the nucleus.
   (a) What happens to the amount of electrostatic repulsion existing between the electrons?
   (b) What happens to the volume occupied by the electrons due to the change in repulsion?
   (c) Fill in the appropriate word.

POSITIVE IONS are _____ than the corresponding neutral atom.

67. Examine the diagram below, which shows a section of a crystal of NaCl.

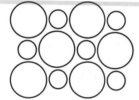

Which circles represent Na $^+$:
the larger or smaller ones?

(b) COVALENT BONDING

Definition: A **COVALENT BOND** is a bond which involves the **equal sharing of electrons.**

A covalent bond is formed when two atoms having less than full shells of electrons are able to share one or more of their electrons with each other to attain full electron shells.

Definition: The **OCTET RULE** states that atoms in columns 14 to 17 of the periodic table tend to form covalent bonds so as to have eight electrons in their valence shells.

The Lewis Structures below show how fluorine atoms gain an octet of valence electrons by forming covalent bonds.

EXAMPLE:

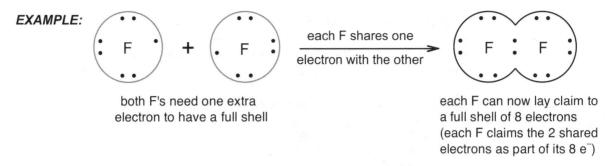

both F's need one extra
electron to have a full shell

each F shares one
electron with the other

each F can now lay claim to
a full shell of 8 electrons
(each F claims the 2 shared
electrons as part of its 8 e⁻)

The shared electrons in a F–F covalent bond can be visualized as follows.

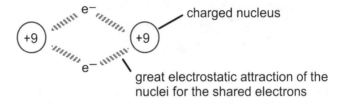

great electrostatic attraction of the
nuclei for the shared electrons

How to predict when a COVALENT BOND will form.

COVALENT BONDS are formed when a **nonmetal** combines with a **nonmetal.**

Covalent bonds form when both atoms involved have relatively large electronegativities. In general, nonmetals have large to very large electronegativities, attract each other's electrons strongly and will not let go of their own electrons. Since both F atoms (above) have the same ELECTRONEGATIVITY, they attract the shared electrons equally and neither wins the "tug of war" for the electrons. Therefore they **MUST SHARE** the electrons in the bond.

EXERCISE:

68. Which of the following atom pairs would you expect to form covalent bonds when they join?
    (a) S and O
    (b) Ba and O
    (c) Fe and Cl
    (d) N and O
    (e) H and S
    (f) C and H

The following melting points have been found experimentally.

$$BN \text{ (boron nitride)} = \text{about } 3000^{\circ}C$$
$$SiC \text{ (silicon carbide)} = \text{about } 2700^{\circ}C$$
$$C \text{ (diamond)} = \text{about } 3550^{\circ}C$$

All of these materials form crystals which are held together by a **network of covalent bonds** extending between every atom in the crystal. This network makes each crystal one huge "molecule" held together by identical bonds. The high melting points are interpreted as evidence that the bonds in the crystals are very strong.

COVALENT BONDS are VERY STRONG.

It is very tempting to say that "covalent compounds have high melting points", but look at the melting points of the following covalent compounds.

$$CH_4 = -182^{\circ}C$$
$$O_2 = -218^{\circ}C$$
$$F_2 = -220^{\circ}C$$

Each of these compounds consists of INDIVIDUAL molecules which contain covalent bonds. Because the bonds are strong, it requires a great deal of energy to break the covalent bond connecting an atom to the rest of a molecule. On the other hand, the **individual molecules** of CH_4, O_2 and F_2 in a solid are held next to each other by much weaker bonds. (More will be said later about these weak bonds.)

EXAMPLE: The diagram below represents part of a crystal of solid I_2.

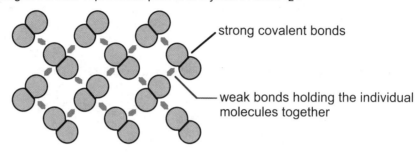

When solid iodine melts only the weak bonds holding individual I_2 molecules next to each other are broken. The covalent bonds are very strong and are not affected by the melting process.

$$I_2(s) + heat \longrightarrow I_2(l)$$

Oxygen atoms are 2 electrons short of a full shell. By each donating 2 electrons into a covalent bond, the atoms attain a full octet (4 shared electrons and 4 unshared electrons) and produce a molecule of O_2.

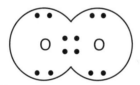

Atoms of N are 3 electrons short of a closed shell; that is, an octet of electrons. They each contribute 3 electrons to a covalent bond in order to form N_2 and gain a closed shell. (Each has 6 shared electrons and 2 unshared electrons.)

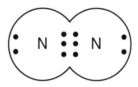

EXERCISES:

69. (a) When the distance between two covalently–bonded atoms increases, what happens to the electrostatic attraction of their nuclei to the shared electrons in a covalent bond?
    (b) What would you expect to happen to the strength of the covalent bond between two identical halogen atoms when going down the halogen family from F_2 to I_2?

70. What would you expect to happen to the strength of a covalent bond when the number of shared electrons increases?

71. The distance between the nuclei of two atoms involved in a bond is called the **BOND LENGTH**. What should happen to the bond length as the number of shared electrons in the bond increases? Why will this happen?

PREDICTING THE FORMULA OF COVALENT COMPOUNDS

Predicting the formulae of covalently–bonded binary compounds (compounds made from two different elements) is a very simple process. In fact, the process is almost identical to the process used to predict the formulae of ionic compounds.

Instead of using the charge on an ion to decide the formula, the "combining capacity" is used. The combining capacity is the number of bonds which an atom is expected to form when involved in covalent bonding, and is equal to the *valence* of the atom.

Column	1	2	13	14	15	16	17	18
Valence	1	2	3	4	3	2	1	0

EXAMPLES: Predict the formula of the compound formed from N and F.

N has a valence of 3 and F has a valence of 1. "Criss–cross" the valences.

$$\overset{3}{N_1}\diagup\!\!\!\!\diagdown\overset{1}{F_3}$$ gives the formula N_1F_3 or simply   **NF_3**

Predict the formula of the compound formed from C and O.

C has a valence of 4 and O has a valence of 2. "Criss–cross" the valences.

$$\overset{4}{C_2}\diagup\!\!\!\!\diagdown\overset{2}{O_4}$$ gives the formula C_2O_4 or more simply   **CO_2**

EXERCISE:

72. Predict the formula of the compound formed by bonding together the following.
     (a) P and Cl   (d) P and O   (g) H and O   (j) C and Cl
     (b) B and O   (e) H and Se   (h) N and I   (k) Si and P
     (c) C and S   (f) F and O   (i) B and C   (l) Si and S

(c) LONDON FORCES

Individual molecules are held together by covalent bonds between the atoms in the molecule. Such bonds are STRONG and are called **INTRAMOLECULAR FORCES** ("intra" means "within"). In addition to the bonds holding atoms together into molecular units, there are weak forces which hold one complete, neutrally–charged molecule next to another such molecule. These **INTERMOLECULAR FORCES** ("inter" means "between") are called **van der Waals forces.**

There are two main types of van der Waals forces. This section only deals with a special type of van der Waals force called the **London force** (also called the Heitler–London force or London dispersion force). The topic of van der Waals forces will come up again in the next unit, which examines the role that van der Waals forces play in solubility.

Definitions: A **DIPOLE** is a partial separation of charge which exists when one end of a molecule (or bond) has a slight excess of positive charge and the other end of the molecule (or bond) has a slight excess of negative charge.

LONDON FORCES are weak attractive forces which arise as a result of temporary dipolar attractions between neighbouring atoms. The atoms may exist individually or as parts of molecules.

The Origin of London Forces

The electrons around an atom tend to avoid each other (negative charges repel) and at the same time are attracted to positively charged regions. When two atoms are close to each other, the electrons on one atom repel the electrons on the other atom and also experience an attraction to the nucleus of the other atom (in addition to the attraction to their own nucleus). This process of repelling the electrons on a nearby atom is called "**polarization**" and atoms which can be polarized easily are said to have a "**high polarizability**". The polarization process sets up a very short–lived dipole. In the diagram, two adjacent helium atoms find themselves with a greater electron "density" on one side than the other, creating a slight excess of negative charge, $\delta-$, on one side and a slight excess of positive charge, $\delta+$, on the other side. ("δ" is the Greek symbol for "d" and stands for "slightly" or "a little bit.") These dipoles are extremely short–lived because the overall distribution of the charges of the electrons within the atom is constantly changing; in one instant there may be more negative charge on one side of an atom while in the next instant the distribution of charge may be more to another side. As a result of these temporary dipoles, a weak attractive force exists between the atoms.

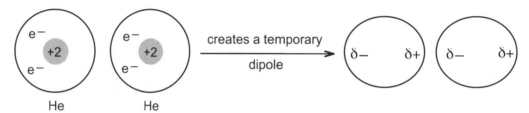

electron charge distribution is
temporarily more to one side
of the atoms than the other

In small atoms such as helium, the electrons are tightly held by the nucleus and are not easily polarized so that helium experiences very weak London forces and melts below -272°C. Similarly, the hydrogen molecule (H_2) has only two tightly–held electrons engaged in a covalent bond. The low polarizability of these electrons again gives rise to very weak London forces between adjacent H_2 molecules so that H_2(s) melts at -259°C.

LONDON FORCES ARE THE WEAKEST TYPE OF BONDING FORCE KNOWN. The rule governing the strength of London forces is simple and without any exceptions.

> The **more** electrons an atom or molecule has altogether, the **stronger** the London forces existing between it and a neighbouring atom or molecule.
>
> In other words: **the greater the atomic number of an atom, the stronger the London forces it experiences.**

SPECIAL NOTE: London forces are ALWAYS present, even in species which have covalent or ionic bonding.

EXERCISE:

73. What happens to the strength of the London forces between two identical atoms going
    (a) down a column in the periodic table?   (b) left to right across the periodic table?

HOW CAN I TELL WHEN LONDON FORCES ARE IMPORTANT?

London forces are always present, but are much weaker than covalent and ionic bonds. Hence, London forces are important when they are the **ONLY** force of attraction existing between two species. That is, London forces are important between the following closed–shell species:

a) adjacent noble gas atoms, and
b) adjacent covalently–bonded molecules (made up of atoms having a full shell after bonding).

EXAMPLE: London forces hold the following species together in the solid or liquid phase.

$$Kr(s), H_2(l), H_2(s), Cl_2(s), O_2(l), He(l), CH_4(l)$$

Notice that in each case the species are either noble gases (He & Kr), or molecules made up of covalently–bonded atoms having filled shells (H_2, Cl_2, O_2 & CH_4). In the case of liquid hydrogen, the bonding present resembles the figure below.

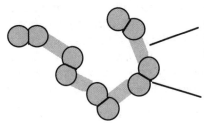

weak London forces hold the hydrogen molecules next to each other to form the liquid phase

strong covalent bonds hold the H atoms together to form hydrogen molecules

EXERCISES:

74. Are London forces INTERMOLECULAR or INTRAMOLECULAR forces?

75. The F atoms in a single molecule of F_2 are held together by covalent bonding. A sample of $F_2(l)$ consists of F_2 molecules held next to each other by London forces. When a sample of $F_2(l)$ boils and becomes $F_2(g)$, are the covalent bonds between F atoms or the London forces between F_2 molecules broken? Why does this occur?

76. What should happen to the melting and boiling temperatures of atoms held together by London forces when the atomic number of the atoms increases?

77. The following substances rely on London forces to hold them in the liquid phase. Which substance in each pair should have a higher boiling temperature?
    (a) Ne or Ar   (b) Br_2 or Cl_2 (c) CH_4 or CF_4 (d) CBr_4 or CCl_4

78. In response to a request to "write an equation showing what happens when $H_2(s)$ melts", a student writes the following:

$$H_2(s) \longrightarrow 2 H(l).$$

What does this equation incorrectly imply about the bonds and forces in a sample of $H_2(s)$?

SUMMARY II : IONIC BONDING, COVALENT BONDING & LONDON FORCES

Ionic Bonding

Ionic bonds involve the electrostatic attraction of positive ions for negative ions.
Ionic bonds exist between metals and nonmetals.
Ionic bonds are very strong and ionic compounds have high melting points.
The greater the radius of the ions, the weaker the ionic bond strength.
The greater the charge on the ions, the stronger the ionic bond strength.

Electronegativity is the tendency of an atom to attract the electrons of a neighbouring atom.
Electronegativity increases going from left to right across each period of the periodic table.
Electronegativity decreases going down each family of the periodic table.
Atoms with high electronegativities have high ionization energies; atoms with low electronegativities have low ionization energies.

Positive ions are smaller in size than the corresponding neutral atoms; negative ions are larger.

Covalent Bonding

Covalent bonds involve the sharing of electrons by two nonmetal atoms.
Covalent bonds are very strong; compounds with only covalent bonds have high melting points.
Covalent bonding allows atoms to attain the same number of electrons as a noble gas.
The more electrons shared in a covalent bond, the stronger the bond.
The larger the atoms involved in a covalent bond, the weaker the bond.
The larger the number of shared electrons in a covalent bond, the shorter the bond length.

Comparing and Contrasting Covalent and Ionic Bonds

IONIC and COVALENT bonds are *similar* in that:
   • their bonds are strong (generally).
   • their bond strength DECREASES going down a family of the periodic table.
   • their bond strength INCREASES as the VALENCE of the atoms increases.

IONIC and COVALENT bonds are *different* in that:
   • IONIC bonds are formed between a METAL and a NONMETAL.
   • COVALENT bonds are formed between two NONMETALS.

London Forces

London forces are extremely weak intermolecular forces.
London forces increase as the number of electrons in an atom or molecule increase.
London forces are important between two closed–shell species.

SUMMARY EXERCISES:

79. What type of bond would be expected to form between atoms of each of the following?
    (a) H and O   (c) Ni and Cl   (e) Ca and Br   (g) I and F
    (b) K and I   (d) P and O   (f) N and F

80. Which of the following should have a higher electronegativity?
    (a) F or I   (b) Rb or Li   (c) Si or Cl   (d) Na or Si   (e) Sn or S   (f) N or Sb

81. Which of the following would be expected to form a stronger bond?
    (a) Na^+Cl^- or K^+Br^- (c) K^+F^- or $Ca^{2+}O^{2-}$ (e) C–C or Si–Si
    (b) C–O or Si–S   (d) Cs^+I^- or $Mg^{2+}O^{2-}$ (f) B–F or $N \equiv N$ ($N \equiv N$ shares 6 electrons)

82. Which of ionic bonding, covalent bonding and London forces does NOT involve the sharing of electrons in some way?

83. Which is expected to be larger?
    (a) Na^+ or Na^- (c) As or As^{3-} (e) Se^- or S   (g) Ca^{2+} or Se^{2-} (i) K^+ or Cl^-
    (b) I or I^+ (d) Na^+ or Cs^+ (f) S^{2-} or S (h) O^{2-} or S^{2-}

84. Which of ionic bonding, covalent bonding or London forces are most important in holding each
of the following substances together in the solid phase?

(a) $N_2(s)$; melts at $-210^{\circ}C$ (c) $CS_2(s)$; melts at $-111^{\circ}C$ (e) $CaCl_2(s)$; melts at $782^{\circ}C$

(b) RbBr; melts at $693^{\circ}C$ (d) Ge(s); a network structure   (f) Xe(s); melts at $-112^{\circ}C$
which melts at $937^{\circ}C$

C. WRITING LEWIS STRUCTURES

a) The Lewis Structures of Simple Ionic Compounds

The Lewis Structure of an ionic compound is simple to construct. You previously have been shown
some example structures for such compounds; this section extends the previous work.

EXAMPLE: Draw the Lewis Structure of $MgCl_2$.

First, determine the charge expected for each ion. In this case, the ions are Mg^{2+}
and Cl^-.

For the purposes of Chemistry 11, the nonmetal ions are symmetrically arranged
around the metal ion. Remove the two electrons from the Mg atom to form the Mg^{2+}
ion. Add one electron to each Cl atom to form the Cl^- ion.

$$\overset{\displaystyle ..}{\underset{\displaystyle ..}{:\ Cl^-\ :}} \qquad Mg^{2+} \qquad \overset{\displaystyle ..}{\underset{\displaystyle ..}{:\ Cl^-\ :}}$$

EXERCISE:

85. Draw the Lewis Structure of each of the following ionic compounds.

(a) KBr   (b) $AlCl_3$ (c) MgO   (d) Li_2S (e) K_3P

b) The Lewis Structures of Covalent Compounds that Obey the Octet Rule

Lewis Structures show how the *VALENCE* electrons are distributed in a molecule. The octet rule
states that most atoms, other than hydrogen, tend to attain an octet of electrons as a result of
forming covalent bonds.

EXAMPLE: The Lewis structure of H_2O is shown below.

$$\overset{\displaystyle ..}{\underset{\displaystyle ..}{H:O:}}$$
$$H$$

For water, above, H and O contribute one electron each to the covalent bonds between them and
share the two electrons in the bond. Each H can then "lay claim" to a *closed shell* of 2 electrons.
The O atom has 4 electrons which it does not share with the H's in addition to the 4 electrons
shared with the H's, for a total of 8 electrons: a closed shell and a "full octet".

Drawing the Lewis Structures of molecules follows a simple set of rules.

THE "RULES OF THE GAME"

A. Count up the total number of **valence** electrons in the molecule. Adjust this number by SUBTRACTING one electron for every POSITIVE charge and ADDING one electron for every NEGATIVE charge on the molecule.

B. Determine which atoms are bonded together and put 2 electrons into each bond.
    Note: You will always be shown which atoms are connected to which other atoms.

C. Use the remaining valence electrons to complete the octets of the atoms surrounding the central atom(s). Then place any remaining electrons, in pairs, on the central atom(s).

D. If a central atom has less than an octet of electrons, have a neighbour share electrons with the "deficient" atom by putting an extra pair (or pairs) of electrons into the shared bond.

E. Tidy up: replace each pair of electrons engaged in a bond with a dash, "—".

EXAMPLES:

NH_4^+ This molecule has 8 valence electrons: N has 5, each of the 4 H's have 1, and one electron is removed to make a +1 charge.

The atoms connected together are shown below ("""" indicates a bond).

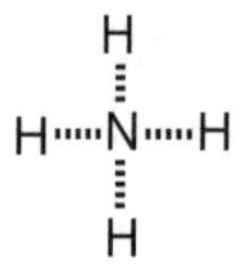

$$\begin{array}{c} H \\ \vdots \\ H\cdots N\cdots H \\ \vdots \\ H \end{array}$$

First, assign 2 electrons to each bond.

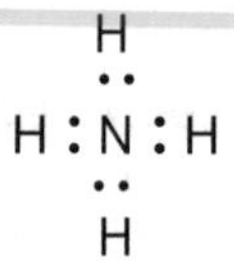

$$\begin{array}{c} H \\ \cdot\cdot \\ H : N : H \\ \cdot\cdot \\ H \end{array}$$

A check shows that each H has its required 2 electrons (2 electrons is a full shell for H) and the N has an octet of 8 electrons. The structure is finished, apart from tidying up by replacing each pair of electrons in a bond with a "dash" and adding the charge.

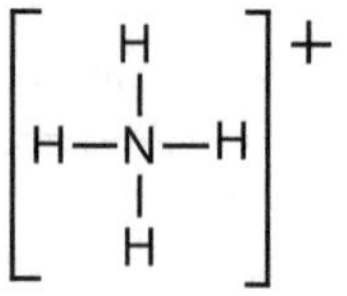

$$\left[\begin{array}{c} H \\ | \\ H-N-H \\ | \\ H \end{array} \right]^+$$

CHO_2^- This molecule has 18 valence electrons: C has 4, H has 1, each of the 2 O's have 6, and one extra electron is added to make a –1 charge.

The atoms which are connected are shown below.

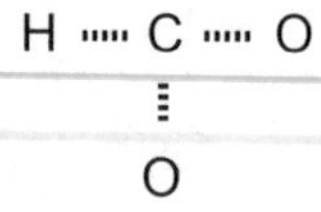

$$\begin{array}{c} H \cdots C \cdots O \\ \vdots \\ O \end{array}$$

First, assign 2 electrons to each bond.

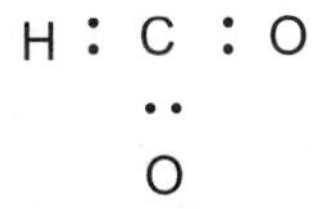

$$H : C : O$$
$$\overset{..}{O}$$

Second, fill the octets on each O attached to the central C.

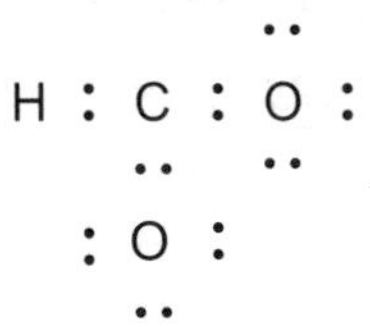

$$\overset{..}{H : C : \overset{..}{O} :}$$
$$: \overset{..}{O} :$$

All of the 18 available electrons have been distributed, but the central carbon atom does not yet have a full octet (it only has 6 electrons). Arbitrarily let one of the oxygens donate an extra 2 electrons to a bond shared with carbon.

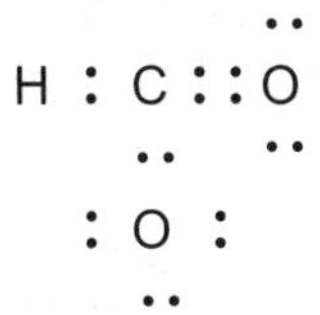

$$H : C :: \overset{..}{O} \qquad \text{or, alternately} \qquad H : C : \overset{..}{O} :$$
$$: \overset{..}{O} : \qquad\qquad\qquad\qquad\qquad : \overset{..}{O} :$$

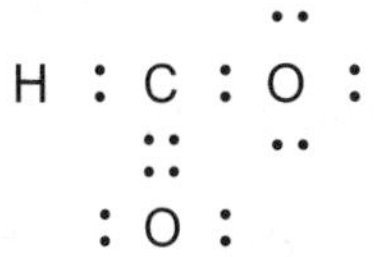

Replacing each pair of electrons in a bond with a "dash" and adding the charge gives the finished structure.

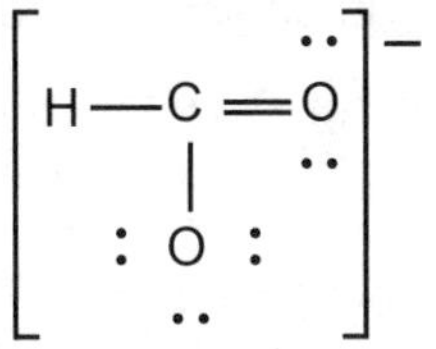

$$\left[H - C = \overset{..}{O} \atop : \overset{..}{O} : \right]^{-} \qquad \text{or, alternately} \qquad \left[H - C - \overset{..}{O} : \atop : \overset{..}{O} : \right]^{-}$$

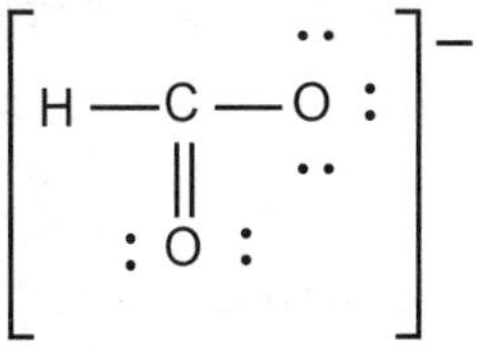

HOPO   This molecule has 18 valence electrons: H has 1, P has 5 and each O has 6.

The atoms are connected as shown below.

$$H \cdots O \cdots P \cdots O$$

First, assign 2 electrons to each bond.

$$H : O : P : O$$

Second, fill the octets on the outer O's attached to the "central" P.

$$H : \overset{..}{\underset{..}{O}} : P : \overset{..}{\underset{..}{O}} :$$

At this point, 16 out of the 18 electrons available are now used. The remaining 2 electrons are put on the central P atom.

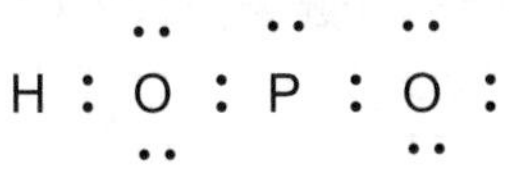

$$H : \overset{..}{\underset{..}{O}} : \overset{..}{P} : \overset{..}{\underset{..}{O}} :$$

The central P atom only has 6 electrons and needs another 2 electrons to be donated by one or the other of the attached oxygens.

• If the left oxygen donates 2 electrons the structure below results.

$$H : \overset{..}{\underset{..}{O}} :: \overset{..}{P} : \overset{..}{\underset{..}{O}} :$$

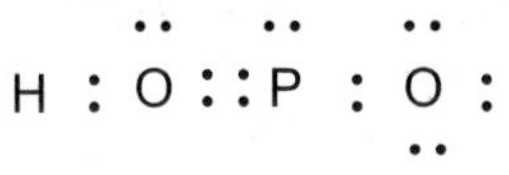

• If the right oxygen donates 2 electrons the structure below results.

$$\overset{\displaystyle \cdot\cdot \quad\quad \cdot\cdot \quad\quad \cdot\cdot}{H \; : \; O \; : \; P \; :: \; O}$$
$$\underset{\displaystyle \cdot\cdot \quad\quad\quad\quad \cdot\cdot}{}$$

Note: Either answer is considered to be correct; they are alternate ways to represent the Lewis structure and the actual situation within the molecule will act as if it were an average of the two structures.

Tidy up by substituting a "dash" for each pair of bond electrons.

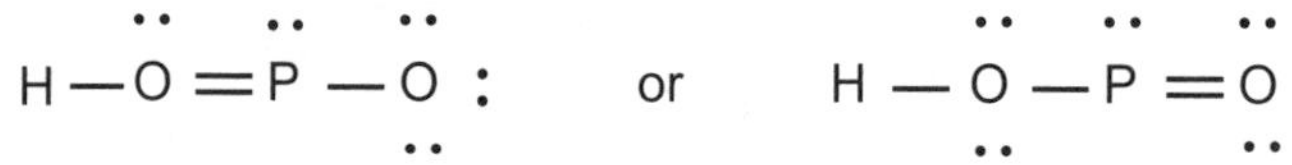

$$H—O = P — O : \qquad \text{or} \qquad H — O — P = O$$

c) EXTENSION: The Lewis Structures of Covalent Compounds that Violate the Octet Rule

Electron–Deficient Molecules

In addition to **H**, the atoms **Be, B** and **Al** are exceptions to the tendency for covalently–bonded atoms to complete their octets. These atoms have such low electronegativities that the best that they can do is to **GAIN ONE EXTRA ELECTRON IN A COVALENT BOND FOR EVERY ELECTRON THEY CAN CONTRIBUTE TO THE BOND.** (They do not have sufficient electronegativity to pull extra electrons on an adjacent atom into covalent bonds.) Therefore:

Be has 2 valence electrons and can share a maximum of 4 electrons, and
B and Al have 3 valence electrons and can share a maximum of 6 electrons.

Definition: A molecule in which one or more atoms (other than hydrogen) does not possess a full octet of electrons is called an **ELECTRON–DEFICIENT** molecule.

BF_3, below, is an example of an electron-deficient molecule because the central B atom only has 6 valence electrons after bonding.

EXAMPLE: Draw the Lewis Structure of **BF_3**.

This molecule has   3 (B) + 3 x 7 (F) = 24 valence electrons.

The atoms are connected as shown below.

$$F \;\text{''''}\; B \;\text{''''}\; F$$
$$\vdots$$
$$F$$

First, assign 2 electrons to each bond.

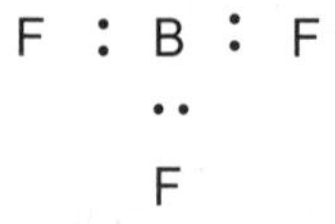

$$F \; : \; B \; \overset{\displaystyle \cdot}{:} \; F$$
$$\underset{\displaystyle \cdot\cdot}{}$$
$$F$$

Second, complete the octets of the outer fluorines attached to the central B.

$$: \overset{\bullet\bullet}{\underset{\bullet\bullet}{F}} : B : \overset{\bullet\bullet}{\underset{\bullet\bullet}{F}} :$$

$$: \overset{}{\underset{\bullet\bullet}{F}} :$$

All 24 of the available valence electrons have now been assigned. **No attempt is made to try to fill the octet of the central boron: recall that atoms in column 3 have 3 valence electrons and only get up to a maximum of 6 electrons after bonding occurs. The low electronegativity of B prevents it from attracting extra electrons from F.**

The structure is completed by substituting a dash for every pair of bond electrons.

$$: \overset{\bullet\bullet}{\underset{\bullet\bullet}{F}} — B — \overset{\bullet\bullet}{\underset{\bullet\bullet}{F}} :$$

$$| $$

$$: \overset{}{\underset{\bullet\bullet}{F}} :$$

Atoms Having an Expanded Octet of Valence Electrons

Elements in the third and fourth periods of the periodic table frequently attain more than an octet of valence electrons when they form covalent compounds. (The extra electrons are placed in low–lying d–orbitals.) Other than the fact that the central atom will end up with more than eight valence electrons, the same rules are used for forming the Lewis Structures.

EXAMPLE: Draw the Lewis Structure for PCl_5.

The chlorine atoms are connected to the central phosphorus atom.

The molecule has a total of 40 valence electrons. Two electrons are assigned to each bond and the octet of each Cl is filled.

$$:\overset{\bullet\bullet}{\underset{\bullet}{Cl}}\bullet \quad \bullet\overset{\bullet\bullet}{\underset{\bullet}{Cl}}\bullet$$

$$:\overset{\bullet\bullet}{\underset{\bullet\bullet}{Cl}}— P —\overset{\bullet\bullet}{\underset{\bullet\bullet}{Cl}}:$$

$$|$$

$$:\overset{}{\underset{\bullet\bullet}{Cl}}:$$

The phosphorus atom has an expanded octet of 10 valence electrons.

EXERCISE:

86. Assign Lewis structures to the following molecules.

(a)   H ⸺ Cl   (b)   I ⸺ I   (c)   I ⸺ Cl

(d) 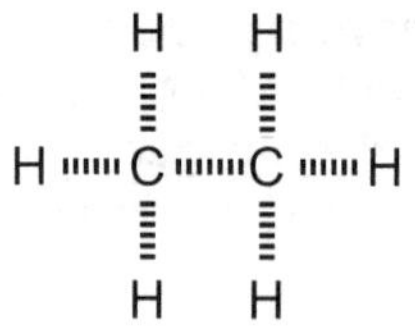
```
      H   H
      |   |
 H ── C ──C ── H
      |   |
      H   H
```

(e) 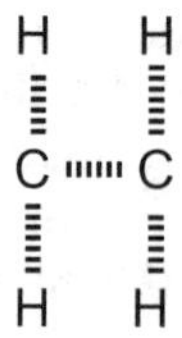
```
      H   H
      |   |
      C ──C
      |   |
      H   H
```

(f)   H ⸺ C ⸺ C ⸺ H

(g)   F ⸺ Be ⸺ F   (h)   O ⸺ O   (i)   Cl ⸺ S ⸺ Cl

(j)   N ⸺ N

(k) 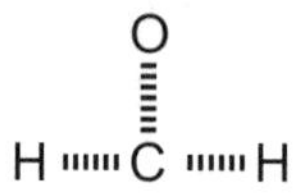
```
      O
      ‖
 H ── C ── H
```

(l) 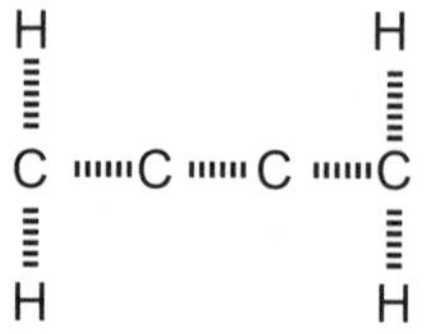
```
  H               H
  |               |
  C ──C ──C ──C
  |               |
  H               H
```

(m)   H ⸺ C ⸺ N

(n) 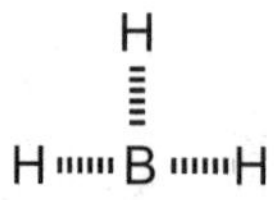
```
      H
      |
 H ── B ── H
```

(o) 
```
      S
      ‖
 H ── C ── Cl
```

(p)   [O ⸺ N ⸺ O]⁻   (q)   [N ⸺ O]⁺   (r)   H ⸺ O ⸺ N ⸺ C

(s)   [H ⸺ N ⸺ H]⁻   (t)   O ⸺ S ⸺ O   (u)   Cl ⸺ S ⸺ S ⸺ Cl

(v) 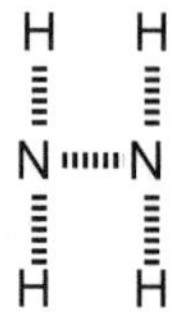
```
  H   H
  |   |
  N ──N
  |   |
  H   H
```

(w) 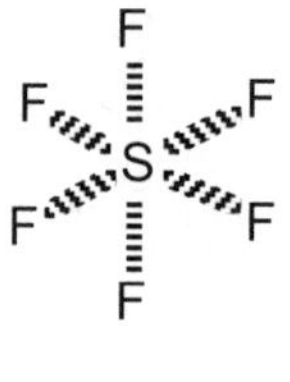
```
         F
    F    |    F
     \   |   /
      \  S  /
     /  | |  \
    F   | |   F
        F
```

(x)   [C ⸺ N ⸺ O]⁻

(y) 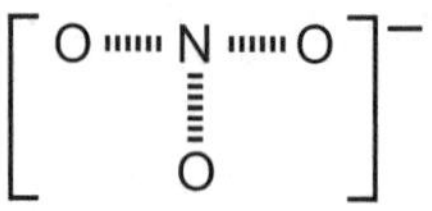
```
 ⎡          ⎤⁻
 ⎢ O ──N ──O ⎢
 ⎢     |     ⎢
 ⎢     O     ⎢
 ⎣          ⎦
```

(z) 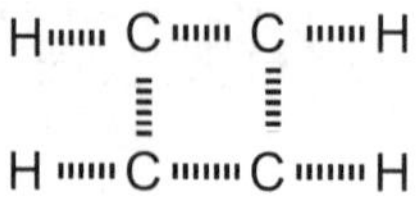
```
 H ── C ── C ── H
      |    |
 H ── C ── C ── H
```

(aa) 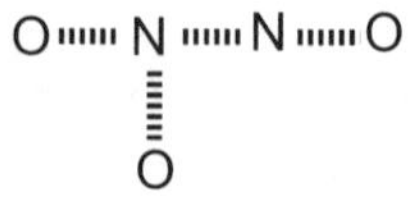
```
 O ── N ── N ── O
      |
      O
```

(bb) 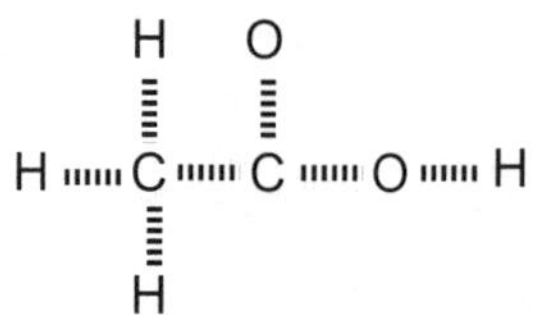
```
      H   O
      |   ‖
 H ── C ── C ── O ── H
      |
      H
```

(cc) 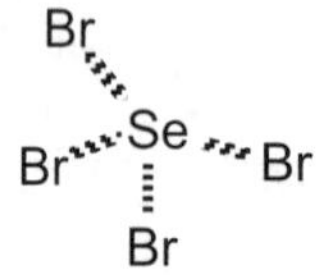
```
      Br
       \
 Br ─── Se ── Br
       |
       Br
```

VIII.4. CHEMICAL FAMILIES

Our knowledge of bonding allows us to systematically examine and review the properties of the major families/groups in the periodic table.

A. THE NOBLE GASES : He, Ne, Ar, Kr, Xe and Rn

The single most important fact regarding the noble gases is their almost total lack of chemical reactivity. The following exercises examine the properties of these gases.

EXERCISES:

87. Write the electron configurations for each of He, Ne, Ar, Kr and Xe using core notation.

88. Why are the noble gases unreactive? (Hint: how many valence electrons do they have?)

89. What type of bonding must be present to hold the noble gas atoms next to one another in the liquid or solid phase? Would you expect the melting or boiling temperatures of these elements to be high or low? Why?

90. The melting points (MP's) and boiling points (BP's) of the noble gases are shown below.

Element	MP (^{o}C)	BP (^{o}C)	Element	MP (^{o}C)	BP (^{o}C)
He	−272 (*)	−269	Kr	−157	−153
Ne	−249	−246	Xe	−112	−108
Ar	−189	−186	Rn	−71	−62

* He only forms a solid at −272°C and 26 atm pressure

How can the type of bonding suggested in the previous exercise account for the observed melting/boiling temperatures?

91. What should happen to the ionization energy of the noble gases going down the periodic table from He to Rn?

92. Some of the noble gases can be made to react with fluorine gas. Which noble gas: He or Rn, would you expect to be more likely to react? Why?

93. Suggest a reason why the noble gases were among the last naturally−occurring elements to be discovered.

B. THE ALKALI METALS : Li, Na, K, Rb, Cs and Fr

The bonding occurring in metals is extremely complicated and well beyond the scope of Chemistry 11. A reasonable, but rough, approximation to the bonding situation existing in metals is to think of metals as being a regular array of atomic nuclei (and their core electrons) surrounded by a "sea" of communally−shared valence electrons which may be simultaneously attracted to several nuclei at one time. (I told you it was complicated!)

For the purposes of predicting trends in selected properties of the alkali metals (and the alkaline earth metals in the next section), it is only necessary to understand the following concepts.
  • The greater the atomic radius the less the valence electrons are attracted to adjacent nuclei.
  • Alkaline earth metals have more valence electrons than alkali metals and hence stronger bonding.

The ease with which the ALKALI METALS lose an electron dominates their physical and chemical properties.

As with the noble gases, the chemical and physical properties of the alkali metals are examined in a set of exercises (below).

EXERCISES:

94. Write the electron configurations for Li, Na, K, Rb, Cs and Fr using core notation.

95. What happens to the ease with which the alkali metals lose an electron, going down the periodic table from Li to Cs? Why?

96. What happens to an atom of lithium when it reacts; that is, what is produced? What trend in reactivity should exist going down the periodic table from Li to Fr?

97. What trend in ionization energy should exist going down the periodic table from Li to Fr?

98. The electrical conductivity of a metal is governed by the ability of its valence electrons to move freely from one atom to the next. Would you expect the alkali metals to be good or poor electrical conductors? Why?

99. Do the following observed temperatures agree with the expected trend? Why?

Element	MP (^{o}C)	BP (^{o}C)	Element	MP (^{o}C)	BP (^{o}C)
Li	181	1342	Rb	39	688
Na	98	883	Cs	28	671
K	64	759			

C. THE ALKALINE EARTH METALS : Be, Mg, Ca, Sr, Ba and Ra

The properties of the alkaline earth metals are similar to those of the alkali metals. The differences between the properties of the two related families are due to the fact that the alkaline earth metals form +2 ions, rather than +1 ions.

EXERCISES:

100. Would you expect the alkaline earth metals to be more or less reactive than their alkali metal counterparts? Hint: what has to be done to form the ions of the metals in each family?

101. Suggest the trends for the alkaline earth metals which should occur in the following properties when going down the table.
(a) melting/boiling temperature   (b) reactivity   (c) ionization energy

The observed melting/boiling temperatures for the alkaline earth metals are shown below.

Element	MP (^{o}C)	BP (^{o}C)	Element	MP (^{o}C)	BP (^{o}C)
Be	1289	2472	Sr	769	1384
Mg	650	1090	Ba	729	1805
Ca	842	1494	Ra	700	1140

Which metal or metals seem to be exceptions to the predicted trend?

D. THE HALOGENS : F_2, Cl_2, Br_2 and I_2

The following properties are observed for the halogens at room temperature.

- Fluorine is a pale green–yellow gas having the highest reactivity of any element: it reacts with every element except some of the noble gases.
- Chlorine is highly reactive, but less so than fluorine, and has a pale green–yellow colour.
- Bromine is a dark red–brown liquid having a reactivity less than that of chlorine.
- Iodine is a violet–black solid having a slightly metallic lustre and a reactivity substantially less than that of bromine.

EXERCISES:

102. Based on the phases of the halogens at room temperature, described above, what can you conclude about the trend in melting/boiling temperatures going down the halogens?

103. The observed melting/boiling temperatures are as follows.

Element	MP ($^{\circ}$C)	BP ($^{\circ}$C)	Element	MP ($^{\circ}$C)	BP ($^{\circ}$C)
F_2	−220	−188	Br_2	−7	59
Cl_2	−101	−35	I_2	114	184

Based on the melting/boiling temperatures, what type of INTERMOLECULAR bonding must exist between individual halogen molecules?

104. What ion is formed when a halogen atom reacts? How could you explain the observed reactivity of the halogens?

105. What trend in ionization energy should exist going down the halogen family in the periodic table? Why?

COMBINED EXERCISES FOR "CHEMICAL BONDING" and "CHEMICAL FAMILIES"

The following set of exercises gives you a chance to work on the material from previous sections in a "jumbled" manner, without clues gained from knowing that a given exercise must relate to a particular section.

106. Define the following terms.
    (a) valence electron
    (b) open shell
    (c) intermolecular bond
    (d) electronegativity
    (e) covalent bond
    (f) intramolecular bond
    (g) valence (as a noun)
    (h) ionic bond
    (i) London force

107. Which atom is bigger: Pb or Si? Why?

108. Why does the melting temperature **increase** going down the halogen family, whereas the melting temperature **decreases** going down the alkali metals?

109. Molecules of N_2 and O_2 both have closed shells after the atoms bond together to form a molecule. Would you expect $N_2(s)$ or $O_2(s)$ to have a higher melting temperature? Why?

110. Is it easier to break the O=O bond in O_2 or the S=S bond in S_2? Why?

111. Which atom is more electronegative: S or Te?

112. What is an ion?

113. Which ionic solid should have the higher melting temperature: AlN(s) or NaF(s)? Why?

114. Experimentally it is found that F_2 is a green-yellow gas and I_2 is a shiny blue–black solid at room temperature. Why does I_2 have a higher melting and boiling temperature than F_2?

115. How many valence electrons are possessed by each of: Se, K^-, Sn, Ge^{2+}, Br?

116. Which substance has a lower melting temperature: RbI(s) or KBr(s)? Why?

117. What is the valence of each of: S, B, Ca, Xe, Ga, Bi?

118. What is the *total* number of electrons contained in molecules of: Cl_2, O_2, CH_4, S_4, H_2SO_4?

119. How many shells (closed and open, altogether) do each of the following have? Rn, Sr^{2+}, P, I^+, Sb, Na^-, Ga^{2+}

120. Although O_2 and F_2 are about the same size, each oxygen shares 4 electrons with its neighbour while each fluorine shares 2 electrons. Which bond should be stronger: O=O or F–F? Why?

121. Which types of bonds increase in strength going down a family in the periodic table?

122. Which types of bonds decrease in strength going down a family in the periodic table?

123. Write a complete and detailed explanation of why:
    (a) the melting temperatures of the noble gases increase going down the periodic table.
    (b) the reactivity of the alkali metals increases going down the periodic table.
    (c) the reactivity of the noble gases increases going down the periodic table.
    (d) the melting temperature of the alkali metals decreases going down the periodic table.
    (e) the melting temperature of an ionic solid made from an alkali metal ion and a halide ion decreases going down the periodic table.
    (f) the reactivity of the halogens decreases going down the periodic table.

124. How many unpaired electrons are there on each of: H, C, O, He, S, N, F, Kr?

125. *If* a noble gas *could* form a +1 ion, which of the noble gases would form a +1 ion most easily?

126. What is the valence of each of: O, P, Al, Xe, Cl, Na, Ba, Ga, Se, He?

127. Which substance has the lower melting temperature: $S_4(s)$ or $S_8(s)$?

128. How many covalent bonds are atoms of each of the following expected to form: Xe, I, N, Se, B, P, C, O?

129. If all the atoms in a molecule of "X" can obtain a closed shell as a result of covalent bonding, what type of bond would hold one molecule of "X" next to another?

130. Predict the formula of the compound formed by joining each of the following?
    (a) Pb and I   (c) Al and Si   (e) Si and C
    (b) In and As   (d) N and F   (f) P and H

UNIT IX : SOLUTION CHEMISTRY

IX.1. SOLUTIONS AND SOLUBILITY

SOLUTION CHEMISTRY is the study of chemical reactions that occur in solutions. Such reactions are of great interest to chemists (and others) because solutions are frequently encountered and convenient to handle. In contrast

- reactions in the gas phase are complicated by the need to have special containers which are "air–tight".
- reactions in the solid state are generally very slow or do not occur at all.
- reactions between pure liquids are quite common, but frequently the liquids used will not mix with each other, or are too "concentrated" and react in an uncontrolled manner.

The nature of solutions allows their concentrations to be changed to suit our needs, the concentrations of the materials in solution to be determined accurately, and different solvents to be used.

The terms **solution**, **solute** and **solvent** were defined in the unit "The Physical Properties and Physical Changes of Substances", and are repeated below to aid the following discussions.

Definitions: A **SOLUTION** is a homogeneous mixture.

A **SOLVENT** is the component in a solution which exists in the greater quantity.

A **SOLUTE** is the component in a solution which exists in the smaller quantity.

This unit deals with liquid or solid SOLUTES dissolved in liquid SOLVENTS. In PURE solids, liquids and gases, the properties of each phase are governed by the interactions existing between the IDENTICAL particles which make up the phase. Solutions are more complicated than pure solids, liquids or gases because of the additional ways the solute and solvent can interact with each other. In addition, the properties of a solution can vary greatly because the concentration of the solute in a solvent can be changed.

A solute is **SOLUBLE** in a solvent if the solute and the solvent mix to form a homogeneous mixture. Once two substances are mixed and form a single phase, you know that dissolving has occurred. A solute is INSOLUBLE in a solvent if little or no solute is able to dissolve in the solvent.

Definitions: A solvent is said to be **SATURATED** with a particular solute if the solvent has dissolved as much of the solute as possible.

A solution is said to be **UNSATURATED** if it can dissolve more of the solute being added.

In a solution saturated with a solute, *there MUST be a constant amount of undissolved solute present if the solution is kept in a sealed container at a constant temperature*. (The amount of undissolved solute present is unimportant just as long as some undissolved solute is present.) If the temperature is increased, more solute usually dissolves and the solution becomes UNSATURATED.

Definition: The **SOLUBILITY** of a solute is the maximum amount of the solute which can dissolve in a given amount of solvent at a given temperature.

In other words, the solubility of a substance is the amount of substance needed to saturate a solution.

EXAMPLE: The solubility of $Ba(NO_2)_2 \cdot H_2O$ is: 63 g/100 mL of H_2O at $20^{\circ}C$,
109.6 g/100 mL of H_2O at $80^{\circ}C$, and
1.6 g/100 mL of alcohol at $20^{\circ}C$.

Therefore, when defining solubility you MUST specify the following information.
- the solute being used
- the amount of solute used
- the solvent being used
- the amount of solvent used
- the temperature of the solution

EXERCISES:

1. You have a solution of NaCl in water. The solution was made a week before being given to you. How could you tell if the solution is saturated? Would your answer change if the salt is added to the water only a few seconds before being given to you? Why?

2. Based on your own experiences, can you dissolve more of a substance in cold or hot water? If you had a saturated solution, would you expect to have to heat or cool the saturated solution to make it unsaturated?

3. Give 3 examples of solutions which exist in nature.

4. Glass containers are frequently used when making and storing solutions. Two important properties which explain the usefulness of glass are its transparency and its ability to be molded into various useful shapes. What other important property does glass have which makes it useful for dealing with aqueous solutions? [HINT: Why can't you make a suitable container from melted and molded SUGAR?]

HOME EXPERIMENT

Part 1: Add 3 teaspoons of room temperature water to a clear drinking glass and let the water sit for a minute until air bubbles have left the water. Then add one teaspoon of salt to the water WITHOUT STIRRING. Wait three minutes, then hold the glass up to a light, level with your eyes, so that you can see through the solution with the light behind. Gently tilt the glass back and forth and record what you see.

_____

_____

This effect is called "schlieren" and is related to heat waves you see above a hot road. The schlieren are caused by light passing through regions having different densities.

Question: Why should there be regions of different densities in the salt water?

_____

_____

Part 2: Take the mixture from Part 1 and stir it occasionally for ten minutes, to make an almost saturated solution. (Hint: if the mixture has been standing for a while and you CANNOT observe any schlieren effect when the glass is tilted, then the solution is saturated. The less the schlieren effect, the closer to saturation.) Pour off the liquid into a separate clear drinking glass.

Problem: If this solution is saturated, will it dissolve some sugar? Add a "pinch" of sugar, stir occasionally for a few minutes and check to see if any sugar seems to have dissolved. Bring your results to class next day.

Summary of Classroom Discussion:

_____

_____

_____

_____

_____

_____

_____

IX.2. THE CONDUCTIVITY OF AQUEOUS SOLUTIONS

Recall that atoms or molecules having an electric charge are called IONS. This section examines the evidence for the existence of ions and the effects which ions have on solutions.

The next exercise summarizes the results of actual experiments and asks you to draw several conclusions.

EXERCISE:

5. **Part A. Conductors versus Non-Conductors**

The following apparatus is used to test the electrical conductivity of a solution.

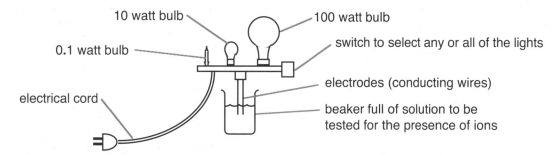

Electrical conduction in a solution requires the transferring of electrically–charged ions through the solution.

In a sample of distilled water a very small amount of the water breaks up into ions.

$$H_2O(l) \longrightarrow H^+(aq) + OH^-(aq)$$

The concentrations of the $H^+(aq)$ and $OH^-(aq)$ are both 1×10^{-7} M.

Observations:

#	Substance tested	Result
1	distilled water	only the smallest bulb glows
2	pure alcohol (C_2H_5OH)	no light on even the smallest bulb
3	1 M NaSCN	all bulbs glow brightly
4	1 M HCl	all bulbs glow brightly
5	1 M NaOH	all bulbs glow brightly
6	1 M sugar ($C_{12}H_{22}O_{11}$)	only the smallest bulb glows
7	1 M H_2SO_4	all bulbs glow brightly
8	1 M Na_3PO_4	all bulbs glow brightly
9	pure glycerine ($C_3H_5(OH)_3$)	no light on even the smallest bulb
10	1 M KOH	all bulbs glow brightly
11	pure acetone (CH_3COCH_3)	no light on even the smallest bulb

Questions:

i)   How do the observations show that pure water contains only a tiny concentration of ions?

ii) Which of compounds 1 to 11 produce **substantial** amounts of ions in solution?

iii) Does 1 M sugar appear to contain more ions than pure water? Does it appear that sugar produces ions when in water?

iv) What is true about the chemical formula of the non–conducting compounds (except H_2O)?

v) HCl and H_2SO_4 are examples of what special type of compound? KOH and NaOH are examples of what special type of compound?

vi) Based on the way you classified HCl, H_2SO_4 , KOH and NaOH, how could you classify NaCl and NH_4NO_3?

Part B. The Phase Requirements for Conductivity

Observations:

#	Substance tested	Result
1	crystals of sugar ($C_{12}H_{22}O_{11}$)	no light on even the smallest bulb
2	melted sugar	no light on even the smallest bulb
3	crystals of NaSCN	no light on even the smallest bulb
4	melted NaSCN	all bulbs glow brightly
5	solid NaOH pellets	no light on even the smallest bulb
6	melted NaOH	all bulbs glow brightly
7	solid paradichlorobenzene ($C_6H_4Cl_2$)	no light on even the smallest bulb
8	melted paradichlorobenzene	no light on even the smallest bulb
9	crystals of Na_3PO_4	no light on even the smallest bulb
10	melted Na_3PO_4	all bulbs glow brightly
11	pure liquid alcohol (C_2H_5OH)	no light on even the smallest bulb

Questions:

vii) Which compounds form conducting **solutions** in Part A **and** conducting **liquids** in Part B?

viii) What can you conclude regarding which phase **does NOT** conduct electricity? (Note that this section is only concerned with ionic conduction, not metallic conduction.)

ix) What additional requirement must be met, other than ions being present, before electrical conductivity can occur?

Part C. The Effect of Ion Concentration on Conductivity

Observations:

#	Substance tested	Result
1	1 M NaCl	all bulbs glow brightly
2	0.01 M NaCl	medium bulb glows weakly
3	0.0001 M NaCl	only smallest bulb glows

Question:

x) What relationship appears to exist between the concentration of ions in a solution and the conductivity of the solution?

Part D. The Role of Water in Conducting Solutions

Observations:

When pure acetic acid is tested for conductivity, there is no light from even the smallest bulb. As water is slowly added to the acetic acid with stirring, the smallest bulb starts to glow brighter and brighter (although the medium bulb does not glow). Continued addition of water causes the medium bulb to glow brighter and brighter and eventually the large bulb is able to glow weakly. Continued addition of water causes first the glow in the large bulb and then the glow in the medium bulb to diminish.

Questions:

xi) According to the above observations, what must happen when acetic acid is mixed with water?

xii) Why does the conductivity start to decrease after substantial amounts of water have been added?

The manner in which an ionic solution allows the conduction of electricity is discussed in detail in Chem 12. For the purposes of Chem 11, the following simplified explanation of ionic conduction can be used.

In order for electricity to flow through an electrical circuit, there must be a flow of electrical charges. When a device such as the conductivity tester shown in exercise 5 is plugged in with no electrically–conducting material filling the gap between the electrodes, no lights go on. The electrical circuit is "open" between the two electrodes, similar to an electrical switch in the "off" position. If the electrodes are placed in a solution containing ions, positively–charged ions flow toward one electrode and negatively–charged ions flow toward the other electrode. This flow of electrical charge completes the circuit and the light bulbs glow.

The following generalizations can be made with respect to the types of substances which do and do not form conducting solutions. (There are exceptions to some of these rules, but the generalities are still very useful.)

- A conducting solution contains ions; the greater the concentration of ions, the greater the conductivity.

- If a substance is made up of a METAL and a NONMETAL, the substance will form an ionic solution in water. That is, a compound made up of a METAL and a NONMETAL is **ionic**.

  Example: NaCl forms ionic solutions. Na is a metal found on the left side of the table and Cl is a nonmetal found on the right side.

- If a substance is made up of a NONMETAL and a NONMETAL, the substance will NOT form an ionic solution in water.

  Example: CS_2 does not form a conducting solution. Both C and S are found on the right hand side of the table.

- Compounds whose formulae start with a carbon atom ("organic compounds") NORMALLY do NOT form an ionic solution in water. An exception is organic acids such as acetic acid, CH_3COOH, which end in "COOH". (There are other exceptions but they will be ignored for our purposes.)

  Example: $C_{12}H_{22}O_{11}$, CH_3CH_2OH, $C_3H_5(OH)_3$ and CH_3COCH_3 are organic (their formulae start with a carbon atom) and they do not form conducting solutions.

- Acids and bases form conducting solutions in water.

  Example: HCl(aq) and NaOH(aq) form ionic solutions.

How to Decide if a Substance will be Conducting or Nonconducting	
First, is the substance a **METAL**?	If so, it conducts.
Next, is the phase a **SOLID**?	If so, it doesn't conduct.
The following assume that the substance is a liquid or in aqueous solution.	
Is the substance an **ACID** or a **BASE** (*)?	If so, it conducts.
Is the substance **IONIC**? (Is it made of a metal and a nonmetal or two known ions?)	If so, it conducts.
If none of the above	It doesn't conduct.

* Note that an organic molecule ending in OH, such as C_2H_5OH, is not a base (it is an alcohol).

EXERCISES:

6. Which of the following would you expect to form conducting ("ionic") solutions and which would form non–conducting ("non–ionic") solutions?
   (a) KI   (c) HBr   (e) CH_4 (g) CsF   (i) H_2CO_3
   (b) ICl   (d) $CaBr_2$ (f) LiOH   (h) CH_3OCH_3 (j) N_2O

7. When a compound is dissolved in water, the resulting solution DOES NOT conduct electricity. What types of compounds will produce such results?

8. Which of the following would you expect to conduct electricity? Note: some metals are included to remind you that both metals and ionic solutions conduct electricity.
   (a) KBr(s)   (e) $CH_3OH(l)$ (i) $HNO_3(aq)$ (m) $NaNO_3(s)$ (q) Hg(l)   (u) LiOH(l)
   (b) N_2 (l)   (f) Ag(s)   (j) $Ba(OH)_2(s)$ (n) HBr(s)   (r) $C_{14}H_{10}(s)$ (v) $H_3PO_4(aq)$
   (c) LiCl(aq)   (g) $HNO_3(s)$ (k) Na(l)   (o) Cu(s)   (s) $FeCl_3$ (l)   (w) $C_4H_9OH(aq)$
   (d) $AgNO_3$ (l)   (h) $Cl_2(aq)$ (l) $BaBr_2(aq)$ (p) $CO_2(s)$ (t) LiOH(aq)   (x) $K_2CrO_4(aq)$

IX.3. MOLECULAR POLARITY

The previous unit, "Atoms and the Periodic Table", discussed the role of London forces in holding together species such as the noble gases in the liquid and solid state. London forces are examples of intermolecular forces called van der Waals forces. This section examines the role of van der Waals forces in the dissolving process and the formation of solutions.

A. DIPOLE-DIPOLE FORCES

There are two main types of van der Waals forces.

- London forces (also called Heitler–London forces or London dispersion forces)
- Dipole–dipole forces

The distinction between the two types of forces is due to the *presence* or *absence* of PERMANENT DIPOLES.

Recall that: A **DIPOLE** is a partial separation of charge which exists when one end of a molecule (or bond) has a slight excess of positive charge and the other end of the molecule (or bond) has a slight excess of negative charge.

LONDON FORCES are weak attractive forces which arise as a result of temporary dipolar attractions between neighbouring atoms.

Definitions: **DIPOLE–DIPOLE FORCES** are bonding forces which exist as a result of an electrostatic attraction between molecules having permanent dipoles.

A molecule is said to be **POLAR** if there is a partial positive charge at one end of a molecule and a partial negative charge at the other end. (A molecule which is not polar is said to be "**NONPOLAR**".)

If a permanent dipole is **ABSENT** then only London forces are present.
In *dipole–dipole forces*, a permanent dipole is **PRESENT**.

The two types of intermolecular forces occur in different ways and give rise to specific effects. The previous unit discussed London forces and when they are present.

REMINDER: London forces are ALWAYS present, even in species which have dipoles and even if the species is ionic.

> A bond between two atoms with different electronegativities gives rise to a dipole. (Usually, a bond between two different atoms involves a dipole; only rarely do two different atoms in a bond have the same electronegativity.)

EXAMPLE: In the molecule H–Cl, the H has a relatively small electronegativity while Cl has a high electronegativity. As a result, the electrons in the bond are shared unequally: chlorine has a greater tendency to attract electrons than does hydrogen so that the shared electrons are preferentially attracted more toward the chlorine end.

$$H \text{——} Cl$$
$$\delta+ \quad \delta-$$

(recall that $\delta+$ means "a slight excess of positive charge" and $\delta-$ means "a slight excess of negative charge")

EXERCISE:

9. Which of the following are expected to be polar and which are expected to be nonpolar?
    (a) H–H   (b) H–O   (c) O–Cl   (d) Cl–Cl

Atoms which have very low electronegativities tend to form positive ions and are said to be "*electropositive*". For example, the alkali metals and alkaline earth metals are electropositive.

The table below shows the electronegativities of the elements. As can be seen, there is a general trend to increasing electronegativity going up a column of the periodic table and to the right along a period of the table. (There are some exceptions to this trend among the transition metals.)

ELECTRONEGATIVITIES OF THE ELEMENTS

H 2.2																
Li 1.0	Be 1.5											B 2.0	C 2.5	N 3.0	O 3.5	F 3.9
Na 0.9	Mg 1.2											Al 1.5	Si 1.8	P 2.1	S 2.4	Cl 2.8
K 0.9	Ca 1.0	Sc 1.3	Ti 1.5	V 1.6	Cr 1.6	Mn 1.5	Fe 1.8	Co 1.8	Ni 1.8	Cu 1.9	Zn 1.7	Ga 1.6	Ge 1.8	As 2.0	Se 2.4	Br 2.7
Rb 0.8	Sr 1.0	Y 1.2	Zr 1.4	Nb 1.6	Mo 1.8	Tc 1.9	Ru 2.2	Rh 2.2	Pd 2.2	Ag 1.9	Cd 1.5	In 1.7	Sn 1.8	Sb 1.9	Te 2.1	I 2.2
Cs 0.7	Ba 0.9	La-Lu 1.1	Hf 1.3	Ta 1.5	W 1.7	Re 1.9	Os 2.2	Ir 2.2	Pt 2.2	Au 2.4	Hg 1.4	Tl 1.8	Pb 1.9	Bi 1.9	Po 2.0	At 2.2
Fr 0.7	Ra 0.9															

Source: L. Pauling, The Nature of the Chemical Bond and the Structure of Molecules and Crystals, Cornell University Press, Ithica, New York, 1960. **Used by permission of the publisher**.

In addition to having dipoles present, a molecule must also possess one other property in order to be a polar molecule: *THE MOLECULE MUST BE ASYMMETRICAL.*

Definition: A molecule is **ASYMMETRICAL** if one end of the molecule differs from the other end.

EXAMPLE: The following molecules all have at least one dipole present and are *asymmetrical*, so they are **POLAR MOLECULES.**

The following molecules all have at least one dipolar bond *but* are *symmetrical*, so they are **NONPOLAR MOLECULES.**

Note that the borane molecule is actually symmetrical although it might appear that one "end" of the molecule has 2 H's and the other "end" only has one. (The 3 H's are symmetrically attached at $120°$ angles around the B.) **An intuitive way to think of symmetry is as follows.**

Pretend the central atom is a rock and each bond is a rope pulling outwards from the rock. If attached atoms have the same electronegativity, then the ropes are pulled with equal force. If the attached atoms are symmetrically arranged around the central atom, each attached atom's "pull" on the central "rock" CANCELS the pull from other "ropes" and the central rock/atom doesn't move. This complete cancellation of the "pull" by the electrons in the molecule gives rise to a NONPOLAR MOLECULE.

Using the above analogy, you should be able so see why the presence of three hydrogen atoms symmetrically arranged around the central boron of borane produce a NONPOLAR MOLECULE.

EXERCISE:

10. Which of the following molecules will be polar and which will be nonpolar?

(a) $Cl-S-Cl$ (bent)

(b) $\begin{matrix} Cl \\ | \\ B-Cl \\ | \\ Cl \end{matrix}$

(c) $\begin{matrix} H \\ | \\ H-C-Cl \\ | \\ H \end{matrix}$

(d) $H-Mg-H$

(e) $\begin{matrix} H \\ | \\ H-C-O-H \\ | \\ H \end{matrix}$

(f) $\begin{matrix} H \\ | \\ C-O \\ | \\ H \end{matrix}$

(g) $H-C\equiv C-H$

(h) $\begin{matrix} O & O-H \\ & S \\ O & O-H \end{matrix}$

Dipole–dipole forces are weak intermolecular equivalents of ionic bonds.

In an ionic bond, an electrostatic attraction exists between a positively charged ion and a neighbouring negatively charged ion. Because there is at least a full +1 charge attracting a full −1 charge, the attraction is quite strong and ionic compounds have high melting temperatures.

Dipole–dipole forces exist within any collection of polar molecules. Since a dipole–dipole force is a weak, but permanent, attraction between the slightly positive end of one molecule to the slightly negative end of another, the attraction between polar molecules is much less than the attraction between ions.

The relative strengths of interaction are: **ionic bond >> dipole–dipole force ≈ London force.**

Both dipole–dipole and London forces are weak, but if a molecule experiences a dipole–dipole force then this force is added to the London forces which are always present so that the dipole–dipole force leads to an overall increase in the attraction between molecules.

EXAMPLE: The following boiling temperatures are observed.

$$N_2(l) \quad = -196°C \quad (14 \text{ electrons, nonpolar})$$
$$O_2(l) \quad = -183°C \quad (16 \text{ electrons, nonpolar})$$
$$NO(l) = -152°C \quad (15 \text{ electrons, polar})$$

$$ICl(l) \quad = 97°C \quad (70 \text{ electrons, polar})$$
$$Br_2(l) \quad = 59°C \quad (70 \text{ electrons, nonpolar})$$

Notice that the London forces involved in the N_2, O_2 and NO are all about the same (they all have roughly the same number of electrons), while the polar NO molecule has a higher boiling temperature due to the added strength of the dipole–dipole attraction. Similarly, ICl and Br_2 have identical numbers of electrons but the added strength of the dipole– dipole attraction in ICl increases the boiling temperature.

EXERCISES:

11. Both HCl and F_2 have 18 electrons. Which substance would you expect to have a higher boiling temperature, and why?

12. Although CF_4 has 42 electrons and CHF_3 has only 34 electrons, the boiling temperature of CF_4 is $-129°C$ while that of CHF_3 is $-82°C$. Why is the boiling temperature higher for CHF_3?

B. HYDROGEN BONDING

A relatively strong type of dipole–dipole attraction exists in the case where a *hydrogen atom is covalently bonded to one of N, O or F* (each of which is highly electronegative). The strong dipole–dipole attractions between molecules containing a H–N, H–O or H–F bond are called **HYDROGEN BONDS.**

Predicting when a HYDROGEN BOND will form

HYDROGEN BONDS are formed whenever a molecule contains one or more of the bonds N–H, O–H or F–H. The formula will include one of:
 (a) HF [this is the ONLY example containing F–H],
 (b) NH_3, NH_2 or NH [for example: CH_3–NH_2, $(CH_3)_2NH$], or
 (c) H_2O, H_2O_2, or OH [for example: CH_3–OH].

EXAMPLES:

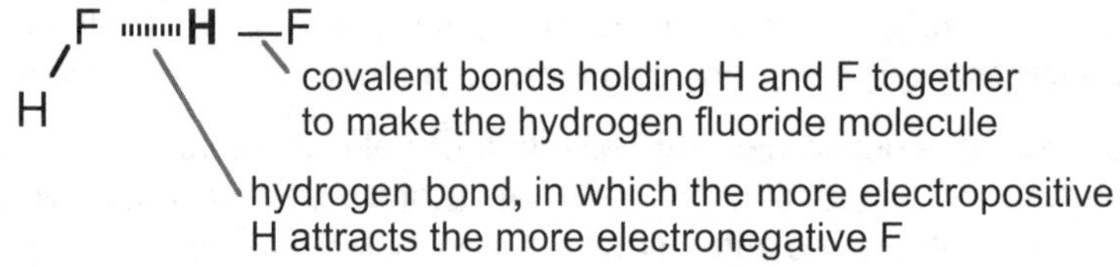

covalent bonds holding H and F together to make the hydrogen fluoride molecule

hydrogen bond, in which the more electropositive H attracts the more electronegative F

Notice that the bold H atom above is more or less *centred* between the two fluorine atoms. This central position is evidence that a hydrogen bond is quite strong. Although covalent bonds are much stronger, the hydrogen bonds are able to hold adjacent molecules closely together.

The structure of ice is shown below. The six sided structure of ice crystals can be seen as a consequence of the hexagonal arrangement of the oxygens (larger circles). This diagram shows the bonding as lying in a flat plane, whereas the structure is actually three dimensional, with alternate oxygen atoms lying above and below the plane of the paper. The hydrogen bonds are shown as broad dotted bonds.

The following diagram shows how hydrogen bonds form between two organic bases called cytosine and guanine. These molecules form part of the DNA structure present in all living things.

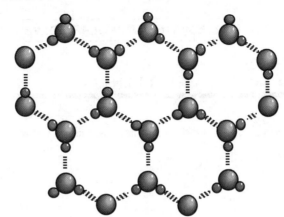

Cytosine   **Guanine**

EXERCISES:

13. Examine the following melting temperatures. All the molecules are polar.

$$NH_3 = -78^{\circ}C$$
$$PH_3 = -133^{\circ}C$$
$$AsH_3 = -116^{\circ}C$$
$$SbH_3 = -88^{\circ}C$$

(a) Why do the melting temperatures of SbH_3, AsH_3 and PH_3 steadily decrease?

(b) Why does the melting temperature of NH_3 suddenly increase going from PH_3 up to NH_3?

14. Which of the following substances would you expect to involve hydrogen bonds?

(a) CH_4 (c) H_2O (e) CH_3-NH_2 (g) CH_3-CH_2-OH
(b) HCl (d) H_2S (f) CH_3-SH (h) HF

15. Suggest a reason why liquid propane has a very low viscosity, whereas liquid glycerine has a very high viscosity.

propane = $CH_3-CH_2-CH_3$ glycerine = $\begin{array}{ccc} CH_2 & CH & CH_2 \\ | & | & | \\ OH & OH & OH \end{array}$

16. Which of the following would you expect to have the higher boiling temperature?
    (a) $CH_3–CH_2–SH$ or $CH_3–CH_2–OH$
    (b) H_2O or H_2S
    (c) CH_3NH_2 or CH_3CH_3

IS "ICE WATER" A "*POLAR* SOLVENT"?

IX.4. POLAR AND NONPOLAR SOLVENTS

Some of the more common solvents used in chemistry are listed below.

water (H_2O) =

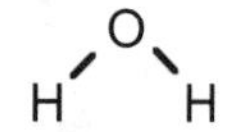

methanol (CH_3OH)

ethanol (CH_3CH_2OH)

benzene (C_6H_6) =

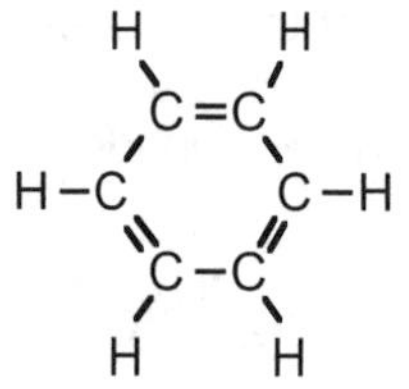

ethoxyethane (also known as diethyl ether or "hospital ether") =

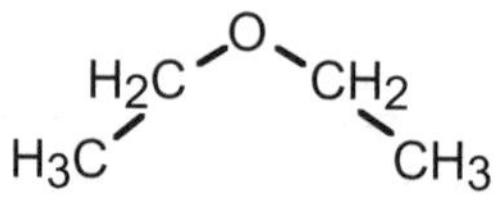

acetone (CH_3COCH_3) =

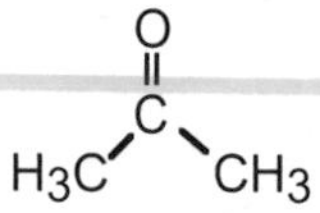

acetic acid (CH_3COOH)

chloroform ($CHCl_3$) =

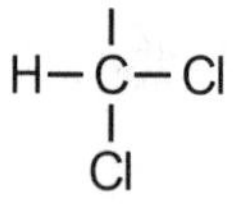

carbon tetrachloride (CCl_4) =

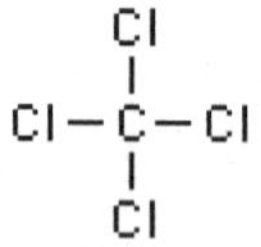

heptane (C_7H_{16}) =

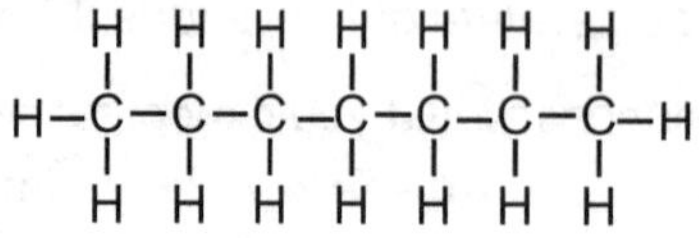

liquid ammonia (NH_3) =

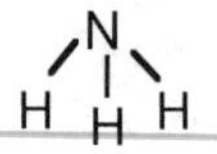

EXERCISE:

17. Classify each of the above solvents as either polar or nonpolar.

Solvent	Polar or nonpolar?	Solvent	Polar or nonpolar?	Solvent	Polar or nonpolar?
water		ethoxyethane		carbon tetrachloride	
methanol		acetone		heptane	
ethanol		acetic acid		liquid ammonia	
benzene		chloroform			

The results of extensive experiments concerned with the mixing of polar and nonpolar **solvents** with polar and nonpolar **solutes** point to the following general conclusion.

> **LIKE DISSOLVES LIKE.**

This summary statement is interpreted to mean:

- **Polar or ionic solutes tend to dissolve in polar solvents.**
- **Nonpolar solutes tend to dissolve in nonpolar solvents.**

The Reasons for "Like Dissolves Like"

A typical ionic solid is made up of alternating positive and negative ions as shown below.

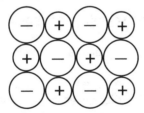

The "dissolving process" involves the interplay of three different attractions:
- the attraction of a solvent molecule to surrounding solvent molecules,
- the attraction of a solvent molecule to particles of the solute, and
- the attraction of one solute particle to other solute particles.

You know that energy must be added in order to break a bond and therefore energy is released when a bond forms. If the solvent forms sufficiently strong bonds to the solute, enough energy is produced to allow solute particles to separate from one another. The attraction of the solvent molecules to each other then allows solvent molecules attached to solute particles to be mixed into the general population of solvent molecules and dissolving occurs.

THE SOLUBILITY OF POLAR AND IONIC SOLUTES

The ionic forces holding an ionic crystal together are very strong and polar molecules in the solid phase are held next to each other by relatively strong bonds. The weak London forces of nonpolar solvents cannot exert a strong pull on the particles in crystals made up of ions or polar molecules. The weak bonds formed cannot release enough energy to overcome the strong forces holding one ion next to another in the crystal. Therefore, little or no dissolving occurs.

CONCLUSION: In general, polar and ionic solutes have low solubilities in nonpolar solvents.

Only if a solvent is polar can it strongly attract the ions or polar molecules in a crystal and perhaps release sufficient energy to overcome the forces holding the particles together in the crystal.

CONCLUSION: In general, polar and ionic solutes tend to dissolve in polar solvents.

THE SOLUBILITY OF NONPOLAR SOLUTES

Because nonpolar species do not possess positive and negative ends, there is no attraction to polar or ionic species as a result of dipole–dipole forces (or attractions between ions). Nonpolar solvents are only attracted to solute particles by London forces.

The diagram below shows $I_2(s)$, a nonpolar solid, in the solid phase and $I_2(s)$ dissolved in pentane, a nonpolar solvent.

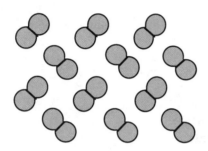   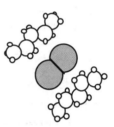

crystal of solid I_2 I_2 molecule "solvated" by pentane, C_5H_{12}

The nonpolar solvent molecule attaches itself to the nonpolar I_2 by London forces. Although the London forces are weak, they are strong enough to overcome the equally weak London forces holding the I_2 molecules to each other in the crystal.

CONCLUSION: Nonpolar solutes tend to be soluble in nonpolar solvents.

As mentioned above, nonpolar solutes cannot "feel" dipole–dipole forces. The most polar solvents, such as water, tend to have very weak London forces because they are small and possess few electrons. The weak London force of attraction between the solvent and solute is generally less than the London forces holding the solute particles together. Therefore, little or no dissolving occurs.

CONCLUSION: Nonpolar substances tend to have at most a low solubility in polar solvents.

Note: Water is one of the most polar solvents known and tends to dissolve both polar and ionic solutes. Ionic solutes are held in the solid phase by stronger bonds than polar solutes so that only the most polar solvents, such as water, are able to dissolve most ionic solutes.

Methanol, CH_3OH, has a nonpolar CH_3 group at one end and a polar OH group at the other end. Since methanol is less polar than water, ionic and polar solutes tend to be much less soluble in methanol than in water. On the other hand, because methanol is a larger molecule than H_2O and gives rise to more London forces, methanol is better able to dissolve nonpolar solutes.

Ethanol, CH_3CH_2OH, has a larger nonpolar group (CH_3CH_2) than methanol and is less polar than both water and methanol. Ionic and polar solutes are usually insoluble in ethanol while nonpolar solutes tend to be more soluble in ethanol than methanol.

EXERCISES:

18. Bromine, Br_2, is highly soluble in hexane ($C_6H_{14} = CH_3CH_2CH_2CH_2CH_2CH_3$) but only slightly soluble in water. Why might this situation occur?

19. What advantage might a molecule have as a solvent if it had a long nonpolar carbon chain ending with an ionic group, such as $CH_3CH_2CH_2CH_2CH_2CH_2CH_2COO^-Na^+$?

20. Why can't a nonpolar solvent dissolve an ionic compound?

21. Why is the polar solvent water able to dissolve small amounts of nonpolar liquid pentane, $C_5H_{12}(l)$?

22. You have water, methanol (CH_3OH) and ethanol (CH_3CH_2OH) available to act as solvents. Which of these three solvents do you expect to dissolve the greatest amount of each of the following?
    (a) KCl   (b) $CH_3CH_2CH_2CH_2Br$ (c) octane ($CH_3CH_2CH_2CH_2CH_2CH_2CH_2CH_3$)

SUMMARY: "MOLECULAR POLARITY" and "POLAR and NONPOLAR SOLVENTS"

London forces

London forces arise from temporary dipoles existing when electrons on one atom temporarily repel the electrons and attract the nucleus of an adjacent atom: the more electrons in an atom or molecule, the stronger the London forces.

London forces are weak intermolecular attractions. (Substances bonded together with London forces melt and boil at low temperatures. If individual **covalently–bonded** molecules are held together by **LONDON FORCES**, then melting and boiling involve breaking the London attraction rather than the stronger covalent bonds.)

London forces are always present but are most important if no other bond exists between two particles.

Dipole–Dipole Forces

Dipole–dipole forces arise when a permanent dipole on one molecule experiences electrostatic attraction for a permanent dipole on another molecule.

Dipole–dipole forces are about as strong as London forces, but weaker than hydrogen bonds and much weaker than covalent or ionic bonds.

A bond dipole arises when two atoms with different electronegativities are covalently bonded. The negative end of the dipole exists at the more electronegative atom and the positive end at the more electropositive atom.

A polar molecule exists whenever the molecule has bond dipoles and is ASYMMETRICAL.

Hydrogen Bonding

Hydrogen bonds only exist between molecules possessing NH, OH or HF bonds.

Hydrogen bonds are simply strong dipole–dipole bonds.

Hydrogen bonds are the strongest van der Waals bonds but still weaker than covalent or ionic bonds.

Polar and Nonpolar Solvents

"Like–dissolves–like" means polar and ionic solutes are most soluble in polar solvents, and nonpolar solutes are most soluble in nonpolar solvents.

Polar and ionic solutes have relatively strong bonds holding the solid together and only polar solvents have sufficient attraction to the solute to be able to pull the solute out of a crystal and into solution.

Nonpolar solutes require solvents with sufficient London forces to remove the solute from the crystal and into solution; polar solvents tend to have small London forces while nonpolar solvents tend to have large London forces.

How to Distinguish the Most Important Bonds or Forces Holding Substances Together

IONIC BOND – the substance is an ionic crystal (made of metal and nonmetal atoms or recognizable ions)
eg. $NaCl(s)$, $NH_4NO_3(s)$

COVALENT BOND – the bond in question is intramolecular (bond holds two atoms together IN a molecule)
eg. C–H in CH_4

The remaining types of bonding are all intermolecular (bonds **between** existing molecules)

HYDROGEN BONDS – look for HF or any molecule having OH or NH in its formula

If not present then

DIPOLE–DIPOLE FORCE – look for an asymmetric molecule

If not present then

LONDON FORCE is all that is present

SUMMARY EXERCISES:

23. Classify each of the following with respect to the *most important* type(s) of bonding or force(s) existing **between** the particles.
    (a) 2 molecules of O_2 in $O_2(s)$
    (b) 2 atoms of Xe in Xe(s)
    (c) 2 molecules of BrCl in BrCl(l)
    (d) 2 molecules of $CH_3CH_2NH_2$ in $CH_3CH_2NH_2(l)$
    (e) an atom of C and an atom of Cl in CCl_4
    (f) 2 molecules of BF_3 (symmetric) in $BF_3(l)$
    (g) 2 molecules of CH_3F in $CH_3F(l)$
    (h) 2 molecules of CCl_4 (symmetric) in $CCl_4(l)$
    (i) 2 molecules of NOCl in NOCl(s)
    (j) F and Cs in CsF(s)
    (k) 2 molecules of NH_2OH in $NH_2OH(l)$
    (l) atoms of He and Kr

24. Which should melt at a higher temperature?
    (a) He or Xe
    (b) HBr or Kr
    (c) CH_3-CH_3 or HO-CH_2CH_2-OH
    (d) F_2 or Br_2
    (e) CH_4 or CCl_4
    (f) H_2O or H_2Te
    (g) CH_4 or CH_3F
    (h) HI or HCl

25. Octane, $CH_3CH_2CH_2CH_2CH_2CH_2CH_2CH_3$, should be a good solvent for which of the following?
    (a) $I_2(s)$ (b) NaCl(s)   (c) $H_2O(l)$ (d) $C_{10}H_8(s)$ (symmetric)

26. You have the task of preparing several different solutions, each of which must contain at least moderate amounts of one of the following chemicals: iodine (I_2), sodium nitrate ($NaNO_3$), carbon disulphide (S=C=S), formaldehyde (H_2C=O; polar) and sulphur (S_8 ; forms a ring of sulphur atoms). The solvents available are: water, ethanol, acetone, heptane and carbon tetrachloride – see the section "Polar and Nonpolar Solvents" for the structures and polar versus nonpolar characteristics. Which of the solvents would you expect to be solvents for each of the chemicals?

27. You have three beakers labelled A, B and C and three flasks labelled X, Y and Z. The beakers contain, in no particular order: naphthalene (nonpolar), benzoic acid (polar) and sodium chloride (ionic). **Flask X is known to contain water** and flasks Y and Z contain different unknown liquids. Each entry in the body of the table below shows the effect of mixing the powder at the top of each column with the liquid at the left of each row.

	Powder "A"	Powder "B"	Powder "C"
Liquid "X"	Soluble	Slightly soluble	Insoluble
Liquid "Y"	Insoluble	Fairly soluble	Soluble
Liquid "Z"	Insoluble	Soluble	Soluble

Identify each of A, B and C and classify each of solvents X, Y and Z as being nonpolar or polar.

IX.5. THE NATURE OF SOLUTIONS OF IONS

The process of dissolving is actually quite complex at the molecular level. You may see salt or sugar dissolving and say that they have "gone into solution", but young children may say that the salt or sugar "disappeared". A quick taste of the salt or sugar solution reminds you that the salt or sugar still exists. What is happening in the solution? In order to answer that question with any accuracy, a bit of additional background information will be needed.

The formation of a solution depends on the ability of the solute to dissolve in the solvent.

Definitions: **SOLVATION** is the interaction between a solute and a solvent.

An **IONIC SOLID** is a solid whose crystal structure is made up of ions.

A **MOLECULAR SOLID** is a solid whose crystal structure is made of neutral molecules.

As was shown in the section "Polar and Nonpolar Solvents", the nature of the interaction between the solvent and the solute determines the extent to which the solute dissolves in the solvent.

The dissolving of an ionic solid such as NaCl by a solvent such as H_2O occurs as a result of solvent molecules attaching themselves to ions in the **CRYSTAL LATTICE** (that is, the orderly arrangement of particles which exists within a crystal.)

EXAMPLE: In a crystal of NaCl(s), each Na^+ is surrounded by Cl^- ions, and each Cl^- is in turn surrounded by Na^+ ions, so as to form an ionic crystal as shown in the figure below.

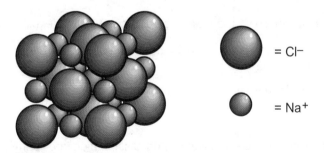

Water molecules are "V–shaped", as shown below. The polarity of the dipoles is also shown.

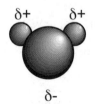

The "negative ends" of the polar H_2O molecules are attracted to the positive ions in an ionic crystal and the "positive ends" of molecules are attracted to the negative ions in the crystal. When water is added to NaCl crystals, many water molecules bond to the ions and release sufficient energy to pull one ion after another away from the rest of the ions in the crystal, causing the crystal to dissolve. In the figure below, a "dotted line" indicates a bond between a water molecule and an ion. (The ions and molecules are shown to scale.)

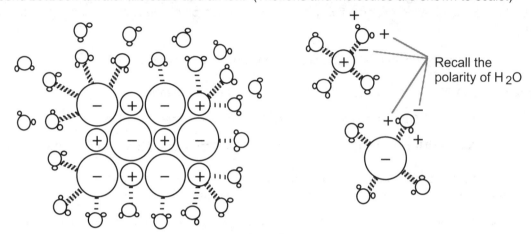

Recall the polarity of H_2O

Definitions: A **DISSOCIATION** reaction involves separating previously–existing ions in an ionic solid.

> Since the ions already exist in a dissociation reaction, the solvent is merely separating the ions from one another.

> *Example:* $NaCl(s) \longrightarrow Na^+(aq) + Cl^-(aq)$

An **IONIZATION** reaction involves the breaking up of a neutral molecule into ions.

> In an ionization reaction, ions do not exist until the solvent is able to react with the molecule and break it apart into ions.

> *Example:* $CH_3COOH(l) \longrightarrow CH_3COO^-(aq) + H^+(aq)$

Both dissociation and ionization reactions produce electrically–conducting ionic solutions.

The actual form of the equations used to show ionization and dissociation are identical. In both cases the species to be ionized or dissociated are shown on the reactant side and the resulting ions are shown on the product side. You are not required to predict whether a substance undergoes dissociation versus ionization.

EXAMPLES: Write an equation to show the dissociation of $FeBr_3(s)$ in water.

> Because $FeBr_3$ is composed of Fe^{3+} and three Br^- ions, the dissociation reaction is:

> $FeBr_3(s) \longrightarrow Fe^{3+}(aq) + 3\ Br^-(aq)$.

> Write an equation to show the ionization of $HCN(g)$ in water.

> When HCN ionizes, H^+ and CN^- are formed.

> $HCN(g) \longrightarrow H^+(aq) + CN^-(aq)$

EXERCISE:

28. Write an equation to show the dissociation/ionization of each of the following.
   (a) $KBr(s)$ (c) $Na_2SO_4(s)$ (e) $Al_2(SO_4)_3(s)$ (g) $AlCl_3(s)$
   (b) $HCl(g)$ (d) $Ca(OH)_2(s)$ (f) $K_3PO_4(s)$ (h) $(NH_4)_2S(s)$

29. The most commonly used solvent in chemistry is water. Suggest some reasons why water is such a common solvent.

IX.6. CALCULATING THE CONCENTRATIONS OF IONS IN SOLUTION

You have previously seen how to calculate the molarity of substances in solution and how to calculate the molarity of substances after dilution occurs. This section will extend your knowledge so you will be able to calculate the concentrations of ions in solutions.

EXAMPLE: What is the molar concentration of the chloride ions in 0.25 M $AlCl_3(aq)$?

$AlCl_3(aq)$ is an ionic compound which releases 3 Cl^- ions in water for every molecule of $AlCl_3$ which dissolves.

$$AlCl_3(s) \longrightarrow Al^{3+}(aq) + 3\ Cl^-(aq)$$

Therefore: $[Cl^-] = 0.25\ \dfrac{mol\ AlCl_3}{1\ L}\ \times\ \dfrac{3\ mol\ Cl^-}{1\ mol\ AlCl_3} = \mathbf{0.75\ M}$

An alternate way to carry out this calculation is as follows. Since 1 mol of $AlCl_3$ produces 1 mol of Al^{3+} and 3 moles of Cl^-:

$$AlCl_3(s) \longrightarrow Al^{3+}(aq) + 3\ Cl^-(aq)$$
$$1\ mol \qquad 1\ mol \qquad 3\ mol$$

you can simply state that the $[Cl^-]$ in solution is three times the dissolved $[AlCl_3]$.

$$[Cl^-] = 3 \times [AlCl_3] = 3 \times 0.25\ M = \mathbf{0.75\ M}$$

EXAMPLE: What is the concentration of each type of ion in a solution made by mixing 50.0 mL of 0.240 M $AlBr_3$ and 25.0 mL of 0.300 M $CaBr_2$?

When $AlBr_3$ and $CaBr_2$ dissolve in water, they undergo dissociation.

$$AlBr_3 \longrightarrow Al^{3+} + 3\ Br^- \quad and \quad CaBr_2 \longrightarrow Ca^{2+} + 2\ Br^-$$

First perform a dilution calculation on each of the starting solutions.

$$[AlBr_3]_{DIL} = 0.240\ M \times \frac{50.0\ mL}{75.0\ mL} = 0.160\ M$$

$$[CaBr_2]_{DIL} = 0.300\ M \times \frac{25.0\ mL}{75.0\ mL} = 0.100\ M$$

Below each dissociation equation, indicate each ion's concentration.

$$AlBr_3 \longrightarrow Al^{3+} + 3\ Br^-$$
$$0.160\ M \qquad 0.160\ M \quad 0.480\ M$$

$$CaBr_2 \longrightarrow Ca^{2+} + 2\ Br^-$$
$$0.100\ M \qquad 0.100\ M \quad 0.200\ M$$

Since 1 mol of $AlBr_3$ produces 3 mol of Br^-, then
0.160 M $AlBr_3$ produces 3 x 0.160 M = 0.480 M Br^-.
Similarly, 1 mol of $CaBr_2$ gives 2 mol of Br^-, so that
0.100 M $CaBr_2$ produces 2 x 0.100 M = 0.200 M Br^-.
The mixture therefore has two sources of Br^-, which add to give a total $[Br^-]$.

In summary: $[Al^{3+}]$ = **0.160 M**
$[Ca^{2+}]$ = **0.100 M**
$[Br^-]$ = 0.480 + 0.200 = **0.680 M**

EXERCISES:

30. What is the concentration of SO_4^{2-} present in 0.135 M $Al_2(SO_4)_3$?

31. What is the $[Cl^-]$ formed when 10.0 g of $BaCl_2(s)$ is dissolved and diluted to 0.600 L?

32. What is the concentration of Cl^- produced when 55.0 mL of 0.300 M HCl is mixed with 80.0 mL of 0.550 M $CaCl_2$?

33. When 350.0 mL of 0.250 M $MgCl_2$ is boiled down to a final volume of 275.0 mL, what is the $[Cl^-]$ in the resulting solution?

34. Calculate the number of moles of all aqueous ions in the following solutions, assuming that each dissolved substance dissociates completely in solution.
    (a) 0.60 L of 0.20 M K_2SO_4 (c) 75.0 mL of 0.160 M $MnCl_2$
    (b) 0.450 L of 0.300 M Na_3PO_4 (d) 0.0950 L of 0.235 M $Al_2(SO_4)_3$

35. A solution is made by mixing 100.0 mL of 0.200 M $BaCl_2$ and 150.0 mL of 0.400 M NaCl. What is the concentration of each ionic species in the final solution?

36. If 75.0 mL of 0.200 M Na_3PO_4 is added to 25.0 mL of 0.800 M K_3PO_4, what is the final concentration of each ion in solution?

37. What is the concentration of all the ions in a solution produced by mixing 15.0 mL of 0.325 M Na_3PO_4 with 35.0 mL of 0.225 M K_2SO_4.

38. A chemistry student dissolves 3.25 g of K_2CrO_4 and 1.75 g of $K_2Cr_2O_7$ in water and dilutes the mixture to a total volume of 100.0 mL. What is the concentration of all the ions in the solution?

UNIT X : ORGANIC CHEMISTRY

X.1. INTRODUCTION

Organic chemistry is defined as the chemistry of **CARBON** compounds. Because of the immense number of organic compounds, organic chemistry is considered to be one of the major branches of chemistry.

In spite of the fact that carbon is the focus of organic chemistry, hydrogen atoms are usually, but not always, present in organic molecules. Compounds containing only carbon and hydrogen atoms number in the hundreds of thousands and the option of adding other atoms such as oxygen, nitrogen, chlorine and so on, extends the number of known organic compounds to over 8 million.

The key to this huge number of organic compounds is the fact that carbon forms chains involving several carbon atoms linked to each other in a straight–line fashion, in a "circular" pattern, or in a branched pattern. In addition, the carbon atoms may form single, double or triple bonds to neighbouring atoms, which further extends the range of possible molecules.

Why is organic chemistry so important? A partial answer is found by looking at the organic compounds below.

C_8H_{18}	= iso–octane (the chief ingredient in gasoline)
CH_4	= methane ("natural gas")
$C_{18}H_{21}NO_3$	= codeine (pain reliever)
$C_{22}H_{25}NO_6$	= colchicine (anti–leukemia drug)
$C_8H_6O_3Cl_2$	= 2,4–D (a herbicide)
$C_{14}H_9Cl_5$	= DDT (a banned pesticide)
$C_{10}H_{19}O_6S_2P$	= malathion (an insecticide)
$C_{19}H_{28}O_2$	= testosterone (a male sex hormone)
$C_{17}H_{21}NO_4$	= cocaine
$C_{10}H_{14}N_2$	= nicotine
$C_6H_{12}O_6$	= glucose (a sugar)
C_2H_4	= ethene (a plant hormone which causes ripening of fruit)
$C_{20}H_{12}$	= 1,2–benzpyrene (a cancer–causing ingredient of cigarette smoke)
$C_{40}H_{56}$	= beta–carotene (the yellow colour in carrots; used as the colouring agent in margarine)
$[C_2H_4]_x$	= polyethylene (plastic) ["x" implies a multiply–repeated unit]
$[C_2F_4]_x$	= Teflon

Looking down the list, you may notice that all these organic compounds contain carbon, and most also contain hydrogen. Organic chemicals have an extensive range of uses and properties. Some organic chemicals occur naturally and some are produced synthetically; some are beneficial and some are hazardous.

Where do we find organic compounds? Look around you! They are found in petroleum, natural gas and all living things including trees, grasses, vegetables, insects, animals and people.

The largest industry involving organic chemistry is the manufacture of petrochemicals. Petroleum is presently the starting material for a vast range of products. Part of the complicated mixture of organic chemicals which makes up petroleum is separated ("fractionated") and refined for use in gasoline and oil, while other "fractions" of petroleum are chemically altered to serve as raw materials for a huge array of industrial processes such as the manufacture of plastics, solvents, pharmaceuticals and personal care products. The food and beverage industry alone uses a substantial amount of organic chemicals in the form of "food additives" — look at the ingredients listed on a package of your favourite "junk food" (most of those unpronouncable names are organic chemicals).

This unit starts by looking at compounds containing only carbon and hydrogen and then looks at the effects of introducing other kinds of atoms.

X.2. ALKANES

Definition: A **HYDROCARBON** is a compound containing only hydrogen and carbon.

A carbon atom, such as the one shown in bold below on the left, can form bonds to four other atoms (carbon has a valence of four) — and this is the key to the wide variety of possible carbon compounds. If one or more of the four bonds connect to other carbon atoms, each of these attached carbons can connect to three other atoms, and so on. The possible variety and complexity of the molecules increases with each carbon added.

A. UNBRANCHED ("STRAIGHT CHAIN") ALKANES

There is more than one way to represent a hydrocarbon formula, depending on how compact one wants to write the formula.

EXAMPLE: The structure of propane, C_3H_8, can be shown in three ways.

full structure:

$$
\begin{array}{c}
\quad\ \text{H}\ \ \text{H}\ \ \text{H} \\
\quad\ |\ \ \ |\ \ \ | \\
\text{H}-\text{C}-\text{C}-\text{C}-\text{H} \\
\quad\ |\ \ \ |\ \ \ | \\
\quad\ \text{H}\ \ \text{H}\ \ \text{H}
\end{array}
$$

or   condensed structure: $CH_3-CH_2-CH_3$ (or even $CH_3CH_2CH_3$)

or   molecular formula: C_3H_8

In the following sequence of hydrocarbons, each molecule differs by the number of carbon atoms linked to one another to form a "carbon chain". Because the chain of carbon atoms extends in a straight–line fashion, the hydrocarbons in this section are call "straight–chain" or "unbranched" hydrocarbons.

$$
\text{methane} = CH_4 = \begin{array}{c} \text{H} \\ | \\ \text{H}-\text{C}-\text{H} \\ | \\ \text{H} \end{array}
$$

$$
\text{ethane} = C_2H_6 = \begin{array}{c} \text{H}\ \ \text{H} \\ |\ \ \ | \\ \text{H}-\text{C}-\text{C}-\text{H} \\ |\ \ \ | \\ \text{H}\ \ \text{H} \end{array} = CH_3-CH_3
$$

$$
\text{propane} = C_3H_8 = \begin{array}{c} \text{H}\ \ \text{H}\ \ \text{H} \\ |\ \ \ |\ \ \ | \\ \text{H}-\text{C}-\text{C}-\text{C}-\text{H} \\ |\ \ \ |\ \ \ | \\ \text{H}\ \ \text{H}\ \ \text{H} \end{array} = CH_3-CH_2-CH_3
$$

$$
\text{butane} = C_4H_{10} = \begin{array}{c} \text{H}\ \ \text{H}\ \ \text{H}\ \ \text{H} \\ |\ \ \ |\ \ \ |\ \ \ | \\ \text{H}-\text{C}-\text{C}-\text{C}-\text{C}-\text{H} \\ |\ \ \ |\ \ \ |\ \ \ | \\ \text{H}\ \ \text{H}\ \ \text{H}\ \ \text{H} \end{array} = CH_3-CH_2-CH_2-CH_3
$$

and similarly   pentane $= C_5H_{12}$ $= CH_3-CH_2-CH_2-CH_2-CH_3$

hexane $= C_6H_{14}$ $= CH_3-CH_2-CH_2-CH_2-CH_2-CH_3$

heptane $= C_7H_{16}$ $= CH_3-CH_2-CH_2-CH_2-CH_2-CH_2-CH_3$

octane $= C_8H_{18}$ $= CH_3-CH_2-CH_2-CH_2-CH_2-CH_2-CH_2-CH_3$

nonane $= C_9H_{20}$ $= CH_3-CH_2-CH_2-CH_2-CH_2-CH_2-CH_2-CH_2-CH_3$

decane $= C_{10}H_{22}$ $= CH_3-CH_2-CH_2-CH_2-CH_2-CH_2-CH_2-CH_2-CH_2-CH_3$

Definition: An **ALKANE** is a hydrocarbon in which all the carbon atoms are connected by **single** bonds.

Note: 1.   The names of the above hydrocarbons end in "ane" because they are "alkanes".

2.   An alkane is also called a "**SATURATED**" hydrocarbon because each carbon atom is bonded to the maximum possible number of other atoms; that is, the carbon's ability to bond to other atoms is "saturated".

EXERCISE:

1. Look at the sequence of hydrogen atoms connected to carbon atoms in the list below.

    CH_4, C_2H_6, C_3H_8, C_4H_{10}, C_5H_{12}, etc.

    Suggest a general formula for all straight–chain alkanes. That is, if there are "N" carbons, how many hydrogens will be present?

THE GEOMETRY OF ALKANES

Although the bonds on a carbon atom are usually drawn as if they were run over by a steam roller, lying flat on a page at right angles to each other, the bonds are actually arranged in the shape of a 4–cornered pyramid (a "TETRAHEDRON") as shown below. All the bonds have equal lengths and all the H–C–H angles are 109°.

these H's lie in the plane of the paper

this H is receding into the background

this H is coming out of the plane of the paper

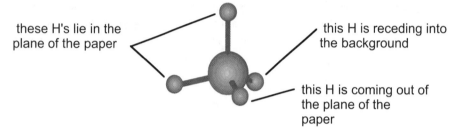

Therefore the actual shape of the propane molecule can be shown as

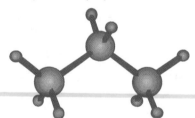

and a molecule of hexane might look something like the following.

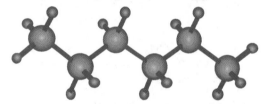

Each of the single bonds between the carbon atoms is able to rotate freely, leading to a highly flexible chain which can wave about and take many shapes. The above arrangement is one shape hexane can assume; another might be the arrangement shown below.

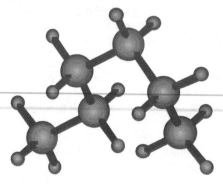

B. ALKYL GROUPS AND BRANCHED HYDROCARBONS

A hydrocarbon chain can have "side branches" which are also hydrocarbon chains.

EXAMPLE: $CH_3–CH_2–CH–CH_2–CH_2–CH_3$
                                   |
                                 CH_2
                                   |
                                 CH_3

These attached "groups" are called ALKYL GROUPS.

A short digression on the "organic language"

This unit introduces some complicated words which seem like a foreign language to an outsider. In fact, the words ARE part of another language — the "organic language". As in other languages, the basic "words" are placed together to make complete names for organic molecules, similar to the way in which basic words are placed together to make complete sentences in English. The "organic" words can have their endings modified and be used like adjectives, verbs or adverbs. As you proceed, always be sure you know the "syntax" or set of rules for constructing the organic "sentences" which make up the complete organic names of molecules. The rules are simple .... and there are NO IRREGULAR VERBS!

Definition: An **ALKYL GROUP** is an alkane which has lost one hydrogen atom.

EXAMPLE: $CH_4 \xrightarrow{\text{remove one H}} CH_3–$

$CH_3–CH_3 \xrightarrow{\text{remove one H}} CH_3–CH_2–$

$CH_3–CH_2–CH_3 \xrightarrow{\text{remove one H}} CH_3–CH_2–CH_2–$ or $CH_3–CH–CH_3$
                                                                                                  |
                                         (remove end H)   (remove middle H)

The "unused" bond on the carbon atom can be connected to another hydrocarbon chain. **This unit only uses alkyl groups formed by taking a hydrogen off the END carbon of a hydrocarbon chain.**

An alkyl group is named by changing the "ane" ending of the original hydrocarbon to "yl".

EXAMPLES:

Original hydrocarbon	Alkyl group
methane = CH_4	methyl = $CH_3–$
ethane = $CH_3–CH_3$	ethyl = $CH_3–CH_2–$
propane = $CH_3–CH_2–CH_3$	propyl = $CH_3–CH_2–CH_2–$
butane = $CH_3–CH_2–CH_2–CH_3$	butyl = $CH_3–CH_2–CH_2–CH_2–$

When an alkyl group is attached to another hydrocarbon, the resulting molecule is called a **SUBSTITUTED HYDROCARBON** or a **BRANCHED HYDROCARBON.**

RULE: The first step in naming a substituted hydrocarbon is to find the longest continuous chain of
carbon atoms. This longest chain is called the "**PARENT**" hydrocarbon.

EXAMPLES: To find the longest carbon chain, look at every "branch point" carbon (in a box in the
examples below) and decide which TWO branches create the longest overall path (shown in
bold). Only carbons are shown so as to make the various branches easier to see.

a) 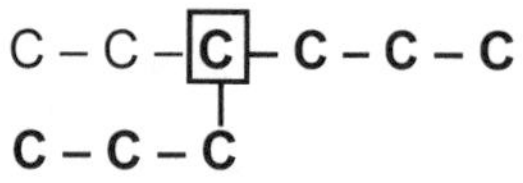   C – C –│C│– C – C – C   The carbon in the box has 3 branches:
     　　　　　　　│　　　　　　the longest route involves the right branch
     C – C – C   (3 carbons) and the lower branch (3 carbons).
     Longest path length = 7 carbons = **heptane**

b) 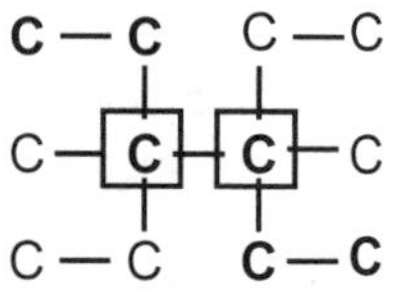   **C — C**　　C —C   Here, no unique "longest path" exists. The longest
     　　│　　　　　│　　　　　chain involves either the upper or lower pair of carbons
     C—│C│—│C│—C   on the left side and either the upper or lower group of
     　　│　　　　　│　　　　　two carbons on the right. The bold path shown was
     C — C　　**C—C**   selected randomly from the 4 possible choices.
     Longest path length = 6 carbons = **hexane**

c) 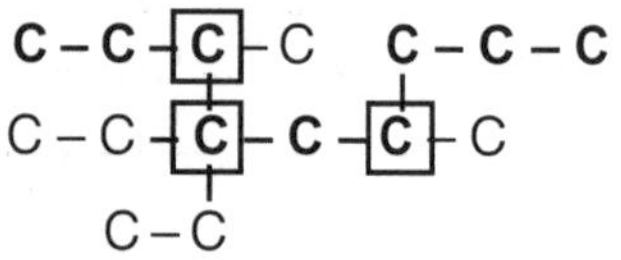   **C – C –│C│– C**　 C – C – C   Do you agree with the bold path shown?
     C – C –│C│– **C** –│C│– C
     　　　　　│
     　　　　C – C
     Longest path length = 9 carbons = **nonane**

EXERCISE:

2. Determine the number of carbon atoms in the longest chain of each of the following, and name the
    parent hydrocarbon represented by the longest chain.

(a) 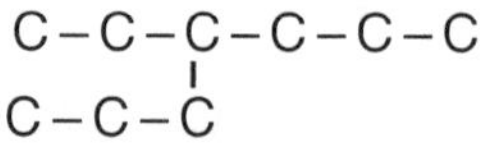 C – C – C – C – C – C   (b) C – C – C – C – C
     　　　　　│　　　　　　　　　　　　　　　│
     　　　　C – C – C   C – C – C – C – C
     　　　　　　　　　　　　　　　　　　　　│
     　　　　　　　　　　　　　　　C – C – C – C – C

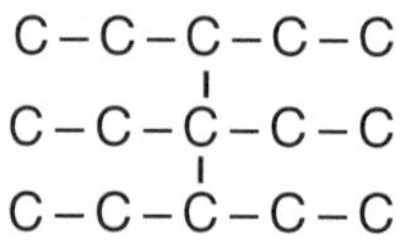

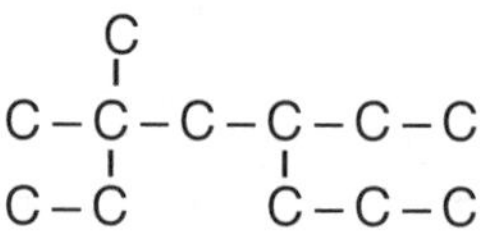

(c) 　　　　C   (d) 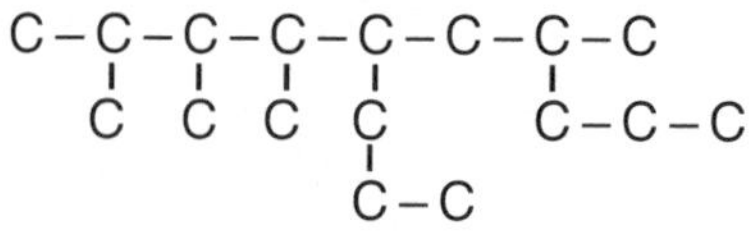 C – C – C – C – C – C – C – C
     　　　　│   　│　 │　 │　 │　　　 │
     C – C – C – C – C – C   C　 C　 C　 C　　 C – C – C
     　　│　　　　　│   　　　　　 │
     　C – C　　 C – C – C   　　　　 C – C

To name a substituted hydrocarbon, the basic idea is to name the longest (parent) hydrocarbon chain and
then name the various alkyl groups which are attached to the parent hydrocarbon.

RULE: A substituted hydrocarbon is named by writing the following one after another
     • the carbon number at which the alkyl group is attached,
     • a dash,
     • the name of the alkyl group, and finally
     • the name of the longest or "parent" hydrocarbon chain, to which the alkyl
       group is attached.

Note: The carbon atoms in the parent hydrocarbon are numbered consecutively from
     the end of the hydrocarbon which gives the LOWEST POSSIBLE SET OF
     NUMBERS to the attached groups.

EXAMPLES:

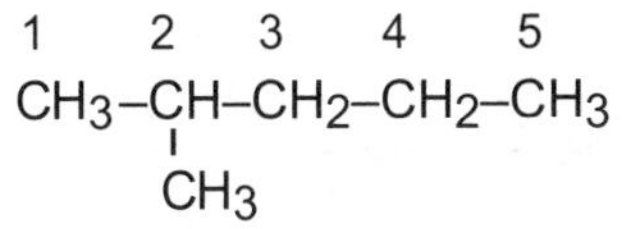

$$1 \quad 2 \quad 3 \quad 4 \quad 5$$
$$CH_3-CH-CH_2-CH_2-CH_3 = 2\text{-methylpentane}$$
$$|$$
$$CH_3$$

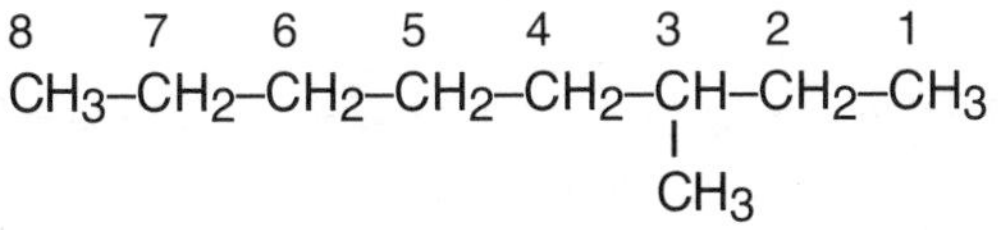

$$8 \quad 7 \quad 6 \quad 5 \quad 4 \quad 3 \quad 2 \quad 1$$
$$CH_3-CH_2-CH_2-CH_2-CH_2-CH-CH_2-CH_3 = 3\text{-methyloctane}$$
$$|$$
$$CH_3$$

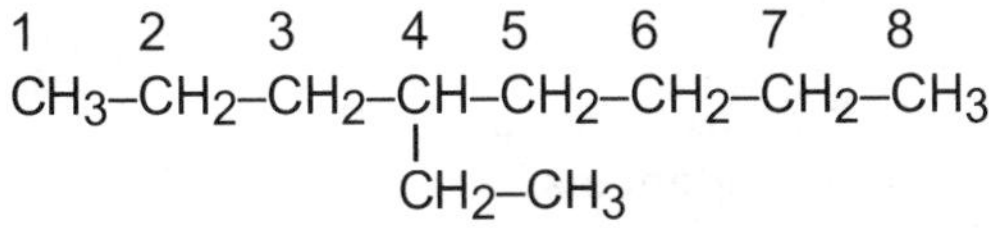

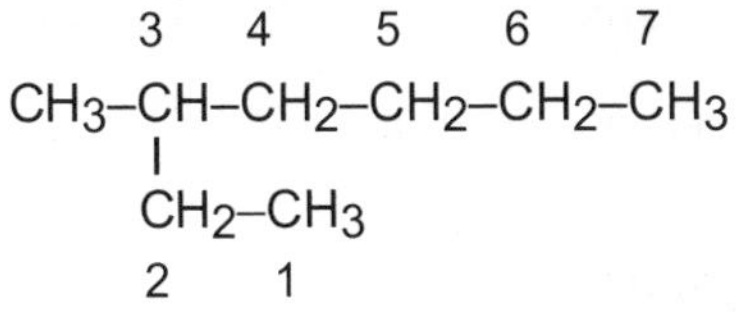

$$1 \quad 2 \quad 3 \quad 4 \quad 5 \quad 6 \quad 7 \quad 8$$
$$CH_3-CH_2-CH_2-CH-CH_2-CH_2-CH_2-CH_3 = 4\text{-ethyloctane}$$
$$|$$
$$CH_2-CH_3$$

$$3 \quad 4 \quad 5 \quad 6 \quad 7$$
$$CH_3-CH-CH_2-CH_2-CH_2-CH_3 = 3\text{-methylheptane}$$
$$|$$
$$CH_2-CH_3$$
$$2 \quad 1$$

EXERCISE:

3. Name the following hydrocarbons. Care: e and f are tricky!

(a) 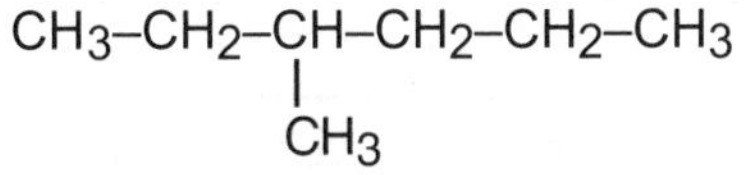 $CH_3-CH_2-CH-CH_2-CH_2-CH_3$
$$|$$
$$CH_3$$

(b) 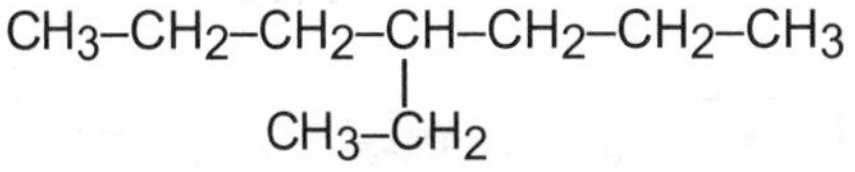 $CH_3-CH_2-CH_2-CH-CH_2-CH_2-CH_3$
$$|$$
$$CH_3-CH_2$$

(c) 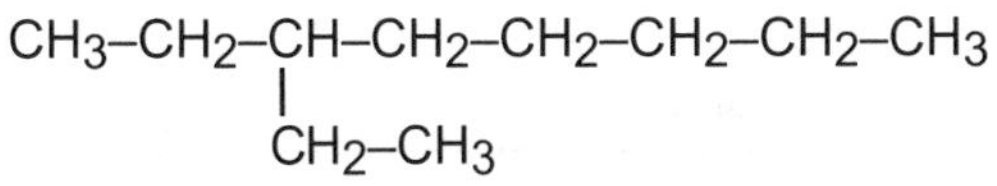 $CH_3-CH_2-CH-CH_2-CH_2-CH_2-CH_2-CH_3$
$$|$$
$$CH_2-CH_3$$

(d) 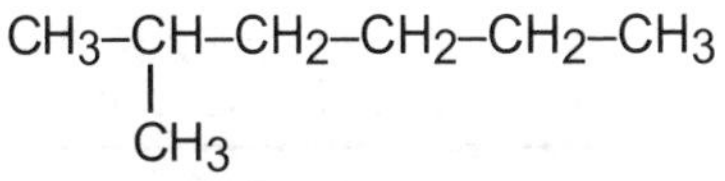 $CH_3-CH-CH_2-CH_2-CH_2-CH_3$
$$|$$
$$CH_3$$

(e) 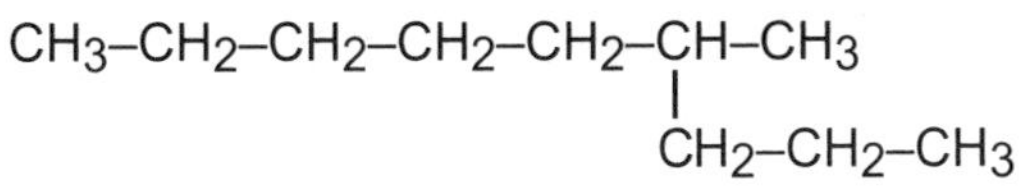 $CH_3-CH_2-CH_2-CH_2-CH_2-CH-CH_3$
$$|$$
$$CH_2-CH_2-CH_3$$

(f) 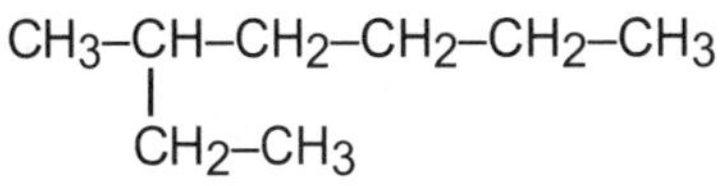 $CH_3-CH-CH_2-CH_2-CH_2-CH_3$
$$|$$
$$CH_2-CH_3$$

Since carbons have FOUR bonds, count the bonds between a given carbon atom and its neighbours and subtract that number from 4. The difference equals the number of hydrogen atoms which must be attached to each carbon. That is, the number of bonds to hydrogens PLUS the number of bonds to other carbons equals four. The required number of hydrogens is then written into the formula.

EXAMPLES: When a carbon is attached to ONE other carbon —

4 bonds – 1 bond used = 3 H's added and $C - CH_3$ becomes $\mathbf{CH_3} - CH_3$

When a carbon is attached to TWO other carbons —

4 bonds – 2 bonds used = 2 H's added and $CH_3 - C - CH_3$ becomes $CH_3 - \mathbf{CH_2} - CH_3$

When a carbon is attached to THREE other carbons —

4 bonds – 3 bonds used = 1 H added and $CH_3 - \mathbf{C} - CH_3$ becomes $CH_3 - \mathbf{CH} - CH_3$
$$|\qquad\qquad\qquad\qquad |$$
$$CH_3 \qquad\qquad\qquad CH_3$$

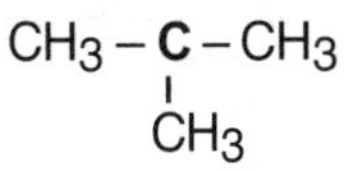

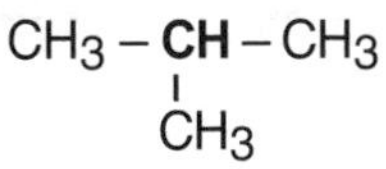

When a carbon is attached to FOUR other carbons —

$$CH_3$$
$$|$$
4 bonds – 4 bonds used = **NO** H's added and $CH_3 - \mathbf{C} - CH_3$ needs **no** extra H's
$$|\qquad\qquad\qquad$$ on the central C
$$CH_3$$

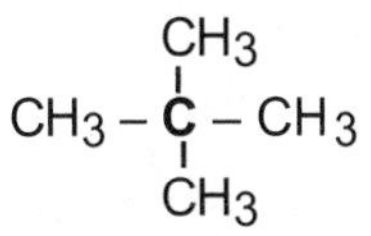

EXERCISES:

4. Re–write the following structures to show the hydrogens attached.

(a) 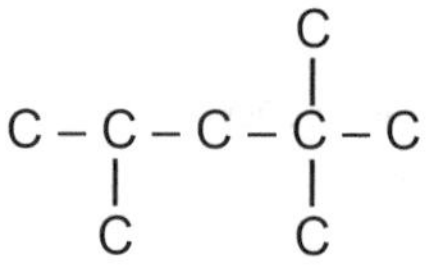
```
            C
            |
    C – C – C – C – C
        |       |
        C       C
```
(b) 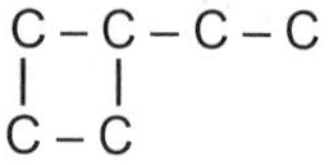
```
    C – C – C – C
        |   |
        C – C
```
(c)
```
                        C
                        |
    C – C – C – C – C – C – C – C – C
        |       |       |
        C – C   C       C
               / \
              C — C
```

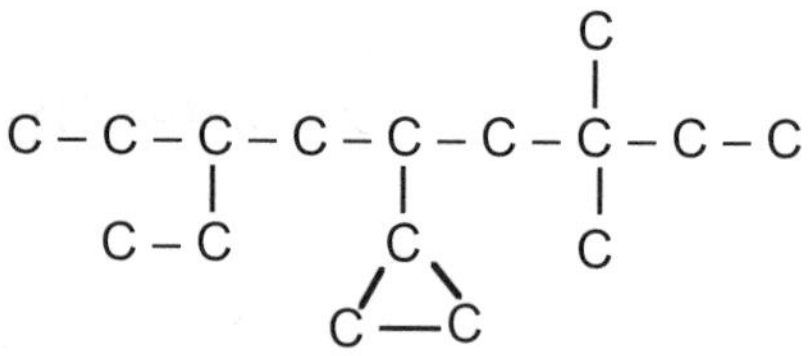

5. Draw the following hydrocarbons. Include all hydrogens.
    (a) 3–methylhexane   (c) 2–methylpentane   (e) 3–ethylheptane
    (b) 4–ethyloctane   (d) 4–propylnonane   (f) 5–propyldecane

6. What is wrong with each of the following?   (You may have to sketch the molecule to see the error in some cases.)

    (a) 6–methylheptane   (b) 1–ethylbutane

```
             CH3                            CH3
              |                              |
[c]  CH3–CH3–CH–CH3          (d)  CH3–CH–CH3
                                            |
                                           CH3
```

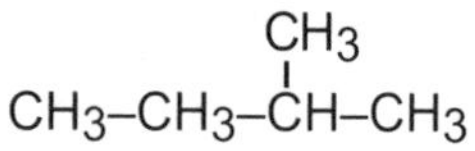

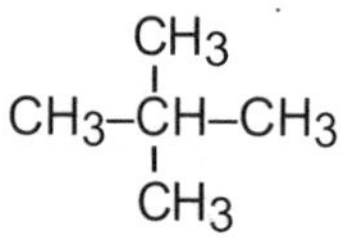

> **RULE:** If more than one DIFFERENT alkyl group is attached to a hydrocarbon, then
> • list the alkyl groups alphabetically,
> • precede each alkyl group by its number, and
> • put a dash between each alkyl group and its number.

EXAMPLES: 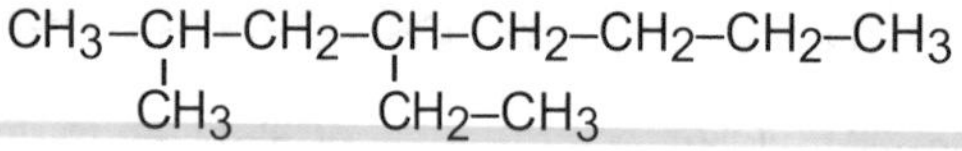
```
CH3–CH–CH2–CH–CH2–CH2–CH2–CH3  = 4–ethyl–2–methyloctane
    CH3        CH2–CH3
```
```
          CH3
           |
CH3–CH2–C–CH2–CH2–CH2–CH2–CH3  = 3–ethyl–3–methyloctane
           |
          CH2–CH3                (note that there can be 2 groups
                                  attached to the same carbon)
```
```
          CH2–CH3
           |
CH3–CH–CH2–CH–CH–CH2–CH2–CH2–CH3  = 5–ethyl–3–methyl–6–propyldecane
    |           |                    (TRICKY!  Can you see why?)
    CH2–CH3   CH2–CH2–CH3
```

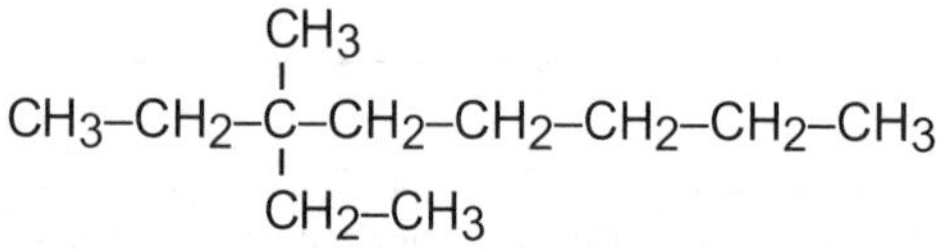

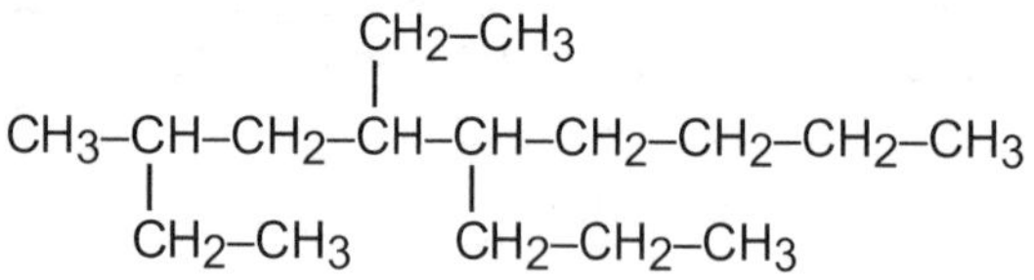

> **RULE:** If an alkyl group is repeated, then
> • list each carbon number where the repeated group is attached, separated by commas, and
> • prefix the repeated group name by **di, tri, tetra,** etc. to show how many identical groups are attached.

EXAMPLES: CH₃–CH–CH₂–CH–CH₂–CH–CH₂–CH₃ = 2,4,6–trimethyloctane

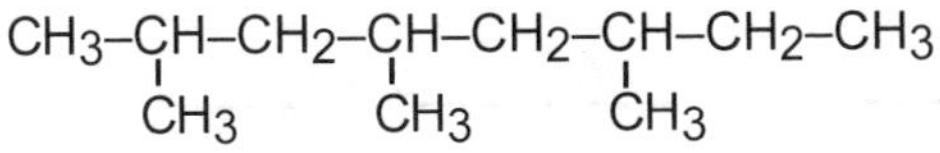

$$CH_3\text{–}CH\text{–}CH_2\text{–}CH\text{–}CH_2\text{–}CH\text{–}CH_2\text{–}CH_3 = 2,4,6\text{–trimethyloctane}$$

with CH₃, CH₃, CH₃ branches

$$CH_3\text{–}C\text{–}CH_2\text{–}C\text{–}CH_2\text{–}CH_2\text{–}C\text{–}CH_2\text{–}CH_2\text{–}CH_3$$

with CH₃, CH₂–CH₃, CH₃ above and CH₃, CH₂–CH₃, CH₂–CH2–CH₃ below

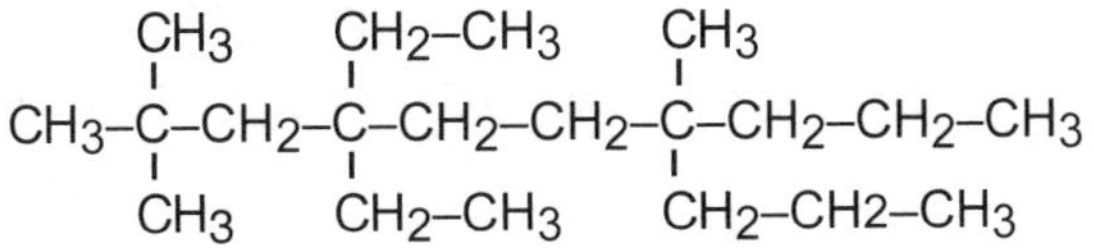

= 4,4–diethyl–2,2,7–trimethyl–7–propyldecane

EXERCISES:

7. Count up the number of carbons and hydrogens in the two example molecules above. The general formula for a simple straight–chain hydrocarbon (methane, ethane, etc.) is C_NH_{2N+2}. What is the general formula for a branched hydrocarbon?

8. Name the following molecules.

(a)   CH₃ –CH – CH–CH₃
         CH₃–CH₂–CH₂ CH₂–CH₃

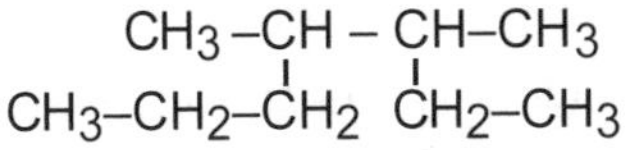

(b)   CH₃–CH₂–CH–CH₂–CH₃
       CH3–CH₂–C–CH₂–CH₃
       CH3–CH₂–CH–CH₂–CH₃

(c)   CH₃–C–CH₂–CH₂–CH₂–CH₂–C–CH₃ with CH₃, CH₃ above and CH₃, CH₃ below

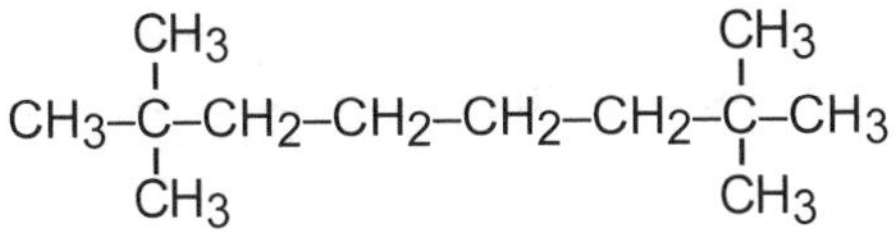

(d)   CH₃–CH–CH–CH–CH₂–CH₃ with CH₃ above and CH₃–CH₂, CH₂–CH₃ below

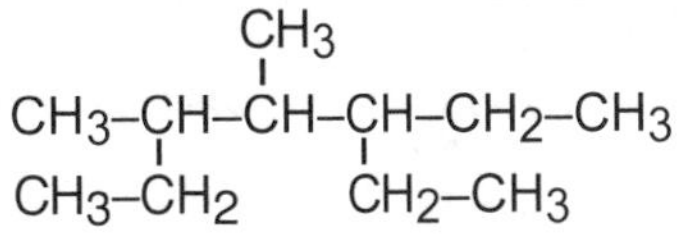

(e)   CH₃–CH₂–CH₂–C–CH₂–CH₃ with CH₃ above and CH₂–CH₂–CH₂–CH₃ below

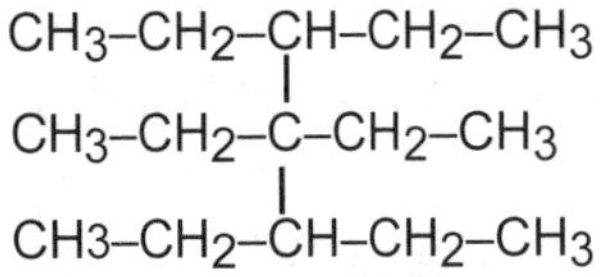

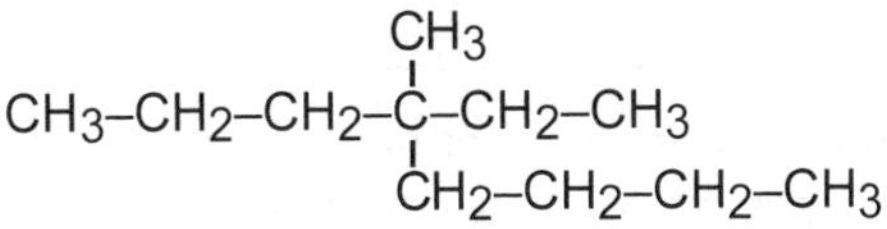

(f)   CH₂–CH₂–CH–CH₂–CH₂–C–CH₃ with CH₃, CH₃ above and CH₃, CH₃ below

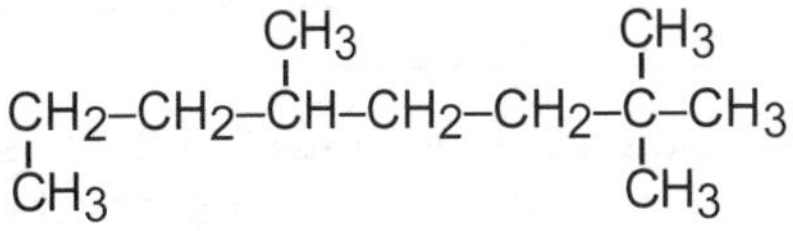

(g)   CH3–CH–CH2–CH–CH₃ with CH₂–CH₂–CH₃ above and CH₃–CH₂–CH₂ below

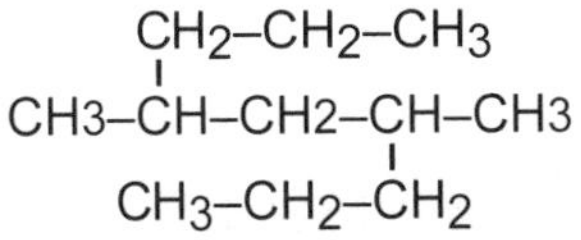

(h)   CH2–CH2–CH2–CH2–CH2–CH2 with CH₂–CH₃ and CH3–CH2 below

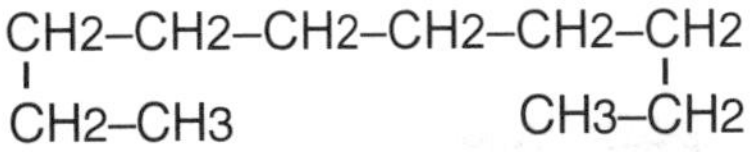

(i)   CH₃–CH₂–CH–CH–CH₂–CH₃ with CH₃–CH–CH₂–CH₃ above and CH₂–CH–CH₂–CH₃ and CH₃ below

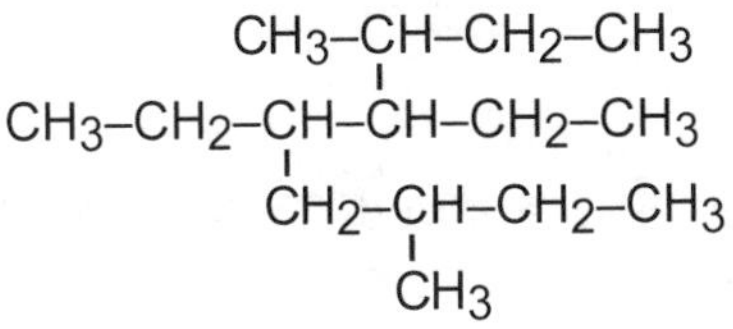

(j)   CH₃–CH₂–CH₂–CH–CH – C–CH₃ with CH₃, CH₃ above and CH₃, CH₂–CH₃ below

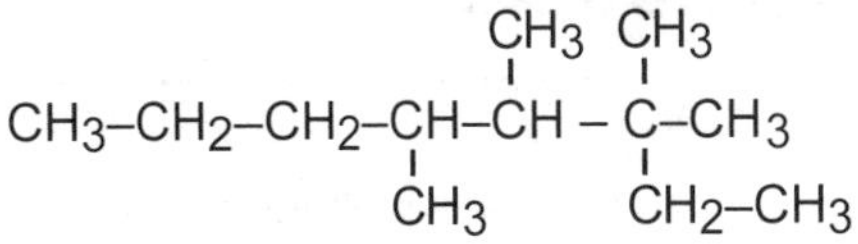

(k)   CH₃–CH₂–CH₂–CH–CH–CH–CH₃ with CH₂–CH₃ above and CH₃–CH₂–CH₂, CH₂–CH₃ below

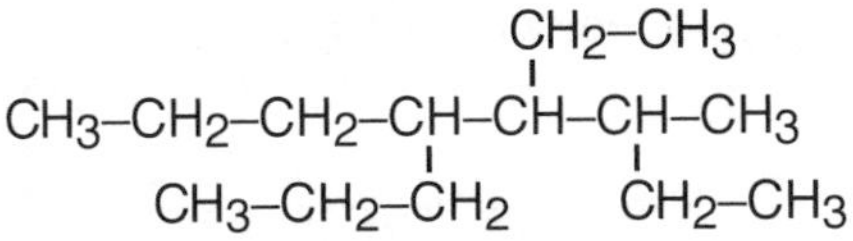

(l)   CH₃–CH–CH₂ with CH₃–CH₂ above; CH₃–CH₂–CH–CH–CH₃ with CH₂–CH–CH₂–CH₃ and CH₂–CH₃ below

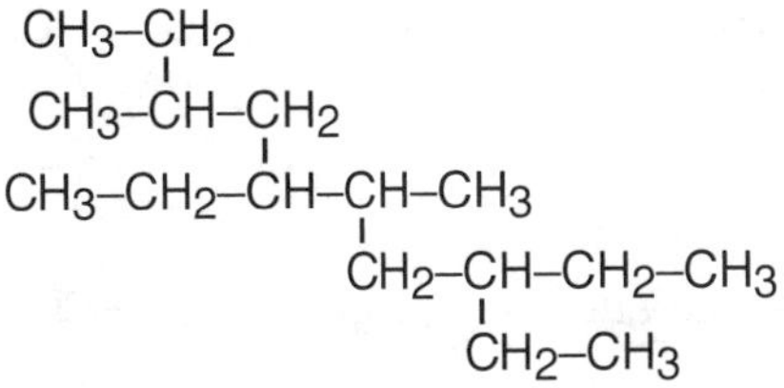

9. Sketch the following molecules.
    (a) 3–ethyl–2,3–dimethylhexane
    (b) 2,2–dimethyl–5,6–dipropylnonane
    (c) 4–ethyl–3–methyl–5–propyloctane
    (d) 2,2,3,3–tetramethylpentane
    (e) 3,4–diethylhexane
    (f) 5–butyl–6,6–diethyl–3,3,7–trimethyldecane
    (g) dimethylpropane (why were no numbers used?)
    (h) 4–ethyl–2–methyloctane
    (i) hexamethylpentane
    (j) 3,6–diethyl–4–methyl–5–propyloctane

STRUCTURAL ISOMERS

Definition: **STRUCTURAL ISOMERS** are compounds which have the same molecular formula but a different arrangement of atoms.

EXAMPLE: C_4H_{10} can refer to either $CH_3 - CH_2 - CH_2 - CH_3$ or $CH_3 - CH - CH_3$
$$| \quad\quad CH_3$$

Each structural isomer has a set of chemical and physical properties which differ from those of other isomers with the same chemical formula.

EXERCISES:

10. Write the condensed structure and name for the three structural isomers having the molecular formula C_5H_{12}.

11. Write the condensed structure and name for the two structural isomers that involve a single methyl group attached to hexane.

12. Write the condensed structure and name of the four structural isomers that involve two methyl groups attached to pentane.

13. How many isomers of C_8H_{18} contain no side chains other than a single methyl group?

THE PROPERTIES OF ALKANES

- Alkanes are very unreactive because C–C and C–H bonds are strong and not easily broken.
- Methane, ethane, propane and butane are gases at room temperature (butane is easily liquified under pressure). Pentane and longer chains are liquids.
- Very long chains ($C_{16}H_{34}$ and longer) are solids and are commonly called WAXES or PARAFFINS.

C. CYCLOALKANES

Hydrocarbon chains which connect in a head–to–tail "circle" are called CYCLIC HYDROCARBONS or CYCLOALKANES. The first members of the cycloalkane series are shown below.

cyclopropane = C_3H_6 = H_2C——CH_2
                                    $\diagdown \diagup$
                                    CH_2

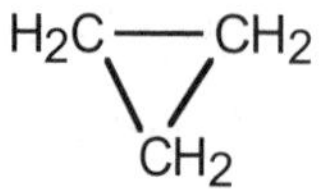

cyclopentane = C_5H_{10} = H_2C $\diagup$ CH_2 $\diagdown$ CH_2
H_2C — CH_2

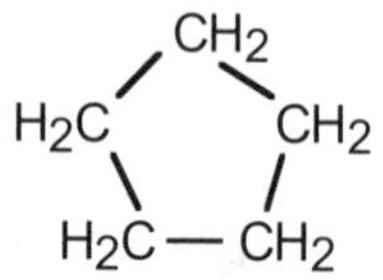

cyclobutane = C_4H_8 = H_2C — CH_2
                          H_2C — CH_2

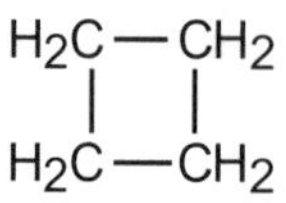

cyclohexane = C_6H_{12} = H_2C CH_2 CH_2
H_2C CH_2
CH_2

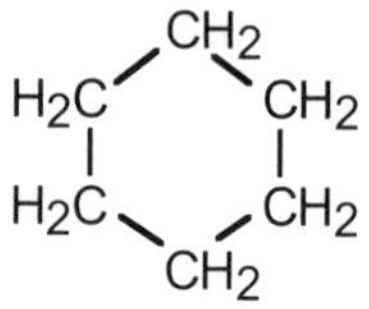

EXERCISE:

14. What is the general formula for a cycloalkane?

SUBSTITUTED CYCLOALKANES

RULE: Substituted cycloalkanes follow the same rules as straight–chain alkanes, except that
- a **single** substituent does not use a number to indicate the position of attachment (all carbons in the cycloalkyl group are identical).
- if there is more than one substituent, the first substituent is assumed to be at the "1" position and the remaining substituents are numbered either clockwise or anticlockwise so as to have the lowest set of overall values.

EXAMPLE:

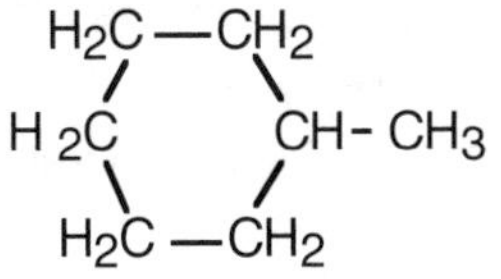

H_2C —CH_2
H_2C CH- CH_3 = methylcyclohexane
H_2C —CH_2

H_2C — CH_2
H_2C CH - CH_3 = 1–ethyl–2–methylcyclohexane 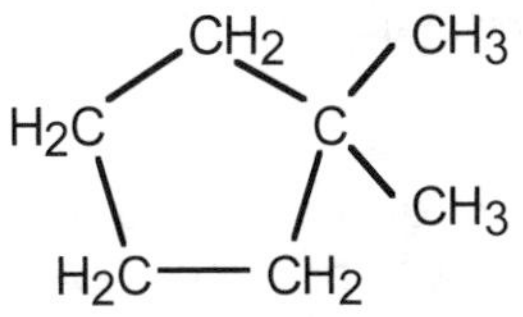
H_2C — CH
           CH_2–CH_3

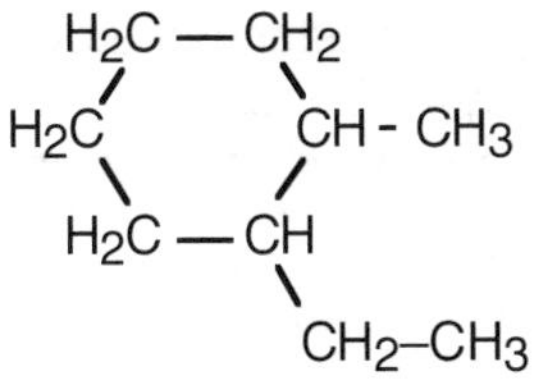

CH_2 CH_3
H_2C C = 1,1–dimethylcyclopentane
           CH_3
H_2C — CH_2

EXERCISES:

15. Name the following compounds.

(a)
CH_2
H_2C CH–CH_2–CH_3
H_2C CH_2
    CH_2

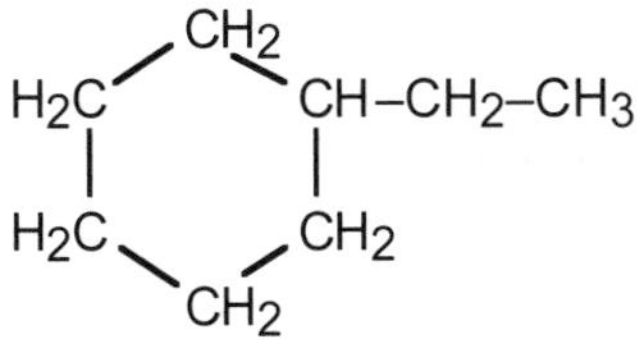

(b)
H_2C — CH —CH_3
H_3C—HC — CH_2

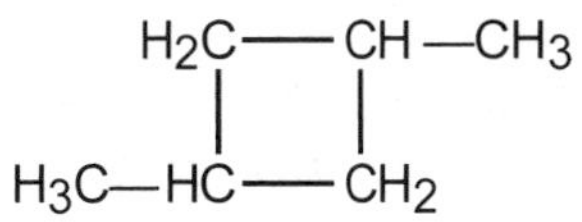

(c)
H_2C
   CH- CH_3
H_2C

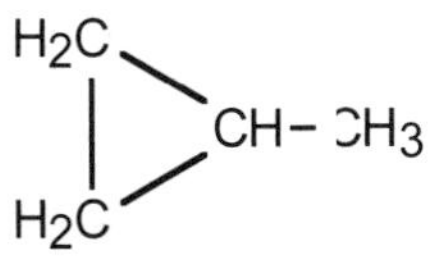

(d)
           CH_2 CH_3
H_3C—HC C
                  CH_2–CH_3
        H_2C — CH_2

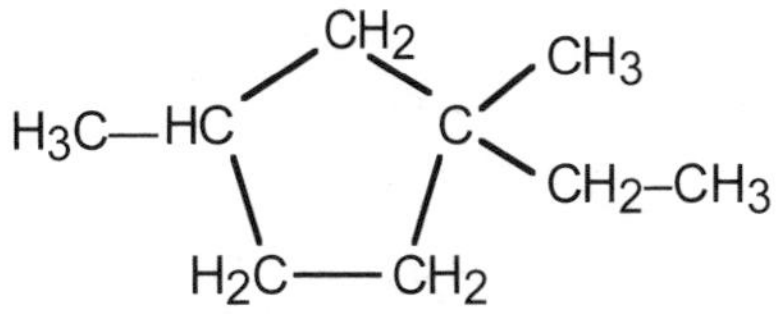

(e)
H_2C — CH_2
H_2C CH CH_3
H_2C CH
H_2C — CH CH_2–CH_3
        CH_3

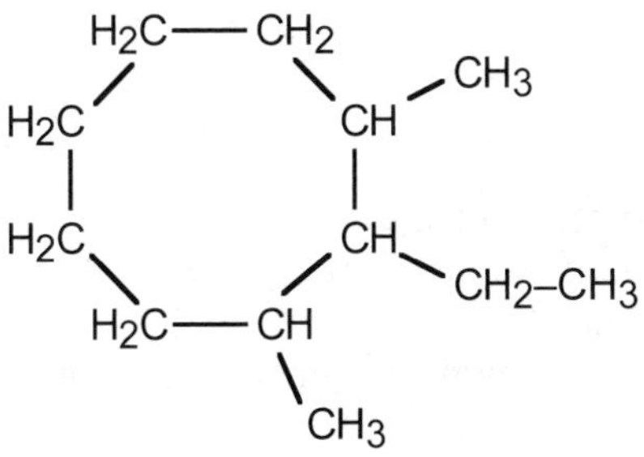

16. Sketch the following compounds.
    (a) 1,2–dimethylcyclobutane
    (b) 1,1,2–trimethylcyclopropane
    (c) 1,3–dipropylcyclopentane
    (d) propylcyclopropane
    (e) 1,3–diethyl–2,2–dimethylcyclooctane
    (f) 1,2,4–triethylcycloheptane

X.3 ALKYL HALIDES

The naming of alkyl halides (halogens – F, Cl, Br or I – attached to alkanes) is straightforward.

RULE: Name **alkyl halides** in the same manner used for alkyl groups.
- Attached F, Cl, Br and I atoms are called "fluoro", "chloro","bromo" and "iodo" groups. (The general term for an attached halogen atom is a "halo" group.) Use a number to indicate the position of attachment on the hydrocarbon chain.
- If more than one of the same kind of halogen is present, use the prefixes di, tri, etc.
- If a compound contains both alkyl and halo groups, list the attached groups in alphabetical order. Start numbering from the end which gives the lowest set of numbers.

EXAMPLES: $CH_3–Cl$ = chloromethane

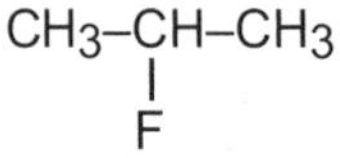

$CH_3–CH–CH_3$ (or $CH_3–CHF–CH_3$) = 2–fluoropropane
         |
         F

Note: Unlike the situation involving the addition of alkyl groups to a straight–chain hydrocarbon, halo groups can be placed at the 1–position.

$CCl_3–CF_3$ = 1,1,1–trichloro–2,2,2–trifluoroethane

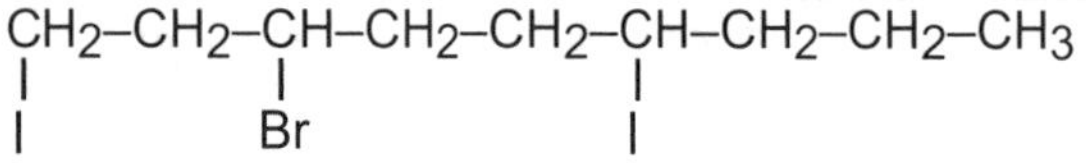

$CH_2–CH_2–CH–CH_2–CH_2–CH–CH_2–CH_2–CH_3$ = 3–bromo–1,6–diiodononane 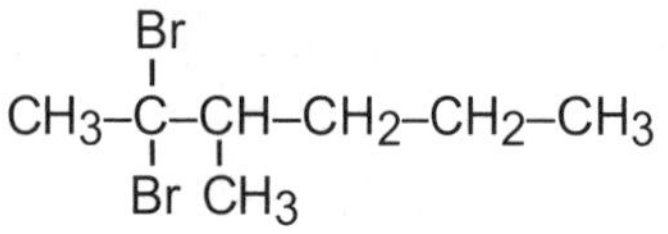
| | |
I   Br   I

    Br
    |
$CH_3–C–CH–CH_2–CH_2–CH_3$ = 2,2–dibromo–3–methylhexane
    | |
    Br CH_3

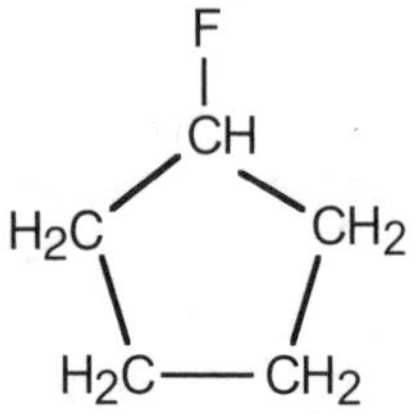

       F
       |
       CH
H_2C CH_2 = fluorocyclopentane
  H_2C——CH_2

PROPERTIES OF ALKYL HALIDES

- Alkyl halides tend to be insoluble in water (similar to alkanes).
- Compounds with many fluorine atoms tend to be unreactive ("inert"). "Teflon" is a highly fluorinated hydrocarbon which is inert to almost all chemical attack.
- Chloro and bromo compounds are susceptible to chemical attack, but require relatively drastic conditions. Iodo compounds are more reactive.

EXERCISES:

17. Name the following molecules.

(a) $CH_3–CH_2–Cl$

(b) $Br–CH_2–CH_2–CH_2–Br$

(c) $CH_3–CH–CH_2–CH_2–CH_2–I$
        |
        CH_3

(d) $CH_2F–CHCl_2$

(e)

18. Draw the following molecules.
(a) trichloromethane (common name = chloroform)
(b) 1,2–dichloroethane
(c) 1,3,5–tribromocyclohexane
(d) 4–bromo–2–chloro–3–ethyloctane
(e) 1,1,1–trifluoro–2–methylpentane

19. Draw and name the 8 structural isomers of $C_5H_{11}Cl$.

20. Draw and name the 9 structural isomers of $C_5H_{10}Cl_2$ that have no methyl groups.

X.4. MULTIPLE BONDS ("ALKENES and ALKYNES")

Definitions: An **ALKENE** is an organic compound containing a carbon–carbon double bond.

An **ALKYNE** is an organic compound containing a carbon–carbon triple bond.

(Double and triple bonds can be either at the end of a carbon chain or in the middle.)

EXAMPLES:

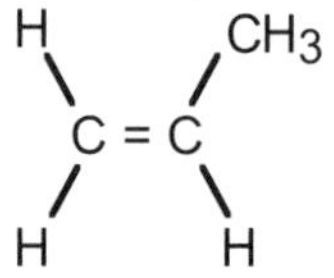

$$\begin{matrix} H & & CH_3 \\ & C = C & \\ H & & H \end{matrix}$$ or simply $CH_2 = CH{-}CH_3$

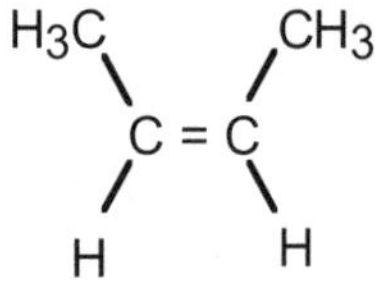

$$\begin{matrix} H_3C & & CH_3 \\ & C = C & \\ H & & H \end{matrix}$$ or simply $CH_3{-}CH = CH{-}CH_3$

$H - C \equiv C - CH_3$ or simply $CH \equiv C{-}CH_3$

$CH_3 - C \equiv C - CH_3$ or simply $CH_3C \equiv CCH_3$

The naming of compounds with double and triple bonds is quite straightforward.

RULE: If a double bond is present, change the "ane" ending of the parent hydrocarbon to "ene".
If a triple bond is present, change the "ane" ending of the parent hydrocarbon to "yne".
- Use a number to indicate the lower numbered carbon atom involved in the bond (the bond goes FROM the lower numbered carbon TO the higher numbered one). The number goes immediately in front of the name of the parent hydrocarbon, separated by a hyphen.
- Number the parent hydrocarbon to give the double/triple bond the lowest possible number. If the number is the same starting from either end, start the numbering from the end closest to the 1st branch point (where a group is attached).

Note: 1.   There is an easy way to remember the bond endings.

single bonds	double bonds	triple bonds
<u>A</u>NE	<u>E</u>NE	<u>Y</u>NE

The 1st letters (underlined) are in alphabetical order and sound like the long vowels a, e and i. (We can't use "ine" since this is used to indicate the presence of an amine group, $-NH_2$.)

2.   Alkenes and alkynes are called **UNSATURATED** hydrocarbons because they have less hydrogen atoms than equivalent alkanes. Alkanes are said to be **SATURATED** hydrocarbons because they contain the maximum number of hydrogens possible.

WRITING THE CONDENSED STRUCTURE OF ALKENES AND ALKYNES

When you are given the name of an alkene or alkyne, the following process is used to arrive at the correct condensed structure.

EXAMPLES: Write the condensed formula for 2–hexene.

- Since "hex" means 6 carbon atoms are present, start by writing 6 carbons in a row.

$$C \quad C \quad C \quad C \quad C \quad C$$

- The "ene" ending means a C=C bond is present, and the "2" means the bond **starts** at carbon #2 and goes to carbon #3. The other carbon–carbon bonds are single.

$$C - C = C - C - C - C$$

- Since all carbons have FOUR bonds, count the bonds between each carbon and its neighbours and subtract that number from 4. The difference is the number of hydrogens attached to each carbon. The appropriate number of hydrogens are now written into the formula.

$$CH_3-CH=CH-CH_2-CH_2-CH_3$$

3 bonds between carbons so 4th bond is to a hydrogen

Write the condensed formula for 1–pentyne.

- Similar to the reasoning above, the "yne" ending means a triple bond is present and the "1" indicates that the bond starts at carbon #1 and goes to carbon #2.

$$HC \equiv C-CH_2-CH_2-CH_3$$

4 bonds to carbons so no extra H's

3 bonds to carbons so one bond to H

EXAMPLES: $H_2C=CH_2$ (or, $CH_2=CH_2$) = ethene (common name = ethylene)

$CH_2=CH-CH_3$ = propene

$CH_3-CH=CH-CH_3$ = 2–butene

$CH_2=C-CH_2-CH_3$ = 2–methyl–1–butene
     |
     CH_3

            CH_3
            |
$CH_2=CH-C-CH_2-CH_3$ = 3,3–dimethyl–1–pentene
            |
            CH_3

$HC \equiv CH$ = ethyne (common name = acetylene)

$HC \equiv C - CH_3$ = propyne

$CH_3-C \equiv C-CH_3$ = 2–butyne

$HC \equiv C-CH_2-CH-CH_3$ = 4–methyl–1–pentyne
                 |
                 CH_3

H3C   CH3
    \   /
     C
H2C   CH   = 3,3–dimethyl–1–cyclopentene
   \   ‖
   H2C——CH

Note: the double (or triple) bond starts at carbon #1 and attached groups are numbered so as to have the lowest possible numbers

EXERCISES:

21. Look at the examples above (except for the cyclopentene) and decide on the general formula relating the ratio of carbons to hydrogens for each of the following.
    (a) an alkene   (b) an alkyne
    Express your answer in a form similar to the expression C_NH_{2N+2} which was found for alkanes.

22. Draw the condensed structure for the following.
    (a) 1–hexene   (c) 3–decene   (e) 2–octene
    (b) 4–nonyne   (d) 2–heptyne   (f) 1–octyne

23. Name the following.

    (a) $CH_3–CH_2–CH=CH–CH_2–CH_3$

    (b) $CH_3–CH_2–CH_2–CH_2–CH_2–C\equiv CH$

    (c) $CH_3–CH_2–CH_2–C\equiv C–CH_2–CH_2–CH_2–CH_2–CH_3$

    (d) $CH_3–CH_2–CH=CH–CH_2–CH_2–CH_3$

24. Draw the condensed structure for each of the following.
    (a) 4–ethyl–3–methyl–2–hexene   (e) dimethyl–2–butene
    (b) 3–methyl–4–octyne   (f) 3,6–dimethyl–1–cyclohexene
    (c) 1–ethyl–1–cyclononene   (g) cyclopropyne
    (d) 3–ethyl–4–methyl–1–hexyne   (h) 1,3–dimethyl–1–cyclopentene

25. Name the following compounds.

    (a)
    $$CH_3–\overset{\overset{\displaystyle H_3C}{|}}{\underset{\underset{\displaystyle H_3C\ \ CH_2–CH_3}{|\ \ \ \ |}}{C}}–CH–CH=CH–CH_2–CH_3$$

    (b)
    $$CH_3–CH_2–\underset{\underset{\displaystyle CH_2–CH_3}{|}}{CH}–C\equiv C–\overset{\overset{\displaystyle CH_2–CH_3}{|}}{CH}–\underset{\underset{\displaystyle CH_3}{|}}{CH}–CH_3$$

    (c)
    H3C   CH3
       \   /
      HC——CH
       | |
      HC====C
              \
              CH3

    (d)
            CH3 CH3
            | |
            CH——CH
           /   \
        H2C   CH2
         | |
        H2C   CH2
           \   /
            C≡≡≡C

    (e) $CH_3–CH_2–CH=\underset{\underset{\displaystyle CH_3}{|}}{C}–CH_2–CH_3$

    (f)
              HC═══
           /   \
        H2C   CH
         | |
        H2C   CH–CH3
           \   /
            CH2

THE GEOMETRY OF ALKENES AND ALKYNES

In alkanes, each carbon atom is bonded to four other atoms in a tetrahedral shape. The resulting structure is very flexible as a result of atoms being able to rotate freely around the axis of each single bond.

Alkenes have a geometry in which the three atoms connected to each carbon lie flat, arranged 120° from each other in a plane.

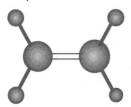

which looks like this from the side:

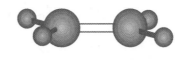

Alkynes have a geometry in which the two atoms attached to the central carbon lie in a straight line, such that the attached atoms are 180° from each other.

Whereas alkanes have flexible structures, alkenes have very rigid structures. The double bonds effectively "lock" the structure to prevent the attached atoms from "twisting" around the double bond.

The triple bond in alkynes is also very rigid, and a series of triple bonds will form straight "needle–like" structures. For example, molecules similar to the following have been detected in interstellar space, where the molecules act as radio antennae.

$$H - C \equiv C - C \equiv C - C \equiv C - C \equiv C - C \equiv C - C \equiv C - C \equiv C - H$$

On the other hand, in a molecule such as

$$CH_3 - C \equiv C - CH_3$$

the carbons involved in the triple bond are locked to each other, but the single bonds extending from the triply–bonded carbons to the methyl carbons allow free rotation of the methyl groups.

The rigid structure of the alkene carbons has an immediate and important consequence: a new kind of isomerism.

This kind of isomerism, called **CIS–TRANS ISOMERISM**, is possible whenever a molecule has:
- a double bond present, AND
- groups (other than a hydrogen atom) which are attached to each of the carbons involved in the double bond. (The attached groups do not have to be identical; all that is required is that they not be hydrogen atoms.)

EXAMPLE: 2–pentene has two different isomers possible.

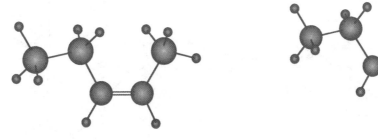

cis–2–pentene   trans–2–pentene

In the above example, the methyl and ethyl groups on opposite ends of the double bond are either "cis" or "trans" to each other.

Note: In a "**CIS**" isomer, the two groups are on the **SAME SIDE** of the double bond.

$$H_3C \quad\quad CH_3 \quad\longleftarrow \text{both } CH_3\text{'s are on the upper side}$$

$$C = C$$

$$H \quad\quad H$$

In a "**TRANS**" isomer, the two groups are "**TRANSVERSE**" to each other (that is, on opposite sides of the double bond).

$$H \quad\quad CH_3$$

$$C = C$$

$$H_3C \quad\quad H$$

the CH_3's are on opposite sides

EXERCISES:

26.   Draw the actual shape of the following molecules using condensed structures.
   (a) trans–2–hexene   (c) cis–3–octene   (e) 2–butyne
   (b) 3–hexyne   (d) trans–4–decene   (f) 4–methyl–cis–2–pentene

27.   Which of the following molecules can exhibit cis–trans isomerism?
   (a) 1–butene   (c) 4–heptyne   (e) 3–ethyl–3–hexene
   (b) 3–hexene   (d) 2–octene   (f) 2,5–dimethyloctane

28.   Name the following as "cis" or "trans" isomers.

(a) $CH_3–CH_2 \quad CH_2–CH_3$
         $C = C$
         $H \quad\quad H$

(b) $H \quad\quad CH_2–CH_3$
         $C = C$
    $CH_3–CH_2–CH_2–CH_2 \quad H$

(c) $H \quad\quad CH_2–CH_2–CH_2–CH_3$
         $C = C$
      $CH_3 \quad H$

(d) $H \quad\quad H$
         $C = C$
    $CH_3–CH_2–CH_2 \quad CH_2–CH_2–CH_3$

X.5. AROMATIC COMPOUNDS

Benzene, C_6H_6 , is an important molecule having the following structure.

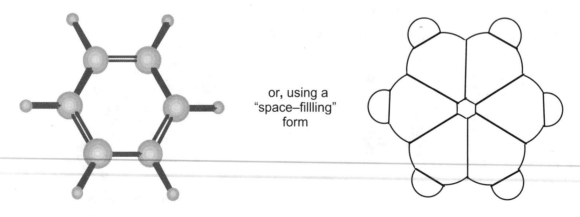

or, using a
"space–filling"
form

The ring–like structure of benzene can be written in either of two **RESONANCE STRUCTURES,** differing only in the placement of the double bonds. Each resonance structure consists of alternating single and double bonds between carbon atoms.

Strictly speaking, drawing benzene in either of its two resonance structures is not correct. The actual arrangement of electrons in the carbon ring is a mixture of both resonance structures. In order to better show the situation which occurs, benzene is frequently represented as follows.

Benzene's resonance structures give it unusual stability; that is, it is highly resistant to chemical attack. Atoms attached to the benzene ring can be replaced, but only the strongest chemical attack (such as combustion) will affect the ring itself.

The benzene ring, also known as an "aromatic ring", is present in a large number of molecules and many molecules contain two or more aromatic rings joined together.

Definition: An **AROMATIC MOLECULE** is a molecule containing one or more benzene rings.

The aromatic ring (benzene ring) is frequently shown as: 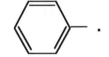 .

The origin of the term "aromatic" comes from the fact that many molecules containing benzene rings are quite fragrant and pleasant smelling (although many others are quite disagreeable). In the past, aromatic molecules were obtained primarily from the distillation of coal, but modern industry obtains them from a process called the **catalytic reforming** of petroleum.

The naming of simple aromatic compounds formed by adding groups to a benzene ring is almost identical to the naming procedure used for other cyclic hydrocarbons. Two exercises on the next page allow you to apply what you know to naming aromatic compounds.

The example molecules which follow do not have to be memorized; they are shown for your information.

EXAMPLES:

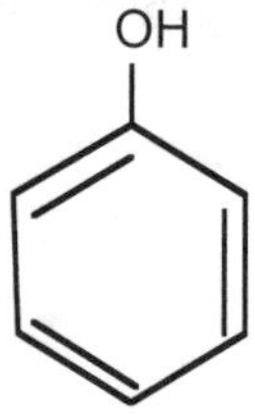

hydroxybenzene
or "phenol"

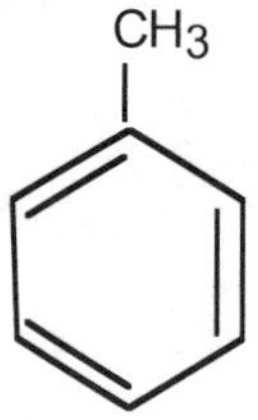

methylbenzene
or "toluene"

1,4–dichlorobenzene
or "paradichlorobenzene"

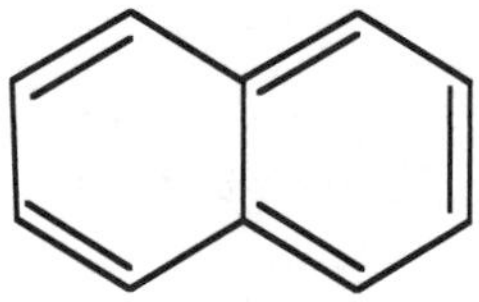

naphthalene

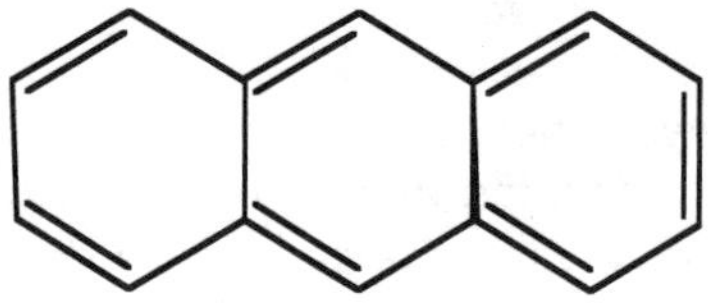

anthracene

EXERCISES:

29. (a) One resonance structure was drawn for naphthalene (above). Draw two other resonance structures.
    (b) One resonance structure was drawn for anthracene (above). Draw three other resonance structures.

30. Draw the structures of the following compounds.
    (a) 1,3,5–trimethylbenzene
    (b) 1–bromo–4–chlorobenzene
    (c) fluorobenzene
    (d) 1,4–dibromo–2–methylbenzene
    (e) 1,3–diethylbenzene
    (f) hexylbenzene

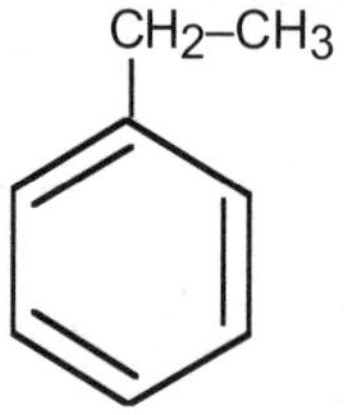

31. Name the following compounds.

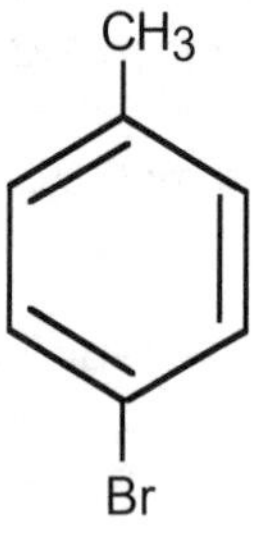

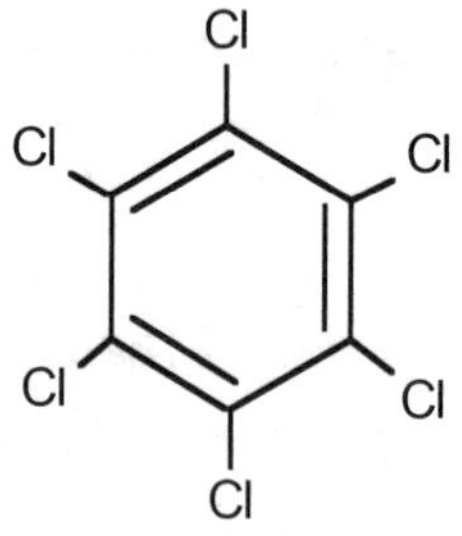

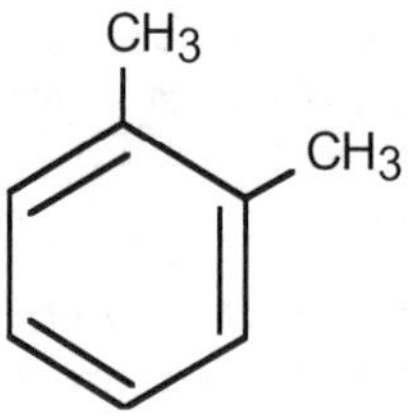

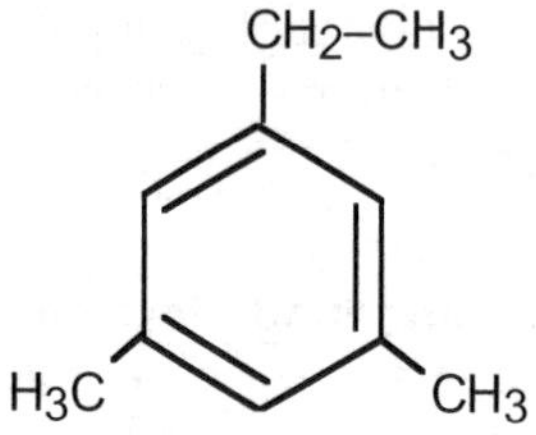

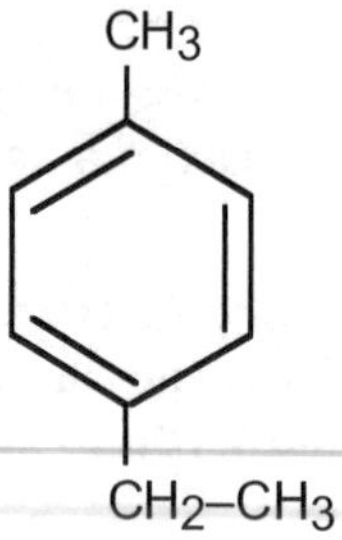

X.6. FUNCTIONAL GROUPS

Definition: A **FUNCTIONAL GROUP** is a specific group of atoms which exists in a molecule and gives a molecule an ability to react in a specific manner or gives it special properties.

Hydrocarbons have a limited range of properties and uses. Functional groups allow the addition of specific properties to a molecule. For example, by carefully choosing the functional groups present in a molecule, a chemist can
  • make a molecule act as a base, an acid, or both;   • make a molecule react with specific chemicals;
  • give the molecule a particular solubility;   • make a molecule explosive.
  • give a molecule a pleasant or unpleasant smell;

The previous sections have already introduced some functional groups: halides, carbon–carbon double bonds (in alkenes) and carbon–carbon triple bonds (in alkynes). This section examines some other important functional groups and how their presence changes the properties of the parent hydrocarbon.

A. ALCOHOLS

Definition: An **ALCOHOL** is an organic compound containing an OH group.

> **RULE:** When naming an **ALCOHOL**
> • number the hydrocarbon chain to give the LOWEST possible number to the OH group.
> • place the number immediately before the name of the parent hydrocarbon, separated by a dash. Alkyl groups (and their numbers) are placed in front of the number for the OH.
> • indicate the presence of an OH group by changing the "e" ending of the hydrocarbon chain to "ol". (The ending "ol" comes from "alcoh*ol* ".)

EXAMPLES: $CH_3–OH$ = methanol (commercial name = methyl hydrate)

$CH_3–CH_2–OH$ = ethanol ("beverage alcohol")

$CH_3–CH–CH_2–CH_3$ = 2–butanol
      |
      OH

$CH_3–CH–CH_2–CH–CH_2–CH_3$ = 5–methyl–3–hexanol
      | |
      CH_3 OH

PROPERTIES OF ALCOHOLS

• There are two opposing solubility tendencies which exist in all alcohols.
    – the OH group tends to make alcohols soluble in water
    – the non–polar hydrocarbon chain tends to make alcohols insoluble in water

Methanol, ethanol and propanol are highly soluble in water ("miscible") because the hydrocarbon chain is small and the hydrogen–bonding of the OH group to water molecules "wins out".

Butanol is moderately soluble in water as a result of a "tie" between the tendency of the OH group to promote solubility and the tendency of the longer hydrocarbon chain to resist dissolving.

Pentanol and higher alcohols are effectively insoluble in water as a result of the increasing dominance of the hydrocarbon chain.

• All alcohols are poisonous; ethanol is no exception – it is simply less poisonous than other alcohols.

EXERCISES:

32. Draw the following compounds.
    (a) 1–butanol
    (b) 2–methyl–1–cyclopentanol
    (c) 2,2–dichloro–3–methyl–4–nonanol
    (d) 2,5–diethyl–1–cyclohexanol
    (e) 3–methyl–1–pentanol
    (f) 1,1,1–trifluoro–2–propanol

33. Name the following compounds.

(a) CH_3–CH–CH_3
               |
               OH

(b) CF_3–CH2–CH–CH_3
                      |
                      OH

(c) CH_2–CH_2–CH–CH_3
          | |
          OH CH_3

(d) CH_3–C–OH
                 |
               CH_3
         (with CH_3 above)

(e) CH_2–CH–OH
          | |
         CH_2–CH–Cl

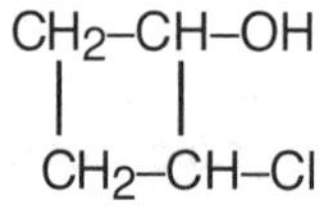

(f) CH_3–HC
                    \
                     | CH–OH
                    /
         CH_3–HC

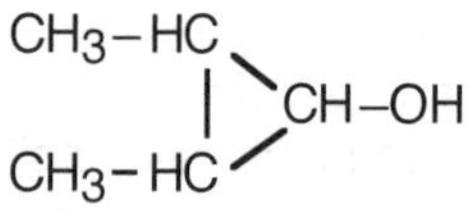

B. OTHER FUNCTIONAL GROUPS

In addition to alcohols there are several other functional groups which can change the properties of a hydrocarbon chain. You are not required to know how to name compounds containing the functional groups listed below. It is sufficient that you can recognize and name the groups present in a given compound. (The names of the compounds in the examples are given for your interest only.)

In section C, you will be shown how to name an additional functional group called an "ester".

ALDEHYDES

An *aldehyde* is an organic compound containing a C=O group at the end of a hydrocarbon chain.

The aldehyde group actually looks like
$$\overset{O}{\underset{}{\overset{\|}{-C-H}}}$$
or simply   –CHO

EXAMPLES: Some typical aldehydes are shown below.

$$H-\overset{O}{\overset{\|}{C}}-H$$ or   HCHO   (name = methanal;   common name = formaldehyde)

CH_3–CHO   (name = ethanal)

CH_3–CH_2–CH_2–CH–CHO   (name = 2–methylpentanal)
                         |
                       CH_3

CHO

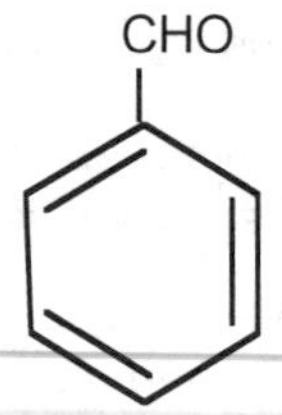

(name = benzaldehyde)

KETONES

A *ketone* is an organic compound containing a C=O group at a position OTHER THAN AT THE END OF A HYDROCARBON CHAIN.

EXAMPLES: Some typical ketones are shown below.

$$CH_3-\overset{\overset{\displaystyle O}{\|}}{C}-CH_3 \quad or \quad CH_3COCH_3 \quad (name = propanone; common name = acetone)$$

$CH_3CH_2COCH_2CH_2CH_3$ (name = 3–hexanone)

$$\begin{array}{ccc} H_2C & \!\!\!\!\!\!\!\!\!\!\!\! & CH_2 \\ & & \\ H_2C & & C=O \qquad (name = cyclohexanone) \\ & & \\ H_2C & \!\!\!\!\!\!\!\!\!\!\!\! & CH_2 \end{array}$$

ETHERS

An *ether* is a compound in which an oxygen joins two hydrocarbon groups.

Several ethers have anaesthetic properties: ethoxyethane was formerly used in hospitals and is still used by biologists to "quiet" or anaesthetize insects.

EXAMPLES: Some typical ethers are shown below.

$CH_3CH_2-O-CH_2CH_3$ (name = ethoxyethane; common name is "hospital ether")

$CH_3-O-CH_2CH_2\,CH_3$ (name = 1–methoxypropane; an anaesthetic)

$$\begin{array}{l} \quad\;\; CH_3 \\ \quad\;\; | \\ CH_3-C-CH_2-CH_2-O-CH_3 \qquad (name = 1-methoxy-3,3-dimethylbutane) \\ \quad\;\; | \\ \quad\;\; CH_3 \end{array}$$

THE ETHER BUNNY

–Zimbabwe

AMINES

An *amine* is an organic compound containing an NH_2 group. Amines are organic bases and react with acids. Typically, amines have a "fish–like" odour.

EXAMPLES: Some typical amines are shown below.

$CH_3–CH_2–NH_2$ (name = aminoethane)

$H_2N–CH_2–CH_2–CH_2–CH_2–NH_2$ (name = 1,4–diaminobutane; common name is putrescine, produced by decomposing meat)

$CH_3–CH–CH_2–CH_2–CH_3$ (name = 2–aminopentane)
$|$
NH_2

AMIDES

An *amide* is an organic compound containing a $CONH_2$ group. The $CONH_2$ group is also some–times shown as

$$\underset{\displaystyle -C-NH_2}{\overset{\displaystyle O \atop \displaystyle \|}{}} .$$

EXAMPLES: Some typical amides are shown below.

$CH_3–CONH_2$ (name = ethanamide)

$CH_3–CH_2–CH_2–CH_2–CH_2–CONH_2$ (name = hexanamide)

$$CH_3 \atop | \atop CH_3–C–CH_2–CONH_2 \quad (name = 3,3–dimethylbutanamide) \atop | \atop CH_3$$

CARBOXYLIC ACIDS

A *carboxylic acid* is an organic compound which contains a COOH group. The COOH group is also sometimes shown as

$$\underset{\displaystyle -C-O-H}{\overset{\displaystyle O \atop \displaystyle \|}{}} .$$

Carboxylic acids are commonly referred to as "organic acids".

EXAMPLES: Some typical carboxylic acids are shown below.

CH_3COOH (name = ethanoic acid; commonly called acetic acid)

$HCOOH$ (name = methanoic acid; common name = formic acid, found in red ant venom)

$CH_3–CH_2–CH_2–COOH$ (name = butanoic acid; common name = butyric acid, responsible for the odour of "smelly feet")

A Digression on Amino Acids

An *amino acid* is a carboxylic acid with an amine group at the 2–position. Although there are numerous amino acids, only 20 different amino acids are essential biological "building blocks".

EXAMPLE: $CH_3-CH-COOH$ = 2–aminopropanoic acid (common name = alanine)
             |
             NH_2

Amino acids can react with both acids and bases.

EXAMPLE   Reaction with acids – $CH_3-CH-COOH + H^+$ $\longrightarrow$ $CH_3-CH-COOH$
                                          | |
                                          NH_2 $^+NH_3$

Reaction with bases – $CH_3-CH-COOH + OH^-$ $\longrightarrow$ $CH_3-CH-COO^- + H_2O$
                              | |
                              NH_2 NH_2

After reacting with either an acid or base the amino acid is ionic and remains soluble in water.

There are two properties of amino acids which are especially important.

a) **Amino acids are highly soluble in water** because amino acids have both acid and base groups arranged such that the acid and base groups can "neutralize" each other.

or, using space–filling models

The resulting ionic compound is highly soluble in water.

b) **Amino acids link with each other to form "dipeptides" and "polypeptides".**

a "dipeptide"

The shaded oval, above, shows how water is removed from two molecules and allows the molecules to link together. The box indicates that the molecules are now joined together by an "amide linkage" (or "peptide bond" or "peptide linkage")

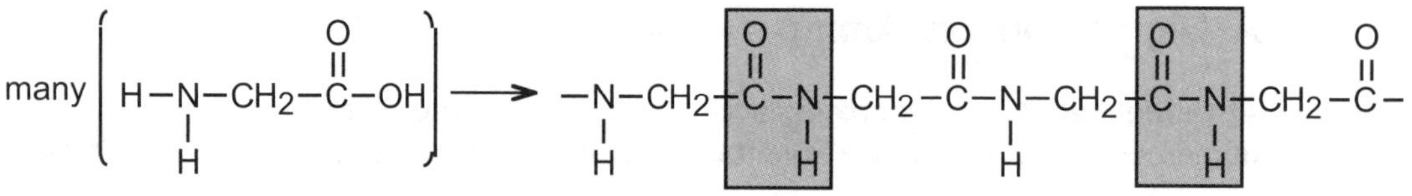

$$\text{many} \left(\text{H} - \text{N} - \text{CH}_2 - \overset{\overset{\displaystyle O}{\|}}{\text{C}} - \text{OH} \right) \longrightarrow -\text{N} - \text{CH}_2 - \overset{\overset{\displaystyle O}{\|}}{\text{C}} - \text{N} - \text{CH}_2 - \overset{\overset{\displaystyle O}{\|}}{\text{C}} - \text{N} - \text{CH}_2 - \overset{\overset{\displaystyle O}{\|}}{\text{C}} - \text{N} - \text{CH}_2 - \overset{\overset{\displaystyle O}{\|}}{\text{C}} -$$

a "polypeptide"

As seen above, a series of amino acid molecules can be joined by a series of amide linkages to form a polypeptide.

C. ESTERS

An **ester** is a compound in which a COO group ($-\text{C} \overset{\displaystyle \nearrow O}{\underset{\displaystyle \searrow O}{}}$) joins two hydrocarbon chains.

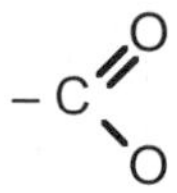

> **RULE:** To name an **ESTER**
> - the hydrocarbon chain attached directly to the carbon side of the COO group has its "e" ending changed to "oate". The C in the COO group is considered to be part of the parent hydrocarbon chain.
> - the hydrocarbon chain attached to the oxygen side of the COO group is named as an alkyl group; the name of the alkyl group is used as a separate, initial word.

EXAMPLES: Some typical esters are shown below.

$\text{CH}_3-\text{CH}_2-\text{CH}_2-\text{COO}-\text{CH}_3$ = methyl butanoate

$\text{HCOO}-\text{CH}_2-\text{CH}_2-\text{CH}_2-\text{CH}_3$ = butyl methanoate

$\text{CH}_3-\text{CH}_2-\text{COO}-\text{CH}_2-\text{CH}_3$ = ethyl propanoate

$\text{CH}_3-\text{COO}-\text{CH}_2-\text{CH}_2-\text{CH}_3$ = propyl ethanoate

Preparation and Properties of Esters

Esters are prepared by reacting an organic acid and an alcohol in the presence of an inorganic acid such as HCl or H_2SO_4. In the example below, ethanoic acid reacts with methanol (written backwards); the "H^+" over the reaction arrow indicates that H^+ is used as a catalyst.

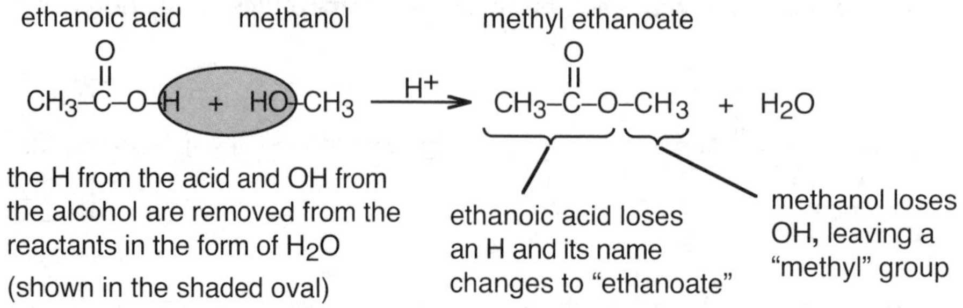

ethanoic acid   methanol   methyl ethanoate

$$\text{CH}_3-\overset{\overset{\displaystyle O}{\|}}{\text{C}}-\text{O} - \text{H} \; + \; \text{HO} - \text{CH}_3 \xrightarrow{\;H^+\;} \text{CH}_3-\overset{\overset{\displaystyle O}{\|}}{\text{C}}-\text{O}-\text{CH}_3 \; + \; H_2O$$

the H from the acid and OH from the alcohol are removed from the reactants in the form of H_2O (shown in the shaded oval)

ethanoic acid loses an H and its name changes to "ethanoate"

methanol loses OH, leaving a "methyl" group

The actual experimental procedure for producing small amounts of impure esters is quite simple.

Mix a few millilitres of the desired carboxylic acid and a few millilitres of the desired alcohol in a test tube. Add a few drops of concentrated sulphuric acid and heat over a bunsen burner for a minute or so. Be sure not to overheat the liquid and cause it to spurt out the end of the tube. [The distinctive presence of the ester is detected by cautiously smelling the contents of the tube.]

Organic acids have a "sharp, pungent and biting" odour which is often quite unpleasant. (Butanoic acid has the odour of "rancid sneakers", only FAR MORE CONCENTRATED!) Alcohols also have a "sharp" odour, although generally less so than that of acids having a similar number of carbon atoms. Methanol and ethanol have very little odour but their smell tends to "catch" in the nasal passage. Propanol and higher alcohols have more intense and often unpleasant odours which also tend to "catch" in the nasal passage.

The odour of esters, on the other hand, is generally very pleasant. In small amounts, esters form the basis of many fragrant fruit and flower smells.

EXAMPLE:

Ester	Odour	Ester	Odour
methyl butanoate	pineapples	pentyl propanoate	apricots
pentyl ethanoate	bananas	ethyl methanoate	rum
octyl ethanoate	orange rind		

EXERCISES:

34. Name the following molecules.
   (a) $CH_3-CH_2-COO-CH_3$
   (b) $HCOO-CH_2-CH_2-CH_3$
   (c) $CH_3-CH_2-CH_2-COO-CH_2-CH_3$
   (d) $CH_3-COO-CH_2-CH_2-CH_2-CH_2-CH_2-CH_3$
   (e) $CH_3-CH_2-CH_2-CH_2-COO-CH_2-CH_2-CH_2-CH_3$

35. Draw the following molecules.
   (a) propyl pentanoate
   (b) methyl hexanoate
   (c) ethyl propanoate
   (d) butyl butanoate
   (e) hexyl methanoate

36. Draw the carboxylic acid molecule and alcohol molecule which are used to make each ester in exercise 34.

The new Chemistry 11 teacher is about to find that not all esters have a pleasant smell.

D. A SUMMARY OF THE FUNCTIONAL GROUPS

The functional groups which have been introduced in this unit are shown in the table below. The exercise which follows is designed to help you learn to recognize the presence of specific functional groups in a given molecule.

Name	Functional Group	Name	Functional Group
alkene	$C = C$	ether	$-O-$
alkyne	$C \equiv C$	amine	$-NH_2$
halide	$-F, -Cl, -Br$ or $-I$	amide	$-CONH_2$
alcohol	$-OH$	carboxylic acid	$-COOH$
aldehyde	$-CHO$	ester	$-COO-$
ketone	$-CO-$	aromatic ring	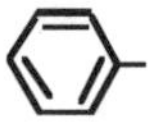

EXERCISE:

37. Circle the functional groups which exist in each of the following molecules and label each group as one of:

    DOU = double bond , TRI = triple bond , ARO = aromatic ring ,   HAL = halide ,
    ALC = alcohol ,   ALD = aldehyde ,   KET = ketone ,   ETH = ether ,
    AMN = amine ,   AMD = amide ,   CAR = carboxylic acid , EST = ester.

(a) $Br-CH_2CH_2CH_2CHCH_3$
                         |
                        CH_3

(b) $HC \equiv CCH_2C \equiv CH$

                     OH
                      |
(c) $HOCH_2CHCHCH_2OH$
                    |
                   OH

(d) $CH_3CH_2CH=CHCHCH_3$
                            |
                           Cl

                CH_3
                  |
(e) $CH_3-C-CO-CH_3$
                  |
                CH_3

                CH_2OH
                  |
(f) CH_3-C-NH_2
                  |
                CH_2OH

(g)

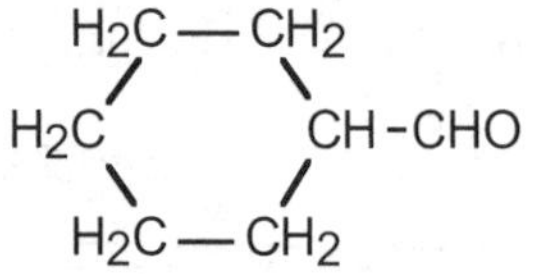

(h)

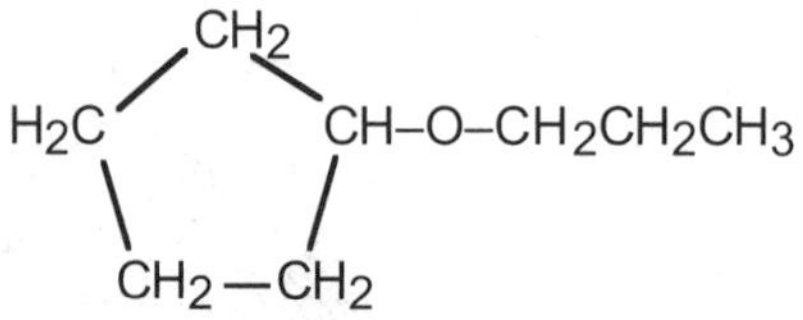

(i) $CH_3-CO-CHCH_2CH_2CH-CO-CH_3$
                    | |
                 $COOCH_3$ $COOCH_3$

(j) $CH_2=CHCHC \equiv CH$
                    |
                  CH_3

(k)

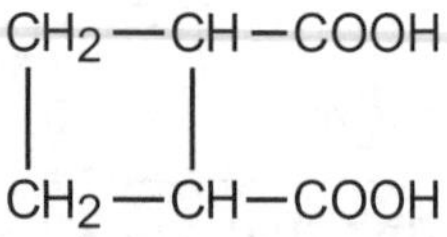

(l)

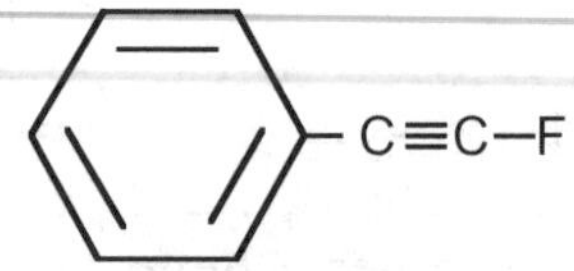

(m) 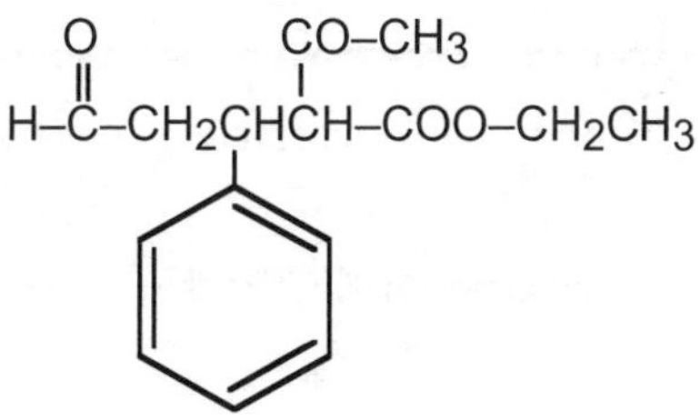
$$\text{H}-\overset{\displaystyle O}{\overset{\|}{\text{C}}}-\text{CH}_2\overset{\text{CO}-\text{CH}_3}{\overset{|}{\text{CH}}}\text{CH}-\text{COO}-\text{CH}_2\text{CH}_3$$

(with a phenyl ring attached below)

(n)
$$\text{O}=\text{C}-\text{CH}-\text{O}-\text{CH}-\text{OCH}_3$$
with CH$_2$OH above CH, H below first C=O, and O=C—H group

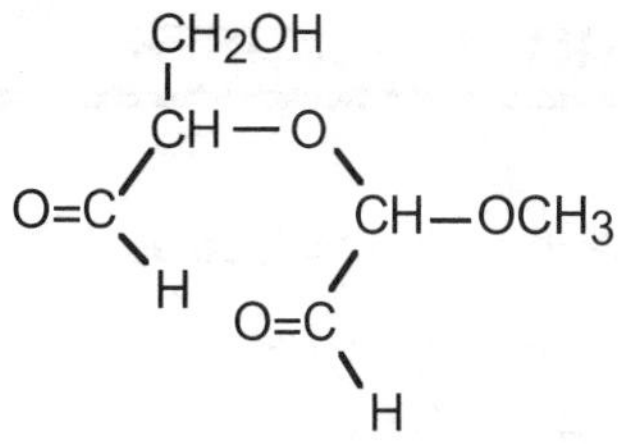

(o)
$$\text{H}_2\text{N}-\overset{\displaystyle O}{\overset{\|}{\text{C}}}-\text{CH}_2\overset{}{\underset{\text{NH}_2}{\text{CH}}}-\text{COOH}$$

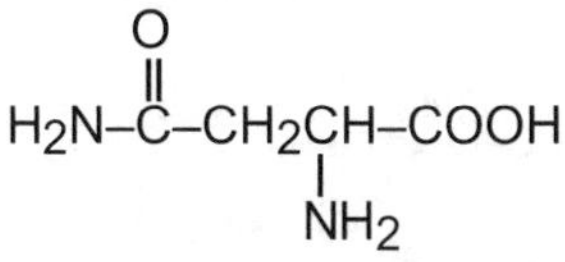

(p) 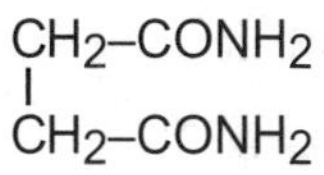
$$\overset{\text{CH}_2-\text{CONH}_2}{\underset{\text{CH}_2-\text{CONH}_2}{|}}$$

(q) 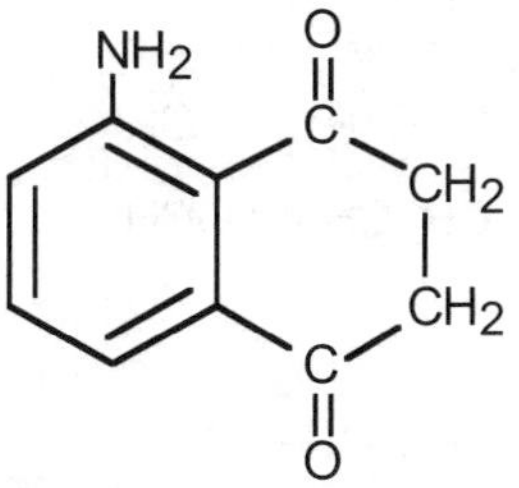 structure: benzene ring with NH$_2$, fused ring containing C=O, CH$_2$, CH$_2$, C=O

(r) 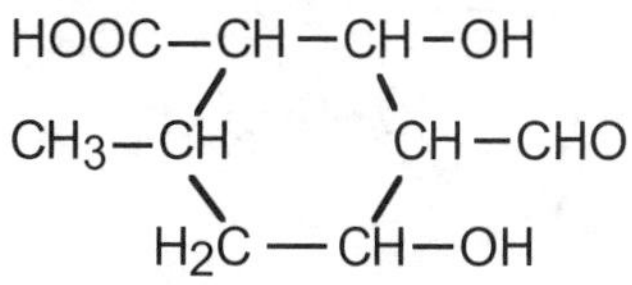
HOOC—CH—CH—OH
CH$_3$—CH   CH—CHO
H$_2$C—CH—OH

(s) 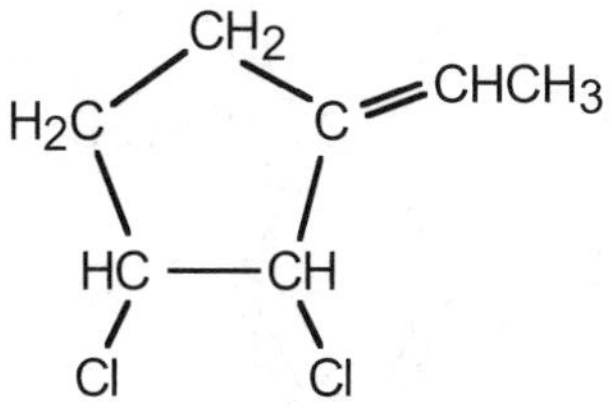
H$_2$C—CH$_2$—C=CHCH$_3$ ring with HC—CH, Cl, Cl

(t) 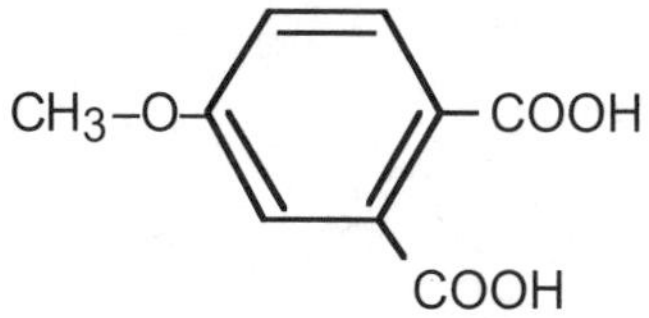
CH$_3$—O— (benzene ring) —COOH
COOH

(u) 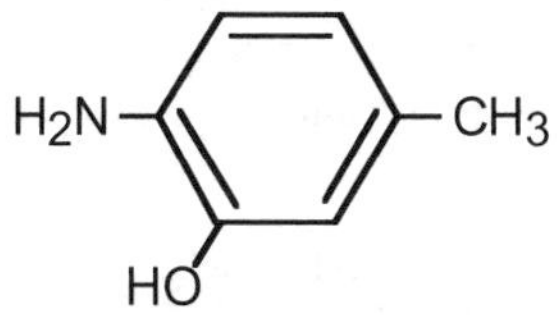
H$_2$N— (benzene ring) —CH$_3$
HO

(v) 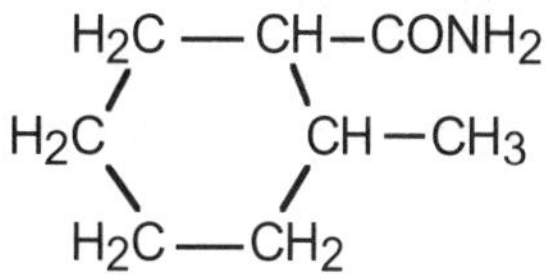
H$_2$C—CH—CONH$_2$
H$_2$C   CH—CH$_3$
H$_2$C—CH$_2$

(w) 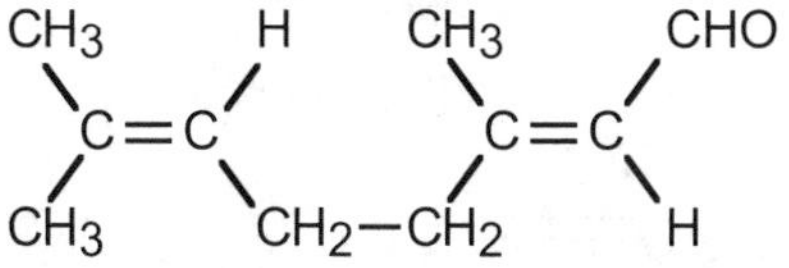
$$\overset{\text{CH}_3}{\underset{\text{CH}_3}{}}\text{C}=\text{C}\overset{\text{H}}{\underset{\text{CH}_2-\text{CH}_2}{}}\overset{\text{CH}_3}{}\text{C}=\text{C}\overset{\text{CHO}}{\underset{\text{H}}{}}$$

(x) 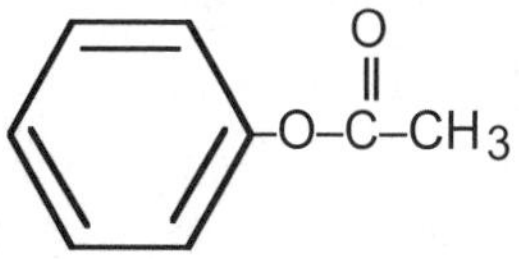
(benzene ring)—O—C(=O)—CH$_3$

(y) 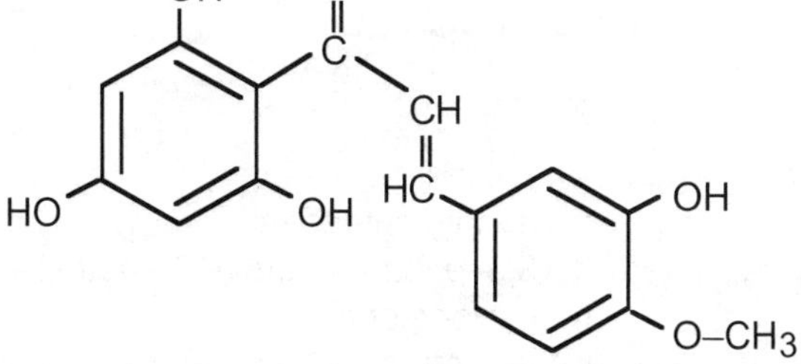
OH, C=O, HO, (benzene ring) with OH, OH, CH, HC=, (benzene ring) OH, O—CH$_3$

X.7. SUMMARY EXERCISES

38. Name the following molecules.

(a) 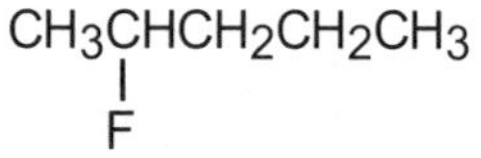 CH₃CHCH₂CH₂CH₃
           |
           F

(b) 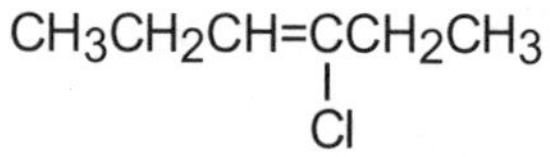 CH₃CH₂CH=CCH₂CH₃
                    |
                    Cl

(c) I–CH₂C≡CCH₂–I

(d) HCOOCH₂CH₂CH₂CH₂CH₃

(e) 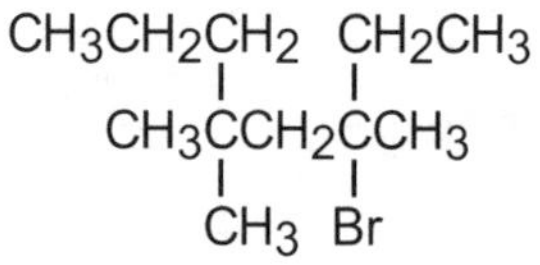 CH₃CH₂CH₂ CH₂CH₃
           | |
      CH₃CCH₂CCH₃
           | |
         CH₃   Br

(f) 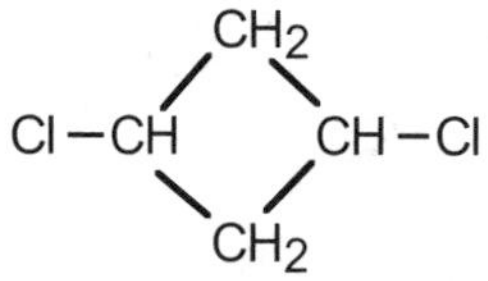 Cl–CH / CH₂ \ CH–Cl with CH₂ below forming ring

(g) 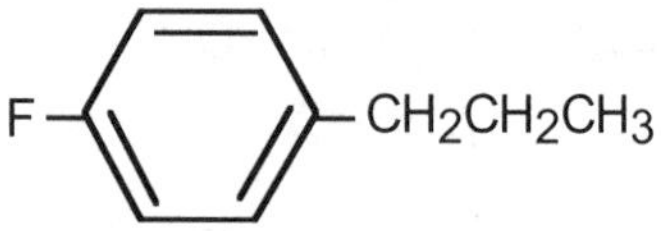 F– [benzene ring] –CH₂CH₂CH₃

(h) 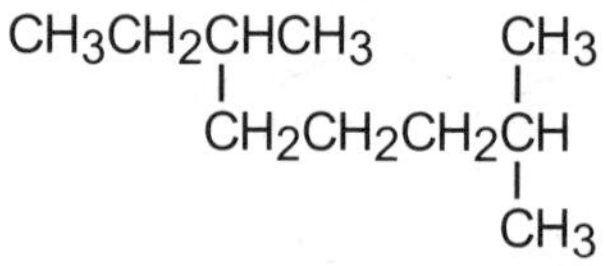 CH₃CH₂CHCH₃   CH₃
              | |
         CH₂CH₂CH₂CH
                         |
                        CH₃

(i) 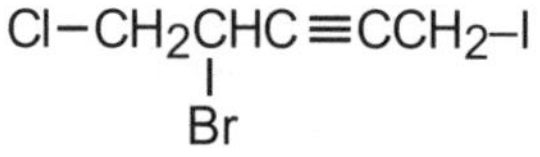 Cl–CH₂CHC≡CCH₂–I
              |
              Br

(j) 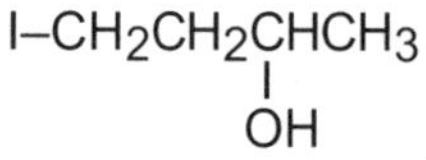 I–CH₂CH₂CHCH₃
                 |
                 OH

(k) 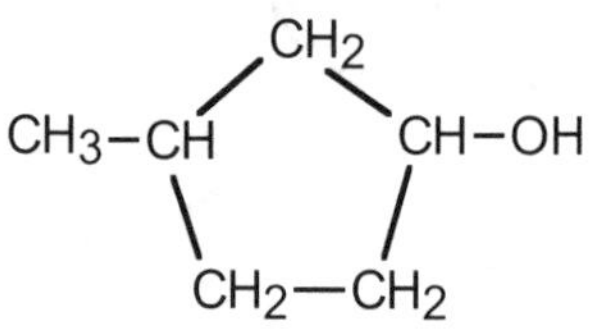   CH₂
      CH₃–CH   CH–OH
          CH₂—CH₂

(l) 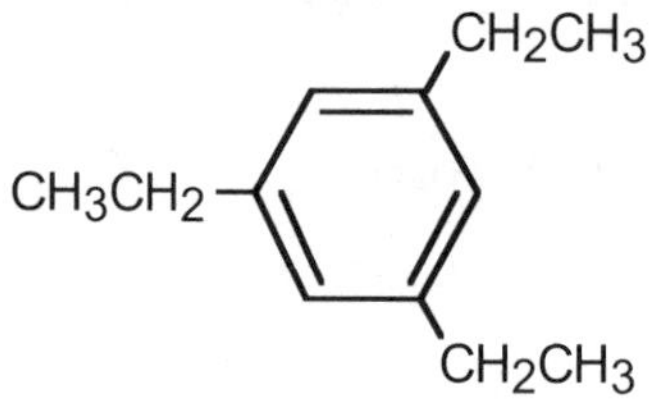 CH₃CH₂– [benzene ring] with CH₂CH₃ and CH₂CH₃ substituents

(m) Br–CH₂CH=CH₂

(n) CH₃COOCH₂CH₂CH₂CH₂CH₃

(o) 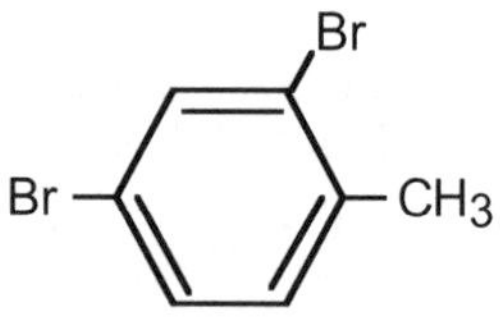 Br– [benzene ring with Br and CH₃]

(p) 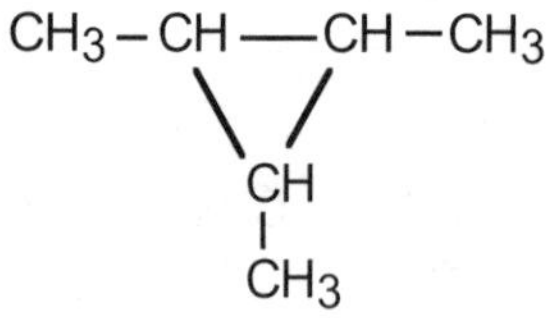 CH₃–CH—CH–CH₃
            \ /
             CH
             |
             CH₃

(q) 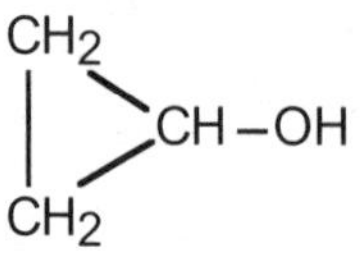 CH₂
      | \ CH–OH
     CH₂

(r) 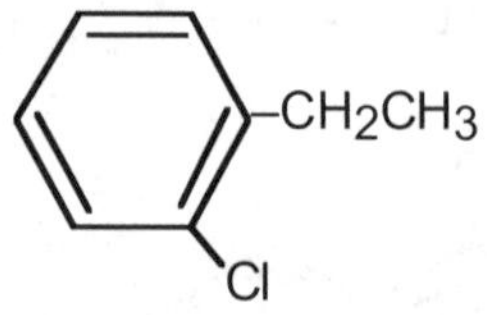 [benzene ring] –CH₂CH₃ with Cl

39. Draw the following molecules.

(a) 1,4,4–trifluoro–2–pentanol
(b) 4–chloro–2–hexyne
(c) ethyl pentanoate
(d) 3,4,5,6–tetramethylnonane
(e) 3–octyne
(f) 1,3–diethylbenzene
(g) 1,3–dibromo–3–hexene
(h) 3,5–diethyl–4,4–dimethylheptane
(i) 2,3–dichloro–2–butene
(j) methyl octanoate
(k) 3,3–diiodo–4–ethyl–2–methyl–1–hexene
(l) cyclooctene
(m) 2–methyl–3–heptyne
(n) 3–methyl–1–cyclobutanol
(o) 1–ethyl–3–propylbenzene
(p) cyclohexyne
(q) 2–methyl–2–butanol
(r) 2,2,3,3–tetrabromobutane

40. A hydrocarbon has the formula C_NH_{2N-2}. Which of the following are possible?
    (a) The compound is branched but has no multiple bonds or cyclic groups.
    (b) The compound has a single double bond.
    (c) The compound has a single triple bond.
    (d) The compound has a single cyclic group.
    (e) The compound has two double bonds.
    (f) The compound has two triple bonds.
    (g) The compound has two cyclic groups.
    (h) The compound has a double bond and a triple bond.
    (i) The compound has a double bond and a single cyclic group.
    (j) The compound has a cyclic group and a triple bond.

41. Draw and name the 9 isomers of C_5H_{10}. (Hint: think what you were doing in the previous exercise.)

42. What class of organic compounds
    (a) can neutralize bases?   (d) form waxes?
    (b) often smell "fishy"?   (e) can form polypeptides?
    (c) can be prepared by combining an acid and an alcohol?   (f) have fruity odours?

43. Draw the following cis and trans isomers.
    (a) trans–3,4–dichloro–3–hexene   (d) trans–1,1,1–trifluoro–2–pentene
    (b) trans–2–octene   (e) cis–1,1,1,7,7,7–hexachloro–3–heptene
    (c) cis–2,3–dibromo–2–butene   (f) cis–2–nonene

44. Circle the functional groups in each of the following molecules and label each group as one of:
    DOU = double bond ,   TRI = triple bond ,   ARO = aromatic ring ,   HAL = halide ,
    ALC = alcohol ,   ALD = aldehyde ,   KET = ketone ,   ETH = ether ,
    AMN = amine ,   AMD = amide ,   CAR = carboxylic acid , EST = ester.

    (a) $F_3CCOOCH_3$ (b) $CH_3COCH_2CH_2OH$

    (c)   (d)

    (e) $CH_3C=CHCHC{\equiv}CH$ (f) $H_2NCOCH_2CHCH_2CONH_2$
        $\quad\ \ \ |\quad\ \ |$ $\qquad\qquad\quad |$
        $\quad\ \ CH_3\ \ CH_3$ $\qquad\qquad\ NH_2$

    (g)   (h)

    (i) $CH_3CHCH_2–O–CH_3$ (j) $H_2NCOCH_2CHC{\equiv}CCHCHO$
        $\qquad\ |$ $\qquad\qquad\quad |\qquad\ |$
        $\qquad OH$ $\qquad\qquad\ Cl\qquad Cl$

    (k) $HOCH_2CH$ (l)

(m) $\text{C}_6\text{H}_5\text{–CH}_2\text{CONH}_2$ (benzene ring)–CH₂CONH₂

(n)
$$\begin{array}{c} \text{CH}_2\text{–CH}_2 \\ \text{O} \qquad \text{O} \\ \text{CH}_2\text{–CH}_2 \end{array}$$

(o)
$$\underset{\text{OH}\quad\text{OH}\;\text{OH}\qquad\text{OH}}{\text{CH}_2\text{–CH–CH–}\overset{\text{OH}}{\text{CH}}\text{–CH–CHO}}$$

(p)
$$\text{CH}_3\text{CH}_2\text{CH}_2\underset{\text{COOCH}_2\text{CH}_3}{\overset{\text{CH}_3}{\text{C}}}\text{—}\overset{\text{O}}{\text{C}}\text{–CH}_3$$

(q) HO–(benzene ring)$\text{–CH}_2\underset{\text{NH}_2}{\text{CH}}\text{COOH}$

(r)
$$\underset{\text{O}}{\overset{\text{H}}{\text{C}}}\text{-}\overset{\text{O}}{\underset{\text{H}}{\text{C}}}$$

(s)
$$\begin{array}{c} \text{CH=CH} \\ \text{O=C} \qquad \text{C=O} \\ \text{CH=CH} \end{array}$$

(t) HO–(benzene ring)–CHO, $\text{CH}_3\text{O–}$

(u)
$$\begin{array}{c} \qquad\qquad \overset{\text{O}}{\parallel} \\ \text{H}_2\text{C–C} \\ \text{C} \qquad\quad \text{O} \\ \text{C–CH}_2 \end{array}$$

(v)
$$\begin{array}{c} \text{H}_3\text{C} \qquad \text{CH}_3 \\ \text{C} \\ \text{CH}_3 \qquad \text{CH—CH} \\ \text{C=C} \qquad\qquad \text{O} \\ \text{CH}_3 \quad\; \text{H} \qquad \text{C} \\ \qquad\qquad\qquad \text{O} \end{array}$$

ANSWERS TO UNIT I : SAFETY IN THE CHEMICAL LABORATORY

1. (a) Yell to alert others that you have a problem and immediately "stop, drop and roll". In other words, don't run around (you can't escape the flames); just roll on the floor to put out the flames. If a large amount of chemical has landed on you, other students should quickly get the fire blanket to cover you.
   (b) Yell to alert others that you have a problem and get to the eyewash fountain or station as soon as possible. You may need someone to guide you to the eyewash fountain.
   (c) Immediately stand back out of harm's way, yell to alert others that you have a problem, and then assess the situation to decide if the fire is controlled and can be put out by smothering the fire.
   (d) Alert other students in the vicinity and notify the teacher for specific cleanup instructions.
   (e) Quickly wash the acid or base off your hands and then rinse with some neutralizing solution.

2. Turn off the gas! Then, while waiting for the gas to dissipate, check that the device used to ignite the gas is working correctly and that the air collar of the bunsen burner is closed. If necessary, seek help from the teacher.

3. The spray is swept back and forth across the base of the flames.

4. If the flame is in a container such as a beaker of test tube, smother the flames by placing a watch glass or inverted beaker over the top. If a somewhat larger area is involved, smother the flame with the fire blanket.

5. Emergency equipment needs to be used as soon as possible; wasting time trying to get the teacher's permission might worsen the situation.

6. About 10 s; (larger ones spray for about 20 s)

7. Save the life, save the sight, save the skin. First extinguish the flames by rolling the student on the floor because the flames are life–threatening. Then wash the eyes to try to save the eyesight. Only then should you worry about washing chemicals off the rest of the skin.

8. If you cut yourself on the glass you might get the chemical on the glass into the cut.

ANSWERS TO UNIT II : INTRODUCTION TO CHEMISTRY

1. (a) unknown amount = cost in dollars   or   # of dollars
initial amount = 100 g
conversion factor = $50/g, or 1 g/$50

   (b) unknown amount = # of disks
initial amount = $36.00
conversion factor = $6.00/10 disks, or 10 disks/$6.00

   (c) unknown amount = volume in millilitres   or   # of millilitres
initial amount = 20 g
conversion factor = 0.35 g/mL, or 1 mL/0.35 g

   (d) unknown amount = # of kiwi fruit
initial amount = $5
conversion factor = 3 kiwi fruit/$1, or $1/3 kiwi fruit

   (e) unknown amount = # of bims
initial amount = 30 tuds
conversion factor = 4 bims/5 tuds, or 5 tuds/4 bims

   (f) unknown amount = # of goats
initial amount = 10 cows
conversion factor = 2 cows/7 goats, or 7 goats/2 cows

   (g) unknown amount = mass of oxygen   or   # of grams
initial amount = 5.5 moles
conversion factor = 32 g/mole, or 1 mole/32 g

   (h) unknown amount = # of sulphur molecules
initial amount = 104 sulphur atoms
conversion factor = 8 sulphur atoms/1 sulphur molecule,   or 1 sulphur molecule/8 sulphur atoms

   (i) unknown amount = length of time   or   # of seconds
initial amount = 200 coulombs
conversion factor = 35 coulombs/s, or 1 s/35 coulombs

   (j) unknown amount = temperature increase   or   # of $^\circ$C
initial amount = 100 kJ
conversion factor = 4.18 kJ/1°C, or 1°C/4.18 kJ

2. (a) # of atoms = 5.5 mol x $\dfrac{6.02 \times 10^{23} \text{ atoms}}{1 \text{ mol}}$ = **3.3 x 10^{24} atoms**

   (b) # of moles = 25.0 L x $\dfrac{1 \text{ mol}}{22.4 \text{ L}}$ = **1.12 mol**

   (c) # of moles = 7.0 g x $\dfrac{1 \text{ mol}}{28g}$ = **0.25 mol**

   (d) # of seconds = 200.0 coulombs x $\dfrac{1 \text{ s}}{35 \text{ coulombs}}$ = **5.7 s**

   (e) # of atmospheres = 4 x 10^{-8} kPa x $\dfrac{1 \text{ atm}}{101.3 \text{ kPa}}$ = **4 x 10^{-10} atmospheres**

   (f) # of kilograms = 3.20 x 10^4 troy ounce x $\dfrac{0.0311 \text{kg}}{1 \text{ troy ounce}}$ = **995 kg**

   (g) # of milliseconds = 5.0 x 10^{-4} s x $\dfrac{1 \text{ ms}}{10^{-3} \text{ s}}$ = **0.50 ms**

   (h) # of moles = 15 100 kJ x $\dfrac{1 \text{ mol}}{5450 \text{ kJ}}$ = **2.77 mol**

(i)   # of millimetres = 0.05 micron x $\dfrac{10^{-3}\ mm}{1\ micron}$ = **5 x 10^{-5} mm**

(j)   # of litres = 0.0358 mol x $\dfrac{1\ L}{11.7\ mol}$ = **0.00306 L**

3.   # of kilopascals = 27.0 inches x $\dfrac{0.0334\ atm}{1\ inch}$ x $\dfrac{101.3\ kPa}{1\ atm}$ = 91.4 kPa

4.   (a) amount of heat = 3.1 x 10^{13} m^3 x $\dfrac{917\ kg}{1\ m^3}$ x $\dfrac{334\ kJ}{1\ kg}$ = **9.5 x 10^{18} kJ**

   (b) # of kilograms = 9.5 x 10^{18} kJ x $\dfrac{1\ kg}{1.51 \times 10^4\ kJ}$ = **6.3 x 10^{14} kg**

5.   # of tonnes = \$350 x $\dfrac{1\ kg}{\$0.980}$ x $\dfrac{1\ t}{1000\ kg}$ = **0.357 t**

6.   # of carats = 177 mL x $\dfrac{3.51g}{1\ mL}$ x $\dfrac{1\ carat}{0.200\ g}$ = **3110 carats**

7.   (a) # of kilometres = 0.25 h x $\dfrac{120\ km}{h}$ = **30 km**

   (b) # of kilometres = 12 min x $\dfrac{1\ h}{60\ min}$ x $\dfrac{120\ km}{1\ h}$ = **24 km**

8.   (a)   # of dollars = 3 doz x $\dfrac{\$8.40}{1\ doz}$ = **\$25.20**

   (b) # of hamburgers = 5 doz x $\dfrac{\$8.40}{1\ doz}$ x $\dfrac{1\ hamburger}{\$1.50}$ = **28 hamburgers**

   (c) # of beakers = \$13.30 x $\dfrac{1\ doz}{\$8.40}$ x $\dfrac{12\ beakers}{1\ doz}$ = **19 beakers**

9.   # of chickens = 1 gift x $\dfrac{2\ horses}{1\ gift}$ x $\dfrac{5\ cows}{3\ horses}$ x $\dfrac{4\ hogs}{1\ cow}$ x $\dfrac{4\ goats}{3\ hogs}$ x $\dfrac{9\ chickens}{1\ goat}$ = **160 chickens**

10. # of centimetres = 5 yard x $\dfrac{3\ feet}{1\ yard}$ x $\dfrac{12\ inches}{1\ foot}$ x $\dfrac{1\ cm}{0.3937\ inch}$ = **457.2 cm**

11. (a) 2.5 cm ; 2.5 x 10^{-2} m   (d) 5.1 dg ; 5.1 x 10^{-1} g
   (b) 1.3 kg ; 1.3 x 10^3 g   (e) 0.25 ML ; 0.25 x 10^6 L (or 2.5 x 10^5 L)
   (c) 25.2 mmol ; 25.2 x 10^{-3} mol (or 2.52 x 10^{-2} mol)   (f) 6.38 μg ; 6.38 x 10^{-6} g

12. (a) 2.5 millimetres ; 2.5 x 10^{-3} m   (d) 4 megatonnes ; 4 x 10^6 t
   (b) 6.5 decilitres ; 6.5 x 10^{-1} L   (e) 9.94 centigrams ; 9.94 x 10^{-2} g
   (c) 1.9 kilomoles ; 1.9 x 10^3 mol   (f) 1.25 microseconds ; 1.25 x 10^{-6} s

13. (a) 4.5 mmol ; 4.5 millimoles   (d) 2.68 dg ; 2.68 decigrams
   (b) 1.6 km ; 1.6 kilometres   (e) 8.85 Mt; 8.85 megatonnes
   (c) 0.50 μL ; 0.50 microlitre   (f) 7.25 cm ; 7.25 centimetres

14. (a) 50 mL
   (b) 22.5 x 10^3 kg (or 2.25 x 10^4 kg)
   (c) 0.125 x 10^3 L (or 1.25 x 10^2 L)

15. (a) 1 kg = 10^3 g   (d) 1 dm = 10^{-1} m   (g) 1 kL = 10^3 L   (j) 1 cL = 10^{-2} L
   (b) 1 Mm = 10^6 m   (e) 1 cs = 10^{-2} s   (h) 1 μs = 10^{-6} s   (k) 1 dmol = 10^{-1} mol
   (c) 1 μL = 10^{-6} L   (f)   1 mmol = 10^{-3} mol (i) 1 Mg = 10^6 g   (l) 1 mg = 10^{-3} g

16. (a) # of milligrams = 0.25 Mg x $\dfrac{10^6\text{ g}}{1\text{ Mg}}$ x $\dfrac{1\text{ mg}}{10^{-3}\text{ g}}$ = **2.5 x 10^8 mg**

(b) # of centiseconds = 10 μs x $\dfrac{10^{-6}\text{ s}}{1\text{ }\mu\text{s}}$ x $\dfrac{1\text{ cs}}{10^{-2}\text{ s}}$ = **1 x 10^{-3} cs**

(c) # of millimetres = 15.8 cm x $\dfrac{10^{-2}\text{ m}}{1\text{ cm}}$ x $\dfrac{1\text{ mm}}{10^{-3}\text{ m}}$ = **158 mm**

(d) # of kilograms = 250 mg x $\dfrac{10^{-3}\text{ g}}{1\text{ mg}}$ x $\dfrac{1\text{ kg}}{10^3\text{ g}}$ = **2.5 x 10^{-4} kg**

(e) # of decilitres = 0.5 kL x $\dfrac{10^3\text{ L}}{1\text{ kL}}$ x $\dfrac{1\text{ dL}}{10^{-1}\text{L}}$ = **5 x 10^3 dL**

17. (a) # of milliseconds = 3 s x $\dfrac{1\text{ ms}}{10^{-3}\text{ s}}$ = **3 x 10^3 ms**

(b) # of litres = 50.0 mL x $\dfrac{10^{-3}\text{ L}}{1\text{ mL}}$ = **5.0 x 10^{-2} L**

(c) # of microlitres = 2 L x $\dfrac{1\text{ }\mu\text{L}}{10^{-6}\text{ L}}$ = **2 x 10^6 µL**

(d) # of grams = 25 kg x $\dfrac{10^3\text{ g}}{1\text{ kg}}$ = **2.5 x 10^4 g**

(e) # of metres = 3 Mm x $\dfrac{10^6\text{ m}}{1\text{ Mm}}$ = **3 x 10^6 m**

(f) # of decilitres = 2 L x $\dfrac{1\text{ dL}}{10^{-1}\text{L}}$ = **2 x 10^1 dL**

(g) # of milliseconds = 7 μs x $\dfrac{10^{-6}\text{ s}}{1\text{ }\mu\text{s}}$ x $\dfrac{1\text{ ms}}{10^{-3}\text{ s}}$ = **7 x 10^{-3} ms**

(h) # of milligrams = 51 kg x $\dfrac{10^3\text{ g}}{1\text{ kg}}$ x $\dfrac{1\text{ mg}}{10^{-3}\text{ g}}$ = **5.1 x 10^7 mg**

(i) # of kilolitres = 3125 μL x $\dfrac{10^{-6}\text{ L}}{1\text{ }\mu\text{L}}$ x $\dfrac{1\text{ kL}}{10^3\text{ L}}$ = **3.125 x 10^{-6} kL**

(j) # of centigrams = 1.7 μg x $\dfrac{10^{-6}\text{ g}}{1\text{ }\mu\text{g}}$ x $\dfrac{1\text{ cg}}{10^{-2}\text{ g}}$ = **1.7 x 10^{-4} cg**

(k) # of seconds = 1 y x $\dfrac{365\text{ d}}{1\text{ y}}$ x $\dfrac{24\text{ h}}{1\text{ d}}$ x $\dfrac{60\,\text{min}}{1\text{ h}}$ x $\dfrac{60\text{ s}}{1\text{ min}}$ = **3.15 x 10^7 s**

(l) # of $\dfrac{\text{grams}}{\text{litre}}$ = $\dfrac{1\text{ mg}}{\text{dL}}$ x $\dfrac{10^{-3}\text{ g}}{1\text{ mg}}$ x $\dfrac{1\text{ dL}}{10^{-1}\text{L}}$ = **1 x 10^{-2} $\dfrac{\text{g}}{\text{L}}$**

(m) # of $\dfrac{\text{kilometres}}{\text{second}}$ = $\dfrac{1\text{ cm}}{\mu\text{s}}$ x $\dfrac{10^{-2}\text{ m}}{1\text{ cm}}$ x $\dfrac{1\text{ km}}{10^3\text{ m}}$ x $\dfrac{1\text{ }\mu\text{s}}{10^{-6}\text{ s}}$ = **1 x 10^1 $\dfrac{\text{km}}{\text{s}}$**

(n) # of $\dfrac{\text{decigrams}}{\text{litre}}$ = $\dfrac{1\text{ cg}}{\text{mL}}$ x $\dfrac{10^{-2}\text{ g}}{1\text{ cg}}$ x $\dfrac{1\text{ dg}}{10^{-1}\text{ g}}$ x $\dfrac{1\text{ mL}}{10^{-3}\text{ L}}$ = **1 x 10^2 $\dfrac{\text{dg}}{\text{L}}$**

(o) # of $\dfrac{\text{mg}}{\text{s}}$ = $\dfrac{5\text{ cg}}{\text{ds}}$ x $\dfrac{10^{-2}\text{ g}}{\text{cg}}$ x $\dfrac{1\text{ mg}}{10^{-3}\text{ g}}$ x $\dfrac{1\text{ ds}}{10^{-1}\text{ s}}$ = **5 x 10^2 $\dfrac{\text{mg}}{\text{s}}$**

18. (a) # of metres = 8.3 min x $\dfrac{60\ s}{1\ min}$ x $\dfrac{3.00 \times 10^8\ m}{1\ s}$ = **1.5 x 10^{11} m**

   (b) # of seconds = 3.8 x 10^5 km x $\dfrac{10^3\ m}{1\ km}$ x $\dfrac{1\ s}{3.00 \times 10^8\ m}$ = **1.3 s**

   (c) # of minutes = 7.83 x 10^7 km x $\dfrac{10^3\ m}{1\ km}$ x $\dfrac{1\ s}{3.00 \times 10^8\ m}$ x $\dfrac{1\ min}{60\ s}$ = **4.35 min**

19. # of $\dfrac{kg}{m^3}$ = $\dfrac{9.0\ lb}{in^3}$ x $\dfrac{1\ kg}{2.2\ lb}$ x $\left(\dfrac{39\ in}{1\ m}\right)^3$ = **2.4 x 10^5 $\dfrac{kg}{m^3}$**

20. (a) # of dollars = 90.0 kg x $\dfrac{\$9.80}{10\ kg}$ = **\$88.2**

   (b) # of dollars = 6.00 t x $\dfrac{10^3\ kg}{1\ t}$ x $\dfrac{\$9.80}{10\ kg}$ = **\$5880**

21. (a) # of centimetres = 20.0 inch x $\dfrac{2.54\ cm}{1\ inch}$ = **50.8 cm**

   (b) # of metres = 36 inch x $\dfrac{2.54\ cm}{1\ inch}$ x $\dfrac{10^{-2}\ m}{1\ cm}$ = **0.914 m**

22. # of centigrams = 90 μg x $\dfrac{10^{-6}\ g}{1\ \mu g}$ x $\dfrac{1\ cg}{10^{-2}\ g}$ = **9 x 10^{-3} cg**

23. (a) # of hours = 450 km x $\dfrac{1\ h}{105\ km}$ = **4.3 h**

   (b) # of seconds = 2.0 x 10^2 m x $\dfrac{1\ km}{10^3\ m}$ x $\dfrac{1\ h}{105\ km}$ x $\dfrac{60\ min}{1\ h}$ x $\dfrac{60\ s}{1\ min}$ = **6.9 s**

   (c) # of kilometres = 10.0 min x $\dfrac{1\ h}{60\ min}$ x $\dfrac{105\ km}{1\ h}$ = **17.5 km**

   (d) # of centimetres = 1.00 ms x $\dfrac{10^{-3}\ s}{1\ ms}$ x $\dfrac{1\ min}{60\ s}$ x $\dfrac{1\ h}{60\ min}$ x $\dfrac{105\ km}{1\ h}$ x $\dfrac{10^3\ m}{1\ km}$ x $\dfrac{1\ cm}{10^{-2}\ m}$ = **2.92 cm**

24. (a) # of kilograms = 7.00 L x $\dfrac{5.50\ kg}{1\ L}$ = **38.5 kg**

   (b) # of litres = 22 kg x $\dfrac{1\ L}{5.50\ kg}$ = **4.0 L**

   (c) # of grams = 5.00 mL x $\dfrac{10^{-3}\ L}{1\ mL}$ x $\dfrac{5.50\ kg}{1\ L}$ x $\dfrac{10^3\ g}{1\ kg}$ = **27.5 g**

25. (a) # of grams = 10.0 kJ x $\dfrac{1.00\ g}{0.334\ kJ}$ = **29.9 g**

   (b) # of kilojoules = 50.0 g x $\dfrac{0.334\ kJ}{1.00\ g}$ = **16.7 kJ**

   (c) # of joules = 2.00 kg x $\dfrac{10^3\ g}{1\ kg}$ x $\dfrac{0.334\ kJ}{1.00\ g}$ x $\dfrac{1000\ J}{kJ}$ = **6.68 x 10^5 J**

26. # of micrograms = 80 Mg x $\dfrac{10^6 \text{ g}}{1 \text{ Mg}}$ x $\dfrac{1 \text{ μg}}{10^{-6} \text{ g}}$ = **8 x 10^{13} μg**

27. # of $\dfrac{\text{kilolitres}}{\text{second}}$ = $\dfrac{2 \text{ cL}}{\text{ms}}$ x $\dfrac{10^{-2} \text{ L}}{1 \text{ cL}}$ x $\dfrac{1 \text{ kL}}{10^3 \text{ L}}$ x $\dfrac{1 \text{ ms}}{10^{-3} \text{ s}}$ = **2 x 10^{-2} $\dfrac{\text{kL}}{\text{s}}$**

28. # of $\dfrac{\text{microlitres}}{\text{second}}$ = $\dfrac{50.0 \text{ mL}}{\text{min}}$ x $\dfrac{10^{-3} \text{ L}}{1 \text{ mL}}$ x $\dfrac{1 \text{ μL}}{10^{-6} \text{ L}}$ x $\dfrac{1 \text{ min}}{60 \text{ s}}$ = **833 $\dfrac{\text{μL}}{\text{s}}$**

29. (a) $c = \dfrac{n}{V} = \dfrac{0.250 \text{ mol}}{0.500 \text{ L}}$ = **0.500 $\dfrac{\text{mol}}{\text{L}}$**

(b) i) $R = \dfrac{P \cdot V}{n \cdot T} = \dfrac{1 \text{ atm} \times 22.4 \text{ L}}{1 \text{ mol} \times 273 \text{ K}}$ = **0.0821 $\dfrac{\text{atm} \cdot \text{L}}{\text{mol} \cdot \text{K}}$**

ii) $R = \dfrac{P \cdot V}{n \cdot T} = \dfrac{202.6 \text{ kPa} \times 24.45 \text{ L}}{2 \text{ mol} \times 298 \text{ K}}$ = **8.31 $\dfrac{\text{kPa} \cdot \text{L}}{\text{mol} \cdot \text{K}}$**

(c) $\Delta S = \dfrac{\Delta H}{T} = \dfrac{44.0 \text{ kJ}}{373 \text{ K}}$ = **0.118 $\dfrac{\text{kJ}}{\text{K}}$**

(d) KE = $\frac{1}{2}$ m·v^2 = $\frac{1}{2}$ (3.35 x 10^{-27} kg) x (1692 $\frac{\text{m}}{\text{s}}$)^2 = **4.80 x 10^{-21} $\dfrac{\text{kg} \cdot \text{m}^2}{\text{s}^2}$**

30. $d = \dfrac{m}{V} = \dfrac{(\text{g})}{(\text{L})}$, and the units of d are g/L.

31. $d = \dfrac{m}{V} = \dfrac{8.19 \text{ g}}{3.50 \text{ mL}}$ = **2.34 $\dfrac{\text{g}}{\text{mL}}$**,   or: $d = \dfrac{8.19 \text{ g}}{3.50 \times 10^{-3} \text{ L}}$ = **2.34 x 10^3 $\dfrac{\text{g}}{\text{L}}$**

32. $V = \dfrac{m}{d} = \dfrac{125 \text{ g}}{7.86 \times 10^3 \text{ g/L}}$ = **0.0159 L**

33. $m = d \cdot V = 961 \dfrac{\text{g}}{\text{L}}$ x 0.2000 L = **192 g**

34. $V = \dfrac{m}{d} = \dfrac{46 \text{ g}}{789 \text{ g/L}}$ = **0.058 L**

35. $m = d \cdot V = 0.900 \dfrac{\text{g}}{\text{L}}$ x 22.4 L = **20.2 g**

36. $V_{\text{SPHERE}} = \dfrac{m}{d} = \dfrac{70.0 \text{ g}}{7.20 \times 10^3 \text{ g/L}}$ = 0.00972 L = 9.72 mL

$V_{\text{TOTAL}} = V_{\text{SPHERE}} + V_{\text{START}}$ = 9.72 + 54.0 = **63.7 mL**

37. Since less dense liquids float on more dense liquids, the least dense layer will be at the top and the most dense layer will be at the bottom, as shown below. The order is: Z, Y, W and X on the bottom.

$d_Z = \dfrac{m}{V} = \dfrac{74.8 \text{ g}}{115.0 \text{ mL}}$ = 0.650 $\dfrac{\text{g}}{\text{mL}}$ $d_W = \dfrac{m}{V} = \dfrac{107.3 \text{ g}}{55.0 \text{ mL}}$ = 1.95 $\dfrac{\text{g}}{\text{mL}}$

$d_Y = \dfrac{m}{V} = \dfrac{46.8 \text{ g}}{42.5 \text{ mL}}$ = 1.10 $\dfrac{\text{g}}{\text{mL}}$ $d_X = \dfrac{m}{V} = \dfrac{51.8 \text{ g}}{12.0 \text{ mL}}$ = 4.32 $\dfrac{\text{g}}{\text{mL}}$

38. Although the density of iron is greater than the density of water, the fact that the boat floats means the density of the boat must be less than the density of the water. Since $d = m/V$, then in order for the density of the boat to be less than 1 g/mL (water's density), the volume occupied by the boat must be quite large, relative to its mass. This situation is obtained by having a shape which keeps water out of

the center of the boat, allowing most of the interior volume to be air (and other stuff inside the boat). The AVERAGE density of the entire boat, including iron hull, air, etc. is then less than 1 g/mL.

39.　$V_{COPPER} = \dfrac{m}{d} = \dfrac{100.0 \text{ g}}{8.92 \times 10^3 \text{ g/L}} = 0.01121 \text{ L} = V_{MAGNESIUM}$

$m_{MAGNESIUM} = d \cdot V = 1.74 \times 10^3 \dfrac{g}{L} \times 0.01121 \text{ L} = \mathbf{19.5 \text{ g}}$

40.　mass of sun $= d \cdot V = 1.407 \dfrac{g}{mL} \times \dfrac{1 \text{ kg}}{10^3 \text{ g}} \times \dfrac{1 \text{ t}}{10^3 \text{ kg}} \times \dfrac{1 \text{ mL}}{10^{-3} \text{ L}} \times 1.41 \times 10^{30} \text{ L} = 1.98 \times 10^{27} \text{ t}$

time required $= 1.98 \times 10^{27} \text{ t} \times \dfrac{1 \text{ s}}{4.0 \times 10^6 \text{ t}} \times \dfrac{1 \text{ y}}{3.15 \times 10^7 \text{ s}} = 1.6 \times 10^{13} \text{ y}$

41.　$V_{SODIUM} = \dfrac{m}{d} = \dfrac{90.0 \text{ g}}{970.0 \text{ g/L}} = 0.0928 \text{ L} = 92.8 \text{ mL}$

After inserting the cube, the remaining volume is less.

$V_{REMAINING} = V_{START} - V_{SODIUM} = 250.0 - 92.8 = 157.2 \text{ mL}; \quad d_{ARGON} = \dfrac{m}{V} = \dfrac{4.60 \text{ g}}{157.2 \text{ mL}} = \mathbf{0.0293 \dfrac{g}{mL}}$

42.　(a) 3　　　(b) 4　　　(c) 2　　　(d) 2　　　(e) 4　　　(f) 6　　　(g) 1　　　(h) 4

43.　The balanced has been damaged or mis–calibrated in such a way that all the readings are a few grams too high or too low, for example.

44.　(a) A, B　　　(b) A, D　　　(c) A

45.　(a) A time reading with lots of digits, most of which are incorrect; for example: 75.987 654 s
　　　(b) A time reading with few digits, but the digits are close to the correct time; for example: 121.3 s
　　　(c) A time reading with few digits, most of which are incorrect; for example: 88 s
　　　(d) A time reading with lots of digits, and a value which is quite close to the accepted value; for example: 121.315 593 s

46.　(a) 2　　　(b) 4　　　(c) 2　　　(d) 5

47.　(a) C　　　(b) M　　　(c) M　　　(d) C　　　(e) M

48.　(a) Numbered division difference = 1 cm ;　Unnumbered subdivision difference = $\dfrac{1 \text{ cm}}{10} = 0.1 \text{ cm}$

　　　Reading A:　Pointer is $^4/_{10}$ of the way from one subdivision to the next: $^4/_{10} \times 0.1 \text{ cm} = 0.04 \text{ cm}$
　　　　　　　　　　The reading is　15.20 + 0.04 = **15.24 cm.**

　　　Reading B:　Pointer is $^7/_{10}$ of the way from one subdivision to the next: $^7/_{10} \times 0.1 \text{ cm} = 0.07 \text{ cm}$
　　　　　　　　　　The reading is　15.80 + 0.07 = **15.87 cm.**

　　　(b) Numbered division difference = 10 cm ;　Unnumbered subdivision difference = $\dfrac{10 \text{ cm}}{5} = 2 \text{ cm}$

　　　Reading A:　Pointer is $^3/_{10}$ of the way from one subdivision to the next: $^3/_{10} \times 2 \text{ cm} = 0.6 \text{ cm}$
　　　　　　　　　　The reading is　10.0 + 0.6 = **10.6 cm.**

　　　Reading B:　Pointer is $^5/_{10}$ of the way from one subdivision to the next: $^5/_{10} \times 2 \text{ cm} = 1.0 \text{ cm}$
　　　　　　　　　　The reading is　14.0 + 1.0 = **15.0 cm.**

　　　(c) Numbered division difference = 1 cm ;　Unnumbered subdivision difference = $\dfrac{1 \text{ cm}}{2} = 0.5 \text{ cm}$

　　　Reading A:　Pointer is $^5/_{10}$ of the way from one subdivision to the next: $^5/_{10} \times 0.5 \text{ cm} = 0.25 \text{ cm}$
　　　　　　　　　　The reading is　5.50 + 0.25 = **5.75 cm.**

　　　Reading B:　Pointer is $^3/_{10}$ of the way from one subdivision to the next: $^3/_{10} \times 0.5 \text{ cm} = 0.15 \text{ cm}$
　　　　　　　　　　The reading is　7.00 + 0.15 = **7.15 cm.**

(d) Numbered division difference = 10 cm ; Unnumbered subdivision difference = $\dfrac{10\ cm}{5}$ = 2 cm

    Reading A: Pointer is $^8/_{10}$ of the way from one subdivision to the next: $^8/_{10}$ x 2 cm = 1.6 cm
        The reading is   114.0 + 1.6 = **115.6 cm.**

    Reading B: Pointer is $^4/_{10}$ of the way from one subdivision to the next: $^4/_{10}$ x 2 cm = 0.8 cm
        The reading is   122.0 + 0.8 = **122.8 cm.**

(e) Numbered division difference = 0.1 cm ; Unnumbered subdivision difference = $\dfrac{0.1\ cm}{10}$ = 0.01 cm

    Reading A: Pointer is $^7/_{10}$ of the way from one subdivision to the next: $^7/_{10}$ x 0.01 cm = 0.007 cm
        The reading is   0.410 + 0.007 = **0.417 cm.**

    Reading B: Pointer is $^4/_{10}$ of the way from one subdivision to the next: $^4/_{10}$ x 0.01 cm = 0.004 cm
        The reading is   0.450 + 0.004 = **0.454 cm.**

49. (a) i = 2.00 cm   ii = 3.20 cm   iii = 4.60 cm   iv = 5.00 cm
    (b) i = 99.16 cm   ii = 99.60 cm   iii = 100.00 cm   iv = 100.50 cm

50. (a) 20.32 mL   (c) 24.11 mL   (e) 43.80 mL   (g) 0.01 mL
    (b) 10.50 mL   (d) 8.00 mL   (f) 17.54 mL   (h) 30.30 mL

51. (a) 51.32 ± 0.01 g   (c) 455 ± 3 g   (e) 98.9 ± 0.7 s
    (b) 55 ± 1 mL   (d) 0.5130 ± 0.0002 g   (f) 49.8 ± 0.9 g

52. (a) 15.24 mL to 15.26 mL   (b) 109.8 mL to 110.2 mL   (c) 1.523 x 10^{-6} s to 1.533 x 10^{-6} s

53. The contents of the table will depend on the equipment available.

54. #48 (a) A = 15.24 ± 0.01 cm , B = 15.87 ± 0.01 cm
        (b) A = 10.6 ± 0.2 cm   , B = 15.0 ± 0.2 cm
        (c) A = 5.75 ± 0.05 cm   , B = 7.15 ± 0.05 cm
        (d) A = 115.6 ± 0.2 cm   , B = 122.8 ± 0.2 cm
        (e) A = 0.417 ± 0.001 cm , B = 0.454 ± 0.001 cm

     #49 (a) i = 2.00 ± 0.02 cm   (b) i = 99.16 ± 0.01 cm
              ii = 3.20 ± 0.02 cm   ii = 99.60 ± 0.01 cm
              iii = 4.60 ± 0.02 cm   iii = 100.00 ± 0.01 cm
              iv = 5.00 ± 0.02 cm   iv = 100.50 ± 0.01 cm

     #50 (a) 20.32 ± 0.01 mL   (e) 43.80 ± 0.01 mL
           (b) 10.50 ± 0.01 mL   (f) 17.54 ± 0.01 mL
           (c) 24.11 ± 0.01 mL   (g) 0.01 ± 0.01 mL
           (d) 8.00 ± 0.01 mL   (h) 30.30 ± 0.01 mL

55. (a) 3   (b) 5   (c) 5   (d) 2   (e) 3   (f) 3   (g) 4   (h) 4   (i) 6   (j) 4

56. (a) 6.3   (c) 1.33   (e) 3 x 10^{14} (g) 202   (i) 20   (k) 2
    (b) 0.000 24   (d) 1.3 x 10^2 (f) 5.11 x 10^5 (h) 90   (j) 1 x 10^{-4} (l) 2.2 x 10^{-6}

57. (a) 90.4   (f) –0.000 769
    (b) 53.0991   (g) 7.002 x 10^5
    (c) 7.7 x 10^{-5} (h) –35.55
    (d) 4.0076   (i) 0.1368 x 10^{-6} or 1.368 x 10^{-7}
    (e) 1.864 x 10^4 (j) 6.2055 x 10^{-9}

58. (a) 8.53   (c) –29.7   (e) 1.67 x 10^4 (g) 5.6 x 10^2 (i) 3.1 x 10^2
    (b) 0.64   (d) 4.0 x 10^2 (f) 30.9   (h) –8.72 x 10^{-3} (j) 0.004 000

59. (a) 0.856   (c) 0.69   (e) –23.9   (g) 1.1
    (b) 102.1   (d) 610   (f) 96   (h) 0.109

ANSWERS TO UNIT III : THE PHYSICAL PROPERTIES AND PHYSICAL CHANGES OF SUBSTANCES

1. (a) any description using a **number**; for example: 5 s, 10 min, 3 h, 2 d.
    (b) any description using a **number**; for example: 5°C, 10 degrees hotter than room temperature.

2. (a) any **non–numerical** description; for example: in a moment, after a short while, a lifetime, quickly.
    (b) any **non–numerical** description; for example: hot, cold, room temperature.

3. The quantitative descriptions are in bold and the qualitative descriptions are underlined.

    Copper is a reddish–coloured element with a metallic lustre. It is an excellent conductor of heat and electricity, **melts at 1085°C and boils at 2563°C**. Archeological evidence shows that it has been mined for the past **5000 years** and presently is considered to be one of the most important metals available. Copper is insoluble in water and virtually all other solvents, reacts easily with nitric acid but only slightly with sulphuric and hydrochloric acids. It has a **density of 8.92 g/mL**, which makes it more dense than iron.

4. The tube could have been white–hot, **or** the tube could have been illuminated by a spotlight, **or** the tube could have been covered with a fluorescent white paint, **or** the tube could have been an operating fluorescent light bulb. You could cautiously feel if the tube is giving off heat **or** you could see if the tube still glows when shaded from light **or** investigate whether the tube has a source of electrical power.

5. (a) Observations are qualitative (non–numerical) facts whereas data are quantitative (numerical) facts.
    (b) An "observation" is a single qualitative fact whereas a "description" is a series of observations used to characterize something.
    (c) An observation is a fact recorded by our senses whereas an interpretation is the meaning which our mind gives to an observation.

6. Any of the terms listed can be wrong; even observations can be incorrect because our senses can be tricked (as magicians will tell you).

7. You might be biased in the way you interpret some of the observations. In fact, you might see only what you expect to see, even if something different actually occurred. Also, you might tend to use only data which agrees with your pre–conceived ideas and disregard data which contradicts your ideas.

8. A hypothesis; it is called an "assumption" and it is only a single idea.

9. This statement is not testable and makes no predictions. It could be a "belief" but not a scientific theory.

10. A law; the statement simply says what always occurs in a given situation.

11. (a) *Hypothesis* – a temporary idea put forward to explain the results of an experiment and based on initial experiments; intended to explain a narrow set of experimental results; initial confidence in a hypothesis may be low.
        Theory – a refined and extensively tested explanation of how and why related results are found; intended to explain a wide–ranging set of experimental results; level of confidence in a theory is generally very high.

    (b) *Theory* – attempts to explain why something occurs and to predict what is expected to happen in new circumstances; does not attempt to summarize past results of experiments.
        Law – summarizes experiments by describing what happens if a known situation occurs; does not predict what will happen in new situations and makes no attempt to explain **why** something occurs.

12. (a) & (b) – ask your Chem teacher to let you set up such an experiment. Science doesn't give "THE ANSWER" and you aren't going to get one here either. What happens inside an atom cannot be seen directly so scientists must be satisfied with their models. It can be tough on people who must have a "definite answer", but one has to get used to intrinsic uncertainties in science. No; whining won't help!

13. (a) physical property (The glass is not altered when light passes through it.)
    (b) physical property (Melted salt is still salt and solidifies to exhibit the same properties it had originally.)
    (c) chemical property (The properties of soap differ from those of lye and fat; soap is a new substance.)
    (d) physical property (Copper is not changed when electricity passes through it.)
    (e) chemical property (The white smoke is a new substance.)

14. light, heat, sound, etc. – in other words **ENERGY**!

15. Intensive = b, d, e, g   Extensive = a, c, f

16. (a) density, melting temperature, lustre, malleability, ductility, electrical and heat conductivity, hardness, smell, taste
     (b) density, boiling temperature, freezing temperature, diffusion rate, viscosity, vapour pressure, electrical and heat conductivity, smell, taste
     (c) density, condensation temperature, diffusion rate, heat conductivity, smell, viscosity

17. (a) acetone
     (b) The lower the boiling temperature of a liquid, the higher its vapour pressure.
     (c) The higher the vapour pressure of a liquid, the faster its evaporation rate.
     (d) Iron is known to melt at a very high temperature and to boil at an even higher temperature. The relationship for part (b), above, implies that iron has a very low vapour pressure.
     (e) Since diethyl ether boils at a lower temperature than acetone, the relationship for parts (b) and (c) implies that diethyl ether has a higher vapour pressure and evaporation rate than acetone.

18. (a) The higher the temperature, the greater the diffusion rate.
     (b) ammonia
     (c) The smaller the mass of a molecule, the faster the diffusion rate.

19. (a) viscosity: hexane < carbon tetrachloride < glycerol
     (b) density: hexane < glycerol < carbon tetrachloride
     (c) There is no relationship between viscosity and density.

20. (a) the pressure increases
     (b) the volume decreases
     (c) When the pressure exerted on a gas increases, the volume of the gas **decreases.**
     (d) i) the volume decreases   ii) the volume stays small when the pressure is released
     (e) i) the volume decreases   ii) the volume increases back to its original value
     (f) The volume of a gas "recovers" back to its original value when an applied pressure is released.

21. Corn syrup has a HIGH viscosity because it has a high RESISTANCE to flow.
     Gasoline has a LOW viscosity because it has a low RESISTANCE to flow.
     If you heat a glass of syrup, the viscosity of the syrup decreases.

22. (a) intensive   (b) extensive   (c) extensive

23. The vapour pressure is quite low since very little ice evaporates and forms a vapour.

24. (a) liquid and gas   (b) solid, liquid and gas   (c) gas   (d) solid   (e) solid and liquid

25. liquid

26. (a) 22.4 mL   (b) 22.4 L

27. (a) The pressure inside the balloon is equal to the pressure exerted by the atmosphere.
     (b) The balloon should expand because the pressure inside the balloon (pushing outward) is greater than the pressure outside (pushing inward).

28. Nothing regarding the densities can be predicted from a knowledge of the viscosities.

29. (a) According to exercise 18, the higher the temperature the greater the diffusion rate of a fluid (in this case the gaseous "scent" of the aftershave lotion). Therefore the scent of John's aftershave should travel faster to Juanita because of the higher temperature of the air carrying the scent.
     (b) According to exercise 18, lighter particles travel faster than heavier ones at the same temperature. Therefore, if the particles having a scent in John's aftershave are lighter in **mass**, Juanita will smell them first. (The property will be "diffusion rate" or "mass of particle".)

30. The sphere falls faster in chlorine gas. Chlorine has a lower viscosity, that is, a lower resistance to flow, and therefore the sphere will fall ("flow") faster in the chlorine.

31. Chloroform forms a VAPOUR because it boils above room temperature ($20^{\circ}C$).

32. According to exercise 17, since ethanol has a higher vapour pressure it has a lower boiling point.

33. (a) ion   (b) molecule   (c) atom   (d) atom   (e) ion   (f) molecule

34. Four phases are mentioned: 1 = white sand, 2 = nails, 3 = salt water with some dye in it, 4 = gasoline. A 5th phase (air) may be above the phases described but is not mentioned as part of "this system".

35. Visible boundaries separating one phase from another must be present in a heterogeneous system. In a homogeneous system everything must look the same no matter which part of the system is examined.

36. (a) homogeneous   (c) heterogeneous (shell, yolk, white)
    (b) heterogeneous (bark, leaves, roots, etc.)   (d) homogeneous

37. An element; the term "atom" is reserved for the smallest possible particle of gold and a 10 g piece of gold can be extensively subdivided.

38. They are similar in being homogeneous; they differ in that a compound is a pure substance while a solution is made of two or more pure substances.

39. (a) true solution
    (b) mechanical mixture
    (c) element, compound or true solution (a solid solution in this case)
    (d) element, compound or true solution (such as air)
    (e) element, compound or true solution (such as salt water)
    (f) The first statement implies we have either an element or a compound. The second statement shows that at least two different substances can be produced and therefore we have at least two different types of atoms present. Conclusion: the substance was a COMPOUND.

40. (a) acetic acid   (c) chloroform (present in smaller amount)
    (b) iodine   (d) silver nitrate (water is always the solvent, if present)

41. Sugar is a pure substance; dirt and air are mixtures

42. KCl(aq) refers to aqueous KCl or KCl dissolved in water

43. 6 (wood, lead, 2 colours of paint, metal end, eraser)

44. (a) compound (a single type of molecule)   (d) compound (single type of molecule)
    (b) mixture (crust, cheese, etc.)   (e) mixture (two types of molecules)
    (c) mixture (water, carbonation, flavouring, etc.)

45. The layer having the lower density will be on the top; that is, the water.

46. (a) distillation   (b) evaporation, recrystallization, distillation (distillate can be discarded)

47. (a) distillation; solvent extraction may also work
    (b) hand separation (pour off the top layer or use a separatory funnel), distillation (but why bother?)
    (c) filtration, gravity separation (using a centrifuge)
    (d) paper, column or thin–layer chromatography; you might try solvent extraction
    (e) Filtration (separate sand from salt water); distillation (separate water from salt)

48. Recrystallization

49. amount left after one extraction = 0.10 = 10 %
    amount left after two extractions = 0.10 x 0.10 = 0.010 = **1 %**

50. amount left after one extraction = 0.40 = 40 %
    amount left after four extractions = 0.40 x 0.40 x 0.40 x 0.40 = 0.0256 = 2.6 %
    therefore, amount removed = 100 % – 2.6 % = **97.4 %**

51. The idea is to let only one substance form crystals while the others remain in solution. If all the solvent evaporates, all the solids are deposited together and no separation occurs.

52. hand separation (pick out the good crystals by hand)

53. There may be more than one way to do this, but one way is:
    • use filtration to remove the liquids from the sand and iron filings
    • use a magnet to separate the iron filings from the sand
    • use hand separation to pour off the gasoline from the water (or use a separatory funnel)
    • distil off the water, leaving a mixture of dyes
    • re–dissolve the dyes and use chromatography to separate them.

54. There may be more than one way to do this, but one way is:
    · use filtration to separate the liquids from the solids
    · use a gravity separation method to separate the two types of sand (put in a mechanical shaker and shake the dry sand; the heavier black sand will accumulate at the bottom of the container)
    · distil the methanol–hexanol mixture to separate the liquids.

55. · Solvent extract the mixture with alcohol. Only the naphthalene will dissolve. The alcohol can later be distilled off or evaporated to leave solid naphthalene.
    · Solvent extract the remaining solids with water. Only the potassium sulphate will dissolve. The water can then be distilled off or evaporated to leave solid potassium sulphate.
    · The calcium carbonate is the only solid left in the original mixture.

56. The mixture will appear as separate layers of aluminum powder, a solution of benzene and chloroform and a final layer consisting of a solution of sugar and water.
    · Filter off the aluminum, leaving two layers: benzene–chloroform solution and sugar–water solution.
    · Use hand separation or a separatory funnel to remove the benzene–chloroform layer from the sugar–water layer.
    · Distil the benzene–chloroform solution; the chloroform will come off first, leaving the benzene behind.
    · Distil the water, leaving the sugar behind (if the water was not wanted, the sugar–water solution could just be left in the open or on a hot plate to let the water evaporate.

57. Dissolve the powdered crystals in an appropriate solvent and use chromatography to separate the coloured chemicals from each other. This is appropriate because there is only a little of each chemical.

58. · First, use a magnet to remove the nails.
    · Next, put the remaining mixture through a sieve which allows the white sand and platinum to pass through while holding back the pennies.
    · Finally, use a mechanical shaker to allow the high density platinum to settle to the bottom while the white sand stays on top.

59. (a) physical change (water vapour condenses into droplets of moisture)
    (b) chemical change (new substances are formed: smoke and various cancer–causing chemicals)
    (c) chemical change (growth involves chemicals being produced and used up)
    (d) chemical change (rust is a new substance formed by the combination of iron, air and water)
    (e) physical change (no reaction has occurred to make new substances)
    (f) physical change (we are only separating substances, not producing new ones)

60.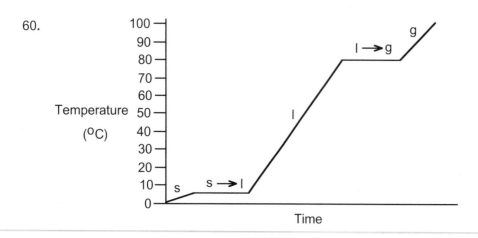

61.

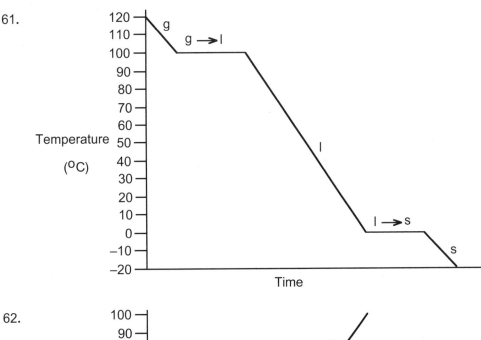

62.

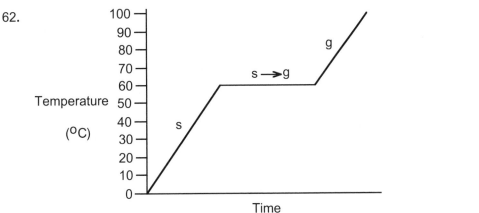

63. (a) At 5 minutes, the sample was about 75% ice and 25% water.
    (b) At 10 minutes, the sample was about 50% ice and 50% water.

64. The kinetic energy of the particles increases.

65. translational

66. translational

67. translational and rotational

68. rotational and translational

69. The viscosity should decrease as the temperature increases. As temperature increases, the transla-
    tional energy increases. This allows the molecules to move past one another faster and therefore they
    must have less resistance to "flow" past one another and possess a lower viscosity.

70. Many bonds in the molecules are identical to each other, so those parts of their spectra are identical.

71. The volume increases (recall that as the translational energy increases we change phase from solid to
    liquid to gas, and that the volume increases as we go from solid to liquid to gas).

ANSWERS TO UNIT IV : INORGANIC NOMENCLATURE

Self–Test (a) Na   (e) Si   (i) S   (m) As   (q) W
         (b) potassium (f) krypton (j) cesium   (n) molybdenum   (r) lead
         (c) Tl   (g) F   (k) Cd   (o) Pt   (s) At
         (d) mercury   (h) chromium (l) beryllium (p) copper   (t) boron

1. (a) A, P   (b) N, T, P   (c) C, M   (d) A, D, P   (e) C, P   (f) N, M

2. (a) copper(I) ion   (b) chromium(III) ion   (c) tungsten(VI) ion

3. (a) Co^{3+} (b) Ni^{2+} (c) V^{5+}

4. (a) $Sn(SO_4)_2$ (e) $Hg_2(NO_2)_2$ (i) Cr_2O_3 (m) $(NH_4)_2Cr_2O_7$ (q) $Mg(MnO_4)_2$
    (b) $(NH_4)_2C_2O_4$ (f) $Fe(OH)_3$ (j) MnF_2 (n) Cu_3PO_4 (r) WBr_5
    (c) Li_2O (g) Ag_2SO_4 (k) KH_2PO_4 (o) $Ca(ClO)_2$ (s) $(NH_4)_3PO_4$
    (d) Cu_3N (h) $Pb(ClO_4)_2$ (l) $U(SO_4)_2$ (p) $NaHSO_3$ (t) $Hg(CH_3COO)_2$

5. (a) silver phosphate   (h) copper(II) sulphate   (o) aluminum hydroxide
    (b) aluminum sulphate   (i) ammonium sulphide   (p) chromium(III) iodide
    (c) iron(III) sulphide   (j) ammonium hydrogen carbonate   (q) tin(IV) oxide
    (d) copper(I) chloride   (k) iron(II) oxalate   (r) zinc dichromate
    (e) ammonium carbonate   (l) magnesium hydrogen sulphite   (s) vanadium(V) oxide
    (f) vanadium(III) chloride   (m) lithium chlorite   (t) strontium nitride
    (g) mercury(I) carbonate   (n) sodium monohydrogen phosphate

6. (a) iron(III) bromide hexahydrate   (f) sodium sulphide nonahydrate
    (b) lithium dichromate dihydrate   (g) sodium sulphate decahydrate
    (c) aluminum oxide trihydrate   (h) nickel(II) phosphate octahydrate
    (d) cobalt(II) fluoride tetrahydrate   (i) magnesium monohydrogen phosphate heptahydrate
    (e) sodium carbonate monohydrate

7. (a) $FePO_4 \cdot 8H_2O$ (c) $Cu_3(PO_4)_2 \cdot 3H_2O$ (e) $NiCl_2 \cdot 6H_2O$
    (b) $Cd(NO_3)_2 \cdot 4H_2O$ (d) $CrC_2O_4 \cdot H_2O$ (f) $Al(NO_3)_3 \cdot 9H_2O$

8. (a) nitrogen dioxide   (d) diphosphorus hexoxide   (g) bromine monofluoride
    (b) chlorine trifluoride   (e) dinitrogen trioxide   (h) sulphur hexafluoride
    (c) tetrasulphur dinitride   (f) sulphur tetrafluoride

9. (a) SO_3 (b) PCl_5 (c) XeF_6 (d) OF_2 (e) CO (f) CCl_4 (g) P_4S_3 (h) N_2S_5 (i) Si_3N_4

10. yellow = chromate; blue = copper(II). Therefore: $CuCrO_4$ = copper(II) chromate

11. iron(II) became iron(III)

12. (a) colourless   (b) purple   (c) blue   (d) colourless   (e) orange   (f) pale pink

13. bright green = nickel(II); this positive ion will have to react with the negative ion, carbonate, in the potassium carbonate solution. Therefore: nickel carbonate = $NiCO_3$

14. magnesium oxide   27. sodium sulphite
15. copper(II) sulphate   28. lead(IV) hydrogen sulphate
16. sodium acetate   29. tungsten(VI) fluoride
17. ammonium nitrite   30. sodium dihydrogen phosphate
18. molybdenum(V) chloride   31. barium sulphide
19. lithium hydroxide monohydrate   32. ammonium chlorite
20. platinum(IV) chloride   33. iron(II) hypochlorite
21. ammonium perchlorate   34. tin(II) cyanide
22. aluminum nitride   35. krypton difluoride
23. potassium permanganate   36. sodium phosphate
24. copper(I) sulphate   37. calcium sulphide
25. sulphuric acid   38. manganese(II) thiocyanate
26. sodium carbonate decahydrate   39. silver permanganate

40. platinum(III) oxide trihydrate
41. phophorus pentabromide
42. copper(II) acetate
43. aluminum perchlorate
44. ammonia
45. aluminum sulphide
46. sodium hydroxide
47. barium hydrogen sulphide tetrahydrate
48. dinitrogen monoxide
49. nitric acid
50. cesium hydrogen carbonate
51. copper(I) sulphide
52. tricarbon disulphide
53. copper(II) nitrate hexahydrate
54. cobalt(II) chlorate
55. manganese(III) oxide
56. zinc acetate
57. acetic acid
58. manganese(III) phosphate
59. chromium(III) nitrate nonahydrate
60. strontium hypochlorite
61. vanadium(III) nitride
62. lead(IV) oxalate
63. cobalt(III) fluoride
64. barium sulphite

65. copper(II) dichromate
66. nitrogen triiodide
67. chromium(II) bromide
68. magnesium phosphide
69. iron(II) sulphate pentahydrate
70. calcium hydroxide
71. phosphoric acid
72. radium sulphate
73. potassium hydrogen oxalate
74. dichlorine monoxide
75. titanium(IV) oxide
76. nickel(II) sulphate heptahydrate
77. magnesium chlorite
78. lead(IV) chloride
79. iron(III) hydrogen oxalate
80. diiodine pentoxide
81. mercury(II) nitrate
82. zinc hydroxide
83. hydrogen sulphide
84. xenon trioxide
85. titanium(II) chloride
86. hydrofluoric acid
87. tin(IV) chromate
88. cobalt(II) phosphate octahydrate
89. platinum(IV) sulphide

90. $AgCl$
91. SO_2
92. $Fe_2(C_2O_4)_3$
93. BeO
94. $Pb(CH_3COO)_2 \cdot 10H_2O$
95. K_2CrO_4
96. $Hg_2(CH_3COO)_2$
97. $MoCl_3$
98. NH_3
99. Au_2S_3
100. $Ag_2Cr_2O_7$
101. $Ca(CH_3COO)_2$
102. $Cr_2(C_2O_4)_3$
103. $Ca(NO_2)_2$
104. F_2O_2
105. Mo_2O_5
106. SiF_4
107. $Cd(CH_3COO)_2$
108. $HgCl_2$
109. $LiHSO_3$
110. CH_3COOH
111. $Mg(ClO_3)_2 \cdot 6H_2O$
112. PF_3
113. CuI_2
114. Ca_3N_2

115. $Mg(OH)_2$
116. $Mo_2S_5 \cdot 3H_2O$
117. $Fe(H_2PO_4)_2$
118. CI_4
119. $ZnSO_4$
120. Hg_2S
121. H_2SO_3
122. $FeF_2 \cdot 8H_2O$
123. $Mg(HSO_4)_2$
124. Al_2S_3
125. $RaCO_3$
126. XeF_4
127. Na_2O
128. $Ba_3(PO_4)_2$
129. $Hg_2(NO_3)_2 \cdot 2H_2O$
130. $NaClO$
131. $AuCN$
132. $SnBr_4$
133. HI
134. S_4N_4
135. $Fe(OH)_2$
136. CuF
137. $Sn(HCO_3)_2$
138. N_2O_5
139. $Zn(HSO_3)_2$

140. $Zn(ClO_4)_2 \cdot 6H_2O$
141. $Au(NO_3)_3$
142. $Mn_2(SO_4)_3$
143. HCl
144. CrO
145. $Zn(HS)_2$
146. MoS_3
147. $Fe_2(CO_3)_3$
148. IF_5
149. MnO_2
150. HCN
151. $Fe_2(SO_4)_3 \cdot 9H_2O$
152. KNO_2
153. CrP
154. $Ni(OH)_2$
155. ClO_4
156. $Hg(SCN)_2$
157. HNO_2
158. $PbCO_3$
159. $NaHC_2O_4$
160. $AlBr_3 \cdot 6H_2O$
161. PbI_2
162. Ag_2O
163. $Mn(HPO_4)_2$

ANSWERS TO UNIT V : THE MOLE CONCEPT

1. Since oxygen is $\dfrac{88.9 \text{ g}}{11.1 \text{ g}}$ = 8 times heavier than hydrogen (which has a mass of 1), oxygen has a mass of

   8. Since nitrogen is $\dfrac{46.7 \text{ g}}{53.3 \text{ g}}$ = 0.876 times heavier than oxygen, nitrogen has a mass of 0.876 x 8 = 7.

   Finally, since carbon is $\dfrac{42.9 \text{ g}}{57.1 \text{ g}}$ = 0.751 times heavier than oxygen, carbon has a mass of 0.751 x 8 = 6.

2. Since there is 3 times the volume of chlorine gas compared to nitrogen, the reaction involves 3 times as many chlorine molecules as nitrogen molecules. Therefore, the formula is **NCl_3**. The name of the compound is nitrogen trichloride.

3. The volume of oxygen is twice the volume of sulphur so that the product contains twice as many oxygen atoms as sulphur atoms. The formula of the product is SO_2, sulphur dioxide.

4. The volume of fluorine is three times the volume of chlorine so that the formula contains three times as many fluorine atoms as chlorine atoms: ClF_3, chlorine trifluoride.

5. Since the volume of oxygen is five times the volume of unknown gas X, there are five times as many oxygen molecules as gas X molecules; that is, 5 x 3.0 x 10^{23} = 1.5 x 10^{24} molecules.

6. (a) 1 N = 1 x 14.0 = 14.0 g
        1 O = 1 x 16.0 = 16.0 g
        _____
        molar mass   = **30.0 g**

   (b) 2 H = 2 x 1.0 = 2.0 g
        1 O = 1 x 16.0 = 16.0 g
        _____
        molar mass   = **18.0 g**

   (c) 1 N = 1 x 14.0 = 14.0 g
        3 H = 3 x 1.0 = 3.0 g
        _____
        molar mass   = **17.0 g**

   (d) 1 C = 1 x 12.0 = 12.0 g
        2 O = 2 x 16.0 = 32.0 g
        _____
        molar mass   = **44.0 g**

   (e) 1 C = 1 x 12.0 = 12.0 g
        4 H = 4 x 1.0 = 4.0 g
        _____
        molar mass   = **16.0 g**

   (f) 1 Ag = 1 x 107.9 = 107.9 g
        1 N = 1 x 14.0 = 14.0 g
        3 O = 3 x 16.0 = 48.0 g
        _____
        molar mass   = **169.9 g**

   (g) 1 Ca = 1 x 40.1 = 40.1 g
        2 O = 2 x 16.0 = 32.0 g
        2 H = 2 x 1.0 = 2.0 g
        _____
        molar mass   = **74.1 g**

   (h) 1 Al = 1 x 27.0 = 27.0 g
        3 N = 3 x 14.0 = 42.0 g
        9 O = 9 x 16.0 = 144.0 g
        _____
        molar mass   = **213.0 g**

   (i) 1 Fe = 1 x 55.8 = 55.8 g
        3 Cl = 3 x 35.5 = 106.5 g
        _____
        molar mass   = **162.3 g**

   (j) 1 Sn = 1 x 118.7 = 118.7 g
        2 C = 2 x 12.0 = 24.0 g
        4 O = 4 x 16.0 = 64.0 g
        _____
        molar mass   = **206.7 g**

   (k) 1 Sn = 1 x 118.7 = 118.7 g
        4 C = 4 x 12.0 = 48.0 g
        8 O = 8 x 16.0 = 128.0 g
        _____
        molar mass   = **294.7 g**

   (l) 3 N = 3 x 14.0 = 42.0 g
        12 H = 12 x 1.0 = 12.0 g
        1 P = 1 x 31.0 = 31.0 g
        4 O = 4 x 16.0 = 64.0 g
        _____
        molar mass   = **149.0 g**

   (m) 2 C = 2 x 12.0 = 24.0 g
        4 H = 4 x 1.0 = 4.0 g
        2 O = 2 x 16.0 = 32.0 g
        _____
        molar mass   = **60.0 g**

   (n) 4 C = 4 x 12.0 = 48.0 g
        10 H = 10 x 1.0 = 10.0 g
        _____
        molar mass   = **58.0 g**

   (o) 1 Ni = 1 x 58.7 = 58.7 g
        16 H = 16 x 1.0 = 16.0 g
        2 O = 2 x 16.0 = 32.0 g
        4 N = 4 x 14.0 = 56.0 g
        2 Cl = 2 x 35.5 = 71.0 g
        _____
        molar mass   = **233.7 g**

   (p) 2 Al = 2 x 27.0 = 54.0 g
        3 S = 3 x 32.1 = 96.3 g
        12 O = 12 x 16.0 = 192.0 g
        _____
        molar mass   = **342.3 g**

7. (a)

$$3 \text{ Co} = 3 \times 58.9 = 176.7 \text{ g}$$
$$2 \text{ As} = 2 \times 74.9 = 149.8 \text{ g}$$
$$16 \text{ O} = 16 \times 16.0 = 256.0 \text{ g}$$
$$16 \text{ H} = 16 \times 1.0 = 16.0 \text{ g}$$

molar mass   = **598.5 g**

(b)

$$1 \text{ Pb} = 1 \times 207.2 = 207.2 \text{ g}$$
$$4 \text{ C} = 4 \times 12.0 = 48.0 \text{ g}$$
$$12 \text{ H} = 12 \times 1.0 = 12.0 \text{ g}$$
$$7 \text{ O} = 7 \times 16.0 = 112.0 \text{ g}$$

molar mass   = **379.2 g**

(c)

$$1 \text{ Mg} = 1 \times 24.3 = 24.3 \text{ g}$$
$$1 \text{ S} = 1 \times 32.1 = 32.1 \text{ g}$$
$$11 \text{ O} = 11 \times 16.0 = 176.0 \text{ g}$$
$$14 \text{ H} = 14 \times 1.0 = 14.0 \text{ g}$$

molar mass   = **246.4 g**

(d)

$$1 \text{ K} = 1 \times 39.1 = 39.1 \text{ g}$$
$$1 \text{ Al} = 1 \times 27.0 = 27.0 \text{ g}$$
$$2 \text{ S} = 2 \times 32.1 = 64.2 \text{ g}$$
$$20 \text{ O} = 20 \times 16.0 = 320.0 \text{ g}$$
$$24 \text{ H} = 24 \times 1.0 = 24.0 \text{ g}$$

molar mass   = **474.3 g**

8. (a) $\text{mass} = 1.00 \text{ mol} \times \dfrac{53.5 \text{ g}}{1 \text{ mol}} = \textbf{53.5 g}$

(f) $\text{mass} = 2.60 \text{ mol} \times \dfrac{30.0 \text{ g}}{1 \text{ mol}} = \textbf{78.0 g}$

(b) $\text{mass} = 4.50 \text{ mol} \times \dfrac{53.5 \text{ g}}{1 \text{ mol}} = \textbf{241 g}$

(g) $\text{mass} = 3.25 \times 10^2 \text{ mol} \times \dfrac{17.0 \text{ g}}{1 \text{ mol}} = \textbf{5.53} \times \textbf{10}^3 \textbf{ g}$

(c) $\text{mass} = 3.25 \text{ mol} \times \dfrac{137.5 \text{ g}}{1 \text{ mol}} = \textbf{447 g}$

(h) $\text{mass} = 7.90 \times 10^{-4} \text{ mol} \times \dfrac{82.1 \text{ g}}{1 \text{ mol}} = \textbf{0.0649 g}$

(d) $\text{mass} = 0.00355 \text{ mol} \times \dfrac{142.0 \text{ g}}{1 \text{ mol}} = \textbf{0.504 g}$

(i) $\text{mass} = 1.00 \times 10^{-3} \text{ mol} \times \dfrac{40.0 \text{ g}}{1 \text{ mol}} = \textbf{0.0400 g}$

(e) $\text{mass} = 0.0125 \text{ mol} \times \dfrac{207.3 \text{ g}}{1 \text{ mol}} = \textbf{2.59 g}$

(j) $\text{mass} = 1.75 \times 10^{-4} \text{ mol} \times \dfrac{55.8 \text{ g}}{1 \text{ mol}} = \textbf{9.77} \times \textbf{10}^{-3} \textbf{ g}$

9. (a) $\text{\# of moles} = 17.0 \text{ g} \times \dfrac{1 \text{ mol}}{98.1 \text{ g}} = \textbf{0.173 mol}$

(b) $\text{\# of moles} = 91.5 \text{ g} \times \dfrac{1 \text{ mol}}{18.0 \text{ g}} = \textbf{5.08 mol}$

(c) $\text{\# of moles} = 53.0 \text{ g} \times \dfrac{1 \text{ mol}}{12.0 \text{ g}} = \textbf{4.42 mol}$

(d) $\text{\# of moles} = 1.25 \times 10^{-4} \text{ g} \times \dfrac{1 \text{ mol}}{95.6 \text{ g}} = \textbf{1.31} \times \textbf{10}^{-6} \textbf{ mol}$

(e) $\text{\# of moles} = 4.50 \text{ kg} \times \dfrac{10^3 \text{ g}}{1 \text{ kg}} \times \dfrac{1 \text{ mol}}{16.0 \text{ g}} = \textbf{281 mol}$

(f) $\text{\# of moles} = 225 \text{ g} \times \dfrac{1 \text{ mol}}{132.1 \text{ g}} = \textbf{1.70 mol}$

(g) $\text{\# of moles} = 55.2 \text{ mg} \times \dfrac{10^{-3} \text{ g}}{1 \text{ mg}} \times \dfrac{1 \text{ mol}}{71.0 \text{ g}} = \textbf{7.77} \times \textbf{10}^{-4} \textbf{ mol}$

(h) $\text{\# of moles} = 128.2 \text{ g} \times \dfrac{1 \text{ mol}}{64.1 \text{ g}} = \textbf{2.00 mol}$

(i) $\text{\# of moles} = 2955 \text{ kg} \times \dfrac{10^3 \text{ g}}{1 \text{ kg}} \times \dfrac{1 \text{ mol}}{107.9 \text{ g}} = \textbf{2.739} \times \textbf{10}^4 \textbf{ mol}$

(j) $\text{\# of moles} = 0.0845 \text{ g} \times \dfrac{1 \text{ mol}}{158.0 \text{ g}} = \textbf{5.35} \times \textbf{10}^{-4} \textbf{ mol}$

10. (a) molar mass = $\dfrac{4.00 \text{ g}}{0.250 \text{ mol}}$ = **16.0 g/mol**   (c) molar mass = $\dfrac{7.76 \times 10^{-3} \text{ g}}{6.47 \times 10^{-4} \text{ mol}}$ = **12.0 g/mol**

   (b) molar mass = $\dfrac{0.947 \text{ g}}{0.00248 \text{ mol}}$ = **382 g/mol**   (d) molar mass = $\dfrac{74.8 \text{ g}}{3.44 \times 10^{-5} \text{ mol}}$ = **2.17 x 10^6 g/mol**

11. (a) volume = 12.5 mol x $\dfrac{22.4 \text{ L}}{1 \text{ mol}}$ = **2.80 x 10^2 L**   (c) volume = 4.25 mol x $\dfrac{22.4 \text{ L}}{1 \text{ mol}}$ = **95.2 L**

   (b) volume = 0.350 mol x $\dfrac{22.4 \text{ L}}{1 \text{ mol}}$ = **7.84 L**

12. (a) # of moles = 85.9 L x $\dfrac{1 \text{ mol}}{22.4 \text{ L}}$ = **3.83 mol**

   (b) # of moles = 375 mL x $\dfrac{10^{-3} \text{ L}}{1 \text{ mL}}$ x $\dfrac{1 \text{ mol}}{22.4 \text{ L}}$ = **0.0167 mol**

   (c) # of moles = 5.00 mL x $\dfrac{10^{-3} \text{ L}}{1 \text{ mL}}$ x $\dfrac{1 \text{ mol}}{22.4 \text{ L}}$ = **2.23 x 10^{-4} mol**

13. # of seconds in 1 year = 365 x 24 x 60 x 60 = 3.15 x 10^7 s

   amount spent in 1 yr = 3.15 x 10^7 s x $\dfrac{\$10^3}{1 \text{ s}}$ = \$3.15 x 10^{10}

   amount given to each person = $\dfrac{\$6.02 \times 10^{23}}{4.5 \times 10^9}$ = \$1.34 x 10^{14}

   percentage spent = $\dfrac{\$3.15 \times 10^{10}}{\$1.34 \times 10^{14}}$ x 100 % = **0.024 %**

14. # of pennies/layer = $\dfrac{1 \text{ penny}}{3.61 \text{ cm}^2}$ x $\dfrac{10^{10} \text{ cm}^2}{1 \text{ km}^2}$ x 1.49 x 10^8 km^2 = 4.13 x 10^{17}

   thickness = 6.02 x 10^{23} pennies x $\dfrac{1 \text{ layer}}{4.13 \times 10^{17} \text{ pennies}}$ x $\dfrac{1.50 \text{ mm}}{1 \text{ layer}}$ x $\dfrac{10^{-3} \text{ m}}{1 \text{ mm}}$ x $\dfrac{1 \text{ km}}{10^3 \text{ m}}$ = **2.19 km**

15. (a) # of moles = 10.6 L x $\dfrac{1 \text{ mol}}{22.4 \text{ L}}$ = **0.473 mol**

   (b) # of moles = 7.50 x 10^{21} molecules x $\dfrac{1 \text{ mol molecules}}{6.02 \times 10^{23} \text{ molecules}}$ = **0.0125 mol**

   (c) # of moles = 425 mg x $\dfrac{10^{-3} \text{ g}}{1 \text{ mg}}$ x $\dfrac{1 \text{ mol}}{74.1 \text{ g}}$ = **5.74 x 10^{-3} mol**

   (d) # of moles = 4.25 x 10^{12} molecule x $\dfrac{1 \text{ mol molecules}}{6.02 \times 10^{23} \text{ molecules}}$ = **7.06 x 10^{-12} mol**

   (e) # of moles = 0.950 kg x $\dfrac{10^3 \text{ g}}{1 \text{ kg}}$ x $\dfrac{1 \text{ mol}}{40.0 \text{ g}}$ = **23.8 mol**

   (f) # of moles = 25.0 mL x $\dfrac{10^{-3} \text{ L}}{1 \text{ mL}}$ x $\dfrac{1 \text{ mol}}{22.4 \text{ L}}$ = **1.12 x 10^{-3} mol**

   (g) # of moles = 5.50 x 10^{25} molecules x $\dfrac{1 \text{ mol molecules}}{6.02 \times 10^{23} \text{ molecules}}$ = **91.4 mol**

(h) # of moles = 0.120 L x $\dfrac{1 \text{ mol}}{22.4 \text{ L}}$ = **5.36 x 10^{-3} mol**

16. (a) volume = 0.235 mol x $\dfrac{22.4 \text{ L}}{1 \text{ mol}}$ = **5.26 L**   (c) volume = 2.55 x 10^3 mol x $\dfrac{22.4 \text{ L}}{1 \text{ mol}}$ = **5.71 x 10^4 L**

(b) volume = 9.36 mol x $\dfrac{22.4 \text{ L}}{1 \text{ mol}}$ = **2.10 x 10^2 L**

17. (a) mass = 0.125 mol x $\dfrac{44.0 \text{ g}}{1 \text{ mol}}$ = **5.50 g**   (c) mass = 6.54 x 10^{-4} mol x $\dfrac{27.0 \text{ g}}{1 \text{ mol}}$ = **0.0177 g**

(b) mass = 5.48 mol x $\dfrac{162.3 \text{ g}}{1 \text{ mol}}$ = **889 g**   (d) mass = 15.4 mol x $\dfrac{92.7 \text{ g}}{1 \text{ mol}}$ = **1.43 x 10^3 g**

18. (a)   2 Na = 2 x 23.0 =   46.0 g
        4 B = 4 x 10.8 =   43.2 g
       17 O = 17 x 16.0 = 272.0 g
       20 H = 20 x 1.0 =   20.0 g
       _____

       molar mass   = **381.2 g**

(b) mass of 1 mol of grannies = 6.02 x 10^{23} x 52 kg = **3.1 x 10^{25} kg**

(c) mass of 1 mol = 3.52 x 10^{-22} g x 6.02 x 10^{23} = **212 g**

(d) mass of 1 mol of electrons = 6.02 x 10^{23} x 9.1 x 10^{-28} g = **5.5 x 10^{-4} g**

(e)   3 Cu = 3 x 63.5 = 190.5 g
       8 O = 8 x 16.0 = 128.0 g
       2 H = 2 x   1.0 =   2.0 g
       2 C = 2 x 12.0 =   24.0 g
       _____

       molar mass   = **344.5 g**

(f)   mass of 1 mol of books = 6.02 x 10^{23} x 1.34 kg = **8.07 x 10^{23} kg**

19. mass of 1 mol of unknown = 6.02 x 10^{23} x 1.18 x 10^{-22} g = 71.0 g

    molar masses of known gases: SO_3 = 80.1 g
                                       CH_4 = 16.0 g
                                       NF_3 = 71.0 g   (this is the unknown)
                                       C_2H_2 = 26.0 g

20. (a) # of drumsticks = 2 mol x $\dfrac{6.02 \text{ x } 10^{23} \text{ chickens}}{1 \text{ mol chickens}}$ x $\dfrac{2 \text{ drumsticks}}{1 \text{ chicken}}$ = **2.41 x 10^{24} drumsticks**

(b) each chicken has 2 drumsticks + 2 wings + 2 thighs = 6 "parts"

    # of parts = 2 mol x $\dfrac{6.02 \text{ x } 10^{23} \text{ chickens}}{1 \text{ mol chickens}}$ x $\dfrac{6 \text{ parts}}{1 \text{ chicken}}$ = **7.22 x 10^{24} parts**

21. (a) 8   (b) 6   (c) 10   (d) 15   (e) 46   (f)   23

22. (a) mass = 2 x 10^6 molecules x $\dfrac{1 \text{ mol}}{6.02 \text{ x } 10^{23} \text{ molecules}}$ x $\dfrac{28.0 \text{ g}}{1 \text{ mol}}$ = **9 x 10^{-17} g**

(b) mass = 1.25 L x $\dfrac{1 \text{ mol}}{22.4 \text{ L}}$ x $\dfrac{17.0 \text{ g}}{1 \text{ mol}}$ = **0.949 g**

(c) mass = 5 x 10^{14} molecules x $\dfrac{1 \text{ mol}}{6.02 \text{ x } 10^{23} \text{ molecules}}$ x $\dfrac{28.0 \text{ g}}{1 \text{ mol}}$ = **2 x 10^{-8} g**

(d) mass = 1 molecule x $\dfrac{1 \text{ mol}}{6.02 \times 10^{23} \text{ molecules}}$ x $\dfrac{56.1 \text{ g}}{1 \text{ mol}}$ = **9.32 x 10^{-23} g**

(e) mass = 125 atoms x $\dfrac{1 \text{ mol}}{6.02 \times 10^{23} \text{ atoms}}$ x $\dfrac{4.0 \text{ g}}{1 \text{ mol}}$ = **8.3 x 10^{-22} g**

(f) mass = 1 atom x $\dfrac{1 \text{ mol}}{6.02 \times 10^{23} \text{ atoms}}$ x $\dfrac{107.9 \text{ g}}{1 \text{ mol}}$ = **1.79 x 10^{-22} g**

(g) mass = 4.15 x 10^{15} molec x $\dfrac{1 \text{ mol}}{6.02 \times 10^{23} \text{ molecules}}$ x $\dfrac{16.0 \text{ g}}{1 \text{ mol}}$ = **1.10 x 10^{-7} g**

(h) mass = 175 atoms x $\dfrac{1 \text{ mol}}{6.02 \times 10^{23} \text{ atoms}}$ x $\dfrac{14.0 \text{ g}}{1 \text{ mol}}$ = **4.07 x 10^{-21} g**

(i) mass = 3.45 mL x $\dfrac{10^{-3} \text{ L}}{1 \text{ mL}}$ x $\dfrac{1 \text{ mol}}{22.4 \text{ L}}$ x $\dfrac{32.0 \text{ g}}{1 \text{ mol}}$ = **4.93 x 10^{-3} g**

(j) mass = 1.00 x 10^{8} L x $\dfrac{1 \text{ mol}}{22.4 \text{ L}}$ x $\dfrac{2.0 \text{ g}}{1 \text{ mol}}$ = **8.93 x 10^{6} g**

23. (a) # of atoms = 1.00 mol x $\dfrac{6.02 \times 10^{23} \text{ molecules}}{1 \text{ mol}}$ x $\dfrac{6 \text{ atoms}}{1 \text{ molecule}}$ = **3.61 x 10^{24} atoms**

(b) # of atoms = 2.5 mol x $\dfrac{6.02 \times 10^{23} \text{ molecules}}{1 \text{ mol}}$ x $\dfrac{3 \text{ atoms}}{1 \text{ molecule}}$ = **4.5 x 10^{24} atoms**

(c) # of atoms = 8.00 g x $\dfrac{1 \text{ mol}}{55.8 \text{ g}}$ x $\dfrac{6.02 \times 10^{23} \text{ atoms}}{1 \text{ mol}}$ = **8.63 x 10^{22} atoms**

(d) # of atoms = 15.0 L x $\dfrac{1 \text{ mol}}{22.4 \text{ L}}$ x $\dfrac{6.02 \times 10^{23} \text{ atoms}}{1 \text{ mol}}$ = **4.03 x 10^{23} atoms**

(e) # of atoms = 12 g x $\dfrac{1 \text{ mol}}{34.0 \text{ g}}$ x $\dfrac{6.02 \times 10^{23} \text{ molecules}}{1 \text{ mol}}$ x $\dfrac{4 \text{ atoms}}{1 \text{ molecule}}$ = **8.5 x 10^{23} atoms**

(f) # of atoms = 55.0 mL x $\dfrac{10^{-3} \text{ L}}{1 \text{ mL}}$ x $\dfrac{1 \text{ mol}}{22.4 \text{ L}}$ x $\dfrac{6.02 \times 10^{23} \text{ molecules}}{1 \text{ mol}}$ x $\dfrac{3 \text{ atoms}}{1 \text{ molecule}}$

= **4.43 x 10^{21} atoms**

(g) # of atoms = 40.0 g x $\dfrac{1 \text{ mol}}{39.1 \text{ g}}$ x $\dfrac{6.02 \times 10^{23} \text{ atoms}}{1 \text{ mol}}$ = **6.16 x 10^{23} atoms**

(h) # of atoms = 5.0 g x $\dfrac{1 \text{ mol}}{58.5 \text{ g}}$ x $\dfrac{6.02 \times 10^{23} \text{ molecules}}{1 \text{ mol}}$ x $\dfrac{2 \text{ atoms}}{1 \text{ molecule}}$ = **1.0 x 10^{23} atoms**

(i) # of atoms = 125 g x $\dfrac{1 \text{ mol}}{50.5 \text{ g}}$ x $\dfrac{6.02 \times 10^{23} \text{ molecules}}{1 \text{ mol}}$ x $\dfrac{5 \text{ atoms}}{1 \text{ molecule}}$ = **7.45 x 10^{24} atoms**

(j) # of atoms = 8.30 x 10^{-4} mL x $\dfrac{10^{-3} \text{ L}}{1 \text{ mL}}$ x $\dfrac{1 \text{ mol}}{22.4 \text{ L}}$ x $\dfrac{6.02 \times 10^{23} \text{ molecules}}{1 \text{ mol}}$ x $\dfrac{4 \text{ atoms}}{1 \text{ molecule}}$

= **8.92 x 10^{16} atoms**

(k) # of atoms = 6.5 x 10^{-6} g x $\dfrac{1 \text{ mol}}{83.8 \text{ g}}$ x $\dfrac{6.02 \times 10^{23} \text{ atoms}}{1 \text{ mol}}$ = **4.7 x 10^{16} atoms**

(l) # of atoms = 9.5 x 10^{-3} g x $\dfrac{1 \text{ mol}}{17.0 \text{ g}}$ x $\dfrac{6.02 \times 10^{23} \text{ molecules}}{1 \text{ mol}}$ x $\dfrac{4 \text{ atoms}}{1 \text{ molecule}}$ = **1.3 x 10^{21} atoms**

24. (a) volume = $16.5 \text{ g} \times \dfrac{1 \text{ mol}}{77.9 \text{ g}} \times \dfrac{22.4 \text{ L}}{1 \text{ mol}}$ = **4.74 L**

(b) volume = $5.65 \times 10^{22} \text{ molecules} \times \dfrac{1 \text{ mol}}{6.02 \times 10^{23} \text{ molecules}} \times \dfrac{22.4 \text{ L}}{1 \text{ mol}}$ = **2.10 L**

(c) volume = $0.750 \text{ g} \times \dfrac{1 \text{ mol}}{48.0 \text{ g}} \times \dfrac{22.4 \text{ L}}{1 \text{ mol}}$ = **0.350 L**

(d) volume = $9.04 \times 10^{24} \text{ atoms} \times \dfrac{1 \text{ mol}}{6.02 \times 10^{23} \text{ atoms}} \times \dfrac{22.4 \text{ L}}{1 \text{ mol}}$ = **336 L**

(e) volume = $8.65 \times 10^{21} \text{ molecules} \times \dfrac{1 \text{ mol}}{6.02 \times 10^{23} \text{ molecules}} \times \dfrac{22.4 \text{ L}}{1 \text{ mol}}$ = **0.322 L**

(f) volume = $6.98 \times 10^{15} \text{ atoms} \times \dfrac{1 \text{ mol}}{6.02 \times 10^{23} \text{ atoms}} \times \dfrac{22.4 \text{ L}}{1 \text{ mol}}$ = **2.60×10^{-7} L**

(g) volume = $28.4 \text{ mg} \times \dfrac{10^{-3} \text{ g}}{1 \text{ mg}} \times \dfrac{1 \text{ mol}}{129.6 \text{ g}} \times \dfrac{22.4 \text{ L}}{1 \text{ mol}}$ = **4.91×10^{-3} L**

(h) volume = $3.25 \text{ kg} \times \dfrac{10^{3} \text{ g}}{1 \text{ kg}} \times \dfrac{1 \text{ mol}}{30.0 \text{ g}} \times \dfrac{22.4 \text{ L}}{1 \text{ mol}}$ = **2.43×10^{3} L**

25. density of $CO_2(g)$ = $\dfrac{44.0 \text{ g}}{22.4 \text{ L}}$ = **1.96 $\dfrac{g}{L}$**

26. # of N atoms = $30.0 \text{ g} \times \dfrac{1 \text{ mol}}{80.0 \text{ g}} \times \dfrac{6.02 \times 10^{23} \text{ molecules}}{1 \text{ mol}} \times \dfrac{2 \text{ N– atoms}}{1 \text{ molecule}}$ = **4.52×10^{23} atoms**

27. # of molecules = $2.50 \text{ L} \times \dfrac{1.59 \text{ g}}{10^{-3} \text{ L}} \times \dfrac{1 \text{ mol}}{154.0 \text{ g}} \times \dfrac{6.02 \times 10^{23} \text{ molecules}}{1 \text{ mol}}$ = **1.55×10^{25} molecules**

28. density = $\dfrac{1.67 \text{ g}}{1.35 \text{ L}}$ = 1.237 g/L , and mass of 1 mol = 1.237 $\dfrac{g}{L} \times 22.4 \text{ L}$ = **27.7 g**

29. density = $\dfrac{30.0 \text{ g}}{22.4 \text{ L}}$ = **1.34 $\dfrac{g}{L}$**

30. volume = $8.50 \times 10^{24} \text{ C–atoms} \times \dfrac{1 \text{ molecule}}{6 \text{ C – atoms}} \times \dfrac{1 \text{ mol}}{6.02 \times 10^{23} \text{ molecules}} \times \dfrac{78.0 \text{ g}}{1 \text{ mol}} \times \dfrac{1 \text{ mL}}{0.877 \text{ g}}$ = **209 mL**

31. density = $\dfrac{0.358 \text{ g}}{0.2500 \text{ L}}$ = 1.432 g/L , and mass of 1 mol = 1.432 $\dfrac{g}{L} \times 22.4 \text{ L}$ = **32.1 g**

Silane molecules have at least one Si and one H atom. The molar mass of Si is 28.1 g and of H is 1.0 g. Silane has a molar mass of 32.1 g, which is not big enough to allow 2 atoms of Si per molecule. Hence, there is exactly 1 Si per molecule and 32.1 – 28.1 = 4.0 H atoms. The formula must be **SiH_4**.

32. volume = $4.50 \times 10^{22} \text{ molecules} \times \dfrac{1 \text{ mol}}{6.02 \times 10^{23} \text{ molecules}} \times \dfrac{76.2 \text{ g}}{1 \text{ mol}} \times \dfrac{1 \text{ mL}}{1.26 \text{ g}}$ = **4.52 mL**

33. molar mass = 60.1 g; volume of 1 mol = $60.1 \text{ g} \times \dfrac{1 \text{ mL}}{2.64 \text{ g}}$ = **22.8 mL**

34. density = $\dfrac{0.02780 \text{ mol}}{0.2836 \times 10^{-3} \text{ L}} \times \dfrac{197.0 \text{ g}}{1 \text{ mol}}$ = **1.931×10^{4} g/L**

35. (a) 60   (b) 290

36. (a) # of molecules = $0.0500 \text{ L} \times \dfrac{1 \text{ mol}}{22.4 \text{ L}} \times \dfrac{6.02 \times 10^{23} \text{ molecules}}{1 \text{ mol}}$ = **1.34 x 10^{21} molecules**

    (b) # of molecules = $25.0 \text{ L} \times \dfrac{1 \text{ mol}}{22.4 \text{ L}} \times \dfrac{6.02 \times 10^{23} \text{ molecules}}{1 \text{ mol}}$ = **6.72 x 10^{23} molecules**

    (c) # of molecules = $75.0 \text{ g} \times \dfrac{1 \text{ mol}}{342.0 \text{ g}} \times \dfrac{6.02 \times 10^{23} \text{ molecules}}{1 \text{ mol}}$ = **1.32 x 10^{23} molecules**

    (d) # of molecules = $0.125 \text{ g} \times \dfrac{1 \text{ mol}}{124.0 \text{ g}} \times \dfrac{6.02 \times 10^{23} \text{ molecules}}{1 \text{ mol}}$ = **6.07 x 10^{20} molecules**

37. (a) volume = $10.0 \text{ g} \times \dfrac{1 \text{ mol}}{34.1 \text{ g}} \times \dfrac{22.4 \text{ L}}{1 \text{ mol}}$ = **6.57 L**

    (b) volume = $0.0150 \text{ g} \times \dfrac{1 \text{ mol}}{124.0 \text{ g}} \times \dfrac{22.4 \text{ L}}{1 \text{ mol}}$ = **0.00269 L**

    (c) volume = $5.0 \times 10^{20} \text{ molecules} \times \dfrac{1 \text{ mol}}{6.02 \times 10^{23} \text{ molecules}} \times \dfrac{22.4 \text{ L}}{1 \text{ mol}}$ = **0.019 L**

    (d) volume = $8.5 \times 10^{25} \text{ molecules} \times \dfrac{1 \text{ mol}}{6.02 \times 10^{23} \text{ molecules}} \times \dfrac{22.4 \text{ L}}{1 \text{ mol}}$ = **3.2 x 10^{3} L**

38. (a) mass = $1 \text{ atom} \times \dfrac{1 \text{ mol}}{6.02 \times 10^{23} \text{ atoms}} \times \dfrac{197.0 \text{ g}}{1 \text{ mol}}$ = **3.27 x 10^{-22} g**

    (b) mass = $1.5 \times 10^{15} \text{ molecules} \times \dfrac{1 \text{ mol}}{6.02 \times 10^{23} \text{ molecules}} \times \dfrac{143.4 \text{ g}}{1 \text{ mol}}$ = **3.6 x 10^{-7} g**

    (c) mass = $0.2500 \text{ L} \times \dfrac{1 \text{ mol}}{22.4 \text{ L}} \times \dfrac{42.0 \text{ g}}{1 \text{ mol}}$ = **0.469 g**

    (d) mass = $2.00 \text{ L} \times \dfrac{1 \text{ mol}}{22.4 \text{ L}} \times \dfrac{146.1 \text{ g}}{1 \text{ mol}}$ = **13.0 g**

39. (a) # of moles = $5.00 \text{ g} \times \dfrac{1 \text{ mol}}{128.0 \text{ g}}$ = **0.0391 mol**

    (b) # of moles = $0.525 \text{ g} \times \dfrac{1 \text{ mol}}{212.3 \text{ g}}$ = **0.00247 mol**

    (c) # of moles = $6.00 \text{ L} \times \dfrac{1 \text{ mol}}{22.4 \text{ L}}$ = **0.268 mol**

    (d) # of moles = $1.00 \times 10^{-3} \text{ L} \times \dfrac{1 \text{ mol}}{22.4 \text{ L}}$ = **4.46 x 10^{-5} mol**

    (e) # of moles = $4.55 \times 10^{12} \text{ atoms} \times \dfrac{1 \text{ mol}}{6.02 \times 10^{23} \text{ atoms}}$ = **7.56 x 10^{-12} mol**

    (f) # of moles = $6.02 \times 10^{16} \text{ molecules} \times \dfrac{1 \text{ mol}}{6.02 \times 10^{23} \text{ molecules}}$ = **1.00 x 10^{-7} mol**

40. (a) molar mass = 6.02 x 10^{23} molecules x $\dfrac{1.25 \times 10^{-17} \text{ g}}{\text{molecule}}$ = **7.53 x 10^6 g**

(b) molar mass = $\dfrac{74.0 \text{ g}}{0.179 \text{ mol}}$ = **413 g/mol**

(c) molar mass = 6.02 x 10^{23} molecules x $\dfrac{2.96 \times 10^{-22} \text{ g}}{\text{molecule}}$ = **178 g**

(d) molar mass = 248.2 g

(e) molar mass = $\dfrac{2.13 \text{ g}}{0.0229 \text{ mol}}$ = **93.0 g/mol**

(f) molar mass = 329.6 g

41. (a) density = $\dfrac{34.0 \text{ g}}{22.4 \text{ L}}$ = **1.52 g/L**

(b) volume of 1 mol = 197.0 g x $\dfrac{1 \text{ mL}}{19.31 \text{ g}}$ = **10.2 mL**

(c) # of moles = 1.25 mL x $\dfrac{1.26 \text{ g}}{\text{mL}}$ x $\dfrac{1 \text{ mol}}{76.2 \text{ g}}$ = **0.0207 mol**

(d) density = $\dfrac{0.100 \text{ mol}}{16.2 \text{ mL}}$ x $\dfrac{114.0 \text{ g}}{1 \text{ mol}}$ = **0.704 g/mL**

(e) density = $\dfrac{65.5 \text{ g}}{22.4 \text{ L}}$ = **2.92 g/L**

(f) volume = 0.0875 mol x $\dfrac{107.9 \text{ g}}{1 \text{ mol}}$ x $\dfrac{1 \text{ mL}}{10.5 \text{ g}}$ = **0.899 mL**

(g) density = $\dfrac{0.0275 \text{ mol}}{3.01 \text{ mL}}$ x $\dfrac{249.6 \text{ g}}{1 \text{ mol}}$ = **2.28 g/mL**

(h) # of moles = 7.50 L x $\dfrac{1 \text{ mL}}{10^{-3} \text{ L}}$ x $\dfrac{0.789 \text{ g}}{1 \text{ mL}}$ x $\dfrac{1 \text{ mol}}{46.0 \text{ g}}$ = **129 mol**

(i) density = $\dfrac{1.14 \text{ g}}{0.7500 \text{ L}}$ = 1.52 g/L   and   mass of 1 mol = 1.52 $\dfrac{\text{g}}{\text{L}}$ x 22.4 L = **34.0 g**

(j) volume = 0.0155 mol x $\dfrac{58.5 \text{ g}}{1 \text{ mol}}$ x $\dfrac{1 \text{ mL}}{2.17 \text{ g}}$ = **0.418 mL**

(k) density = $\dfrac{3.47 \text{ g}}{1.25 \text{ L}}$ = 2.776 g/L   and   mass of 1 mol = 2.776 $\dfrac{\text{g}}{\text{L}}$ x 22.4 L = **62.2 g**

(l) volume of 1 mol = 6.9 g x $\dfrac{1 \text{ L}}{534 \text{ g}}$ = **0.013 L**

42. (a) # of atoms = 2 molecules x $\dfrac{9 \text{ atoms}}{1 \text{ molecule}}$ = **18 atoms**

(b) volume = 1.45 x 10^{30} molecules x $\dfrac{1 \text{ mol}}{6.02 \times 10^{23} \text{ molecules}}$ x $\dfrac{22.4 \text{ L}}{1 \text{ mol}}$ = **5.40 x 10^7 L**

(c) # of molecules = 64.0 g x $\dfrac{1 \text{ mol}}{87.9 \text{ g}}$ x $\dfrac{6.02 \times 10^{23} \text{ molecules}}{1 \text{ mol}}$ = **4.38 x 10^{23} molecules**

(d) # of moles = 0.0250 L x $\dfrac{1 \text{ mol}}{22.4 \text{ L}}$ = **1.12 x 10^{-3} mol**

(e) volume = 43.5 g x $\dfrac{1 \text{ mol}}{92.5 \text{ g}}$ x $\dfrac{22.4 \text{ L}}{1 \text{ mol}}$ = **10.5 L**

(f) # of moles = 2.75 x 10^{23} atoms x $\dfrac{1 \text{ mol}}{6.02 \times 10^{23} \text{ atoms}}$ = **0.457 mol**

(g) # of molecules = 0.125 L x $\dfrac{1 \text{ mol}}{22.4 \text{ L}}$ x $\dfrac{6.02 \times 10^{23} \text{ molecules}}{1 \text{ mol}}$ = **3.36 x 10^{21} molecules**

(h) mass = 3.01 x 10^{22} atoms x $\dfrac{1 \text{ mol}}{6.02 \times 10^{23} \text{ atoms}}$ x $\dfrac{195.1 \text{ g}}{1 \text{ mol}}$ = **9.76 g**

(i) molar mass = 136.5 g

(j) density = $\dfrac{52.0 \text{ g}}{22.4 \text{ L}}$ = **2.32 g/L**

(k) mass = 0.0250 L x $\dfrac{1 \text{ mol}}{22.4 \text{ L}}$ x $\dfrac{83.8 \text{ g}}{1 \text{ mol}}$ = **0.0935 g**

(l) volume of 1 mol = 192.2 g x $\dfrac{1 \text{ mL}}{22.42 \text{ g}}$ = **8.573 mL**

(m) molar mass = $\dfrac{0.888 \text{ g}}{0.0139 \text{ mol}}$ = **63.9 g/mol**

(n) density = $\dfrac{0.250 \text{ mol}}{14.3 \text{ mL}}$ x $\dfrac{60.0 \text{ g}}{1 \text{ mol}}$ = **1.05 g/mL**

(o) # of moles = 0.0850 g x $\dfrac{1 \text{ mol}}{121.6 \text{ g}}$ = **6.99 x 10^{-4} mol**

(p) volume = 0.145 mol x $\dfrac{102.0 \text{ g}}{1 \text{ mol}}$ x $\dfrac{1 \text{ mL}}{3.97 \text{ g}}$ = **3.73 mL**

(q) molar mass = 6.02 x 10^{23} particles x $\dfrac{9.11 \times 10^{-28} \text{ g}}{\text{particle}}$ = **5.48 x 10^{-4} g**

(r) density = $\dfrac{313 \text{ g}}{135 \text{ L}}$ = 2.319 g/L   and   mass of 1 mol = 2.319 $\dfrac{\text{g}}{\text{L}}$ x 22.4 L = **51.9 g**

(s) # of moles = 50.0 mL x $\dfrac{8.10 \text{ g}}{1 \text{ mL}}$ x $\dfrac{1 \text{ mol}}{232.7 \text{ g}}$ = **1.74 mol**

43. (a) volume = 5.75 x 10^{10} molecules x $\dfrac{1 \text{ mol}}{6.02 \times 10^{23} \text{ molecules}}$ x $\dfrac{22.4 \text{ L}}{1 \text{ mol}}$ = **2.14 x 10^{-12} L**

(b) # of molecules = 75.0 L x $\dfrac{1 \text{ mol}}{22.4 \text{ L}}$ x $\dfrac{6.02 \times 10^{23} \text{ molecules}}{1 \text{ mol}}$ = **2.02 x 10^{24} molecules**

(c) mass = 2.50 L x $\dfrac{1 \text{ mol}}{22.4 \text{ L}}$ x $\dfrac{126.0 \text{ g}}{1 \text{ mol}}$ = **14.1 g**

(d) molar mass = 390.0 g

(e) # of moles = 15.0 L x $\dfrac{1 \text{ mol}}{22.4 \text{ L}}$ = **0.670 mol**

(f) mass = 1 molecule x $\dfrac{1 \text{ mol}}{6.02 \times 10^{23} \text{ molecules}}$ x $\dfrac{132.1 \text{ g}}{1 \text{ mol}}$ = **2.19 x 10^{-22} g**

(g) density = $\dfrac{56.0 \text{ g}}{22.4 \text{ L}}$ = **2.50 g/L**

(h) molar mass = 6.02 x 10^{23} molecules x $\dfrac{6.23 \times 10^{-22} \text{ g}}{\text{molecule}}$ = **375 g**

(i) # of atoms = 3 molecules x $\dfrac{14 \text{ atoms}}{1 \text{ molecule}}$ = **42 atoms**

(j) density = $\dfrac{0.0149 \text{ g}}{0.00554 \text{ L}}$ = 2.690 g/L   and   mass of 1 mol = 2.690 $\dfrac{\text{g}}{\text{L}}$ x 22.4 L = **60.2 g**

(k) # of moles = 125 g x $\dfrac{1 \text{ mol}}{295.2 \text{ g}}$ = **0.423 mol**

(l) molar mass = $\dfrac{73.1 \text{ g}}{0.546 \text{ mol}}$ = **134 g/mol**

(m) # of moles = 1.85 x 10^{24} molecules x $\dfrac{1 \text{ mol}}{6.02 \times 10^{23} \text{ molecules}}$ = **3.07 mol**

(n) volume = 0.0694 mol x $\dfrac{160.1 \text{ g}}{1 \text{ mol}}$ x $\dfrac{1 \text{ mL}}{4.80 \text{ g}}$ = **2.31 mL**

(o) # of molecules = 5.00 g x $\dfrac{1 \text{ mol}}{54.0 \text{ g}}$ x $\dfrac{6.02 \times 10^{23} \text{ molecules}}{1 \text{ mol}}$ = **5.57 x 10^{22} molecules**

(p) density = $\dfrac{0.0316 \text{ mol}}{1.167 \text{ mL}}$ x $\dfrac{100.1 \text{ g}}{1 \text{ mol}}$ = **2.71 g/mL**

(q) # of moles = 100.0 mL x $\dfrac{1.58 \text{ g}}{1 \text{ mL}}$ x $\dfrac{1 \text{ mol}}{342.0 \text{ g}}$ = **0.462 mol**

(r) volume = 0.275 g x $\dfrac{1 \text{ mol}}{76.6 \text{ g}}$ x $\dfrac{22.4 \text{ L}}{1 \text{ mol}}$ = **0.0804 L**

(s) volume of 1 mol = 200.6 g x $\dfrac{1 \text{ mL}}{13.55 \text{ g}}$ = **14.80 mL**

44. (a) molar mass = 30.0 g

%C = $\dfrac{24.0 \text{ g}}{30.0 \text{ g}}$ x 100 % = 80.0 %

%H = $\dfrac{6.0 \text{ g}}{30.0 \text{ g}}$ x 100 % = 20.0 %

(b) molar mass = 126.8 g

%Fe = $\dfrac{55.8 \text{ g}}{126.8 \text{ g}}$ x 100 % = 44.0 %

%Cl = $\dfrac{71.0 \text{ g}}{126.8 \text{ g}}$ x 100 % = 56.0 %

(c) molar mass = 162.3 g

%Fe = $\dfrac{55.8 \text{ g}}{162.3 \text{ g}}$ x 100 % = 34.4 %

%Cl = $\dfrac{106.5 \text{ g}}{162.3 \text{ g}}$ x 100 % = 65.6 %

(d) molar mass = 60.0 g

%C = $\dfrac{24.0 \text{ g}}{60.0 \text{ g}}$ x 100 % = 40.0 %

%H = $\dfrac{4.0 \text{ g}}{60.0 \text{ g}}$ x 100 % = 6.7 %

%O = $\dfrac{32.0 \text{ g}}{60.0 \text{ g}}$ x 100 % = 53.3 %

(e) molar mass = 100.1 g

%Ca = $\dfrac{40.1 \text{ g}}{100.1 \text{ g}}$ x 100 % = 40.0 %

%C = $\dfrac{12.0 \text{ g}}{100.1 \text{ g}}$ x 100 % = 12.0 %

%O = $\dfrac{48.0 \text{ g}}{100.1 \text{ g}}$ x 100 % = 48.0 %

(f) molar mass = 40.0 g

%Na = $\dfrac{23.0 \text{ g}}{40.0 \text{ g}}$ x 100 % = 57.5 %

%O = $\dfrac{16.0 \text{ g}}{40.0 \text{ g}}$ x 100 % = 40.0 %

%H = $\dfrac{1.0 \text{ g}}{40.0 \text{ g}}$ x 100 % = 2.5 %

(g) molar mass = 147.1 g

$$\% \ Ca = \frac{40.1 \ g}{147.1 \ g} \times 100 \ \% = 27.3 \ \%$$

$$\% \ Cl = \frac{71.0 \ g}{147.1 \ g} \times 100 \ \% = 48.3 \ \%$$

$$\% \ H \ = \frac{4.0 \ g}{147.1 \ g} \times 100 \ \% = 2.7 \ \%$$

$$\% \ O \ = \frac{32.0 \ g}{147.1 \ g} \times 100 \ \% = 21.8 \ \%$$

(h) molar mass = 149.0 g

$$\% \ N = \frac{42.0 \ g}{149.0 \ g} \times 100 \ \% = 28.2 \ \%$$

$$\% \ H = \frac{12.0 \ g}{149.0 \ g} \times 100 \ \% = 8.1 \ \%$$

$$\% \ P = \frac{31.0 \ g}{149.0 \ g} \times 100 \ \% = 20.8 \ \%$$

$$\% \ O = \frac{64.0 \ g}{149.0 \ g} \times 100 \ \% = 43.0 \ \%$$

(i) molar mass = 177.4 g

$$\% \ Ag = \frac{107.9 \ g}{177.4 \ g} \times 100 \ \% = 60.8 \ \%$$

$$\% \ N \ = \frac{28.0 \ g}{177.4 \ g} \times 100 \ \% = 15.8 \ \%$$

$$\% \ H \ = \frac{6.0 \ g}{177.4 \ g} \times 100 \ \% = 3.4 \ \%$$

$$\% \ Cl = \frac{35.5 \ g}{177.4 \ g} \times 100 \ \% = 20.0 \ \%$$

(j) molar mass = 328.5 g

$$\% \ C \ = \frac{204.0 \ g}{328.5 \ g} \times 100 \ \% = 62.1 \ \%$$

$$\% \ H \ = \frac{15.0 \ g}{328.5 \ g} \times 100 \ \% = 4.6 \ \%$$

$$\% \ N \ = \frac{42.0 \ g}{328.5 \ g} \times 100 \ \% = 12.8 \ \%$$

$$\% \ O \ = \frac{32.0 \ g}{328.5 \ g} \times 100 \ \% = 9.7 \ \%$$

$$\% \ Cl = \frac{35.5 \ g}{328.5 \ g} \times 100 \ \% = 10.8 \ \%$$

(k) molar mass = 346.9 g

$$\% \ Sn = \frac{118.7 \ g}{346.9 \ g} \times 100 \ \% = 34.2 \ \%$$

$$\% \ S \ = \frac{64.2 \ g}{346.9 \ g} \times 100 \ \% = 18.5 \ \%$$

$$\% \ O \ = \frac{160.0 \ g}{346.9 \ g} \times 100 \ \% = 46.1 \ \%$$

$$\% \ H \ = \frac{4.0 \ g}{346.9 \ g} \times 100 \ \% = 1.2 \ \%$$

(l) molar mass = 256.7 g

$$\% \ N \ = \frac{28.0 \ g}{256.7 \ g} \times 100 \ \% = 10.9 \ \%$$

$$\% \ H \ = \frac{14.0 \ g}{256.7 \ g} \times 100 \ \% = 5.4 \ \%$$

$$\% \ Sn = \frac{118.7 \ g}{256.7 \ g} \times 100 \ \% = 46.2 \ \%$$

$$\% \ O \ = \frac{96.0 \ g}{256.7 \ g} \times 100 \ \% = 37.4 \ \%$$

(m) molar mass = 120.0 g

$$\% \ C = \frac{24.0 \ g}{120.0 \ g} \times 100 \ \% = 20.0 \ \%$$

$$\% \ H = \frac{4.0 \ g}{120.0 \ g} \times 100 \ \% = 3.3 \ \%$$

$$\% \ N = \frac{28.0 \ g}{120.0 \ g} \times 100 \ \% = 23.3 \ \%$$

$$\% \ O = \frac{64.0 \ g}{120.0 \ g} \times 100 \ \% = 53.3 \ \%$$

(n) molar mass = 329.1 g

$$\% \ K \ = \frac{117.3 \ g}{329.1 \ g} \times 100 \ \% = 35.6 \ \%$$

$$\% \ Fe = \frac{55.8 \ g}{329.1 \ g} \times 100 \ \% = 17.0 \ \%$$

$$\% \ C \ = \frac{72.0 \ g}{329.1 \ g} \times 100 \ \% = 21.9 \ \%$$

$$\% \ N \ = \frac{84.0 \ g}{329.1 \ g} \times 100 \ \% = 25.5 \ \%$$

45. (a) $\% \ H_2O = \dfrac{36.0 \ g}{147.1 \ g} \times 100 \ \% = 24.5 \ \%$

(b) $\% \ H_2O = \dfrac{126.0 \ g}{280.8 \ g} \times 100 \ \% = 44.9 \ \%$

(c) $\% \ H_2O = \dfrac{162.0 \ g}{706.2 \ g} \times 100 \ \% = 22.9 \ \%$

(d) $\% \ H_2O = \dfrac{324.0 \ g}{666.3 \ g} \times 100 \ \% = 48.6 \ \%$

(e) % NH_3 = $\dfrac{102.0\ g}{278.5\ g}$ x 100 % = 36.6 %   (f) % H_2O = $\dfrac{18.0\ g}{278.5\ g}$ x 100 % = 6.46 %

(g) % $C_2H_3O_2$ = $\dfrac{118.0\ g}{215.5\ g}$ x 100 % = 54.8 %   (h) % SO_4 = $\dfrac{288.3\ g}{561.9\ g}$ x 100 % = 51.3 %

46. (a) moles B = 15.9 g x $\dfrac{1\ mol}{10.8\ g}$ = 1.47 mol $\bigg|$ 1

    moles F = 84.1 g x $\dfrac{1\ mol}{19.0\ g}$ = 4.43 mol $\bigg|$ 3

    and empirical formula = **BF$_3$**

(b) moles Si = 87.5 g x $\dfrac{1\ mol}{28.1\ g}$ = 3.11 mol $\bigg|$ 1

    moles H = 12.5 g x $\dfrac{1\ mol}{1.0\ g}$ = 12.5 mol $\bigg|$ 4

    and empirical formula = **SiH$_4$**

(c) moles P = 43.7 g x $\dfrac{1\ mol}{31.0\ g}$ = 1.41 mol $\bigg|$ 1 $\bigg|$ 2

    moles O = 56.3 g x $\dfrac{1\ mol}{16.0\ g}$ = 3.52 mol $\bigg|$ 2.50 $\bigg|$ 5

    and empirical formula = **P$_2$O$_5$**

(d) moles I = 77.9 g x $\dfrac{1\ mol}{126.9\ g}$ = 0.614 mol $\bigg|$ 1 $\bigg|$ 4

    moles O = 22.1 g x $\dfrac{1\ mol}{16.0\ g}$ = 1.38 mol $\bigg|$ 2.25 $\bigg|$ 9

    and empirical formula = **I$_4$O$_9$**

(e) moles Fe = 77.7 g x $\dfrac{1\ mol}{55.8\ g}$ = 1.39 mol $\bigg|$ 1

    moles O = 22.3 g x $\dfrac{1\ mol}{16.0\ g}$ = 1.39 mol $\bigg|$ 1

    and empirical formula = **FeO**

(f) moles Fe = 70.0 g x $\dfrac{1\ mol}{55.8\ g}$ = 1.25 mol $\bigg|$ 1 $\bigg|$ 2

    moles O = 30.0 g x $\dfrac{1\ mol}{16.0\ g}$ = 1.875 mol $\bigg|$ 1.5 $\bigg|$ 3

    and empirical formula = **Fe$_2$O$_3$**

(g) moles Fe = 72.4 g x $\dfrac{1\ mol}{55.8\ g}$ = 1.30 mol $\bigg|$ 1 $\bigg|$ 3

    moles O = 27.6 g x $\dfrac{1\ mol}{16.0\ g}$ = 1.725 mol $\bigg|$ 1.33 $\bigg|$ 4

    and empirical formula = **Fe$_3$O$_4$**

(h) moles Li = 46.3 g x $\dfrac{1\ mol}{6.9\ g}$ = 6.71 mol $\bigg|$ 2

    moles O = 53.7 x $\dfrac{1\ mol}{16.0\ g}$ = 3.36 mol $\bigg|$ 1

    and empirical formula = **Li$_2$O**

(i)   moles C = 24.4 g x $\dfrac{1 \text{ mol}}{12.0 \text{ g}}$ = 2.03 mol | 1 | 3

moles H = 3.39 g x $\dfrac{1 \text{ mol}}{1.0 \text{ g}}$ = 3.39 mol | 1.67 | 5   and empirical formula = $C_3H_5Cl_3$

moles Cl = 72.2 g x $\dfrac{1 \text{ mol}}{35.5 \text{ g}}$ = 2.03 mol | 1 | 3

(i)   moles K = 26.6 g x $\dfrac{1 \text{ mol}}{39.1 \text{ g}}$ = 0.680 mol | 1 | 2

moles Cr = 35.4 g x $\dfrac{1 \text{ mol}}{52.0 \text{ g}}$ = 0.681 mol | 1 | 2   and empirical formula = $K_2Cr_2O_7$

moles O = 38.0 g x $\dfrac{1 \text{ mol}}{16.0 \text{ g}}$ = 2.375 mol | 3.49 | 7

(k)   moles Mg = 21.8 g x $\dfrac{1 \text{ mol}}{24.3 \text{ g}}$ = 0.897 mol | 1 | 2

moles P = 27.9 g x $\dfrac{1 \text{ mol}}{31.0 \text{ g}}$ = 0.900 mol | 1 | 2   and empirical formula = $Mg_2P_2O_7$

moles O = 50.3 g x $\dfrac{1 \text{ mol}}{16.0 \text{ g}}$ = 3.14 mol | 3.5 | 7

(l)   moles H = 3.66 g x $\dfrac{1 \text{ mol}}{1.0 \text{ g}}$ = 3.66 mol | 3

moles P = 37.8 g x $\dfrac{1 \text{ mol}}{31.0 \text{ g}}$ = 1.22 mol | 1   and empirical formula = H_3PO_3

moles O = 58.4 g x $\dfrac{1 \text{ mol}}{16.0 \text{ g}}$ = 3.65 mol | 3

(m)   moles C = 46.2 g x $\dfrac{1 \text{ mol}}{12.0 \text{ g}}$ = 3.85 mol | 1.33 | 4

moles H = 7.69 g x $\dfrac{1 \text{ mol}}{1.0 \text{ g}}$ = 7.69 mol | 2.66 | 8   and empirical formula = $C_4H_8O_3$

moles O = 46.2 g x $\dfrac{1 \text{ mol}}{16.0 \text{ g}}$ = 2.89 mol | 1 | 3

(n)   moles C = 50.5 g x $\dfrac{1 \text{ mol}}{12.0 \text{ g}}$ = 4.21 mol | 1.33 | 4

moles H = 5.26 g x $\dfrac{1 \text{ mol}}{1.0 \text{ g}}$ = 5.26 mol | 1.66 | 5   and empirical formula = $C_4H_5N_3$

moles N = 44.2 g x $\dfrac{1 \text{ mol}}{14.0 \text{ g}}$ = 3.16 mol | 1 | 3

47.   density = $\dfrac{1.59 \text{ g}}{0.850 \text{ L}}$ = 1.871 g/L,   and   mass of 1 mol = 1.871 $\dfrac{\text{g}}{\text{L}}$ x 22.4 L = 41.9 g

empirical mass of CH_2 = 12.0 + 2 x 1.0 = 14.0 g

N = $\dfrac{41.9 \text{ g}}{14.0 \text{ g}}$ = 2.99 .   Therefore the molecular formula = 3 x (CH_2) = C_3H_6 .

48.   moles N = 30.4 g x $\dfrac{1 \text{ mol}}{14.0 \text{ g}}$ = 2.17 mol $\Big|$ 1

      moles O = 69.6 g x $\dfrac{1 \text{ mol}}{16.0 \text{ g}}$ = 4.35 mol $\Big|$ 2

      and empirical formula = NO_2 ,   empirical mass = 14.0 + 2 x 16.0 = 46.0 g

      molar mass = 4.11 $\dfrac{g}{L}$ x 22.4 L = 92.1 g

      N = $\dfrac{92.1 \text{ g}}{46.0 \text{ g}}$ = 2.0 . Therefore the molecular formula = 2 x (NO_2) = N_2O_4 .

49.   Empirical mass of C_5H_{11} = 71.0 g

      molar mass = $\dfrac{3.91 \text{ g}}{0.0275 \text{ mol}}$ = 142 g/mol

      N = $\dfrac{142 \text{ g}}{71.0 \text{ g}}$ = 2.0. Therefore the molecular formula = 2 x (C_5H_{11}) = $C_{10}H_{22}$.

50.   density = $\dfrac{0.522 \text{ g}}{0.450 \text{ L}}$ = 1.16 g/L ,   and   mass of 1 mol = 1.16 $\dfrac{g}{L}$ x 22.4 L = 26.0 g

      empirical mass = 1 x 12.0 + 1 x 1.0 = 13.0 g

      N = $\dfrac{26.0 \text{ g}}{13.0 \text{ g}}$ = 2.0 . Therefore the molecular formula = 2 x (CH) = C_2H_2 .

51.   Percentage O = 100% – 42.9% = 57.1%

      moles C = 42.9 g x $\dfrac{1 \text{ mol}}{12.0 \text{ g}}$ = 3.58 mol $\Big|$ 1

      moles O = 57.1 g x $\dfrac{1 \text{ mol}}{16.0 \text{ g}}$ = 3.57 mol $\Big|$ 1

                                                                empirical formula = CO and empirical mass = 28.0 g

      molar mass = $\dfrac{1.68 \text{ g}}{0.0600 \text{ mol}}$ = 28.0 g/mol

      N = $\dfrac{28.0 \text{ g}}{28.0 \text{ g}}$ = 1   and the molecular formula is **CO**

52.   moles Si = 33.0 g x $\dfrac{1 \text{ mol}}{28.1 \text{ g}}$ = 1.17 mol $\Big|$ 1

      moles F = 67.0 g x $\dfrac{1 \text{ mol}}{19.0 \text{ g}}$ = 3.53 mol $\Big|$ 3

                                                                empirical formula = SiF_3 and empirical mass = 85.1 g

      molar mass = 7.60 $\dfrac{g}{L}$ x 22.4 L = 1.70 x 10^2 g

      N = $\dfrac{1.70 \text{ x } 10^2 \text{ g}}{85.1 \text{ g}}$ = 2.0   and the molecular formula = 2 x (SiF_3) = Si_2F_6

53.   moles B = 78.3 g x $\dfrac{1 \text{ mol}}{10.8 \text{ g}}$ = 7.25 mol $\Big|$ 1

      moles H = 21.7 g x $\dfrac{1 \text{ mol}}{1.0 \text{ g}}$ = 21.7 mol $\Big|$ 3

                                                                empirical formula = BH_3 and empirical mass = 13.8 g

      molar mass = 0.986 x 28.0 g = 27.6 g

      N = $\dfrac{27.6 \text{ g}}{13.8 \text{ g}}$ = 2.0   and the molecular formula = 2 x (BH_3) = B_2H_6

54. empirical mass = 14.0 g

$$\text{density} = \frac{0.938 \text{ g}}{0.500 \text{ L}} = 1.876 \text{ g/L} \quad \text{and} \quad \text{mass of 1 mol} = 1.876 \frac{g}{L} \times 22.4 \text{ L} = 42.0 \text{ g}$$

$$N = \frac{42.0 \text{ g}}{14.0 \text{ g}} = 3.0 \quad \text{and molecular formula} = 3 \times (CH_2) = \textbf{C}_3\textbf{H}_6$$

55. empirical mass = 16.0 g ; molar mass = 3 × 16.0 g = 48.0 g

$$N = \frac{48.0 \text{ g}}{16.0 \text{ g}} = 3.0 \quad \text{and} \quad \text{molecular formula} = 3 \times (O) = \textbf{O}_3$$

56. The total volume of water plus dissolved salt would be greater than 1.000 L.

57. Ask for instructions regarding disposal of the solution. There is no quick way to "save" the solution and be sure of the concentration.

58. When pouring samples from the volumetric flask, some of the samples will have different concentrations from other samples. The samples taken from the top of the flask will be less concentrated than those taken from the bottom.

59. (a) $[HCl] = \dfrac{0.26 \text{ mol}}{1.0 \text{ L}} = \textbf{0.26 M}$

(b) $[HNO_3] = \dfrac{2.8 \text{ mol}}{4.0 \text{ L}} = \textbf{0.70 M}$

(c) $[NH_4Cl] = \dfrac{0.0700 \text{ mol}}{0.0500 \text{ L}} = \textbf{1.40 M}$

(d) $[NaCl] = \dfrac{25.0 \text{ g}}{0.2500 \text{ L}} \times \dfrac{1 \text{ mol}}{58.5 \text{ g}} = \textbf{1.71 M}$

(e) $[CoBr_2 \cdot 6H_2O] = \dfrac{1.50 \text{ g}}{0.6000 \text{ L}} \times \dfrac{1 \text{ mol}}{326.7 \text{ g}} = \textbf{0.00765 M}$

(f) $[Cr(NO_3)_3 \cdot 9H_2O] = \dfrac{10.0 \text{ g}}{0.325 \text{ L}} \times \dfrac{1 \text{ mol}}{400.0 \text{ g}} = \textbf{0.0769 M}$

60. (a) moles $NH_4Cl = 3.00 \dfrac{mol}{L} \times 1.00 \text{ L} = 3.00 \text{ mol}$

mass $NH_4Cl = 3.00 \text{ mol} \times \dfrac{53.5 \text{ g}}{1 \text{ mol}} = 161 \text{ g}$

Dissolve 161 g of NH_4Cl in less than 1.00 L of water and dilute to 1.00 L.

(b) moles $Hg(NO_3)_2 = 0.250 \dfrac{mol}{L} \times 0.5000 \text{ L} = 0.125 \text{ mol}$

mass $Hg(NO_3)_2 = 0.125 \text{ mol} \times \dfrac{324.6 \text{ g}}{1 \text{ mol}} = 40.6 \text{ g}$

Dissolve 40.6 g of $Hg(NO_3)_2$ in less than 500 mL of water and dilute to 500.0 mL.

(c) moles $Ba(NO_3)_2 = 0.500 \dfrac{mol}{L} \times 0.125 \text{ L} = 0.0625 \text{ mol}$

mass $Ba(NO_3)_2 = 0.0625 \text{ mol} \times \dfrac{261.3 \text{ g}}{1 \text{ mol}} = 16.3 \text{ g}$

Dissolve 16.3 g of $Ba(NO_3)_2$ in less than 125 mL of water and dilute to 125 mL.

(d) moles $SbCl_3$ = 0.100 $\frac{mol}{L}$ x 0.2500 L = 0.0250 mol

mass $SbCl_3$ = 0.0250 mol x $\frac{228.3\ g}{1\ mol}$ = 5.71 g

Dissolve 5.71 g of $SbCl_3$ in less than 250 mL of water and then dilute to 250 mL.

(e) moles NaOH = 0.0120 $\frac{mol}{L}$ x 2.75 L = 0.0330 mol

mass NaOH = 0.0330 mol x $\frac{40.0\ g}{1\ mol}$ = 1.32 g

Dissolve 1.32 g of NaOH in less than 2.75 L of water and then dilute to 2.75 L.

(f) moles $CuSO_4 \cdot 5H_2O$ = moles $CuSO_4$ = 0.0300 $\frac{mol}{L}$ x 2.00 L = 0.0600 mol

mass $CuSO_4 \cdot 5H_2O$ = 0.0600 mol x $\frac{249.6\ g}{1\ mol}$ = 15.0 g

Dissolve 15.0 g of $CuSO_4 \cdot 5H_2O$ in less than 2.00 L of water and then dilute to 2.00 L.

(g) moles $BaI_2 \cdot 2H_2O$ = moles BaI_2 = 0.225 $\frac{mol}{L}$ x 0.0500 L = 0.01125 mol

mass $BaI_2 \cdot 2H_2O$ = 0.01125 mol x $\frac{427.1\ g}{1\ mol}$ = 4.80 g

Dissolve 4.80 g of $BaI_2 \cdot 2H_2O$ in less than 50.0 mL of water and then dilute to 50.0 mL.

61. moles $AlCl_3$ = 0.250 $\frac{mol}{L}$ x 0.3500 L = **0.0875 M**

62. moles HCl = 100.0 g x $\frac{1\ mol}{36.5\ g}$ = 2.74 mol

$c = \frac{n}{V}$,   so $V = \frac{n}{c} = \frac{2.74\ mol}{2.40\ mol/L}$ = **1.14 L**

63. moles $Sr(NO_3)_2$ = 1.30 x 10^{-3} $\frac{mol}{L}$ x 0.0550 L = **7.15 x 10^{-5} mol**

64. moles NaF = 0.15 g x $\frac{1\ mol}{42.0\ g}$ = 3.57 x 10^{-3} mol

$c = \frac{n}{V}$,   so $V = \frac{n}{c} = \frac{3.57\ x\ 10^{-3}\ mol}{2.8\ x\ 10^{-2}\ mol/L}$ = **0.13 L**

65. $[H_2O]$ = 1000 $\frac{g}{L}$ x $\frac{1\ mol}{18.0\ g}$ = **55.6 M**

66. $[CH_3COOH]$ = 1049 $\frac{g}{L}$ x $\frac{1\ mol}{60.0\ g}$ = **17.5 M**

67. d = 17.6 $\frac{mol}{L}$ x $\frac{100.5\ g}{1\ mol}$ = **1.77 x 10^3 $\frac{g}{L}$**

68. d = 16.6 $\frac{mol}{L}$ x $\frac{76.2\ g}{1\ mol}$ = **1.26 x 10^3 $\frac{g}{L}$**

69. moles $CaCl_2$ = 0.0350 $\frac{mol}{L}$ x 0.225 L = 7.88 x 10^{-3} mol

mass = 7.88 x 10^{-3} mol x $\frac{111.1 \text{ g}}{1 \text{ mol}}$ = **0.875 g**

70. moles Na_3PO_4 = moles $Na_3PO_4 \cdot 12H_2O$ = 0.175 $\frac{mol}{L}$ x 3.45 L = 0.604 mol

mass Na_3PO_4 = 0.604 mol x $\frac{164.0 \text{ g}}{1 \text{ mol}}$ = **99.0 g**

71. moles C_6H_5COOH = 0.0100 $\frac{mol}{L}$ x 0.3500 L = 3.50 x 10^{-3} mol

mass C_6H_5COOH = 3.50 x 10^{-3} mol x $\frac{122.0 \text{ g}}{1 \text{ mol}}$ = **0.427 g**

Now to find the mass of the acetone. Since $d = \frac{m}{V}$, then $m = d \cdot V$

and   mass acetone = 0.790 $\frac{g}{mL}$ x 350.0 mL = **277 g.**

Since the volume of solvent used was 350 mL (about a "pop-can-full"), the addition of less than half a gram of solid (about a "pinch") would not appreciably change the volume.

72. (a) $\frac{1}{3}$ OJ   (b) $\frac{1}{4}$ OJ   (c) $\frac{1}{10}$ OJ   (d) $\frac{2}{4}$ OJ = $\frac{1}{2}$ OJ   (e) $\frac{1}{5}$ OJ   (f) $\frac{3}{8}$ OJ

73. diluted concentration = $\frac{C}{C + W}$ OJ

74. (a) The amount of orange juice is not changed and the total volume is unchanged from that produced when water is used instead of apple juice. Therefore the orange juice is diluted to the same extent, regardless of whether apple juice or water is added.

(b)   diluted concentration of apple juice = $\frac{1}{2}$ AJ

(c) i)   diluted orange = $\frac{1}{2}$ OJ ; diluted apple = $\frac{1}{2}$ AJ

ii)   diluted orange = $\frac{1}{3}$ OJ ; diluted apple = $\frac{2}{3}$ AJ

iii)   diluted orange = $\frac{1}{4}$ OJ ; diluted apple = $\frac{3}{4}$ AJ

iv)   diluted orange = $\frac{2}{5}$ OJ ; diluted apple = $\frac{3}{5}$ AJ

v)   diluted orange = $\frac{1}{2}$ OJ ; diluted apple = $\frac{1}{2}$ AJ

vi)   diluted orange = $\frac{2}{5}$ OJ ; diluted apple = $\frac{3}{5}$ AJ

75. diluted orange = $\frac{O}{O + A}$ OJ ; diluted apple = $\frac{A}{O + A}$ AJ

76. diluted orange = $\frac{O}{O + A}$ x 0.8 OJ ; diluted apple = $\frac{A}{O + A}$ x 0.7 AJ

77. (a) diluted El Cheapo = $\frac{2}{5}$ x 0.5 OJ = 0.20 OJ

(b) diluted Expensive = $\frac{3}{5}$ X 1.0 OJ = 0.60 OJ

(c) total concentration = 0.20 OJ + 0.60 OJ = 0.80 OJ

(d) total concentration = $\frac{5}{8}$ x 1.0 OJ + $\frac{3}{8}$ x 0.50 OJ = 0.81 OJ

(e) total concentration = $\frac{4}{11}$ x 1.0 OJ + $\frac{7}{11}$ x 0.50 OJ = 0.68 OJ

78. $[HBr]$ = 0.75 M x $\dfrac{20.0 \text{ mL}}{90.0 \text{ mL}}$ = **0.17 M**

79. $[KOH]_{DIL}$ (#1) = 0.15 M x $\dfrac{55 \text{ mL}}{130 \text{ mL}}$ = 0.063 M

$[KOH]_{DIL}$ (#2) = 0.25 M x $\dfrac{75 \text{ mL}}{130 \text{ mL}}$ = 0.14 M

$[KOH]$ (total) = 0.063 + 0.14 = **0.21 M**

80. $[NaBr]$ = 0.20 M x $\dfrac{0.050 \text{ mL}}{100.05 \text{ mL}}$ = **1.0 x 10^{-4} M**

81. $[HNO_3]_{DIL}$ (#1) = 3.5 M x $\dfrac{5.0 \text{ mL}}{100 \text{ mL}}$ = 0.18 M

$[HNO_3]_{DIL}$ (#2) = 0.20 M x $\dfrac{95 \text{ mL}}{100 \text{ mL}}$ = 0.19 M

$[HNO_3]$ (total) = 0.18 + 0.19 = **0.37 M**

82. $V_{CONC} = \dfrac{c_{DIL} \times V_{DIL}}{c_{CONC}} = \dfrac{0.375 \text{ M X } 2.50 \text{ L}}{15.4 \text{ M}}$ = 0.0609 L

Dilute 0.0609 L of concentrated HNO_3 to a total volume of 2.50 L.

83. $V_{CONC} = \dfrac{c_{DIL} \times V_{DIL}}{c_{CONC}} = \dfrac{0.0600 \text{ M X } 45.0 \text{ L}}{14.6 \text{ M}}$ = 0.185 L

Dilute 0.185 L of concentrated H_3PO_4 to a total volume of 45.0 L.

84. $[KCl] = \dfrac{\text{total moles}}{\text{total volume}}$,   total mass KCl = 25.0 + 60.0 = 85.0 g

$[KCl] = \dfrac{85.0 \text{ g}}{0.5500 \text{ L}}$ x $\dfrac{1 \text{ mol}}{74.6 \text{ g}}$ = **2.07 M**

85. $[NaCl]$ = 0.750 M x $\dfrac{500.0 \text{ mL}}{300.0 \text{ mL}}$ = **1.25 M**

86. $V_{CONC} = \dfrac{c_{DIL} \times V_{DIL}}{c_{CONC}} = \dfrac{0.350 \text{M} \times 0.2500 \text{ L}}{6.00 \text{ M}}$ = 0.0146 L = 14.6 mL

Dilute 14.6 mL of concentrated HCl to a total volume of 250.0 mL.

87. moles NaCl needed = 0.400 $\dfrac{\text{mol}}{\text{L}}$ x 0.5000 L = 0.200 mol

mass NaCl = 0.200 mol x $\dfrac{58.5 \text{ g}}{1 \text{ mol}}$ = **11.7 g**

88. $[NaOH]_{DIL}$ (#1) = 0.250 M x $\dfrac{125.0 \text{ mL}}{325.0 \text{ mL}}$ = 0.0962 M

$[NaOH]_{DIL}$ (#2) = 0.175 M x $\dfrac{200.0 \text{ mL}}{325.0 \text{ mL}}$ = 0.108 M

[NaOH] (total) = 0.0962 + 0.108 = **0.204 M**

89. $V_{CONC} = \dfrac{c_{DIL} \times V_{DIL}}{c_{CONC}} = \dfrac{0.750 \text{ M} \times 3.00 \text{ L}}{12.0 \text{ M}}$ = **0.188 L**

90. $[CaCl_2]$ = 0.550 M x $\dfrac{80.0 \text{ mL}}{135.0 \text{ mL}}$ = **0.326 M**

91. $[MgCl_2]$ = 0.250 M x $\dfrac{350.0 \text{ mL}}{275.0 \text{ mL}}$ = **0.318 M**

92. $[NaCl]_{DIL}$ (#1) = 0.350 M x $\dfrac{20.0 \text{ mL}}{60.0 \text{ mL}}$ = 0.117 M

$[NaCl]_{DIL}$ (#2) = 0.875 M x $\dfrac{75.0 \text{ mL}}{60.0 \text{ mL}}$ = 1.09 M

[NaCl] (total) = 0.117 M + 1.09 M = **1.21 M**

93. [NaCl] = 0.400 M x $\dfrac{150.0 \text{ mL}}{250.0 \text{ mL}}$ = **0.240 M**

94. $[Na_3PO_4]$ = 0.200 M x $\dfrac{75.0 \text{ mL}}{100.0 \text{ mL}}$ = **0.150 M**

95. (a) $[NaHCO_3]$ = $\dfrac{5.62 \text{ g}}{0.2500 \text{ L}}$ x $\dfrac{1 \text{ mol}}{84.0 \text{ g}}$ = **0.268 M**

(b) $[K_2CrO_4]$ = $\dfrac{0.1846 \text{ g}}{0.5000 \text{ L}}$ x $\dfrac{1 \text{ mol}}{194.2 \text{ g}}$ = **1.901 x 10^{-3} M**

(c) $[H_2C_2O_4]$ = $\dfrac{0.584 \text{ g}}{0.1000 \text{ L}}$ x $\dfrac{1 \text{ mol}}{90.0 \text{ g}}$ = **0.0649 M**

96. (a) moles NaCl = 0.100 $\dfrac{\text{mol}}{\text{L}}$ x 1.00 L = 0.100 mol

mass NaCl = 0.100 mol x $\dfrac{58.5 \text{ g}}{1 \text{ mol}}$ = 5.85 g

Dissolve 5.85 g of NaCl in less than 1 L and then dilute to 1.00 L.

(b) moles KBr = 0.09000 $\dfrac{\text{mol}}{\text{L}}$ x 0.2500 L = 0.02250 mol

mass KBr = 0.02250 mol x $\dfrac{119.0 \text{ g}}{1 \text{ mol}}$ = 2.678 g

Dissolve 2.678 g of KBr in less than 250 mL and then dilute to 250.0 mL.

(c) moles $Ca(NO_3)_2$ = 0.125 $\dfrac{\text{mol}}{\text{L}}$ x 0.5000 L = 0.0625 mol = moles $Ca(NO_3)_2 \cdot 3H_2O$

mass $Ca(NO_3)_2 \cdot 3H_2O$ = 0.0625 mol x $\dfrac{218.1 \text{ g}}{1 \text{ mol}}$ = 13.6 g

Dissolve 13.6 g of $Ca(NO_3)_2 \cdot 3H_2O$ in less than 500 mL and dilute to 500.0 mL.

97. (a) $[LiOH]_{DIL}$ (#1) = 3.55 M x $\dfrac{125\ mL}{600\ mL}$ = 0.740 M

   $[LiOH]_{DIL}$ (#2) = 2.42 M x $\dfrac{475\ mL}{600\ mL}$ = 1.92 M

   [LiOH] (total) = 0.740 M + 1.92 M = **2.66 M**

(b) [NaCl] = 0.250 M x $\dfrac{200.0\ mL}{350.0\ mL}$ = **0.143 M**

(c) $[KBr]_{DIL}$ (#1) = 12.0 M x $\dfrac{100.0\ mL}{1050.0\ mL}$ = 1.14 M

   $[KBr]_{DIL}$ (#2) = 0.200 M x $\dfrac{950.0\ mL}{1050.0\ mL}$ = 0.181 M

   [KBr] (total) = 1.14 M + 0.181 M = **1.32 M**

(d) [KBr] = 2.50 M x $\dfrac{5.0\ mL}{80\ mL}$ = **0.16 M**

(e) [HCl] = 0.1105 M x $\dfrac{850.0\ mL}{900.0\ mL}$ = **0.1044 M**

(f) $[HCl]_{DIL}$ (#1) = 0.125 M x $\dfrac{50.0\ mL}{125.0\ mL}$ = 0.0500 M

   $[HCl]_{DIL}$ (#2) = 0.350 M x $\dfrac{75.0\ mL}{125.0\ mL}$ = 0.210 M

   [HCl] (total) = 0.0500 M + 0.210 M = **0.260 M**

98. (a) [KBr] = 0.750 M x $\dfrac{250.0\ mL}{175.0\ mL}$ = **1.07 M**

(b) $[NaNO_3]$ = 0.125 M x $\dfrac{75.0\ mL}{325.0\ mL}$ = **0.0288 M**

(c) $[LiBr]_{DIL}$ (#1) = 0.325 M x $\dfrac{150.0\ mL}{275.0\ mL}$ = 0.177 M

   $[LiBr]_{DIL}$ (#2) = 0.500 M x $\dfrac{225.0\ mL}{275.0\ mL}$ = 0.409 M

   [LiBr] (total) = 0.177 M + 0.409 M = **0.586 M**

99. (a) moles KBr = 2.5 $\dfrac{mol}{L}$ x 5.0 L = 12.5 mol

   mass KBr = 12.5 mol x $\dfrac{119.0\ g}{1\ mol}$ = **1.5 x 10^3 g**

(b) moles MgI_2 = 0.135 $\dfrac{mol}{L}$ x 0.225 L = 0.0304 mol

   mass MgI_2 = 0.0304 mol x $\dfrac{278.1\ g}{1\ mol}$ = **8.45 g**

(c) moles NaCl = 0.250 $\dfrac{mol}{L}$ x 0.3500 L = 0.0875 mol

   mass NaCl = 0.0875 mol x $\dfrac{58.5\ g}{1\ mol}$ = **5.12 g**

100. (a) $[C_8H_{18}] = 702.5 \frac{g}{L} \times \frac{1 \text{ mol}}{114.0 \text{ g}} = $ **6.162 M**

(b) $[CH_3COCH_3] = 789.9 \frac{g}{L} \times \frac{1 \text{ mol}}{58.0 \text{ g}} = $ **13.6 M**

(c) $[POCl_3] = 1675 \frac{g}{L} \times \frac{1 \text{ mol}}{153.5 \text{ g}} = $ **10.91 M**

101. (a) $d = 13.8 \frac{\text{mol}}{L} \times \frac{216.8 \text{ g}}{1 \text{ mol}} = $ **2.99 x 10³ g/L** or **2.99 g/mL**

(b) $d = 12.73 \frac{\text{mol}}{L} \times \frac{135.2 \text{ g}}{1 \text{ mol}} = $ **1721 g/L** or **1.721 g/mL**

(c) $d = 9.825 \frac{\text{mol}}{L} \times \frac{106.0 \text{ g}}{1 \text{ mol}} = $ **1041 g/L** or **1.041 g/mL**

102. (a) $V_{CONC} = \frac{c_{DIL} \times V_{DIL}}{c_{CONC}} = \frac{0.250 \text{ M} \times 5.00 \text{ L}}{3.00 \text{ M}} = $ **0.417 L**

(b) $V_{CONC} = \frac{c_{DIL} \times V_{DIL}}{c_{CONC}} = \frac{0.100 \text{ M} \times 0.5000 \text{ L}}{15.4 \text{ M}} = 0.00325 \text{ L} = $ **3.25 mL**

(c) $V_{DIL} = \frac{c_{CONC} \times V_{CONC}}{c_{DIL}} = \frac{5.00 \text{ M} \times 0.2500 \text{ L}}{0.150 \text{ M}} = $ **8.33 L**

(d) $c_{DIL} = \frac{c_{CONC} \times V_{CONC}}{V_{DIL}} = \frac{0.850 \text{ M} \times 3.00 \text{ L}}{12.5 \text{ L}} = $ **0.204 M**

(e) $c_{CONC} = \frac{c_{DIL} \times V_{DIL}}{V_{CONC}} = \frac{0.100 \text{ M} \times 5.00 \text{ L}}{0.1000 \text{ L}} = $ **5.00 M**

(f) moles KBr $= 0.235 \frac{\text{mol}}{L} \times 0.5000 \text{ L} = 0.118 \text{ mol}$

mass KBr $= 0.118 \text{ mol} \times \frac{119.0 \text{ g}}{1 \text{ mol}} = $ **14.0 g**

(g) moles HCl $= 50.0 \text{ g} \times \frac{1 \text{ mol}}{36.5 \text{ g}} = 1.37 \text{ mol}$

volume $= \frac{1.37 \text{ mol}}{0.550 \text{ mol/L}} = $ **2.49 L**

(h) moles LiCl $= 0.850 \frac{\text{mol}}{L} \times 5.50 \text{ L} = $ **4.68 mol**

(i) $[CaCl_2] = \frac{75.0 \text{ g}}{0.9500 \text{ L}} \times \frac{1 \text{ mol}}{111.1 \text{ g}} = $ **0.710 M**

(j) density $= 11.4 \frac{\text{mol}}{L} \times \frac{252.7 \text{ g}}{1 \text{ mol}} = $ **2.88 x 10³ g/L** or **2.88 g/mL**

(k) moles $Ba(NO_3)_2 = 2.55 \text{ g} \times \frac{1 \text{ mol}}{261.3 \text{ g}} = 9.76 \times 10^{-3} \text{ mol}$

volume $= \frac{9.76 \times 10^{-3} \text{ mol}}{0.0675 \text{ mol/L}} = $ **0.144 L**

(l)   moles $FeCl_3$ = 0.368 $\dfrac{mol}{L}$ x 1.50 L = **0.552 mol**

(m) $[SnCl_2]$ = $\dfrac{25.00\ g}{0.7500\ L}$ x $\dfrac{1\ mol}{225.7\ g}$ = **0.1477 M**

(n) V_{CONC} = $\dfrac{c_{DIL}\ \times\ V_{DIL}}{c_{CONC}}$ = $\dfrac{0.0450\ M\ \times\ 3.50\ L}{0.995\ M}$ = **0.158 M**

(o) $[NaCl]$ = 0.543 M x $\dfrac{55.0\ mL}{240.0\ mL}$ = **0.124 M**

(p)   moles $BaCl_2 \cdot 2H_2O$ = moles $BaCl_2$ = 0.250 $\dfrac{mol}{L}$ x 1.35 L = 0.338 mol

   mass $BaCl_2 \cdot 2H_2O$ = 0.338 mol x $\dfrac{244.3\ g}{1\ mol}$ = **82.4 g**

(q) $[CaCl_2]_{DIL}$ (#1) = 0.550 M x $\dfrac{145\ mL}{200\ mL}$ = 0.399 M

   $[CaCl_2]_{DIL}$ (#2) = 0.135 M x $\dfrac{55\ mL}{200\ mL}$ = 0.0371 M

   $[CaCl_2]$ (total) = 0.399 M + 0.0371 M = **0.436 M**

(r) $[C_6H_6]$ = 878.7 $\dfrac{g}{L}$ x $\dfrac{1\ mol}{78.0\ g}$ = **11.3 M**

ANSWERS TO UNIT VI : CHEMICAL REACTIONS

1. (a) A system that is enclosed by an opaque box. (Light can't get in.)
    (b) A system that is enclosed by a transparent box. (Material can't get in or out, but light can.)
    (c) A system that is enclosed by a sound–absorbing box (transparent or opaque).
    (d) A system that, for example, is surrounded by two boxes, one that is open at the top and one that is open at the bottom, as shown below.

    (e) A system in a container with heat–insulation. (This is not truly "closed"; see exercise 2; below.)

2. The only system which might be closed is the universe itself (and astronomers are still arguing about this point). In general approximately closed systems can be made; but even the best heat insulation cannot keep a liquid hot forever. The problem is making a container through which energy cannot pass.

3. (a) What is CONSERVED: the composition (the material is still paper); total mass and properties such as colour, volume and density
    (b) What is NOT CONSERVED: the number of pieces present, shape
    (c) What is CONSERVED: composition and properties such as colour and density
       What is NOT CONSERVED: total mass; volume, surface area, shape and number of pieces

4. (a) Conservation of atoms (primarily) and conservation of mass will also be violated since Fe atoms have a different mass from Cu atoms.
    (b) Conservation of mass (15 g of reactants cannot make 16 g of products)
    (c) Conservation of charge: total charge on left = +1; total charge on right = 0.
    (d) No conservation laws violated.
    (e) Conservation of atoms (different numbers of Cr's and O's on either side). Conservation of mass will also be violated as a result.
    (f) No conservation laws violated

5. Only (b) is **always** conserved. The others occasionally may be conserved in particular reactions.

6. (a) Left hand side contains: 1 C + 4 H + 4 O ;   molar mass of reactants = 1 x 16.0 + 2 x 32.0 = 80.0 g
       Right hand side contains: 1 C + 4 O + 4 H ; molar mass of products = 1 x 44.0 + 2 x 18.0 = 80.0 g
       Since left and right sides have the same number and types of atoms and the same mass, atoms and mass are conserved.

    (b) Left hand side contains: 1 Na + 1 O + 2 H + 1 Cl ; molar mass of reactants = 40.0 + 36.5 = 76.5 g
       Right hand side contains: 1 Na + 1 Cl + 2 H + 1 O ; molar mass of products = 58.5 + 18.0 = 76.5 g
       Since left and right sides have the same number and types of atoms and the same mass, atoms and mass are conserved.

7. $2 Sn + O_2 \longrightarrow 2 SnO$

8. $H_2 + Cl_2 \longrightarrow 2 HCl$

9. $N_2 + 3 H_2 \longrightarrow 2 NH_3$

10. $2 Na + 2 H_2O \longrightarrow 2 NaOH + H_2$

11. $4 NH_3 + 3 O_2 \longrightarrow 2 N_2 + 6 H_2O$

12. $2 C_6H_{14} + 19 O_2 \longrightarrow 12 CO_2 + 14 H_2O$

13. $2 KNO_3 \longrightarrow 2 KNO_2 + O_2$

14. $CaC_2 + 2 O_2 \longrightarrow Ca + 2 CO_2$

15. $C_5H_{12} + 8 O_2 \longrightarrow 5 CO_2 + 6 H_2O$

16. $K_2SO_4 + BaCl_2 \longrightarrow 2 KCl + BaSO_4$

17. $2 KOH + H_2SO_4 \longrightarrow K_2SO_4 + 2 H_2O$

18. $Ca(OH)_2 + 2 NH_4Cl \longrightarrow 2 NH_3 + CaCl_2 + 2 H_2O$

19. $5 C + 2 SO_2 \longrightarrow CS_2 + 4 CO$

20. $Mg_3N_2 + 6\,H_2O \longrightarrow 3\,Mg(OH)_2 + 2\,NH_3$

21. $V_2O_5 + 5\,Ca \longrightarrow 5\,CaO + 2\,V$

22. $2\,Na_2O_2 + 2\,H_2O \longrightarrow 4\,NaOH + O_2$

23. $Fe_3O_4 + 4\,H_2 \longrightarrow 3\,Fe + 4\,H_2O$

24. $Cu + 2\,H_2SO_4 \longrightarrow CuSO_4 + 2\,H_2O + SO_2$

25. $2\,Al + 3\,H_2SO_4 \longrightarrow 3\,H_2 + Al_2(SO_4)_3$

26. $2\,Si_4H_{10} + 13\,O_2 \longrightarrow 8\,SiO_2 + 10\,H_2O$

27. $4\,NH_3 + O_2 \longrightarrow 2\,N_2H_4 + 2\,H_2O$

28. $2\,C_{15}H_{30} + 45\,O_2 \longrightarrow 30\,CO_2 + 30\,H_2O$

29. $2\,BN + 3\,F_2 \longrightarrow 2\,BF_3 + N_2$

30. $CaSO_4{\cdot}2H_2O + 2\,SO_3 \longrightarrow CaSO_4 + 2\,H_2SO_4$

31. $4\,C_3H_7N_2O_7 + 5\,O_2 \longrightarrow 12\,CO_2 + 14\,H_2O + 4\,N_2$

32. $C_7H_{16}O_4S_2 + 11\,O_2 \longrightarrow 7\,CO_2 + 8\,H_2O + 2\,SO_2$

33. $9\,Na + 4\,ZnI_2 \longrightarrow 8\,NaI + NaZn_4$

34. $HBrO_3 + 5\,HBr \longrightarrow 3\,H_2O + 3\,Br_2$

35. $Al_4C_3 + 12\,H_2O \longrightarrow 4\,Al(OH)_3 + 3\,CH_4$

36. $2\,Ca(NO_3)_2{\cdot}3H_2O + 3\,LaC_2 \longrightarrow 2\,Ca(NO_3)_2 + 3\,La(OH)_2 + 3\,C_2H_2$

37. $CH_3NO_2 + 3\,Cl_2 \longrightarrow CCl_3NO_2 + 3\,HCl$

38. $Ca_3(PO_4)_2 + 3\,SiO_2 + 5\,C \longrightarrow 3\,CaSiO_3 + 5\,CO + 2\,P$

39. $Al_2C_6 + 6\,H_2O \longrightarrow 2\,Al(OH)_3 + 3\,C_2H_2$

40. $2\,NaF + CaO + H_2O \longrightarrow CaF_2 + 2\,NaOH$

41. $4\,LiH + AlCl_3 \longrightarrow LiAlH_4 + 3\,LiCl$

42. $2\,CaF_2 + 2\,H_2SO_4 + SiO_2 \longrightarrow 2\,CaSO_4 + SiF_4 + 2\,H_2O$

43. $3\,CaSi_2 + 2\,SbCl_3 \longrightarrow 6\,Si + 2\,Sb + 3\,CaCl_2$

44. $2\,TiO_2 + B_4C + 3\,C \longrightarrow 2\,TiB_2 + 4\,CO$

45. $4\,NH_3 + 5\,O_2 \longrightarrow 4\,NO + 6\,H_2O$

46. $SiF_4 + 8\,NaOH \longrightarrow Na_4SiO_4 + 4\,NaF + 4\,H_2O$

47. $2\,NH_4Cl + CaO \longrightarrow 2\,NH_3 + CaCl_2 + H_2O$

48. $4\,NaPb + 4\,C_2H_5Cl \longrightarrow Pb(C_2H_5)_4 + 3\,Pb + 4\,NaCl$

49. $Be_2C + 4\,H_2O \longrightarrow 2\,Be(OH)_2 + CH_4$

50. $4\,NpF_3 + O_2 + 4\,HF \longrightarrow 4\,NpF_4 + 2\,H_2O$

51. $3\,NO_2 + H_2O \longrightarrow 2\,HNO_3 + NO$

52. $3\,LiAlH_4 + 4\,BF_3 \longrightarrow 3\,LiF + 3\,AlF_3 + 2\,B_2H_6$

53. $3\,Cu + 8\,HNO_3 \longrightarrow 3\,Cu(NO_3)_2 + 2\,NO + 4\,H_2O$

54. $3\,FeCl_2 + KNO_3 + 4\,HCl \longrightarrow 3\,FeCl_3 + NO + 2\,H_2O + KCl$

55. $2\,KMnO_4 + 16\,HBr \longrightarrow 2\,MnBr_2 + 5\,Br_2 + 2\,KBr + 8\,H_2O$

56. $K_2Cr_2O_7 + 14\,HCl \longrightarrow 2\,KCl + 2\,CrCl_3 + 7\,H_2O + 3\,Cl_2$

57. (a) $2\,K + 2\,H_2O \longrightarrow 2\,KOH + H_2$ (d) $2\,Cu_2O + C \longrightarrow 4\,Cu + CO_2$

   (b) $Sr + 2\,H_2O \longrightarrow Sr(OH)_2 + H_2$ (e) $2\,NH_3 + H_2SO_4 \longrightarrow (NH_4)_2SO_4$

   (c) $2\,Al + 3\,Cl_2 \longrightarrow 2\,AlCl_3$

58. $2\,H_3PO_4(l) + 3\,Ba(OH)_2(aq) \longrightarrow Ba_3(PO_4)_2(s) + 6\,H_2O(l)$

59. $Al_2O_3(s) + 3\,H_2SO_4(aq) \longrightarrow 3\,H_2O(l) + Al_2(SO_4)_3(aq)$

60. $2\,NF_3(g) + 3\,H_2(g) \longrightarrow N_2(g) + 6\,HF(g)$

61. $Na_2CO_3(s) + 2\,HBr(aq) \longrightarrow CO_2(g) + 2\,NaBr(aq) + H_2O(l)$

62. $2 NaNO_3(s) + 10 Na(s) \longrightarrow 6 Na_2O(s) + N_2(g)$

63. $BCl_3(g) + 3 H_2O(g) \longrightarrow B(OH)_3(s) + 3 HCl(g)$

64. $XeF_6(g) + 3 H_2O(l) \longrightarrow XeO_3(s) + 6 HF(g)$

65. (a) $H_2SO_4 + 2 NaOH \longrightarrow Na_2SO_4 + 2 H_2O$

    (b) $H_3PO_4 + 3 KOH \longrightarrow K_3PO_4 + 3 H_2O$

    (c) $3 H_2SO_4 + 2 Fe(OH)_3 \longrightarrow Fe_2(SO_4)_3 + 6 H_2O$

    (d) $H_4P_2O_7 + 2 Ca(OH)_2 \longrightarrow Ca_2P_2O_7 + 4 H_2O$

    (e) $H_2SO_4 + Ba(OH)_2 \longrightarrow BaSO_4 + 2 H_2O$

66. (a) $2 C_2H_2 + 5 O_2 \longrightarrow 4 CO_2 + 2 H_2O$ (combustion)

    (b) $Mg + CuSO_4 \longrightarrow MgSO_4 + Cu$ (single replacement)

    (c) $4 Na + O_2 \longrightarrow 2 Na_2O$ (synthesis)

    (d) $2 Fe(NO_3)_3 + 3 MgS \longrightarrow Fe_2S_3 + 3 Mg(NO_3)_2$ (double replacement)

    (e) $2 N_2O \longrightarrow 2 N_2 + O_2$ (decomposition)

    (f) $Sn(OH)_4 + 4 HBr \longrightarrow 4 H_2O + SnBr_4$ (neutralization)

    (g) $Cl_2 + 2 KI \longrightarrow 2 KCl + I_2$ (single replacement)

    (h) $2 Al + 3 S \longrightarrow Al_2S_3$ (synthesis)

    (i) $C_6H_{12}O_6 + 6 O_2 \longrightarrow 6 CO_2 + 6 H_2O$ (combustion)

    (j) $3 HF + Fe(OH)_3 \longrightarrow FeF_3 + 3 H_2O$ (neutralization)

    (k) $2 H_2O_2 \longrightarrow 2 H_2O + O_2$ (decomposition)

    (l) $FeCl_2 + K_2S \longrightarrow FeS + 2 KCl$ (double replacement)

    (m) $2 Ca + O_2 \longrightarrow 2 CaO$ (synthesis)

    (n) $H_2SO_4 + 2 NaOH \longrightarrow Na_2SO_4 + 2 H_2O$ (neutralization)

    (o) $C_2H_5OH + 3 O_2 \longrightarrow 2 CO_2 + 3 H_2O$ (combustion)

    (p) $4 Cr + 3 SnCl_4 \longrightarrow 4 CrCl_3 + 3 Sn$ (single replacement)

    (q) $Pb(NO_3)_2 + K_2CrO_4 \longrightarrow PbCrO_4 + 2 KNO_3$ (double replacement)

    (r) $Fe + I_2 \longrightarrow FeI_2$ (synthesis)

    (s) $C_3H_6OS_2 + 6 O_2 \longrightarrow 3 CO_2 + 3 H_2O + 2 SO_2$ (combustion)

    (t) $MgCl_2 \longrightarrow Mg + Cl_2$ (decomposition)

    (u) $Co(NO_3)_2 + H_2S \longrightarrow CoS + 2 HNO_3$ (double replacement)

    (v) $H_4P_2O_7 + 4 KOH \longrightarrow K_4P_2O_7 + 4 H_2O$ (neutralization)

    (w) $Mg + 2 HCl \longrightarrow H_2 + MgCl_2$ (single replacement)

    (x) $2 HI \longrightarrow H_2 + I_2$ (decomposition)

67. (a) $2 HNO_3 + Sr(OH)_2 \longrightarrow Sr(NO_3)_2 + 2 H_2O$ (neutralization)

    (b) $2 C_6H_4(OH)_2 + 13 O_2 \longrightarrow 12 CO_2 + 6 H_2O$ (combustion)

    (c) $Zn + Ni(NO_3)_2 \longrightarrow Ni + Zn(NO_3)_2$ (single replacement)

    (d) $2 AlCl_3 + 3 Na_2CO_3 \longrightarrow Al_2(CO_3)_3 + 6 NaCl$ (double replacement)

    (e) $4 Al + 3 O_2 \longrightarrow 2 Al_2O_3$ (synthesis)

    (f) $Ba(OH)_2 + H_2SO_4 \longrightarrow BaSO_4 + 2 H_2O$ (neutralization)

    (g) $2 NO_2 \longrightarrow N_2 + 2 O_2$ (decomposition)

    (h) $Cl_2 + CaBr_2 \longrightarrow Br_2 + CaCl_2$ (single replacement)

    (i) $C_9H_{20}O_4S_2 + 14 O_2 \longrightarrow 9 CO_2 + 10 H_2O + 2 SO_2$ (combustion)

    (j) $ZnSO_4 + SrCl_2 \longrightarrow SrSO_4 + ZnCl_2$ (double replacement)

    (k) $8 Zn + S_8 \longrightarrow 8 ZnS$ (synthesis)

    (l) $2 NH_3 \longrightarrow N_2 + 3 H_2$ (decomposition)

    (m) $HCl + KOH \longrightarrow KCl + H_2O$ (neutralization)

    (n) $2 ICl \longrightarrow I_2 + Cl_2$ (decomposition)

(o) $2\ Na_3PO_4 + 3\ Ca(OH)_2 \longrightarrow Ca_3(PO_4)_2 + 6\ NaOH$ (double replacement)

(p) $C_4H_8S + 7\ O_2 \longrightarrow 4CO_2 + 4\ H_2O + SO_2$ (combustion)

(q) $Mg + ZnSO_4 \longrightarrow Zn + MgSO_4$ (single replacement)

(r) $4\ Li + O_2 \longrightarrow 2\ Li_2O$ (synthesis)

68. (a) Step 1 absorbs energy to break bonds.
    (b) Step 2 gives off energy as bonds are made.
    (c) Step 2 gives off more energy than step 1 absorbs.

69. $H + Cl \longrightarrow HCl + 432\ kJ$. The two reactions are exact opposites of each other, including the heat term.

70. Exothermic; heat is produced

71. Endothermic; heat is absorbed by the sugar in order to melt

72. Chemicals are **losing** energy to the surrounding beaker. The reaction is exothermic.

73. Products. The reactants gain energy and become high energy products.

74. Energy is removed from reactants as lower energy products are formed.

75. Since $H_{REACTANTS} < H_{PRODUCTS}$; then $\Delta H = H_{PRODUCTS} - H_{REACTANTS} > 0$ for an endothermic reaction.
    Since $H_{REACTANTS} > H_{PRODUCTS}$; then $\Delta H = H_{PRODUCTS} - H_{REACTANTS} < 0$ for an exothermic reaction.

76. The actual energies of the reactants and products are not important; only the energy difference matters.

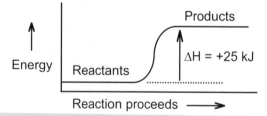

77. Again; only the energy difference of the reactants and products matters.

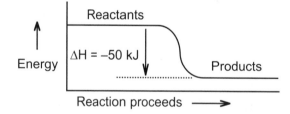

78. $F \longrightarrow G + 50\ kJ$

79. $\Delta H = +30\ kJ$

80. $\Delta H = -25\ kJ$; the reactants have more energy.

1. (a) # of O_2 molecules = 6 molecules C_2H_6 x $\dfrac{7 \text{ molecules } O_2}{2 \text{ molecules } C_2H_6}$ = **21 molecules**

   (b) # of H_2O molecules = 12 molecules C_2H_6 x $\dfrac{6 \text{ molecules } H_2O}{2 \text{ molecules } C_2H_6}$ = **36 molecules**

   (c) # of moles of O_2 = 18 mol CO_2 x $\dfrac{7 \text{ mol } O_2}{4 \text{ mol } CO_2}$ = **31.5 mol**

   (d) # of moles of CO_2 = 13 mol C_2H_6 x $\dfrac{4 \text{ mol } CO_2}{2 \text{ mol } C_2H_6}$ = **26 mol**

2. (a) # of molecules Fe_3O_4 = 12 atoms Fe x $\dfrac{1 \text{ molecule } Fe_3O_4}{3 \text{ atoms Fe}}$ = **4 molecules**

   (b) of moles of Fe = 16 mol H_2 x $\dfrac{3 \text{ mol Fe}}{4 \text{ mol } H_2}$ = **12 mol**

   (c) # of molecules H_2 = 40 molecules Fe_3O_4 x $\dfrac{4 \text{ molecules } H_2}{1 \text{ molecule } Fe_3O_4}$ = **160 molecules**

   (d) # of moles H_2O = 14.5 mol Fe x $\dfrac{4 \text{ mol } H_2O}{3 \text{ mol Fe}}$ = **19.3 mol**

3. # of moles of H_2O = 9.6 mol O_2 x $\dfrac{2 \text{ mol } H_2O}{1 \text{ mol } O_2}$ = **19 mol**

4. (a) # of moles of I_4F_2 = 5.40 mol F_2 x $\dfrac{1 \text{ mol } I_4F_2}{6 \text{ mol } F_2}$ = **0.900 mol**

   (b) # of moles of F_2 = 4.50 mol IF_5 x $\dfrac{6 \text{ mol } F_2}{2 \text{ mol } IF_5}$ = **13.5 mol**

   (c) # of moles of I_2 = 7.60 mol F_2 x $\dfrac{3 \text{ mol } I_2}{6 \text{ mol } F_2}$ = **3.80 mol**

5. Since 2 mol of reactants make a total of 3 mol of products, then O_2 represents $^1/_5$ of the total moles involved. Therefore:

   $$\text{\# of moles of } O_2 = \dfrac{0.125 \text{ mol}}{5} = \textbf{0.025 mol}$$

   Alternately: # of moles of O_2 = 0.125 mol molecules x $\dfrac{1 \text{ mol } O_2}{5 \text{ mol molecules}}$ = **0.025 mol**

6. (a) mass of NO = 2.00 mol NH_3 x $\dfrac{4 \text{ mol NO}}{4 \text{ mol } NH_3}$ x $\dfrac{30.0 \text{ g NO}}{1 \text{ mol NO}}$ = **60.0 g**

   (b) mass of H_2O = 4.00 mol O_2 x $\dfrac{6 \text{ mol } H_2O}{5 \text{ mol } O_2}$ x $\dfrac{18.0 \text{ g } H_2O}{1 \text{ mol } H_2O}$ = **86.4 g**

   (c) volume of NH_3 = 3.00 mol O_2 x $\dfrac{4 \text{ mol } NH_3}{5 \text{ mol } O_2}$ x $\dfrac{22.4 \text{ L } NH_3}{1 \text{ mol } NH_3}$ = **53.8 L**

   (d) volume NH_3 = 0.750 mol H_2O x $\dfrac{4 \text{ mol } NH_3}{6 \text{ mol } H_2O}$ x $\dfrac{22.4 \text{ L } NH_3}{1 \text{ mol } NH_3}$ = **11.2 L**

7. (a) mass of CO_2 = 100.0 g C_5H_{12} x $\dfrac{1 \text{ mol } C_5H_{12}}{72.0 \text{ g } C_5H_{12}}$ x $\dfrac{5 \text{ mol } CO_2}{1 \text{ mol } C_5H_{12}}$ x $\dfrac{44.0 \text{ g } CO_2}{1 \text{ mol } CO_2}$ = **306 g**

(b) mass of O_2 = 60.0 g H_2O x $\dfrac{1 \text{ mol } H_2O}{18.0 \text{ g } H_2O}$ x $\dfrac{8 \text{ mol } O_2}{6 \text{ mol } H_2O}$ x $\dfrac{32.0 \text{ g } O_2}{1 \text{ mol } O_2}$ = **142 g**

(c) mass of C_5H_{12} = 90.0 L CO_2 x $\dfrac{1 \text{ mol } CO_2}{22.4 \text{ L } CO_2}$ x $\dfrac{1 \text{ mol } C_5H_{12}}{5 \text{ mol } CO_2}$ x $\dfrac{72.0 \text{ g } C_5H_{12}}{1 \text{ mol } C_5H_{12}}$ = **57.9 g**

(d) volume of O_2 = 70.0 g CO_2 x $\dfrac{1 \text{ mol } CO_2}{44.0 \text{ g } CO_2}$ x $\dfrac{8 \text{ mol } O_2}{5 \text{ mol } CO_2}$ x $\dfrac{22.4 \text{ L } O_2}{1 \text{ mol } O_2}$ = **57.0 L**

(e) volume of O_2 = 48.0 L CO_2 x $\dfrac{1 \text{ mol } CO_2}{22.4 \text{ L } CO_2}$ x $\dfrac{8 \text{ mol } O_2}{5 \text{ mol } CO_2}$ x $\dfrac{22.4 \text{ L } O_2}{1 \text{ mol } O_2}$ = **76.8 L**

(f) mass of H_2O = 106 L CO_2 x $\dfrac{1 \text{ mol } CO_2}{22.4 \text{ L } CO_2}$ x $\dfrac{6 \text{ mol } H_2O}{5 \text{ mol } CO_2}$ x $\dfrac{18.0 \text{ g } H_2O}{1 \text{ mol } H_2O}$ = **102 g**

8. (a) volume of O_2 = 100.0 g PbO x $\dfrac{1 \text{ mol PbO}}{223.2 \text{ g PbO}}$ x $\dfrac{27 \text{ mol } O_2}{2 \text{ mol PbO}}$ x $\dfrac{22.4 \text{ L } O_2}{1 \text{ mol } O_2}$ = **135 L**

(b) # of molecules of CO_2 = 1.00 x 10^{-6} g $Pb(C_2H_5)_4$ x $\dfrac{1 \text{ mol } Pb(C_2H_5)_4}{323.2 \text{ g } Pb(C_2H_5)_4}$ x $\dfrac{16 \text{ mol } CO_2}{2 \text{ mol } Pb(C_2H_5)_4}$

       x $\dfrac{6.02 \times 10^{23} \text{ molecules } CO_2}{1 \text{ mol } CO_2}$ = **1.49 x 10^{16} molecules**

(c) # of molecules of H_2O = 135 molecules O_2 x $\dfrac{20 \text{ molecules } H_2O}{27 \text{ molecules } O_2}$ = **100 molecules**

(d) volume of O_2 = 1.00 x 10^{15} molec $Pb(C_2H_5)_4$ x $\dfrac{1 \text{ mol } Pb(C_2H_5)_4}{6.02 \times 10^{23} \text{ molec } Pb(C_2H_5)_4}$ x $\dfrac{27 \text{ mol } O_2}{2 \text{ mol } Pb(C_2H_5)_4}$

       x $\dfrac{22.4 \text{ L } O_2}{1 \text{ mol } O_2}$ x $\dfrac{1 \text{ mL}}{10^{-3} \text{ L}}$ = **5.02 x 10^{-4} mL**

9. (a) mass of H_2O = 0.150 g CH_3NO_2 x $\dfrac{1 \text{ mol } CH_3NO_2}{61.0 \text{ g } CH_3NO_2}$ x $\dfrac{6 \text{ mol } H_2O}{4 \text{ mol } CH_3NO_2}$ x $\dfrac{18.0 \text{ g } H_2O}{1 \text{ mol } H_2O}$

       = **0.0664 g**

(b) First, note that 4 mol of CH_3NO_2 produce 4 mol CO_2(g) and 2 mol N_2(g); that is, 6 mol of gas.

       volume of gas = 0.316 g CH_3NO_2 x $\dfrac{1 \text{ mol } CH_3NO_2}{61.0 \text{ g } CH_3NO_2}$ x $\dfrac{6 \text{ mol gas}}{4 \text{ mol } CH_3NO_2}$ x $\dfrac{22.4 \text{ L gas}}{1 \text{ mol gas}}$ = **0.174 L**

(c) volume of O_2 = 0.250 g CO_2 x $\dfrac{1 \text{ mol } CO_2}{44.0 \text{ g } CO_2}$ x $\dfrac{3 \text{ mol } O_2}{4 \text{ mol } CO_2}$ x $\dfrac{22.4 \text{ L } O_2}{1 \text{ mol } O_2}$ = **0.0955 L**

(d) mass of H_2O = 0.410 g CO_2 x $\dfrac{1 \text{ mol } CO_2}{44.0 \text{ g } CO_2}$ x $\dfrac{6 \text{ mol } H_2O}{4 \text{ mol } CO_2}$ x $\dfrac{18.0 \text{ g } H_2O}{1 \text{ mol } H_2O}$ = **0.252 g**

10. mass of $SiCl_4$ = 1.00 g Si x $\dfrac{1 \text{ mol Si}}{28.1 \text{ g Si}}$ x $\dfrac{1 \text{ mol } SiCl_4}{1 \text{ mol Si}}$ x $\dfrac{170.1 \text{ g } SiCl_4}{1 \text{ mol } SiCl_4}$ = **6.05 g**

       mass of H_2 = 1.00 g Si x $\dfrac{1 \text{ mol Si}}{28.1 \text{ g Si}}$ x $\dfrac{2 \text{ mol } H_2}{1 \text{ mol Si}}$ x $\dfrac{2.0 \text{ g } H_2}{1 \text{ mol } H_2}$ = **0.14 g**

11. volume of NH_3 $= 1.25 \times 10^4$ kg $N_2H_4 \times \dfrac{10^3 \text{ g } N_2H_4}{1 \text{ kg } N_2H_4} \times \dfrac{1 \text{ mol } N_2H_4}{32.0 \text{ g } N_2H_4} \times \dfrac{2 \text{ mol } NH_3}{1 \text{ mol } N_2H_4} \times \dfrac{22.4 \text{ L } NH_3}{1 \text{ mol } NH_3}$

$= \mathbf{1.75 \times 10^7 \text{ L}}$

12. mass of $H_2SO_4 = 25.0$ mL $\times 1.84 \dfrac{g}{mL} = 46.0$ g

mass of $P_4O_{10} = 46.0$ g $H_2SO_4 \times \dfrac{1 \text{ mol } H_2SO_4}{98.1 \text{ g } H_2SO_4} \times \dfrac{1 \text{ mol } P_4O_{10}}{6 \text{ mol } H_2SO_4} \times \dfrac{284.0 \text{ g } P_4O_{10}}{1 \text{ mol } P_4O_{10}} = \mathbf{22.2 \text{ g}}$

volume of $SO_3 = 46.0$ g $H_2SO_4 \times \dfrac{1 \text{ mol } H_2SO_4}{98.1 \text{ g } H_2SO_4} \times \dfrac{6 \text{ mol } SO_3}{6 \text{ mol } H_2SO_4} \times \dfrac{22.4 \text{ L } SO_3}{1 \text{ mol } SO_3} = \mathbf{10.5 \text{ L}}$

13. mass of $Cl = 1.5 \times 10^{15}$ L $O_3 \times \dfrac{1 \text{ mol } O_3}{22.4 \text{ L } O_3} \times \dfrac{1 \text{ mol } Cl}{1.0 \times 10^5 \text{ mol } O_3} \times \dfrac{35.5 \text{ g } Cl}{1 \text{ mol } Cl} = \mathbf{2.4 \times 10^{10} \text{ g}}$

14. We know that 0.150 mol of R_4 reacts with 143.8 g of Q_2, but the reaction $(R_4 + 6 Q_2 \longrightarrow 4 RQ_3)$ shows 1 mol of R_4 reacting with 6 mol of Q_2. The amount of Q_2 formed by 0.150 mol of R_4 is

moles of $Q_2 = 0.150$ mol $R_4 \times \dfrac{6 \text{ mol } Q_2}{1 \text{ mol } R_4} = 0.900$ mol.

But, if 0.15 mol of R_4 reacts with 0.900 mol of Q_2 and with 143.8 g of Q_2, then
0.900 mol $Q_2 = 143.8$ g Q_2, so that: 1 mol $Q_2 = 159.8$ g.
Hence, the molar mass of Q is 159.8 g / 2 = **79.9 g.** (A check of the periodic chart shows that Q is "Br".)

15. First find how many MOLES of atoms are in 100.0 g of Ne.

moles of Ne $= 100.0$ g $\times \dfrac{1 \text{ mol Ne}}{20.2 \text{ g Ne}} = 4.95$ mol

moles of atoms from decomposing HgO = 4.95 mol / 3 = 1.65 mol.
Now, 2 HgO molecules decompose to form 4 atoms of products (2 Hg atoms and 2 O atoms).

moles of HgO needed = 1.65 moles products $\times \dfrac{2 \text{ mol HgO}}{4 \text{ mol products}} = 0.825$ mol

and: mass of HgO $= 0.825$ mol $\times \dfrac{216.6 \text{ g}}{1 \text{ mol}} = \mathbf{179 \text{ g}}$

16. Balance the equation: $2 XZO_3 \longrightarrow 3 O_2 + 2 XZ$. Using the mass of O_2, find the moles of XZ produced.

moles of XZ $= 2.208$ g $O_2 \times \dfrac{1 \text{ mol } O_2}{32.0 \text{ g } O_2} \times \dfrac{2 \text{ mol XZ}}{3 \text{ mol } O_2} = 0.0460$ mol

Now: molar mass of XZ $= \dfrac{5.474 \text{ g}}{0.0460 \text{ mol}} = 119$ g/mol

Balance the double replacement equation: $XZ + AgNO_3 \longrightarrow AgZ + XNO_3$. The double replacement implies that 1 mol XZ produces 1 mol AgZ (or that 0.0460 mol XZ produces 0.0460 mol AgZ). Hence: 0.0460 mol AgZ = 8.639 g (from problem statement) and

molar mass of AgZ $= \dfrac{8.639 \text{ g}}{0.0460 \text{ mol}} = 188$ g/mol

Since the molar mass of Ag is 107.9, then molar mass of Z = 188 − 107.9 = **8.0 × 10¹ g/mol** (= Br)
and: molar mass X = molar mass XZ − molar mass Z = 119 − 8.0 × 10¹ = **39 g/mol** (= K)

17. Moles of NaOH $= 50.0$ L $H_2 \times \dfrac{1 \text{ mol } H_2}{22.4 \text{ L } H_2} \times \dfrac{2 \text{ mol NaOH}}{3 \text{ mol } H_2} = 1.488$ mol

volume of NaOH $= \dfrac{n}{c} = \dfrac{1.488 \text{ mol}}{3.00 \text{ mol/L}} = \mathbf{0.496 \text{ L}}$

neutralization equation is: $HCl + NaOH \longrightarrow NaCl + H_2O$.

moles of NaOH = 0.318 $\frac{mol}{L}$ x 0.0250 L = 7.95 x 10^{-3} mol = moles HCl

volume of HCl = $\frac{n}{c}$ = $\frac{0.00795 \text{ mol}}{0.250 \text{ mol/L}}$ = **0.0318 L** (**31.8 mL**)

19. (a) moles of Cl^- = 0.0148 $\frac{mol}{L}$ x 0.0154 L = 2.279 x 10^{-4} mol

    moles of Hg^{2+} = 2.279 x 10^{-4} mol Cl^- x $\frac{1 \text{ mol } Hg^{2+}}{2 \text{ mol } Cl^-}$ = 1.140 x 10^{-4} mol

    = moles $HgCl_2$ (for second part of problem)

    $[Hg^{2+}]$ = $\frac{n}{V}$ = $\frac{1.140 \times 10^{-4} \text{ mol}}{0.0250 \text{ L}}$ = **4.56 x 10^{-3} M**

    (b) mass of $HgCl_2$ = 1.140 x 10^{-4} mol x $\frac{271.6 \text{ g}}{1 \text{ mol}}$ = **0.0310 g**

20. (a) The neutralization reaction is: $Ca(OH)_2 + 2 HCl \longrightarrow CaCl_2 + 2 H_2O$.

    moles of HCl = 0.0156 $\frac{mol}{L}$ x 0.0235 L = 3.666 x 10^{-4} mol

    moles of $Ca(OH)_2$ = 3.666 x 10^{-4} mol HCl x $\frac{1 \text{ mol } Ca(OH)_2}{2 \text{ mol } HCl}$ = 1.833 x 10^{-4} mol

    $[Ca(OH)_2]$ = $\frac{n}{V}$ = $\frac{1.833 \times 10^{-4} \text{ mol}}{0.0100 \text{ L}}$ = **0.0183 M**

    (b) mass of $Ca(OH)_2$ = 0.01833 $\frac{mol}{L}$ x 0.2500 L x $\frac{74.1 \text{ g}}{1 \text{ mol}}$ = **0.340 g**

21. (a) moles of H_2O_2 = 1.24 $\frac{mol}{L}$ x 0.00200 L = 2.48 x 10^{-3} mol

    moles of MnO_4^- = 2.48 x 10^{-3} H_2O_2 x $\frac{2 \text{ mol } MnO_4^-}{5 \text{ mol } H_2O_2}$ = 9.92 x 10^{-4} mol

    volume of MnO_4^- = $\frac{n}{c}$ = $\frac{9.92 \times 10^{-4} \text{ mol}}{0.0496 \text{ mol/L}}$ = **0.0200 L** (**20.0 mL**)

    (b) volume of O_2 = 9.92 x 10^{-4} mol MnO_4^- x $\frac{5 \text{ mol } O_2}{2 \text{ mol } MnO_4^-}$ x $\frac{22.4 \text{ L } O_2}{1 \text{ mol } O_2}$ = **0.0556 L**

22. (a) moles of NaOH = 0.853 $\frac{mol}{L}$ x 0.0438 L = 0.03736 mol

    moles of H_3PO_4 = 0.03736 mol NaOH x $\frac{1 \text{ mol } H_3PO_4}{2 \text{ mol } NaOH}$ = 0.01868 mol

    $[H_3PO_4]$ = $\frac{n}{V}$ = $\frac{0.01868 \text{ mol}}{0.00100 \text{ L}}$ = **18.7 M**

    (b) density = 18.68 $\frac{mol}{L}$ x $\frac{98.0 \text{ g}}{1 \text{ mol}}$ = **1.83 x 10^3** $\frac{g}{L}$

23. (a) moles of $Cr_2O_7^{2-}$ = 0.125 $\frac{mol}{L}$ x 0.0176 L = 2.20 x 10^{-3} mol

moles of Fe^{2+} = 2.20 x 10^{-3} mol $Cr_2O_7^{2-}$ x $\frac{6 \ mol \ Fe^{2+}}{1 \ mol \ Cr_2O_7^{2-}}$ = 0.0132 mol

$[Fe^{2+}] = \frac{n}{V} = \frac{0.0132 \ mol}{0.0250 \ L}$ = **0.528 M**

(b) mass of Fe = mass of Fe^{2+} = 0.01320 mol x $\frac{55.8 \ g}{1 \ mol}$ = **0.737 g**

24. (a) $[NH_4NO_3] = \frac{15.5 \ g}{0.5000 \ L}$ x $\frac{1 \ mol}{80.0 \ g}$ = 0.3875 M

moles of NH_4NO_3 = 0.3875 $\frac{mol}{L}$ x 0.0100 L = 3.875 x 10^{-3} mol = moles NaOH

$[NaOH] = \frac{n}{V} = \frac{3.875 \times 10^{-3} \ mol}{0.0250 \ L}$ = **0.155 M**

(b) volume of NH_3 = 3.875 x 10^{-3} mol NaOH x $\frac{1 \ mol \ NH_3}{1 \ mol \ NaOH}$ x $\frac{22.4 \ L \ NH_3}{1 \ mol \ NH_3}$ = **0.0868 L**

25. (a) moles of $Ba(OH)_2$ (at start) = 0.0538 $\frac{mol}{L}$ x 0.0250 L = **1.345 x 10^{-3} mol**

(b) moles of HCl = 0.104 $\frac{mol}{L}$ x 0.0230 L = 2.392 x 10^{-3} mol

moles of $Ba(OH)_2$ (remaining) = 2.392 x 10^{-3} mol HCl x $\frac{1 \ mol \ Ba(OH)_2}{2 \ mol \ HCl}$ = **1.196 x 10^{-3} mol**

(c) moles of $Ba(OH)_2$ (reacted) = moles $Ba(OH)_2$ (at start) – moles $Ba(OH)_2$ (remaining)
= 1.345 x 10^{-3} – 1.196 x 10^{-3} = **1.49 x 10^{-4} mol**

(d) moles of CO_2 = 1.49 x 10^{-4} mol $Ba(OH)_2$ x $\frac{1 \ mol \ CO_2}{1 \ mol \ Ba(OH)_2}$ = **1.49 x 10^{-4} mol**

(e) volume of CO_2 = 1.49 x 10^{-4} mol x $\frac{22.4 \ L}{1 \ mol}$ = 3.34 x 10^{-3} L

% CO_2 in air = $\frac{3.34 \times 10^{-3} \ L}{10.0 \ L}$ x 100% = **0.0334%**

26. mass of CS_2 (based on C) = 17.5 g C x $\frac{1 \ mol \ C}{12.0 \ g \ C}$ x $\frac{1 \ mol \ CS_2}{5 \ mol \ C}$ x $\frac{76.2 \ g \ CS_2}{1 \ mol \ CS_2}$ = 22.2g

mass of CS_2 (based on SO_2) = 39.5 g SO_2 x $\frac{1 \ mol \ SO_2}{64.1 \ g \ SO_2}$ x $\frac{1 \ mol \ CS_2}{2 \ mol \ SO_2}$ x $\frac{76.2 \ g \ CS_2}{1 \ mol \ CS_2}$ = 23.5 g

Since C produces the least amount of CS_2, then the mass of CS_2 produced is **22.2 g.** The SO_2 is present in excess, so the mass of SO_2 used can be calculated arbitrarily based on the mass of C.

mass of SO_2 used = 17.5 g C x $\frac{1 \ mol \ C}{12.0 \ g \ C}$ x $\frac{2 \ mol \ SO_2}{5 \ mol \ C}$ x $\frac{64.1 \ g \ SO_2}{1 \ mol \ SO_2}$ = 37.4 g

mass of SO_2 in excess = 39.5 – 37.4 = **2.1 g**

27. mass of NO (based on Cu) = 87.0 g Cu x $\dfrac{\text{1 mol Cu}}{\text{63.5 g Cu}}$ x $\dfrac{\text{2 mol NO}}{\text{3 mol Cu}}$ x $\dfrac{\text{30.0 g NO}}{\text{1 mol NO}}$ = 27.4 g

mass of NO (based on HNO_3) = 225 g HNO_3 x $\dfrac{\text{1 mol } HNO_3}{\text{63.0 g } HNO_3}$ x $\dfrac{\text{2 mol NO}}{\text{8 mol } HNO_3}$ x $\dfrac{\text{30.0 g NO}}{\text{1 mol NO}}$ = 26.8 g

Since HNO_3 produces the least amount of NO, then the mass of NO produced is **26.8 g.**

Now find the mass of Cu in excess, based on the amount of HNO_3 used.

mass of Cu used = 225 g HNO_3 x $\dfrac{\text{1 mol } HNO_3}{\text{63.0 g } HNO_3}$ x $\dfrac{\text{3 mol Cu}}{\text{8 mol } HNO_3}$ x $\dfrac{\text{63.5 g Cu}}{\text{1 mol Cu}}$ = 85.0 g

mass of Cu in excess = 87.0 − 85.0 = **2.0 g**

28. mass of P_4 [based on $Ca_3(PO_4)_2$] = 41.5 g $Ca_3(PO_4)_2$ x $\dfrac{\text{1 mol } Ca_3(PO_4)_2}{\text{310.3 g } Ca_3(PO_4)_2}$ x $\dfrac{\text{1 mol } P_4}{\text{2 mol } Ca_3(PO_4)_2}$

x $\dfrac{\text{124.0 g } P_4}{\text{1 mol } P_4}$ = 8.29 g

mass of P_4 (based on SiO_2) = 26.5 g SiO_2 x $\dfrac{\text{1 mol } SiO_2}{\text{60.1 g } SiO_2}$ x $\dfrac{\text{1 mol } P_4}{\text{6 mol } SiO_2}$ x $\dfrac{\text{124.0 g } P_4}{\text{1 mol } P_4}$ = 9.11 g

mass of P_4 (based on C) = 7.80 g C x $\dfrac{\text{1 mol C}}{\text{12.0 g C}}$ x $\dfrac{\text{1 mol } P_4}{\text{10 mol C}}$ x $\dfrac{\text{124.0 g } P_4}{\text{1 mol } P_4}$ = 8.06 g

Since C produces the least amount of P_4 , then the mass of P_4 produced is **8.06 g.**

Next, calculate the masses of both $Ca_3(PO_4)_2$ and SiO_2 used by the C:

mass of $Ca_3(PO_4)_2$ used = 7.80 g C x $\dfrac{\text{1 mol C}}{\text{12.0 g C}}$ x $\dfrac{\text{2 mol } Ca_3(PO_4)_2}{\text{10 mol C}}$ x $\dfrac{\text{310.3 g } Ca_3(PO_4)_2}{\text{1 mol } Ca_3(PO_4)_2}$ = 40.3 g

mass of $Ca_3(PO_4)_2$ in excess = 41.5 − 40.3 = **1.2 g**

mass of SiO_2 used = 7.80 g C x $\dfrac{\text{1 mol C}}{\text{12.0 g C}}$ x $\dfrac{\text{6 mol } SiO_2}{\text{10 mol C}}$ x $\dfrac{\text{60.1 g } SiO_2}{\text{1 mol } SiO_2}$ = 23.4 g

mass of SiO_2 in excess = 26.5 − 23.4 = **3.1 g**

29. mass of Br_2 (based on $K_2Cr_2O_7$) = 25.0 g $K_2Cr_2O_7$ x $\dfrac{\text{1 mol } K_2Cr_2O_7}{\text{294.2 g } K_2Cr_2O_7}$ x $\dfrac{\text{3 mol } Br_2}{\text{1 mol } K_2Cr_2O_7}$ x $\dfrac{\text{159.8 g } Br_2}{\text{1 mol } Br_2}$

= 40.7 g

mass of Br_2 (based on KBr) = 55.0 g KBr x $\dfrac{\text{1 mol KBr}}{\text{119.0 g KBr}}$ x $\dfrac{\text{3 mol } Br_2}{\text{6 mol KBr}}$ x $\dfrac{\text{159.8 g } Br_2}{\text{1 mol } Br_2}$ = 36.9 g

mass of Br_2 (based on H_2SO_4) = 60.0 g H_2SO_4 x $\dfrac{\text{1 mol } H_2SO_4}{\text{98.1 g } H_2SO_4}$ x $\dfrac{\text{3 mol } Br_2}{\text{7 mol } H_2SO_4}$ x $\dfrac{\text{159.8 g } Br_2}{\text{1 mol } Br_2}$

= 41.9 g

KBr is the limiting reactant (it produces the least amount of Br_2). $K_2Cr_2O_7$ and H_2SO_4 are in excess.
Calculate the mass of $K_2Cr_2O_7$ and H_2SO_4 present in excess, arbitrarily based on the mass of KBr.

mass of $K_2Cr_2O_7$ used = 55.0 g KBr x $\dfrac{\text{1 mol KBr}}{\text{119.0 g KBr}}$ x $\dfrac{\text{1 mol } K_2Cr_2O_7}{\text{6 mol KBr}}$ x $\dfrac{\text{294.2 g } K_2Cr_2O_7}{\text{1 mol } K_2Cr_2O_7}$ = 22.7 g

mass of $K_2Cr_2O_7$ in excess = 25.0 − 22.7 = **2.3 g**

mass of H_2SO_4 used = 55.0 g KBr x $\dfrac{\text{1 mol KBr}}{\text{119.0 g KBr}}$ x $\dfrac{\text{7 mol } H_2SO_4}{\text{6 mol KBr}}$ x $\dfrac{\text{98.1 g } H_2SO_4}{\text{1 mol } H_2SO_4}$ = 52.9 g

mass of H_2SO_4 in excess = 60.0 − 52.9 = **7.1 g**

30. volume of CO_2 (based on C_5H_{12}) = 0.0250 L C_5H_{12} x $\dfrac{626.0 \text{ g } C_5H_{12}}{1 \text{ L } C_5H_{12}}$ x $\dfrac{1 \text{ mol } C_5H_{12}}{72.0 \text{ g } C_5H_{12}}$ x $\dfrac{5 \text{ mol } CO_2}{1 \text{ mol } C_5H_{12}}$

x $\dfrac{22.4 \text{ L } CO_2}{1 \text{ mol } CO_2}$ = 24.3 L

volume of CO_2 (based on O_2) = 40.0 L O_2 x $\dfrac{1 \text{ mol } O_2}{22.4 \text{ L } O_2}$ x $\dfrac{5 \text{ mol } CO_2}{8 \text{ mol } O_2}$ x $\dfrac{22.4 \text{ L } CO_2}{1 \text{ mol } CO_2}$ = 25.0 L

Hence, the C_5H_{12} is the limiting reactant and **24.3 L** of CO_2(g) will be produced.

31. moles of HCl = 0.100 $\dfrac{\text{mol}}{\text{L}}$ x 0.0500 L = 5.00 x 10^{-3} mol

moles of NaCl (based on HCl) = 5.00 x 10^{-3} mol HCl x $\dfrac{1 \text{ mol NaCl}}{1 \text{ mol HCl}}$ = 5.00 x 10^{-3} mol

moles of NaOH = 0.200 $\dfrac{\text{mol}}{\text{L}}$ x 0.0300 L = 6.00 x 10^{-3} mol

moles of NaCl (based on NaOH) = 6.00 x 10^{-3} mol NaOH x $\dfrac{1 \text{ mol NaCl}}{1 \text{ mol NaOH}}$ = 6.00 x 10^{-3} mol

Since the NaOH can produce more NaCl, the **NaOH** is in excess.

32. mass of $BaBr_2$ [based on $Ba(OH)_2$] = 0.250 g $Ba(OH)_2$ x $\dfrac{1 \text{ mol } Ba(OH)_2}{171.3 \text{ g } Ba(OH)_2}$ x $\dfrac{1 \text{ mol } BaBr_2}{1 \text{ mol } Ba(OH)_2}$

x $\dfrac{297.1 \text{ g } BaBr_2}{1 \text{ mol } BaBr_2}$ = 0.434 g

moles of HBr = 0.125 $\dfrac{\text{mol}}{\text{L}}$ x 0.0150 L = 1.875 x 10^{-3} mol

mass of $BaBr_2$ (based on HBr) = 1.875 x 10^{-3} mol HBr x $\dfrac{1 \text{ mol } BaBr_2}{2 \text{ mol HBr}}$ x $\dfrac{297.1 \text{ g } BaBr_2}{1 \text{ mol } BaBr_2}$ = 0.279 g

Since HBr is the limiting reactant, **0.279 g** of $BaBr_2$ can be formed.

33. (a) First assume the $FeCO_3$ is 100 % pure.

mass of Fe_2O_3 = 15.0 g $FeCO_3$ x $\dfrac{1 \text{ mol } FeCO_3}{115.8 \text{ g } FeCO_3}$ x $\dfrac{2 \text{ mol } Fe_2O_3}{4 \text{ mol } FeCO_3}$ x $\dfrac{159.6 \text{ g } Fe_2O_3}{1 \text{ mol } Fe_2O_3}$ = 10.3 g

Since the $FeCO_3$ is only 42.0 % pure there will be less than 10.3 g.

mass of pure $FeCO_3$ = 0.420 x 10.3 g = **4.34 g**

(b) First calculate the mass of pure $FeCO_3$ required to produce 37.0 g of Fe_2O_3.

mass of $FeCO_3$ = 37.0 g Fe_2O_3 x $\dfrac{1 \text{ mol } Fe_2O_3}{159.6 \text{ g } Fe_2O_3}$ x $\dfrac{4 \text{ mol } FeCO_3}{2 \text{ mol } Fe_2O_3}$ x $\dfrac{115.8 \text{ g } FeCO_3}{1 \text{ mol } FeCO_3}$ = 53.69 g

Then: % purity = $\dfrac{\text{mass of pure } FeCO_3}{\text{mass of impure } FeCO_3}$ x 100% = $\dfrac{53.69 \text{ g}}{55.0 \text{ g}}$ x 100% = **97.6%**

(c) First calculate the mass of Fe_2O_3 EXPECTED from the reaction.

mass of Fe_2O_3 = 35.0 g $FeCO_3$ x $\dfrac{1 \text{ mol } FeCO_3}{115.8 \text{ g } FeCO_3}$ x $\dfrac{2 \text{ mol } Fe_2O_3}{4 \text{ mol } FeCO_3}$ x $\dfrac{159.6 \text{ g } Fe_2O_3}{1 \text{ mol } Fe_2O_3}$ = 24.12 g

Now: % yield = $\dfrac{\text{mass obtained}}{\text{mass expected}}$ x 100% = $\dfrac{22.5 \text{ g}}{24.12 \text{ g}}$ x 100% = **93.3%**

(d) First find the mass of 100% pure $FeCO_3$ required to make 1.00×10^3 g of Fe_2O_3.

$$\text{mass of } FeCO_3 \;=\; 1.00 \times 10^3 \text{ g } Fe_2O_3 \times \frac{1 \text{ mol } Fe_2O_3}{159.6 \text{ g } Fe_2O_3} \times \frac{4 \text{ mol } FeCO_3}{2 \text{ mol } Fe_2O_3} \times \frac{115.8 \text{ g } FeCO_3}{1 \text{ mol } FeCO_3}$$

$$= 1451 \text{ g}$$

Since not all the ore was pure $FeCO_3$, dividing by the percentage purity will increase the amount of ore to be used and allow for losses in forming products.

$$\text{mass of ore} = \frac{1451 \text{ g}}{0.628} = \mathbf{2.31 \times 10^3 \text{ g}}$$

34. First calculate the mass of pure FeS_2 required to produce 4.50 L of SO_2.

$$\text{mass of } FeS_2 = 4.50 \text{ L } SO_2 \times \frac{1 \text{ mol } SO_2}{22.4 \text{ L } SO_2} \times \frac{4 \text{ mol } FeS_2}{8 \text{ mol } SO_2} \times \frac{120.0 \text{ g } FeS_2}{1 \text{ mol } FeS_2} = 12.05 \text{ g}$$

$$\text{\% purity} = \frac{\text{mass of pure } FeS_2}{\text{mass of impure } FeS_2} \times 100\% = \frac{12.05 \text{ g}}{100.0 \text{ g}} \times 100\% = \mathbf{12.1\%}$$

35. (a) volume of $C_6H_5NO_2$ EXPECTED $= 25.0 \text{ mL } C_6H_6 \times \dfrac{0.879 \text{ g } C_6H_6}{1 \text{ mL } C_6H_6} \times \dfrac{1 \text{ mol } C_6H_6}{78.0 \text{ g } C_6H_6} \times$

$$\frac{1 \text{ mol } C_6H_5NO_2}{1 \text{ mol } C_6H_6} \times \frac{123.0 \text{ g } C_6H_5NO_2}{1 \text{ mol } C_6H_5NO_2} \times \frac{1 \text{ mL } C_6H_5NO_2}{1.204 \text{ g } C_6H_5NO_2} = 28.781 \text{ mL}$$

$$\text{\% yield} = \frac{\text{volume obtained}}{\text{volume expected}} \times 100\% = \frac{18.0 \text{ mL}}{28.781 \text{ mL}} \times 100\% = 62.54\% \text{ (which rounds to } \mathbf{62.5\%})$$

(b) mass of C_6H_6 reacted $= 18.0 \text{ mL } C_6H_5NO_2 \times \dfrac{1.204 \text{ g } C_6H_5NO_2}{1 \text{ mL } C_6H_5NO_2} \times \dfrac{1 \text{ mol } C_6H_5NO_2}{123.0 \text{ g } C_6H_5NO_2} \times$

$$\frac{1 \text{ mol } C_6H_6}{1 \text{ mol } C_6H_5NO_2} \times \frac{78.0 \text{ g } C_6H_6}{1 \text{ mol } C_6H_6} = 13.743 \text{ g}$$

$$\text{mass of } C_6H_6 \text{ (originally)} = 25.0 \text{ mL} \times \frac{0.879 \text{ g}}{1 \text{ mL}} = 21.975 \text{ g}$$

mass of C_6H_6 (unreacted) $= 21.975 \text{ g} - 13.743 \text{ g} = \mathbf{8.23 \text{ g}}$

Alternately: if the reaction has a 62.54% yield, then $100.0 - 62.54 = 37.46\%$ of the C_6H_6 is unreacted.

$$\text{mass of } C_6H_6 \text{ (originally)} = 21.975 \text{ g (as calculated above)}$$

and: mass of C_6H_6 (unreacted) $= 21.975 \text{ g} \times 0.3746 = \mathbf{8.23 \text{ g}}$

36. (a) mass of SiF_4 formed $= 2.50 \text{ g } H_2O \times \dfrac{1 \text{ mol } H_2O}{18.0 \text{ g } H_2O} \times \dfrac{1 \text{ mol } SiF_4}{2 \text{ mol } H_2O} \times \dfrac{104.1 \text{ g } SiF_4}{1 \text{ mol } SiF_4} = \mathbf{7.23 \text{ g}}$

(b) mass of SiO_2 used $= 2.50 \text{ g } H_2O \times \dfrac{1 \text{ mol } H_2O}{18.0 \text{ g } H_2O} \times \dfrac{1 \text{ mol } SiO_2}{2 \text{ mol } H_2O} \times \dfrac{60.1 \text{ g } SiO_2}{1 \text{ mol } SiO_2} = 4.17 \text{ g}$

mass of SiO_2 (unreacted) $= 12.20 - 4.17 = \mathbf{8.03 \text{ g}}$

(c) $\text{\% yield} = \dfrac{\text{mass of } SiO_2 \text{ used}}{\text{mass of } SiO_2 \text{ available}} \times 100\% = \dfrac{4.17 \text{ g}}{12.20 \text{ g}} \times 100\% = \mathbf{34.2\%}$

or: mass of SiF_4 expected $= 12.20 \text{ g } SiO_2 \times \dfrac{1 \text{ mol } SiO_2}{60.1 \text{ g } SiO_2} \times \dfrac{1 \text{ mol } SiF_4}{1 \text{ mol } SiO_2} \times \dfrac{104.1 \text{ g } SiF_4}{1 \text{ mol } SiF_4} = 21.13 \text{ g}$

$$\text{\% yield} = \frac{\text{mass of } SiF_4 \text{ obtained}}{\text{mass of } SiF_4 \text{ expected}} \times 100\% = \frac{7.23 \text{ g}}{21.13 \text{ g}} \times 100\% = \mathbf{34.2\%}$$

37. (a) First find the mass of CuO produced if the purity and yield are both 100%.

mass of CuO = 5.00×10^3 g malach x $\dfrac{1\ mol\ malach}{221.0\ g\ malach}$ x $\dfrac{2\ mol\ CuO}{1\ mol\ malach}$ x $\dfrac{79.5\ g\ CuO}{1\ mol\ CuO}$ = 3597 g

Next allow for a purity of 4.30 % and a yield of 84.0 % by decreasing the mass of products formed.

mass of CuO formed = $0.0430 \times 0.840 \times 3597$ g = **1.30×10^2 g**

(b) First find the mass of pure malachite required to produce 100.0 g of CuO, assuming 100 % yield.

mass of malachite = 100.0 g CuO x $\dfrac{1\ mol\ CuO}{79.5\ g\ CuO}$ x $\dfrac{1\ mol\ malachite}{2\ mol\ CuO}$ x $\dfrac{221.0\ g\ malachite}{1\ mol\ malachite}$ = 139.0 g

Both percent purity and percentage yield decrease the mass of products so that the mass of malachite ore used must be increased to compensate for these losses. Dividing the mass of pure malachite by the percent purity and percent yield gives the required increased mass.

mass of ore used = $\dfrac{139.0\ g}{0.870\ \times\ 0.0370}$ = **4.32×10^3 g**

38. (a) First find the mass of Ag produced if the ore is 100% pure Ag_2S.

mass of Ag = 250.0×10^3 g Ag_2S x $\dfrac{1\ mol\ Ag_2S}{247.9\ g\ Ag_2S}$ x $\dfrac{2\ mol\ Ag}{1\ mol\ Ag_2S}$ x $\dfrac{107.9\ g\ Ag}{1\ mol\ Ag}$ = 2.18×10^5 g

Now find the mass of silver if the ore is only 0.135% pure.

mass of Ag = $0.00135 \times 2.18 \times 10^5$ g = **294 g**

(b) Find the mass of Ag_2S which produces 0.261 g of silver.

mass of Ag_2S = 0.261 g Ag x $\dfrac{1\ mol\ Ag}{107.9\ g\ Ag}$ x $\dfrac{1\ mol\ Ag_2S}{2\ mol\ Ag}$ x $\dfrac{247.9\ g\ Ag_2S}{1\ mol\ Ag_2S}$ = 0.300 g

Hence: % purity = $\dfrac{mass\ of\ pure\ Ag_2S}{mass\ of\ impure\ ore}$ x 100% = $\dfrac{0.300\ g}{76.4\ g}$ x 100% = **0.392%**

c) First find the mass of pure Ag which is produced by 152.6 g of pure Ag_2S.

mass of Ag = 152.6 g Ag_2S x $\dfrac{1\ mol\ Ag_2S}{247.9\ g\ Ag_2S}$ x $\dfrac{2\ mol\ Ag}{1\ mol\ Ag_2S}$ x $\dfrac{107.9\ g\ Ag}{1\ mol\ Ag}$ = 132.8 g

Hence: % yield = $\dfrac{actual\ mass\ of\ pure\ Ag}{expected\ mass\ of\ pure\ Ag}$ x 100% = $\dfrac{117.4\ g}{132.8\ g}$ x 100% = 88.38%

(d) First find the mass of pure Ag_2S required to produce 50.0 kg of pure Ag.

mass of pure Ag_2S = 50.0×10^3 g Ag x $\dfrac{1\ mol\ Ag}{107.9\ g\ Ag}$ x $\dfrac{1\ mol\ Ag_2S}{2\ mol\ Ag}$ x $\dfrac{247.9\ g\ Ag_2S}{1\ mol\ Ag_2S}$

= 5.744×10^4 g

Now find the mass of ore needed if the ore only contains 0.795% Ag_2S.

mass of ore = $\dfrac{5.744 \times 10^4\ g}{0.00795}$ = 7.22×10^6 g

(e) First find the mass of Ag produced if the purity and yield are both 100%.

mass of Ag expected = 3.50×10^7 g Ag_2S x $\dfrac{1\ mol\ Ag_2S}{247.9\ g\ Ag_2S}$ x $\dfrac{2\ mol\ Ag}{1\ mol\ Ag_2S}$ x $\dfrac{107.9\ g\ Ag}{1\ mol\ Ag}$

= 3.047×10^7 g

Now, the ore is only 1.86% pure Ag_2S and only 89.2% of the Ag_2S is extracted.

actual mass of Ag produced = 3.047×10^7 g x 0.0186×0.892 = **5.05×10^5 g**

1. Contradict. The Greek view of nature assumed that experimental work could be misleading an ...ut philosophy should be used to reveal how nature worked.

2. Metals were immediately recognizable, valuable and useful in everyday life.

3. Dalton's work allowed the composition of chemicals to be known more accurately and compounds to be made efficiently without wasting reactants.

4. Thomson's work showed that atoms contained different particles having positive and negative charges.

5. The Law of Definite Proportions

6. The last column in the table below gives the result of dividing the mass of oxygen in each compound by the mass of oxygen in compound #1.

Compound #	Mass of N (g)	Mass of O (g)	Ratio
1	0.3160	0.0903	1
2	0.3160	0.3611	4
3	0.3160	0.7223	8
4	0.3160	0.5417	6

7. The "plum pudding" model assumed that the protons and electrons were uniformly distributed throughout the volume of the atom, such that the mass associated with the protons was distributed throughout the atom. When Rutherford found that most of the atom was empty space except for a tiny nucleus containing almost all the atom's mass, the even distribution of proton mass throughout the atom assumed by J.J. Thomson was seen to be incorrect.

8. Rutherford had found that the presence of protons in the nucleus could account for the charge on the nucleus but it could not account for all of the mass present in the nucleus.

9. Dalton's model is not in conflict with Rutherford's model because Rutherford accepted the idea that atoms exist and concerned himself with the internal structure of the atom. Dalton was concerned with the manner in which atoms had constant properties and were able to combine in specific ways.

10. Protons (but he suspected that some particle like the neutron existed in the nucleus).

11. (a) beta and gamma (alpha is stopped by a piece of paper)   (b) gamma

12. Protons and neutrons exist in the nucleus and have a substantial mass while the region outside the nucleus consists only of electrons, which are almost massless. Therefore, most of the mass of the atom is concentrated in the nucleus.

13. (a) 4   (b) 92   (c) 25

14. (a) 6   (b) 26   (c) 18

15. (a) 10   (c) 20   (e) 18   (g) 54   (i) 2
    (b) 10   (d) 10   (f) 10   (h) 24   (j) 36

16. (a) S^{2-} (c) Cl^- (e) Cr^{2+} (g) V^{5+} (i) O^-
    (b) Ca^{2+} (d) Al^{3+} (f) Mn^{4+} (h) Sb^{3-}

17. (a) +12   (b) +10   (c) +19   (d) +16

18. Proton = ^1_1p , neutron = ^1_0n , electron = $^{\;0}_{-1}e$

19.

Particle	Atomic Number	Atomic Mass	Number of protons	Number of neutrons	Number of electrons
$^{52}_{24}Cr$	**24**	**52**	**24**	**28**	**24**
$^{222}_{86}Rn$	**86**	**222**	**86**	**136**	**86**
$^{70}_{31}Ga$	31	**70**	**31**	39	31
$^{27}_{13}Al$	**13**	**27**	13	14	13
$^{197}_{79}Au^{3+}$	**79**	197	**79**	118	76
$^{75}_{33}As^{3-}$	**33**	75	33	**42**	36
$^{209}_{83}Bi^{5+}$	**83**	**209**	83	126	78

20. (a) heavy water is $\dfrac{27.65}{25.00}$ = **1.106** times heavier than ordinary water

(b) molar mass of ordinary water = 18.0 g, so heavy water's molar mass = 1.106 x 18.0 g = **19.908 g.**

(c) heavy water = D_2O = 2 D + O = 19.908 g , so that: 2 D + 16.0 g = 19.908 g   and: D = **1.95 g**

(d) ^2_1D

(e) For D: # of e^- = 1, # of p = 1, # of n = 1   For H: # of e^- = 1, # of p = 1, # of n = 0
Since both H and D have one proton, they are both "hydrogen" but the extra neutron makes D a heavier version of hydrogen.

21. Sample 2 is $\dfrac{1.670}{1.539}$ = 1.085 times heavier than Sample 1

molar mass of Sample 1 = 2 x 1.008 + 32.066 = 34.082 g
molar mass of Sample 2 = 34.082 g x 1.085 = 36.983 g
mass of artificial S–isotope = 36.983 – 2 x 1.008 = **34.97 g**

22.

	Symbol	Atomic Mass	Atomic Number	Number of protons	Number of neutrons	Number of electrons
(a)	$^{84}_{36}Kr$	84	36	**36**	**48**	36
(b)	$^{80}_{35}Br$	**80**	**35**	35	45	35
(c)	$^{127}_{53}I^-$	127	53	**53**	**74**	54
(d)	$^{59}_{27}Co$	**59**	27	**27**	32	27
(e)	$^{66}_{30}Zn$	66	**30**	**30**	36	**30**
(f)	$^{112}_{48}Cd^{2+}$	112	**48**	**48**	**64**	**46**
(g)	$^{88}_{38}Sr^{2+}$	**88**	**38**	38	50	36
(h)	$X^{2-} = ^{127}_{52}Te^{2-}$	**127**	**52**	**52**	75	54
(i)	$X^{3+} = ^{103}_{45}Rh^{3+}$	103	**45**	**45**	**58**	42
(j)	$X^{3-} = ^{75}_{33}As^{3-}$	**75**	33	**33**	42	**36**

23. (a) 10.8 g   (c) 108.0 g   (e) 65.4 g   (g) 95.9 g
    (b) 69.8 g   (d) 72.7 g   (f) 91.3 g

24. Average mass = 0.9890 x 12.000 000 + 0.0110 x 13.003 355 = **12.011 g**

25. Average mass = 0.9223 x 27.976 927 + 0.0467 x 28.976 495 + 0.0310 x 29.973 770 = **28.0855 g**

26. (a) P ($1s^2 2s^2 2p^6 3s^2 3p^3$)

    (b) Ti ($1s^2 2s^2 2p^6 3s^2 3p^6 4s^2 3d^2$)

    (c) Co ($1s^2 2s^2 2p^6 3s^2 3p^6 4s^2 3d^7$)

    (d) Br ($1s^2 2s^2 2p^6 3s^2 3p^6 4s^2 3d^{10} 4p^5$)

    (e) Sr ($1s^2 2s^2 2p^6 3s^2 3p^6 4s^2 3d^{10} 4p^6 5s^2$)

    (f) Ar ($1s^2 2s^2 2p^6 3s^2 3p^6$)

    (g) K ($1s^2 2s^2 2p^6 3s^2 3p^6 4s^1$)

    (h) Cd ($1s^2 2s^2 2p^6 3s^2 3p^6 4s^2 3d^{10} 4p^6 5s^2 4d^{10}$)

    (i) Ca ($1s^2 2s^2 2p^6 3s^2 3p^6 4s^2$)

    (j) Xe ($1s^2 2s^2 2p^6 3s^2 3p^6 4s^2 3d^{10} 4p^6 5s^2 4d^{10} 5p^6$)

    (k) Cs ($1s^2 2s^2 2p^6 3s^2 3p^6 4s^2 3d^{10} 4p^6 5s^2 4d^{10} 5p^6 6s^1$)

    (l) Pb ($1s^2 2s^2 2p^6 3s^2 3p^6 4s^2 3d^{10} 4p^6 5s^2 4d^{10} 5p^6 6s^2 4f^{14} 5d^{10} 6p^2$)

    (m) Ga ($1s^2 2s^2 2p^6 3s^2 3p^6 4s^2 3d^{10} 4p^1$)

    (n) Mn ($1s^2 2s^2 2p^6 3s^2 3p^6 4s^2 3d^5$)

    (o) Zr ($1s^2 2s^2 2p^6 3s^2 3p^6 4s^2 3d^{10} 4p^6 5s^2 4d^2$)

27. (a) P ([Ne] $3s^2 3p^3$)   (f) Ar ([Ne] $3s^2 3p^6$)   (k) Cs ([Xe] $6s^1$)

    (b) Ti ([Ar] $4s^2 3d^2$)   (g) K ([Ar] $4s^1$)   (l) Pb ([Xe] $6s^2 4f^{14} 5d^{10} 6p^2$)

    (c) Co ([Ar] $4s^2 3d^7$)   (h) Cd ([Kr] $5s^2 4d^{10}$)   (m) Ga ([Ar] $4s^2 3d^{10} 4p^1$)

    (d) Br ([Ar] $4s^2 3d^{10} 4p^5$)   (i) Ca ([Ar] $4s^2$)   (n) Mn ([Ar] $4s^2 3d^5$)

    (e) Sr ([Kr] $5s^2$)   (j) Xe ([Kr] $5s^2 4d^{10} 5p^6$)   (o) Zr ([Kr] $5s^2 4d^2$)

28. (a) H^- ($1s^2$)   (e) Ti^{2+} ([Ar] $3d^2$)   (i) Fe^{3+} ([Ar] $3d^5$)

    (b) Sr^{2+} ([Ar] $4s^2 3d^{10} 4p^6$)   (f) N^{2-} ([He] $2s^2 2p^5$)   (j) Ge^{2+} ([Ar] $4s^2 3d^{10}$)

    (c) Br^- ([Ar] $4s^2 3d^{10} 4p^6$)   (g) Mn^{2+} ([Ar] $3d^5$)   (k) Ru^{3+} ([Kr] $4d^5$)

    (d) N^{3+} ([He] $2s^2$)   (h) Ge^{4+} ([Ar] $3d^{10}$)   (l) Sb^{3+} ([Kr] $5s^2 4d^{10}$)

29. (a) 6   (c) 5   (e) 0   (g) 6   (i) 2   (k) 0   (m) 3   (o) 7
    (b) 5   (d) 2   (f) 2   (h) 0   (j) 6   (l) 0   (n) 2   (p) 2

30. The actual properties of Germanium are as follows. How close were your estimates?
    atomic mass = 72.6 ; density = 5.35 ; density of oxide = 4.23 ; formula of chloride = $GeCl_4$;
    density of chloride = 1.84 ; color = greyish white ; lustre = metallic

31. (a) noble gases   (d) alkali metals   (g) alkali metals
    (b) alkaline earth metals   (e) halogens   (h) halogens
    (c) transition metals   (f) transitions metals

32. (a) two of Li, K, Rb, Cs and Fr   (c) two of Be, Ca, Sr, Ba and Ra
    (b) two of He, Ne, Kr, Xe and Rn   (d) two of F, Cl, I and At

33. (a) two of Li, Be, B, N, O, F and Ne   (b) two of Na, Mg, Al, Si, P, Cl and Ar

34.

SAMPLE	PROPERTIES	CLASSIFICATION
A	pale yellow gas, non–conductor	NONMETAL
B	conductor, shiny, hard, silvery, malleable	METAL
C	non–conductor, yellow, looks waxy, soft, brittle	NONMETAL
D	hard, silvery–grey, brittle, somewhat shiny, fair conductor	MIXTURE
E	liquid, shiny, silvery, conductor	METAL
F	dark red, liquid, non–conductor	NONMETAL
G	fair conductor, brittle, dull grey	MIXTURE

35.   On the right side.

36.   (a) Ga   (b) Ge   (c) Sn   (d) Mg   (e) Bi

37.   Ca, Ge, Si, P, F

38.   (a) Sb   (b) K   (c) Ge   (d) Al   (e) Tl   (f) Sb

39.   P = iii , Ba = ii , Sb = iv , Ar = v , As = i

40.   The atomic radius increases. The more electrons around the nucleus, the greater the volume needed to contain them (since electrons repel each other and can't easily be "compacted"). Therefore, going down a group the atomic radius of the elements in the group should increase.

41.   Going across a row, the positive charge on the nucleus increases, and each electron experiences a greater attraction to the nucleus. This results in a smaller distance between the individual electrons and the nucleus, which causes the atomic radius to decrease going across each period of the table.

42.

If an atom has:	Then its outermost shell is:	If an atom has:	Then its outermost shell is:
1 electron	**OPEN**	10 electrons	**CLOSED**
2 electrons	**CLOSED**	11 electrons	**OPEN**
3 electrons	**OPEN**	16 electrons	**OPEN**
8 electrons	**OPEN**	18 electrons	**CLOSED**

43.   The NOBLE GASES have CLOSED SHELLS.   All other elements have OPEN SHELLS.

44.   (a) Cl : open   (c) Mg : open   (e) Na^+ : closed   (g) O^- : open   (i) I : open
      (b) Ne : closed   (d) Si : open   (f) Cl^- : closed   (h) Ca^{2+} : closed   (j) Al^+ : open

45.

atom	# of valence electrons	atom	# of valence electrons
F	7	Pb	4
Ne	0	Pb^{2+}	2
Na	1	S^-	7
Ne^+	7	S^{2-}	0

46. (a, b)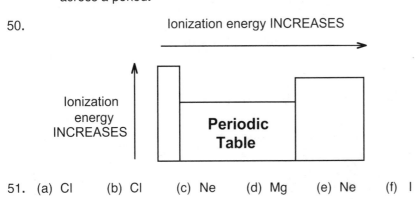

47.

atom	H	He						
valence	1	0						
atom	Li	Be	B	C	N	O	F	Ne
valence	1	2	3	4	3	2	1	0
atom	Na	Mg	Al	Si	P	S	Cl	Ar
valence	1	2	3	4	3	2	1	0

48. (a) The distance between the nucleus and the outermost electrons increases. The greater the number of electrons, the larger the atomic radius.
    (b) The nucleus has a decreasing hold on the outer electrons because of the increasing nucleus–electron distance.
    (c) The ionization energy will decrease going down a family. The less hold the nucleus has on the outer electrons, the easier it is to remove one of them.

49. (a) The distance decreases as the increasing nuclear charge pulls the electrons in closer.
    (b) increases
    (c) The nucleus can hold more strongly to a given outer electron because of the greater charge and the smaller electron–nucleus distance.
    (d) The ionization energy (energy required to remove an outer electron) will therefore increase going across a period.

50.   Ionization energy INCREASES

Ionization
energy
INCREASES

Periodic
Table

51. (a) Cl   (b) Cl   (c) Ne   (d) Mg   (e) Ne   (f) I

52.

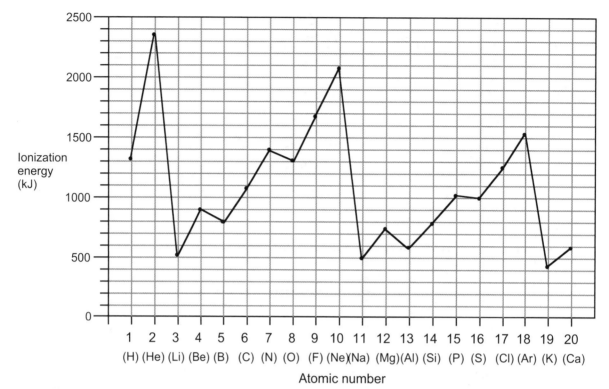

(a) Electrons are being removed from full shells, which is very difficult to do.
(b) The outermost electrons are farther from the nucleus, so that the attraction between the nucleus and outer electrons is decreased and less energy is required for electron removal.
(c) The outer electrons are drawn closer to the nucleus (recall exercise 40), causing an increased attraction between the larger nuclear charge and the outermost electrons. The increased attraction requires a greater energy to be applied before an electron can be removed.
(d) Be and Mg have filled s–subshells, so that their ionization energies are higher than those of the elements immediately before and after them. Similarly, N and P have half–filled p–subshells and their ionization energies are higher than those of the elements immediately before and after them. The filling of the p–subshells (Ne and Ar) is a special case of increased stability leading to increased ionization energy.

53. (a) Te   (b) O   (c) Te   (d) 6   (e) 2   (f) O

54. Li^+ and F^- (smaller ions are closer together)

55. (a) Ga   (b) Br   (c) same   (d) Ga = 3, Br = 7   (e) Ga = 3, Br = 1   (f) Br

56. Se, Sr^+, Kr^+ and Ge

57. (a) Ba and S = ionic   (d) Rb and I = ionic
    (b) P and Cl = non–ionic   (e) O and H = non–ionic
    (c) Ca and O = ionic   (f) S and O = non–ionic

58. (a) Li   (b) F   (c) F   (d) F
    (e) IN GENERAL, going from left to right across the periodic table the electronegativity of the atoms will INCREASE.

59. (a) I (more electron shells)   (b) F
    (c) IN GENERAL, going down a family of the periodic table the electronegativity of the atoms will DECREASE.

60.

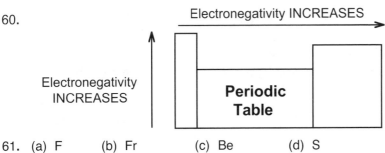

61. (a) F   (b) Fr   (c) Be   (d) S

62. (a) NaCl
    (b) The smaller the ions, the smaller the distance between the + and − charges and the greater the force of attraction between the ions.
    (c) The smaller the ions involved, the greater the ionic bond strength and the higher the melting temperature. This is confirmed by the fact that the melting temperatures of NaCl and KBr are $801^{\circ}C$ and $734^{\circ}C$ respectively.

63. Although the ions are about the same size, there is more charge on both O^{2-} and Mg^{2+}. Recall that the greater the charge, the greater the force of attraction. The increased attraction between O^{2-} and Mg^{2+} requires a greater energy to separate the ions and therefore a higher melting point. This is confirmed by the fact that the melting temperatures of MgO and NaF are $2852^{\circ}C$ and $993^{\circ}C$ respectively.

64. (a) CaO   (b) BN   (c) LiF   (d) BaS   (e) KCl   (f) BeO

65. (a) amount of repulsion INCREASES
    (b) volume INCREASES
    (c) Negative ions are LARGER than the corresponding neutral atom.

66. (a) amount of repulsion DECREASES
    (b) volume DECREASES
    (c) Positive ions are SMALLER than the corresponding neutral atom.

67. Na^{+} = smaller circles

68. (a) SO = covalent   (c) FeCl = (ionic)   (e) HS = covalent
    (b) BaO = (ionic)   (d) NO   = covalent   (f) CH = covalent

69. (a) As the size of the atoms increases, the distance between the nuclei and the shared electrons increases, and the electrostatic attraction between the nuclei and the shared electrons decreases.
    (b) Going down the halogens, the distance between the nuclei and the shared electrons increases and the strength of the covalent bond should decrease. (F_2 actually doesn't follow the trend.)

70. The more electrons shared in a bond, the greater the electrostatic attraction between the nuclei and the shared electrons and the stronger the bond.

71. The more electrons shared between two atoms, the greater the electrostatic attraction between the nuclei and the electrons (pulling the electrons closer to the nucleus) and the shorter the bond length.

72. (a) PCl_3 (c) CS_2 (e) H_2Se (g) H_2O (i) B_4C_3 (k) Si_3P_4
    (b) B_2O_3 (d) P_2O_3 (f) F_2O (h) NI_3 (j) CCl_4 (l) SiS_2

73. (a) increases   (b) increases

74. intermolecular

75. The London forces between F_2 molecules are broken because London forces are much weaker than the covalent bonds involved.

76. Both melting and boiling points increase

77. (a) Ar   (b) Br_2 (c) CF_4 (d) CBr_4

78. The student's answer incorrectly implies that covalent bonds are broken when melting occurs and that London forces are absent.

79. (a) covalent (c) ionic (e) ionic (g) covalent
(b) ionic (d) covalent (f) covalent

80. (a) F (b) Li (c) Cl (d) Si (e) S (f) N

81. (a) Na^+Cl^- (b) C–O (c) $Ca^{2+}O^{2-}$ (d) $Mg^{2+}O^{2-}$ (e) C–C (f) $N \equiv N$

82. ionic bonding and London forces

83. (a) Na^- (c) As^{3-} (e) Se^- (g) Se^{2-} (i) Cl^-
(b) I (d) Cs^+ (f) S^{2-} (h) S^{2-}

84. (a) London (b) ionic (c) London (d) covalent (e) ionic (f) London

85. (a) K^+ :Br⁻:   (b) :Cl⁻: Al^{3+} :Cl⁻:   (c) Mg^{2+} :O²⁻:
    :Cl⁻:

(d) Li^+ :S²⁻: Li^+ (e) K^+ :P³⁻: K^+
    K^+

86. (a) H—Cl: (b) :I—I: (c) :I—Cl:

(d) H—C—C—H (with H's)   (e) C=C (with H's)   (f) H—C≡C—H

(g) :F—Be—F: (h) O=O   (i) :Cl—S—Cl:

(j) :N≡N: (k) H—C—H with O double bonded   (l) C=C=C=C (with H's)

(m) H—C≡N: (n) H—B—H with H   (o) H—C—Cl: with S double bonded

(p) [:O—N=O]⁻ or [O=N—O:]⁻   (q) [:N≡O:]⁺

(r) H—O=N=C or H—O≡N—C: or H—O—N≡C:

(s) [H—N—H]⁻   (t) O=S—O: or :O—S=O

(u) :Cl—S—S—Cl: (v) :N—N: (with H's)   (w) SF_6 structure

(x) $[\ddot{C}=N=\ddot{O}]^-$ or $[:\ddot{C}-N\equiv O:]^-$ or $[:C\equiv N-\ddot{O}:]^-$

(y) $\ddot{O}=N-\ddot{O}:$ with $:\ddot{O}:$ below   or $:\ddot{O}-N=\ddot{O}$ with $:\ddot{O}:$ below   or $:\ddot{O}-N-\ddot{O}:$ with $:O:$ below

(z)   H—C=C—H / H—C=C—H (with H substituents)   or   H—C—C—H with double bonds to lower carbons

(aa) $\ddot{O}=N-N=\ddot{O}$ with $:\ddot{O}:$ below   or $:\ddot{O}-N-N=\ddot{O}$ with $:O:$ below   or $:\ddot{O}-N=N=\ddot{O}$ with $:\ddot{O}:$ below

or $:\ddot{O}-N-N\equiv O:$ with $:\ddot{O}:$ below

(bb)   acetic acid structures   (cc)   SeBr structure

87. He($1s^2$) ; Ne([He] $2s^2\,2p^6$) ; Ar([Ne] $3s^2\,3p^6$) ; Kr ([Ar] $4s^2\,3d^{10}\,4p^6$) ; Xe ([Kr] $5s^2\,4d^{10}\,5p^6$)

88. The full valence shells of the inert gases make them unreactive.

89. Since no other type of bond is possible, due to the full valence shells, the inert gases are held next to one another by London forces. The melting/boiling temperatures will be very low because London forces are very weak.

90. The more electrons on an atom or molecule, the greater the London forces involved. Hence, the London forces should increase going down a family in the periodic table and the melting/boiling temperatures should increase.

91. The farther down a family in the periodic table, the larger the atoms and the farther the outermost electrons are from the nucleus. As a result, the farther down the table the easier to remove an electron (the lower the ionization energy).

92. The reaction of a noble gas will involve the removal of an electron from the outer shell (since it would have no tendency to gain an extra electron), so the question is really asking about the ionization energy. As seen earlier, the lower the atom on the table the lower the ionization energy and the easier for the atom to react. Rn will be more reactive.

93. The noble gases form no naturally–occurring compounds from which they can be extracted. Also, the gases are relatively rare and do not liquify easily so the noble gases were only found when samples of air were liquified and different portions of the sample were boiled off and analyzed.

94. Li ([He] $2s^1$) ; Na ([Ne] $3s^1$) ; K ([Ar] $4s^1$) ; Rb ([Kr] $5s^1$) ; Cs ([Xe] $6s^1$) ; Fr ([Rn] $7s^1$)

95. All families show the same trend: going down the periodic table the outermost electrons are farther from the nucleus, less strongly held by electrostatic forces and easier to remove.

96. Li^+ is produced when Li reacts. The ease of removing an outer electron (tendency to react) increases going down the periodic table.

97. This is essentially the same as the previous exercise: the ionization energy decreases going down the periodic table because the electrons being removed are farther from the nucleus and less strongly held by electrostatic forces.

98. The alkali metals are good electrical conductors because they have a single valence electron which is easily removed and able to move freely from atom to atom. (Recall from exercise 52 that the ionization energies of the alkali metals are very low, indicating loosely–held valence electrons.)

99. Going down the alkali metals in the periodic table, the outer electrons are farther from the nuclei and adjacent nuclei are not as tightly held together, causing a lowered melting/boiling temperature.

100. Electrons are removed when both the alkali metals and alkaline earth metals react. Since it is easier to remove one electron from an atom (alkali metals) than to remove two electrons (alkaline earth metals), the alkaline earth metals should be less reactive. (This is experimentally observed to be true.)

101. (a) The melting/boiling temperature decreases. (The larger distances between valence electrons and nuclei decrease the attractions holding metal atoms together in solid and liquid phases.)
     (b) The reactivity increases. (Larger atoms have decreased attractions between valence electrons and nuclei, allowing easier removal of electrons. Since the reaction of the alkaline earth metals involves the removal of electrons, the reactivity should increase.)
     (c) The ionization energy decreases. (see reasons for part b)

     Mg is an exception to the MP/BP trend; Ba is also an exception to the BP trend.

102. Since Cl_2 is a gas, bromine is a liquid and iodine is a solid, the melting/boiling temperatures must increase going down the table.

103. Only London forces can explain such low melting/boiling temperatures.

104. Halogen molecules form halide ions having a -1 charge. Since the halogens must attract or gain an extra electron, the electronegativity (electron-attracting tendency) must dictate the ease with which the halogens gain an electron. Since the electronegativity decreases going down the periodic table, the halogens will have less tendency to react by gaining an electron.

105. As with all families, the halogen atoms are larger going down the periodic table, the outer electrons are less tightly held and the ionization energy decreases.

106. (a) A valence electron is an electron in an open shell.
     (b) An open shell is an electron shell which contains less than its maximum number of electrons.
     (c) An intermolecular bond is a bond which occurs between adjacent molecules.
     (d) Electronegativity is the tendency of an atom to attract an extra electron.
     (e) A covalent bond is a bond in which electrons are shared equally by the atoms being joined.
     (f) An intramolecular bond is a bond which occurs within a given molecule.
     (g) The valence of an atom is the number of unpaired electrons in an atom.
     (h) An ionic bond is a bond resulting from a positive ion being held next to a negative ion by the electrostatic attraction of the negative electrical charge for the positive charge.
     (i) The London force is a force of attraction which exists between species having closed shells and which exists as a result of a temporary dipolar attraction between the species.

107. Pb is bigger than Si since Pb has more electron shells.

108. Halogen molecules are held next to one another by London forces, which increase in strength as the number of electrons increases going down the periodic table. The alkali metals are held together by bonds which decrease in strength as the size of the atoms (and distance between the valence electrons and nuclei) increases going down the periodic table.

109. Both N_2 and O_2 are held together in the solid phase by London forces. Since London forces increase as the number of electrons increases, and since O_2 has more electrons than N_2, O_2 should have the higher melting temperature.

110. Both O_2 and S_2 are held together with covalent bonds. Since S is larger than O, the shared electrons in S_2 are farther from the nuclei so that it is easier to separate the nuclei and break the bond in S_2.

111. Both S and Te have the same number of valence electrons, but S is a smaller atom than Te and therefore more electronegative.

112. An ion is an atom which has more or less electrons than its atomic number.

113. AlN has a greater electrostatic attraction between the ions (+3 and –3 charge) than does NaF (+1 and –1), so a greater melting temperature is required to separate the ions.

114. Molecules of F_2 and I_2 are held next to one another in the solid phase by London forces. Since I_2 has more electrons than F_2, and since London forces increase as the number of electrons increases, F_2 will melt at a lower temperature than I_2.

115. # of valence electrons: Se = 6 , K^- = 2 , Sn = 4 , Ge^{2+} = 2 , Br = 7

116. Both substances have the same number of charges attracting each other but the ions in RbI are larger than the atoms in KBr, so the greater separation of the ions in RbI lowers the electrostatic attraction between the ions and lowers the melting temperature.

117. the valences are: S = 2 , B = 3 , Ca = 2 , Xe = 0 , Ga = 3 , Bi = 3

118. total numbers of electrons:
$$Cl_2 = 2 \times 17\ (Cl) = 34$$
$$O_2 = 2 \times 8\ (O) = 16$$
$$CH_4 = 6\ (C) + 4 \times 1\ (H) = 10$$
$$S_4 = 4 \times 16\ (S) = 64$$
$$H_2SO_4 = 2 \times 1\ (H) + 16\ (S) + 4 \times 8\ (O) = 50$$

119. # of shells:

Rn	= 6 (closed)	= 6 (total) ;	Sb	= 4 (closed) + 1 (open)	= 5 (total)
Sr^{2+}	= 4 (closed)	= 4 (total) ;	Na^-	= 2 (closed) + 1 (open)	= 3 (total)
P	= 2 (closed) + 1 (open)	= 3 (total) ;	Ga^{2+}	= 3 (closed) + 1 (open)	= 4 (total)
I^+	= 4 (closed) + 1 (open)	= 5 (total)			

120. O_2 has the stronger bond because the greater number of shared electrons in O_2 holds the nuclei together more strongly.

121. London forces increase in strength going down the periodic table.

122. Ionic and covalent bonds decrease in strength going down the periodic table.

123. (a) The noble gases are held together by London forces. Going down the periodic table, the number of electrons in the atoms increases and the strength of the London forces increases, leading to an increased melting temperature.
    (b) When alkali metals react, they lose an electron. As the alkali metal atoms increase in size, their valence electrons are farther from the nuclei, less tightly held, and easier to remove.
    (c) Since the noble gases have no tendency to attract extra electrons, the only way they can react is to lose an electron or allow one or more of the outer electrons to be attracted to another atom and engage in covalent bonding. Going down the periodic table, the outermost electrons are further from the nucleus and the electrostatic attraction between the electrons and nucleus decreases, increasing the reactivity of the noble gases.
    (d) As the alkali metals increase in size, their valence electrons are farther from the nuclei and therefore are not able to hold the nuclei together as strongly, resulting in a lowered melting temperature.
    (e) Going down the periodic table, the size of the ions involved in the ionic bond increases and the distance between the charges increases. As a result, the electrostatic attraction between the charges decreases and the melting temperature decreases.
    (f) The halogens react by attracting an electron to form a negative charge. This tendency to attract extra electrons is just the electronegativity and electronegativity decreases going down the periodic table due to the increased distance between the nucleus and electrons outside the atom.

124. The number of unpaired electrons is just the valence, so:
     H = 1 , C = 4 , O = 2 , He = 0 , S = 2 , N = 3 , F = 1 , Kr = 0 .

125. Rn is the largest noble gas atom, so its outermost electrons are farther from its nucleus than is the case with the other noble gases. This increased distance makes it easier to remove an outer electron and form a +1 charge.

126. O = 2, P = 3, Al = 3, Xe = 0, Cl = 1, Na = 1, Ba = 2, Ga = 3, Se = 2, He = 0

127. The molecules are held in the solid phase by London forces. Since S_8 has more electrons than S_4, S_8 should have stronger London forces and a higher melting temperature.

128. The number of covalent bonds will be the same as the valence of the atom, so:
     Xe = 0 , I = 1 , N = 3 , Se = 2 , B = 3 , P = 3 , C = 4 , O = 2

129. London forces

130. (a) PbI_4 (b) InAs   (c) Al_4Si_3 (d) NF_3 (e) SiC   (f) PH_3

ANSWERS TO UNIT IX : SOLUTION CHEMISTRY

1. The solution is saturated if a visible amount of solid NaCl is present. The solution is NOT saturated if the NaCl was added only a few seconds before, because the salt hasn't had enough time to completely dissolve. If the newly–made salt water mixture is constantly stirred the resulting solution might or might not be saturated — only the eventual observation of undissolved NaCl allows you to say the solution is saturated.

2. Normally, the hotter a solvent is the more solute it can dissolve. Therefore, you would expect warming of a saturated solution to allow the solution to dissolve more solute and become "unsaturated".

3. Some solutions found in nature are: sea, lake and river waters, the air (oxygen and nitrogen), rocks (solid solutions of minerals), water lying in puddles on soil (contains dissolved minerals from the soil), fruit juices, tree sap (such as maple syrup) and various biological fluids.

4. Glass is not soluble in water.

5. i) Only the smallest bulb glows so there is very little conductivity and very low ion concentration.
   ii) Compounds 3, 4, 5, 7, 8, 10
   iii) It has the same conductivity as pure water and therefore the same concentration of ions. This can be interpreted to mean glucose does not produce ions.
   iv) The non–conducting compounds start with a carbon atom (are organic).
   v) HCl and H_2SO_4 are acids; KOH and NaOH are bases.
   vi) NaCl and NH_4NO_3 are salts.
   vii) NaSCN, NaOH, Na_3PO_4
   viii) Substances in the solid phase do not conduct electricity.
   ix) The phase must be a liquid (melted substance or aqueous solution).
   x) The greater the concentration of ions, the greater the conductivity.
   xi) A reaction occurs between water and acetic acid to produce ions.
   xii) The acetic acid solution, and its ions, are being diluted in concentration.

6. Conducting = a, c, d, f, g, i ;   Non–conducting = b, e, h, j

7. Organic compounds and nonpolar compounds (which can be the same compound in some cases)

8. c, d, f, i, k, l, o, q, s, t, u, v, x

9. (a) nonpolar   (b) polar   (c) polar   (d) nonpolar

10. (a) polar   (c) polar   (e) polar   (g) nonpolar
    (b) nonpolar   (d) nonpolar   (f) polar   (h) polar

11. HCl is expected to have a higher boiling temperature than F_2 because HCl is a polar molecule and experiences dipole–dipole forces in addition to London forces. F_2 experiences only London forces.

12. The low boiling temperature of CF_4 is expected because only London forces are involved. The higher boiling temperature of CHF_3 is explained by the fact that the molecule is polar. The dipole–dipole forces in CHF_3 hold the molecules together to a greater degree and raise the boiling temperature.

13. (a) Going up column 15 of the periodic table, the atoms Sb, As and P have fewer and fewer electrons and therefore smaller London forces hold molecules to their neighbours. As a result, it is easier to melt the compounds. (Although the molecules are all polar, the dipole–dipole forces are almost the same for each molecule because the electronegativity of Sb, As and P are almost identical.)
    (b) NH_3 contains the N–H bond, which means that hydrogen bonding is present in NH_3 but not in the others. Since hydrogen bonds are much stronger than London forces, the melting temperature is higher than otherwise expected.

14. c, e, g, h

15. Propane molecules are held next to neighbouring molecules in the liquid phase by weak London forces. Such forces are not very "sticky" and freely allow one molecule to "slide" or "flow" past one another, leading to a low viscosity (low resistance to flow). Glycerine has three O–H groups which can hydrogen bond strongly to neighbouring molecules, preventing the molecules from sliding freely past each other and leading to a high viscosity.

16. The molecule with the higher boiling temperature is the one with hydrogen bonding in addition to London forces. Hence, molecules with N, O or F bonded to H have higher boiling temperatures.
    (a) $CH_3–CH_2–OH$ (b) H_2O (c) CH_3NH_2

17.

Solvent	Polar or nonpolar?	Solvent	Polar or nonpolar?
water	Polar	acetic acid	Polar
methanol	Polar	chloroform	Polar
ethanol	Polar	carbon tetrachloride	Nonpolar
benzene	Nonpolar	heptane	Nonpolar
ethoxyethane	Polar	liquid ammonia	Polar
acetone	Polar		

18. Both hexane and Br_2 are nonpolar; "like dissolves like". Water is polar and does not dissolve nonpolar Br_2 to a great extent.

19. The long carbon chain can help dissolve nonpolar solutes, while the ionic end helps to dissolve polar solutes.

20. Nonpolar solvents can only attach to solutes using weak London forces; these forces are unable to overcome the strong bonds holding an ionic compound together so that nonpolar solvents are unable to dissolve ionic compounds.

21. Pentane is held together in the liquid phase by weak London forces. Pentane is not affected by the polar character of water, or its potential for hydrogen bonding, but water **does** exert weak London forces which to a certain extent are able to overcome the London forces holding $C_5H_{12}(l)$ together .

22. (a) Only the highly polar water can dissolve appreciable amounts of ionic KCl(s).
    (b) The large "nonpolar" part of $CH_3CH_2CH_2CH_2$ Br is dissolved to the greatest extent by the greater London forces available with CH_3CH_2OH.
    (c) The large nonpolar octane molecule is dissolved to the greatest extent by the greater London forces available with CH_3CH_2OH.

23. (a) London force   (g) Dipole–dipole and London forces
    (b) London force   (h) London force
    (c) Dipole–dipole and London forces   (i) Dipole–dipole and London forces
    (d) Hydrogen bonding   (j) Ionic bond
    (e) Covalent bond   (k) Hydrogen bond
    (f) London force   (l) London force

24. (a) Xe   (c) $HO-CH_2CH_2-OH$ (e) CCl_4 (g) CH_3F
    (b) HBr   (d) Br_2 (f) H_2O (h) HI

25. a, d

26. For $I_2(s)$ try any of ethanol, acetone, heptane or carbon tetrachloride.
    For $NaNO_3$ try water.
    For carbon disulphide try any of ethanol, acetone, heptane or carbon tetrachloride.
    For $H_2C=O$ try any of water, ethanol, acetone, heptane or carbon tetrachloride.
    For sulphur try any of ethanol, acetone, heptane or carbon tetrachloride.

27. X is water (polar). A is sodium chloride (soluble in water). Liquids Y and Z must be nonpolar solvents (do not dissolve NaCl). Nonpolar naphthalene must be C (insoluble in polar water). Polar benzoic acid must be B (slightly soluble in polar water; fairly soluble to soluble in the nonpolar solvents).

28. (a) $KBr(s) \longrightarrow K^+(aq) + Br^-(aq)$

    (b) $HCl(g) \longrightarrow H^+(aq) + Cl^-(aq)$

    (c) $Na_2SO_4(s) \longrightarrow 2Na^+(aq) + SO_4^{2-}(aq)$

    (d) $Ca(OH)_2(s) \longrightarrow Ca^{2+}(aq) + 2 OH^-(aq)$

    (e) $Al_2(SO_4)_3(s) \longrightarrow 2 Al^{3+}(aq) + 3 SO_4^{2-}(aq)$

    (f) $K_3PO_4(s) \longrightarrow 3 K^+(aq) + PO_4^{3-}(aq)$

    (g) $AlCl_3(s) \longrightarrow Al^{3+}(aq) + 3Cl^-(aq)$

    (h) $(NH_4)_2S(s) \longrightarrow 2 NH_4^+(aq) + S^{2-}(aq)$

29. Water is plentiful, cheap, nontoxic/nonpolluting and an excellent solvent for many ionic and polar solutes.

30. $[SO_4^{2-}] = 3 \times 0.135\ M = \textbf{0.405 M}$

31. $[BaCl_2] = \dfrac{10.0\ g}{0.600\ L} \times \dfrac{1\ mol\ BaCl_2}{208.3\ g} = 0.0800\ M\ ;\quad [Cl^-] = 2 \times [BaCl_2] = 2 \times 0.0800\ M = \textbf{0.160 M}$

32. $[HCl] = 0.300\ M \times \dfrac{55.0\ mL}{135.0\ mL} = 0.1222\ M\ ;\quad [Cl^-] = [HCl] = 0.1222\ M$

    $[CaCl_2] = 0.550\ M \times \dfrac{80.0\ mL}{135.0\ mL} = 0.3259\ M\ ;\quad [Cl^-] = 2 \times [CaCl_2] = 2 \times 0.3259\ M = 0.6519\ M$

    total $[Cl^-] = 0.1222\ M + 0.6519\ M = \textbf{0.774 M}$

33. $[MgCl_2] = 0.250\ M \times \dfrac{350.0\ mL}{275.0\ mL} = 0.3182\ M\ ;\quad [Cl^-] = 2 \times [MgCl_2] = 2 \times 0.3182\ M = \textbf{0.636 M}$

34. (a) moles $K_2SO_4 = 0.20\ \dfrac{mol}{L} \times 0.60\ L = 0.12\ mol$

    so that: # of moles $K^+ = 2 \times$ moles $K_2SO_4 = \textbf{0.24 mol}$,
    and: # of moles $SO_4^{2-} =$ moles $K_2SO_4 = \textbf{0.12 mol}$

    (b) moles $Na_3PO_4 = 0.300\ \dfrac{mol}{L} \times 0.450\ L = 0.135\ mol$

    so that: # of moles $Na^+ = 3 \times$ moles $Na_3PO_4 = \textbf{0.405 mol}$,
    and: # of moles $PO_4^{3-} =$ moles $Na_3PO_4 = \textbf{0.135 mol}$

    (c) moles $MnCl_2 = 0.160\ \dfrac{mol}{L} \times 0.0750\ L = 0.0120\ mol$

    so that: # of moles $Mn^{2+} =$ moles $MnCl_2 = \textbf{0.0120 mol}$,
    and: # of moles $Cl^- = 2 \times$ moles $MnCl_2 = \textbf{0.0240 mol}$

    (d) moles $Al_2(SO_4)_3 = 0.235\ \dfrac{mol}{L} \times 0.0950\ L = 0.022\ 33\ mol$

    so that: # of moles $Al^{3+} = 2 \times$ moles $Al_2(SO_4)_3 = 2 \times 0.022\ 33\ mol = \textbf{0.0447 mol}$,
    and: # of moles $SO_4^{2-} = 3 \times$ moles $Al_2(SO_4)_3 = 3 \times 0.022\ 33\ mol = \textbf{0.0670 mol}$

35. $[BaCl_2] = 0.200 \text{ M} \times \dfrac{100.0 \text{ mL}}{250.0 \text{ mL}} = 0.0800 \text{ M}$; $[Ba^{2+}] = [BaCl_2] = \textbf{0.0800 M}$

                                                          $[Cl^-] = 2 \times [BaCl_2] = 2 \times 0.0800 \text{ M} = 0.160 \text{ M}$

      $[NaCl] = 0.400 \text{ M} \times \dfrac{150.0 \text{ mL}}{250.0 \text{ mL}} = 0.240 \text{ M}$; $[Na^+] = [NaCl] = \textbf{0.240 M}$; $[Cl^-] = [NaCl] = 0.240 \text{ M}$

      total $[Cl^-] = 0.160 \text{ M} + 0.240 \text{ M} = \textbf{0.400 M}$

36. $[Na_3PO_4] = 0.200 \text{ M} \times \dfrac{75.0 \text{ mL}}{100.0 \text{ mL}} = 0.150 \text{ M}$; $[Na^+] = 3 \times [Na_3PO_4] = 3 \times 0.150 \text{ M} = \textbf{0.450 M}$

                                                   $[PO_4^{3-}] = [Na_3PO_4] = 0.150 \text{ M}$

      $[K_3PO_4] = 0.800 \text{ M} \times \dfrac{25.0 \text{ mL}}{100.0 \text{ mL}} = 0.200 \text{ M}$; $[K^+] = 3 \times [K_3PO_4] = 3 \times 0.200 \text{ M} = \textbf{0.600 M}$

                                                   $[PO_4^{3-}] = [Na_3PO_4] = 0.200 \text{ M}$

      $[PO_4^{3-}]$ (total) $= 0.150 \text{ M} + 0.200 \text{ M} = \textbf{0.350 M}$

37. $[Na_3PO_4] = 0.325 \text{ M} \times \dfrac{15.0 \text{ mL}}{50.0 \text{ mL}} = 0.0975 \text{ M}$; $[Na^+] = 3 \times [Na_3PO_4] = 3 \times 0.0975 \text{ M} = \textbf{0.293 M}$

                                                   $[PO_4^{3-}] = [Na_3PO_4] = \textbf{0.0975 M}$

      $[K_2SO_4] = 0.225 \text{ M} \times \dfrac{35.0 \text{ mL}}{50.0 \text{ mL}} = 0.1575 \text{ M}$; $[K^+] = 2 \times [K_2SO_4] = 2 \times 0.1575 \text{ M} = \textbf{0.315 M}$

                                                   $[SO_4^{2-}] = [K_2SO_4] = \textbf{0.158 M}$

38. $[K_2CrO_4] = \dfrac{3.25 \text{ g}}{0.1000 \text{ L}} \times \dfrac{1 \text{ mol}}{194.0 \text{ g}} = 0.1675 \text{ M}$; $[K^+] = 2 \times [K_2CrO_4] = 2 \times 0.1675 \text{ M} = 0.3351 \text{ M}$

                                                   $[CrO_4^{2-}] = [K_2CrO_4] = \textbf{0.168 M}$

      $[K_2Cr_2O_7] = \dfrac{1.75 \text{ g}}{0.1000 \text{ L}} \times \dfrac{1 \text{ mol}}{294.0 \text{ g}} = 0.059 \, 52 \text{ M}$; $[K^+] = 2 \times [K_2Cr_2O_7] = 2 \times 0.059 \, 52 \text{ M} = 0.1190 \text{ M}$

                                                   $[Cr_2O_7^{2-}] = [K_2Cr_2O_7] = \textbf{0.0595 M}$

      total $[K^+] = 0.3351 + 0.1190 = \textbf{0.454 M}$

1. C_NH_{2N+2}

2. (a) 7 carbons; heptane   (c) 8 carbons; octane
   (b) 7 carbons; heptane   (d) 10 carbons; decane

3. (a) 3–methylhexane   (d) 2–methylhexane
   (b) 4-ethylheptane   (e) 4–methylnonane
   (c) 3-ethyloctane   (f) 3–methylheptane

4. (a)
$$\begin{array}{c} \qquad\qquad CH_3 \\ \qquad\qquad | \\ CH_3-CH-CH_2-C-CH_3 \\ \quad\;\; | \qquad\quad | \\ \quad\;\; CH_3 \qquad CH_3 \end{array}$$

   (b)
$$\begin{array}{c} H_2C-CH-CH_2-CH_3 \\ \quad\;\; | \quad\;\; | \\ \quad\; H_2C-CH_2 \end{array}$$

   (c)
$$\begin{array}{c} \qquad\qquad\qquad\qquad\qquad CH_3 \\ \qquad\qquad\qquad\qquad\qquad | \\ CH_3-CH_2-CH-CH_2-CH-CH_2-C-CH_2-CH_3 \\ \qquad\quad | \qquad\qquad\quad | \qquad\qquad | \\ \qquad CH_3-CH_2 \qquad CH \qquad\; CH_3 \\ \qquad\qquad\qquad\quad / \;\; \backslash \\ \qquad\qquad\quad H_2C-CH_2 \end{array}$$

5. (a)
$$\begin{array}{c} CH_3-CH_2-CH-CH_2-CH_2-CH_3 \\ \qquad\qquad | \\ \qquad\qquad CH_3 \end{array}$$

   (b)
$$\begin{array}{c} CH_3-CH_2-CH_2-CH-CH_2-CH_2-CH_2-CH_3 \\ \qquad\qquad\qquad | \\ \qquad\qquad\quad CH_3-CH_2 \end{array}$$

   (c)
$$\begin{array}{c} CH_3-CH-CH_2-CH_2-CH_3 \\ \quad\;\; | \\ \quad\;\; CH_3 \end{array}$$

   (d)
$$\begin{array}{c} CH_3-CH_2-CH_2-CH-CH_2-CH_2-CH_2-CH_2-CH_3 \\ \qquad\qquad\qquad | \\ \qquad\qquad\; CH_3-CH_2-CH_2 \end{array}$$

   (e)
$$\begin{array}{c} CH_3-CH_2-CH-CH_2-CH_2-CH_2-CH_3 \\ \qquad\qquad | \\ \qquad\quad CH_3-CH_2 \end{array}$$

   (f)
$$\begin{array}{c} CH_3CH_2CH_2CH_2CHCH_2CH_2CH_2CH_2CH_3 \\ \qquad\qquad\qquad | \\ \qquad\qquad CH_3CH_2CH_2 \end{array}$$

6. (a) the molecule is numbered from the wrong end; it should be 2–methylheptane

   (b) 1–ethylbutane is
$$\begin{array}{c} CH_2-CH_2-CH_2-CH_3 \\ | \\ CH_2-CH_3 \end{array}$$
   which is just hexane

   (c)
$$\begin{array}{c} \qquad\qquad CH_3 \\ \qquad\qquad | \\ CH_3-CH_2-CH-CH_3 \end{array}$$
   this carbon has the subscript "2"

   (d) the carbon at the 2–position of the propane chain should have NO hydrogens

7. C_NH_{2N+2} (unchanged from straight–chain alkanes)

8. (a) 3,4–dimethylheptane   (g) 4,6–dimethylnonane
   (b) 3,4,4,5–tetraethylheptane   (h) decane
   (c) 2,2,7,7–tetramethyloctane   (i) 4,5–diethyl–3,7–dimethylnonane
   (d) 5–ethyl–3,4–dimethylheptane   (j) 3,3,4,5–tetramethyloctane
       or 3–ethyl–4,5–dimethylheptane   (k) 4–ethyl–3–methyl–5–propyloctane
   (e) 4–methyl–4–ethyloctane   (l) 3,6–diethyl–5,8–dimethyldecane
   (f) 2,2,5–trimethyloctane   or 5,8–diethyl–3,6–dimethyldecane

9. (a) 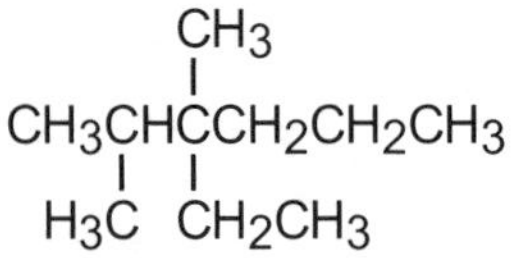

(b) 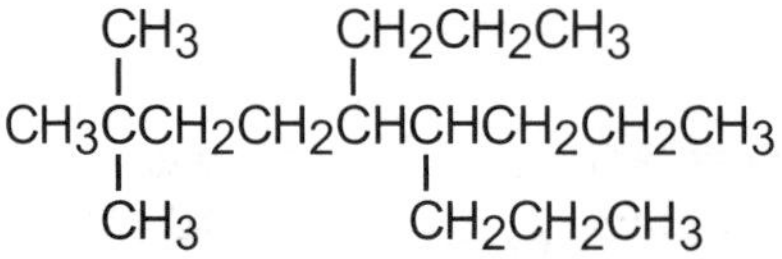

(c) 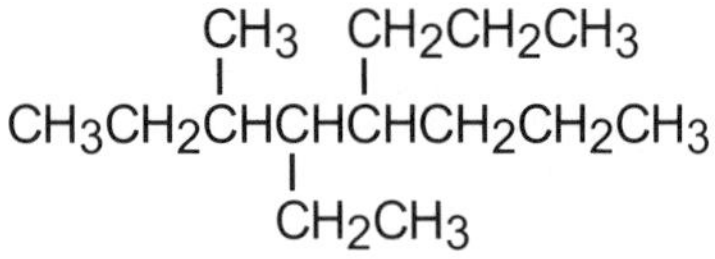

(d) 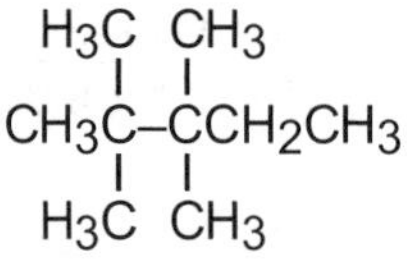

(e) 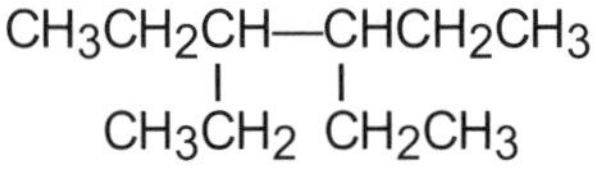

(f) 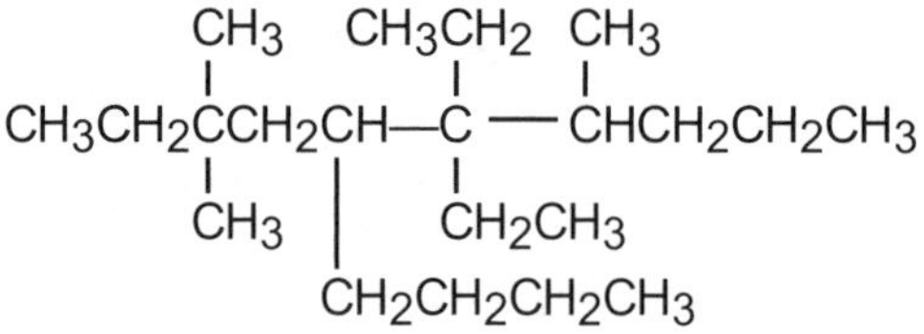

(g) 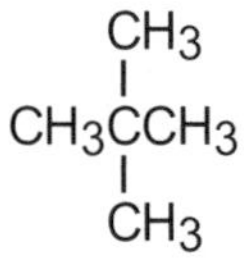

(h) 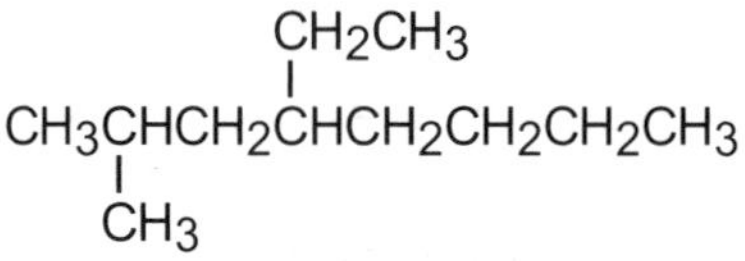

(i) 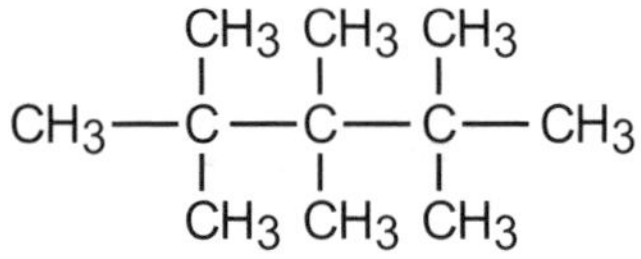

(j) 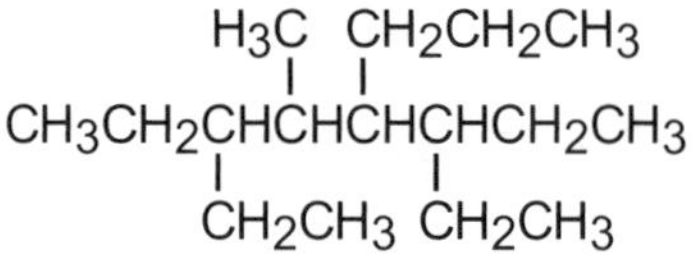

10. pentane = $CH_3CH_2CH_2CH_2CH_3$

methylbutane = 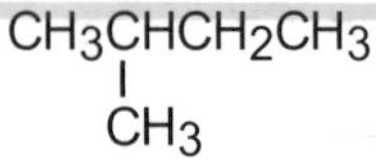

dimethylpropane = 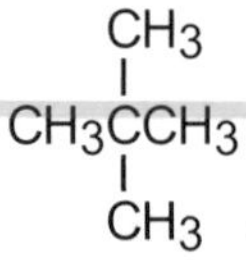

11. 2–methylhexane = 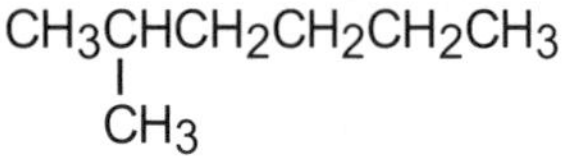

3–methylhexane = 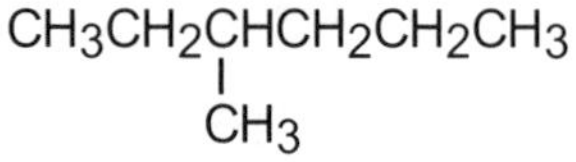

12. 2,2–dimethylpentane = 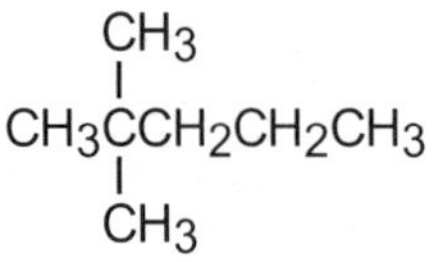

2,3–dimethylpentane = 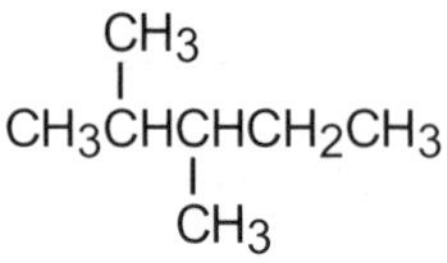

2,4–dimethylpentane = 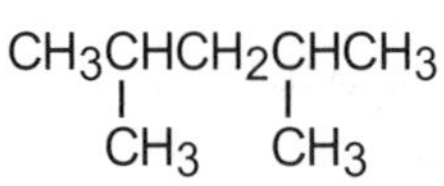

3,3–dimethylpentane = 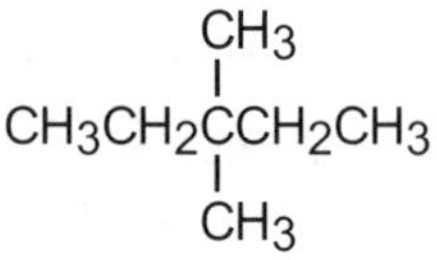

13. 3 – having methyl groups at the 2, 3 or 4 position

14. C_NH_{2N}

15. (a) ethylcyclohexane
(b) 1,3–dimethylcyclobutane
(c) methylcyclopropane
(d) 1–ethyl–1,3–dimethylcyclopentane
(e) 2–ethyl–1,3–dimethylcyclooctane

16. (a)

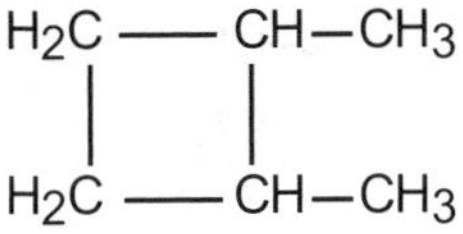

H₂C —— CH–CH₃
| |
H₂C —— CH–CH₃

(b)

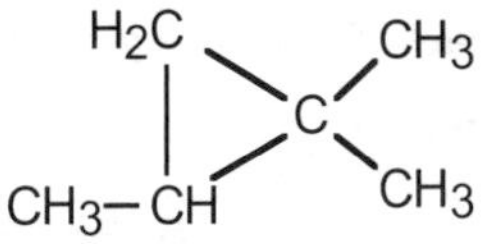

H₂C   CH₃
  \   /
   | C 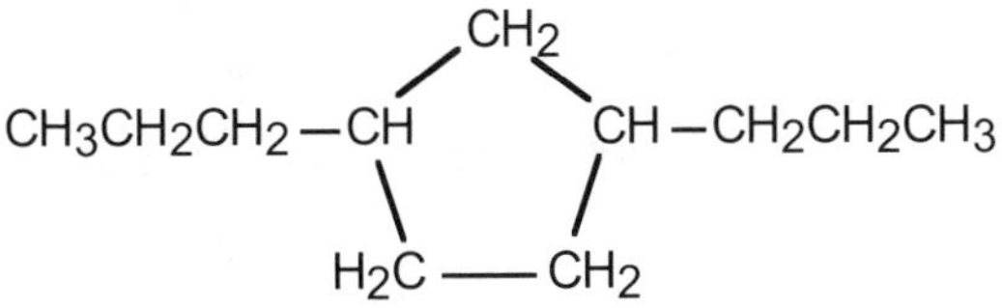
  /   \
CH₃–CH   CH₃

(c) CH₃CH₂CH₂–CH ⟨ring⟩ CH–CH₂CH₂CH₃ (cyclopentane ring with CH₂ top and H₂C—CH₂ bottom)

(d)

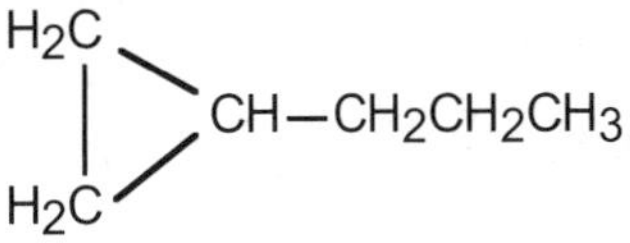

H₂C
  \
   | CH–CH₂CH₂CH₃
  /
H₂C

(e)

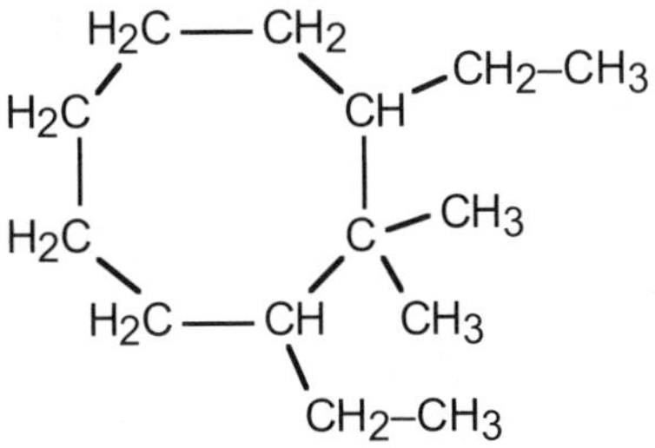

H₂C —— CH₂
| \
H₂C   CH–CH₂–CH₃
| |
H₂C   C ⟨CH₃, CH₃⟩
| |
H₂C —— CH
|
CH₂–CH₃

(f)

H₂C —— CH₂
/   \
H₂C   CH–CH₂–CH₃
| |
CH₃–CH₂–CH   CH–CH₂–CH₃
\   /
CH₂

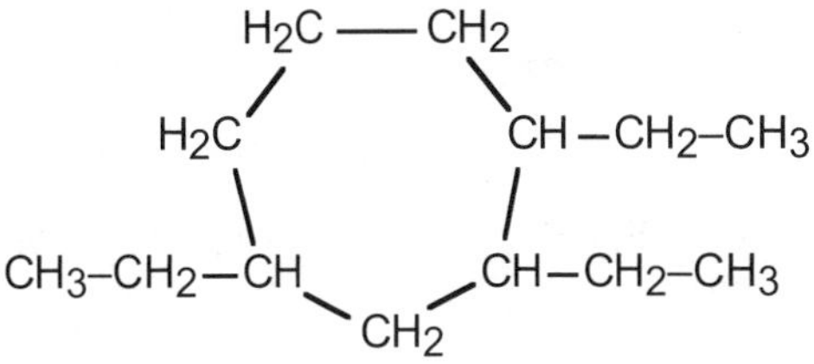

17. (a) chloroethane
(b) 1,3–dibromopropane
(c) 1–iodo–4–methylpentane

(d) 1,1–dichloro–2–fluoroethane
(e) 1,1–dichloro–2–ethylcyclohexane

18. (a) CHCl₃

(b) ClCH₂CH₂Cl

(c)

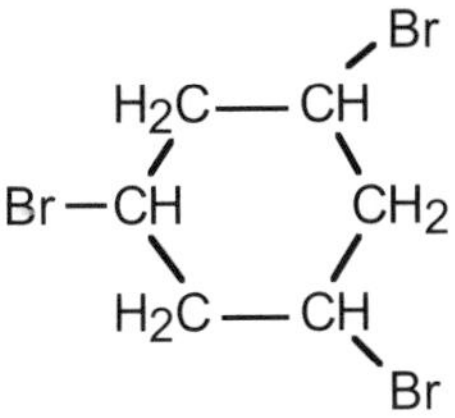

        Br
        |
H₂C —— CH
/   \
Br–CH   CH₂
\   /
H₂C —— CH
        |
        Br

(d)

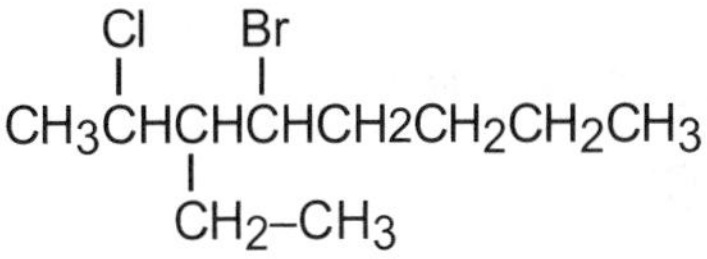

        Cl   Br
        | |
CH₃CHCHCHCH2CH₂CH₂CH₃
        |
        CH₂–CH₃

(e) 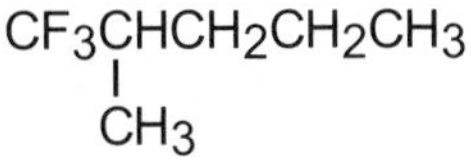 CF₃CHCH₂CH₂CH₃
          |
          CH₃

19. 1–chloropentane = Cl–CH₂CH₂CH₂CH₂CH₃

2–chloropentane = CH₃CHCH₂CH₂CH₃
                            |
                            Cl

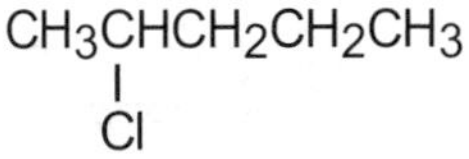

3–chloropentane = CH₃CH₂CHCH₂CH₃
                              |
                              Cl

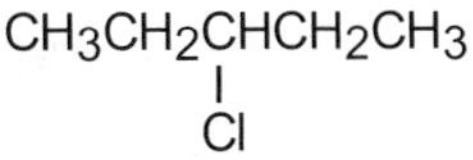

1–chloro–2–methylbutane = ClCH₂CHCH₂CH₃
                                      |
                                      CH₃

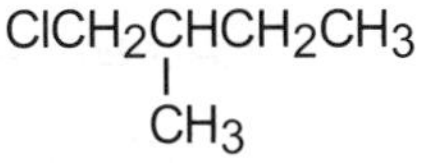

2–chloro–2–methylbutane = CH₃CCH₂CH₃
                                    Cl (top)
                                    |
                                    CH₃

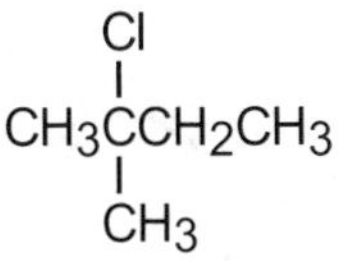

chlorodimethylpropane = ClCH₂CCH₃
                                  CH₃ (top)
                                  |
                                  CH₃

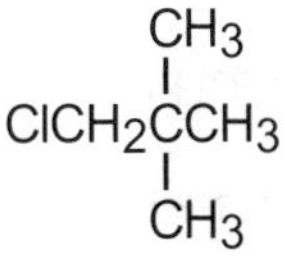

3–chloro–2–methylbutane = CH₃CHCHCH₃
(or 2–chloro–3–methylbutane)   Cl (top)
                                      |
                                      CH₃

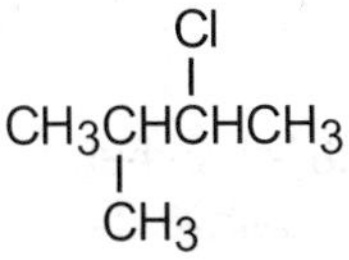

1–chloro–3–methylbutane = ClCH₂CH₂CHCH₃
                                        |
                                        CH₃

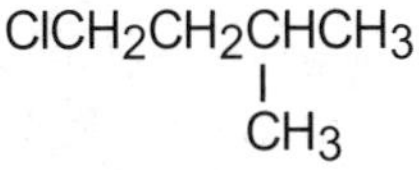

20. 1,1–dichloropentane = $Cl_2CHCH_2CH_2CH_2CH_3$ 1,2–dichloropentane = $ClCH_2CHCH_2CH_2CH_3$
$\overset{|}{Cl}$

  1,3–dichloropentane = $ClCH_2CH_2CHCH_2CH_3$ 1,4–dichloropentane = $ClCH_2CH_2CH_2CHCH_3$
$\overset{|}{Cl}\overset{|}{Cl}$

  1,5–dichloropentane = $ClCH_2CH_2CH_2CH_2CH_2Cl$ 2,2–dichloropentane = $CH_3\overset{\overset{Cl}{|}}{\underset{\underset{Cl}{|}}{C}}CH_2CH_2CH_3$

  2,3–dichloropentane = $CH_3\underset{\underset{Cl}{|}}{C}H\underset{\underset{Cl}{|}}{C}HCH_2CH_3$ 2,4–dichloropentane = $CH_3\underset{\underset{Cl}{|}}{C}HCH_2\underset{\underset{Cl}{|}}{C}HCH_3$

  3,3–dichloropentane = $CH_3CH_2\overset{\overset{Cl}{|}}{\underset{\underset{Cl}{|}}{C}}CH_2CH_3$

21. (a) alkene = C_NH_{2N} (same as cycloalkane)   (b) alkyne = C_NH_{2N-2}

22. (a) $CH_2=CHCH_2CH_2CH_2CH_3$ (b) $CH_3CH_2CH_2C\equiv CCH_2CH_2CH_2CH_3$
    (c) $CH_3CH_2CH=CHCH_2CH_2CH_2CH_2CH_3$ (d) $CH_3C\equiv CCH_2CH_2CH_2CH_3$
    (e) $CH_3CH=CHCH_2CH_2CH_2CH_3$ (f) $HC\equiv CCH_2CH_2CH_2CH_2CH_2CH_3$

23. (a) 3–hexene   (b) 1–heptyne   (c) 4–decyne   (d) 3–heptene

24. (a) $CH_3CH=\overset{\overset{CH_2CH_3}{|}}{\underset{\underset{CH_3}{|}}{C}}CHCH_2CH_3$ (b) $CH_3CH_2\underset{\underset{CH_3}{|}}{C}HC\equiv CCH_2CH_2CH_3$

(c)   (d) $HC\equiv C\underset{\underset{CH_2CH_3}{|}}{C}H\overset{\overset{CH_3}{|}}{C}HCH_2CH_3$

(e) $CH_3\underset{\underset{H_3C}{|}}{C}=\underset{\underset{CH_3}{|}}{C}CH_3$ (f)

(g)   (h)

25. (a) 5–ethyl–6,6–dimethyl–3–heptene   (d) 5,6–dimethyl–1–cyclooctyne
    (b) 3,6–diethyl–2–methyl–4–octyne   (e) 3–methyl–3–hexene
    (c) 1,3,4–trimethyl–1–cyclobutene   (f) 3–methyl–1–cyclohexene

26. (a)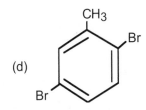

   (b) $CH_3CH_2C \equiv CCH_2CH_3$

   (c)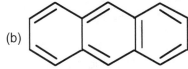

   (d)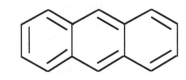

   (e) $CH_3C \equiv CCH_3$

   (f)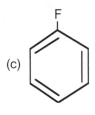

27. (a) no   (b) yes   (c) no   (d) yes   (e) no   (f) no

28. (a) cis–3–hexene   (b) trans–3–octene   (c) trans–2–heptene   (d) cis–4–octene

29. (a)

   (b)

30. (a)   (b)   (c)

   (d)   (e)   (f)

31. (a) ethylbenzene
   (b) 1–bromo–4–methylbenzene
       or 4–bromo–1–methylbenzene
   (c) hexachlorobenzene
   (d) 1,2–dimethylbenzene

   (e) 1–ethyl–3,5–dimethylbenzene
       or 3–ethyl–1,5–dimethylbenzene
       or 5–ethyl–1,3–dimethylbenzene
   (f) 1–ethyl–4–methylbenzene
       or 4–ethyl–1–methylbenzene

32. (a) $CH_3CH_2CH_2CH_2OH$

(b)

$$
\begin{array}{c}
OH \\
| \\
CH \\
H_2C \quad\quad CH-CH_3 \\
H_2C - CH_2
\end{array}
$$

(c) $CH_3CCl_2CHCHCH_2CH_2CH_2CH_2CH_3$
               H_3C OH

(d)
$$
\begin{array}{c}
OH \\
| \\
H_2C - CH \\
CH_3CH_2 - HC \quad\quad CH-CH_2CH_3 \\
H_2C - CH_2
\end{array}
$$

(e) $CH_3CH_2CHCH_2CH_2OH$
           CH_3

(f) CF_3CHCH_3
       OH

33. (a) 2–propanol
   (b) 4,4,4–trifluoro–2–butanol
   (c) 3–methyl–1–butanol
   (d) 2–methyl–2–propanol
   (e) 2–chloro–1–cyclobutanol
   (f) 2,3–dimethyl–1–cyclopropanol

34. (a) methyl propanoate
   (b) propyl methanoate
   (c) ethyl butanoate
   (d) hexyl ethanoate
   (e) butyl pentanoate

35. (a) $CH_3CH_2CH_2CH_2COOCH_2CH_2CH_3$
   (b) $CH_3CH_2CH_2CH_2CH_2COOCH_3$
   (c) $CH_3CH_2COOCH_2CH_3$
   (d) $CH_3CH_2CH_2COOCH_2CH_2CH_2CH_3$
   (e) $HCOOCH_2CH_2CH_2CH_2CH_2CH_3$

36. (a) CH_3OH and CH_3CH_2COOH
   (b) $CH_3CH_2CH_2OH$ and $HCOOH$
   (c) CH_3CH_2OH and $CH_3CH_2CH_2COOH$
   (d) $CH_3CH_2CH_2CH_2CH_2CH_2OH$ and CH_3COOH
   (e) $CH_3CH_2CH_2CH_2OH$ and $CH_3CH_2CH_2CH_2COOH$

37. (a) Br–CH$_2$CH$_2$CH$_2$CHCH$_3$
                       CH_3
     HAL

(b) HC≡CCH$_2$C≡CH
      TRI   TRI

(c)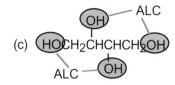

(d) $CH_3CH_2CH=CHCHCH_3$
     DOU   Cl
               HAL

(e)
$$
\begin{array}{c}
CH_3 \\
| \\
CH_3-C-CO-CH_3 \\
| \\
CH_3 \quad KET
\end{array}
$$

(f)
$$
\begin{array}{c}
CH_2OH - ALC \\
| \\
CH_3-C-NH_2 - AMN \\
| \\
CH_2OH - ALC
\end{array}
$$

(g)
$$
\begin{array}{c}
H_2C - CH_2 \\
H_2C \quad\quad CH-CHO \\
H_2C - CH_2 \quad ALD
\end{array}
$$

(h)
$$
\begin{array}{c}
CH_2 \\
H_2C \quad\quad CH-O-CH_2CH_2CH_3 \\
H_2C - CH_2 \quad ETH
\end{array}
$$

(i)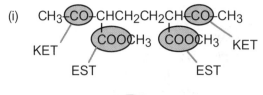

(j)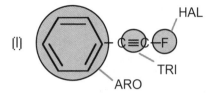

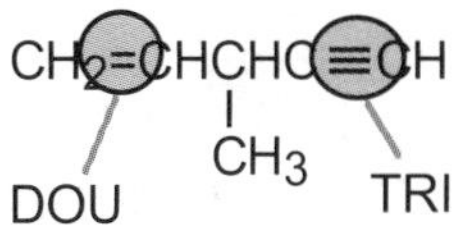

(k)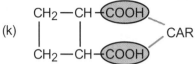

(l)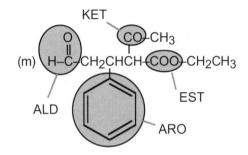

(m)

(n)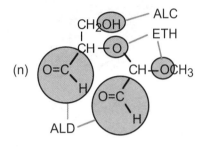

(o)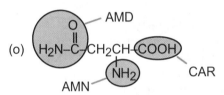

(p)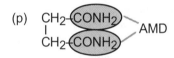

(q)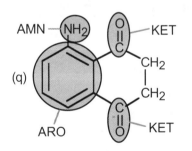

(r)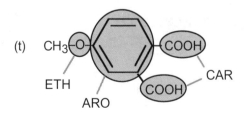

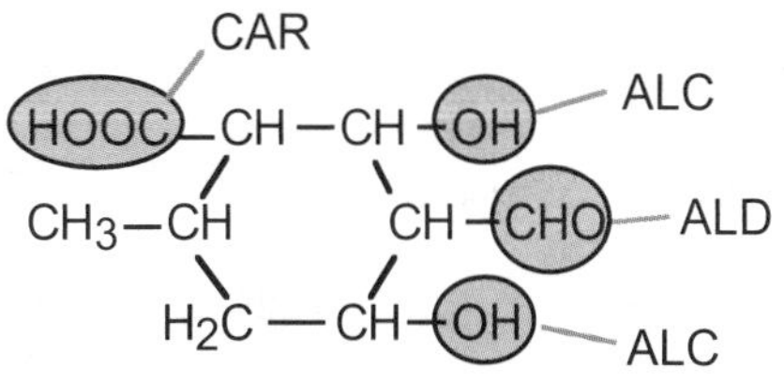

(s)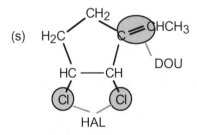

(t)

(u)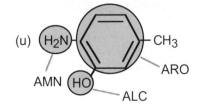

(v)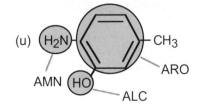

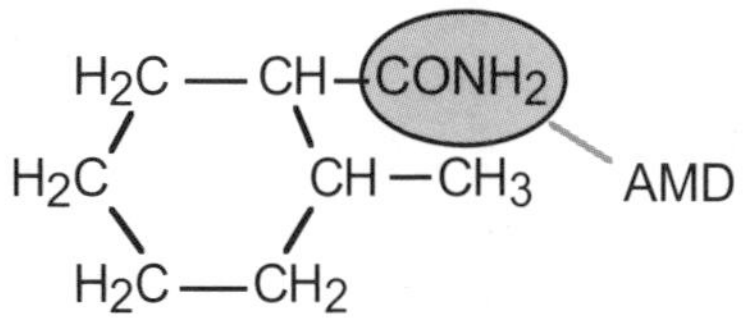

(w) 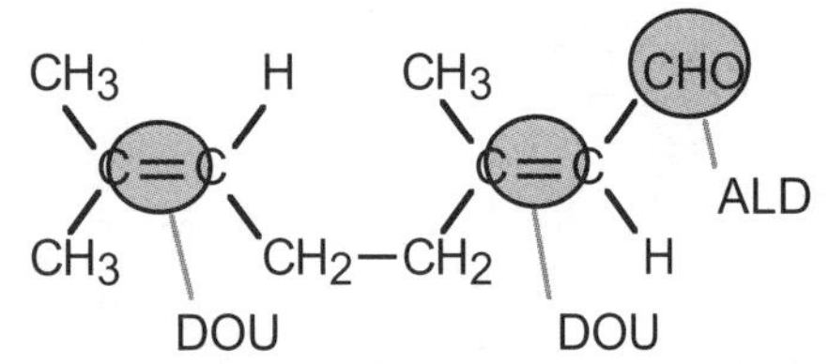
CH3
H
CH3
CHO
ALD
CH3
CH2—CH2
H
DOU
DOU

(x) 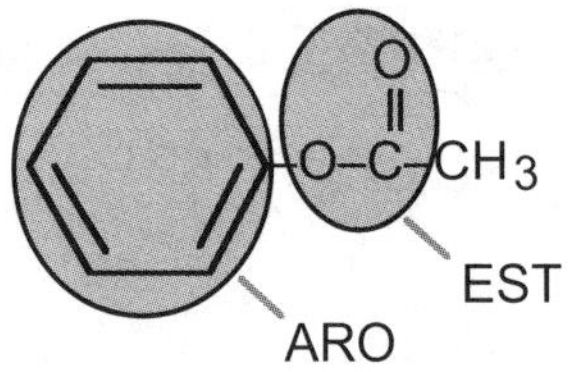
O
O–C–CH3
EST
ARO

(y) 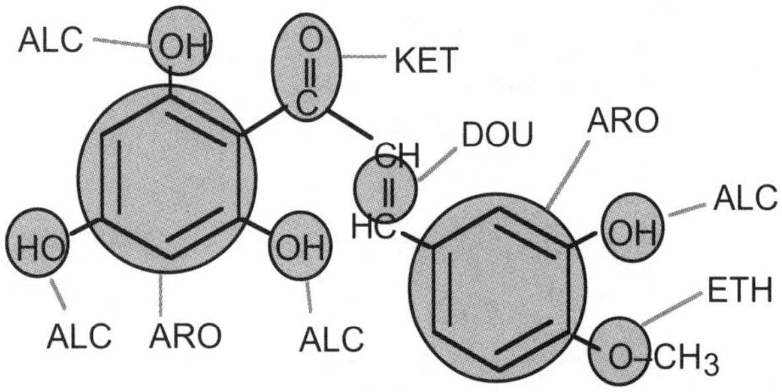
ALC
OH
O
C
KET
CH
DOU
ARO
HC
HO
OH
OH
ALC
ETH
ALC
ARO
ALC
O–CH3

38. (a) 2–fluoropentane
(b) 3–chloro–3–hexene
(c) 1,4–diiodo–2–butyne
(d) pentyl methanoate
(e) 3–bromo–3,5,5–trimethyloctane
(f) 1,3–dichlorocyclobutane
(g) 1–fluoro–4–propylbenzene
or 4–fluoro–1–propylbenzene
(h) 2,6–dimethyloctane
(i) 4–bromo–5–chloro–1–iodo–2–pentyne
(j) 4–iodo–2–butanol
(k) 3–methyl–1–cyclopentanol
(l) 1,3,5–triethylbenzene
(m) 3–bromo–1–propene
(n) pentyl ethanoate
(o) 2,4–dibromo–1–methylbenzene
(p) 1,2,3–trimethylcyclopropane
(q) cyclopropanol
(r) 1–chloro–2–ethylbenzene
or 2–chloro–1–ethylbenzene

39. (a) 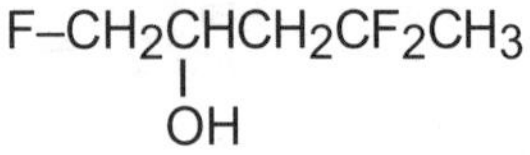
F–CH2CHCH2CF2CH3
OH

(b) $CH_3C\equiv CCHClCH_2CH_3$

(c) $CH_3CH_2CH_2CH_2COOCH_2CH_3$

(d) 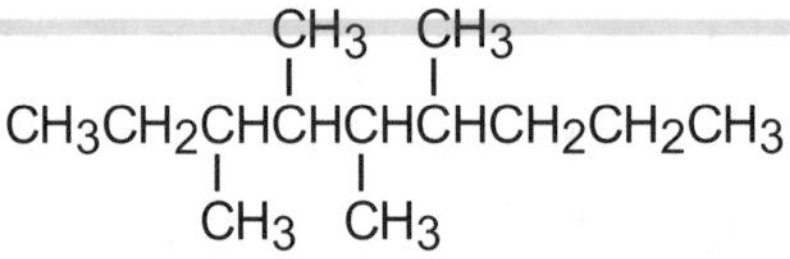
CH3 CH3
CH3CH2CHCHCHCHCH2CH2CH3
CH3 CH3

(e) $CH_3CH_2C\equiv CCH_2CH_2CH_2CH_3$

(f) 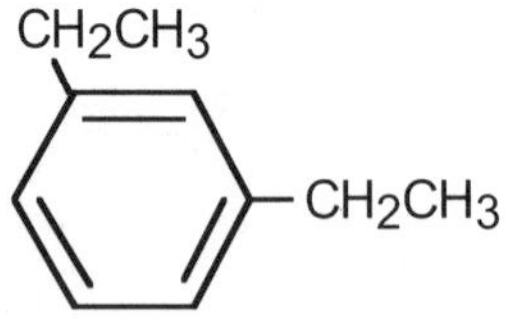
CH2CH3
CH2CH3

(g) 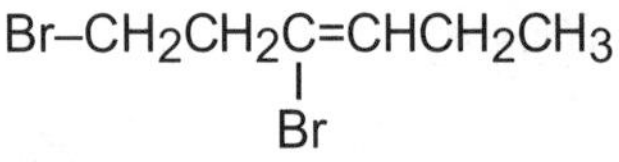
Br–CH2CH2C=CHCH2CH3
Br

(h) 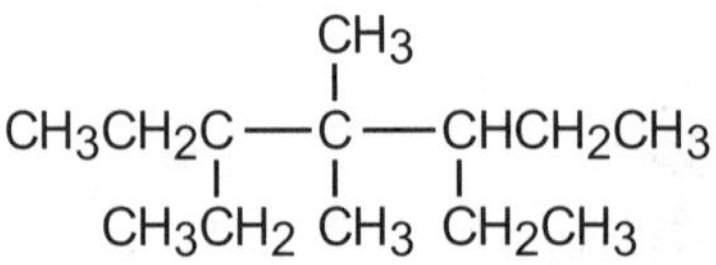
CH3
CH3CH2C—C—CHCH2CH3
CH3CH2 CH3 CH2CH3

(i) 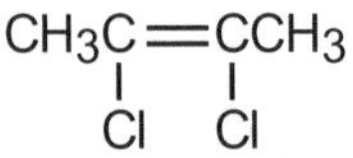
CH3C=CCH3
Cl Cl

(j) $CH_3CH_2CH_2CH_2CH_2CH_2CH_2COOCH_3$

(k) 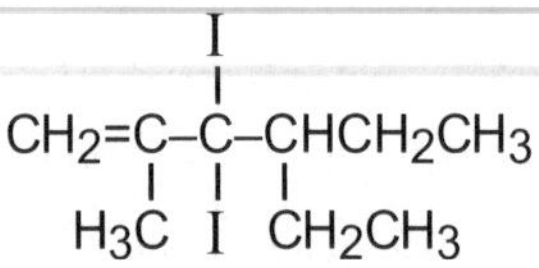
I
CH2=C–C–CHCH2CH3
H3C I CH2CH3

(l) 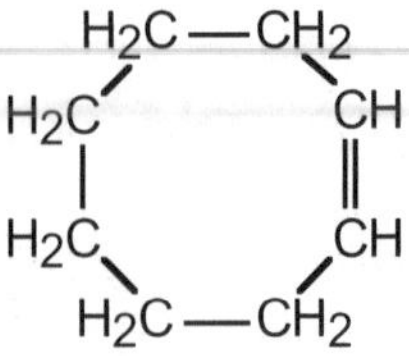
H2C—CH2
H2C
CH
CH
H2C
H2C—CH2

(m) $CH_3CHC \equiv CCH_2CH_2CH_3$
      |
     CH_3

(n) 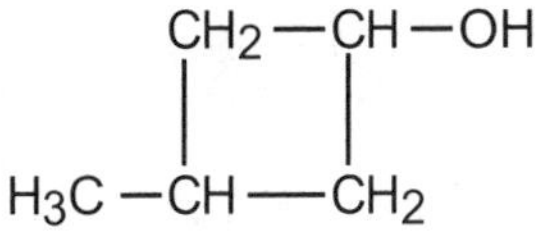
$$CH_2 - CH - OH$$
$$|\qquad\ \ |$$
$$H_3C - CH - CH_2$$

(o) 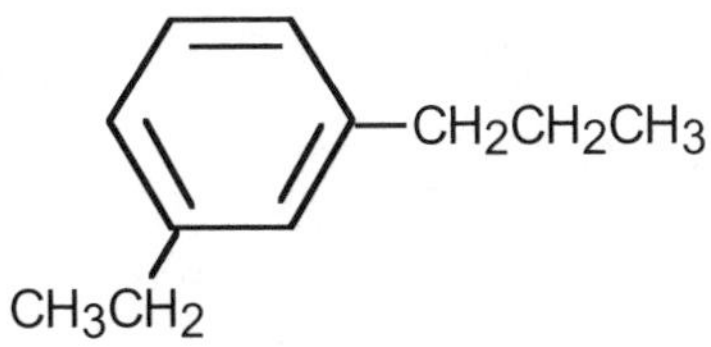
—$CH_2CH_2CH_3$
CH_3CH_2

(p) 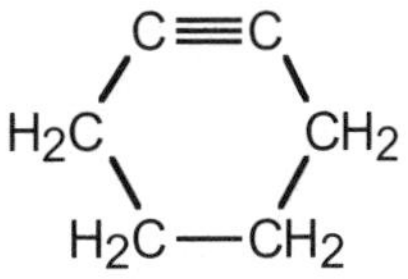 H_2C
$C \equiv C$
CH_2
$H_2C - CH_2$

(q)
    CH_3
     |
$CH_3CCH_2CH_3$
     |
    OH

(r) $CH_3CBr_2CBr_2CH_3$

40. C_NH_{2N+2} implies no loss of H's (no multiple bonds; no ring present which joins one end of a chain back onto itself).

C_NH_{2N} implies the loss of 2 H's due to either a ring present **OR** a double bond.

C_NH_{2N-2} implies the loss of 4 H's due to either a triple bond **OR** two double bonds **OR** two rings present **OR** a double bond AND a ring present.

Answers: c, e, g, i

41. Structures involving a double bond:

$CH_2=CH–CH_2–CH_2–CH_3$ = 1–pentene $CH_3–CH=CH–CH_2–CH_3$ = 2–pentene

$CH_2=CCH_2CH_3$ = 2–methyl–1–butene $CH_3C=CHCH_3$ = 2–methyl–2–butene
    | |
   CH_3 CH_3

$CH_3CHCH=CH_2$ = 3–methyl–1–butene
    |
   CH_3

Structures involving a ring:

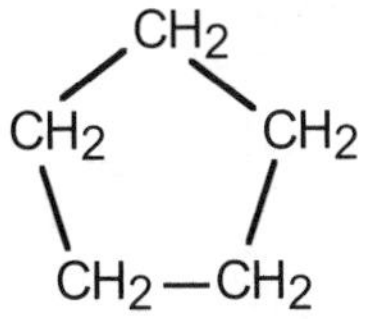

= cyclopentane

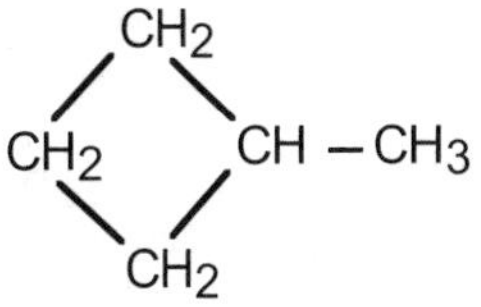

= methylcyclobutane

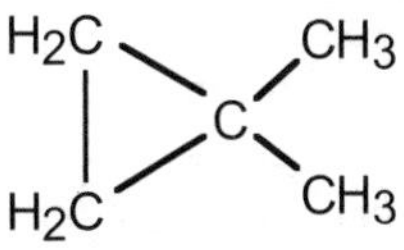

= 1,1–dimethylcyclopropane

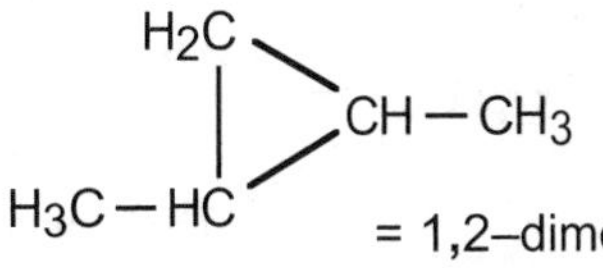

= 1,2–dimethylcyclopropane

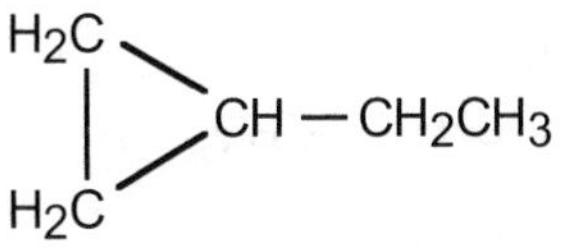

= ethylcyclopropane

42. (a) carboxylic acids, amino acids   (d) alkanes
   (b) amines   (e) amino acids
   (c) esters   (f) esters

43. (a)
$$CH_3CH_2 \quad Cl$$
$$C=C$$
$$Cl \quad CH_2CH_3$$

(b)
$$H_3C \quad H$$
$$C=C$$
$$H \quad CH_2CH_2CH_2CH_2CH_3$$

(c)
$$H_3C \quad CH_3$$
$$C=C$$
$$Br \quad Br$$

(d)
$$F_3C \quad H$$
$$C=C$$
$$H \quad CH_2CH_3$$

(e)
$$CCl_3CH_2 \quad CH_2CH_2CCl_3$$
$$C=C$$
$$H \quad H$$

(f)
$$H_3C \quad CH_2CH_2CH_2CH_2CH_2CH_3$$
$$C=C$$
$$H \quad H$$

44. (a) $F_3CCOOCH_3$
    HAL   EST

(b) $CH_3COCH_2CH_2OH$
    KET   ALC

(c)
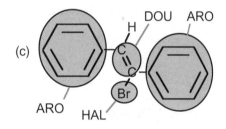
DOU ARO
ARO HAL

(d)
$$CH_2$$
$$CH_2 \quad CH-O-CH_3$$
$$CH_2-CH_2 \quad ETH$$

(e) $CH_3C=CHCHC\equiv CH$
    DOU CH_3 CH_3 TRI

(f) $H_2NCOCH_2CHCH_2CONH_2$
    AMD   NH_2   AMD
             AMN

(g)
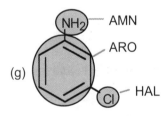
NH_2 — AMN
ARO
Cl — HAL

(h)
$$CH_2$$
$$CH_2 \quad CH_2 \quad CH \quad COOH — CAR$$
$$CH_2 \quad C \quad DOU$$
$$CH_2 \quad CH_2 \quad CH_2$$
$$CH_2$$

(i) $CH_3CHCH_2-O-CH_3$
    OH   ETH
        ALC

(j) $H_2NCOCH_2CHC\equiv CCHCHO$
    AMD   Cl   Cl   ALD
         HAL   TRI   HAL

(k)
$$O$$
$$C-OH — CAR$$
$$HOCH_2CH$$
$$C-OH — CAR$$
$$O$$
ALC

(l)
$$CH_3 \quad CH_2$$
$$CH \quad CH_3 CH_2 \quad DOU$$
$$CH_2 \quad C \quad CH \quad CH_3$$
$$O=C \quad C \quad CH_2$$
$$CH \quad CH_2$$
KET   DOU

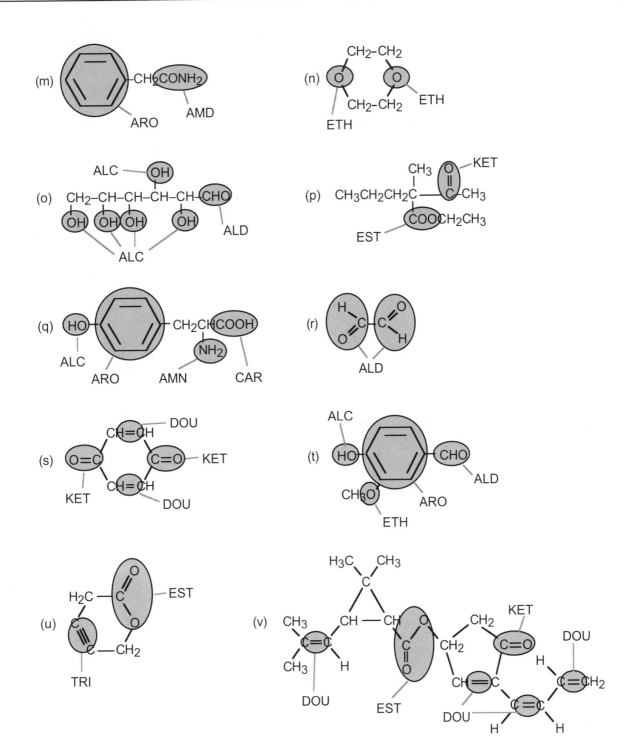

GLOSSARY

The number following each entry is the page number where the term is defined or first mentioned.

ACCURATE MEASUREMENT – a measurement that is close to the CORRECT or ACCEPTED value (28)

ACID – a compound whose formula starts with "H" (74)

ACTINIDE – an element in the row underneath the main part of the table, starting with actinium (161)

ALCOHOL– an organic compound containing an OH group (233)

ALDEHYDE – an organic compound containing a CHO group at the end of a hydrocarbon chain (234)

ALKALI METAL – an element in the first column of the periodic table (except hydrogen) (161)

ALKALINE EARTH METAL – an element in the second column of the periodic table (161)

ALKANE – a hydrocarbon in which all the carbon atoms are connected by single bonds (215)

ALKENE – an organic compound containing a carbon–carbon double bond (226)

ALKYL GROUP – an alkane which has lost one hydrogen atom (217)

ALKYL HALIDE – an alkane having a halogen attached (224)

ALKYNE – an organic compound containing a carbon–carbon triple bond (226)

ALPHA PARTICLE – a He^{2+} ion which is given off by a radioactive atom (142, 143)

AMIDE – an organic compound containing a $CONH_2$ group (236)

AMINE – an organic compound containing an NH_2 group (236)

AMINO ACID – a carboxylic acid with an amine group at the 2–position (237)

ANION – an ion with a NEGATIVE charge (68)

AQUEOUS SOLUTION – a solution in which the solvent is WATER (51)

AROMATIC MOLECULE – a molecule containing one or more benzene rings (231)

ASYMMETRICAL MOLECULE – a molecule in which one end is different than the other (200)

ATOM – the smallest possible unit of an element which retains the fundamental properties of the element (49)

ATOMIC MASS – the total number of protons and neutrons in an atom (146)

ATOMIC NUMBER – the number of protons in the nucleus of an atom; also, the charge on the nucleus (145)

AVOGADRO'S HYPOTHESIS – equal volumes of gases, at the same temperature and pressure, contain the same number of particles (77)

AVOGADRO'S NUMBER – the number of particles in 1 mol of a substance = 6.02×10^{23} (83)

BALANCED EQUATION – a chemical reaction equation in which mass, atoms, and electrical charge are conserved (107)

BASE – a compound that has a chemical formula ending with OH (116)

BASE UNIT – one of the basic units in SI measurement (such as gram, metre, second and mole) (16)

BETA PARTICLE – a high energy electron emitted directly from an atomic nucleus (142)

BINARY COMPOUND – a compound made of two different types of atom (73)

BOHR MODEL (OF THE ATOM) – a model in which the electrons in an atom are restricted to having certain specific energies and are restricted to following specific paths at a fixed distance from the nucleus (144)

BOILING TEMPERATURE– the temperature at which a liquid changes into the gas phase. At the boiling temperature the liquid and gas phases co–exist. (60)

CARBOXYLIC ACID – an organic compound which contains a COOH group (236)

CATION – an ion with a POSITIVE charge (68)

CHEMICAL CHANGE – a change in which new substances are formed (59)

CHEMICAL PROPERTY – the ability of a substance to undergo chemical reactions and change into new substances, either by itself or with other substances (44)

CHEMICAL REACTION EQUATION – an equation that shows the chemicals used up and produced during a chemical reaction (105)

CHEMICAL WORD EQUATION – uses words to describe the REACTANTS and PRODUCTS (105)

CHEMISTRY – the science concerned with the properties, composition and behaviour of matter (44)

CHROMATOGRAPHY – a separation process in which different dissolved substances in a solution (the mobile phase) preferentially move through an absorbent material (the stationary phase) and are separated according to the relative attractions of the dissolved solids to the mobile phase or stationary phase (57)

CIS ISOMER – an isomer in which attached groups are on the same side of a double bond (230)

CLOSED SHELL – an electron shell which contains its maximum number of electrons (154)

CLOSED SYSTEM – a system is closed if nothing can enter or leave it (105)

COEFFICIENT – the number shown in front of each species involved in a chemical reaction (105)

COMBINATION REACTION – see SYNTHESIS

COMBINING CAPACITY – see VALENCE (as a noun)

COMBUSTION – a general term referring to the rapid reaction of a substance with oxygen to produce substantial amounts of heat, and usually a flame (116)

COMPOUND – a pure substance made of two or more types of atoms (51)

CONCENTRATED SOLUTION – a solution with a relatively high concentration of a particular substance (96)

CONCENTRATION (of a substance in solution) – the amount of the substance which exists in a given volume of the solution (96)

CONDENSATION TEMPERATURE – the temperature at which a gas changes into the liquid phase. At the condensation temperature the liquid and gas phases co–exist. (60)

CONSERVATION LAW – an experimentally observed law which states what is CONSERVED (unchanged) in a special set of circumstances (106)

CONSERVED QUANTITY – a quantity which does not change during a closed system reaction (106)

CONTROLLED FIRE – a fire which is contained in a beaker, flask or test tube, such that the fire can be put out by placing a watch glass or inverted beaker over the top of the container and smothering the fire (5)

CONVERSION FACTOR – is a fractional expression relating or connecting two different units (9)

CORE – the set of electrons with the configuration of the nearest noble gas having an atomic number LESS than that of the atom being considered (155)

COVALENT BOND – a bond which involves the equal sharing of electrons (176)

CRYSTAL LATTICE – the orderly arrangement of particles which exists within a crystal (209)

CYCLOALKANE – a hydrocarbon chain which is connected in a head–to–tail "circle"; also called a cyclic hydrocarbon (222)

DATA – quantitative information which is experimentally–determined or obtained from references (41)

DECOMPOSITION REACTION – involves breaking down a molecule into simpler substances (114)

DENSITY – the mass contained in a given volume of a substance, calculated from the formula $d = \dfrac{m}{V}$ (24)

DERIVED QUANTITY – a number made by combining two or more other values (23)

DERIVED UNIT – a unit which is made by combining two or more other units (23)

DESCRIPTION – a list of the properties of something (41)

DEUTERIUM – an isotope of hydrogen having an atomic mass of 2; sometimes call "heavy hydrogen" (148)

DIATOMIC SPECIES – a chemical species that is made up of two atoms (which may be the same or different types) (68)

DIFFUSION – the intermingling of fluids as a result of motion within the fluid (this applies to both gases and liquids) (46)

DILUTE SOLUTION – a solution with a relatively low concentration of a particular substance (96)

DIPOLE – a partial charge separation existing when one end of a molecule (or bond) has a slight excess of positive charge and the other end of the molecule (or bond) has a slight excess of negative charge (179)

DIPOLE–DIPOLE FORCE – a bonding force which exists as a result of an electrostatic attraction between molecules having permanent dipoles (199)

DISSOCIATION REACTION – a reaction involving separating previously–existing ions in an ionic solid (210)

DISTILLATION – a separation process in which a liquid is boiled and the resulting vapour is condensed to a liquid by being passed through a condenser. Since different liquids boil at different temperatures, mixtures of liquids can be separated by the distillation process. (53)

DOUBLE REPLACEMENT or **METATHESIS REACTION** – a reaction which involves an exchange of atoms or groups between two different compounds (115)

DUCTILITY – the ability of a substance to be stretched or drawn into wires (46)

ELECTRON CONFIGURATION – a description of which orbitals in an atom contain electrons and how many electrons are in each orbital (154)

ELECTRON–DEFICIENT MOLECULE – a molecule in which one or more atoms (other than hydrogen) does not possess a full octet of electrons (186)

ELECTRON DOT DIAGRAM – see LEWIS STRUCTURE

ELECTRONEGATIVITY – the tendency of the atom to attract electrons from a neighbouring atom (173)

ELECTROSTATIC FORCE – a force existing as a result of the attraction or repulsion between two charged particles (165)

ELEMENT – a substance which cannot be separated into simpler substances as a result of any chemical process (49)

EMERGENCY EQUIPMENT – equipment which is intended to be used only in the event of an emergency (1)

EMPIRICAL FORMULA (sometimes called the **SIMPLEST FORMULA**) – the smallest whole–number ratio of atoms which represents the molecular composition of a species (91)

ENDOTHERMIC REACTION – a reaction which absorbs heat from its surroundings (120)

ENERGY LEVEL – a specific amount of energy which an electron in an atom can possess (151)

ENTHALPY – the heat contained in a system (121)

EQUIVALENCE POINT or **STOICHIOMETRIC POINT** – the point in a titration where the mole ratio of the reacting species equals the ratio of the coefficients of the species in the balanced reaction equation (130)

ESTER – an organic compound in which a COO group connects two hydrocarbon chains (238)

ETHER – a compound in which an oxygen joins two hydrocarbon groups (235)

EVAPORATION (as a method of physical separation) – the process of allowing the liquid in a solid–in–liquid solution to evaporate or to be boiled away, leaving the solid (53)

EXCESS REACTANT – a reactant which is not completely used up in a reaction (132)

EXOTHERMIC REACTION – a reaction which gives off heat to its surroundings (119)

EXPERIMENT – a test or a procedure that is carried out in order to discover a result (41)

EXPERIMENTAL UNCERTAINTY – the estimated amount by which a measurement might be in error (34)

EXPONENTIAL EQUIVALENT – an exponential number which can replace an SI prefix symbol (for example, "10^3" is the exponential equivalent of "k") (17)

EXTENSIVE PROPERTY – a physical property which depends on the amount of the substance present (44)

FAMILY – see GROUP

FILTRATE – the liquid which passes through a filter paper (53)

FILTRATION – the separation of an undissolved solid from a liquid by passing the liquid through a filter paper, so as to leave the solid behind (53)

FREEZING TEMPERATURE – the temperature at which a liquid changes into the solid phase. At the freezing temperature the solid and liquid phases co–exist. (60)

FUNCTIONAL GROUP – a specific group of atoms which exists in a molecule and gives a molecule an ability to react in a specific manner or gives it special properties (233)

GAMMA PARTICLE – high energy radiation given off by the nucleus (142)

GRAVITY SEPARATION – any of several separation methods which separate the components of a mechanical mixture according to their densities. The methods include gold panning, mechanical shaking, froth flotation and centrifugation. (56)

GROUP or **FAMILY** – the set of all the elements in a given column going down the table (161)

HALOGEN – an element in the 17th column of the periodic table (headed by fluorine) (161)

HAND SEPARATION – the separation of a mechanical mixture by bare hand, sieve or magnet (53)

HARDNESS – the ability of a solid to resist abrasion or scratching (46)

HETEROGENEOUS SUBSTANCE – a substance consisting of more than one phase (50)

HOMOGENEOUS SUBSTANCE – a substance consisting of only one phase (50)

HYDRATE – a molecule which includes one or more water molecules in its crystal structures (72)

HYDROCARBON – a compound made of carbon and hydrogen (116)

HYDROGEN BOND – a bond which exists as a result of a strong dipole–dipole attraction between molecules having H–F, H–O or H–N bonds (202)

HYPOTHESIS – a SINGLE, UNPROVEN assumption or idea which attempts to explain why nature behaves in a specific manner. When initially put forward, hypotheses are tentative but, if they survive testing, eventually gain general acceptance. (41)

IMMISCIBLE LIQUIDS – liquids which are insoluble in each other (54)

INDICATOR – a coloured dye which changes colour when an acidic solution has been exactly neutralized by a basic solution, or vice versa (130)

INORGANIC NOMENCLATURE – the naming of elements and inorganic compounds (65)

INTENSIVE PROPERTY – a physical property which depends solely on the nature of a substance, and NOT on how much of a substance is present (44)

INTERMOLECULAR FORCE – a force which holds complete, neutral molecules next to one another (179)

INTERPRETATION (or "inference") – an attempt to put meaning into an observation (41)

INTRAMOLECULAR FORCE – a force which holds atoms together to make a molecule (179)

ION – an atom or molecule which possesses an electrical charge (49)

IONIC BOND – a bond formed by the attraction of positive ions to negative ions (172)

IONIC COMPOUND – a compound made up of ions (70)

IONIC SOLID – a solid whose crystal structure is made up of ions (209)

IONIZATION ENERGY – the energy required to remove an electron from a neutral atom (168)

IONIZATION REACTION – a reaction which involves the breaking up of a neutral molecule into ions (210)

ISOTOPES – atomic species having the same atomic number but different atomic masses (148)

KETONE – an organic compound containing a C=O group at a position other than at the end of a hydrocarbon chain (235)

KINETIC ENERGY – the energy that molecules possess as a result of their motion (62)

LANTHANIDE – an element in the row underneath the main part of the table, starting with lanthanum (161)

LAW – a broad generalization or summary statement which describes a large amount of experimental evidence stating how nature behaves when a particular situation occurs (41)

LAW OF CONSERVATION OF ATOMS – the total number and type of atoms in a closed system does not change during a chemical reaction (106)

LAW OF CONSERVATION OF ELECTRICAL CHARGE – the total electrical charge in a closed system does not change during a chemical reaction (106)

LAW OF CONSERVATION OF ENERGY – the total energy in a closed system does not change during a chemical reaction (106)

LAW OF CONSERVATION OF MASS – the total mass in a closed system does not change during a chemical reaction; that is, the mass of the reactants equals the mass of the products (106)

LAW OF CONSTANT COMPOSITION – see LAW OF DEFINITE PROPORTIONS

LAW OF DEFINITE PROPORTIONS (or LAW OF CONSTANT COMPOSITION) – every pure sample of a particular compound always contains the same proportion by mass of the elements in the compound (140)

LAW OF MULTIPLE PROPORTIONS – when different masses of one element combine with a specific mass of a second element, the mass ratios of the first element are small whole number ratios (141)

LEADING ZERO – a zero digit which is not significant and only serves to hold the place value of the following digits (37)

LEWIS STRUCTURE – a diagram showing how the valence electrons are distributed in an atom, ion or molecule; also called an electron dot diagram (172)

LIMITING REACTANT – a reactant which sets a limit on the amount of product which can be formed (132)

LONDON FORCES – weak attractive forces which arise as a result of temporary dipolar attractions between neighbouring atoms (179)

LUSTRE – the manner in which a solid surface reflects light (46)

MALLEABILITY – the ability of a substance to be rolled or hammered into thin sheets (46)

MASS – the quantity of matter in an object (24)

MATTER – anything that has mass and occupies space (44)

MECHANICAL MIXTURE – a heterogeneous mixture of two or more substances (50)

MELTING TEMPERATURE – the temperature at which a solid changes into the liquid phase. At the melting temperature the solid and liquid phases co–exist. (60)

METALLOID – see semiconductor

METATHESIS REACTION – see DOUBLE REPLACEMENT REACTION

METRIC CONVERSION – a unit conversion between a prefix symbol and its exponential equivalent (19)

MISCIBLE LIQUIDS – liquids that are mutually soluble in each other in all proportions (54)

MIXTURE – a system made up of two or more substances, such that the relative amounts of each substance can be varied (50)

MOLAR CONCENTRATION or **MOLARITY** (of a substance in solution) – the number of moles of the substance contained in 1 L of solution (96)

MOLARITY – see MOLAR CONCENTRATION

MOLAR MASS – the mass of ONE MOLE of particles. The molar mass of an element is the mass shown on the periodic table, expressed in grams (79)

MOLAR VOLUME (of a substance) – the volume occupied by one mole of the substance. The molar volume of any gas at STP is 22.4 L. (82)

MOLE – the fundamental unit used for measuring amount. One mole of particles is 6.02×10^{23} particles. (Strictly speaking, one mole is the number of carbon atoms in exactly 12 g of carbon–12.) (79, 83)

MOLECULAR SOLID – a solid whose crystal structure is made of neutral molecules (209)

MOLECULE – a cluster of two or more atoms, held together strongly by electrical forces (49)

MONATOMIC SPECIES – a chemical species that is made up of only ONE atom (68)

NEUTRALIZATION REACTION – the reaction between **H** in an acid and **OH** in a base to make H_2O (116)

NEUTRAL SOLUTION – a solution which has no excess of either an acid or a base (116)

NOBLE GAS– an element in the 18th column of the periodic table (headed by helium) (161)

OBSERVATION – *qualitative* information collected through the direct use of our senses (41)

OCTET RULE – states that atoms in columns 14 to 17 of the periodic table tend to form covalent bonds so as to have eight electrons in their valence shells (176)

OPEN SHELL – a shell containing less than its maximum number of electrons (166)

OPEN SYSTEM – a system is OPEN if things can enter and leave it (105)

ORBITAL – the actual region of space occupied by an electron in a particular energy level (152)

ORGANIC CHEMISTRY – the chemistry of carbon compounds (213)

OUTER ELECTRON– see VALENCE ELECTRON

PARTICLE – a general term used to describe a small bit of matter such as an atom, molecule or ion (49)

PERCENTAGE COMPOSITION – the percentage (by mass) of the species in a chemical formula (90)

PERCENTAGE PURITY – the amount of pure chemical actually present in a sample as a percentage of the amount of the impure chemical present; calculated from the expression:
Percentage Purity = (mass of pure chemical / mass of impure chemical) x 100% (134)

PERCENTAGE YIELD – the amount of a product actually produced as a percentage of the expected amount; calculated from the expression:
Percentage Yield = (mass of product obtained / mass of product expected) x 100% (134)

PERIOD – the set of all the elements in a given row going across the table (161)

PERIODIC LAW – the properties of the chemical elements recur periodically when the elements are arranged from lowest to highest atomic numbers (160)

PHASE – any part of a system which is uniform in both its composition and properties (49)

PHYSICAL CHANGE – a change in a substance's phase, such that no new substances are formed (59)

PHYSICAL PROPERTY – a property that can be found without creating a new substance (44)

POLARIZATION – the repulsion of the electrons on one atom by the electrons on a second atom, combined with the simultaneous attraction of the electrons on one atom for the nucleus of a second atom (180)

POLAR MOLECULE – a molecule which has a partial positive charge at one end and a partial negative charge at the other end (199)

POLYATOMIC SPECIES – a general term for a chemical species made up of many atoms (68)

POLYELECTRONIC ATOM – an atom having more than one electron (153)

PRECIPITATE – a solid formed when two liquids or aqueous solutions react (113)

PRECISE MEASUREMENT – a reproducible measurement. In general, the more precise a measurement, the more SIGNIFICANT DIGITS it possesses. (28)

PREFIX–NAMING SYSTEM – a method of naming binary compounds made of nonmetals in which the number of each type of atom in the molecule is indicated by a prefix such as mono, di, tri, tetra, etc. (73)

PREFIX SYMBOL – a symbol which stands for a power of 10 (for example "c" stands for "10^{-2}") (17)

PRODUCT – a chemical which is formed as a result of a chemical reaction (105)

PROTECTIVE EQUIPMENT – equipment which is used to protect you from the effects of hazardous chemicals or material BEFORE any problems arise (5)

PURE SUBSTANCE – a substance that is homogeneous and has an unchangeable composition (50)

QUALITATIVE INFORMATION – NON–NUMERICAL information (41)

QUANTITATIVE INFORMATION – NUMERICAL information (41)

QUANTUM OF ENERGY – the energy difference between two particular energy levels in an atom (151)

RADIOACTIVITY – the ability of an atom to give off energy and nuclear particles (142)

REACTANT – a chemical which is present at the start of a chemical reaction (105)

RECRYSTALLIZATION – a purification and separation process in which a solid is dissolved in a suitable solvent and the mixture is allowed to cool or evaporate until purified crystals of the solid are deposited in the mixture (55)

REPRESENTATIVE ELEMENTS – the groups of elements which includes columns 1, 2 and 13 to 18 of the periodic table (161)

RESIDUE – the solid which remains behind on a filter paper after a filtration (53)

RESONANCE STRUCTURES – structures differing only in the placement of alternating double bonds (231)

ROTATIONAL ENERGY – kinetic energy which a molecule possesses as a result of rotation about one of its molecular axes (62)

RUTHERFORD MODEL (OF THE ATOM) – a model in which the atom consists of a tiny, positively–charged nucleus surrounded by a cloud of negatively–charged electrons (143)

SALT – an ionic compound that is neither an acid nor a base (116)

SATURATED HYDROCARBON – a hydrocarbon in which the carbon atoms are connected by single bonds; in other words, an alkane (215)

SATURATED SOLUTION – a solution which has dissolved as much of a particular solute as possible (193)

SEMICONDUCTOR – a nonmetal having an electrical conductivity which increases with temperature. Semiconductors were formerly called metalloids or semimetals. (163)

SEMIMETAL – see semiconductor

SHELL – the set of all orbitals having the same n–value. For example, the four orbitals consisting of the 2 s and three 2 p orbitals is a shell. (152)

SIGNIFICANT FIGURE – a measured or meaningful digit (27)

SINGLE REPLACEMENT REACTION – involves replacing **one** atom in a compound by another atom (114)

SOLUBILITY (of a solute) – the maximum amount of a solute which can dissolve in a given amount of solvent at a given temperature (193)

SOLUTE – the component in a solution which exists in the smaller quantity (51)

SOLUTION – a homogeneous mixture of two or more substances (50)

SOLUTION CHEMISTRY– the study of chemical reactions that occur in solutions (193)

SOLVATION – the interaction between a solute and a solvent (209)

SOLVENT – the component in a solution which exists in the greater quantity (51)

SOLVENT EXTRACTION – a separation process in which one of more components of a mixture are prefer-entially dissolved by the addition of a solvent. The added solvent and the dissolved substances are then removed, leaving the remainder of the original mixture behind. (54)

STOCK SYSTEM (of naming ions) – a method of naming metal ions in which the charge is indicated by a Roman numeral, in parentheses, immediately following the name (69)

STOICHIOMETRIC POINT – see EQUIVALENCE POINT

STOICHIOMETRY – the relationship between the amounts of reactants used in a chemical reaction and the amounts of products produced by the reaction (123)

STP – Standard Temperature and Pressure = $0^{\circ}C$ and 101.3 kPa (82)

STRUCTURAL ISOMERS – compounds which have the same molecular formula but a different arrangement of atoms (222)

SUBSHELL – a set of orbitals of the same type. For example, the set of three 2 p orbitals is a subshell. (152)

SUBSTANCE – something with a unique and identifiable set of properties (44)

SYNTHESIS or **COMBINATION REACTION** – involves the combination of two or more substances to form (or "synthesize") a compound (114)

SYSTEM – the part of the universe being studied in a given situation (49)

TERNARY COMPOUND – a compound made of three different types of atoms (73)

THEORY – a set of hypotheses that ties together a large number of observations of the real world into a logically consistent and understandable pattern. In other words, a theory is a TESTED, REFINED and EXPANDED explanation of why nature behaves in a given way. (41)

THOMSON MODEL (OF THE ATOM) – a model which proposed that an atom consisted of a ball of positive charge having negative charges distributed through the ball (141)

TITRATION – a process by which a measured amount of a solution is reacted with a known volume of another solution (one of the solutions has an unknown concentration) until a desired equivalence point is reached (130)

TRAILING ZERO – a zero digit which is significant (37)

TRANSLATIONAL ENERGY – kinetic energy which a molecule or atom possesses as a result of motion in a straight line (62)

TRANS ISOMER – an isomer in which attached groups are on opposite sides of a double bond (230)

TRANSITION METAL – an element in columns 3 to 12 of the periodic table (161)

TRIATOMIC SPECIES – a chemical species that is made up of three atoms (which may be the same or different types) (68)

TRITIUM – an isotope of hydrogen with an atomic mass of 3; sometimes called "radioactive hydrogen" (148)

UNCONTROLLED FIRE – a fire which is not minor and will possibly continue to spread (6)

UNIT CONVERSION – a calculation method which uses conversion factors to change the units associated with an expression to a different set of units (10)

UNIT SYMBOL – a symbol which stands for one of the SI base units (for example, **g** stands for grams) (16)

UNSATURATED HYDROCARBON – a general term for alkenes and alkynes (226)

VALENCE (as a noun) – the number of unpaired electrons on the atom; also called combining capacity (168)

VALENCE ELECTRON – an electron which can take part in a chemical reaction; also, any electron in an atom except those in the core, or in filled d– or f–subshells. In other words, electrons in OPEN shells. (157)

VAN DER WAALS FORCE – a general term referring to any of three types of weak intermolecular force, including the London force, dipole–dipole force and hydrogen bonding (179)

VAPOUR – the gaseous material formed by the evaporation of a substance which boils above room temperature (47)

VAPOUR PRESSURE – the pressure created by the vapour evaporating from a liquid (47)

VIBRATIONAL ENERGY – kinetic energy which a molecule possesses as a result of changes in its bond lengths and/or angles (62)

VISCOSITY – the *resistance* of a fluid to flow (46)

VOLUMETRIC FLASK – a special flask used to make up an exact volume of a solution. The flask has a narrow neck with a line etched around the neck. When filled to the etched line, the flask holds its exact rated volume. (97)

PERIODIC TABLE OF THE ELEMENTS

Legend:
- 14 — Atomic number
- Si — Symbol
- Silicon — Name
- 28.1 — Atomic mass

1	2	3	4	5	6	7	8	9	10	11	12	13	14	15	16	17	18
1 H Hydrogen 1.0																	2 He Helium 4.0
3 Li Lithium 6.9	4 Be Beryllium 9.0											5 B Boron 10.8	6 C Carbon 12.0	7 N Nitrogen 14.0	8 O Oxygen 16.0	9 F Fluorine 19.0	10 Ne Neon 20.2
11 Na Sodium 23.0	12 Mg Magnesium 24.3											13 Al Aluminum 27.0	14 Si Silicon 28.1	15 P Phosphorus 31.0	16 S Sulphur 32.1	17 Cl Chlorine 35.5	18 Ar Argon 39.9
19 K Potassium 39.1	20 Ca Calcium 40.1	21 Sc Scandium 45.0	22 Ti Titanium 47.9	23 V Vanadium 50.9	24 Cr Chromium 52.0	25 Mn Manganese 54.9	26 Fe Iron 55.8	27 Co Cobalt 58.9	28 Ni Nickel 58.7	29 Cu Copper 63.5	30 Zn Zinc 65.4	31 Ga Gallium 69.7	32 Ge Germanium 72.6	33 As Arsenic 74.9	34 Se Selenium 79.0	35 Br Bromine 79.9	36 Kr Krypton 83.8
37 Rb Rubidium 85.5	38 Sr Strontium 87.6	39 Y Yttrium 88.9	40 Zr Zirconium 91.2	41 Nb Niobium 92.9	42 Mo Molybdenum 95.9	43 Tc Technetium (98)	44 Ru Ruthenium 101.1	45 Rh Rhodium 102.9	46 Pd Palladium 106.4	47 Ag Silver 107.9	48 Cd Cadmium 112.4	49 In Indium 114.8	50 Sn Tin 118.7	51 Sb Antimony 121.8	52 Te Tellurium 127.6	53 I Iodine 126.9	54 Xe Xenon 131.3
55 Cs Cesium 132.9	56 Ba Barium 137.3	57 La Lanthanum 138.9	72 Hf Hafnium 178.5	73 Ta Tantalum 180.9	74 W Tungsten 183.8	75 Re Rhenium 186.2	76 Os Osmium 190.2	77 Ir Iridium 192.2	78 Pt Platinum 195.1	79 Au Gold 197.0	80 Hg Mercury 200.6	81 Tl Thallium 204.4	82 Pb Lead 207.2	83 Bi Bismuth 209.0	84 Po Polonium (209)	85 At Astatine (210)	86 Rn Radon (222)
87 Fr Francium (223)	88 Ra Radium (226)	89 Ac Actinium (227)	104 Rf Rutherfordium (261)	105 Ha Hahnium (262)	106 Sg Seaborgium (263)	107 Uns Unnilseptium (262)	108 Uno Unniloctium (265)	109 Une Unnilennium (266)									

Lanthanide series:

58 Ce Cerium 140.1	59 Pr Praseodymium 140.9	60 Nd Neodymium 144.2	61 Pm Promethium (145)	62 Sm Samarium 150.4	63 Eu Europium 152.0	64 Gd Gadolinium 157.3	65 Tb Terbium 158.9	66 Dy Dysprosium 162.5	67 Ho Holmium 164.9	68 Er Erbium 167.3	69 Tm Thulium 168.9	70 Yb Ytterbium 173.0	71 Lu Lutetium 175.0

Actinide series:

90 Th Thorium 232.0	91 Pa Protactinium 231.0	92 U Uranium 238.0	93 Np Neptunium (237)	94 Pu Plutonium (244)	95 Am Americium (243)	96 Cm Curium (247)	97 Bk Berkelium (247)	98 Cf Californium (251)	99 Es Einsteinium (252)	100 Fm Fermium (257)	101 Md Mendelevium (258)	102 No Nobelium (259)	103 Lr Lawrencium (262)

Based on mass of C^{12} at 12.00

Values in parenthesis are the masses of the most stable or best known isotopes for elements which do not occur naturally.

ATOMIC MASSES OF THE ELEMENTS

Based on mass of C^{12} at 12.00. Values in parentheses are the mass of the most stable or best known isotopes for elements which do not occur naturally.

Element	Symbol	Atomic Number	Atomic Mass	Element	Symbol	Atomic Number	Atomic Mass
Actinium	Ac	89	(227)	Mercury	Hg	80	200.6
Aluminum	Al	13	27.0	Molybdenum	Mo	42	95.9
Americium	Am	95	(243)	Neodymium	Nd	60	144.2
Antimony	Sb	51	121.8	Neon	Ne	10	20.2
Argon	Ar	18	39.9	Neptunium	Np	93	(237)
Arsenic	As	33	74.9	Nickel	Ni	28	58.7
Astatine	At	85	(210)	Niobium	Nb	41	92.9
Barium	Ba	56	137.3	Nitrogen	N	7	14.0
Berkelium	Bk	97	(247)	Nobelium	No	102	(259)
Beryllium	Be	4	9.0	Osmium	Os	76	190.2
Bismuth	Bi	83	209.0	Oxygen	O	8	16.0
Boron	B	5	10.8	Palladium	Pd	46	106.4
Bromine	Br	35	79.9	Phosphorus	P	15	31.0
Cadmium	Cd	48	112.4	Platinum	Pt	78	195.1
Calcium	Ca	20	40.1	Plutonium	Pu	94	(244)
Californium	Cf	98	(251)	Polonium	Po	84	(209)
Carbon	C	6	12.0	Potassium	K	19	39.1
Cerium	Ce	58	140.1	Praseodymium	Pr	59	140.9
Cesium	Cs	55	132.9	Promethium	Pm	61	(145)
Chlorine	Cl	17	35.5	Protactinium	Pa	91	231.0
Chromium	Cr	24	52.0	Radium	Ra	88	(226)
Cobalt	Co	27	58.9	Radon	Rn	86	(222)
Copper	Cu	29	63.5	Rhenium	Re	75	186.2
Curium	Cm	96	(247)	Rhodium	Rh	45	102.9
Dysprosium	Dy	66	162.5	Rubidium	Rb	37	85.5
Einsteinium	Es	99	(252)	Ruthenium	Ru	44	101.1
Erbium	Er	68	167.3	Rutherfordium	Rf	104	(261)
Europium	Eu	63	152.0	Samarium	Sm	62	150.4
Fermium	Fm	100	(257)	Scandium	Sc	21	45.0
Fluorine	F	9	19.0	Selenium	Se	34	79.0
Francium	Fr	87	(223)	Silicon	Si	14	28.1
Gadolinium	Gd	64	157.3	Silver	Ag	47	107.9
Gallium	Ga	31	69.7	Sodium	Na	11	23.0
Germanium	Ge	32	72.6	Strontium	Sr	38	87.6
Gold	Au	79	197.0	Sulphur	S	16	32.1
Hafnium	Hf	72	178.5	Tantalum	Ta	73	180.9
Hahnium	Ha	105	(262)	Technetium	Tc	43	(98)
Helium	He	2	4.0	Tellurium	Te	52	127.6
Holmium	Ho	67	164.9	Terbium	Tb	65	158.9
Hydrogen	H	1	1.0	Thallium	Tl	81	204.4
Indium	In	49	114.8	Thorium	Th	90	232.0
Iodine	I	53	126.9	Thulium	Tm	69	168.9
Iridium	Ir	77	192.2	Tin	Sn	50	118.7
Iron	Fe	26	55.8	Titanium	Ti	22	47.9
Krypton	Kr	36	83.8	Tungsten	W	74	183.8
Lanthanum	La	57	138.9	Uranium	U	92	238.0
Lawrencium	Lr	103	(262)	Vanadium	V	23	50.9
Lead	Pb	82	207.2	Xenon	Xe	54	131.3
Lithium	Li	3	6.9	Ytterbium	Yb	70	173.0
Lutetium	Lu	71	175.0	Yttrium	Y	39	88.9
Magnesium	Mg	12	24.3	Zinc	Zn	30	65.4
Manganese	Mn	25	54.9	Zirconium	Zr	40	91.2
Mendelevium	Md	101	(258)				

Names, Formulae and Charges of some Common Ions

Positive ions (cations)		Negative ions (anions)	
Aluminum	Al^{3+}	Bromide	Br^-
Ammonium	NH_4^+	Carbonate	CO_3^{2-}
Barium	Ba^{2+}	Chlorate	ClO_3^-
Calcium	Ca^{2+}	Chloride	Cl^-
Chromium(II), chromous	Cr^{2+}	Chlorite	ClO_2^-
Chromium(III), chromic	Cr^{3+}	Chromate	CrO_4^{2-}
Copper(I)*, cuprous	Cu^+	Cyanide	CN^-
Copper(II), cupric	Cu^{2+}	Dichromate	$Cr_2O_7^{2-}$
Hydrogen	H^+	Dihydrogen phosphate	$H_2PO_4^-$
Hydronium	H_3O^+	Ethanoate, acetate	CH_3COO^-
Iron(II)*, ferrous	Fe^{2+}	Fluoride	F^-
Iron(III), ferric	Fe^{3+}	Hydrogen carbonate, bicarbonate	HCO_3^-
Lead(II), plumbous	Pb^{2+}	Hydrogen oxalate, binoxalate	$H_2CO_4^-$
Lead(IV), plumbic	Pb^{4+}	Hydrogen sulphate, bisulphate	HSO_4^-
Lithium	Li^+	Hydrogen sulphide, bisulphide	HS^-
Magnesium	Mg^{2+}	Hydrogen sulphite, bisulphite	HSO_3^-
Manganese(II), manganous	Mn^{2+}	Hydroxide	OH^-
Manganese(IV)	Mn^{4+}	Hypochlorite	ClO^-
Mercury(I)*, mercurous	Hg_2^{2+}	Iodide	I^-
Mercury(II), mercuric	Hg^{2+}	Monohydrogen phosphate	HPO_4^{2-}
Potassium	K^+	Nitrate	NO_3^-
Silver	Ag^+	Nitrite	NO_2^-
Sodium	Na^+	Oxalate	$C_2O_4^{2-}$
Tin(II)*, stannous	Sn^{2+}	Oxide †	O^{2-}
Tin(IV), stannic	Sn^{4+}	Perchlorate	ClO_4^-
Zinc	Zn^{2+}	Permanganate	MnO_4^-
		Phosphate	PO_4^{3-}
		Sulphate	SO_4^{2-}
		Sulphide	S^{2-}
		Sulphite	SO_3^{2-}
		Thiocyanate	SCN^-

* Aqueous solutions are readily oxidized by air.

† Not stable in aqueous solutions.